Psychiatry in Law/
Law in Psychiatry

Psychiatry in Law/
Law in Psychiatry

Law in Psychiatry

RALPH SLOVENKO

Brunner-Routledge
New York • *London*

Published in 2002 by
Brunner-Routledge
29 West 35th Street
New York, NY 10001

Published in Great Britain by
Brunner-Routledge
27 Church Road
Hove, East Sussex, BN3 2FA

10 9 8 7 6 5 4 3 2 1

Library of Congress Cataloging-in-Publication Data

Slovenko, Ralph.
    Psychiatry in law/law in psychiatry / Ralph Slovenko.
        p.   cm.
    Includes bibliographical references and indexes.
    ISBN 0-415-93365-X (set)—ISBN 0-415-93363-3 (vol. 1)—
    ISBN 0-415-93364-1 (vol. 2)
        1. Forensic psychiatry—United States. 2. Psychiatrists—Legal status,
    laws, etc.—United States. I. Title.

KF8965 .S59 2002
614′.1—dc21

                                                      2002018494

Contents

PART I

Hospitalization of the Mentally Ill

1

Civil Commitment (Involuntary Hospitalization)

Views held by the medical profession and the surrounding culture about insanity (or *mental illness*, as now called) and what to do about it have changed over the years. For centuries the idea of "demonic possession," reflecting the biblical explanation of insanity, held sway. In the late eighteenth and early nineteenth centuries insanity came to be regarded as a disease rather than as divine retribution or demonic possession. At this time, a convergence of popular indignation, growing medical interest, and several examples seemed to prove that, with humane treatment, insanity could be cured. In this context laymen and physicians developed a system that they called *moral treatment*. It was considered revolutionary in the history of psychiatry.[1]

Most prominently, two years after the French Revolution, Philippe Pinel in 1793 in France introduced humanitarian principles in the care and treatment of the mentally ill. Pinel's classic work *A Treatise on Insanity* was first published in French in 1801; the English translation appeared in 1806. As director of two psychiatric hospitals in Paris, he ordered the unchaining of the inmates. He advocated "moral medicine," directed at the mind and emotions, advising physicians to approach patients with "gentleness" and "consoling words, the happy expedient of reviving the hope of the lunatic and gaining his confidence." No longer would the devil be beaten out of a person (as was done to King George III). In the early years of the nineteenth century Jean-Etienne-Dominique Esquirol, Pinel's disciple, and others demanded an end to bleedings and purgings, which were standard treatments for mental illness.

In America this philosophy of moral treatment was championed by Dr. Benjamin Rush, the renowned political leader of the Revolutionary War period, and the father of American psychiatry. Later, during the 1800s, the cause of moral treatment for the mentally ill was taken up by Dorothea Dix, who carried on a campaign to build state institutions after it had become generally apparent that private philanthropy could not cope unaided with so large a burden.[2]

The philosophy of moral treatment espoused by these pioneers prevailed in the United States in the early part of the nineteenth century. At that time, in part reflecting the positive results of humane treatment of the mentally disordered, and in part reflecting the stresses arising out of the burgeoning industrial era, there was considerable social pressure to take care of the mentally ill on a larger scale. Palatial manors to house the mentally ill were built at considerable expense in rustic, attractive (though remote) parts of the states. Constructed at a cost unparalleled in the world, these facilities were designed with the premise that madness might be soothed in a setting of architectural and environmental beauty. This progressive thinking as well as the building efforts it engendered became a model for the whole world.[3]

In Europe, before the eighteenth century, only a small proportion of individuals deemed to be mentally ill were put in a special institution. People who were a menace to others or utterly incapable of looking after themselves were taken care of by their family, or by charity, or by their parish, or occasionally locked away in a jail. Systematic confinement of the mentally ill instigated by the state developed in France from the mid-seventeenth century as part of the "great confinement" of troublemakers launched by Louis XIV's absolutism. In England, the biggest growth sector for the confinement of the mentally ill before the nineteenth century lay within the market economy, where a trade in lunacy grew up, centered upon the private madhouse. These institutions might be run by physicians or laymen; some were big, others small, all of a private nature. They were accused of shady practices, above all the iniquitous confinement of sane people. Daniel Defoe, among others, alleged that they were tailor-made for husbands who wished to put away their wives. As historian Roy Porter observed, "It is not surprising then that so many of the earliest autobiographical writings of English 'mad people' raise a howl of protest against the private asylum and its abuses."[4]

In 1842 Charles Dickens noted approvingly that American mental hospitals were supported by the state, a fact that made the government, in his view, a merciful and benevolent protector of people in distress.[5] With increasing numbers of the seriously mentally ill on the streets and in the jails, the various state governments in the United States came to accept full responsibility for their care and built the large public mental hospitals. The constitutions of the various states mandated state-sponsored care of the mentally ill.[6] In England, on the other hand, where public charity was minimal, the government offered the mentally ill, as Dickens said, "very little shelter or relief beyond that which is to be found in the workhouse and the jail."[7]

This era of moral treatment in America, however, soon came to an end. As the population increased with the influx of immigrants, the public mental hospitals were turned into welfare institutions. Previously, every state hospital had a farm or dairy that provided meaningful work and activity for the residents. Beginning in the late nineteenth century, business interests seeking to sell supplies to these big institutions, however, effectively pressured the state to have the farms and dairies closed. As a result, once meaningful work experiences in the hospital were replaced with a state of idleness.[8] The hospital degenerated into the "snake pit," a place of chaotic disorder and distress; its motto became: "Abandon hope, all ye who enter here."[9]

During this period Mrs. E. P. W. Packard began her crusade for the enactment of laws on the hospitalization of the mentally ill as well as laws for the protection of patient rights.[10] Her crusade had its genesis in her hospitalization. Her husband, the Reverend Theophilus Packard, stating that he could not "manage" her at home, had her committed, utilizing a state statute that provided that married women could be involuntarily committed on the request of the husband without the evidentiary standard applicable in other cases.[11] Upon her discharge she went on a crusade for the adoption of mental health codes that became the foundation of modern codes.[12] She claimed that sane persons were illegally incarcerated and maltreated. Her attacks, along with exposés by other former patients, resulted in the passage of legislation that would more effectively safeguard the rights of patients and circumscribe the powers of hospital officials.[13]

At the turn of the twentieth century a second revolution in psychiatry was brought about by Sigmund Freud. Like Pinel, Freud engendered hope and enthusiasm in the treatment of the mentally ill. On the basis of the new learning, laws were enacted on sexual psychopathology, alcoholism, and drug addiction that would divert individuals out of the criminal law process and into the hospital system. These behaviors came to be regarded as mental illness rather than as crime.[14] Much of the impetus for these new laws came from the success achieved in treating battle-fatigued soldiers during World War I.

Following World War II, in the 1950s, a third revolution in psychiatry occurred with the development of psychotropic medication. These chemical agents resulted in a decrease in the use of physical restraints, psychosurgery, electroshock, hydrotherapy, insulin coma, and other physical means of treatment. These chemical agents would control the voices and delusional thinking of schizophrenia, and the mania of manic-depressive psychosis. For the first time, the number of persons admitted to mental hospitals declined.

With this decline, a new philosophy began to emerge, which had as a goal the abandonment of state mental hospitals altogether. First of all, proponents of this philosophy argued, hospitalization while reducing stress produces institutional dependency, which offers not mental health, but mental death, and robs the individual of all incentive. Sociologist Erving Goffman, who had worked for a time as an occupational therapist in a large mental hospital, crystallized this thinking. He wrote that "chronic schizophrenia" is merely an adaptation to the social system of the hospital. In his 1961 book *Asylums*, Goffman presented a scathing critique, not only of the conditions prevailing in mental hospitals but also of the basic philosophical premises on which such institutions were founded.[15] Thereafter, the word *asylum* became a derogatory term.

In fiction, in the novel *One Flew Over the Cuckoo's Nest*, Ken Kesey described the hospital staff as a tyrannical, sadistic group that forced patients into total submission.[16] In still another dramatic view, Dr. Thomas Szasz in his book *The Manufacture of Madness* drew a parallel between the persecution of witches in the thirteenth through the seventeenth centuries and what he termed our persecution of people labeled mentally ill in the twentieth century.[17] In his view, modern psychiatry has led not to more enlightenment, but only to different victims for persecution.[18]

During the tumultuous 1960s and 1970s, Bruce Ennis, an attorney for the American Civil Liberties Union, led the Mental Health Bar in litigation to close all mental hospitals. These efforts were unlike those of Mrs. Packard, who, a century earlier, sought hospital safeguards and regulations instead of outright closings. In 1972, Ennis and three other young attorneys (Charles Halpern, Paul Friedman, and Margaret Ewing) formed the Mental Health Law Project (MHLP), which rapidly became—and has remained (it changed its name in 1993 to the Bazelon Center for Mental Health Law)—the ideological and logistical center of the mental patient liberation bar, as it was called. They were abolitionists, not reformers, who challenged every assumption of the mental health system.[19] An observation by the U.S. Supreme Court in 1972 in a criminal case gave impetus to litigation on the commitment power of the state: "Considering the number of persons affected, it is perhaps remarkable that the substantive constitutional limitations [on a state's commitment] power have not been more frequently litigated."[20] On another occasion the Supreme Court commented that there is more stigma to mental hospitalization than to imprisonment.[21]

Ennis wrote a polemic against mental hospitalization, *Prisoners of Psychiatry*, which also appeared in 1972.[22] In an introduction, Szasz praised Ennis for recognizing "that individuals incriminated as mentally ill do not need guarantees of 'treatment' but protection against their enemies—the legislators, judges, and psychiatrists who persecute them in the name of mental health."[23] In this book, Ennis portrayed psychiatry as a means to control or dispose of people who annoy others. As Ennis wrote: "How would we tame our rebellious youth, or rid ourselves of doddering parents, or clear the streets of the offensive poor, without it?" For Ennis, hospitals were places "where sick people get sicker and sane people go mad."[24] In 1974, in an interview published in *Madness Network News*, Ennis stated: "My personal goal is either to abolish involuntary commitment or to set up so many procedural roadblocks and hurdles that it will be difficult, if not impossible, for the state to commit people against their will."[25]

Ironically, in the 1960s and 1970s, with some notorious exceptions, mental hospitals were at their best in staffing and conditions since the era of moral treatment of the early 1800s.[26] In the 1960s, when the allegations of abuse at mental health facilities began to mount, Senator Sam Ervin (later of Watergate fame) held hearings and uncovered no cases of "railroading."[27] The American Bar Association also commissioned a field investigation of mental hospitals in six states, and it concluded that railroading was a myth.[28] In general, a patient in a mental hospital who wanted to leave simply had to put one foot in front of the other and walk out. Professor Gerald Grob, the prizewinning historian of mental hospitals, has written that the hospitals provided an asylum nowhere else available.[29]

With liberty said to be at stake, the MHLP urged that the substantive and procedural due process requirements of criminal justice be applied to the civil commitment process—which would make it more difficult to achieve a commitment. For the substantive criterion, the police power of the state (dangerousness) rather than *parens patriae* (need of care) would become the primary focus of civil commitment.[30] By 1985, dangerousness was a necessary prerequisite in twenty-five jurisdictions—that involves prediction, and prediction is always problematical.[31] Massachusetts legislation requires that the harm necessary to justify commitment must be manifested by behavior that is suicidal, homicidal, or places others in reasonable fear of serious physical harm.[32] With community-based services, it became difficult to justify, except in the case of a dangerous individual, the institutionalization of the gravely disabled or of those unable to render a competent judgment for the need of treatment. In any event, quite often, rather than leave it to the court to decide on commitment, psychiatrists prejudge whether an individual is committable under what they understand about the dangerousness criterion and do not certify, though the tendency of courts is to commit when the family appears in court pleading for hospitalization of a distraught family member.

Another restriction on hospital commitment has been the development of the concept of the *least restrictive alternative* (LRA), also known as the *least restrictive environment.* Under this doctrine, state intervention resulting from commitment is to take place in the least restrictive manner. The basis for the doctrine is the constitutional requirement that the state may restrict the exercise of fundamental liberties only to the extent necessary to effectuate the state's interest.[33] Under this scheme, the state hospital is posited as the most restrictive environment, with community-based services and outpatient care seen as less restrictive.

Thinking in terms of liberty, proponents of LRA did not use the phrase "most beneficial alternative." Under the LRA concept, any feasible alternative must be implemented in lieu of involuntary hospitalization. The trial court must find "by clear and convincing evidence that alternative treatment is not adequate or hospitalization is the least restrictive alternative."[34] The first enunciation of LRA in the law on civil commitment was in 1966 in a case involving Catherine Lake—a sixty-year-old woman who wandered about in the downtown crime-ridden district of the nation's capital, appearing disoriented and carrying her worldly possessions around with her in a shopping bag.[35] She was placed in a mental hospital. In assessing a habeas corpus petition brought on her behalf the D.C. Circuit Court of Appeals ruled that whatever is done should not exceed the minimum necessary to ensure the patient's protection. Writing for the majority, Judge David Bazelon, with Warren Burger (later to become chief justice of the Supreme Court) dissenting, ruled that the trial court is to make the determination, not the department of mental health.[36]

In a case that came before the U.S. Supreme Court, *Addington v. Texas,*[37] the MHLP sought to invoke the *proof beyond a reasonable doubt* procedural standard of criminal justice in the civil commitment process.[38] The case involved a man whose mother filed a petition to have him involuntarily committed to a state mental hospital. Writing the opinion of the Court, Chief Justice Burger wrote that to require proof beyond a reasonable doubt of the mental illness or dangerousness criteria of civil commitment would be well-nigh impossible, and thereby would do away with involuntary commitment.[39] In the opinion, handed down in 1979, he said that the criminal-law beyond a reasonable doubt standard was inappropriate because, "[g]iven the lack of certainty and the fallibility of psychiatric diagnosis, there is a serious question as to whether a state could ever prove beyond a reasonable doubt that an individual is both mentally ill and likely to be dangerous."[40] However, he called for a *clear and convincing evidence* standard in commitment hearings, which is more than the *preponderance of the evidence* standard of the ordinary civil case and less than proof beyond a reasonable doubt of criminal cases.[41]

Approved, SCAO

OSM CODE-crT

STATE OF MICHIGAN
    PROBATE COURT   **CLINICAL CERTIFICATE**
    COUNTY

FILE NO.

CIRCUIT COURT - FAMILY DIVISION

In the matter **of** _____

1. **TO THE EXAMINER:** The following is a statement that must be read to the individual before proceeding with any questions.

> I am authorized by law to examine you for the purpose of advising the court if you have a mental condition which needs treatment and whether such treatment should take place in a hospital or in some other place. I am also here to determine **if** you should be hospitalized, or remain hospitalized, before a court hearing is held. I may be required to tell the court what I observe and what you tell me.

> I certify that on this date I read the above statement to the individual before asking any questions or conducting any examination.

2. I further certify that I, _____, personally examined _____

    at _____, on _____

    Starting at _____m. and continuing **for** _____ minutes.

INSTRUCTIONS: In answering describe in detail the specific actions statements, demeanor, and appearance of the individual, together with other information in reasonable detail ,which underlie your conclusion. **Indicate the source of any information not personally known or observed.** If this certificate is to accompany a petition of discharge, also state why the individual continues to **be** or is no longer a person requiring treatment or in need **of** hospitalization.

3. my determination is that the person is :

    _____ mentally ill (has a substantial disorder of thought or mood that significantly impairs judgment, behavior, capacity to recognize reality, or ability to cope with the ordinary demands of life).

    _____ not mentally ill,

4. if applicable) The person has

    _____ convulsive disorder   _____ alcoholism   _____ other drug dependence.

    _____ mental processes weakened by reason of advanced years,

    _____ other (specify):

    _____

    _____ been hospitalized involuntarily two or more times within the two year period immediately preceding the filing of the petition and has rejected after care programs and treatment

5. My diagnosis is. _____

6. Facts serving as the basis for my determination are:

_____

_____

_____

(PLEASE SEE OTHER SIDE)

Figure 1.1 *Typical Certification Form.*

6. (Continued) _____

_____

_____

7. Explain in the space below the facts which lead you to believe that future conduct may result in (check applicable box)

_____ **a. likelihood of injury to self. Facts:**

Therefore, I believe the person can reasonably be expected within the near future to intentionally or unintentionally seriously physically injure self.

_____ **b. likelihood in injury to others. Facts:**

Therefore, I believe the person can reasonably be expected within the near future to intentionally or unintentionally seriously physically injure others.

_____ **c. inability to attend to basic physical needs. Facts:**

Therefore, I believe that as a result of mental illness the examined person is unable to attend to those basic physical needs (such as food, clothing or shelter) that must be attended to in order to avoid serious harm in the near future.

_____ **d. inability to understand need for treatment. Facts:**

Therefore, I believe that as a result of mental illness the examined person is unable to understand the need for treatment, and continued behavior can reasonably be expected to result in significant physical harm to self or others.

8. I conclude the individual _____ is _____ is not a person requiring treatment.

9. (optional) I recommend _____ hospitalization _____ alternative treatment

as follows: _____

_____

I certify that I am a person authorized by law to certify as to the individual's mental condition. I am not related by blood or marriage either to the person about whom this certificate is concerned or to any person who has filed, or whom I know to be planning to file, a petition in this proceeding. I declare that this certificate has been examined by me and that its contents are true to the best of my information knowledge, and belief.

Date _____ **Time** _____ **Signature** _____

Title (physician, psychiatrist)

Figure 1.1 *Typical Certification Form (continued).*

Over the years mental health associations have urged voluntary mental hospitalization in preference to involuntary commitment, while recognizing that there are times (as with suicidal or violent mentally ill individuals) when an involuntary commitment is in order. Admission practices were promoted by these associations that would encourage individuals to sign themselves into the hospital as voluntary patients (some were known as "coerced voluntaries"). That process would lessen the stigma of civil commitment. In recent years, however, the courts have tilted in the direction of hospitalization by way of a judicial proceeding. In 1990, in *Zinermon v. Burch*,[42] the U.S. Supreme Court ruled that patient competency must be considered in regard to hospital admission as well as to treatment. The Court said that "even if the state usually might be justified in taking at face value a person's request for admission to a hospital for medical treatment, it might not be justified in doing so without further inquiry as to a mentally ill person's request for admission and treatment at a mental hospital."

The case involved Darrell Burch, who was seen bruised and bloodied wandering on a Florida highway, and was brought by a concerned citizen to a community mental health service. He was hallucinating, confused, and disoriented. At the hospital he thought he was entering heaven. He signed a form for voluntary admission and another authorizing treatment. After three days of treatment with psychotropic medication he was transferred to Florida State Hospital, where he again signed voluntary admission and treatment forms. As a voluntary patient, he was free to leave at any time. He remained there for about five months.

Upon discharge, he complained that he had been improperly admitted to both facilities and had thus been confined and treated against his will. He was brought to the hospital, he did not appear there on his own motion. He claimed that because he had not been competent to sign any legal documents, he had a constitutional right to a judicial commitment before being admitted and treated, and that since there was no such hearing, he had been deprived of his liberty without due process of law. The Supreme Court agreed. In a 5–4 ruling, the Court held that before being admitted and treated he was entitled to a judicial hearing, or at least some other hearing that would be a safeguard against arbitrary action by the state, to determine either that he was competent to consent to admission or that he met the statutory standard for involuntary commitment. The Court acknowledged that persons who are mentally ill and incapable of giving informed consent to admission would not necessarily meet the statutory standard for involuntary placement, which requires either that they are likely to injure themselves or others, or that their neglect or refusal to care for themselves threatens their well-being. The Court said:

> The involuntary placement process serves to guard against the confinement of a person who, though mentally ill, is harmless and can live safely outside an institution. Confinement of such a person not only violates Florida law, but also is unconstitutional. . . . Thus, it is at least possible that if Burch had an involuntary placement hearing, he would not have been confined at FSH. Moreover, even assuming that Burch would have met the statutory requirements or involuntary placement, he still could have been harmed by being deprived of other protections built into the involuntary placement procedure, such as the appointment of a guardian

advocate to make treatment decisions, and periodic judicial review of placement.[43]

As a result of the decision, a psychiatric facility faces liability for false imprisonment if it admits an individual of questionable competence on a voluntary basis without providing some procedure, possibly an adversarial judicial hearing. Most patients brought to a psychiatric facility are in such a condition that their competence to admit themselves voluntarily or to consent to treatment is questionable. Actually, while it may be argued that he was deprived of his liberty without due process, there was little in the way of damages to Burch, and he had been helped by his hospitalization. Accordingly, a nominal settlement was negotiated, giving Burch some money and making a contribution to his lawyer.[44]

Because a voluntary mental patient does not enjoy the same due process protections as an involuntary patient, it thus becomes prudent that a patient enter a hospital via the judicial route. In *Kennedy v. Schafer*,[45] the Eighth Circuit ruled that a teenage patient who committed suicide while under treatment at a state psychiatric facility did not have a constitutionally protected liberty interest in a safe and humane environment under the due process clause of the Fourteenth Amendment. Because the patient was voluntarily admitted to the state facility by her parents, the court held that she was not entitled to the same due process right to a safe and humane environment as would be a patient under the same circumstances who had been involuntarily committed to the facility. Her parents brought suit for infringement of rights conferred by the Constitution.[46]

The Eighth Circuit noted, "The due process clause of the Fourteenth Amendment ensures that '[n]o *State* shall . . . deprive any person of life, liberty, or property, without due process of law,'" (emphasis added).[47] Quoting the U.S. Supreme Court in *DeShaney v. Winnebago County Dept. Soc. Servs.*,[48] the "deprivation of liberty" that triggers "the protection of the Due Process Clause" is "the State's affirmative act of restraining the individual's freedom to act on his own behalf—through incarceration, institutionalization, or other similar restraint of personal liberty."[49] Thus from the perspective of both the hospital and the patient, the judicial route becomes preferable, but one may wonder about it. In these cases, the judicial commitment process is usually a rubber-stamping. Assuredly, Darrell Burch (and the others) would have been committed had he been presented to a court, but he got a monetary award because he was not.

Passage of Commitment Laws

Mrs. Packard, outraged by her experience, persuaded the various states to enact broad commitment laws, not simply to do away with the commitment power of a husband. Were the laws warranted, distinguishing the care of the mentally ill from that of physically ill? Was she railroaded? In the book *The Private War of Mrs. Packard*,[50] Barbara Sapinsley contends that Mrs. Packard's husband, a rigid, fundamentalist clergyman, had her confined in an insane asylum because she questioned his beliefs, but the evidence indicates that she was in need of hospitalization. According to the historian Albert Deutsch, Mrs. Packard claimed to be the mother of Christ and the Third Person of the Blessed Trinity.[51] Her doctor at the hospital,

Andrew McFarland, was driven to despair treating her, and he vowed never again to treat a woman.

As a general principle, under the common law, there is no duty to come to the aid of another, but family members owe a duty of providing care to each other, and anyone may come to the assistance of the mentally ill. Unwarranted inter-meddling, however, could result in a tort action for false arrest or false imprison-ment.[52] In 1869 Isaac Ray, the prominent forensic psychiatrist, suggested that fam-ilies should be left to their own "sense of duty and affection" in determining appropriate care for ill relatives.[53] The early laws in America focused on need for care under *parens patriae*.[54]

Until the 1990s, Poland did not have commitment laws. Individuals went or were brought into a mental hospital no differently than into other hospitals. There were no complaints, as the care was fairly decent, particularly if a *lapowka* (pay-ment under the table) were given the doctor. But the history of the misuse of psychiatry in the USSR, just as it had an impact on commitment laws in the United States, prompted the enactment of commitment laws in Poland, although it did not have a history of abuse of psychiatry. The law in Poland was pushed by Dr. Stanislaw Dabrowski, who was in tune with U.S. laws. In many countries, for better or worse, the United States has become the model.[55]

The United States and Russia (USSR): Each a Catalyst for the Other

In a subway station in today's Russia I heard a man shout, "The country is in danger. The leaders are crooked." The populace would agree with him, but was he sane or mad in shouting it out in public? In the days of the Soviet Union, whether sane or mad, that individual would likely have been put in a mental institution. Those were the days when psychiatry was used to quash dissent. At the same time, psychiatry was not abused in nonpolitical cases. Mental health care was decent, especially at Moscow Hospital No. 1. There was no need to force anyone into it. The problem, if any, was to get patients to leave. Treatment was competent, the food was good, housing was attractive, and the grounds—trees, grass, and benches— were inviting.

In reaction to the misuse of psychiatry, Russia has now enacted commitment laws similar to those in the United States.[56] Actually, the crucial issue was really not *how* something was accomplished but rather *what* was accomplished. The political dissidents who were put in a mental institution could have readily been prosecuted under its criminal laws. For some dissenters, the worst penalty was the psychiatric hospital; for others, the labor camp; for still others, exile to the West. The issue was the quashing of dissent, not how it was done. There is a saying, "If your intention is to beat a dog, you can always find a stick," but psychiatrists worldwide were concerned about the misuse of psychiatry, not about other ways of quashing dissent. Like a man looking through the wrong end of a telescope, psychiatrists, with some exception, indulged in what might be called a perspective fallacy.[57]

The Soviet Union's use of psychiatric hospitalization as a means of social con-trol gave impetus to the view in the United States that the population of American mental hospitals is composed of social or political critics. Indeed, the antipsychiatry movement in the 1960s and 1970s claimed that so-called schizophrenics are in fact social dissenters. That was implicit in the statement in 1973 by Jerome J. Shestack, chairman of the American Bar Association Commission on the Mentally Disabled, that the United States must prevent "the kind of situation which is developing in Russia in which a diagnosis of anti-state conduct is equated with being deviate and subject to commitment to a mental institution."[58]

The result was a change in focus of civil commitment in the United States from *parens patriae* to police power. Criminal justice criteria were invoked in civil commitment, mental hospitals were closed, and jails housed the mentally ill.[59] Those concerned over the misuse of psychiatry ignored various safeguards in the United States that did not exist in the Soviet Union. In the United States the state is not the only source of employment for psychiatrists, an outside (privately employed) psychiatrist may evaluate a patient, there is judicial review by writ of habeas corpus, an unfounded or malicious petition may result in liability, and volunteers and relatives and friends who visit in mental hospitals may report any abuses.

Today, with the economic collapse of the country, Russia's health care has deteriorated. As in the United States, the mentally ill now sleep on the streets and shout in public places, or they are in jail. Many do not know who or where they are. No one cares. A family seeking help will likely be told that under the new commitment laws nothing can be done when an individual resists going to a hospital. Moreover, hospital staff is not interested in treating an uncooperative patient. Why bother, when there are many others needing care?

There has been a rash of suicides in Russia committed by jumping in the path of a subway train. In St. Petersburg, just after there were three deaths on the subway rails within a period of twelve days, the head of the subway police said, "I would not recommend that anyone commit suicide on the subway rails. If it is urgent, jumping from a tall building is better. Death under a train is not necessarily a quick one, and can be very tortuous." What else could have been suggested? To suggest social services or psychiatric care would have been fanciful, given their disappearance.[60] In the United States supporters of Jack Kevorkian have proposed legislation to allow the prescription of lethal drugs to terminally ill persons for the purpose of committing suicide.

Who Benefits from Commitment Laws?

Who really benefits from commitment laws? For one thing, the laws provide a rationale not to provide care when the individual does not meet the standard of involuntary commitment (now essentially based on dangerousness). For another, these laws stigmatize, as they regard the mentally ill as though they were criminals. Moreover, in a country like the United States, where malpractice litigation is commonplace, commitment laws more or less provide a safeguard against liability, now that sovereign immunity has generally fallen by the wayside.[61] In that regard, commitment laws are a plus for the hospital staff, not the patient. For patients, the writ of habeas corpus and tort remedies provide a better safeguard in the case of malicious confinement.

The bill of rights in U.S. mental health codes, a section of the code following provisions on admission and discharge, actually add nothing to the law. Commitment to a hospital is neither a determination of incompetency nor a deprivation of civil or political rights. At one time, when hospitalization was lifelong, an incompetency proceeding was joined with a commitment proceeding, in effect rendering the hospital the legal guardian of the patient. Without an adjudication of incompetency, the status of a mental patient is, or should be, the same as that of any individual, and he should have all the rights listed in the mental patient's bill of rights without their enumeration. Indeed, a special bill of rights implies that the mental patient has only these rights and no more. Safeguards against inappropriate treatment lie in the writ of habeas corpus, a malpractice action, or the appointment of an ombudsman.

The focus on commitment laws may draw attention to the conditions of institutions, but lest the tail wag the dog, it must be emphasized that the quality of institutions determines public attitudes, the commitment laws, and their interpretation. In cases of an involuntary hospitalization, the individual almost always in a few days is grateful for it, so one must question the merit of a judicial proceeding. Posttreatment reports of changed beliefs by patients in their need for hospitalization and their saying "thank you" would indicate that excessive value ought not to be placed on an initial refusal of hospitalization.[62]

A number of courts have pointed out certain benefits that accrue to a proposed patient in delaying a judicial determination on hospitalization. They note that the stigma of a court record is avoided when treatment can begin immediately, and the length of hospitalization is shortened.[63] At least until the 1970s, when control of the commitment process was taken over by the courts, two physicians (including a psychiatrist) who had no financial interest in the treatment of the patient or the medical examiner had authority, for all practical purposes, to admit a mentally disordered person to an institution. Before the 1970s, physicians and families would usually call the medical examiner (the coroner in Louisiana), who when appropriate would bring the disturbed individual to a hospital. Nowadays they do not know whom to call—perhaps emergency or the police, who would take the individual in a paddy wagon, likely to jail. By and large, when encountering a person acting out because of mental illness, the police find that trying to get the person into treatment means taking hours away from other vital work to transport the person and fill out paper, and it does not guarantee the person will be admitted, so they take the person to jail and book him for a criminal offense.[64] Nowadays, with the closure of mental hospitals, the police may have no alternative but to bring the mentally disordered person to jail. In Florida, where all but two of the public mental hospitals have been closed, sheriffs protest about the number of mentally ill in jail.[65]

Mental health and criminal justice systems often deal with the same groups of chronically troubled and troublesome individuals. In practice, however, the two systems of social control rarely exchange cases, information, and resources. The lack of systems coordination is especially apparent in the area of aftercare services. Many seriously mentally ill persons in jail receive psychiatric services during their incarceration but are usually discharged with no referrals to community treatment.[66]

In any event, the development of pharmacological drugs and community-based programs cause laws on commitment to a hospital to be regarded as archaic vestiges of a bygone era. Perforce, the closure of mental hospitals leads to outpatient commitment (for whatever it may be worth), and the closure of nearby emergency centers leads to the police (even more) taking the mentally ill to jail. With deinstitutionalization, the various states either under the doctrine of least restrictive alternative or by enactment of outpatient commitment laws require the individual to take medication as a condition for living in the community.[67] However, as in the case of institutional care, these states tend to require that the individuals be an imminent danger to themselves or others before they can be involuntarily treated. Psychotic individuals who are merely making threats against others or eating out of garbage cans are not usually considered to meet the criteria for out-patient commitment. Once again, police power rather than *parens patriae* has become the guiding principle of the commitment.

As history shows, nothing could be more meaningless than commitment laws when there are no hospitals, and when there are decent hospitals there is usually no need to turn to the law. The need for commitment laws is in inverse proportion to the quality of care. By and large, when there are decent hospitals, people seek admission. In any event, the terms in civil commitment statutes—*mental illness, need of treatment, danger to self or to others*—cannot be defined with the realistic precision necessary to allow application in a general fashion. They are as elastic as a rubber band. Sympathetic judges can (and do) interpret *dangerousness* when it is the only criterion for commitment to include the "gravely disabled" or those who lack the capacity to make an informed decision concerning treatment. In the case of physical illness, a physician cannot formulate a general rule stating when a person should be admitted to a hospital. Likewise, in the case of emotional dis-order, the decision has to be on a case-by-case basis, after consideration of the degree and kind of disability and the effect the individual will have on the people around him, as well as the resources available at the hospital. Many jurisdictions have enacted legislation that protects those responsible for committal if they acted in good faith and with reasonable care. The role of counsel is an important factor in the disposition of civil commitment cases—some lawyers take a best interest approach, while others litigate as though it were a criminal case (Minnesota and Wisconsin lead the country in the number of appellate decisions involving civil commitment).

Community Mental Health Centers

The emergence of the community mental health center (CMHC) laid the ground-work for a fourth revolution in the care of the mentally ill.[68] The CMHCs were designed to maintain patients in the community, thereby sparing them the alleg-edly dreadful consequences of institutionalization.[69] California's commitment law, the Lanterman-Petris-Short (LPS) Act,[70] was regarded as the "outstanding accom-plishment of the California legislature in its 1967 session."[71] It was designed to keep hospital population down by limiting commitment, thus saving liberty while saving money.[72] The LPS Act was hailed as a model to which all other states could look, and it was even called "the Magna Carta of the mentally ill."[73] The Act was designed to "protect the civil liberties of persons alleged to be mentally ill" and to accelerate the trend toward community treatment of the mentally ill as an alternative to hos-pitalization in remote state institutions.[74] Presumably, the mentally disturbed would be willing to come to the center with small problems before they became big ones, thus shifting the state's role from custodial to preventive.

President Kennedy was impressed with the 1963 Report of the Joint Commis-sion on Mental Illness and Health, *Action for Mental Health*. He endorsed it, and made funds available for its implementation.[75] The CMHC program had the sup-port of both the political right and left. The right wanted to close the mental hospitals to save money, and the left thought it was freeing prisoners of snake-pit psychiatric bureaucracy.[76]

At the time, there was little or no support among policymakers for mental hospitals. Many legislators and judges were persuaded by both the legal and psychiatric professions that mental hospitalization was both outdated and expensive. The state hospitals became expensive because they were no longer run by the patients but rather by the civil servants who were paid prevailing wages; the courts had held that patients could not work without compensation because that was interpreted as exploitation rather than rehabilitation.[77] The community mental health program was sold to legislators on the basis of saving money—and no argument is more appealing to a legislator's heart.[78] The legislators after whom the California commitment law was named (Lanterman-Petris-Short) were members of the Ways and Means Committee—a finance committee—and were, therefore, probably concerned about the state getting its money's worth.

The change in the treatment of mental patients precipitated the change in funding sources for mental health care facilities from the states to the federal government. In 1963, when CMHCs were first funded and deinstitutionalization had just begun, the total amount of public funds spent on the mentally ill was approximately a billion dollars per year. An estimated 96 percent of these funds came from the states. Following passage of the CMHC Act, the configuration of fiscal responsibility changed. The first change was a liberalization of rules making mentally ill individuals living in the community eligible for federal benefits under the Aid to the Disabled program. This program was subsequently incorporated into the federal Supplemental Security Income (SSI) program for individuals who did not qualify for Social Security benefits and into the Social Security Disability Insurance (SSDI) program for those who did qualify. In addition, a federal Food Stamps program, which could also be used by mentally ill individuals in the community, was enacted in 1966.[79]

At the same time, other federal programs were enacted that paid part of the costs for mentally ill patients in nursing homes and in the psychiatric units of general hospitals, but provided relatively little for such patients in state mental hospitals. These programs were Medicaid, enacted in 1965, and Medicare, in 1966. Medicaid and SSI require states to provide some funds to match the federal subsidy, whereas Medicare and SSDI do not have this requirement. Even with the matching funds, however, states saved at least 50 percent of the costs of inpatient and outpatient psychiatric care by the use of such federal programs. As a result of the shifting fund base, the 552,150 beds occupied nationwide in 1955 in state mental hospitals have been reduced by over 85 percent.[80]

Given that economics was the primary motivation in the deinstitutionalization of the mentally ill, the tax dollars not spent on hospitalization did not follow the patient into the community.[81] During these changes, no one seemed to ask about the community in mid-twentieth-century America. In places that might be considered a community, the reaction to the CMHC program has been expressed in an acronym, NIMBY (not in my backyard).[82] The mental hospital may not be a rose garden, but compared to urban America, it smells and looks a whole lot sweeter. Since the 1950s, the saying "Abandon hope, all ye who enter here," applies more appropriately to the inner cities than to the mental hospitals. The sprawl of the suburbs has encroached upon and enhanced the value of the land of the historic asylums resulting in their demolition.[83] The new domicile of mental patients is the jail or the abandoned inner city.

Ironically, when mental hospitals were known as asylums, the environmental pattern of the communities from which the individuals came was close-knit, small-scaled, and personalized. At one time, service and amenity facilities were in pedestrian proximity, but today, when the mental hospital is no longer regarded as an asylum, the environmental pattern of the so-called community is loose-knit, large-scaled, and depersonalized. Service and amenity facilities are only in automobile proximity. For survival, the denizen in today's so-called community must exercise his constitutional right to bear arms to negotiate the hazards of an expressway in order to get around.[84]

The grounds of any state hospital offer more freedom of movement than the streets of the inner cities of America.[85] In 1996, regarding the community placement of Mrs. Lake, the "bag lady," Judge Burger dissented, saying, "This city [the nation's capital] is hardly a safe place for able-bodied men, to say nothing of an infirm, senile, and disoriented woman to wander about with no protection except an identity tag advising police where to take her."[86] The state of the cities remains essentially the same but the process of deinstitutionalization proceeds apace.

In 1999, in *Olmstead v. L.C.*,[87] a divided U.S. Supreme Court held that under Title 2 of the Americans with Disabilities Act, institutionalized persons with mental disabilities have a right to be placed in a community setting if (1) the state's treatment professionals have determined that community placement is appropriate, (2) the transfer from institutional care to a less restrictive setting is not opposed by the affected individual, and (3) the placement can be reasonably accommodating, taking into account the resources available to the state and the needs of others with mental disabilities. Title 2 of the ADA states that "a public entity shall administer services, programs, and activities in the most integrated setting appropriate to the needs of qualified individuals with disabilities."[88]

The decision in *Olmstead* stemmed from a 1995 lawsuit brought by Lois Curtis and Elaine Wilson, two women with mild retardation and mental illness who had been housed in the Georgia Regional Hospital in Atlanta. The two women, known as L. C. and E. W., complained through a legal attorney that Georgia's failure to place them in community-based treatment was a violation of ADA. Appealing an adverse decision, Tommy Olmstead, then commissioner of Georgia's health department, asked the Supreme Court to decide whether the ADA requires states to provide patients with community mental health services when appropriate treatment can also be delivered in institutions.

With the aforementioned qualifications, the majority of the Court embraced the principle that undue institutionalization is a form of prohibited disability discrimination, but in any case a decision is iffy given the qualifications. The first qualification requires the reasonable exercise of professional judgement. The second qualification calls for a decision on placement by the affected individual, but if incompetent to make a decision, who, if anyone, is to make it? The third qualification provides that the states may take into account the "resources available" and the needs of others with mental disabilities when making decisions to deinstitutionalize.

Justice Kennedy, with Justice Breyer, while concurring in the judgment, commented that "[i]t would be unreasonable, it would be a tragic event ... were the

[ADA] to be interpreted so that States had some incentive, for fear of litigation, to drive those in need of medical care and treatment out of appropriate care and into settings with too little assistance and supervision." They quoted from Dr. E. Fuller Torrey's book *Out of the Shadows:* "For a substantial minority . . . deinstitutionalization has been a psychiatric Titanic. Their lives are virtually devoid of 'dignity' or 'integrity of body, mind, and spirit.' 'Self-determination' often means merely that the person has a choice of soup kitchens. The 'least restrictive setting' frequently turns out to be a cardboard box, a jail cell, or terror-filled existence plagued by both real and imaginary enemies."[89]

Mandatory outpatient treatment laws, which have been adopted in some forty-two states and the District of Columbia, would seem superfluous in light of the doctrine of least restrictive alternative. It strains logic to draw a distinction between hospitalization followed by conditional discharge and outpatient commitment straightaway.[90] The outpatient commitment law is usually enacted following a heinous crime committed by a mentally ill person who was not taking medication; the enactment of the law tends to put the public at ease. To implement the law, however, there is rarely any appropriation of new funds to pay the costs of intensive treatment. A subcommittee on mandatory outpatient treatment of the American Psychiatric Association Council on Psychiatry and Law has published a Resource Document that recommends mandatory outpatient treatment for those patients who are unlikely to comply with "needed treatment," even if these individuals would be deemed legally competent. According to the Resource Document, the enactment of mandatory outpatient treatment may prompt the legislature to provide the funding needed to provide enhanced community services for all patients, whether or not they are subject to a commitment.[91] That has not happened, and as a result, the laws are usually considered a dead letter. People resist medication that has adverse side effects, and who is to verify that the medication is taken?[92]

What will substitute for the structure and support afforded in the hospital? Medication? Actually, in appropriate cases, the ADA may be invoked to call for mental hospitalization as the reasonable accommodation for the individual.[93] Psychiatric medication was condemned when used in the hospital, but now its use is even greater in the outpatient setting. The medication is proclaimed to alleviate symptoms and to make possible resocialization, remotivation, rehabilitation, and reemployment. Actually, it may indeed reduce symptoms, but in fact it may not improve effectiveness in living. It causes sedation, and it causes weight gain with an increased risk of diabetes. It increases the rate of morbidity and mortality. Life span is reduced. Patients on medication typically die ten to fifteen years earlier. Due to relapse 300,000 patients are rehospitalized annually (it is a revolving door), and often with every relapse there is brain damage.

The CMHC was supposed to bring about an era without snake pits, without exploitation of patients, and without deprivation of liberty. Unfortunately, it has not turned out that way, and it has resulted in high costs to families and society as well as to the individual. As Los Angeles Superior Court Judge Eric Younger put it:

> Crazy people are now everywhere. Modern notions of civil liberties and fiscal considerations have combined to produce a population of very disturbed people in every city in America. The notion of local treatment alternatives for mentally incapacitated citizens is a cruel hoax. It is clear that

the vast majority of dangerously impaired people are out there on the streets.[94]

The shift from large institutions to nursing home care or other facilities is not deinstitutionalization but reinstitutionalization—a new custodialism replete with its own failures and shortcomings. In 1984, John Talbott, as president-elect of the American Psychiatric Association, pointed out that more than 50 percent of nursing homes were populated by persons with primary or secondary diagnoses of mental disorder; thousands of disturbed persons were wandering the urban landscape without housing; and legions were inhabiting welfare hotels, board and care homes, and adult residences.[95]

Many of the chronic mentally ill, who previously were housed in state hospitals and were working on hospital farms or in laundries, kitchens, and housekeeping services, functioned better, had greater feelings of self-esteem, and contributed more to their own existence than they do now in the so-called community system. Today, time and again, the complaints are countless about the mentally ill running amok in public housing or nursing homes.[96] Now these patients are on their own and they are given low priority in the CHMCs. A hospital bed often is not available when needed, and with increasing frequency these chronic, rejected, and displaced patients end up in jail. Years of progress in state hospital care have been reversed by penal custody, which has often become the treatment of choice.

Those who originally advocated deinstitutionalization and community treatment programs supported the claim that not only would their programs be better (more effective) but that CMHCs would cost less. Now, these advocates bemoan the lack of adequate funds and attribute their failures to that. Their vision of a system of clinics, halfway houses, day care centers, nursing homes, skilled nursing facilities, general hospital beds, and residential facilities would require, by far, a budget that would exceed previous costs.[97] The trend now is to permit for-profit companies to bid against public mental health agencies to provide care to the mentally ill and developmentally disabled and to drug and alcohol abusers.[98]

The asylum concept has been abandoned, and there is little or no mention of therapeutic community. The CMHC system is basically a nonmedical system, without commitment to research or interest in developmental and familial factors. Instead of treating the seriously ill, the CMHCs have turned into counseling centers for marital problems, existential crises, adolescent turmoil, and general unhappiness. The physical disorders of many patients go either unrecognized or untreated, which is evidenced by the fact that many CMHCs do not even have an examining room. Separating psyche from soma, they dichotomize the treatment of sick people. Dr. Donald G. Langsley, past president of the American Psychiatric Association, was prompted to ask, "Does the community mental health center treat patients?"[99]

Often to the dismay and fear of families, neighbors, and others in the community, thousands of psychotic individuals have been discharged from hospitals. In the oft-quoted words of Dr. Donald A. Treffert, these patients are left to "die with their rights on."[100] There are crippling limitations of mental illness that do not yield to current treatment methods. Apathy, withdrawal, submissiveness, and passivity may not be the result of hospitalization, as many have claimed in promoting deinstitutionalization, but symptoms of the illness itself. Patients with these conditions are pushed into communities less able to care for them than the hospitals.

The result is a situation where not only the rights of others are ignored but where patients' rights too have diminished.

In some instances, families, when assisted by the CMHC, have been helpful in the rehabilitation of the patient. Such success is more apt to be with the less severely ill and less disturbed individuals whose behavior is less bizarre and where contact with reality is less impaired. These patients do not impose as much of a burden on families as those who are much sicker, more regressed, more bizarre, more out of contact, and more out of control—but who, despite the severity of their symptoms, were discharged from hospitals because they were not considered homicidal or suicidal and presumably were able to take care of themselves.[101]

In cases where institutionalization is needed, admission to a private hospital under Medicare has often been denied by a hospital utilization review committee, contrary to medical opinion.[102] Other mentally ill patients who seek voluntary treatment in state hospitals may be turned away because there are no beds available. We have nearly come full circle to the days of Patrick Henry. When in 1775 he uttered the famous words, "Give me liberty or give me death," he had his wife, a mother of six, confined in a basement room—she was disturbed and disturbing, and he had no other recourse. His biographer has written:

> An insane asylum had just been established at Williamsburg, but it was hardly a place where Henry would have confined his wife. It does seem that she was kept in the basement with a Negro woman attendant—probably the kindest fate for the unhappy woman, considering the horrors in store for the mentally ill in the eighteenth century, whose families were unable to care for them.[103]

The family physician wrote, "Whilst his towering and master-spirit was arousing a nation to arms, his soul was bowed down and bleeding under the heaviest sorrows and personal distresses. His beloved companion had lost her reason, and could only be restrained from self-destruction by a strait-dress."[104]

Once again, for lack of care and treatment, families lock up a disturbed or disturbing member, or he wanders the streets. The Ik, the mountain people of north Uganda described by Colin Turnbull, put their members who are considered defective on mountain tops to be destroyed by the elements.[105] The state hospitals have been often maligned, but they filled a vital need. Even with the best community support system, there are individuals who need an asylum. The critics of the hospital system in the 1960s and 1970s were acclaimed, but by the end of the 1970s, the failures of deinstitutionalization had become all too apparent.

The families of chronic patients are protesting. In the 1950s and 1960s they were loosely organized, but in the 1970s they formed political action associations with chapters in virtually every state. They remain active in seeking legal reform to make involuntary commitment easier, and they want increased public funding and services for the mentally ill.[106] The overall population of state psychiatric hospitals have been reduced from 559,000 in 1955 to less than 80,000 today. In Michigan, fifteen of the state's twenty-one mental hospitals have been closed, with only one for children still operating.[107] With the virtual demise of public psychiatric hospitals as the caring and treating agency for individuals with debilitating mental illness, many of the seriously mentally ill now walk the streets or sit in jails. In the words of Dr. E. Fuller Torrey, it "mocks our pretense of being a civilized nation."[108]

Notes

1. See J. S. Bockhoven, *Moral Treatment in American Psychiatry* (New York: Springer, 1963); N. Dain, *Concepts of Insanity in the United States, 1789–1865* (New Brunswick, N.J.: Rutgers University Press, 1964); A. Deutsch, *The Mentally Ill in America: A History of Their Care and Treatment from Colonial Times* (New York: Doubleday, 1973); L. Gamwell & N. Tomes, *Madness in America* (Ithaca: Cornell University Press, 1995); D. J. Rothman, *Discovery of the Asylum: Social Order and Disorder in the New Republic* (Boston: Little, Brown, 1990); J. S. Bockhoven, "Moral Treatment in American Psychiatry," *J. Nervous & Mental Disease* 124 (1956): 167; E. T. Carlson & N. Dain, "The Psychotherapy That Was Moral Treatment," *Am J. Psychiatry* 117 (1960): 519.

2. R. B. Caplan, *Psychiatry and the Community in Nineteenth-Century America* (New York: Basic Books, 1969).

3. G. N. Grob, *Mental Institutions in America: Social Policy to 1875* (New York: Free Press, 1973); see also G. N. Grob, "Mental Health Policy in America: Myths and Realities," *Health Affairs* 11 (1992): 7.

4. R. Porter, *A Social History of Madness* (New York: Weidenfeld & Nicolson, 1987), p. 168.

5. C. Dickens, *American Notes and Pictures from Italy* (1842; New York: Oxford University Press, 1957), p. 28.

6. For example, Michigan's constitution, as revised, provides: "Institutions, programs and services for the care, treatment, education or rehabilitation of those inhabitants who are physically, mentally or otherwise seriously handicapped shall always be fostered and supported." Mich. Const., art. 7, sec. 8. The words "programs and services" were added in 1963.

7. C. Dickens, supra note 5.

8. R. B. Caplan, supra note 2.

9. G. N. Grob, *Mental Institutions in America: Social Policy to 1875* (New York: Free Press, 1973), p. 263.

10. B. Sapinsley, *The Private War of Mrs. Packard* (New York: Paragon House, 1991).

11. See S. J. Brakel, J. W. Parry, & B. Weiner, *The Mentally Disabled and the Law* (Chicago: American Bar Foundation, 3d ed. 1985); J. C. Mohr, *Doctors and the Law: Medical Jurisprudence in Nineteenth-Century America* (Baltimore: Johns Hopkins University Press, 1993).

12. E. Packard, "Modern Persecution or Insane Asylums Unveiled: My Abduction" (1869), in C. E. Goshen (ed.), *Documentary History of Psychiatry: A Source Book on Historical Principles* (New York: Philosophical Library, 1967), pp. 640–65; M. S. Himmelhoch & A. H. Shaffer, "Elizabeth Packard: Nineteenth Century Crusader for the Rights of Mental Patients," *J. Am. Studies* 13 (1979): 343. The writ of habeas corpus (brought by her son on her behalf) obtained her release not from the hospital, where she stayed three years, but from the bedroom where her husband confined her after her discharge.

13. A long, unsigned editorial in the October 1869 issue of the *American Journal of Insanity* (now the *American Journal of Psychiatry*), presumably written by the editor, Dr. John Gray, superintendent of the Utica (N.Y.) State Hospital, begins, "For the last two or three years, the state of Illinois has been singularly under the influence of a handsome and talkative crazy woman and of a Legislature prompted by her to be crazy on at least one point," and "an attractive person and a double-springed tongue gave force and persuasion to the direful romance of this fascinating woman, and she was successful enough, by her feminine arts, to bewitch a whole legislature." Quoted in L. Ozarin, "Pioneer for Patients' Rights," *Psychiatric News*, Dec. 7, 2001, p. 40. She published three books which had extensive circulation and sales. Copies of the books are in the APA Library Rare Books Room.

14. See K. M. Bowman & B. Engle, "Sexual Psychopath Laws," in R. Slovenko (ed.), *Sexual Behavior and the Law* (Springfield, Ill.: Thomas, 1965), p. 757.

15. E. Goffman, *Asylums* (New York: Doubleday, 1961). The logical corollary to Goffman's conclusion that most of the patients' behavior was a reaction to being hospitalized, not a result of their illnesses, was that one needed only to open the gates of the hospital and let the patients go free, no strings (or medication) attached, and they would live happily ever after. Calling Goffman's book one of the worst books on schizophrenia, Dr. E. Fuller Torrey, clinical and research psychiatrist specializing in schizophrenia, says that one only wishes today that Goffman could be given a mattress under a bridge or freeway in any American city so that he could observe how deinstitutionalization has worked out. E. F. Torrey, *Surviving Schizophrenia* (New York: HarperCollins, 4th ed. 2001), p. 428.

16. K. Kesey, *One Flew Over the Cuckoo's Nest* (New York: Viking Press, 1962). Made into a popular movie, Kesey's *One Flew Over the Cuckoo's Nest* was a fictional version of Goffman's *Asylums*. (Russian President Putin called the film his favorite.) Kesey, working for a time as a night attendant on the psychiatric ward of a veterans' hospital, became convinced that the patients were locked into a system that was the very opposite of therapeutic. The book describes a man called McMurphy who feigns mental illness to evade a prison sentence, but whose presence proves so cheering to the inmates and so disruptive to the regime of the mental hospital that he is lobotomized. Kesey became well-known not only because of his book but also as the hero of Tom Wolfe's famous nonfiction book about psychedelic drugs, *The Electric Kool-Aid Acid Test*. Kesey, with a group of like-minded friends, self-styled Merry Pranksters, went around the country in a vintage school bus decorated with polychromatic swirls intended to evoke the effects of LSD. Kesey's life is depicted in an obituary by Nicholas Foulkes, "Ken Kesey," *Financial Times*, Nov. 17–18, 2001, p. xxvi, and also by Christopher Lehmann-Haupt, "Ken Kesey, Author of 'Cuckoo's Nest' Who Defined the Psychedelic Era, Is Dead at 66," *New York Times*, Nov. 11, 2001, p. 34. See also J. Leland, "Psychodelia's Middle-Aged Head Trip," *New York Times*, Nov. 18, 2001, WK-2; Editorial, "The Prankster's Death," *New York Times*, Nov. 13, 2001, p. 24. Torrey calls Kesey's book another of the worst books on schizophrenia, and he observes, "Kesey was a guru of psychedelic drugs at the time, and his story also has an hallucinatory ring to it." E. F. Torrey, supra note 15, p. 429.

17. T. S. Szasz, *The Manufacture of Madness* (New York: Harper & Row, 1970). Torrey opines that Szasz has produced more erudite nonsense on the subject of serious mental illness than any writer alive. He wonders whether Szasz has ever seen a patient with schizophrenia. E. F. Torrey, supra note 15, p. 431.

18. T. S. Szasz, *Psychiatric Slavery* (New York: Free Press, 1977). On the occasion of Dr. Thomas Szasz's eightieth birthday, on April 15, 2000, Dr. Abraham Halpern commented, "Indoctrinated by centuries-long teachings that involuntary hospitalization was warranted to isolate or treat persons who were believed to be mentally ill, psychiatrists failed to appreciate the primacy of freedom as a value to be prized in a democratic society. The influence of Thomas Szasz on psychiatrists over the past 37 years has been enormous and has led to the abandonment of involuntary hospitalization of hundreds of thousands of non-dangerous persons seeking psychological help, and to a meaningful respect for fundamental human rights in many countries, especially in the United States."

19. R. J. Isaac & V. C. Armat, *Madness in the Streets* (New York: Free Press, 1990).

20. Jackson v. Indiana, 406 U.S. 715, 737 (1972).

21. Vitek v. Jones, 445 U.S. 480 (1980).

22. New York: Harcourt, Brace & Jovanovich, 1974.

23. Ibid., pp. xi–xix, at xvii.

24. Ibid., p. 215.

25. L. R. Frank, "An Interview with Bruce Ennis," in *Madness Network News Reader* (1974), p. 162. See also C. Steir (ed.), *Blue Jolts: True Stories from the Cuckoo's Nest* (Washington, D.C.: New Republic Books, 1978). In this compilation of stories from the voluminous literature on psychiatric hospitalization, famous writers, poets, and politicians—including Seymour Krim, Louise Bogan, and Tennessee Williams—Russian dissidents, and ordinary individuals describe an agonizing process of admission to, treatment in, and release from a mental hospital. They address the fundamental concerns of mental health activists: What is sanity and what is madness? Do psychiatrists have the right to label a person "insane"? What civil liberties do patients have? Can mental illness be cured by those methods applied to physical disease?

26. G. N. Grob, *Mental Institutions in America: Social Policy to 1875* (New York: Free Press, 1973). To add to the irony, Bruce Ennis later became legal counsel for the American Psychological Association, and Joel Klein, who was allied with Ennis in the Mental Health Law Project, became counsel for the American Psychiatric Association. Thus, in a turnaround, these outspoken attorneys found themselves responding to their own allegations. One might say that Ennis and Klein created their own jobs.

27. *Constitutional Rights of the Mentally Ill*, Hearings before the Subcomm. on Constitutional Rights of Comm. on the Judiciary, 87th Cong., 1st Sess. (1961). Allegedly unjustified hospitalization came to be called *railroading* following the case of Mrs. Packard, who was put on a train when sent to the hospital.

28. R. S. Rock, M. A. Jacobson, & R. M. Janopaul, *Hospitalization and Discharge of the Mentally Ill* (Chicago: University of Chicago Press, 1968), p. 77.

29. G. N. Grob, supra note 24; see also G. N. Grob "Rediscovering Asylums: The Unhistorical History of the Mental Hospital," *Hastings Center Rep.* 7 (1977): 4, 33.

30. In Lessard v. Schmidt, 349 F.Supp. 1078 (E.D. 1972), the court prohibited commitment unless the person is found to be dangerous "based upon findings of a recent overt act, attempt or threat to do substantial harm," and it called for the full panoply of criminal justice procedure and rules of evidence in civil commitment. See B. A. Weiner & D. M. Wettstein, *Legal Issues in Mental Health Care* (New York: Plenum, 1993); Symposium, "Civil Commitment," *Behav. Sci. & Law* 6 (1988): 3–148.

31. In a publication in 1978, Dr. Seymour Halleck wrote:

> Psychiatrists in most states are now required to present evidence of the patient's dangerousness to self or others before initiating commitment. Dangerousness to self is difficult enough to predict; dangerousness to others is almost impossible. The new legal approach to civil commitment has forced us to pretend an illegitimate expertise. We cannot predict dangerousness and we cannot even give reasonable probability statements as to the likelihood of dangerousness. As a result, much psychiatric energy is devoted to obsessing about predictions we are incapable of making. The new laws also hurt patients. In most jurisdictions the new laws are not substantial enough to allow for the involuntary confinement and treatment of an individual who is desperately ill and who would respond to treatment; such a patient cannot be treated because there is no proof of dangerousness to self or others.

S. L. Halleck, "Psychiatry and Social Control: Two Contradictory Scenarios," in S. Smith (ed.), *The Human Mind Revisited* (New York: International Universities Press, 1978), p. 433. Though the observation was made in 1978, it remains the state of affairs notwithstanding the development of risk-assessment scales in recent years. In their book *Violent Offenders: Appraising and Managing Risk* (Washington, D.C.: American Psychological Association, 1999), V. L. Quinsey, G. T. Harris, M. E. Rice, and C. A. Cormier propose the "complete replacement" of clinical assessments of dangerousness with actuarial methods (actuarial instruments are created from empirically established risk factors such as past history of violence, psychopathic tendencies, prior arrest). Others argue that research to date has not demonstrated that actuarial methods of risk assessment are superior to clinical methods, because it is very difficult to meaningfully compare clinical and actuarial assessments of dangerousness. Actuarial or statistical data is for actuarial or collective use, whereas individual assessment calls for an evaluation of the individual. Thus, certain medication may be appropriate in general for certain disorders but it may vary for the individual. See T. R. Litwack, "Actuarial versus Clinical Assessments of Dangerousness," *Psychology, Public Policy, and Law* 7 (2001): 409. The term *dangerousness* is taken to include four elements: (1) magnitude of harm, (2) probability that harm will occur, (3) frequency with which harm will occur, and (4) imminence of harm. *Magnitude of harm* is further divided into harm to the person (further subdivided into physical and mental harm) and harm to property. A. D. Brooks, *Law, Psychiatry, and the Mental Health System* (Boston: Little, Brown, 1974), pp. 680–82. In regard nonphysical danger to others, a few states explicitly permit commitment of a person who may cause emotional or psychic harm to others. See, e.g., Iowa Code Ann. 229.1 (2)(b). Kenneth Donaldson's delusions caused psychic pain to his parents, and he was committed and was institutionalized for fifteen years. O'Connor v. Donaldson, 422 U.S. 563 (1975). Sexual harassment is now a crime and a basis for a lawsuit. See, e.g., Vinson v. Superior Court, 43 Cal.3d 833, 740 P.2d 404, 230 Cal. Rptr. 292 (1987). Some states also explicitly include harm to property as a commitment criterion. A mentally ill person who threatens to kill pets belonging to others could face retaliation, and thus the danger to self criterion under the commitment statute would be satisfied. However, the court in Suzuki v. Yuen, 617 F.2d 173 (9th Cir. 1980), said, "Under the current Hawaii definition of 'danger to property,' a person could be committed if he threatened to shoot a trespassing dog. The state's interest in protecting animals must be outweighed by the individual's interest in personal liberty." In regard frequency of harm, no state statute explicitly requires that the fact finder assess the frequency of the anticipated harm, perhaps because frequency is an integral part of magnitude of harm analysis. See C. J. Fredrick (ed.), *Dangerous Behavior: A Problem in Law and Mental Health*

(Washington, D.C.: Govt. Ptg. Off., 1978); G. H. Morris, "Defining Dangerousness: Risking a Dangerous Definition," *J. Contemp. Legal Issues* 10 (1999): 61. On assessment of violence, See J. Monhan & H. J. Steadman (eds.), *Violence and Mental Disorder: Developments in Risk Assessment* (Chicago: University of Chicago Press, 1994); K. Tardiff, *Concise Guide to the Assessment and Management of Violent Patients* (Washington, D.C.: American Psychiatric Press, 1989); G. T. Harris & M. E. Rice, "Risk Appraisal and Management of Violent Behavior," *Psychiatric Serv.* 48 (1997): 1168; V. A. Hiday, "The Social Context of Mental Illness and Violence," *J. Health Soc. Behav.* 36 (1995): 122.

32. Mass. Gen. Laws Ann., ch. 123, sec. 1 (West Supp. 1999). See also N.Y. Ment. Hyg. L., sec. 9.01 (McKinney 1996).

33. The doctrine developed originally in cases involving the First Amendment. See Shelton v. Tucker, 364 U.S. 479 (1960). See the discussion in chapter 2, on right to treatment and right to refuse treatment.

34. In re J.K., 599 N.W.2d 337 (N.D. 1999).

35. Lake v. Cameron, 364 F.2d 657 (D.C. Cir. 1966).

36. Ibid. at 660. The court remanded the case to the lower court for consideration under the least restrictive means analysis. Id. at 661. See also Lessard v. Schmidt, 349 F.Supp. 1078 (E.D. 1972).

37. 441 U.S. 418 (1979).

38. Ibid. at 427.

39. Ibid. at 428–31.

40. Ibid. at 429.

41. Ibid. at 433. See In re J.K., 599 N.W.2d 337 (N.D. 1999); see also R. Slovenko, "Should Psychiatrists Honor Bazelon or Burger?" *J. Psychiatry & Law* 20 (1952): 635.

42. 494 U.S. 113 (1990).

43. Ibid. at 133–34.

44. Professor Bruce Winick argues that "a low standard of competency is all that should be required. As long as the patient understands that the facility he is seeking admission to is a psychiatric hospital, that he will receive care and treatment there, and that release is not automatic, but can occur if he should change his mind and that in such an event he can obtain help from any staff member to gain his release, he should be deemed competent." B. Winick, "Competency to Consent to Voluntary Hospitalization: A Therapeutic Jurisprudence Analysis of Zinermon v. Burch," *Int'l J. Law & Psychiat.* 14 (1997): 169.

In the event of guardianship, a guardian may not under prevailing law, with the exception of a couple of states, admit the ward into a mental hospital. A guardian is not allowed to bypass the commitment law. Ordinarily, a guardian has the same powers, rights, and duties respecting the ward that a parent has regarding a child. Mich. Comp. Laws Ann. 700.455. A proposal would authorize a limited guardian or other independent decision maker to make decisions about hospitalization for the incompetent person. J. C. Beck & J. W. Parry, "Incompetence, Treatment Refusal, and Hospitalization," *Bull. Am. Acad. Psychiat. & Law* 20 (1992): 261. See J. G. Malcom, "Informed Consent in the Practice of Psychiatry," in R. I. Simon (ed.), *Review of Clinical Psychiatry and the Law* (Washington, D.C.: American Psychiatric Press, 1992), vol. 3, p. 223, 244; R. B. Lacoursiere, "What Became of Darrell Burch," *Newsletter of Am. Acad. Psychiat. & Law* 17 (Sept. 1992): 61.

45. 71 F.3d 292 (8th Cir. 1995).

46. Suit was brought under the Civil Rights Act, 42 U.S.C., sec. 1983.

47. 71 F.3d at 294.

48. 489 U.S. 189 (1989).

49. Ibid. at 200. In Wilson v. Formigoni, 832 F.Supp. 1152 (N.D.Ill. 1993), the court upheld a mental patient's claim that the failure to have her involuntarily committed harmed her by preventing her inclusion in due process protections. She was deemed incompetent to make a decision to remain voluntarily.

50. Supra note 10.

51. *The Mentally Ill in America: A History of Their Care and Treatment from Colonial Times* (New York: Doubleday, 1937), pp. 424–25.

52. Carter v. Landy, 163 Ga. App. 509, 295 S.E.2d 177 (1982); Note, "Civil Liability of Persons Participating in the Detention of the Mentally Ill," *Wash. U.L. Q.* 1966: 193. Texas law provides: "All persons acting in good faith, reasonably and without negligence in con-

nection with examination, certification, apprehension, custody, transportation, detention, treatment or discharge of any person, or in the performance of any other act required or authorized by [the Mental Health Code], shall be free from all liability, civil or criminal, by reason of such action." Tex. Rev. Civ. Stat. Ann., art. 5547-18. In James v. Brown, 637 S.W.2d 914 (Tex. 1982), a suit for damages against three psychiatrists arising out of an involuntary hospitalization, the plaintiff alleged libel, negligent misdiagnosis–medical malpractice, false imprisonment, and malicious prosecution. The Texas Supreme Court rejected a blanket immunity from all civil liability for mental health professionals testifying in mental health proceedings. The court declined to allow a defamation claim for the testimony prior to the hearing. The court noted that "[the plaintiff] is not prevented from recovering from the doctors for negligent misdiagnosis–medical malpractice merely because their diagnoses were later communicated to a court in the due course of judicial proceedings."

53. I. Ray, "The Confinement of the Insane," *Am. L. Rev.* 3 (1869): 193.

54. For example, a Connecticut law adopted in 1702 provided:

> [W]hen and so often as it shall happen, any person to be naturally wanting of understanding, so as to be incapable to provide him, or herself; or by the Providence of God, shall fall into Distraction and become Non Compos Mentis, and no Relations Appear, that will undertake the care of providing for them; or that stand in so near a degree, as that by law they may be compelled thereto; in every such case the selectmen or overseers of the poor of the Town, or Peculiar, where such person was born, or is by law an Inhabitant, be, and hereby are empowered and required, to take effectual care and make necessary Provision, for the relief, support, and safety, of such impotent or distracted person.

Acts and Law of His Majesties Colony of Connecticut in New England (1702).

55. The Soviet Union imposed its model on its satellite countries. Today, in a different way, the United States seeks to turn all countries into its image. Various agencies of the government promote its justice procedures (such as the adversary system and jury trial) and civil commitment procedures. Mikhail Gorbachev comments, "Today the whole world is watching as Washington attempts to impose on others its model of how to approach major political, economic, and social problems. . . . But to copy everything that is done across the ocean is unproductive and dangerous. . . . In each country, each society, at any given time, takes on its own particular features, its own special twists and turns." M. Gorbachev, *On My Country and the World* (New York: Columbia University Press, 2000), pp. 45, 51.

See D. N. Weisstub & J. Arboleda-Florez, "An International Perspective on Mental Health Law Reform," in A. Okasha, J. Arboleda-Florez, & N. Sattorius (eds.), *Ethics, Culture and Psychiatry* (Washington, D.C.: American Psychiatric Press, 2000). See also T. L. Friedman, *The Lexus and the Olive Tree* (New York: Farrar Straus Giroux, 1999); J. H. Langbein, "Cultural Chauvinism in Comparative Law," *Cardozo J. Int. & Comp. L.* 5 (1997): 41.

56. See S. V. Polubinskaya, "Law and Psychiatry in Russia: Looking Backward and Forward," in L. E. Frost & R. J. Bonnie (eds.), *The Evolution of Mental Health Law* (Washington, D.C.: American Psychological Association, 2001), pp. 113–25.

57. Recently Dr. A. L. Halpern observed, "China has many work camps and prisons in which to incarcerate political dissidents and Falun Gong practitioners. But the Chinese government also strives to demonstrate that ideological and philosophical positions not in accord with Communist Party doctrine stem from irrationality or psychosis. As was the case in the former Soviet Union, the mechanism used to attain this objective is involuntary hospitalization of non-mentally-ill political protesters considered to be 'dangerous.'" A. L. Halpern, "Abuse in China" (ltr.), *New York Times*, Feb. 25, 2001, p. WK-14.

58. Quoted in *New York Post*, Dec. 8, 1973, p. 4. See also G. M. Carstairs, "Revolutions and the Rights of Man," *Am. J. Psychiatry* 134 (1977): 979.

59. A. B. Johnson, *Out of Bedlam: The Truth About Deinstitutionalization* (New York: Basic Books, 1991); R. Slovenko, "Criminal Justice Procedures in Civil Commitment," *Wayne L. Rev.* 24 (1977): 1.

60. Cover Story, *Itogi* (Russian weekly), July 21, 1998, pp. 38–48.

61. Failure to follow the statutorily prescribed involuntary commitment standards is evidence of negligence for a fact finder to consider, and not negligence per se. See Fair Oaks Hosp. v. Pocrass, 628 A.2d 829 (N.J. Super. 1993); Moore v. Wyoming Medical Center, 825

F.Supp. 1531 (D.Wyo. 1993). In some countries, and also in some states in the United States, legislation protects persons responsible for the committal if they acted in good faith. The law in Australia is discussed in A. Alston, "Wrongful Committal," *Psychiatry, Psychology & Law* 7 (2000): 71. The law on psychotherapist-patient testimonial privilege protecting patient confidentiality has an exception in proceedings for hospitalization in the event the therapist, in the course of diagnosis or treatment, finds that the patient is in need of hospitalization. See, e.g., Mich. Rules of Evidence, Rule 504(d)(2). In a controversial opinion, the Michigan Court of Appeals held that the issue of whether disclosures by a therapist to a court-appointed examiner were reasonably necessary to protect the interests of the patient or others is one for the jury; hence the court held that the therapist is not entitled to summary disposition. Saur v. Probes, 190 Mich. App. 636 (1991). Texas law provides that "*[a]ll persons* acting in good faith, reasonably and without negligence in connection with examination, certification, apprehension, custody, transportation, detention, treatment or discharge of any person, or in the performance of any other act required or authorized by [the Mental Health Code], shall be free from all liability, civil or criminal, by reason of such action" (emphasis added). Tex. Rev. Civ. Stat. Ann., art. 5547-18. Yet there is a caveat: good faith is not enough in the case of negligent diagnosis. In James v. Brown, 637 S.W.2d 914 (Tex. 1982), the Texas Supreme Court held that a patient is not prevented from recovering from the doctors for negligent misdiagnosis (medical malpractice) merely because their diagnoses were later communicated to a court in the due course of judicial proceedings. 637 S.W.2d at 917.

It is generally recommended that psychiatrists not certify their own patients, but there may not be a reasonable option. For a commitment there must be a petitioner and a certifying physician. Potentially a psychiatrist can fill one role or the other (but not both). The *petitioner* is the person who requests that the patient be committed and has the task of explaining to the court (in writing and in testimony) what he has seen the person do or has heard the person say that leads him to believe the patient is dangerous or unable to take care of himself. The petitioner is a fact witness and cannot give an opinion, but this can get fuzzy if the treating physician is the petitioner. Very often the petitioner is a family member or a police officer. In the next step, a psychiatrist or psychologist certifies the need for treatment (a standard form is usually used). The certifying physician or psychologist is fulfilling the role of an expert and, as such, can give opinions in court. An expert may rely on records or statements of others as well as the interview or first-hand observation of the patient. A "peace officer" (a police officer in many cases) on the basis of a petition and certification can take the person to a hospital. In the case of an involuntary admission it is not recommended that family members bring the individual to a hospital, given the potential for violence and injury.

In Michigan as well as in many other states there are one or more bases to request commitment of a mentally ill individual: (1) danger to self, (2) danger to others, (3) unable to care for self, and (4) does not understand the need for treatment. Michigan defines *mental illness* as "a substantial disorder of thought or mood." Unlike many other states, Michigan legislation excludes substance abuse, dementia, personality disorders, or epilepsy, but these disorders or conditions are sometimes accompanied by conditions that fall under the definition (such as a psychotic episode, a brief but deep suicidal depressive state in someone with impulse control problems). See Mich. Comp. Laws Ann. 330.1400a; P. Campbell, "Commitment Process 101," *Mich. Psychiatric Society Newsletter* 33 (Nov./Dec. 2001): 9. The definition of *mental illness* in the legal system depends on the context. The two most common situations in which a determination of mental illness is necessary are insanity defenses and civil commitment proceedings. For the criminal context, see volume 1, part 3.

62. W. Gardner, C. W. Lidz, S. K. Hoge, J. Monahan, M. M. Eisenberg, N. F. Bennett, E. P. Mulvey, & L. H. Roth, "Patients' Revisions of Their Beliefs about the Need for Hospitalization," *Am. J. Psychiatry* 156 (1999): 1385; A. Wertheimer, "A Philosophical Examination of Coercion for Mental Health Issues," *Behav. Sci. & Law* 11 (1993): 239. The civil commitment hearing is defended in B. J. Winick, "Therapeutic Jurisprudence and the Civil Commitment Hearing," *J. Contemp. Legal Issues* 10 (1999): 37.

63. French v. Blackburn, 428 F.Supp. 1351 (M.D. N.C. 1977); Logan v. Arafeh, 246 F.Supp. 1265 (D.Conn. 1972), *aff'd*, Briggs v. Arafeh, 411 U.S. 911 (1973).

64. Nationally, almost 10 percent of police calls and 10 percent of arrests involve persons with flagrant mental disorders. Despite the frequency of contact with emotionally disturbed persons, police officers often lack adequate training on how to deal safely and effectively with

such individuals. According to the *Los Angeles Times*, the Los Angeles Police Department fatally shot twenty-five mentally disordered individuals in the previous six years. Many of these incidents are written off as "a nut with a knife" or "suicide by cop." J. Meyer & S. Berry, "Lack of Training Blamed in Slayings of Mentally Ill," *Los Angeles Times*, Nov. 8, 1999, p. 1. The police picked up a naked senior citizen (who turned out to be Ernest Hemingway's son) clutching spike-heeled shoes, a black velvet dress, shredded pantyhose, and flowered thong underwear and booked him on charges of indecent exposure and resisting arrest without violence. Five days later, while awaiting a court hearing, he was found dead in his cell of a heart attack. K. Hubbard, "Papa's Boy," *People*, Oct. 22, 2001, p. 131. A symposium on police encounters with persons with mental illness appears in *J. Psychiatry & Law* 28 (2000): 325–47. See also S. S. Janus, B. E. Bess, J. J. Cadden, & H. Greenwald, "Training Police Officers to Distinguish Mental Illness," *Am. J. Psychiatry* 137 (1980): 228; R. D. Miller, "Suicide by Cop and Criminal Responsibility," *J. Psychiatry & Law*, 29 (2001): 295.

65. Congress recently approved funds for pilot programs that emphasize supervision and treatment rather than prison sentences for the mentally ill who commit nonviolent crimes. It provides up to $10 million a year for four years for mental health court programs that give specialized training to law enforcement and court personnel and that foster voluntary treatment that carries the possibility of the dismissal of charges or reduced sentences. Representative Ted Strickland, the main sponsor of the House version, said that as a former consulting psychologist at an Ohio correctional facility he had seen how prisons have become "America's new mental asylums." Senator Mike DeWine, who sponsored the bill in the Senate, said the criminal justice system has been forced into the role of a surrogate mental health care provider, with 16 percent of all inmates in America's state prisons and local jails suffering from mental illness. There are 600,000 to 700,000 seriously mentally ill individuals booked into local jails every year, he noted. J. Abrams, "Congress Approves New Treatment Program for Mentally Ill Criminals" (Associated Press news release), *Detroit Legal News*, Oct. 27, 2000, p. 18. Several mental health courts—modeled on drug courts—have been established but their use is problematical. A. Watson, D. Luchins, P. Hanrahan, M. J. Heyrman, & A. Lurigio, "Mental Health Court: Promises and Limitations," *J. Am. Acad. Psychiatry & Law* 28 (2000): 476.

66. A. J. Lurigio, J. R. Fallon, & J. Dincin, "Helping the Mentally Ill in Jails Adjust to Community Life: A Description of a Postrelease ACT Program and Its Clients," *Int'l J. Offender Therapy & Comparative Criminology* 44 (2000): 532. In August 1999, lawyers representing seven New York City inmates filed a class-action lawsuit, known as *Brad H. et al. v. City of New York*, that challenged the city's practice of not providing discharge planning for mentally ill inmates. L. Lipton, "Suit Seeks Mandatory Discharge Planning for New York Jail Inmates," *Psychiatric News*, Oct. 6, 2000, p. 8.

67. Some forty states and the District of Columbia have adopted outpatient commitment laws. Outpatient commitment does not guarantee patients' compliance with taking medication, but it is considered that it improves patients who are discharged from general hospital psychiatric units but who the treatment team knows will probably not be compliant with their medication and other treatment modalities. M. Kohl, "New York State Moves toward Involuntary Residential Commitment of the Mentally Ill," *Psychiatric Times*, Sept. 1999, p. 30. See R. Miller, *Involuntary Civil Commitment of the Mentally Ill in the Post-Reform Era* (Springfield, Ill.: Thomas, 1987). Outpatient commitment is related to the old idea of paroling mentally ill patients from the hospital, or giving them trial discharges. Patients unable to manage in the community would be recalled to the hospital without further legal proceedings. In its new guise, it is not limited to former inpatients but can serve as a disposition of choice at a commitment hearing (under the theory of least restrictive alternative), but only a few states use it with any frequency, due to the lack of clinical and administrative structures to carry it out, judicial unfamiliarity with the concept, the absence of discrete criteria for it, and the absence of enforcement mechanisms. T. G. Gutheil & P. S. Appelbaum, *Clinical Handbook of Psychiatry and the Law* (Philadelphia: Lippincott Williams & Wilkins, 3d ed. 2000), p. 58.

68. See P. S. Appelbaum, *Almost a Revolution: Mental Health Law and the Limits of Change* (New York: Oxford University Press, 1994); id., "Almost a Revolution: An International Perspective on the Law of Involuntary Commitment," *J. Am. Acad, Psychiatry & Law* 25 (1997): 135; S. Cleveland et al., "Do Dangerousness-Oriented Commitment Laws Restrict Hospitalization of Patients Who Need Treatment? A Test," *Hosp. & Community Psychiatry* 40 (1989): 266.

69. L. L. Bachrach, *Deinstitutionalization: An Analytical Review and Sociological Perspective* (Washington, D.C.: U.S. Govt. Ptg. Off., 1976). In *Almost a Revolution: Mental Health Law and the Limits of Change* (New York: Oxford University Press, 1994), Dr. Paul Appelbaum contends that "highly restrictive [hospital] admission policies" and "the rapid discharge of unstable persons" resulted not from changes in the law, but rather from policies of "indiscriminate deinstitutionalization." Appelbaum describes the converging forces that led to a shift from *parens patriae* to police power as the basis of commitment: the questioning of the factual basis of mental illness, focus on deinstitutionalization due to financial constraints and availability of alternative treatments, and the civil rights movement.

70. Calif. Welfare & Institutions Code, ch. 1, sec. 5000. See F. W. Miller, R. O. Dawson, G. E. Dix, & R. I. Parnas, *The Mental Health Process* (Mineola, N.Y.: Foundation Press, 1976); R. J. Isaac & V. C. Armat, supra note 19, p. 121.

71. R. J. Isaac & V. C. Armat, supra note 19, p. 121.

72. Ibid., p. 15.

73. Ibid., p. 121.

74. Ibid.

75. H. R. Lamb (ed.), *The Homeless Mentally Ill* (Washington, D.C.: American Psychiatric Press, 1984).

76. Ibid.

77. R. Cancro, "Functional Psychoses and the Conceptualization of Mental Illness," in R. W. Menninger & J. C. Nemiah (eds.), *American Psychiatry after World War II* (Washington, D.C.: American Psychiatric Press, 2000), pp. 413–29.

78. See E. F. Torrey, *Nowhere to Go: The Tragic Odyssey of the Homeless Mentally Ill* (New York: Harper & Row, 1988).

79. Ibid.

80. G. N. Grob, "Mental Health Policy in Late Twentieth-Century America," in R. W. Menninger & J. C. Nemiah (eds.), *American Psychiatry after World War II* (Washington, D.C.: American Psychiatric Press, 2000).

81. M. J. Mills & B. D. Cummings, "Deinstitutionalization Reconsidered," *Int'l J. L. & Psychiatry* 5 (1982): 271.

82. S. Sandler, "The Westside Has Lost Patience," *New York Times*, Nov. 7, 1992, p. 15.

83. The large state hospitals, built in the nineteenth century in rural settings, are now being demolished and replaced by resorts. With the spread of the population to the suburbs, the land is prime location. The *New York Times* describes the $155 million resort constructed on a site once occupied by a mental hospital overlooking the Choptank River in Maryland: "The site is the result of the planning of the original 1915 Eastern Shore Hospital, which continued the philosophy of the late nineteenth century that asylums should be built in rural, pastoral settings so patients could enjoy fresh air and a park-like setting. The complex of more than 20 buildings, built in the Tudor Revival style, was demolished in 2000." Said the general manager of the resort built on the site, "You can't find land like this anymore." C. Belfoure, "A Resort Replaces a Hospital in Maryland," *New York Times*, Jan. 6, 2002, p. SP-12. See also A. Beam, *Gracefully Insane: The Rise and Fall of America's Premier Mental Hospital* (New York: Public Affairs, 2001).

84. R. Slovenko, "Mobilopathy," *J. Psychiatry & Law* 12 (1984): 293. "Expecting the chronically ill patient to use the current mental health system is like expecting a paraplegic to use stairs." J. Halpern et al., *The Illusion of Deinstitutionalization* (Denver: Denver Research Institute, 1978).

85. R. Slovenko, "Crime Revisited," *J. Psychiatry & Law* 18 (1990): 485.

86. See Lake v. Cameron, supra note 35.

87. 119 S. Ct. 2176 (1999).

88. 42 U.S.C., sec. 12101. See S. Stefan, "The Americans with Disabilities Act and Mental Health Law: Issues for the Twenty-First Century," *J. Contemp. Legal Issues* 10 (1999): 131.

89. 119 S. Ct. at 2191. See S. Fishman, "*Olmstead v. Zimring*: Unnecessary Institutionalization Constitutes Discrimination under the Americans with Disabilities Act," *J. Health Care Law & Policy* 3 (2000): 430. See also N. K. Rhoden, "The Limits of Liberty: Deinstitutionalization, Homelessness, and Libertarian Theory," *Emory L.J.* 31 (1982): 375.

90. Professor Michael Perlin contends that the least restrictive alternative, the roots of which justified outpatient commitment, was originally seen as a way of limiting the numbers of persons under state control in public psychiatric hospitals but is now frequently suggested

as a means of exerting control over more individuals in community settings. Address at the annual meeting of the Association of American Law Schools on January 6, 2001, in San Francisco. Studies have shown that the clientele of community treatment centers include few chronic patients and is comprised mostly of a new class of patients who formerly either did not seek treatment or received it from the private sector. See R. D. Miller, "Clinical and Legal Aspects of Civil Commitment," in C. P. Ewing (ed.), *Psychology, Psychiatry, and the Law: A Clinical and Forensic Handbook* (Sarasota, Fla.: Professional Resource Exchange, 1985), pp. 149–80. See also K. Kress, "An Argument for Assisted Outpatient Treatment for Persons with Serious Mental Illness Illustrated with Reference to a Proposed Statute for Iowa," *Iowa L. Rev.* 85 (2000): 1269.

91. J. B. Gerbasi, R. J. Bonnie, & R. L. Binder, "Resource Document on Mandatory Outpatient Treatment," *J. Am. Acad. Psychiatry & Law* 28 (2000): 127. Stirring the most controversy is the stance of the American Psychiatric Association on reserving mandatory outpatient treatment for those who meet the longstanding dangerousness measure. The Resource Document broadens the criteria defining which patients are eligible for outpatient commitment to include those who simply are "unlikely to seek or comply with needed treatment unless a court enters an order." "Resource Document on Mandatory Outpatient Treatment Reviewed," *Psychiatric News,* Oct. 6, 2000, p. 16. The American Psychiatric Association has also published a special section on outpatient treatment in the March 2001 issue of its *Psychiatric Services.* An additional resource is a RAND study, completed for the California legislature, "The Effectiveness of Involuntary Outpatient Treatment." M. S. Ridgely, R. Borum, & J. Petrila (Santa Monica, Cal.: RAND, 2001).

In a challenge to New York's outpatient commitment law (known as "Kendra's Law"), in *Urcuyo v. James D.* and *Trachtenberg v. Jonathon S.,* King's County New York Supreme Court Justice Anthony Cutrona upheld the law on constitutional grounds. The law was attacked as amounting to summary arrest. Under the law, the court noted, the individual must have a history of a lack of compliance with mental health treatment, causing the individual to be hospitalized at least twice in the preceding thirty-six months. Also, the individual must have received services from a forensic or other mental health unit of a correctional facility or have a history of mental illness that has resulted in one or more acts of serious violent behavior, or threats or attempts at serious physical harm, to self or others. The individual must be found, by clear and convincing evidence, to be unlikely to participate voluntarily in a recommended treatment plan. Additionally, in light of the individual's treatment history and current behavior, the individual must be found in need of assisted outpatient treatment to prevent a relapse or deterioration that would likely result in serious harm to the individual or others. The law mirrors, in many respects, the APA's Resource Document. J. Rosack, "N.Y. Outpatient Commitment Law Survives Legal Challenge," *Psychiatric News,* Nov. 3, 2000, p. 1. Under Kendra's Law the court may order the patient to self-administer psychotropic medication or accept the administration of such medication by authorized personnel as part of an assisted outpatient treatment program. Such treatment may be ordered for periods of up to one year. N.Y. Ment. Hyg. L., sec. 9.60(K). Forced medication has been aptly described as the "core of outpatient commitment." S. Stefan, "Preventive Commitment: The Concept and Its Pitfalls," *Ment. & Phys. Dis. L. Rep.* 11 (1987): 288. On the closing of the Northville Regional Psychiatric Center, one of the last mental hospitals in Michigan, medication that "helps control mental illness" was cited as the chief reason behind the hospital closing. C. Garrett, "Michigan Will Sell Last Mental Hospital," *Detroit News,* Nov. 9, 2001, p. D-1. Under Kendra's Law, a patient who fails or refuses to comply with a treatment plan authorized by the court cannot be held in contempt of court but can be transported to a hospital and held up to seventy-two hours to determine if the individual is in need of "involuntary care and treatment." N.Y. Ment. Hyg. L., sec. 9.60(N).

92. Questions arise: Does involuntary outpatient treatment work? How has it been implemented in states that currently use it? How does it affect people with severe mental illness? The data suggest that a significant percentage of people with mental illness who need services are not getting them, and those who do get very few. A special section on involuntary outpatient commitment appears in *Psychiatric Services* 52 (Mar. 2001): 323–80. Increasingly, mental health and law-enforcement experts denounce a system that seeks to integrate the mentally ill into neighborhoods without enough safeguards to ensure they take medication to control their illness. W. Wendland-Bowyer & P. Montemurri, "State Mental Illness Policy is Challenged by a Killing," *Detroit Free Press,* Sept. 19, 2000, p. 1. See also E. Mattison,

"Commentary: The Law of Unintended Consequences," *J. Am. Acad. Psychiatry & Law* 28 (2000): 154. A suggested minimum initial period of outpatient commitment is six months. Housing is sometimes used as leverage to ensure adherence to a treatment program. H. Korman, D. Engster, & B. Milstein, "Housing as a Tool of Coercion," in D. Dennis & J. Monahan, *Coercion and Aggressive Community Treatment* (New York: Plenum, 1996). See also C. T. Mowbray, K. L. Grazier, & M. Holter, "Managed Behavioral Health Care in the Public Sector: Will It Become the Third Shame of the States?" *Psychiatric Services* 53 (Feb. 2002): 157.

93. In Helen L. v. DiDario, 46 F.3d 325 (3d Cir. 1995), the Third Circuit ruled that a state welfare department regulation that forced certain patients to receive required care services in a nursing home rather than through a community-based attendant care program violated the ADA. In Kathleen S. v. Dept. of Public Welfare, 10 F.Supp.2d 476 (E.D.Pa. 1998), the Pennsylvania Department of Public Welfare sought a stay enforcement of an order requiring acceleration of the integration into the community of patients at a state mental health facility. The federal district court held that the department failed to satisfy the requirements for a grant of stay, namely, that granting of the stay would inflict substantial injury on the patients in community placement and would not be in the public interest.

94. Quoted in N. Q. Brill, *America's Psychic Malignancy* (Springfield, Ill.: Thomas, 1993), p. 113.

95. A. Talbott, "Psychiatry's Agenda for the 80's," *JAMA* 251 (May 4, 1984): 2250.

96. Ltrs., "Patients Cry for Help; System Cries for Reform," *Detroit Free Press,* Oct. 12, 2000, p. 10.

97. A study in Massachusetts reports that 27 percent of those discharged from state psychiatric hospitals became homeless within six months; a similar study in Ohio found the figure to be 36 percent. And an increasing number of mentally ill people are in jails and prisons. A recent survey found that, on any given day, there are approximately 30,700 persons with schizophrenic or manic-depressive illness among the 426,000 inmates in the nation's local jails. Many of these mentally ill inmates have no charges against them but are merely being held in jail awaiting transportation to or the availability of a bed in a state psychiatric hospital. Reported in E. F. Torrey, "The Mental-Health Mess," *National Review,* Dec. 28, 1992, p. 22. More than 7 percent of people held in the nation's jails are seriously mentally ill, according to a report by the Public Citizen Health Research Group and the National Alliance for the Mentally Ill. "Many Seriously Mentally Ill Confined in Jails, Not Getting Help," *Psychiatric News,* Oct. 2, 1992, p. 7. See R. Blumenthal, "Emotionally Ill Pose Growing Problem to Police," *New York Times,* Nov. 16, 1989, p. 1.

98. W. Wendland, "Mental Health Plan Ready," *Detroit Free Press,* Oct. 2, 1999, p. 10.

99. D. G. Langsley, "The Community Mental Health Centre: Does It Treat Patients?" *Hosp. & Community Psychiatry* 31 (1980): 815.

100. D. A. Treffert, "Dying with Your Rights On," *Prism* (Socio-Econ. Magazine of AMA) 2 (1974): 49.

101. G. N. Grob, "Mental Health Policy in America: Myths and Realities," *Health Affairs* 11 (1992): 7. In this article, Grob writes:

In mid-nineteenth century America, the asylum was widely regarded as the symbol of an enlightened and progressive nation that no longer ignored or mistreated its insane citizens. The justification for asylums appeared self-evident: They benefitted the community by offering effective medical treatment for acute cases and humane custodial care of chronic cases. In providing for the mentally ill, the state met its ethical and moral responsibilities and, at the same time, contributed to the general welfare by limiting, if not eliminating, the spread of disease and dependency. After World War II, by way of contrast, the mental hospital began to be perceived as the vestigial remnant of a bygone age. . . . Before World War II the focus of America's efforts to treat its mentally ill citizens was on those individuals who suffered from the most severe and chronic problems. Since 1960 public policy has emphasized creation of a centralized system of services. In the process, the target populations became diffuse, and services were no longer focused on the most severely ill people.

102. W. Chittenden, "Malpractice Liability and Managed Health Care: History and Prognosis," *Torts & Ins. L.J.* 26 (1991): 451.

103. R. D. Meade, *Patrick Henry: Patriot in the Making* (Philadelphia: Tippincott, 1957), p. 281.

104. Ibid.

105. C. M. Turnbull, *The Mountain People* (New York: Simon & Schuster, 1972).

106. J. Q. LaFond & M. L. Durham, *Back to the Asylum: The Future of Mental Health Law and Policy* (New York: Oxford University Press, 1992); J. T. Carney, "America's Mentally Ill: Tormented without Treatment," *Geo. Mason U. C. R. L.J.* 3 (1992): 18; D. H. J. Hermann, "Barriers to Providing Effective Treatment: A Critique of Revision in Procedural, Substantive, and Dispositional Criteria in Involuntary Civil Commitment," *Vand. L. Rev.* 39 (1986): 83.

107. Faced with reduced revenues resulting from tax cuts and the economic downturn, Michigan drastically cut its funding to two of the state's five psychiatry residency programs. J. Rosack, "Psychiatry Residents Threatened by Michigan's Budget Crisis," *Psychiatric News*, Dec. 21, 2001, p. 1. As elsewhere around the country, the closure of almost all the state mental hospitals in Michigan in the 1990s forced county jails to house a growing number of disturbed people, although lacking the resources to meet their needs. N. Sinclair, "Mentally Ill Crowd Metro Area Jails," *Detroit News*, Aug. 29, 1999, p. 1. See also A. Mullen, "Death in the Lockup," *Detroit Metro Times*, Sept. 15, 1999, p. 14; N. Sinclair, "Disturbed Kids Abandoned," *Detroit News*, Aug. 30, 1999, p. 1. While Michigan has virtually closed all of its mental hospitals, it is in the process of constructing a $120 million forensic center that, believe it or not, promises to have all the features of a luxury hotel. A mentally ill person must commit an offense in order to obtain psychiatric care.

108. Quoted in P. Chodoff, "Jails and Mental Illness" (ltr.), *Psychiatric News*, Dec. 4, 1992, p. 2. See the Symposium, "1950–2000: Reflections on the Past Fifty Years of Psychiatric Services," *Psychiatric Services* 51 (Jan. 2000): 70–118. See also A. B. Klapper, "Finding a Right in State Constitutions for Community Treatment of the Mentally Ill," *U. Pa. L. Rev.* 142 (1993): 739.

2

Right to Treatment and Right to Refuse Treatment

Do the mentally ill have a right to treatment? Do they have a right to refuse treatment? (The *right to refuse treatment* is also known as "medication over objection.") These issues have been the subject of extensive litigation. Beyond the general legal requirements on treatment, a special body of law has developed as to whether the mentally ill have a right to treatment or the right to refuse treatment. The issues are discussed in two sections of this chapter.

Right to Treatment

Nowhere in the world, in either the developed or developing countries, has the care of the mentally ill been given top priority as part of health policy or public policy. Public health authorities have a tendency to dichotomize health into physical and mental health and to neglect the importance of mental health in general health. "Compared with the history of medicine, the history of the treatment of mental illness is characterized by blatant societal prejudices, fear and antipathy, and the methods of treatment clearly derived from those negative feelings," states Edward Shorter in his history of psychiatry.[1] In 1991 the UN General Assembly approved the Principles for Improvement of Mental Health Care, granting all persons the right to the best possible care under their public social welfare and health care systems.[2]

In the year 2000, the White Paper of the Council of Europe on the protection of the human rights and dignity of people suffering from mental disorder, especially of those who are placed as involuntarily committed, was under discussion.[3]

Does an individual in a mental institution in the United States have more of a right to treatment than the ordinary citizen? In the United States the ordinary citizen has, in law, no right to treatment. The indigent in the community are provided a modicum of services, more or less, but others must pay for it, by insurance or otherwise.[4] The individual in a prison has no right to treatment except that the constitutional prohibition on cruel and unusual punishment would require, say, a lifesaving blood transfusion.[5] Is one in a mental institution entitled to a greater right than the ordinary citizen?

In a seminal article published in 1960 in the *American Bar Association Journal*, titled "The Right to Treatment," Dr. Morton Birnbaum proposed that institutionalized mental patients have a constitutionally enforceable right to receive therapeutic treatment.[6] Birnbaum, who is both physician (internal medicine) and attorney, also advocated many institutional reforms previously urged upon the psychiatric profession, such as accreditation of mental hospitals by appropriate agencies, more adequate staffing ratios, and detailed recording of patient treatment and progress, and he later suggested Social Security Administration certification of eligibility for Medicare and Medicaid benefits.[7]

The novelty of Birnbaum's proposal was in the suggestion that adequate treatment of the mentally ill is more than simple government largess sympathetically extended to the disadvantaged indigent. It is not only immoral to put a person in a hospital without providing treatment, he said, it is illegal and unconstitutional. Treatment is a right, he argued, that is implicitly required by the Constitution as the price for the deprivation of liberty accompanying involuntary commitment. Following Birnbaum's seminal article, it was widely theorized that as a quid pro quo for the "massive curtailment of liberty" inherent in involuntary civil commitment (a description of hospitalization found in *Humphrey v. Cady*),[8] each patient must be provided with adequate treatment. Birnbaum wrote "[A]n institution that involuntarily institutionalizes the mentally ill without giving them adequate medical treatment for their mental illness is a mental prison and not a mental hospital."[9] Accordingly, failure to provide treatment would violate due process because the state's basis for institutionalization of the mentally ill disappears. Bruce Ennis of the ACLU put it thus: "[I]f the patient is confined not because he is considered dangerous, but because of a supposed need for treatment, then, failing such treatment, the justification for confinement disappears."[10]

Birnbaum's proposal enjoyed a generally favorable reception at the time of its publication. It was accompanied in the same issue of the *American Bar Association Journal* by a strongly supporting editorial and shortly thereafter by an editorial in the *New York Times*.[11] After some initial reluctance, fearing legal control over treatment practices, the American Psychiatric Association came out in support of the doctrine.[12] Birnbaum was awarded the Manfred Guttmacher Award of the American Psychiatric Association for the outstanding contribution of the year in law and psychiatry. In its 1961 and 1963 hearings on constitutional rights of the mentally ill, the Subcommittee on Constitutional Rights of the Senate Committee on the Judiciary heard his testimony concerning a right to treatment and the desirability of its statutory implementation.[13] Under the direction of its chairman, Senator Sam Ervin, a *right to treatment* provision became the law of the District of Columbia.

That law provides: "A person hospitalized in a public hospital for a mental illness shall, during his hospitalization, be entitled to medical and psychiatric care and treatment."[14]

By coincidence, the first legislative expression of a right to treatment came before a court presided over by a judge who had spoken out often about the care of the mentally ill, Chief Judge David Bazelon of the U.S. Court of Appeals for the District of Columbia. In *Rouse v. Cameron*,[15] Clarence Rouse brought an action pursuant to the District of Columbia statutory provision against the director of St. Elizabeths Hospital, Dr. Dale Cameron. By writ of habeas corpus he claimed that, following an acquittal on misdemeanor charges, he was confined without treatment in the hospital's maximum security unit. Judge Bazelon discharged Rouse on the basis of the statute while recognizing the possibility that continued involuntary institutionalization without adequate treatment portended unconstitutional infringement of liberty. It was the first decision, though based on a statute, to suggest a constitutional underpinning of the proposed right to treatment.

Apart from the right to treatment language, there was actually nothing novel about the remedy sought in *Rouse*. Habeas corpus has always been available to challenge original admission procedure or propriety of continued institutionalization. The traditional manner of challenging substandard institutions in the courts has been to attack the commitment, but simply obtaining a release of a person may not be in his best interests. So in *Wyatt v. Stickney*,[16] Federal District Court Judge Frank Johnson in Alabama was not asked to release a patient on a habeas corpus petition but was urged to set out minimum constitutional standards for adequate treatment of the mentally ill. The suit was actually welcomed and encouraged by Dr. Stonewall Stickney, then Commissioner of Mental Health for Alabama, as a means of requiring the state to take action to improve its institutions. It was what might be called a sweetheart or friendly suit. Prior to the suit, to arouse public concern over hospital conditions, Dr. Stickney had considered sending a letter to the family of every patient in Alabama's hospitals, advising that the patients would be discharged and sent home, but he was dissuaded by Governor Wallace.

In 1971, approximately five years after *Rouse*, Judge Johnson held that involuntarily committed patients "unquestionably have a constitutional right to receive such individual treatment as will give each of them a realistic opportunity to be cured or to improve his or her mental condition." It was held that patients at Bryce Hospital in Tuscaloosa, Alabama, were being denied that right to treatment. The testimony at the trial was out of the ordinary. There were many horror stories about the hospital (and the eerie feeling was enhanced by the various lawyers for the parties and amici all with beards, looking like the Smith Brothers of cough-drop fame). It appeared that Judge Johnson responded more to the facts than to the legal arguments.[17]

A court, to be sure, may find a constitutional rationale much more easily than a psychiatrist can find schizophrenia, but, in general, it tends to avoid a decision on a constitutional ground because that results in inflexibility and uniformity. Indeed, any court-mandated program—much less one based on the Constitution—freezes procedures into current assumptions and methods, and would have the same applicability be it in Topeka or Detroit.[18]

Judge Johnson, however, was so shaken by the conditions at Bryce that he granted extraordinary relief at the conclusion of the hearing. Acting as an overseer of state functions (a unique role for a judge) he ordered the implementation of "minimum constitutional standards for adequate treatment of the mentally ill" as suggested by a number of mental health experts. Among other things, he ordered the hiring of three hundred resident care workers (bypassing cumbersome civil-service requirements), the fireproofing of buildings, the revamping of the drug program, and the commencing of a massive immunization program. As a matter of right under the U.S. Constitution, he ruled, it is necessary to provide these minimum requirements for staffing, specified physical facilities and nutritional standards, individualized treatment plans, and a right to the least restrictive conditions necessary to achieve the purposes of commitment. Presumably, a violation of these rights enshrined as constitutional would constitute a violation of the Civil Rights Act, making the person liable in damages and for the payment of attorney fees.[19]

Judge Johnson's unprecedented court order went in the face of testimony in the case by Dr. Karl Menninger and others who denounced making many of these quantitative standards a matter of law. In part, Menninger testified: "I am very much in disagreement with the computer method that has been developed by some administrators. It's like trying to measure food on a calorie basis instead of the kind of food." Menninger considered the number of clergymen working in mental hospitals more important than the number of psychiatrists. "The patients need friendly human beings to communicate with them."[20] Indeed a cheery hello from a lovely young lady or a bingo game may do more for the spirit than a pill. In fairness, it must be noted, Judge Johnson emphasized that the standards he set out are to be viewed as minimum. The Joint Commission on Accreditation of Healthcare Organizations (JCAHO) has more rigorous standards than those enunciated in *Wyatt*, but these standards are not applied to public hospitals seeking JCAHO accreditation.

On seeing the article in the *New York Times* supporting the proposed right to treatment, Kenneth Donaldson contacted Birnbaum, who in turn enlisted the aid of Bruce Ennis of the ACLU in seeking judicial review of his commitment at the Florida State Hospital at Chattahoochee. Birnbaum and Ennis made odd bedfellows. Birnbaum was seeking a right to treatment and an improvement in the condition of institutions; Ennis on the other hand was seeking to close them down.[21] Ennis, on behalf of Donaldson, talked discharge and damages.

During the 1960s some eighteen attempts, all futile, were made to obtain Donaldson's discharge by habeas corpus on the grounds that he was not dangerous, did not require institutionalization, and was receiving inadequate treatment. A damage suit was brought against several doctors at the state hospital under the Civil Rights Act (the state of Florida enjoyed sovereign immunity), alleging that his confinement constituted an unconstitutional deprivation of liberty because he was nondangerous and because he had been provided no therapeutic treatment. At the trial, the jury found for Donaldson and awarded him $28,500 in compensatory and $10,000 in punitive damages. On appeal the Fifth Circuit, Judge John Minor Wisdom writing the opinion, upheld the verdict and said that "a person involuntarily civilly committed to a state mental hospital has a constitutional right to receive such individual treatment as will give him a reasonable opportunity to be cured or to improve his mental condition."[22] Thus, this federal appellate court not only recognized a right to treatment as constitutionally required, the first time any appellate court did so, but it approved the award of damages against the doctors as a remedy for the violation of this right. In a comment, Birnbaum took pains to note that a money damages award would likely cause an exodus of state hospital doctors out of public mental hospital facilities.[23]

The Supreme Court granted certiorari in the case, its first to deal with the civil rights of an involuntarily committed mental patient who had committed no crime. Adhering to the traditional "judicial practice of dealing with the largest questions in the most narrow way,"[24] Justice Stewart on behalf of a unanimous court concluded that "the difficult issues of constitutional law dealt with by the Court of Appeals are not presented by this case in its present posture." In vacating the Fifth Circuit's decision, the Supreme Court declared: "A State cannot constitutionally confine without more a nondangerous individual who is capable of surviving safely in freedom by himself or with the help of willing and responsible family members or friends."[25] At conferences and in the literature, the law and psychiatric communities have debated the meaning or significance of the words "without more" in the aforementioned statement by the Court. In its decision the majority did not reach the question of the right to treatment, concluding rather that there was simply no showing of a constitutionally adequate basis for the state to confine Donaldson against his will.

In a concurring opinion, Chief Justice Burger rejected the quid pro quo theory as justifying any right to treatment under the U.S. Constitution. He wrote:

> [T]here is no historical basis for imposing such a limitation on state power. Analysis of the sources of the civil commitment power . . . lends no support to that notion. There can be little doubt that in the exercise of its police power a State may confine individuals solely to protect society from the dangers of significant antisocial acts or communicable disease. . . . Additionally, the States are vested with the historic parens patriae power, including the duty to protect "persons under legal disabilities to act for themselves." . . . [But] however the power is implemented, due process requires that it not be invoked indiscriminately. At a minimum, a particular scheme for protection of the mentally ill must rest upon a legislative determination that it is compatible with the best interests of the affected class and that its members are unable to act for themselves.[26]

Those who observed or participated in the debates surrounding the right to treatment in the years immediately before *Donaldson* were rather surprised, and many disappointed, by the opinion, as they had detected hints in prior decisions of the Court indicating it would affirm a right to treatment. There was the "massive curtailment of liberty" language in *Humphrey v. Cady*,[27] a case involving the indefinite commitment of an individual under the Wisconsin Sex Crimes Act. There was the language in the competency to stand trial opinion in *Jackson v. Indiana*,[28] regarding the relationship that must exist between the "nature and duration of commitment" and the "purpose" of such commitment. There was the dicta in *Robinson v. California*,[29] about the commitment of individuals with a drug addiction, that a number of lower courts took as a right to treatment.[30] And there was the juvenile delinquency proceeding in *In re Gault* regarding the quid pro quo that must be extended due to relaxed procedural safeguards.[31]

Donaldson represents the high watermark of a movement that had been developing over a decade and a half. The federal or state governments may provide a right to treatment by legislation (though unlikely), but it would not be impelled under the U.S. Constitution. The economy, one may say, turned the tide. The unenthusiastic tone of the opinion together with Justice Burger's rejection altogether of the notion of a right to treatment in a concurring opinion have not gone unnoticed. In *Morales v. Turman*,[32] the Fifth Circuit overturned a detailed district court ruling finding that conditions in Texas juvenile detention facilities had to be improved in part because they violated juveniles' rights to treatment. Citing the Supreme Court's holding in *Donaldson*, the Fifth Circuit, the same court that earlier had affirmed a right to treatment, said:

> The argument for a right to treatment is even less strong as related to juvenile offenders. Many of the detained juveniles will have committed acts that clearly posed a danger to society. . . . In addition, since many of the acts that result in a juvenile's detention would be crimes if committed by adults and since adult offenders do not have a right to treatment, a right to treatment for juveniles may be less appropriate than a similar right for the mentally ill.[33]

Although the quid pro quo theory went without acceptance in the Supreme Court, the *loss of liberty* rationale has had an impact and will continue to do so. To be sure, some rationale was necessary to promote adequacy of treatment, but ideas or slogans often have unintended consequences. The loss of liberty rationale has given impetus to the view that the mental hospital is not an asylum but rather more a political detention center. Some critics of the hospital system, romanticizing psychosis as a type of individualism (like being a Republican or Democrat or Socialist) have charged that psychiatry is depriving individuals of "the right to be different."[34] Needless to say, this view was abetted by the practice in the Soviet Union and other countries of frequently using psychiatric hospitalization as a means of controlling dissent. With liberty said to be at stake, the substantive and procedural due process requirements of criminal justice procedures have been invoked to control hospital admissions and programs.[35]

The liberty rationale is also the basis of the *least restrictive alternative* concept, also known as the *least restrictive environment* or *least intrusive treatment*, which was enunciated in 1966 in *Lake v. Cameron*.[36] When the terms are those of liberty, the focus is not on the most beneficial alternative but rather on the least restrictive alternative. Now at least thirty-five states explicitly or implicitly refer to the least restrictive alternative in their commitment statutes. In any event, the court serves the doctrine's purposes by dismissal of a petition of hospitalization,[37] and there must be a repetitive (judicial) assessment of the hospitalization.[38] The doctrine assumes an organization of mental health services on a graduated pattern of restrictiveness, in which the hospital is the most restrictive. The community, whenever feasible, is to have the nod over hospitalization; but, pray tell, where is the liberty or community in today's urban areas? The mental hospital provides more of a community, especially for the disabled, than do our urban areas.[39]

In a way, the doctrine of the least restrictive alternative is a valuable expression of society's continuing interest in monitoring the care of the mentally ill, but in practice, family members and friends of the patient as well as any doctor that might be involved have searched out alternatives to hospitalization if for no other reason than to avoid the discomfort and stigma of legal proceedings. As a matter of fact, the long proceeding in the *Lake* case ended in naught—no institution or facility other than the mental hospital offered adequate supervision.

The notion of liberty, however defined, blanks discussion on whether there is any relationship between restrictions and treatment effectiveness, or that one variable can be influenced by the other. Positing a simple relationship between restrictiveness and treatment effectiveness merely poses dilemmas. The least restrictive alternative has resulted in a rather rigid hierarchy of therapies, ranging from what is called intrusive to nonintrusive therapies. In this pattern, focusing on the physical characteristics of treatment modalities, medication has the nod over electroshock.[40]

Is it reasonable or workable to involve a court in the daily management of a patient? Management varies from day-to-day or hour-to-hour. At times, for instance, it may be necessary to keep a patient in restraints or seclusion. At other times, it may be necessary to proscribe telephone calls, letters, or other communication with family members. At times, electroshock may be preferable to medication. What is best for a patient therapeutically is constantly shifting; no court (unless it is located on the hospital premises) can keep up with it. The court here (as in the school desegregation and prison cases) departs from its traditional role of looking to the past and providing a one-time remedy, and enters into the field of ongoing administration.[41]

As a rule, there is resort to the courts because other efforts to achieve change have gone nowhere, but there are marked limitations and consequences of judicial activism. The judiciary tends to run aground when it tries to substitute itself for the legislative branch of government. Judicial orders have to be precise to be enforceable, but that very precision of necessity limits innovation and flexibility. A hospital director who is ordered to hire more nurses might better use recreation therapists. Moreover, the court order is most effective when put in the negative. A doctor affirmatively ordered to see a patient a certain number of times per week might undercut the order in a passive-aggressive way by merely taking a peek in the door. And it is hardly consistent with federalism and balance of powers for a federal court to try to determine state budget priorities. Following Judge Johnson's decree, Alabama did an end run around it by closing down many of its hospitals and, at best, complied with the mandated standards on very reduced facilities. Finally, litigation involves defendants. When the institution has charitable or governmental immunity, the doctors are personally blamed and take the consequences, often unfairly, for conditions they themselves have deplored but that have been beyond their power to correct. The time, energy, and expense involved in litigation, the ill-feeling that it arouses, the effect on recruitment of staff, and the effect on patients and families are issues not to be ignored.

In a time of diminished resources, or in the face of other demands, the state looks most sympathetically at any justification for getting out of the mental hospital business. The aggregation of fiscal demands, railroading allegations, and other anti-hospital ideology combined to produce an impetus to close the institution and transfer the population to the community.[42] Over the years the states have taken care of the mentally ill—beginning in the early 1800s the various states built asylums for the care of the mentally ill. The providing of resources and services by the states to the individual, and the underlying determination of the allocation of public funds, have generally been considered a matter of legislative prerogative, not of constitutional command. Michigan's constitution sets out a guarantee of state support of the mentally ill and developmentally disabled. In any event, the various states have gradually transferred the caretaking burden to the federal government, when the central government became the main source of funding, by a process of deinstitutionalization. State legislators were easy to convince that fewer state tax dollars would be needed to care for long-term patients if they were placed in nursing homes rather than in the state hospital. The idea found ready acceptance following the passage of amendments to the Social Security Act in 1965, which provided federal support for long-term patients in nursing homes. The economic reality underlying deinstitutionalization has been couched in the rhetoric of liberty and improved care. As often reported, patients do not receive appropriate care or treatment in the inpatient or outpatient community alternatives.[43] In New York State 13 percent of those discharged from state hospitals were dead within two months.[44] Prisons are being privatized, and the state too is opting out of the care of the mentally ill, turning the task over to the private sector.[45]

Is there a right to treatment in the community facilities? Is there a legal obligation to create community care facilities and programs? By what rationale? A rationale is needed more now than in the preceding years. Some 70 percent of institutionalized people have been moved from hospitals to the cheaper nursing or boarding homes, where there is little or no psychiatric or other care. Home operators, finding it lucrative, have come with large vehicles to transport patients from the hospital to their facilities. Often appointed as guardian, or de facto, the operator provides consent for the medication of the population. For ease in management, chemical straitjacketing is the order of the day. A doctor comes by about once a week, sees each person for a minute or two, charging a fee for each, and out of the visit makes more than a lawyer would hope for as monthly compensation. To be sure, there is not much asylum in these homes.[46]

By what rationale can families be assisted? The old asylum was an asylum not only for the patient but also for the patient's family. The question must be asked: Is a family entitled to assistance or protection from a troublesome member? The family may be driven asunder by one of its members. The focus on liberty or deinstitutionalization has resulted in heavy emotional and social costs to families.[47]

In search of a theory, Birnbaum used the *treatment in exchange for liberty* argument in order to improve the quality of the asylum. In a turnaround, others have used the rationale to achieve the very opposite of what was intended. The theoretical underpinning of the right to treatment has become a euphemism for the liquidation, in part or whole, of the public mental hospital. Would things have been any different without the concept? Given the economic decline of the country at the time, quite likely some other cosmetic covering would have been used to the same end. Reasons are readily at hand to support our predilections.

Right to Refuse Treatment

Over two decades of litigation and regulation on the right of the mentally ill to refuse treatment have left psychiatrists bewildered as to the state of the law. Attorneys general of various states have usually declined or avoided giving an advisory opinion. Foreign-born therapists are particularly confused—they constitute the staff of many state hospitals—and they shy away from treating nonconsenting patients. The end result has benefited no one—neither the individual, the profession, nor society. It has proven to be low benefit, high cost. Time is wasted, at unnecessary expense, and time is limited (hospitalization now is very short, on average about fourteen days).

Does involuntary commitment do away, wholly and entirely, with the usual obligation of a doctor to obtain consent to treatment? Logic would seem to dictate that if people can be hospitalized involuntarily, they can be treated without their consent by appropriate treatment, subject to some kind of review. In 1976, in a decision later narrowed, the Minnesota Supreme Court said: "If [the] interest of the state is sufficiently important to deprive an individual of his physical liberty, it would seem to follow that it would be sufficiently important for the state to assume the treatment decision."[48] It went on to say, quoting from an article in the *Harvard Law Review*:

> Under the *parens patriae* rationale, an individual may be committed when he lacks capacity to make a rational decision concerning hospitalization; and the treatment or custodial care available would be beneficial enough to outweigh the deprivations which commitment would impose on him. Inherent in an adjudication that an individual should be committed under the state's *parens patriae* power is the decision that he can be forced to accept the treatments found to be in his best interest; it would be incongruous if an individual who lacks capacity to make a treatment decision could frustrate the very justification for the state's action by refusing such treatments.[49]

In this area of controversy, a federal district court in Wisconsin said in no uncertain terms, "[A]n involuntary commitment is a finding of incompetency with respect to treatment decisions. Nonconsensual treatment is what involuntary commitment is all about."[50] District court rulings, be it noted, are binding only in that jurisdiction but may be persuasive elsewhere.

Generally speaking, unless authorized, therapeutic intervention is a tort even if the intrusion is for the patient's welfare and actually accomplishes some benefit. It is a trespass, a battery. The saving grace in everyday medical care is consent, or "informed consent." Under classical tort theory, any unauthorized touching outside of conventional social intercourse constitutes a battery. It is an offense to the dignity of the person, an invasion of the right of self-determination for which punitive and actual damages may be imposed. As Justice Cardozo observed in a famous statement:

> Every human being of adult years and *sound mind* has a right to determine what shall be done with his own body. A surgeon who performs an operation without his patient's consent commits [a battery] for which he is liable in damages. (emphasis added)[51]

This oft-quoted statement carries a qualification: "sound mind." A valid consent requires competency, and without it, a guardian would have to be appointed. The law allows an exception in an emergency where the therapist is entitled to assume that, if the patient were competent and understood the situation, he would consent. The law also allows a *therapeutic privilege*, which recognizes that a physician may reasonably take into account the emotional state of a patient and need not disclose matters that would upset the patient and unduly interfere with care and treatment. In the event of litigation, the physician has the burden of justifying the exercise of the privilege.

When an individual is civilly committed, the loss of civil or political rights is not theoretically an integral part of the process although it has been in criminal law. However, in hospitalizing, the various states at one time combined commitment and competency proceedings.[52] At that time, commitment spelled the end of an individual's contact with the outside world. The hospital, in effect, became the guardian and handled the various affairs of the patient. To avoid controversy, the courts in some states have returned to ruling a person incompetent at the time of commitment, at least with regard to treatment, as a time-saving way of allowing the hospital to treat without returning to court for approval. Utah by legislation in 1979 provided that an involuntary patient is incompetent to make treatment decisions.[53] In the application of an outpatient commitment law, the question is raised whether it is legal to administer medication forcibly to an outpatient without a competency inquiry.[54]

Questions persist: Is it necessary to have an incompetency ruling, or treatment order, at the time of commitment? Can treatment, without a hearing or without an informed consent, be forced on a patient who has been committed? Since the patient will bear the risks of mischances, should anyone else make the decision? Is medication or ECT the only available treatment? Does a patient have a choice of treatments? Should the therapist be obliged to justify the value of the proposed treatment?

In making a decision, would the judge be practicing medicine without a license?[55] Perhaps the ultimate request made of a psychiatrist by a judge was, "We don't understand these medications. If I got all of the judges together, could you give us a 15-minute lecture on the topic?"[56] Dr. Stephen Rachlin gives examples of judges in New York making specific treatment decisions, such as specifying the particular antipsychotic medication to be prescribed; limiting the clinicians to one drug at a time, with a new review required for each change; prescribing acceptable schedules for dose changes; and requiring anti-Parkinson medication at the first sign of any side effects.[57]

Nowadays, under typical legislation, commitment or a treatment order does not operate as a general adjudication of legal incompetence.[58] Thus, the civilly committed patient now retains the civil rights of the ordinary citizen, including the right to dispose of property, to make contracts, and to vote. Hence, the status of a civilly committed patient is the same as that of any individual, so the provisions in mental health codes of a bill of rights is surplusage.[59] Is the right to refuse treatment also retained notwithstanding commitment? Members of the Mental Health Bar argue such a right absent consent or present dangerousness.

Under mental health codes, *hospitalize* or *hospitalization* means "to provide treatment for a person as an inpatient in a hospital."[60] *Treatment* includes "diagnostic, and therapeutic services including the administration of drugs and any other service for the treatment of an individual."[61] In many states, we have noted, treatment orders are often issued at the time of commitment, which can be taken to mean that commitment entails a limited abridgement of competency and thereby obviates any need to obtain court approval for forced medication.

As a practical matter, hospital staffs of public hospitals usually require individuals seeking admission to proceed via involuntary commitment so that they cannot refuse treatment. Hospitals tend to refuse voluntary admissions. The Supreme Court's decision in *Zinermon v. Burch*—that an incompetent person cannot consent to admission and treatment—encourages that policy.[62] And even in states where commitment includes incompetency regarding decisions on treatment, psychiatrists want a guardian appointed to approve the treatment when the patient refuses.

The criteria for commitment lend to a finding of incompetency in regard decision making for treatment. Arguably, the criteria—"dangerousness" or "gravely disabled"—satisfy the *emergency* exception in the law on consent. The Michigan law on commitment also includes an *impaired judgment* criterion.[63] As of this writing, there is no appellate case law in Michigan on right to refuse treatment.[64] Michigan is typical.[65]

The abuse that occurs by overmedication or the type of medication may be unrelated to the reasons of those who object to medication. Approximately 5 percent of patients object to medication; why do they object? The reasons vary, some rational, others not. Some patients (notably the paranoid schizophrenic) may think the medication is poison, others may not like the side effects, and still others may want a ride to the courthouse. Still others are willing to take medication but one different from that prescribed. Better compliance in taking medication is linked to better-tolerated side effects. Of those who object to medication, it is estimated that the vast majority end up taking it. Most often the psychiatrist, nurses, or family can persuade the patient to take medication.[66]

Medication is often derided because of its side effects, but it must be kept in perspective. What is its cost-benefit, to use that formula? Before the development of psychotropic medication in the mid-twentieth century, mental hospitals had back wards crowded with psychotic patients. Today, as a result of medication, catatonia has disappeared from the scene, not to mention the benefits of medication in the treatment of other disorders.

In cases of treatment refusal, the aim of intervention by the courts has been to achieve appropriate treatment of patients, not to bar all involuntary treatment. It is argued that the right to refuse treatment provides protection against the overuse of medication to manage understaffed wards and requires psychiatrists to talk to their patients about the prescribed medications and potential risks and side effects of these medications.[67]

In state hospitals, quite often, patients have been given medication, often suffering adverse reactions, on standing orders. Patients have been infrequently seen by a physician, although health codes provide that a licensed physician is to see an inpatient on a daily basis. Moreover, for inpatients or outpatients, the states balk at providing the newer but more expensive medications, which have less side effects such as tardive dyskinesia. Various states restrict Medicaid access to expensive drugs, or they require drug companies participating in a Medicaid program to provide special rebates. In Michigan, a committee of eleven physicians and pharmacists, meeting privately, chose so-called best-in-class drugs in forty categories that would get special treatment in the $1.1 billion the state spends each year on prescription medicines.[68]

The two most discussed decisions in this area, handed down in the early 1980s, are *Rogers v. Okin*, later known as *Mills v. Rogers* (involving the Boston State Hospital),[69] and *Rennie v. Klein* (involving a state institution in New Jersey).[70] The trial and appellate courts faced the issue: Under what circumstances may state hospital doctors forcibly administer antipsychotic drugs to mental patients without violating the Fourteenth Amendment? The trial judge in *Rogers* described psychotropic drugs as "mind-controlling" and ruled that, before a refusing patient could be given treatment, a guardian would need to be appointed in the usual legal manner and that the guardian would then decide whether treatment was to be rendered against the patient's wishes. The trial judge also gave a narrow definition of *emergency*, which would allow treatment of the refusing patient, as "circumstances in which a failure to forcibly medicate would bring about a substantial likelihood of physical harm to the patient or others." In so restricting the definition to instances in which immediate action is required to prevent physical harm, the trial judge rejected the medical claim that an emergency should also include situations in which the immediate administration of drugs is reasonably believed to be necessary to prevent further deterioration in the patient's mental health.

The trial judge in *Rennie*, on the other hand, allowed medical review of the treatment of a refusing patient. On appeal, in a lengthy opinion, the Third Circuit Federal Court of Appeals set out a least intrusive means standard of care and an elaborate procedural mechanism to override a civilly committed patient's refusal of antipsychotic medication. The court emphasized that the "decision to administer drugs depends upon a medical judgment based upon a variety of facts" and that "[d]ue process procedures must therefore provide an opportunity for the exercise of professional judgment in these circumstances."[71] The court further stated that a factor for consideration is "the governmental interest, including fiscal and administrative burdens that other procedural requirements would impose."[72]

The U.S. Supreme Court granted certiorari in *Rennie* and *Rogers* but remanded them for reconsideration in light of other cases. In the process, the Court spurred a wide-ranging debate on the issue. The Court probably abandoned doing anything more for want of a consensus. In *Rogers*, on remand, the First Circuit Federal Court of Appeals certified the questions of state law to the Massachusetts Supreme Judicial Court, which responded by elaborating a strong view of the patient's right to refuse treatment.[73] The court drew no distinction between voluntary patients and involuntarily committed patients; the distinction it made was between competent and incompetent patients. The competent patient has a right to refuse treatment, while for the incompetent patient, the judge, rather than the psychiatrist or a guardian, is the decision maker. It called antipsychotic medication "extraordinary treatment." The court, however, extended the traditional definition of *emergency* to include both life-threatening situations and situations where treatment is needed immediately to prevent the substantial deterioration of the patient's mental illness.[74]

The two approaches are known as the *treatment-driven* model and the *rights-driven* model. The former focuses on treatment, while the latter focuses on legal rights. Under the latter model, a couple of states (Illinois and New York) allow a jury trial. The treatment model has been the most widely adopted, but its application depends on the type of treatment. At first blush it would seem that the rights model would respect the patient's wishes more often than the treatment model, but in actuality, clinicians allow significantly more patients to refuse medications than do courts in jurisdictions requiring judicial hearings.[75] Courts tend to rubber-stamp treatment orders.[76] It may be that applications to the court are made only in the most dire cases; patients who refuse medication are simply discharged or not treated. In the treatment model, on the other hand, a consultant or administrative review board gets more cases for review, with a number not passing muster.

As *Rennie* and *Rogers* were finally decided on state-law grounds, rather than on the Constitution, their precedential value for other jurisdictions was considerably muted. The *Rennie* decision, calling for only a medical review, has been mostly followed, particularly after the U.S. Supreme Court's decision in 1982 in *Youngberg v. Romeo*,[77] which suggested that judicial second-guessing of clinical judgments concerning appropriate treatment of the mentally ill would be disfavored. The Supreme Court said, "It is not appropriate for the courts to specify which of several professionally acceptable choices should have been made."[78] The case involved the restraining of a mentally retarded minor—it did not address nonconsensual use of psychotropic drugs—but its holding is susceptible of broad interpretation. Thus, in a case involving the involuntary treatment with psychotropic drugs, a federal district court said, "[T]he decision in *Youngberg* dictates that deference must be shown to professional judgment."[79]

There is contrary opinion. Professor Bruce Winick suggests that the nature of the intrusion presented by psychotropic drugs may be sufficient to justify more in the way of judicial oversight than was thought appropriate in *Youngberg*.[80] In a 1988 decision involving the forced use of psychotropic medication, *Jarvis v. Levine*,[81] the Minnesota Supreme Court said:

> *Youngberg* did not resolve the question before this court today. The case involved a severely retarded individual committed to a state facility who filed suit for damages and injunctive relief under the federal Constitution. The patient, having the mental capacity of an 18-month-old baby, was obviously unable to participate in any treatment decisions. *Youngberg* also did not raise the issue of forced drug treatment and its potentially devastating effects, but, instead, involved rights to safe physical conditions, habilitation and freedom from bodily restraint. The significant differences between the factual and legal issues addressed in *Youngberg* and those raised today convince us that the case furnishes little guidance.[82]

Moreover, the Minnesota Supreme Court said:

> [W]e are faced with the rights of persons committed to Minnesota institutions, pursuant to Minnesota law, by the courts of this state. Given the significant state law issues involved, we feel it is imperative to assume our obligation to be "independently responsible for safeguarding the rights of [our] citizens." . . . We thus decide the case exclusively under Minnesota statutes and our Minnesota Constitution.[83]

Given the evidence of serious irreversible side effects, the courts have become more receptive to the argument that patients have a right to refuse psychotropic medication. A number of courts in various states have ruled in recent years that civilly committed patients have a right to refuse psychotropic medication, subject to approval only by administrative review or court authorization.[84] Many psychiatrists have argued that public psychiatric patients need psychotherapy as much as or more than medication.[85]

In a criminal case involving pretrial detainees who challenged the forcible administration of antipsychotic drugs, the Tenth Circuit Court of Appeals ruled the least restrictive alternative principle applicable. In the court's view "less restrictive alternatives, such as segregation or the use of less controversial drugs like the tranquilizers or sedatives, should be ruled out before resorting to antipsychotic drugs" when the purpose is protecting the jail staff and other inmates from a violent detainee.[86] The court recognized that the Supreme Court had declined to apply the LRA principle in *Youngberg v. Romeo,* but found that case distinguishable "both because it involved temporary physical restraints rather than mental restraints with potentially long-term effects . . . and because Romeo had been certified as severely retarded and unable to care for himself."[87]

In various states, by regulation of their departments of mental health, LRA is applied not only to the question of the place of commitment—hospital or outpatient facility—but also to treatment. The LRA policy is usually best for psychiatric care as well as in protecting liberty, yet hard and fast rules are not workable. From the hospital's point of view, when the situation requires conventional medication or the separation of a patient from other patients, this is in the realm of treatment and judgment, and is not for a surrogate decision maker to decide. There are things that may not be conceived of as an emergency or as dangerous to life but that are merely uncomfortable or possibly painful, such as loud noise or a punch. The hospital needs to consider not only the individual rights of patients but also the need for a peaceful milieu for other patients and the security of hospital staff. In a ward, screaming or other behavior is disturbing to others. When one is confined with others, the interests of others cannot be ignored.[88]

The mental hospital is society at large in microcosm. All types of people—of different ethnicity and religion plus being mentally disordered—are brought together in a small geographical area, and it cannot be expected that they will get along. Quite often, they present a threat to themselves or to others. The hospital has an obligation to protect patients from causing harm to others or to themselves. If staff is small or its level of training low, premises have to be locked and the patients isolated, restrained, or given strong medication for at least some degree of peace and order to prevail. Then, too, schools have been pushing amphetamines on parents as a way to control disruptive children.

Use of Restraints and Seclusion. The use of restraints or seclusion has been marked by years if not centuries of debate. In a much-noted historical event, Philippe Pinel in 1793 removed the chains from individuals confined in an asylum in Paris. Two hundred years later, the debate about restraint continues in the United States, with government involvement at both the federal and state legislative and regulatory levels. The forms of restraint in common use today in hospitals include manual holding, seclusion, and medication. Manual holding is more expensive than seclusion and, like seclusion, patients tend to perceive it as punitive. Medication, in the form of rapid tranquilization, is usually seen as more humane, as it requires only brief initial restraint during the administration of the injectable medication and before it takes effect. Rapid tranquilization, however, poses the danger of respiratory depression and its use therefore requires medical approval, but a medical doctor may not be at hand.[89]

The therapeutic value of seclusion is explained by the principles of *isolation, decrease in sensory input,* and *sensory deprivation.* On a practical level, the therapeutic basis of seclusion is explained by the principle of *containment* in the safest environment when other forms of intervention have failed. In addition to strapping, the restraint put on patients by Dr. Benjamin Rush, the only psychiatrist to sign the Declaration of Independence, had a headpiece resembling the blinders put on a horse to keep out stimuli; it was called "Rush's tranquilizer." In Escorial, Spain, when a nun would become psychotic, she was put in a box called a "nun's cradle."

Outside the hospital, self-defense or defense of others justify even lethal force in overcoming a person who poses a threat, but inside the hospital, staff are expected to deal with the individual in a nonlethal manner. On a Southwest Airlines flight, Jonathan Burton tried to kick down the door of the cockpit. His behavior cost him his life at the hands of fellow travelers who restrained him. It was deemed that there was no "criminal intent" by those involved and there was no prosecution.[90] In the hospital situation, there likely would be lawsuits for wrongful death on the ground that staff are expected to handle a violent patient without causing physical injury.

In controlling a patient, regulations in some states oblige the therapist to use restraints before medication or seclusion.[91] There is public outcry over reports of injuries and deaths related to the use of seclusion and restraints, and efforts to restrict their use continue in Congress.[92] There is wide variability across the country in the use of seclusion or restraint. The more the medication (often called "chemical restraint"), the less the need for seclusion or (physical) restraint. Another important factor in the variability is the attitude or training of staff in dealing with patients.[93]

State statutes that provide that patients have the right to refuse electroshock treatment and psychosurgery suggest by negative implication that patients in those states do not have the right to refuse drug treatment.[94] Michigan legislation specifically states, as we have noted, that patients admitted on petition can refuse medications before their court hearing unless the patient is physically dangerous to himself or others.[95] Wisconsin also regulates the use of medications statutorily.[96] Some lower courts have restricted the use of seclusion and the forcible administration of psychotropic drugs, even in the case of involuntarily committed patients, except in clear-cut emergencies.

Intrusive Therapies. In general, a line has been drawn between intrusive and non-intrusive therapies, with the intrusive therapies requiring court approval. In 1976, in *Price v. Shepard*,[97] the Minnesota Supreme Court listed drug therapy as more intrusive than milieu therapy or psychotherapy but less intrusive than aversion therapy, ECT, and psychosurgery. The court declined to leave the imposition of "the more intrusive forms of treatment" solely within the discretion of medical personnel.[98] In concluding, the court said:

> We cannot draw a clear line between the more intrusive forms of treatment requiring a procedural hearing and those which do not. Certainly this procedure is not intended to apply to the use of mild tranquilizers or those therapies requiring the cooperation of the patient. On the other hand, given current medical practice, this procedure must be followed where psychosurgery or electroshock therapy is proposed.[99]

In the case of the more intrusive therapies, specific court authorization is required; a guardian would not have authority to consent to the more intrusive therapies.[100] Price, a youth, had been given a course of twenty electroshock treatments.

Within months of the Minnesota Supreme Court's decision in *Price*, two probate courts in the state reached inconsistent decisions on whether the standard set out requires judicial authorization when a patient objects to treatment by a long-acting injectable antipsychotic drug. The drug in each case was Prolixin (fluphenazine hydrochloride), one of the most potent of the antipsychotic drugs. In the first case, the court equated the drug with ECT as an intrusive form of psychiatric treatment. The court determined that the patient was competent to determine for herself whether she wished to accept or refuse the proposed treatment.[101] In the second case, another probate court ruled that absent special circumstances such as an allergic reaction, the usual course of Prolixin therapy would not be reviewable under *Price*. It noted that requiring a formal hearing in such cases would impinge on hospital staff discretion and needlessly delay or frustrate treatment.[102] In a memorandum order, the Minnesota Supreme Court agreed and upheld this second decision. It viewed Prolixin treatment as in accord with standard psychiatric practice and therefore generally immune from routine judicial review.[103]

Complaints about Prolixin and other antipsychotic medication began to mount. The holdings in these Minnesota lower court cases presaged more litigation. Just twelve years after its decision in *Price*, the Minnesota Supreme Court reviewed the authorization procedure set out in that case. In 1988, in aforementioned *Jarvis v. Levine*,[104] the issue was: Does involuntary neuroleptic treatment of involuntarily committed mental patients constitute an intrusive treatment calling for court approval? In *Price*, the 1976 case, the form of treatment was ECT, which the court found to be one of the more intrusive forms of treatment. In *Jarvis*, an intermediate court of appeal concluded that neuroleptics are not intrusive per se, apparently because the side effects can vary widely among patients, type of drug, and dosage.[105] The court found that neuroleptics do "not clearly rise to the level of intrusiveness of electroshock treatments or psychosurgery."[106] The state supreme court disagreed. It said:

> One of the principal considerations in the *Price* holding that ECT was "intrusive" therapy was the risk of side effects and permanent damage to the patient. We noted: "As the techniques increase in severity, so do the risks of serious and long-lasting psychological or neurological damage." . . . The court listed "the risks of adverse side effects" and "the extent of intrusion into the patient's body and the pain connected with the treatment" as factors to be considered in determining whether ECT or psychosurgery is necessary. . . .
>
> Because the privacy interest protected was described by the court as "the concept of personal autonomy," . . . a reasonable starting point in any analysis of "intrusiveness" would be the probable effects of the particular therapy on the patient's body.
>
> In the case of neuroleptics, the likelihood of at least some temporary side effects appears to be undisputed.[107]

The court cited a law review article written by Robert Plotkin, a staff attorney of the Mental Health Law Project, that has the title, "Limiting the Therapeutic Orgy: Mental Patients' Right to Refuse Treatment."[108] As might be expected from the title of the article, Plotkin cites a parade of horrendous side effects, and they are quoted by the court:

> The most common results are the temporary, muscular side effects (extrapyramidal symptoms) which disappear when the drug is terminated; dys-

tonic reactions (muscle spasms, especially in the eyes, neck, face, and arms; irregular flexing, writhing or grimacing movements; protrusion of the tongue); akathesia (inability to stay still, restlessness, agitation); and Parkinsonisms [sic] (mask-like face, drooling, muscle stiffness and rigidity, shuffling gait, tremors). Additionally, there are numerous other nonmuscular effects, including drowsiness, weakness, weight gain, dizziness, fainting, low blood pressure, dry mouth, blurred vision, loss of sexual desire, frigidity, apathy, depression, constipation, diarrhea, and changes in the blood. Infrequent, but serious, nonmuscular side effects, such as skin rash and skin discoloration, ocular changes, cardiovascular changes, and, occasionally, sudden death, have also been documented.[109]

In a number of articles Dr. Paul Appelbaum and Dr. Thomas Gutheil have criticized lawyers and the courts for their misconceptions about medication.[110] The preponderance of data supports a high benefit/risk ratio for psychotropic medications and a safety record commensurate with other powerful pharmacological agents.[111] The decision in the Wisconsin right to refuse treatment case contains over two pages listing side effects but nowhere mentions the fact that medications may help patients.[112]

The Oklahoma Supreme Court has classified psychotropic medication as an "organic therapy," along with ECT and psychosurgery, seeing all three as "intrusive in nature and an invasion of the body."[113] Appellate courts in Alabama and Illinois have held that a patient involuntarily committed does not lose the right to informed consent; like other patients, unless judged incompetent, the courts said, an involuntary patient may refuse treatment unless the patient poses an immediate threat of physical harm to himself or others.[114] The Colorado Supreme Court has ruled that a court order permitting the administration of antipsychotic medication could not continue beyond the patient's commitment certification; subsequent certifications would require renewal of medication orders.[115] As stated at the outset, other courts have held that involuntary commitment means involuntary treatment, and no special order is needed. The Ohio Supreme Court has held that patients who are involuntarily committed can be forced to take antipsychotic medication—even if they do not pose a threat to themselves or others—if it is shown that they lack the capacity to give or withhold informed consent, that no less intrusive means of effective treatment is available, and that the medication is in their best interest.[116]

The Washington Supreme Court has ruled that the court may order ECT in the case of a nonconsenting, involuntarily committed mental patient after considering (1) the nature of the patient's desires, (2) whether the state has a compelling interest in treatment, and (3) whether ECT is necessary and effective to satisfy a state interest.[117] Compelling state interests include the preservation of life, the protection of interests of innocent third parties, the prevention of suicide, and maintenance of the ethical integrity of the medical profession.[118] The court found a compelling state interest for granting treatment in this case. It involved a repeatedly hospitalized person whose admissions constituted a tremendous financial burden on the state. "We hesitate to frustrate professionals' efforts to treat mentally ill individuals as quickly and efficiently as possible," said the court.[119]

On the other hand, faced with the question of whether a person involuntarily admitted to a hospital for treatment, but not adjudicated to be incompetent, may be required to undergo ECT, the Kentucky Court of Appeals ruled in the negative.[120] In Michigan, a class-action suit in 1977 involving Newberry State Hospital ended the involuntary use of ECT in the state. The courts in Michigan, like most other jurisdictions, do not order the use of ECT except in very exceptional circumstances.[121]

ECT has been undone by negative publicity, not to mention by its very name—electroshock. It is widely perceived by patients and others as punishment, not treatment. To have it carried out, state hospitals refer to private hospitals in the case of a patient who is voluntary and capable of informed consent. It is, in fact, the most effective therapy in many cases and without side effects. The American Psychiatric Association stated in a 1990 report on ECT: "Electroconvulsive therapy (ECT) is a safe and effective treatment for certain psychiatric disorders. ECT is most commonly used to treat patients with severe depression. It is often the safest, fastest, and most effective treatment available for this illness. ECT is also sometimes used in the treatment of patients with manic illness and patients with schizophrenia."[122] In 1999 the Surgeon General called ECT "a safe and effective treatment for depression."[123] Annually in the United States an estimated 100,000 patients receive ECT.[124]

Given the publicity about coerced treatment, be it ECT or medication, one would assume that it is the ordinary rather than the extraordinary case. However, given the time and inclination, a doctor is usually able to convince a patient to follow a treatment regime. It is, one might say, a matter of salesmanship. Moreover, in the usual case when a patient refuses treatment, he senses that it is not for him. It is usually in the case of the chronic paranoid schizophrenic or bipolar patient where the treatment goes against the wishes of the patient.[125]

In days of economic difficulties, there is greater emphasis on quick treatments. Today, not only the patient's finances but also utilization reviewers, insurers, and government regulators affect treatment decisions. Fiscal restraints demand the use of medication or ECT; it takes a much shorter time to stabilize a person on medication or ECT than by psychotherapy.[126]

Will increased reliance on somatic therapies give rise to more lawsuits? Malpractice may be alleged in the case of the overuse or misuse of medication or ECT, irrespective of consent of the patient. As state hospitals or their staff usually enjoy immunity from an action in malpractice, an action under the Civil Rights Act is brought, claiming deprivation of due process.[127] The commitment or treatment order by the court safeguards the physician in a civil rights action. In the case of the private hospital, however, the malpractice action may be brought, as it does not enjoy immunity. Quite likely, for inappropriate treatment, the malpractice action provides a safeguard and a remedy far better than treatment orders issued by a court. Judicial review authorizing treatment is a waste of resources.[128] In almost all cases the courts rule in favor of treatment. Patients who object to treatment tend to be discharged, as they are a bad influence on other patients, or only cases of clear incompetency and need of treatment are submitted to the court.

What can be concluded? Are patients who are involuntarily committed excluded from the requirement of consent? Until the courts of a state rule that psychotropic medication is an intrusive therapy, psychiatrists can assume that an involuntary commitment allows it. However, without an appellate holding, psychiatrists (even though insured) are wary, as decisions in tort law are ex post facto. ECT is rarely authorized as an involuntary treatment.[129]

Notes

1. E. Shorter, *A History of Psychiatry* (New York: Wiley, 1997).
2. United Nations General Assembly Resolution 46/119, Dec. 17, 1991.
3. Council of Europe, DIR/JUR (2000)2. See also L. O. Gostin, "Human Rights of Persons with Mental Disabilities," *Int'l J. Law & Psychiatry* 23 (2000): 125.
4. Correspondence, "Medical Care as a Right," *New Eng. J. Med.* 286 (1972): 488. Mental illness as compared to physical illness faces discrimination in insurance or other coverage. Insurance companies often contend that a disability is mental rather than physical and thereby limit benefits. In Patterson v. Hughes Aircraft Co., 11 F.3d 948 (9th Cir. 1993), a claim for disability benefits was filed due to headaches. The appellate court remanded to the district court for a factual determination as to whether the headaches fell within the *mental disorder* limitation in the policy. In Kunin v. Benefit Trust Life Ins. Co., 810 F.2d 534 (9th Cir. 1990), the insurer contended that "autism" is "mental illness" and hence falls outside of coverage. The court ruled against the insurer because the policy contained no definition or explanation of the term *mental illness.* The court noted that insurance contracts generally spell out in inordinate detail the meaning of terms that lack a fixed meaning; hence, ambiguities in a policy are construed against the insurer. In Equitable Life Assurance Soc'y v. Berry, 212 Cal. App.3d 832, 260 Cal. Rptr. 819 (1989), the court ruled against a claimant who had manic depression. The policy defined *mental or nervous treatment* in a way that excluded coverage for its treatment. In Doe v. Guardian Life Ins. Co., 1992 U.S. Dist. Lexis 3214 (N.D.Ill. 1992), the court was asked to determine whether bipolar affective disorder (also known as "manic-depressive disorder") is *mental illness* within the meaning of the disability insurance coverage. The court held it was, and so the claimant would receive fewer benefits. In Fitts v. Fed. Nat'l Mortgage Assn., 2002 U.S. Dist. Lexis 3071, the court classified a claimant's manic depression as a physical malady. In Traynor v. Turnage, 485 U.S. 535 (1988), the U.S. Supreme Court reviewed a Veterans' Administration's decision in regard veterans' educational benefits. Veterans who have been honorably discharged from the armed forces are entitled to receive educational assistance benefits under the G.I. Bill to facilitate their readjustment to civilian life, but these benefits generally must be used within ten years following discharge or release for active duty. The court ruled that "primary alcoholism" otherwise characterized as "willful misconduct" does not excuse the ten-year delimiting period.

Generally speaking, people believe that an individual has more control over a mental illness than a physical one. Moreover, symptoms of psychological ills often seem vaguer, more diffuse than physiological ones. In recent years, however, the medical model of mental illness has gained ground with the discovery of biological, chemical, and even genetic explanations for mental disorders. Proponents of "mental health parity" tend to minimize or deny the differences between physical and mental illnesses. R. Pear, "Minds Over Money," *New York Times,* Dec. 30, 2001, p. WK-4. A former medical director of a health maintenance organization writes: "The insurance industry and employer groups have hidden behind a smokescreen of unfounded concerns about increased costs associated with equal coverage for mental illnesses. . . . People with serious mental illnesses that go untreated miss work, get divorced, abuse drugs, land in jail, live on the streets, commit suicide and use more medical resources. The mental health care system is fragmented, discriminatory and wasteful." B. K. Herman, ltr., *New York Times,* Jan. 1, 2002, p. 22. Critics, however, say that evidence is lacking that psychiatry can make a dent in the various problems associated with mental illness. Moreover, legislators tend to listen to public concerns, but mental illness is not a top concern. USA Today Snapshots, "A Gauge of Top Health Concerns," *USA Today,* Jan. 3, 2002, p. 1. Should parity apply to all mental problems or just the more serious illnesses? Legislation proposed on parity by Senators Pete Domenici and Paul Wellstone would apply to "all categories of mental health conditions" listed in the *DSM,* with the exception of drug and alcohol addiction. The question arises: "Why leave out such a pervasive yet treatable disease?" N. Brach, ltr., *New York Times,* Jan. 1. 2002, p. 22.

5. The Eighth Amendment has been used to control medical services in prison. The Eighth Circuit in Sawyer v. Sigler, 445 F.2d 818 (8th Cir. 1971) ruled that requiring an inmate to take medication that nauseated him violated the Eighth Amendment. In Veals v. Ciccone, 281 F.Supp. 1019 (W.D.Mo. 1968), the court held that medication allegedly causing pain did not amount to cruel and unusual punishment, and in Peek v. Ciccone, 288 F.Supp. 329 (W.D.Mo. 1968), the same court held that forced injection of a tranquilizing drug was legiti-

mate medical treatment and not cruel and unusual punishment. The Supreme Court's opinion in regard to school paddling gave reason for believing that the prohibition on cruel and unusual punishment would regulate conditions of noncriminal confinement as well. Ingraham v. Wright, 430 U.S. 651 (1977), discussed in T. D. Roberts, "Right to Treatment for the Civilly Committed: A New Eighth Amendment Basis," *U. Chi. L. Rev.* 45 (1978): 731.

6. "The purpose of this article is to advocate the recognition and enforcement of the legal right of a mentally ill inmate of a public mental institution to adequate medical treatment for his mental illness. For convenience, this right will be referred to as the right to treatment. At present, our law has not recognized this legal right although our society undoubtedly recognizes a moral right to treatment." M. Birnbaum, "The Right to Treatment," *A. B. A. J.* 46 (1960): 499.

7. Birnbaum followed up and amplified on his seminal article in the *A. B. A. J.* with other articles and a chapter in a book. See M. Birnbaum, "Some Comments on 'The Right to Treatment,'" *Arch. Gen. Psychiatry* 13 (1965): 34; "A Rationale for the Right," *Geo. L. J.* 57 (1969): 752; "The Right to Treatment: Some Comments on its Development" in F. Ayd (ed.), *Medical, Moral and Legal Issues in Mental Health Care* (Baltimore: Williams & Wilkins, 1974), p. 97.

8. 405 U.S. 504, 509 (1972).

9. *A. B. A. J.* 46 at 503. It is not to go unnoticed that Birnbaum, a doctor, looked upon *treatment* in the medical sense.

10. B. Ennis, *Prisoners of Psychiatry* (New York: Harcourt, Brace & Jovanovich, 1972), p. 89.

11. Editorial, "A New Right," *A. B. A. J.* 46 (1960): 516.

12. See J. Katz, "The Right to Treatment—An Enchanting Legal Fiction?" *U. Chi. L. Rev.* 36 (1969): 755, 766.

13. M. Birnbaum, "Statement on the Right to Treatment," presented at Hearings on Constitutional Rights of the Mentally Ill before the Subcommittee on Constitutional Rights of the Senate Committee on Judiciary, 87th Cong., 1st Sess., part 1, p. 273, 1961.

14. D.C. Code Ann., sec. 21-562. Actually, the D.C. statute provides only a precatory or supplicatory right. It does not define *treatment*, it does not say how it is to be enforced, and it does not say anything about funding.

15. 373 F.2d 451 (D.C. Cir. 1966).

16. Later known as Wyatt v. Aderholt, 503 F.2d 1305 (5th Cir. 1974), *aff'g in part*, Wyatt v. Stickney, 344 F.Supp. 387 (M.D.Ala. 1971). See L. R. Jones & R. R. Parlour (eds.), *Wyatt v. Stickney: Retrospect and Prospect* (New York: Grune & Stratton, 1981); M. J. Mills, "The Right to Treatment: Little Law, but Much Impact," in L. Grinspoon (ed.), *Psychiatry 1982: The American Psychiatric Association Annual Review* (Washington, D.C.: American Psychiatric Press, 1982).

17. One may read in Justice William Douglas's account of his thirty-six years on the Supreme Court that he learned the truth of Chief Justice Charles Evans Hughes's remark to him, "At the constitutional level where we work, ninety percent of any decision is emotional. The rational part of us supplies the reasons for supporting our predilections." W. O. Douglas, *The Court Years 1939–1975* (New York: Random House, 1980), p. 8. Professor Laurence Tribe opens his discussion in his treatise on constitutional law of the interplay of structure and substance by noting a cartoon that depicts a ship, perhaps the *Mayflower*, with two pilgrims leaning pensively over its side. As they scan the horizon, one says to the other, "Religious Freedom is my immediate goal, but my long-range plan is to go into real estate." L. Tribe, *American Constitutional Law* (Minneola, N.Y.: Foundation Press, 2000).

18. Thus, the Supreme Court said in declining to articulate a general constitutional doctrine of mens rea: "[F]ormulating a constitutional rule would reduce, if not eliminate, that fruitful experimentation, and freeze the developing productive dialogue between law and psychiatry into a rigid constitutional mold. It is simply not yet the time to write the constitutional formulas in terms whose meaning, let alone relevance, is not yet clear either to doctors or to lawyers." Powell v. Texas, 392 U.S. 514, 537 (1968).

19. 42 U.S.C., sec. 1983.

20. *Montgomery Advertiser*, Feb. 5, 1972, quoting testimony from *Wyatt v. Stickney*, cited supra note 16.

21. Ennis says on the concluding page of his book *Prisoners of Psychiatry*, that the goal should be nothing less than the abolition of involuntary hospitalization and, with it, the larger public mental hospitals. In *Wyatt*, as amici, he suggested to Judge Johnson that the hospitals

be closed down. He has never sought financing of the hospital system by, say, an attack on the bar on Medicaid payments as denial of equal protection of the laws.

22. Donaldson v. O'Connor, 493 F.2d 507 (5th Cir. 1974).

23. M. Birnbaum, "The Right to Treatment: Some Comments on Its Development," supra note 6 at 127.

24. Youngstown Sheet & Tube Co. v. Sawyer, 343 U.S. 579, 635 (1952).

25. O'Connor v. Donaldson, 422 U.S. 563 (1975).

26. 422 U.S. at 578.

27. 405 U.S. 504, 509 (1972).

28. 406 U.S. 715, 738 (1972).

29. 370 U.S. 660 (1962).

30. The U.S. Supreme Court in *Robinson* held that to make criminal the status of being addicted to a drug (as distinguished from being caught in the act of use) constituted cruel and unusual punishment, but it allowed commitment of drug-addicted individuals: "A state might determine that the general health and welfare require that [drug addiction] and other human afflictions be dealt with by compulsory treatment, involving quarantine, confinement, or sequestration." Several cases suggested a right to treatment derived from *Robinson*. In Welsch v. Likins, 373 F.Supp. 487, 496 (D.Minn. 1974), *aff'd in part and vacated in part*, 550 F.2d 1122 (8th Cir. 1977), the court found that *Robinson* supported the right to treatment claim of institutionalized mentally retarded persons. See Hearings before Subcommittee of the Committee on the Judiciary, House of Representatives, *Civil Commitment and Treatment of Narcotic Addicts* (Washington, D.C.: U.S. Govt. Ptg. Off., 1996). Several states (e.g., Michigan) provide that alcoholism or drug addiction is not a "mental illness" and therefore is not of itself a basis for a civil commitment. See chapter 1, on civil commitment.

31. 387 U.S. 1 (1967).

32. 562 F.2d 993 (5th Cir. 1977).

33. 562 F.2d at 998. In a lengthy opinion the U.S. District Court for the Northern District of Ohio ruled that involuntary treatment with psychotropic drugs or the use of restraint and seclusion call for procedural protection. Davis v. Hubbard, 506 F.Supp. 915 (N.D.Ohio 1980).

34. N. Kittrie, *The Right to Be Different* (Baltimore: Johns Hopkins Press, 1971); T. Szasz, *Psychiatric Slavery* (New York: Free Press, 1977); L. Coleman & T. Solomon, "Parens Patriae 'Treatment': Legal Punishment in Disguise," *Hastings Constitutional L. Q.* 3 (1976): 3445. Professor James Jacobs writes: "The primary concern of any mental hygiene law is to empower physicians to imprison innocent citizens, under the rubric of 'civil commitment,' and to justify torturing them by means of a variety of violent acts called 'psychiatric treatments.'" J. B. Jacobs, *Individual Rights and Institutional Authority: Prisons, Mental Hospitals Schools and Military/Cases and Materials* (Indianapolis: Bobbs-Merrill, 1979), p. 246. See also T. Szasz, "The Theology of Therapy: The Breach of the First Amendment through the Medicalization of Morals," *N. Y. U. Soc. Change* 5 (1975): 127. One finds little empirical data supporting these antihospital critics. The underlying concept identifying the mental hospital and the prison is that, in both, freedom (however defined) is denied. It is an identification based on an identification of a predicate, like saying that every man who dresses in black is a priest.

35. R. Slovenko, "Criminal Justice Procedures in Civil Commitment," *Wayne L. Rev.* 24 (1977): 1; G. M. Grant, "Donaldson, Dangerousness, and the Right to Treatment," *Hastings Constitutional L. Q.* 3 (1976): 599.

36. 364 F.2d 657 (D.C. Cir. 1966), discussed in chapter 1, on civil commitment. The World Psychiatric Association's "Ethical Standards for Psychiatric Practice" sets out as its first standard that treatment is to be provided in "the least restrictive setting." That and its other standards as well are taken from American law (such as that on informed consent). A. A. Stone, "The WPA's Declaration of Madrid Has No Foundation in Traditional Medical Ethics," *Psychiatric Times*, Jan. 2002, p. 3. The basis for the doctrine of least restrictive alternative developed in cases involving the First Amendment, which provides that the state may restrict the exercise of fundamental liberties only to the extent necessary to effectuate the state's interest. The doctrine has attained constitutional status in a number of cases involving commitment (see, e.g., Welsch v. Likens, 373 F.Supp. 487 (D.Minn. 1974), but the Supreme Court has not given the doctrine constitutional status (see, e.g., Youngberg v. Romeo, 457 U.S. 307 (1982), where the Court stated, "The Constitution only requires that the courts make certain

that professional judgment in fact was exercised. It is not appropriate for the courts to specify which of several professionally acceptable choices should have been made.").

37. The Michigan Mental Health Code, sec. 469, provides: "Prior to ordering any course of treatment, the court shall determine whether there exists an available program of treatment for the individual which is an alternative to hospitalization. The court shall not order hospitalization without a thorough consideration of available alternatives." MCL, sec. 330.1469. The U.S. Supreme Court ruled that a federal Bill of Rights for the mentally retarded enacted in 1975 does not entitle them to treatment in neighborhood settings rather than large institutions. The Developmentally Disabled Assistance and Bill of Rights Act of 1975 states, "Persons with developmental disabilities have a right to appropriate treatment, service and rehabilitation for such disabilities" and the "treatment . . . should be designed to maximize the developmental potential and should be provided in the setting that is least restrictive of the person's liberty." The Court said that this law was only "advisory" for the states and does not oblige them to provide any particular level of care or training for retarded people. The Court left unanswered whether the Constitution or other federal laws give the mentally retarded a right to least restrictive care. L. Greenhouse, "Justices Restrict a 'Bill if Rights' for the Retarded," *New York Times*, Apr. 21, 1981, p. 1. But see Olmstead v. L. C., 119 S. Ct. 2176 (1999), involving the Americans with Disabilities Act, discussed in chapter 1, on civil commitment.

38. A commitment is no longer open-ended. It is for a period of time, but it can be extended on review. The Michigan Mental Health Code, sec. 482, for example, provides: "Every individual subject to an order of continuing hospitalization has the right to regular, adequate, and prompt review of his current status as a person requiring treatment and in need of hospitalization. Six months from the date of an order of continuing hospitalization, and every six months thereafter, the director of any hospital in which an individual is hospitalized shall review his status as a person requiring treatment and in need of hospitalization." MCL, sec. 330.1482.

39. The community is aptly depicted as a jungle in a liquor advertisement: Tarzan is visiting in New York, returns to his hotel room and says to Jane, "A martini, quick." He downs it and asks for another, and another. "What is it?" asks Jane. Tarzan, shaking his head, says, "It's a jungle out there!" See R. Slovenko & E. Luby, "From Moral Treatment to Railroading out of Hospitals," *Bull. Am. Acad. Psychiatry & Law* 2 (1974): 223.

40. Price v. Shepard, 239 N.W.2d 905 (Minn. 1976).

41. B. Hoffman & L. L. Foust, "Least Restrictive Treatment of the Mentally Ill: A Doctrine in Search of Its Senses," *San Diego L. Rev.* 14 (1977): 1100.

42. It is also to be noted that the Supreme Court ruled that Congress did not violate the constitutional rights of patients in public mental hospitals by excluding them from a federal program that provides $25 a month in personal spending money to indigent patients in other types of public hospitals. A patient in a hospital that receives funds under the Medicaid program can receive the benefit; public mental hospitals are not eligible for Medicaid funds, so their patients are excluded. In a 5–4 decision, the Supreme Court reversed a lower court ruling that the exclusion violated the right of the mentally ill to equal protection of the law. Writing for the majority, Justice Blackmun said, "We cannot say that it was irrational for Congress, in view of budgetary constraints, to decide that it is the Medicaid recipients in public institutions that are the most needy and the most deserving of the small monthly supplement." Schweiker v. Wilson, 101 S. Ct. 1074 (1981); L. Greenhouse, "High Court Rejects Patients' Benefits," *New York Times*, Mar. 5, 1981, p. 12.

43. See P. Dietz & J. Dvoskin, "Quality of Life for the Mentally Disabled," *J. Forensic Sciences* 25 (1980): 926.

44. J. Talbott (ed.), *The Chronic Mental Patient: Problems, Solutions and Recommendations for a Public Policy* (Washington, D.C.: American Psychiatric Association, 1978).

45. B. Meier, "Experiment of Privatized Mental Hospital Shows Benefits," *New York Times*, Dec. 28, 1999, p. 14. The Michigan Department of Community Health has been moving toward an open bid process for Medicaid dollars to provide mental health and substance abuse services that have been provided by community health boards. Dr. Durbin, "Plan to Bid for Mental Health Services Causes County Concern," *Detroit News*, Dec. 17, 1999, p. C-8.

46. See R. B. Saphire, "The Civilly-Committed Public Mental Patient and the Right to Aftercare," *Fla. State U. L. Rev.* 4 (1976): 232, 261. The use of antipsychotic medication in the

private practice of psychiatry in nursing homes and board and care homes is discussed in A. Goode, "Antipsychotic Drugs: Regulating Their Use in the Private Practice of Psychiatry," *Golden Gate U. L. Rev.* 15 (1985): 302.

47. W. Doll, "Family Coping with the Mentally Ill: An Unanticipated Problem of Deinstitutionalization," *Hosp. & Community Psychiatry* 27 (1976): 183; R. Frohboese & B. Sales, "Parental Opposition to Deinstitutionalization," *Law & Human Behavior* 4 (1980): 1. The highlighted cases, spanning nearly two centuries, have been those of Patrick Henry, Mrs. E. P. W. Packard, and Kenneth Donaldson. In all of them, the family—not the state—sought relief. G. Grob, "Rediscovering Asylums: The Unhistorical History of Mental Hospital," *Hastings Center Rep.* 7, no. 4 (1977): 38.

48. Price v. Shepard, 307 Minn. 250, 239 N.W.2d 905, 911 (1976).

49. Note, "Developments in the Law: Civil Commitment of the Mentally Ill," *Harv. L. Rev.* 87 (1974): 1190, 1344.

50. Stensvad v. Reivitz, 601 F.Supp. 128, 131 (W.D.Wis. 1985). See also Dautremont v. Broadlawn Hosp., 827 F.2d 291 (8th Cir. 1987); Johnson v. Silvers, 742 F.2d 823 (4th Cir. 1984); Anderson v. State, 135 Ariz. 578, 663 P.2d 570 (1982); In re Mental Commitment of M. P., 500 N.E.2d 216, *modified*, 510 N.E.2d 645 (Ind. App. 1986). See P. S. Appelbaum, "The Right to Refuse Treatment with Antipsychotic Medication: Retrospect and Prospect," *Am. J. Psychiatry* 145 (1988): 413; A. Brooks, "The Right to Refuse Antipsychotic Medications: Law and Policy," *Rutgers L. Rev.* 39 (1987): 339.

51. Schleoendoff v. Society of New York Hospital, 211 N.Y. 125, 104 N.E. 92 (1914).

52. When ruled incompetent, the individual lost the right to vote and other civil rights. In the small towns where state hospitals are located, the patients, were they allowed to vote, could elect the mayor by virtue of their number.

53. Utah Code Ann., sec. 64-7-36(10)(1979).

54. In re Dowler, No. 9275/00 (N.Y. Sup. Ct., Kings Cy., 2000).

55. K. E. Brooten, "Are the Courts Practicing Medicine?" *Private Practice*, July 1988, p. 14. Responding to Brooten's article, Dr. Abraham L. Halpern commented, "If physicians allow themselves to be intimidated by the courts to violate the Code of Medical Ethics, the blame falls primarily on them, not the judges." A. L. Halpern, "Physicians Should Not Be Intimidated by the Courts" (ltr.), *Private Practice*, Dec. 1988, p. 7.

56. S. Rachlin, "Rethinking the Right to Refuse Treatment," *Psychiatric Annals* 19 (1989): 213.

57. Ibid. See also R. D. Miller, "What Medical School Did You Graduate From? Judicial Prescribing of Medical Treatments," *J. Psychiatry & Law* 28 (2000): 215.

58. MCL 330:1489 provides:

(1) No determination that a person requires treatment, no order of court authorizing hospitalization or alternative treatment, nor any form of admission to a hospital shall give rise to a resumption of, constitute a finding of, or operate as an adjudication of legal incompetence.

(2) No order of commitment under any previous state of this state shall, in the absence of a concomitant appointment of a guardian, constitute a finding of or operate as an adjudication of legal incompetence.

59. It has been held that the patients' bill of rights does not create a higher standard of care for health care providers. The statute is intended "to help insure that patients' rights are protected, not to expand or otherwise change the law of negligence." Erbstoeszer by Leyes v. American Cas. Co., 486 N.W.2d 549, 552 n. 1 (Wis. App. 1992).

60. MCL 330.1400, sec. 400(1)(B).

61. Ibid. at sec. 400(e).

62. 110 S. Ct. 975 (1990); discussed in chapter 1, on civil commitment.

63. The Michigan statute on commitment (MCL 330.1401) provides:

(a) A person who is mentally ill, and who as a result of that mental illness can reasonably be expected within the near future to intentionally or unintentionally seriously physically injure himself or another person, and who has engaged in an act or acts or made significant threats that are substantially supportive of the expectation.

(b) A person who is mentally ill, and who as a result of that mental illness is unable to attend to those of his basic physical needs such as food, clothing, or shelter that must be attended to in order for him to avoid serious harm in the near future, and who has demonstrated that inability by failing to attend to those basic physical needs.

(c) A person who is mentally ill, whose judgment is so impaired that he is unable to understand his need for treatment and whose continued behavior as the result of this mental illness can reasonably be expected, on the basis of competent medical opinion, to result in significant physical harm to himself or others.

64. One case, under a now-repealed statute, is Stowers v. Ardmore Acres Hospital, 19 Mich. App. 115, 172 N.W.2d 497 (1969), *aff'd sub nom*, Stowers v. Wolodzko, 386 Mich. 199, 191 N.W.2d 355 (1971). In this case, which came before the court of appeals in 1969, the plaintiff was sent, under the statute, on temporary commitment to a private psychiatric hospital. MCL 330.21. She was not declared incompetent. She was given two injections of a tranquilizer over her express objection. A jury award of $40,000 in her favor was sustained by the court of appeals and affirmed, in 1971, by the state supreme court. The court held that the circumstances of her involuntary commitment did not change the traditional requirements of informed consent that makes an intrusion privileged. The supreme court noted the distinction made in the statute between private and public hospitals with respect to treatment during prehearing detention. It said (386 Mich. at 134, 191 N.W.2d at 362): "Under the statute a clear distinction is made between referral to a state hospital where custody and treatment are authorized, and a private hospital where a patient is only to be 'detained until such petition can be heard and determined.' If we were to accept defendant's contention that there is no distinction between private and state hospitals, we would be avoiding the clear meaning of the statute and treating a part of the statute as surplusage."

A few years later, in 1974, a federal district court in Michigan ruled that involuntary treatment was authorized in public hospitals, under that statute, during both prehearing detention and temporary commitment. Bell v. Wayne County Gen. Hospital, 384 F.Supp. 1085 (E.D.Mich. 1974). Under prevailing practice, trial courts in Michigan have taken the *provider* approach, that is, involuntary treatment to committed patients.

65. Juxtaposed to the statutory provisions, regulatory provisions of the Michigan Department of Mental Health (as in other states) provide that medication shall not be administered to an involuntary patient unless a treatment order has been issued by probate court, with exceptions: (1) the patient gives informed consent in writing to receive medications, (2) life-saving measure is required (specific documentation must be in the clinical record), or (3) it is necessary to prevent the patient from injuring self or others (specific documentation must be in the clinical record). After the preliminary hearing and issuance of a court order, nonconsensual administration of chemotherapy is authorized in the Michigan Mental Health Code (MCL 330.1718). It provides:

(1) Chemotherapy shall not be administered to an individual who has been hospitalized by medical certification or by petition . . . until after the preliminary court hearing has been held unless the individual consents to such chemotherapy or unless the administration of such chemotherapy is necessary to prevent physical injury to the individual or others.

(2) Chemotherapy shall not be administered to an individual who has been hospitalized by medical certification or by petition . . . on the day preceding and on the day of his full court hearing unless the individual consents to such chemotherapy or unless the administration of such chemotherapy is necessary to prevent physical injury to the individual or others.

66. Dr. Paul Appelbaum and Dr. Thomas Gutheil studied patients' refusal of medication during a three-month period on an inpatient service of a community mental health center. Although refusal of medication was common, most episodes were self-limited. Only five of seventy-two episodes seriously impaired patient care; each of these cases appeared to be delusionally motivated. P. Appelbaum & T. Gutheil, "Drug Refusal: A Study of Psychiatric Inpatients," *Am. J. Psychiatry* 137 (1980): 340. See also P. B. Kraft, "The Right to Refuse Psy-

chiatric Treatment: Professional Self-Esteem and Hopelessness," in C. P. Ewing (ed.), *Psychology, Psychiatry, and the Law: A Clinical and Forensic Handbook* (Sarasota, Fla.: Professional Resource Exchange, 1985), pp. 215–42.

67. The Report of the Third Committee of the Commission on Human Rights of the United Nations provides: "Where any treatment is authorized without the patient's informed consent, every effort shall nevertheless be made to inform the patient about the nature of the treatment and any possible alternatives and to involve the patient as far as practicable in the development of the treatment plan." Report A/46/721, sec. 9 (Dec. 17, 1991).

68. R. Gold, S. Hensley, & A. Caffrey, "States Square Off against Drug Firms in Crusade on Prices," *Wall Street Journal*, Dec. 7, 2001, p. 1. See also E. H. v. Matin, 284 S.E.2d 232 (W.Va. 1981).

69. Rogers v. Okin, 478 F.Supp. 1342, 1386–88 (D.Mass. 1979), *aff'd in part and rev'd in part on other grounds*, 634 F.2d 650 (1st Cir. 1980), *vacated & remanded on other grounds sub nom.* Mills v. Rogers, 457 U.S. 291 (1982); Rogers v. Commissioner, 390 Mass. 489, 458 N.E.3d 308 (1983). In 1986, New York followed the *Rogers* decision in Rivers v. Katz, 67 N.Y.2d 485, 495 N.E.2d 337, 504 N.Y.S.2d 74 (1986). The New York court said,

> We reject any argument that involuntarily committed patients lose their liberty interest in avoiding the unwanted administration of antipsychotic medication. . . . We recognize, however, that the right to reject treatment with antipsychotic medication is not absolute and under circumstances may have to yield to compelling State interests. . . . Where the patient presents a danger to himself or other members of society or engages in dangerous or potentially destructive conduct within the institution, the State may be warranted, in the exercise of its police power, in administering antipsychotic medication over the patient's objections. . . . The most obvious example of this is an emergency situation, such as where there is imminent danger to a patient or others in the immediate vicinity. . . . [I]n situations where the State's police power is not implicated, and the patient refuses to consent to the administration of antipsychotic drugs, there must be a judicial determination of whether the patient has the capacity to make a reasoned decision with respect to proposed treatment before the drugs may be administered pursuant to the State's parens patriae power. The determination should be made at a hearing following exhaustion of the administrative review procedures. . . . The hearing should be de novo, and the patient should be afforded representation by counsel. The State would bear the burden of demonstrating by clear and convincing evidence the patient's incapacity to make a treatment decision. . . . If the court concludes that the patient lacks the capacity to determine the course of his own treatment, the court must determine whether the proposed treatment is narrowly tailored to give substantive effect to the patient's liberty interest, taking into consideration all relevant circumstances, including the patient's best interests, the benefits to be gained from the treatment, the adverse side effects associated with the treatment and any less intrusive alternative treatments. The State would bear the burden to establish by clear and convincing evidence that the proposed treatment meets these criteria.

See Comment, "The Involuntarily Committed Patient's Qualified Right to Refuse Psychotropics in New York," *Albany L. Rev.* 51 (1987): 333.

However, outpatient commitment "already has or will become synonymous with forced medication." S. Schwartz & C. Costanzo, "Compelling Treatment in the Community: Distorted Doctrine and Violated Values," *Loy. L. A. L. Rev.* 20 (1987): 1329. Outpatient commitment laws, including New York's, provide for enforced medication, with institutionalization as a consequence for failing to accept the medication. N.Y. Ment. Hyg. L., sec. 9.60. A petition and hearing process under the Kendra's Law is said to be more cumbersome because it deals with individuals outside the hospital system. Y. Schacher, "Courts, Lawyers Are Gearing Up to Handle Kendra's Law Hearings," *N.Y.L.J.* 222 (Sept. 30, 1999): 1.

70. 653 F.2d 836, 847 n. 12 (3d Cir. 1981) (en banc), *vacated and remanded*, 458 U.S. 1119 (1982). See A. D. Brooks, "The Right to Refuse Antipsychotic Medications: Law and Policy," *Rutgers L. Rev.* 39 (1987): 339; L. H. Roth, "The Right to Refuse Psychiatric Treatment: Law and Medicine at the Interface," *Emory L. J.* 35 (1986): 139. See also C. R. Williams & B. A.

Arrigo, *Law, Psychology, and Justice: Chaos Theory and the New (Dis)order* (Albany: State University of New York Press, 2002), pp. 153–78.

71. 653 F.2d at 848.

72. 653 F.2d at 851. In a concurring opinion, three of the nine-judge court took the position that the state may administer antipsychotic medication in the face of a patient's refusal to accept medication *only* when the state demonstrates either that the medication is necessary to prevent the patient from posing a danger to himself or to others, or that the patient does not have the mental capacity to make a rational decision with respect to medication. 653 F.2d at 858 (emphasis by the judges).

73. The court followed the principles it established in Superintendent of Belchertown State School v. Saikewicz, 373 Mass. 728, 370 N.E.2d 417 (1977), involving cancer chemotherapy for a retarded man, and Guardianship of Roe, 411 Mass. 666, 583 N.E.2d 1282 (1992), involving the involuntary administration of antipsychotic medication to an outpatient diagnosed as paranoid schizophrenic. In these cases the court held that when an individual is incompetent to make a treatment decision, the surrogate decision maker must decide on his or her behalf using a *substituted judgment* analysis; that is, the decision maker is expected to make the decision that the incompetent patient would have made if competent and aware of all the facts of the situation, including his or her own continued incompetence.

74. The Supreme Judicial Court of Massachusetts, in response to questions certified to it by the Court of Appeals for the First Circuit, held that under Massachusetts state law:

(1) a mental patient has the right to make treatment decisions and does not lose that right until the patient is adjudicated incompetent by a judge through incompetence proceedings;

(2) only if a patient poses an imminent threat of harm to himself or others, and only if there is no less intrusive alternative to antipsychotic drugs, may the patient be forcibly medicated under the police power over objection without prior court approval; and

(3) only where necessary as an interim measure to prevent the immediate, substantial and irreversible deterioration of a serious mental illness where even the smallest of avoidable delays would be intolerable may the patient be forcibly medicated under parens patriae power, and then only in the case of a patient who is, or in the exercise of professional judgment is believed to be, incompetent.

Rogers v. Commissioner, 390 Mass. 489, 458 N.E.2d 308 (1983).

75. See J. M. Zito, S. L. Lentz, W. W. Routt, & G. W. Olson, "The Treatment Review Panel: A Solution to Treatment Refusal?" *Bull. Am. Acad. Psychiatry & Law* 12 (1984): 349.

76. In an eighteenth-month study period, of 2,273 petitions filed, 57 were withdrawn for various reasons, and of the others, 1,514 involved incompetent refusers and 702 incompetent acceptors. The court granted 98.6 percent of the petitions for the treatment of incompetent refusers and granted all petitions for incompetent acceptors. Overall, this represents a granting of 99.1 percent of the 2,216 petitions that were actually pursued to judicial decision. Reported in R. Schouten, "Financial Costs of Right-to-Refuse-Treatment Law Assessed," *Psychiatric Times*, Oct. 1991, p. 28.

77. 457 U.S. 307 (1982).

78. 457 U.S. at 322.

79. Stensvad v. Reivitz, 601 F.Supp. 128, 132 (W.D.Wis. 1985). In Dale M. v. Board of Education of Bradley-Bourbonnais High School, 237 F.3d 813 (7th Cir. 2001), the court was asked to spell out what school districts must do to accommodate emotionally troubled children. The Individuals with Disabilities Education Act states that disabled students are entitled to special accommodations at no cost. The act applies to children with mental retardation, specific learning disabilities, emotional disturbances, and other disabilities like deafness. In the case at hand, a school psychologist reported that Dale M. suffered from depression. He was absent from school, drinking up to twelve beers a day, and regularly smoking marijuana. His mother enrolled him in a residential school, where court records showed his discipline problems stopped. The mother contended that the school district where they lived should have to pay for the school, because of his disability. The Seventh Circuit described the school as a "boarding school for difficult children," and it said that because Dale's problems were

not "primarily educational," he did not qualify for reimbursement. The Seventh Circuit, by a 2–1 vote, overturned the trial court's order calling on the school district to pay for the classes. In a dissent, Judge Kenneth Ripple wrote, "[N]one of us who wear black robs are in an institutional position to second guess the Illinois Department of Education that approved the program as a permissible placement for Illinois school children." The U.S. Supreme Court declined to review the case. In Butler v. Evans, 225 F.3d 887 (7th Cir. 2000), the court held that residential treatment at a psychiatric hospital could not be compensable as an educational placement because it was not an accredited educational institution. In Seattle Sch. Dist., No. 1 v. A. S., 82 F.3d 1493 (9th Cir. 1996), the court rejected the school district's argument that it should not be responsible for placement because the facility was "not included as [an] educational placement option for handicapped pupils in that state."

80. B. J. Winick, "The Right to Refuse Psychotropic Medication: Current State of the Law and Beyond," in D. Rapoport & J. Parry (eds.), *The Right to Refuse Antipsychotic Medication* (Washington, D.C.: American Bar Association, 1986), p. 20. See also S. Gelman, *Medicating Schizophrenia: A History* (New Brunswick: Rutgers University Press, 1999); B. J. Winick, *The Right to Refuse Mental Health Treatment* (Washington, D.C.: American Psychological Assn., 1997); S. Gelman, "The Law and Psychiatry Wars, 1960–1980," *Cal. West. L. Rev.* 34 (1997): 153.

81. 418 N.W.2d 139 (Minn. 1988).

82. 418 N.W.2d at 147.

83. Ibid.

84. *Arizona:* Large v. Superior Court, 148 Ariz. 229, 714 P.2d 399 (1986); Anderson v. State, 135 Ariz. 578, 663 P.2d 570 (Ariz. App. 1982). *California:* Keyhea v. Rushen, 178 Cal. App.3d 526, 223 Cal. Rptr. 746 (1986). *Colorado:* Goedecke v. State Department of Institutions, 198 Colo. 407, 603 P.2d 123 (1979); People in Interest of Medina, 662 P.2d 184 (Colo. App. 1982). *District of Columbia:* In re Boyd, 403 A.2d 744 (D.C. 1979). *Indiana:* In re The Mental Commitment of M. P., 500 N.E.2d 216 (Ind. App. 1986). *Iowa:* Clites v. State, 322 N.W.2d 917 (1982). *Massachusetts:* Rogers v. Okin, supra note 69. *Minnesota:* Jarvis v. Levine, supra note 81. *New Hampshire:* Opinion of the Justices, 123 N.H. 554, 465 A.2d 484 (N.H. 1983). *New York:* Rivers v. Katz, 67 N.Y.S.2d 485, 495 N.E.2d 337, 504 N.Y.S.2d 74 (Ct. App. 1986). *Oklahoma:* In re Mental Health of K. B., 609 P.2d 747 (Okla. 1980). *Vermont:* J. L. v. Miller, No. S-418-84-WnC (Vt. Super. Ct., Washington County, May 20, 1985), reported in *Mental & Phys. Disab. L. Rep.* 9 (1985): 261. *Washington:* In re Guardianship of Ingram, 102 Wash.2d 827, 689 P.2d 1363 (1984). *Wisconsin:* State *ex rel.* Jones v. Gerhardstein, 135 Wis.2d 161, 400 N.W.2d 1 (Wis. App. 1986).

In recent years legislatures in various states have enacted legislation that provides for the petitioning by a treatment facility to a court for an order to administer psychotropic medication to an involuntarily committed patient, if, in the opinion of the facility director or attending psychiatrist and the treating physician, psychotropic medication will be medically beneficial to the person and is necessary because (1) the person presents a danger to himself or others, (2) the person cannot improve or his or her condition may deteriorate without the medication, or (3) the person may improve without the medication but only at a significantly slower rate. The legislation further provides that the court may order involuntarily administered psychotropic medications to an involuntarily committed patient if it finds by clear and convincing evidence that the patient is unable to give informed consent for medication treatment due to the inability to make a competent, voluntary, and knowing decision, and that the medication is necessary and would be medically beneficial. The legislation was involved in Rabenberg v. Rigney, 597 N.W.2d 424 (S.D. 1999).

Statutes usually require that an involuntarily committed patient be notified in writing upon arrival at the hospital of the right to immediately make a "reasonable number of calls" to seek counsel or medical or psychiatric assistance. See, e.g., Ohio Rev. Code Ann., sec. 5122.05.

85. See, e.g., F. Lemere, "Psychotherapy" (ltr.), *Psychiatric News*, Sept. 18, 1992, p. 18.

86. Bee v. Greaves, 744 F.2d 1387, 1396 (10th Cir. 1984), *cert. denied*, 105 S. Ct. 1187 (1985).

87. 744 F.2d at 139 n. 7.

88. The primary duty to patients whose judgment is impaired is to prevent them from engaging in harmful behavior. A patient assaulted by another patient at a state hospital may

sue the mental health department for violation of the patient's bill of rights. Texas Dept. of Mental Health & Mental Retardation, 2000 WL 550822 (Tex. App. 2000). What about allegedly consensual sexual behavior among patients? Up until the 1960s, there was total separation of the sexes in psychiatric wards, that is, separate wards for males and females. Later, a tendency began to change this policy and accommodate men and women in the same ward, although in separate rooms. The main rationale for this change was the assumption that male and female patients would neglect themselves less in a mixed ward due to the presence of members of the opposite sex, and that the presence of women in the ward would curb violent behavior among males. Professionals in the field have differing opinions on this issue, with some claiming that the transition to mixed wards has led to improved behavior among patients, while others argue that this improvement is due mainly to the introduction of new medicines.

Whether the danger of sexual assault and abuse is frequent or infrequent is not actually relevant. As these are nonpredictable occurrences, the dangers must be seen to exist at all times for all patients. It is likely that sexual intercourse in a mental hospital with a mentally ill patient would involve exploiting the patient's troubled mental state. Attention must be given to the possibly severe consequences that may result from the sexual activity—pregnancy, HIV, and the possible ruin of the patient's family, as well as creation of mental problems which may require further treatment. The problem is not only a medical issue but also a legal and social one. See Foy & Foy v. Greenblott, 190 Cal. Rptr. 84 (Cal. App. 1983); D. Mossman, M. L. Perlin, & D. A. Dorfman, "Sex on the Wards: Conundra for Clinicians," *J. Am. Acad. Psychiatry & Law* 25 (1997): 441; M. L. Perlin, "Hospitalized Patients and the Right to Sexual Interaction: Beyond the Last Frontier?" *N. Y. U. Rev. L. & Soc'l Change* 20 (1993–94): 517. Can nursing homes cope with their residents' sexuality? See A. H. McLean, "What Kind of Love is This?" *Sciences,* Sept./Oct. 1994, p. 36; M. Purdy, "At Nursing Homes, Intimacy Is Becoming a Matter of Policy," *New York Times,* Nov. 6, 1995, p. 14.

89. See P. H. Soloff, "Physical Controls: The Use of Seclusion and Restraint in Modern Psychiatric Practice," in L. H. Roth (ed.), *Clinical Treatment of the Violent Person* (New York: Guilford, 1987), pp. 119–37; P. Soloff, J. P. McEvoy, R. Gamguli, & M. Gamguli, "Controversies in Psychiatry: Is Seclusion Therapeutic?" *Psychiatric Annals* 19 (Jan. 1989): 45; W. A. Fisher, "Restraint and Seclusion: A Review of the Literature," *Am. J. Psychiatry* 151 (1994): 584; S. S. Kennedy & W. K. Mohr, "A Prolegomenon on Restraint of Children: Implicating Constitutional Rights," *Am. J. Orthopsychiatry* 71 (2001): 26; T. Mason, "Seclusion Theory Reviewed: A Benevolent or Malevolent Intervention?" *Med. Sci. & Law* 33 (1993): 95; F. C. Redmond, "Study on the Use of Seclusion," *Qual. Rev. Bull.* 6 (1980): 20.

90. M. Janofsky, "Neighbors' Gentler View of Man Killed on Plane," *New York Times,* Sept. 23, 2000, p. 8; T. Roche, "Homicide in the Sky," *Time,* Oct. 2, 2000, p. 44.

91. Some, e.g., law professor George Dix, consider medication as more restrictive than restraint or seclusion. G. Dix, "Legal and Ethical Issues in the Treatment and Handling of Violent Behavior," in L. H. Roth (ed.), *Clinical Treatment and Management of the Violent Person* (New York: Guilford Press, 1987), pp. 178–206. But clinician Paul Soloff disagrees. P. H. Soloff, "Physical Controls: The Use of Seclusion and Restraint in Modern Psychiatric Practice," in id., pp. 119–37.

Data on the incidence of deaths and injury in the implementation of seclusion and restraint are not routinely collected, but an investigation published in 1998 in the *Hartford Courant* reported 142 deaths in the previous ten years connected to the use of physical restraint in mental health settings. Those who died were disproportionately young children. The deaths occurred in all fifty states and represent only those that were reported and documented. E. M. Weiss, "Deadly Restraint: A Nationwide Pattern of Death," *Hartford Courant,* Oct. 11–5, 1998. The types of personal injury or death include dehydration, choking, circulatory and skin problems, loss of strength and mobility, incontinence, and injury from other patients. J. Zusman, *Restraint and Seclusion: Improving Practice and Conquering the JCAHO Standards* (Marblehead, Mass.: Opus Communications, 1997).

Litigation involving seclusion and restraint of psychiatric patients has been based on constitutional grounds (violation of civil rights) or malpractice alleging negligent use of seclusion and restraint. In Fleming v. Prince George's County, 277 Md. 655, 358 A.2d 892 (1976), a physician was held to have violated the standard of care by placing the patient in restraints without attempting to determine the cause of her "obstinate and stubborn" behavior. The plaintiff was severely injured when she attempted to escape. The plaintiff's expert expressed the opinion, "[T]he proper standard would have required [the defendant doctor] to ascertain whether this was a personality problem or whether it represented some medical condition which might respond to treatment. . . . [K]nowing that she was obstinate or cantankerous for whatever reason, to her detriment, then [the defendant doctor] should have taken other measures. Whether they would have been successful or not we don't know, but in any event he did not undertake to do something more about it, by enlisting her husband's aid or perhaps other members of the family." In Pisel v. Stamford Hosp., 180 Conn. 314, 430 A.2d 1 (1980), a psychiatric patient, who was locked in a seclusion room in a highly agitated and psychotic condition, was found with her head wedged between a mattress and side railing of a steel bed, unconscious and with no pulse. The evidence showed that the appropriate standard of care required that "no objects or furniture should be left [in the seclusion room] that could cause the patient harm" [e.g., the steel bed frame]. The court awarded $3.6 million in damages. The oft-cited decision by the U.S. Supreme Court in Youngberg v. Romeo, 457 U.S. 307 (1982), that involved a challenge to the "treatment" practices of the Pennhurst State School and Hospital in Pennsylvania, endorsed a *substantial judgment* test in the use of restraints "to provide needed training." In the newsletter of the Michigan Protection and Advocacy Service, *Exchange* (Fall 2001, p. 1), staff attorney Mark Cody writes: "Michigan Protection and Advocacy Service (MPAS) has long fought the use of restraint and seclusion for individuals with disabilities. The use of restraint or seclusion on a human being is a practice that is demeaning, and can be dangerous. MPAS has investigated and substantiated numerous incidents where consumers have been injured while being restrained or secluded."

92. The rules require physicians or other licensed practitioners to evaluate patients face-to-face within one hour of an intervention, which may be difficult to carry out late at night, when a physician may not be on the premises. The new law sets two tiers of standards, one for hospitals and other medical facilities, and another for nonmedical facilities for children and youth (for example, residential treatment centers and group homes). The *medical facility* standards limit the use of seclusion and restraint to interventions required to protect the physical safety of the patient, staff, or others. Drugs can be considered restraints if they are used to control behavior or restrict freedom of movement and are not considered a standard treatment for the patient's medical or psychiatric condition. The second set of standards, applicable to nonmedical facilities serving children and youth, restricts the use of seclusion and restraint to emergency situations and only to ensure the immediate physical safety of the resident, a staff member, or others. Individuals applying seclusion or restraint must be certified by the state in core competencies defined in the legislation. The legislation requires the Secretary of Health and Human Services to develop national guidelines and standards for staff training. "Seclusion and Restraint Law Reflects APA Input to Congress," *Psychiatric News*, Nov. 17, 2000, p. 2. The impulsivity of an individual, which can be assessed by past history of psychological testing, is a criterion for the use of seclusion or restraint. See K. Tardiff (ed.), *The Psychiatric Uses of Seclusion and Restraint* (Washington, D.C.: American Psychiatric Press, 1984). Restrictions on behavior modification are discussed in D. Wexler, "Token and Taboo: Behavior Modification, Token Economics and the Law," *Cal. L. Rev.* 61 (1973): 81.

93. Under the U.S. federal system, both the national government and the state governments have authority to regulate various aspects of health care. The federal government pays for a large percentage of the total national hospital bill through Medicare and Medicaid—so the federal government's power is the power of the purse. The state government has the power to issue or revoke the licenses of health care providers within its boundaries. This gives the state government duties and responsibilities that are concurrent with some of the federal government's duties and responsibilities.

Both the U.S. and state governments have regulations regarding the use of restraints on psychiatric patients. The key features of these regulations are the least restrictive alternative rule, the reasons a person may be restrained, and the documentation required. Health care facilities attempt to comply with these regulations by incorporating their rules into operational policies and procedures. Compliance is monitored by the federal government's designated watchdog, the Joint Commission on Accreditation of Healthcare Organizations, and through the state's periodic licensing regulations.

Federal and state regulations require a written order by a medical professional for restraints. The Michigan Mental Health code requirement can be stretched to allow a patient to be restrained for up to four hours without being examined face-to-face by a physician. It is a reasonable requirement that any average-size city hospital could follow. In rural areas it may be impossible to have a physician respond in person within four hours. The JCAHO approach of allowing licensed independent providers to order restraints may be more workable. Many classifications of Advance Practice Nurses and Physician Assistants, as well as clinical psychologists, would have sufficient knowledge and training to be able to evaluate whether a patient requires, and can tolerate, a specific restraint technique. As with all aspects of practice by paraprofessionals whatever they order would still be subject to review by a supervising physician.

The Michigan Mental Health Code requires the full justification for each instance of restraint be entered promptly into the patient's chart. MCL 330.1740(8). There is a common saying, "If you didn't document it, you didn't do it." The Detroit Medical Center's "Restraint TIP Sheet" reminds staff of the importance of documentation. Not only does it admonish them to write down a "correct" reason for initiating restraints, it tells them to document the less restrictive alternatives they tried first, or at least the less restrictive alternatives they considered using. This will establish that the provider knows of less restrictive measures and thought about using less restrictive alternatives, but in his professional judgment felt the restraint ordered was the least restrictive alternative that would work. There is an educational benefit from this type of requirement, as it constantly reinforces the importance of the least restrictive alternative rule every time a provider orders restraints.

The results of any trial releases must also be documented. Without this information it would be difficult to determine if the restraints were employed longer than needed. The final order to discontinue the restraints must also be written, regardless of the results of the trial releases. Once a restraint is discontinued, a new order, complete with documentation of the full justification for rerestraining the person and less restrictive alternatives that were considered, must be written into the medical chart.

Another feature of the documentation required on the Detroit Medical Center's Restraint Flow Record is "Education Notes." This refers to the education of the patient and family and friends. The provider must document what the patient was told about why the restraint was needed. Visitors to the patient must also be told why the patient is restrained and what must happen before the restraint is discontinued.

The Michigan Mental Health Code does not specify a hierarchy of restraints, but the Children's Hospital of Michigan has a policy that ranks the types of restraints that my be used on pediatric patients. The list is in order of the degree of restriction of movement: jacket restraint, elbow restraints, ankle/waist restraints, mummy restraint, pedi-restraint, Olympic-papoose restraint. Detroit Medical Center, "Restraint/Safety—Pediatrics," Policy No. 2 PCD 260.

As a practical matter, economics play a large factor in the use of restraints. Restraints are often a substitute for adequate staffing levels. The first expense to be cut each time Medicare or Medicaid reimbursement rates are cut is payroll. Even if hospitals are not restraining patients directly due to lack of personnel to control a unit, the understaffing may lead to conditions that cause more disruption and aggression on the unit. Housekeeping that is cut back so that the unit is more cluttered, less attractive, or less comfortable could contribute to situations in which patients have to be retrained. See, in general, J. Luna, "Limiting the Use of Restraint and Seclusion in Psychiatric Treatment Facilities for Patients under 21," downloaded from *www.law. uh.edu/healthlawperspectives/Mental,* Nov. 19, 2001.

The American Psychiatric Association's Task Force on Seclusion and Restraint lists three indications for using seclusion and restraint together: (1) to prevent imminent harm to the patient or other persons where other means of control are not effective or appropriate, (2) to prevent serious disruption of the treatment program or significant damage to the physical environment, and (3) to assist in treatment as part of ongoing behavior therapy. Two additional indications exist for seclusion alone: (1) to decrease the stimulation a patient receives, and (2) to comply with a patient's request. Once a patient's behavior is well-known to staff, restraint or seclusion may be used to prevent loss of control, rather than waiting until the patient has become actively aggressive. The task force cautions that seclusion should not be used when medical conditions exist that require close monitoring, when organic conditions exist that would be exacerbated by sensory deprivation, or merely for the convenience of staff. Full (four—or five—point) restraint should not be used without seclusion, to protect a patient's dignity and safety. See T. Gutheil & K. Tardiff, "Indications and Contradictions for Seclusion and Restraint," in K. Tardiff (ed.), *The Psychiatric Uses of Seclusion and Restraint,* supra note 92; R. D. Miller, "The Continuum of Coercion: Constitutional and Clinical Considerations in the Treatment of Mentally Disordered Persons," *Denver U. L. Rev.* 74 (1997): 1169; H. Bath, "The Physical Restraint of Children: Is It Therapeutic?" *Amer. J. Orthopsychiat.* 64 (1994): 40. For a social structural study of mental hospital functioning, see A. H. Stanton & M. S. (*Tuesdays with Morrie*) Schwartz, *The Mental Hospital* (New York: Basic Books, 1954).

94. See, e.g., Cal. Welf. Inst. Code, sec. 5325(f)(g): Mass. Gen. Laws Ann., ch. 123, sec. 23; N.Y. Ment. Hyg. L., sec. 15.03(b)(4); Wash. Rev. Code Ann., sec. 71.05.370(7). However, the courts even in these states have ruled that a patient may refuse drug treatment. See, e.g., Rivers v. Katz, 67 N.Y.S.2d 485, 495 N.E.2d 337, 504 N.Y.S.2d 74 (Ct. App. 1986).

95. Supra note 37.

96. The Wisconsin legislation provides that patients have the right to refuse *all* types of treatment, not just medication. However, the Wisconsin right to refuse treatment case requiring judicial determination of incompetency before treatment can be administered without patient consent is limited specifically to psychotropic drugs. State *ex rel.* Jones v. Gerhardstein, 141 Wis.2d 710, 416 N.W.2d 888 (1987); R. D. Miller, "The Right to Refuse Treatment: Generic Version," *Newsletter Am. Acad. Psychiat. & Law* 15 (Apr. 1990): 16. Wisconsin legislation also provides for outpatient commitment and for "limited guardianship" to consent to psychotropic medication. Wis. Stat., sec. 880.01 (1989–90). The legislation states that "not competent to refuse psychotropic medication" means that, "because of chronic mental illness. . . . a person is incapable of expressing an understanding of the advantages and disadvantages of accepting treatment, and the alternatives to accepting the particular treatment offered, after the advantage, disadvantages and alternatives have been explained to the person." Id. at sec. 880.01. See R. Miller, *Involuntary Civil Commitment of the Mentally Ill in the Post-Reform Era* (Springfield, Ill.: Thomas, 1987); K. Temple, "The Right to Refuse Treatment," *J. Psychiatry & Law* 14 (1986): 375, 392.

97. 307 Minn. 250, 239 N.W.2d 905 (1976).

98. The court set out the following procedure (239 N.W.2d at 913):

1. If the patient is incompetent to give consent or refuses consent or his guardian other than persons responsible for his commitment also refuses his consent, before more intrusive forms of treatment may be utilized, the medical director of the state hospital must petition the probate division of the county court in the county in which the hospital is located for an order authorizing the prescribed treatment;
2. The court shall appoint a guardian ad litem to represent the interests of the patient;
3. In an adversary proceeding, pursuant to the petition, the court shall determine the necessity and reasonableness of the prescribed treatment.

In making that determination the court should balance the patient's need for treatment against the intrusiveness of the prescribed treatment. Factors which should be considered are (1) the extent and duration of changes in behavior patterns and mental activity affected by the treatment, (2) the risks of adverse side effects, (3) the experimental nature of the treatment, (4) its acceptance by the medical community of this state, (5) the extent of intrusion into the patient's body and the pain connected with the treatment, and (6) the patient's ability to completely determine for himself whether the treatment is desirable.

99. 239 N.W.2d at 913.

100. Washington's guardianship statute specifically denies guardians the power to consent to ECT. In re Schuoler, 106 Wash.2d 500, 723 P.2d 1103, 1107 (1986).

101. In re Lindquist, No. 140151 (Ramsey Co. Minn., Apr. 30, 1976), discussed in *Mental Disabilities L. Rep.* 1 (1976): 190. See also *Psychiatric News,* Apr. 15, 1977, p. 1.

102. In re Fussa, No. 46912 (Minn. June 14, 1976).

103. Noted in L. D. Gaughan & L. H. LaRue, "The Right of a Mental Patient to Refuse Antipsychotic Drugs in an Institution," *Law & Psychology Rev.* 4 (1978): 44, 69. See also the extensive article by D. E. Cichon, "The Right to 'Just Say No': A History and Analysis of the Right to Refuse Antipsychotic Drugs," *La. L. Rev.* 53 (1992): 283.

104. 418 N.W.2d 139 (Minn. 1988).

105. 403 N.W.2d 298 at 308 (Minn. App. 1987).

106. Ibid.

107. 418 N.W.2d at 145.

108. *Nw. U. L. Rev.* 72 (1977): 461.

109. Ibid. at 475–76, quoted in 418 N.W.2d at 145.

110. P. Appelbaum & T. Gutheil, " 'Rotting with Their Rights On,' Constitutional Theory and Clinical Reality in Drug Refusal by Psychiatric Patients," *Bull. Am. Acad. Psychiatry & Law* 7 (1979): 306; T. Gutheil & P. S. Appelbaum, " 'Mind Control,' 'Synthetic Sanity,' 'Artificial Competence,' and Genuine Confusion: Legally Relevant Effects of Antipsychotic Medication," *Hofstra L. Rev.* 1 (1983): 77.

111. J. M. Davis, "Efficacy of Tranquilizing and Antidepressant Drugs," *Arch. Gen. Psychiatry* 13 (1965): 552.

112. State *ex rel.* Jones v. Gerhardstein, 141 Wis.2d 710, 416 N.W.2d 888 (1987). In regard forensic patients, see R. D. Miller, M. R. Gernstein, G. J. VanRybroek, & G. J. Maier, "The Impact of the Right to Refuse Treatment in a Forensic Patient Population: Six-Month Review," *Bull. Am. Acad. Psych. & Law* 17 (1989): 108. The U.S. Supreme Court has said: "While the therapeutic benefits of antipsychotic drugs are well documented, it is also true that the drugs can have serious, even fatal, side effects." Washington v. Harper, 494 U.S. 210 (1990), quoted in Riggins v. Nevada, 112 S. Ct. 1810 (1992). See supra note 5 on medical services in prison.

Experimental medical research on inmates in prison is reportedly on the rise. According to federal regulations, research in prisons must fit into one of four permissible categories; studies of the possible causes and effects of incarceration and criminal behavior; studies of prisons as institutional structures or of prisoners as incarcerated persons; research on conditions affecting prisoners as a group; and research involving a therapy likely to benefit the inmate involved. In all cases, studies are required to present no more than a minimal risk to the prisoner. Yet in many of the clinical trials reported to the federal Office of Human Research Protections, those regulations were clearly violated. HIV-positive prisoners have reportedly been pressured to enroll in clinical trials. Inmates say that they agreed to participate in the studies in order to escape poor medical care, abusive conditions, or lack of access to up-to-date HIV drugs. Inmates who suffer harm as a result of experimental psychiatric programs are limited in seeking redress as a result of the 1996 Prison Litigation Reform Act, which prohibits inmates from bringing lawsuits alleging mental or emotional harm unless they could also prove physical injury. S. J. A. Talvi, "The Prison as Laboratory," *In These Times*, Jan. 7, 2002, p. 10.

113. In re K. K. B., 609 P.2d 747, 749 (Okla. 1980).

114. Nolen v. Peterson, 554 So.2d 863 (Ala. 1989); Matter of Orr, 531 N.E.2d 64 (Ill. App. 1988).

115. People v. Medina, 705 P.2d 961 (Colo. 1985); see also Hopkins v. People, 772 P.2d 624 (Colo. App. 1988).

116. The term *antipsychotic medication* as used in the opinion of the court referred to medications such as Haldol, Prolixin, and Trilafin, which are used in treating psychoses, especially schizophrenia. Steele v. Hamilton Cy. Community Mental Health Board, 90 Ohio St.3d 176, 736 N.E.2d 10 (2000). The Ohio Supreme Court went on to say:

> Additional procedures, such as periodic hearings to reevaluate the patient's capacity and the efficacy of the treatment, will be necessary in those cases where an order is issued permitting the forced administration of drugs. We realize that each forced medication case in unique and, therefore, we do not set specific guidelines other than to state that all court orders permitting the administration of antipsychotic drugs against a patient's wishes should be periodically reviewed, and continued forced medication should be substantiated by competent medical evidence. Appropriate motions to continue forced medication may be filed as the need arises. A motion to continue forced medication is subject to the same procedural safeguards as an original motion for forced medication.

736 N.E.2d at 22.

117. The court said that an individual found incompetent retains the right to choose one type of medical treatment over another, or to refuse medical treatment altogether; a

person involuntarily committed due to a mental disorder retains a fundamental liberty interest in refusing ECT; and that a court in making a substitute judgment for a nonconsenting patient should consider previous and current statements by the patient, the religious and moral values of the patient regarding medical treatment and ECT, and the views of any individuals that might influence the patient's decision. It went on to say, however, that the state can act in derogation of the patient's right to refuse even if the right is constitutionally protected. The court found that an incompetent individual retains the right to choose one type of medical treatment over another or to refuse medical treatment altogether, but that the state can limit this interest by narrowly drawn regulations justified by a compelling state interest. In re Schuoler, 106 Wash.2d 500, 723 P.2d 1103, 1111 (1986).

118. 723 P.2d at 1108.

119. 723 P.2d at 1111.

120. Gundy v. Pauley, 619 S.W.2d 730 (Ky. App. 1981). The court said (619 S.W.2d at 731–32):

> We hold that in the absence of a judicial declaration of incompetence, or an emergency which poses an immediate danger of harm to others or to the patient, a patient who has been involuntarily committed to a mental hospital for treatment cannot be compelled to undergo electroshock therapy against this will simply because it is considered to be in the best interest of the patient.
>
> Electroshock therapy has been shown to be effective in approximately 80% of the cases in which it was used . . . but medical science has no definitive explanation of how or why it works in 80% of the cases or fails in the other 20%. It has potentially harmful side effects.
>
> Under these circumstances the constitution protects the right of a person, who is not otherwise incompetent to do so, to decide for himself whether to submit to electroshock therapy.

In a concurring opinion, Judge McDonald said (619 S.W.2d at 732–33):

> The usefulness of electric-convulsive therapy (ECT) in treating certain types of psychological disorders has grown in recent years, the techniques of administration have been refined so as to avoid some of the horrors associated with earlier treatments. Nevertheless, due to the intrusive nature of ECT, this is one procedure which courts should not order to be performed against the will of a patient under the circumstances presented here.
>
> Lack of consent may be overridden by court order for the taking of blood samples, emptying the contents of the stomach, giving blood transfusions and for performing lifesaving surgery. Whether implicitly or explicitly, the courts in these situations weigh the physical harm to the person against the benefit to be gained by society or the patient by the medical procedure. For example, the needle prick for drawing blood is a slight intrusion and evidence of drugs or intoxicants in the bloodstream will dissipate quickly; therefore, on the basis of relative burden and benefits, the courts have ordered the procedure over the person's objection. The greater the intrusion and assault on the person, however, the greater must be the countervailing need for the procedure. Otherwise, the consent of the person will be required.
>
> To gain a clearer understanding of ECT, I have consulted a recognized medical school text on the topic. 3 Kaplan, Freedman and Sadock, eds., *Comprehensive Textbook of Psychiatry*, Chapter 31.5 (1980). I can envision no greater insult to the person as a whole than the involuntary administration of ECT when the patient is neither suicidal nor dangerous to others. . . .
>
> I cannot take the risk of making such a judgment. Nor can I conclude that the treatment facility's interest in efficiency and convenience outweighs an individual's right to refuse a medical procedure which is potentially harmful and certainly disruptive to both body and psyche. There is no doubt in my mind that the individual's right to the integrity of his person must prevail. Absent appellants' consent or a showing of a risk of harm to self or others, a court should not order the treatment.

121. See, e.g., Dohman v. Richard, 282 So.2d 789 (La. App. 1973); discussed in volume 1, chapter 22, on duty to mitigate damages.

122. American Psychiatric Association, *The Practice of Electroconvulsive Therapy: Recommendations for Treatment, Training, and Privileging* (Washington, D.C.: American Psychiatric Association, 1990), p. 159.

123. A mental health consumers' group accused the surgeon general of doing the public an injustice, it claimed, by ignoring or downplaying many problems linked to ECT. "Consumer Group Criticizes Unpublished ECT Report," *Psychiatric News*, Nov. 5, 1999, p. 1. Additional information on the National Mental Health Consumers' Self-Help Clearinghouse may be found at the Web site *www.mhselfhelp.org*.

124. See M. Fink, *Electroshock: Restoring the Mind* (New York: Oxford University Press, 1999); J. Fawcett, "Maligned, Feared, Misrepresented: Why is ECT Still Alive and Well?" *Psychiatric Annals* 28 (Sept. 1998): 9; C. H. Kellner, "ECT in the Media," *Psychiatric Annals* 28 (Sept. 1998): 528. See the discussion on ECT in part 2, on malpractice.

125. A discussion of the types of factors to be considered in deciding whether to override an incompetent patient's refusal appears in J. Beck, "Right to Refuse Antipsychotic Medication: Psychiatric Assessment and Legal Decision-Making," *Mental & Physical Disability L. Rep.* 11 (1987): 368.

126. Dr. Lawrence Hartmann in his presidential address at the 1992 annual meeting of the American Psychiatric Association said, "This is not a happy era for much of psychiatry. It is a good era for brain research, and a hopeful era for psychopharmacology, but a troublesome era for clinicians, for a great many patients, and for public and private funding." Presidential address, "Reflections on Humane Values and Biopsychosocial Integration," *Am. J. Psychiatry* 149 (1992): 1135.

127. 42 U.S.C., sec. 1983.

128. One study in Massachusetts estimates that a minimum of 10,500 attorney hours and 3,000 paralegal hours were required to process 2,216 petitions. For fiscal years 1985 and 1986, a total of more than $1,888,000 was appropriated by the Massachusetts legislature to set up the system mandated by the *Rogers* decision. These funds were used to hire attorneys, paralegals, and clerks, and also to pay for clinician time devoted to the writing and preparation of *Rogers* petitions. The appropriated funds were not used for clinical purposes. It did not include the cost of hiring independent experts, travel time for attorneys and clinicians, hiring aides to accompany patients to court, judges' salaries, lost income and extra hospital days because patients who were not medicated for psychosis were then hospitalized for extended periods, and the cost to patients' families, not to mention the cost to other patients of having disruptive, agitated, and treatment-refusing patients on the ward. R. Schouten, "Financial Cost of Right-to-Refuse-Treatment Law Assessed," *Psychiatric Times*, Oct. 1991, p. 28.

129. In Matter of W. S., 152 N.J. Super. 298, 377 A.2d 969 (1977), the court, having determined that the patient was incompetent to give an informed consent to ECT, and further finding that the hospital had carried its burden of proving the necessity of the requested treatment on an emergent basis, entered an order appointing the mother special guardian for the purpose of consenting to modes of treatment for her son, including ECT.

In Aden v. Younger, 57 Cal. App.3d 662, 129 Cal. Rptr. 535 (1976), in the hospital, Jane Doe wanted ECT and Betty Roe wanted psychosurgery. They sought the treatments. The state thereupon sought to protect them from themselves, that is, it sought to exercise for them their right to be free from risky treatments even though that freedom was not what they wanted. The court was faced with the question: May the state require a patient to show that the treatment is critically needed and to convince a review board that the patient is competent before the treatment may occur? The court held that if the patient is voluntary and wants ECT, the answer is "no," but if the patient wants psychosurgery, or is an involuntary patient and wants ECT, the answer is "yes."

Kansas legislation (sec. 59-2929 (a)) provides: "Every patient being treated in any treatment facility, in addition to all other rights preserved by the provisions of this act, shall have the following rights: . . . (6) not to be subject to such procedures as psychosurgery, electroshock therapy, experimental medication, aversion therapy or hazardous treatment procedures without the written consent of the patient and the written consent of a parent, guardian or other person in *loco parentis*, if such patient has a living parent or a guardian or other person in *loco parentis*."

PART II
Psychiatric Malpractice

3

Establishing Malpractice Liability

It is textbook knowledge that in any negligence or malpractice action the aggrieved party must establish by a preponderance of the evidence (1) that the defendant has failed to conform to a certain standard of conduct, (2) that there is a reasonable cause-and-effect relationship between that failure and the alleged injury, and (3) that the loss or injury is of a type of concern to the law.[1] The substantive law and the rules of evidence govern the admissibility of evidence at trial, but licensing or administrative boards are not bound by the rules of evidence.[2]

Standard of Care

The public expects that the performance of a professional or a specialist will measure up to the standards of the profession or specialty. A person avowing professional or specialty status is held to the degree of skill claimed by that profession or specialty. The public relies on it. Hence, the test of fault or breach of duty in malpractice cases is determined not by reference to the traditional reasonable or prudent person's standard (as in ordinary personal injury cases), but by whether there was a departure from customary professional conduct. Thus, the legal standard of care for a lawyer is that of the "reasonable and prudent lawyer." The legal standard of care for a doctor is that of a "reasonable and prudent doctor." The legal standard of care for a nurse is that of the "reasonable and prudent nurse." And so on.

But what in the mental health field is the standard of care? What is the competence, avowed or otherwise, of the various practitioners? There are now reportedly over two hundred varieties of psychotherapy, which range from classical psychoanalysis to procedures administered in cultlike surroundings reminiscent of techniques used by preliterate peoples. They are called a "psychotherapy jungle."[3] Indeed, there are books on psychotherapies resembling travel guides.[4]

As a general rule, a practitioner is liable for failure to refer when the circumstances are such that the duly careful practitioner should have known that a problem existed that he was not equipped to handle. Good sense, the law, and professional ethics would all maintain that one should not undertake services in a matter outside of one's competence. And where it turns out services are undertaken by one not competent for them (and who does not expect to become qualified), there is an affirmative duty to seek qualified assistance. With the advent of specialization, a practitioner may not be able to defend against the imposition of higher standards of care by pleading insufficiency of knowledge or lack of expertise in a given area.[5]

Most patients with depressive disorders are seen in primary care settings; only about 10 percent of depressed patients are referred and seen in the mental health specialty sector. Depressed patients come to primary care physicians with such complaints as headaches, fatigue, or gastrointestinal distress, so detection of the depression is thus delayed or missed, sometimes resulting in suicide. In recent decades, the treatment of depressive disorders has progressed from being a mystery and an art to being an array of effective, practical approaches, yet less than 50 percent of patients with depression are properly recognized and adequately treated by practitioners. The primary care physician is today the major dispenser of psychiatric medication, but whether it is properly used is subject to question. Busy primary care practices are not organized to provide the necessary social and psychotherapeutic interventions that may be appropriate.[6]

Every physician or therapist does what he knows best, we may suppose, but in the practice of psychiatry, should the therapist's forte be applied to one and all in distress? Surely, one would say no, but in the mental health field, questions abound, to wit: What is the link, if any, between psychiatric diagnosis and treatment modality?[7] When is there a need to consult or refer to one more competent or specialized?[8] Who is the specialist? What skill does the therapist hold himself out to the public as having? What can the public expect? When may it be said that a psychological problem is caused by a physical problem, and a medical doctor ought to be consulted? What difference does the etiology or pathogenesis of a disorder make as to whether the therapy should be somatic or psychological? How do the therapist's feelings or personality enhance or interfere with the process of psychotherapy? When may it be said that the diagnosis is improper, the prognosis faulty, or the treatment plan inappropriate? Stated differently, is there a statistically preferred treatment? Is psychotherapy, on the other hand, ad hoc or true to nothing but uncertainty, like politics or religion? Psychiatry, like medicine, is known as a healer's art, but it is also said that there is a science to the art of healing. Just about every public lecture in psychiatry begins with the introduction, "Welcome to this *scientific* meeting" (emphasis theirs).

In general, the courts tend not to pass judgment on the appropriate therapy or the efficacy of different forms of treatment. Thus, the courts decline to consider which of two equally reputable methods of psychiatric treatment—psychotherapy as against a physiological approach—would prove efficacious in a particular case.[9] The issue of negligence may be raised, however, where anachronistic therapeutic modes have been applied to psychiatric disorders where newer and more effective therapies are available.

The doctrine that a malpractice action properly lies only where the practitioner has fallen short of the generally accepted standard of the profession itself is a deference to and a reflection of the old Durkheimian insight that each occupational group possesses its own morality.[10] Thus, a practitioner is held to a standard of care that is really defined by his own profession. The standard of the profession is the measuring rod of the standard of care. To put it differently, one's own profession does the fingering.[11] In the usual negligence action, say, in a collision case, the standard of care to which the defendant must conform is that degree of care that, in the jury's view, a reasonable person of ordinary prudence would have exercised in the defendant's place in the same or similar circumstances, but in professional negligence (malpractice) actions the standard of care is that degree of skill and learning that is ordinarily possessed and exercised by members of that profession in good standing.[12] It follows the practice of the early common law, when merchants were judged by the custom of their trade. Hence, an action for malpractice usually requires the plaintiff to produce an expert to establish the standard and that there was a deviation from it.[13]

The treatment or technique need not be the best, it need be acceptable only by respectable professional authority.[14] Negligence is not established simply by proof that the technique used in the particular case was not effective,[15] or that it is not regarded as the best or optimal one by other professionals.[16] Were it otherwise, it might be said that a medical student who does not graduate with a grade of 100 is something of a murderer.[17]

In determining the standard of care, courts take into account the various schools of therapy as well as the many techniques and modes of therapy within each school.[18] Hence, a psychiatrist is entitled to be judged according to his school and the mode of therapy. He may show that his conduct conformed to a minority school within the profession even if most practitioners would not follow his technique.[19] However, this has been somewhat limited by the requirement that "the school . . . be a recognized school of good standing, which has established rules and principles of practice for the guidance of all its members, as respects diagnosis and remedies, which each member is supposed to observe in any given case."[20] A single practitioner adhering to a certain theoretical framework would not constitute a school.[21]

It is not enough for a practitioner to say (in effect), "I belong to the school of mumbo jumbo, and I apply mumbo jumbo therapy." The school may be repudiated at law. Some schools repudiated by the courts include the spiritualist or clairvoyant school, magnetic healers, and Chinese herb doctors.[22] On one occasion the court was called on to decide the question whether one who holds himself out as a clairvoyant physician should be held to the standard that is applicable to ordinary physicians.[23] The court concluded that, there being no recognized school of clairvoyant medicine, the defendant was held liable on the ground that, having held himself out as other physicians, he had not met the requirements of the rule of law applicable to them.[24] So, also, another court held that a magnetic healer was liable to a patient to whom he had administered treatment that, in the opinion of ordinary physicians, could not be justified by the rules of recognized schools, though they knew nothing of the principles of magnetic healing.[25]

Christian Science has fared better. In one of a number of cases,[26] the plaintiff, through her interest in the doctrines of Christian Science and the cures that defendant professed to be able to perfect through the agency of prayer, was induced to employ him to cure her of an attack of appendicitis. He undertook the cure for a reward, but, the malady growing worse, the plaintiff went to a surgeon, had an operation, and was cured. She then brought action against the defendant for damages for malpractice. The court said that one who holds himself out as a Christian Science healer and is employed to give treatment by the methods adopted by such practitioners is required to possess only the knowledge and exercise the care and skill of the ordinary Christian Scientist. Christian Science being a recognized school, the defendant is to be judged by the standard of care, skill, and knowledge of the ordinary Christian Scientist, insofar as he confined himself to those methods.[27]

With the veritable smorgasbord of accepted theories in the mental health field, the defendant will likely always find support from a colleague. A psychiatrist of one school may testify against a psychiatrist of another school, but may a psychiatrist of whatever school testify against a psychologist or social worker, or vice versa, as to standard of care or need for referral? Though separately licensed, they all now fall under the rubric of mental health professionals, but there is among these professionals an intense sibling rivalry that tends to prejudice their testimony. Under the school rule one may testify about another school when the methods of treatment for a particular ailment are generally the same in both schools.[28]

Observers wonder if there is, or ought to be, a uniform standard for mental health care extending beyond the psychiatrist to the traditional clinical disciplines of psychology and social work, perhaps even embracing pastoral counseling, Transactional Analysis, or est.[29] At one time the psychiatrist did the treating, the psychologist did the testing, and the social worker collected the data, but now they are all engaged in the practice of what is called *psychotherapy*.

Given that a professional is entitled to be judged according to his school and mode of therapy, assuming that it at least represents a respectable minority, the question arises as to the qualification of the expert testifying in regard to standard of care. Taking a restrictive view, the Illinois Supreme Court in a malpractice action against a podiatrist, for example, held that the standard of care owed by the podiatrist may not be established by offering the testimony of a physician or another expert other than a podiatrist.[30] Some other courts have taken a similar position.[31]

As a general rule, however, the plaintiff may turn to one outside a school to testify as an expert as to standard of care provided that person is familiar with the practice of the school.[32] Apparently prompted by continued assertions of a conspiracy of silence in malpractice cases, the courts in many jurisdictions have allowed the testimony of experts of other schools. Thus, the court has permitted an orthopedic surgeon to testify as an expert against a psychiatrist who had allegedly negligently administered electroshock. The orthopedist, though he had not ever given electroshock, was familiar with the literature on the subject, had talked with specialists in that field, and had treated fractures sustained in that treatment.[33]

No rule of law is without exceptions. Here, too, in establishing standard of care, there are exceptions to the rule requiring expert testimony in a malpractice case. One exception is where the nature of the alleged negligent conduct is such that inferences to be drawn from the facts are within the range of common experience.[34] A similar exception is where "the very nature of the acts complained of bespeaks improper treatment." *Res ipsa loquitur*—the thing speaks for itself.[35] Thus, a sponge is not ordinarily left in an abdomen in the absence of negligence. This theory was employed in *Hammer v. Rosen,*[36] where ironically the patient's name was Hammer and the psychiatrist (Dr. John Rosen) used beatings as a part of his therapy with catatonic patients. His technique was well known in professional circles. The court held that expert testimony was not necessary to establish negligence in such a case since the treatment used "bespoke" negligence. Actually, "beating the devil out of the afflicted" is an old therapy, but it was not recognized by the court. The court left open the possibility that such a therapy could be properly used if there was evidence that showed that the beatings constituted proper treatment.[37]

Still another exception to the rule requiring expert testimony in a malpractice case is where a statute formulates a standard of care; one example is the use of narcotics in violation of an antinarcotics statute. Under the law of torts, the violation of a statute constitutes negligence. Also, standard of care may be shown by published standards, drug manufacturers' instructions, and under the Federal Rules of Evidence and, in many states, by medical treatises.[38]

What about the role of supervision and the responsibility of the supervisor in safeguarding standard of care? The underlying premise of mental health and other health agencies in seeking to extend care to a larger number of people is that supervision safeguards or improves standard of care.[39] It is said that even paraprofessionals can play an important and increasing role in health care if they have "appropriate training and supervision."[40] The supervisor would establish the overall tone and direction of the agency, develop new treatment programs, and work closely with staff to make sure patients are properly evaluated and treated.

The nature and structure of the outpatient psychiatric clinic (OPC) that prevailed at one time in Michigan warrants examination regarding standards and potential abuses to be found in that pattern of care. Under it, the services of psychologists and social workers were reimbursable only if they were supervised by psychiatrists. Psychiatrists, reasonably enough, expected payment for their services. In many cases, however, what this meant was that the psychologist or social worker actually did the work of treating the patient while the psychiatrist, though spending little time supervising, obtained a substantial portion of the fee that the insurer paid for the therapy. Some called it duplicity, others called it fraud and abuse, still others called it protection money. For the fee, the psychiatrist signed payment forms.

But even assuming that the psychiatrist indeed acted as a supervisor, it was asked, was the supervision needed at all? The Michigan Psychiatric Society took the position that there must be a psychiatrist as medical director who has responsibility for all patients as well as for the quality of their care. On the other hand, the psychologists and social workers argued that each profession should be independently responsible for the mental health personnel in their disciplines.[41] In their words, they said, supervision by one who merely carries the title of psychiatrist served no useful purpose. They would prefer, if needed, the facade of supervision to supervision in fact, as they claimed the latter would merely be a waste of time. In the best-operating OPCs, the arrangement in practice was collegial, not hierarchical; supervision in such cases was essentially an exchange of ideas.

The position of a resident in training changes gradually from that of a novice to that of a professional colleague, and in the latter role he is free to use his own style and orientation.[42] Completion of residency training is something like a bar mitzvah, where the rabbi tells the young lad: "Beginning today you are old enough to be responsible for your own sins. Your father no longer takes them on his shoulders. Today you are a man." In law, a parent is not responsible for the acts of a child arising out of failure of supervision when the child is capable of appreciating a duty of care. But those supervised in the OPC—professionals and paraprofessionals alike—never achieved this level of freedom; they remained supervisees forever. In a psychiatric residency training program, a psychologist may be a teacher or supervisor, but upon completion of the training, a psychiatrist ranked over the psychologist in the OPC hierarchy. After a long struggle, psychologists in Michigan, claiming that they performed equally well in the practice of psychotherapy, obtained legislation requiring insurance companies to pay them on the same basis as they pay psychiatrists. Such laws, called "freedom of choice" laws, have been enacted in a number of states. Licensed psychologists have been recognized as independent providers in CHAMPUS, CHAMPVA, FEHBA, Aetna insurance programs, Medicaid, some BCBS plans, and so forth.[43]

The hierarchy set up in the OPC was the source of controversy. Even more disconcerting was the inadequacy of guidelines and statements concerning the actual providers of services. There was want of delineation of the educational preparation, amount of experience, and kind of quality of training of the providers of services. Within this nonstructure some service providers were prepared, others were not. Inadequately trained persons were allowed to perform services on the theory that supervision would remedy any deficiencies. This expectation placed the supervisor in the role of an educator, a role for which the supervisor may or may not be prepared.[44] There have been many expressions of surprise—given the large number of people who have been treated in these clinics and given the litigiousness of the times—that no lawsuits alleging malpractice were brought against the OPCs.

The Michigan OPC operation points out the potential impact of third-party payment programs. It makes for exploitation of mental health professionals and paraprofessionals, and for poor quality care. It is not a happy picture of cost effectiveness, and it is another example of the corruption of the medical profession by insurance. It sharply poses several questions that have been raised for some time: (1) Who shall be considered a mental health professional? (2) Should there be a hierarchy among the mental health professions? (3) What are the practical guidelines that might be offered insurance carriers? (4) Without practical or just guidelines should there be insurance coverage of outpatient psychotherapy at all? (5) Is hospitalization the alternative to outpatient psychotherapy (hospital practice has the economic attraction—for the physician—of allowing "head in the door" visits)? (6) What is truly the best way of containing costs yet providing best care?[45] Considering, as data seems to suggest, that the mental health professions themselves are not clearly differentiated in terms of professional functions when it comes to psychotherapy, funding agencies and administrators at all levels would have difficulty deciding which professional should engage in which function.[46]

Psychiatrists say that, as physicians, only they are capable of recognizing physical illnesses that mimic mental disorders; a person with a physical illness seen by a psychologist might be in useless therapy while the real illness goes untreated.

Moreover, only they, as physicians, can prescribe medication or other somatic therapy that is sometimes needed in the treatment of mental illness. On the other hand, psychologists argue that the overwhelming majority of people with symptoms of mental illness do not have physical diseases and that requiring psychiatric supervision to screen out the few is an unwarranted expense. Furthermore, they contend, the problem can be solved more cheaply and more effectively by having the client get a physical examination from an internist before psychotherapy begins; a client who needs drugs can then be referred to a psychiatrist or family doctor for a prescription and they can return to the psychologist for continued therapy.[47]

The controversy continues. The class system in some measure prevails, and with it, the concept of supervision. The prophecy made a few years ago that litigation involving supervisors would be the "suit of the future" has materialized in considerable measure. Profiting from an enterprise, the supervisor—like a corporate officer or director—must also bear its perils. That is the underlying principle of vicarious responsibility—"let the superior reply."

For the treatment of many mental disorders, various studies recommend combining psychotherapy and medication (it may be required by the health plan). In carrying out this approach, the treatment is often split between a psychiatrist, who provides the medication, and a nonmedical therapist, who provides the psychotherapy. Managed health plans call for that split.[48] It is a variation of the defunct OPC practice in Michigan. As the patient may assume that the therapists are working together in providing treatment, the legal result may be joint and several liability, that is, each therapist is fully liable for any wrongdoing.[49] To avoid this outcome, patients are advised (often by written contract) of separate responsibility of the therapists. However, when two therapists are involved in the treatment of a mental patient, though acting independently, they may be hard put to argue in the case of the suicide of the patient that they should not be regarded as jointly and severally liable, just as in the cases where a patient is seen by, say, an internist and orthopedist. In any event, joint and several liability has given way in many states to several liability, under which each defendant is responsible for only his share of the total damages, usually defined in terms of causal negligence.[50] In medical practice, a consultant simply proves input, a supervisor oversees and directs all aspects of treatment, and in a collaborative relationship, the clinicians share treatment responsibilities. In litigation, however, whatever the relationship, all of the clinicians are usually joined as defendants. The plaintiff optimizes the chances of a settlement by citing as many defendants as possible and thereby obtaining a contribution from the various insurers that cover the therapists. The term "nuisance value of a lawsuit" describes the amount insurers pay to settle even though they believe there is no merit to the lawsuit. Practitioners who are involved in shared treatment would do well to have a hold-harmless/indemnification agreement. Whatever one may think of split treatment, it is the reality, and what is the reality? Psychotropic medication is mostly dispensed by a primary care physician, with infrequent monitoring, and psychotherapy is carried out by a psychologist or social worker.

Causation

How is a causal relationship established between a psychiatric treatment and patient deterioration? Beyond doubt, it is extremely difficult in a malpractice action to establish causation when a significant segment of the psychiatric community is espousing various treatment modes, albeit solely on an impressionistic basis. This difficulty in establishing causation would particularly characterize the talking therapies where the influence of therapist on patient, whether pernicious or therapeutic, would be virtually impossible to concretize to a court. Many conditions, particularly a psychiatric condition, may have a deteriorating course without treatment, so deterioration in therapy does not of itself establish negligent treatment or causation, but the continuation of a form of treatment over years in the face of deterioration or the absence of improvement may prove to be a case of liability.[51]

As a practical matter, it is often necessary to see a pattern of behavior in order to establish malpractice or fraud. The testimony of one psychiatric patient is often not credible in the eyes of a jury. The testimony is likely to be considered the product of an unstable or infirm mind. Thus, to establish a case, or to impeach credibility, it is often crucial to show a pattern of behavior, but to do this the complainant would have to obtain the names of other patients.

Consider, for example, the suit by Julie Roy against her psychiatrist, Dr. Renatus Hartogs. She claimed that Dr. Hartogs lured her into sex under the guise of therapy. The doctor, denying it, asserted that she was delusional and further testified that he was impotent during the last ten years due to a physical condition. The climax of the trial came when other women, reading about the case in the newspapers, came forward and testified that during this period of time they too were patients of the doctor and that he had had sexual intercourse with them.[52] Without the testimony of these other women, the complainant probably would have been laughed out of court. Suppose instead of publicity that produced other witnesses, the plaintiff had requested the names of other women treated by the doctor in order to interview them? Could their names be obtained? Would their evidence be admissible?

At times, only a pattern may reveal incompetence or abuse, or lack of credibility on the part of the defendant. For example, there may be something amiss when a male psychiatrist at a hospital quickly discharges patients of his sex but holds onto young women for unusually long stays. The tendency to keep a harem would not be revealed by studying the case of a single individual who complains of unnecessary treatment or hospitalization.[53]

Also, only a pattern might establish that a therapist is incompetent to deal with particular classes of people—for example, women, homosexual people, or suicidal individuals. It may be significant, were it known, that an unusually large number of patients of a particular therapist obtain divorces or commit suicide. It may also be significant that an unusually large number of a therapist's patients are pushed onto other therapists. The custom of a profession is admissible evidence to establish standard of care, but generally speaking, to establish either fault or causation, the law on evidence leaves the admissibility of similar facts evidence involving the defendant to a case by case determination.

The law on evidence of past acts or pattern of conduct of the defendant requires convincing proof that the previous acts occurred; a careful comparison of the prior acts with present circumstances, especially with regard to similarity; a clear showing of relevance to a material issue; a showing of necessity; and a weighing of prejudice against probative value. In particular, the prior acts of the defendant must be of like character. Assuming that the test is met, the evidence is weighed in the calculus of probative value versus prejudice or confusion of issues,[54] and, more often than not, it is excluded—but questions of probative value versus other dangers can be resolved only on a case by case basis and not by any rigid rule.[55]

A situation of high probative value of similar incidents was presented in *Carter v. Yardley & Co.*,[56] where the plaintiff alleged that her skin was damaged by the defendant-manufacturer's cosmetic. One of the defenses was that any skin damage resulted from a source or cause other than the defendant's product. To establish what had caused the skin condition, the court allowed the plaintiff to show that two other users of the defendant's preparation sustained similar skin damage. To obtain similar fact evidence, the complainant usually would need to confer with other patients. In the few cases on discovery of the names of other patients, disclosure appears obtainable to establish fiscal fraud,[57] but not malpractice.[58] However, the testimonial privilege covers the content of a communication, and not the fact of a relationship; indeed, a relationship must be established in order to claim the benefit of a privilege. As it turns out, the testimonial privilege does not provide an adequate guideline as to whether a physician or psychotherapist, without the consent of patients who are not a party to litigation, may be compelled to respond to an inquiry in a legal proceeding that would reveal their identity.[59]

An off-label use of drugs or medical products may be the basis for suit against the physician who prescribed it, or it may come up as a defense on the part of the manufacturer. An *off-label use* is one that is not included in labeling approved by the Food and Drug Administration (FDA) for the products. The recent fen-phen (fenfluramine/phentermine) diet drug litigation is an example of off-label use on an enormous scale. Information that a use is one that is not approved by the FDA or that is regarded as experimental may be relevant to a patient's decision regarding treatment options. The FDA has made it clear that although it licenses drugs and devices, it does not purport to regulate the *practice* of medicine. In the agency's view, physicians are free to exercise their medical judgment in prescribing drugs and devices. However, major departure from package insert instructions could be the foundation for a strong malpractice case, especially for failure to obtain informed consent.[60]

In cases alleging improper use of medication resulting in tardive dyskinesia or other serious side effects, the patient must offer proof that the side effect occurred more probably than not as the result of the physician's prescription (in law, there must be proximate cause, but there may be more than one proximate cause, any one of which may justify liability). On the difficulty of proof of causation in TD cases, the *DSM* states, "although [movement disorders] are labeled 'medication induced,' it is often difficult to establish the causal relationship between medication exposure and the development of the movement disorder, especially because some of these movement disorders also occur in the absence of medication exposure."[61]

Even before the advent of the neuroleptic medication that causes TD, TD was not unknown. Schizophrenia is a neurological disorder that has a motor component. Without any exposure to neuroleptics, patients may develop spontaneous neurological disorder associated with schizophrenia, and at a lower rate with other disorders. On the other hand, with exposure to neuroleptics, there is a greater risk of developing TD in the case of mood disorders. In the case of patients with disorders other than schizophrenia, the emergence of a movement disorder is almost always the result of neuroleptics.

In the case of a particular patient with schizophrenia it is not possible to determine whether the involuntary movement was due to the schizophrenia and not neuroleptic induced. So, in either case, the courts tend to rule that the appearance of an involuntary movement is the result of medication.[62] The courts have grappled with the subject of epidemiology and what it means to establish causation. The burden of proof in civil cases is typically "preponderance of the evidence" (i.e., "more likely than not"). In a case where radiation was alleged to be the cause of cancer, the court provided an analysis of statistical significance in establishing causation:

> In a case where a plaintiff tries to establish a factual connection between a particular cause and a delayed, nonspecific effect such as cancer or leukemia, the strongest evidence of relationship is likely to be statistical in form. Where the injuries are causally indistinguishable, and where experts cannot determine whether an individual injury arises from culpable human cause or non-culpable natural causes, evidence that there is an increased incidence of the injury in a population following exposure to defendant's risk-creating conduct may justify an inference of "causal linkage" between defendant's conduct and plaintiff's injuries.[63]

Sometimes the proximate cause of the patient's TD can be attributed to the patient (or the family). Thus, summary judgment was granted in favor of a psychiatrist because the patient had failed to inform him of side effects she was experiencing until it was too late for him to effectively treat them. The court noted that, as under traditional law, the plaintiff has a duty to exercise ordinary care for her own protection by keeping her physician informed of problems she might be having with the prescribed treatment.[64]

There are apparently no direct reports of TD occurring as a result of therapy with the tricyclic antidepressant drugs alone. A few instances have been noted of TD that have occurred in patients who were taking tricyclic antidepressants and antipsychotic medication concurrently. In most of these reports, the antipsychotic drugs used were the phenothiazines. However, the medications associated with the development of TD are not limited to the neuroleptics. TD can be caused or influenced by other pharmacological agents, or it may occur spontaneously. Several drugs have been identified that exacerbate TD.

A study by the research department of the Carrier Foundation reported a significant prevalence of TD among elderly residents of nursing homes who have never received neuroleptics. This study strongly suggested that aging either alone or in combination with senile brain disease may produce a syndrome that may be called *spontaneous dyskinesia,* and that neuroleptics cannot be held solely responsible for dyskinesia.[65] What seemed to be TD, by description, was noted already by Kraepelin in the 1890s in elderly (chronic) patients diagnosed with dementia praecox—this long before the pharmacological revolution.

Damage

Not every human interest or concern has legal protection. The law differentiates between the various kinds of interests for which individuals may claim protection against injury by others. Until the 1960s to 1970s the courts ruled that there was no liability in negligence actions causing emotional distress without physical injury or impact. In a famous dissent, Justice Musmanno of the Pennsylvania Supreme Court protested the continued application of the physical injury or impact rule in a case in which the litigant suffered fright and shock on being chased by a straying bull owned by the defendant. As the bull did not strike or touch the complainant, the suit was dismissed, prompting Justice Musmanno to say he would "continue to dissent from [the logic of such cases] until the cows come home."[66] A Georgia case reduced the impact magic formula to an absurdity by finding impact in a case in which a horse in a circus show evacuated his bowels into the lap of a woman who was sitting near the arena, causing her great embarrassment.[67]

The courts in various states in recent decades have been holding that psychic impairment is compensable without physical injury or impact as a rule of law, but still today, as a practical matter, judges or juries are skeptical of a claim of emotional distress standing alone. In negligence actions, proof of emotional disturbance or of causal connection is considered highly speculative.

Information on Treatment Modalities

It would appear that a psychiatric patient should be told what treatment modalities are available for his particular disorder and how they work, and then be given some approximation of what they may require in time and money. In departing from published standards of care, including drug manufacturers' instructions, the doctor should indicate to the patient that he is doing so. In some instances the patient's cognitive capacity may be so impaired that the information will have to be imparted to a legally responsible member of the family. For example, if a therapist opts to treat a major psychosis like acute schizophrenia with psychotherapy alone, because of some strong antidrug conviction, he is entitled to do so. At the same time he should inform the family what the current consensus of psychiatric literature has to say about results, undesirable consequences, and so on, when various treatment modes are compared. Similarly, if a patient consults a therapist because of acute anxiety related to some stressful life event, he should have the information that will enable him to choose between the intensive long-term psychotherapies and the brief methods, in terms of what he may expect from them and what each will demand of him.

But, properly speaking, let us hasten to ask, can or should accountability of psychiatrists and related professionals be approached in a vacuum? Consider, for example, the state mental health organization. The psychiatrist and other mental health workers are at the bottom of a long chain of authority. What is the responsibility of the legislature, the executive, the judiciary, and the public generally? What type of programs will they support? Economic accountability very much controls the nature or type of treatment. More and more, the fiscal third-party controls who gets what. The third-party payer looks for ways to pay less and less (and, if possible, not to pay a claim at all). The psychoanalytic or long-term approach is under attack by the AMA, with its pill-or-surgery view of medicine, and by government and insurance companies because it is cheaper to control symptoms with drugs.

Economic accountability is increasingly determining the length of treatment, the length of hospitalization, and the kinds of treatment. One California insurer concocted a list of various diagnostic categories that are matched with treatment. This "standard of treatments" was formulated by Blue Shield in consultation with psychiatrists selected by them (not by any psychiatric organization). There are rigid details of what constitutes indications for psychotherapy and hospitalization. This latter includes specifications of when a patient must be discharged. For depression, it is stated that "chemotherapy and electric shock therapy are the treatments of choice." Psychotherapy might be indicated in some cases, but has to be justified.[68]

Psychiatric treatment veering to the cheapest means symptom control with electroshock or drugs (without psychotherapy), patients dumped on the community, and treatment programs that are gestures of doing something rather than meaningful treatment. Rapid bed turnover has resulted in patients being released before they are stabilized.

And many sick patients are not being accepted in a general hospital psychiatric unit for two reasons—they view them as malpractice fodder, or they create problems for the staff that is inadequate for the needs of such patients. Patients are being refused admission because their insurance standing is clouded, and retrograde denial of claims leaves hospitals without payment if they admit them. Families are torn apart because the patient member refuses treatment and there is nothing the family can do to protect itself.

Conclusion

In a psychiatric malpractice action, with the exclusion of similar facts evidence, establishing fault or causation is problematical. The outcome is often like a lottery. And at the same time, tort law fares poorly as a certification service, as it essentially deals with a performance in a particular situation and not with competency to perform a particular function. It is chancy, chancy, chancy whether the competent or the incompetent practitioner is tagged. The board-certified psychiatrist is as often sued and found liable as the non-board-certified. The biggest game of chance is not in Las Vegas but in a courtroom.[69] And so—given the litigious nature of the times, the number of lawyers, and the availability of insurance—lawsuits now are to be considered as an ordinary or unavoidable part of the cost of doing business or carrying on a profession. One must guard against it with insurance as best as one can, as one would guard against a flood or tornado.[70]

Notes

1. Licata v. Spector, 26 Conn. Sup. 378, 225 A.2d 28 (1966).
2. See Federal Rules of Evidence, Rule 1101; State *ex rel.* Lucas v. Board of Education, 277 N.W.2d 524 (Minn. 1979).
3. S. Lesse, Caveat Emptor?: The Cornucopia of Current Psychotherapies" (editorial), *Am. J. Psychotherapy* 33 (1979): 329; Special Section, "The Psychotherapy Jungle: A Guide for the Perplexed," *Saturday Review*, Feb. 21, 1976, p. 12.
4. See, e.g., J. Kovel, *A Complete Guide to Therapy: From Psychoanalysis to Behavior Modification* (New York: Pantheon, 1976); R. B. Stuart, *Trick or Treatment: How and When Psychotherapy Fails* (Champaign, Ill.: Research Press, 1970); D. Sobel, "Freud's Fragmented Legacy: A Bewildering Choice of Therapies for the Anxious American," *New York Times Magazine*, Oct. 26, 1980, p. 28. In the book *The Talking Cures: The Psychoanalyses and the Psychotherapies* (New Haven: Yale University Press, 1995), Dr. Robert Wallerstein discusses the different models of psychoanalysis and dynamic psychotherapies, the formation of these concepts in the post–World War II era and progressive fragmentation in subsequent decades, and the evolution of relational and interactional perspectives.

5. A. R. Holder, *Medical Malpractice Law* (New York: Wiley, 1975); J. D. Peters & D. S. Robinson, "Litigation Errors as a Basis for Legal Malpractice," *Mich. Bar J.* 59 (1980): 22.

6. D. A. Adler & K. M. Bungay, "Treating Depression in Primary Care: 'Best of Times and Worst of Times,'" *Medicine & Behavior*, Oct. 1999, p. 24. When, if ever, should a general practitioner refer to a specialist, say, in a case of appendicitis? What is the standard of care? Does the public expect a different one in such cases? To incur liability, it must appear that breach of duty to refer to a specialist in fact caused patient's injury, and this can be shown only if treatment the plaintiff received was in some way inferior to the treatment he would have received from a specialist. The Minnesota Supreme Court in Larsen v. Uelle, 246 N.W.2d 841 (1976) put it thus:

> [T]he mere breach of duty to refer a patient to a specialist for treatment will not of itself make out a prima facie case of negligence against the general practitioner administers may in fact be the exact treatment which a specialist in good standing would have employed had the case been referred to him, and in that circumstance the general practitioner would be no more liable for injury resulting from the treatment than would be the specialist had he administered the treatment. It must appear that the breach of the duty to refer to a specialist in fact caused the plaintiff's injury, and this can be shown only if the treatment the plaintiff received was in some way inferior to the treatment he would have received from a specialist. Thus, in order to make out a case of negligence based on a breach of duty to refer a patient to a specialist for treatment, the plaintiff must also present evidence from which the trier of fact may determine that in the treatment which he in fact administered, the defendant failed to exercise that degree of skill, care, knowledge, and attention ordinarily possessed and exercised by specialists in good standing under like circumstances.

7. Symposium, "Diagnosis and the Difference it Makes," *Bull. Menninger Clinic* 40 (1976): 411; P. Williams, "Deciding How to Treat: The Relevance of Psychiatric Diagnosis," *Psychological Med.* 9 (1976): 179.

8. In Bogust v. Iverson, 10 Wis.2d 129, 102 N.W.2d 228 (1960), a troubled student sought help from the college guidance counselor (a professor of education with a doctor of philosophy degree). After five months of sessions, the interviews were terminated on the suggestion of the counselor. Six weeks later, the student committed suicide, and her parents brought a claim against the guidance counselor and the college. The court stated that although the individual defendant was a guidance counselor he could not "be charged with the same degree of care . . . as a person trained in medicine or psychiatry." Considering the counselor as a nonexpert, the court found that no facts were alleged that would have apprised him of the student's suicidal tendencies. The court further indicated that even a sufficiently alerted guidance counselor, conceded to have a duty to take some affirmative steps to prevent the suicide of a student, would not be civilly liable for causing suicide unless the suicide was committed in a way that would suggest negligence on the part of the counselor. 10 Wis.2d at 137, 102 N.W.2d at 232.

In a critical comment, Victor Schwartz (then a law professor) wrote that if a college provides a counselor to assist students with personal problems as it did in *Bogust*, it should make sure that the counselor "has sufficient training to recognize suicidal symptoms" and that "[i]f the college's psychiatric facilities are overburdened, there should at least be a duty to refer students to other sources for psychiatric assistance." V. E. Schwartz, "Civil Liability for Causing Suicide: A Synthesis of Law and Psychiatry," *Vand. L. Rev.* 24 (1971): 217, 253–54.

9. See, e.g., United States v. Klien, 325 F.2d 283 (2d Circ. 1963).

10. C. Bock, *Forgive and Remember: Managing Medical Failure* (Chicago: University of Chicago Press, 1979), p. 5.

11. E. D. Shapiro, "Medical Malpractice: History, Diagnosis and Prognosis," *St Louis U. L. J.* 22 (1978): 469. See generally, F. James & D. K. Sigerson, "Particularizing Standards of Conduct in Negligence Trials," *Vand. L. Rev.* 5 (1952): 697; C. Morris, "Custom and Negligence," *Colum. L. Rev.* 42 (1942): 1147. As noted in chapter 4, a precedent-breaking case was Helling v. Carey, 83 Wash.2d 514, 519 P.2d 981 (1974), where the court rather than the profession in a malpractice action set the standard of care for an ophthalmologist. The court required the use, as a matter of routine, of a low-risk but high-benefit procedure. The court

rejected reliance on custom in favor of a reasonability test. The decision generated extensive commentary. In 1996, the Illinois Supreme Court confirmed that compliance with customary standards is not conclusive in actions against medical professionals. Advincula v. United Blood Servs., 678 N.E.2d 1009 (Ill. 1996). In Hood v. Phillips, 554 S.W.2d 160 (Tex. 1977), the Texas Supreme Court defined Texas's new malpractice standard of care as what a "reasonable and prudent" physician would do, rather than what customarily was done. A subsequent case affirmed that "custom or practice . . . is not conclusive on the issue of standard of care. . . . We see no reason for a different rule in medical malpractice cases." Kissinger v. Turner, 727 S.W.2d 750 (Tex. App. 1987). Other notable examples of law-imposed standards of care are informed consent and duty to warn or protect in the event of danger posed by a patient. The *Helling* case is discussed at length in P. G. Peters, "The Quiet Demise of Deference to Custom: Malpractice Law at the Millennium," *Wash. & Lee L. Rev.* 57 (2000): 163.

12. The standard of conduct is what a reasonably careful person engaged in a particular activity, trade, occupation, or profession would do or would refrain from doing under the circumstances then existing. Moreover, medical malpractice must be pled more specifically than other types of negligence. It is not sufficient for a plaintiff to simply describe what a physician did or failed to do and then allege that the action or omission was negligent. The plaintiff must allege the proper or accepted method of diagnosis and treatment. Simonelli v. Cassidy, 336 Mich. 635, 59 N.W.2d 28 (1953). See V. N. Fink, "Medical Malpractice: The Liability of Psychiatrists," *Notre Dame L.* 48 (1973): 693; P. A. Friedman, "Expert Testimony to Establish the Standard of Care in Medical Malpractice," *Am. J. Trial Advocacy* 2 (1979): 213. The standard of care in alternative medicine is discussed in A. Doyle, "Alternative Medicine and Medical Malpractice," *J. Legal Med.* 22 (2201): 533. *Alternative medicine* involves treatments that have not found general acceptance by the mainstream medical community (such as chiropractic, acupuncture, naturopathy, and homeopathy). Alternative practitioners have their own professional organizations and scientific journals an expanded view of the informed consent doctrine would call for disclosure by conventional physicians of safe, effective choices available in alternative therapies. Gemme v. Goldberg, 626 A.2d 318 (Conn. App. 1993).

13. Bivins v. Detroit Osteopathic Hosp., 258 N.W.2d 527 (Mich. App. 1977). However, in a case where there is no informed consent, it is usually not necessary to have expert testimony for the simple reason that such a case hinges on the fact that had the plaintiff been informed of the risks and hazards he would have not agreed to the treatment. The fact that the treatment was properly or improperly performed is immaterial.

14. Foxluger v. State, 23 Misc.2d 933, 203 N.Y.S.2d 985 (1960). For wide-ranging discussion of psychiatric malpractice, see G. J. Alexander & A. W. Scheflin (eds.), *Law and Mental Disorder* (Durham, N.C.: Carolina Academic Press, 1998); R. Reisner, C. Slobogin, & A. Rai (eds.), *Law and the Mental Health System* (St. Paul, Minn.: West, 3d ed. 1999); R. D. Glenn, "Standard of Care in Administering Nontraditional Psychotherapy: Problems in Law and Medicine," *U.C. Davis L. Rev.* 7 (1974): 56; T. E. Shea, "Legal Standard of Care for Psychiatrists and Psychologists," *West. St. U. L. Rev.* 6 (1978): 71. For discussion of medical malpractice in general, see R. E. Shanell & P. Smith, *The Preparation and Trial of Medical Malpractice Cases* (New York: Law Journal Press, rev. ed. 2000).

15. A choice of therapy is not subject to criticism simply because it was not effective in a particular case. Hindsight is always twenty-twenty. Negligence is based not on whether a particular choice of treatment brings about a cure, or was in fact the right treatment with benefit of hindsight, but rather on whether the treatment chosen, based on facts available at the time of treatment, was reasonable. T. F. Campion & J. A. Peck, "Ingredients of a Psychiatric Malpractice Suit," *Psychiatric Q.* 5 (1979): 236. See A. H. Tuma & P. May, "And if That Doesn't Work, What Next . . . ? A Study of Treatment Failures in Schizophrenia," *J. Nerv. Ment. Dis.* 167 (1979): 566.

16. H. B. Rothblatt & D. H. Leroy, "Avoiding Psychiatric Malpractice," *Calif. West. L. Rev.* 9 (1973): 260.

17. "In medical school I was transformed or transformed myself into a straight A student. I had the conscious and continuing thought that, if I failed to learn or comprehend this matter or that, I might kill a patient because of my ignorance. This view was fostered by my teachers. Our professor of pharmacology, for example, began each of his classes with a ten-question written quiz, each requiring a knowledge of the current dosage of drugs. There were

only two grades, written on our quiz papers in bold red letters—either 100% or MURDER." Quip by Dr. John L. Schimel, "Accountability in Psychiatry," *J. Psychiatry & Law* 8 (1980): 191.

18. See A. H. McCoid, "The Care Required of Medical Practitioners," *Vand. L. Rev.* 12 (1959): 549.

19. P. S. Cassidy, "The Liability of Psychiatrists for Malpractice," *U. Pitt. L. Rev.* 36 (1974): 108.

20. The principle is commonly known as the *two schools* or *respectable minority* doctrine. In Jones v. Chidester, 531 Pa. 31, 610 A.2d 964 (1992), the Pennsylvania Supreme Court was called upon to decide whether a school of thought qualifies as such when it is advocated by a "considerable number" of medical experts or when it commands acceptance by "respective, reputable and reasonable" practitioners. The former test calls for a quantitative analysis, while the latter is premised on qualitative grounds. The court ruled that a school of thought should be adopted not only by reputable and respected physicians in order to insure quality but also by a considerable number of medical practitioners for the purpose of meeting general acceptance even if it does not rise to the level of a majority. The court would not place a numerical certainty on what constitutes a considerable number. The burden of proving that there are two schools of thought falls to the defendant. In Tesauro v. Perrige, 437 Pa. Super. 620, 650 A.2d 1079 (1994), the superior court denied the application of the two schools of thought doctrine when holding that "the writings and teachings of one individual are inadequate factual support for the proposition that a considerable number of professionals agree with this treatment." California has defined its standard as one where "a physician chooses one of alternative accepted methods of treatment, with which other physicians agree." Meier v. Ross General Hosp., 69 Cal.2d 420, 71 Cal. Rptr. 903, 445 P.2d 519 (1968). See M. Kowalski, "Applying the 'Two Schools of Thought' Doctrine to the Repressed Memory Controversy," *J. Legal Med.* 19 (1998): 503. Therapists may pay a price for innovation. See A. Scheflin, "The Evolving Standard of Care in the Practice of Trauma and Dissociative Disorder Therapy," *Bull. Menninger Clinic* 64 (2000): 234. See also B. R. Furrow, "Defective Mental Treatment: A Proposal for the Application of Strict Liability to Psychiatric Services," *Boston U. L. Rev.* 58 (1978): 408.

21. In Abraham v. Zaslow, 26 Citation 169 (Cal. Super. Ct., Santa Clara Co., 1972), a psychologist was found liable in the use of an experimental "rage reduction therapy" that resulted in physical and mental injuries to the patient. Note, "Psychiatric Negligence," *Drake L. Rev.* 23 (1974): 640. In a practice regarded as highly unique, the eminent Dr. Harold Searles turned to psychotherapy in the treatment of severely chronic schizophrenic patients. H. Searles, *Collected Papers on Schizophrenia and Related Subjects* (New York: International Universities Press, 1965). See also C. R. Rogers, *The Therapeutic Relationship and Its Impact: A Study of Psychotherapy with Schizophrenics* (Madison: University of Wisconsin Press, 1967); J. S. Strauss et al. (eds.), *The Psychotherapy of Schizophrenia* (New York: Plenum, 1980).

22. Hansen v. Pock, 57 Mont. 51, 187 Pac. 282 (1920) (herb doctor). In an incident making the news, one spiritualist suggested to a wife that she beat her husband, and she did, in order to save their floundering marriage. *Detroit Free Press*, Jan. 18, 1980, p. 3. One may find a parallel in what is called witchcraft in other countries. B. van Niekerk, "A Witch's Brew from Natal: Some Thoughts on Provocation," *So. African L. J.* 89 (1972): 169. Exploitation of the elderly, we know, is commonplace. Members of Washington's House Select Committee on Aging have heard countless reports about quacks peddling fake medical cures to older citizens, along with tales of their physical and mental abuse. Various states have enacted legislation that provides for mandatory reporting of the neglect as well as exploitation or abuse of elderly persons, and grant anonymity and immunity to those investigating or reporting.

23. Nelson v. Harrington, 72 Wis. 599, 40 N.W. 228 (1888).

24. In this case, the court was asked by the defendant to charge that if, at the time defendant was called to treat plaintiff, both parties understood that he would treat him according to the approved practice of clairvoyant physicians, and that he did so treat him with the ordinary skill and knowledge of the clairvoyant system, plaintiff could not recover. The court refused the charge. Instead of the words, "with the ordinary skill and knowledge of the clairvoyant system," the instruction properly was, "with the ordinary skill and knowledge of physicians in good standing."

25. Longan v. Weltmer, 180 Mo. 322, 79 S.W. 655 (1904). See also Ellis v. Newbrough, 6 N.M. 181, 27 Pac. 490 (1891) (misrepresentation); see A. Hill, "Damages for Innocent Misrep-

resentation," *Colum. L. Rev.* 73 (1973): 679; L. H. Rubenstein, "Criminal Aspects of Faith Healing," *New Eng. J. Med.* 224 (1941): 239.

26. Spead v. Tomlinson, 73 N.H. 46, 59 Atl. 376 (1904).

27. The Christian Science practitioner's usual defense is constitutional religious freedom. However, if the practitioner violates the state medical practice act (making a medical diagnosis or manipulating the limbs and body), that defense cannot prevail. I. H. Rubenstein, "Malpractice against Christian Science Practitioners," *Medical Trial Technique Q.*, Spring 1979, p. 372.

"I often wonder," says a character in a novel by Michael Crichton, "about what medicine would be like if the predominant religious feeling in this country was Christian Scientist. For most of history, of course, it wouldn't have mattered; medicine was pretty primitive and ineffective. But, supposing Christian Science was strong in the age of penicillin and antibiotics. Suppose there were pressure groups militating against the administration of these drugs. Suppose there were sick people in a society who *knew* perfectly well that they didn't have to die from their illness, that a simple drug existed which would cure them. Wouldn't there be a roaring black market in these drugs? Wouldn't people die from home administration of overdoses, from impure, smuggled drugs? Wouldn't everything be an unholy mess." M. Crichton, *A Case of Need* (New York: Penguin Books, 1968), p. 31.

28. See Wemmett v. Mount, 134 Ore. 305, 292 Pac. 03 (1930); H. H. Strupp & S. W. Hadley, "Specific vs. Nonspecific Factors in Psychotherapy," *Arch. Gen. Psychiat.* 36 (1979): 1125.

29. B. R. Furrow, *Malpractice in Psychotherapy* (Lexington, Mass.: D. G. Heath, 1980).

30. Dolan v. Galluzzo, 396 N.E.2d 12 (Ill. 1979). The requirement at one time that the testifying expert had to come not only from the same school but also the same locality as the defendant physician made it difficult to obtain an expert. A physician would be reluctant to testify against another physician from the same locality. Medical practice came to be described not as a profession but as a conspiracy. In a book published in 1961, the prominent attorney Louis Nizer wrote: "I do not know whether it is a compliment to the medical profession to say that it is almost impossible in most states to induce a doctor to testify against another doctor. That depends on whether you look at the matter from a social viewpoint and the requirements of justice, or from the viewpoint of professional loyalty and comradeship." L. Nizer, *My Life in Court* (New York: Doubleday, 1961), p. 349.

31. See, e.g., Daniels v. Finney, 262 S.W.2d 431 (Tex. Civ. App. 1953). The Michigan legislature, as in some other states, has enacted legislation that expert witnesses must teach or practice in the same medical specialty as the physician who is being sued. The avowed goal of the legislation is to cut down on the testimony of professional hired guns. In a criticism of the legislation, Dr. Emanuel Tanay said, "The legislation is designed to protect physicians from malpractice litigation, and one cane only be dismayed by its results. I am reminded of a case in Cleveland where a severely depressed patient was admitted to a clinic operated by a nutritional chiropractor. The treatment essentially consisted of starvation. After a few days, the patient committed suicide. It was argued that I could not testify in that case because I was not a nutritional chiropractor, whatever that is. The situation in another case is even more bizarre in my opinion. A dermatologist or a psychiatrist would know that under the facts of the case, a sigmoidoscopic examination was indicated. To exclude the opinion of a gastroenterologist because he is not a colorectal surgeon is unreasonable on the face of it." Tanay adds, "The sub-specialization of medicine is growing exponentially. A group practice of ophthalmology where I have been a patient for years has at least half a dozen subspecialists. If my ophthalmic surgeon failed to diagnose my glaucoma, could I use a general ophthalmologist as an expert witness? I believe that any physician should be able to testify that failure to test for glaucoma when doing any type of eye examination is negligent." Personal communication (Sept. 27, 1999).

32. Thus, under the majority view, the applicable standard of case may be established by other practitioners in the particular field of practice or by other expert witnesses equally familiar and competent to testify with respect to that to limited field of practice. A specialist may testify as to the standard of care of a general practitioner provided the witness is knowledgeable about the general practitioner's standard of care.

33. Quinley v. Cocke, 183 Tenn. 428, 192 S.W.2d 992 (1946).

34. "Expert testimony is generally necessary except where the matters in issue fall within the area of common knowledge and lay comprehension." Olfe v. Gordon, 286 N.W.2d 573

(Minn. 1980). See also Orozco v. Henry Ford Hospital, 290 N.W.2d 363 (Mich. 1980); Christy v. Salterman, 288 Minn. 141, 149 N.W.2d 288 (1970).

35. Comment, "The Application of Res Ipsa Loquitur in Medical Malpractice Cases," *Nw. U. L. Rev.* 40 (1966): 852.

36. 7 N.Y.2d 376, 165 N.E.2d 756, 198 N.Y.S.2d 65 (1960).

37. 198 N.Y.S.2d at 67. However, another New York court ruled against the patient even though allegations of beatings by the therapist were essentially uncontradicted. The court stated that the lower court improperly substituted its judgment for that of the physicians and that there was no medical evidence showing improper procedure. Morgan v. State, 337 N.Y.S.2d 536 (App. Div. 1972).

38. See J. M. Finder, "The Future of Practice Guidelines: Should They Constitute Conclusive Evidence of the Standard of Care?" *Health Matrix: J. Law-Medicine* 10 (2000): 67; Comment, "Substantive Admissibility of Learned Treatises and the Medical Malpractice Plaintiff," *Nw. U. L. Rev.* 71 (1976): 678.

39. W. S. Bell, "Medico-Legal Implications of Recent Legislation Concerning Allied Health Practitioners," *Loyola of Los Angeles L. Rev.* 11 (1978): 379.

40. See E. G. Poser, "The Effect of Therapists' Training on Group Therapeutic Outcome," *J. Consulting Psych.* 30 (1966): 283; H. H. Strupp & S. W. Hadley, "Specific vs. Non-Specific Factors in Psychotherapy," *Arch. Gen. Psychiat.* 36 (1979): 1125; P. G. Bourne, ltr., *Am. J. Psychiatry* 135 (1978): 1113. "Mothers Good Candidates as Counselors," *Clinical Psychiatry News*, Oct. 1979, p. 32.

41. "Psychology: Clinicians Seek Professional Autonomy," *Science* 181 (1973): 117.

42. S. E. Greben, E. R. Markson, & J. Sadovoy, "Resident and Supervisor: An Examination of Their Relationship," *Canadian Psychiat. Assn. J.* 18 (1973): 473.

43. CHAMPUS: Civilian Health and Medical Program of the United States; CHAMPVA: Civilian Health and Medical Program of the Department of Veterans Affairs; FEHBA: Federal Employee Health Benefits Act; BCBS: Blue Cross/Blue Shield.

44. R. Slovenko, "Legal Issues in Psychotherapy Supervision," in A. R. Hess (ed.), *Psychotherapy Supervision: Theory, Research and Practice* (New York: Wiley, 1980), p. 453.

45. P. Chodoff, "Psychiatry and the Fiscal Third Party," *Am. J. Psychiatry* 135 (1978): 1141; S. S. Sharfstein, "Third-Party Payers: To Pay or Not to Pay," *Am. J. Psychiatry* 135 (1978): 1185.

46. W. C. House, S. I. Miller, & R. H. Schlachter, "Role Definitions among Mental Health Professionals," *Comprehensive Psychiatry* 19 (1978): 469. Participation agreements between health insurers and outpatient psychotherapy clinics that set fees for service are not considered in violation of antitrust laws. In Michigan Assn. of Psychotherapy clinics v. Blue Cross & Blue Shield of Michigan, 118 Mich. App. 505, 325 N.W.2d 471 (1982), a clinic sued the insurer because it wanted to give different reimbursements depending on the providers' educational qualifications. The court ruled that this policy is reasonable and does not constitute a restraint of trade or price-fixing. It ruled that fixing a set fee the insurer will pay did not prevent the clinic from charging either over or under the set fee or from charging whatever they wanted.

47. J. P. Brady & H. K. H. Brodie (eds.), *Controversy in Psychiatry* (Philadelphia: Saunders, 1978); J. R. Neill & A. M. Ludwig, "Psychiatry and Psychotherapy: Past and Future," *Am. J. Psychotherapy* 34 (1980): 39. New Mexico recently became the first state to allow psychologists to prescribe psychotropic medication. The passage of the legislation was justified by the small number of psychiatrists outside the major metro areas of the state. E. Goode, "Psychologists Get Prescription Pads and Furor Erupts," *New York Times*, Mar. 26, 2002, p. D-1.

48. In a retrospective study, one HMO found it actually spent less money when it did not split the treatment. W. Goldman et al., "Outpatient Utilization Patterns of Integrated and Split Psychotherapy and Pharmacotherapy for Depression," *Psychiatric Services* 49 (1998): 477. See also A. N. Sabo & L. Havens (eds.), *The Real World Guide to Psychotherapy Practice* (Cambridge: Harvard University Press, 2000).

49. As mental states change, drug treatment needs to be carefully integrated with psychotherapy, which means, it is argued, the person prescribing the drugs should be the same person providing at least some of the psychotherapy and overseeing the patient's care. See J. A. Hobson & J. A. Leonard, *Out of Its Mind: Psychiatry in Crisis* (Cambridge: Perseus, 2001). See also P. S. Appelbaum, "General Guidelines for Psychiatrists Who Prescribe Medication for Patients Treated by Nonmedical Therapists," *Hosp. & Comm. Psych.*

42 (1991): 281; R. S. Goldberg, M. Riba, & A. Tasman, "Psychiatrists' Attitudes toward Prescribing Medication for Patients Treated by Non-medical Psychotherapists," *Hosp. & Comm. Psychiatry* 42 (1991): 276; J. Melonas, "Split Treatment: Does Managed Care Change the Risk to Psychiatrists?" *Psych. Prac. & Managed Care* 5 (May–June 1999): 5; D. J. Meyer & R. I. Simon, "Split Treatment: Clarity between Psychiatrists and Psychotherapists," *Contemp. Psychiatry* 29 (1999): 327; L. K. Sederer, J. Ellison, & S. Keyes, "Guidelines for Prescribing Psychiatrists in Consultative, Collaborative and Supervisory Relationships," *Psychiat. Serv.* 49 (1998): 1197; "Split Treatment: A New Set of Malpractice Risks," *Psychiatric News*, Aug. 24, 2000, p. 9; W. A. Imperio, "Bridging the Professional Divide in Split Therapy," *Clinical Psychiatry News*, Aug. 2000, p. 25. The October 2001 issue of *Psychiatric Annals*, which is on split treatment, includes discussion of the legal aspects and ethics of split treatment.

50. See, e.g., Kan. Stat. Ann. 60-257a(d), as interpreted and defended in Brown v. Keill, 580 P.2d 867 (Kan. 1978).

51. When a patient does not improve or his status deteriorates over the course of long-term therapies, such unfavorable results should prompt referral for consultation and a re-evaluation of diagnosis, psychodynamics, and therapeutic technique. The consultant should probably have a conceptual orientation somewhat at variance with the referring psychiatrist to avoid a validation and simple mirroring of his views. Such consultative help would not only be useful to the patient but to the psychiatrist as well should a malpractice defense ever be necessary.

52. Roy v. Hartogs, 381 N.Y.S.2d 587 (Sup. Ct. N.Y. 1976); see L. Freeman & J. Roy, *Betrayal* (New York: Stein and Day, 1976), W. C. Gentry, "Psychiatric Liability: Abuse of the Therapist-Patient Relationship," *Trial*, May 1980, p. 26; L. Siskin, "Sexual Relations between Psychotherapists and Their Patients: Toward Research or Restraint," *Calif. L. Rev.* 67 (1979): 1000.

53. H. M. Silverberg, "Protecting the Human Rights of Mental Patients," *Barrister*, Fall 1974, p. 46.

54. Federal Rules of Evidence, Rule 403.

55. In lawsuits against a pharmaceutical company, past instances of mishaps are sought to be introduced by the complainant in order to establish causation. In these cases, it is alleged that medication was disinhibiting and resulted in suicide or murder-suicide. It is reported, among other cases, that within weeks of starting Prozac, a dramatic change had occurred in Joe Wesbacker's clinical condition. He became psychotic and severely agitated, with thoughts of violence and suicide, which he carried out. During the trial, attorneys for the survivors in bringing a wrongful death action repeatedly asked the court for permission to introduce evidence of the disinhibiting effects of two other drugs manufactured by the defendant, Oraflex and fialuridine. The attorneys sought to show a larger pattern in which the manufacturer was "a company with a history of flagrant disregard for the safety of the potential patients that are getting their drugs." The defense lawyers argued that the evidence would be too "prejudicial," and on the basis of the rules of evidence, they argued that the defendant was in court to defend Prozac, not the other drugs. The court ruled in defendant's favor. The case is discussed in J. Cornwell, *The Power to Harm* (New York: Viking, 1996); J. Glenmullen, *Prozac Backlash* (New York: Simon & Schuster, 2000). For a discussion of the law on similar facts evidence, see G. C. Lilly, *An Introduction to the Law of Evidence* (St. Paul, Minn.: West, 1978), p. 146; D. Worm, "Similar Facts Evidence: Balancing Probative Value against the Probable Dangers of Mission," *U. Calif. Davis L. Rev.* 9 (1976): 395.

56. 319 Mass. 92, 64 N.E.2d 693 (1946); see Annot., 42 A.L.R.3d 780 (1972).

57. But see Hawaii Psychiatric Society v. Ariyoshi, 481 F.Supp. 1028 (D.Hawaii 1979).

58. Division of Med. Quality v. Gherardini, 156 Cal. Rptr. 55 (Cal. App. 1979).

59. R. Slovenko, *Psychotherapy and Confidentiality* (Springfield, Ill.: Thomas, 1998).

60. One of the drugs most often prescribed for schizophrenia—valproate—has never been approved by the FDA for that indication. Moreover, it has not even been subjected to randomized controlled trials. C. Sherman, "Off-Label Anticonvulsants Useful in Schizophrenia," *Clin. Psychiatry News*, Aug. 2000, p. 17. See P. D. Rheingold & D. B. Rheingold, "Offense or Defense? Managing the Off-Label Use Claim," *Trial*, Mar. 2001, p. 52.

61. *DSM-IV*, pp. 678–79.

62. Accardo v. Cenac, 722 So.2d 302 (La. App. 1998).

63. Allen v. United States, 588 F.Supp. 247 (D.Utah 1984), *reversed on unrelated grounds,* 816 F.2d 1417 (10th Cir. 1987), *cert. denied,* U.S. 1004 (1988). The Autumn 2001 issue (64: 1–323) of *Law & Contemporary Problems* is devoted to the subject of causation in law and science. See also I. Freckelton & D. Mendelson (eds.), *Causation in Law and Medicine* (Burlington, Vt.: Ashgate, 2002).

64. Tisdale v. Johnson, 177 Ga. App. 487. 339 S.E.2d 764 (1989).

65. D. E. Casey, "Managing Tardive Dyskinesia," *J. Clin. Psychiatry* 39 (1978): 748; see also R. Slovenko, "Update on Legal Issues Associated with Tardive Dyskinesia," *J. Clin. Psychiatry* 61 (2000): 45 (supp. 4).

66. Bosley v. Andrews, 393 Pa. 161, 142 A.2d 263 (1958).

67. Christy Bros. Circus v. Turnage, 38 Ga. App. 581, 144 S.E. 680 (1928). The rule requiring physical impact or injury still prevails in a number of states. In Wilson v. Continental Insurance Co., 274 N.W.2d 679 (Wis. 1979), the Wisconsin Supreme Court ruled that a claim of negligence for mental injuries without accompanying physical injury is barred by public policy. On another occasion, the Wisconsin Supreme Court (quoting 64 A.L.R.2d 113) said: "[T]he contention that because of the nature of the evidentiary problems involved, the judicial process is not well adapted to distinguishing valid from fraudulent claims in this area, has been recognized as probably the most substantial of the reasons advanced for denying recovery for mental distress or its physical consequences." Bogust v. Iverson, 10 Wis.2d 129, 102 N.W.2d 228 1960.

68. Dr. Jonas Robitscher in his Isaac Ray Award Lectures said, "The doctor who has a choice of therapies but picks electroshock because the patient's Blue Cross coverage allows for only twenty-one days of in-hospital care, and electroshock can easily be accomplished in that period, will never be criticized for his therapy choice." But in a non sequitur, Robitscher blamed psychiatry for not being good psychiatry, and for abusing its power. J. Robitscher, *The Powers of Psychiatry* (Boston: Houghton Mifflin, 1980), p. 409.

69. E. Osborne, "Courts as Casinos? An Empirical Investigation of Randomness and Efficiency in Civil Litigation," *J. Legal Studies* 28 (1999): 187.

70. Under Michigan Public Act 72 (eff. Jan. 1, 2002), physicians, dentists, and other providers who render uncompensated care to needy individuals are given immunity from civil lawsuits for malpractice. Many retired physicians, especially, were hesitant to volunteer their services because of the expense of liability insurance. Under the legislation there is no immunity for gross negligence or willful and wanton misconduct. The nonemergency health care must be provided inside the premises of, or as a result of a referral from, a health facility that exists for the sole purpose of providing uncompensated, nonemergency health care. Before care can be administered, the provider must give the patient a written disclosure that explains the limitation on liability and the uncompensated nature of the service. The patient must then sign an acknowledgment of receipt of the written disclosure. Under so-called Good Samaritan legislation a physician who provides emergency care at the scene of an emergency is relieved of civil liability except for gross negligence. See F. J. Helminski, "Good Samaritan Statutes: Time for Uniformity," *Wayne L. Rev.* 27 (1980): 217.

4

An Overview of Psychiatric Malpractice

Psychotherapists and nonpsychotherapists alike have expressed concern about the quality of services rendered in the name of treatment. Therapists know about inept or abusive treatment of patients either from other therapists or from their own patients who were treated by a previous therapist, but in either case little or no remedial action is taken. One of a number of law review articles—one of which carries the title, "The Song Is Ended but the Malady Lingers On"—concludes that the solution, if there be one, lies with the judicial system.[1] With regulatory legislation (licensing or certification) said to protect the interests of a professional group rather than those of the public, the tort suit is increasingly looked to as a type of decertification of competency.

To be sure, there is another dimension to litigation. In these litigious times nearly every human or social ill, real or imagined, finds its way to the courthouse. Just about every human problem is now turned into a legal one. And then too there is the big payoff. The public pays for the courts, the attorneys (should they be willing) subsidize the costs of litigation, and the loser does not pay the other's costs—so from the viewpoint of the litigant, why not take a chance at a winning? Approximately one of nine malpractice suits is a judgment rendered against the physician, so the chances are somewhat better than the lottery or the stock market. When asked why he robbed only banks, Willie Sutton replied, "Because that's where the money is."[2] Now, instead of robbing banks, one sues (the wealthy), for that's where the money is.

The word *lawsuit* scares physicians almost as much as their bill scares patients. Being sued evokes unnerving images of grim courtrooms, austere judges, rigid formality, esoteric talk, aggressive lawyers, a hostile complainant, biased witnesses, unknowledgeable jurors, and—win or lose—stigma and loss of time and money. In defending against a claim, it is necessary to devote considerable time to interviews with investigators, meetings with attorneys, depositions before trial, and attendance in court, and notwithstanding all this, judgment may be unfavorable and could exceed insurance coverage.

The ideal behind medical and psychiatric service, like that of other services, is often realized. The individual comes on his own (except in civil commitment), follows a prescribed regimen, and obtains results that he feels justify the trust and the fee. But there are points of tension. The individual may not know of his need for service; or, knowing of his need, he may not want service; or, obtaining it, he may find his situation worsened.

In the usual case, medical or psychiatric tort liability is premised on negligence. There are few instances of intentional wrongdoing. Negligence is conduct that falls below the standard of care established by law for the protection of others against unreasonable risk of harm. Compliance with custom, or what is commonly done, is strong evidence of reasonable conduct but is not conclusive. The standard of care is a hypothetical, objective standard by which the law may necessitate more care, or the use of new procedures or devices that are not commonly used. The narrow and restrictive test using the community in which the defendant practices, or a similar locality, as the measure of the applicable standard of care has been replaced by a national standard for the specialty. The standard is not found through a Gallup poll or in a fashion page, but from logic and experience. In the last analysis, as Judge Learned Hand said, it is for the court to determine the standard.

Definition of Professional Negligence

Professional negligence in general is the adjudged failure of a professional person, evidenced in the results of his activity, to possess the average skill or knowledge of other professionals in like circumstances, or, if he does possess average skill and knowledge, his failure to use them. It is a departure from good, accepted, proper practice. If negligence is proved, there is an obligation to compensate for the damage caused.

The physician's legal responsibility could accurately be termed professional tort liability, but the terms *medical malpractice,* or simply *malpractice,* are embedded in both legal and medical literature and habit of thought. When a person speaks of a malpractice action, it is presumed that it is about a lawsuit against a physician rather than about the negligence of a member of any other professional group. *Malpractice* is even defined in some dictionaries solely as "improper treatment or culpable negligence of a patient by a physician."[3]

The word *malpractice* is misleading, because from *mal-* comes the tendency to think of other words like malicious, malevolent, or malfeasance. It makes the physician sound like a villain. Actually, malpractice has to do with negligence, not deliberate, planned wrongdoing. Less significantly, from the *practice* portion of the word, there may be the tendency to think that one is learning; in common parlance, physicians (and lawyers) have a practice, whereas other people work. The term *professional liability* would be preferable to *malpractice.*

Rate of Malpractice Suits

The rapid increase in the number of medical malpractice suits, to use the prevailing language, following World War II has corresponded with the changing patterns of medical practice and physician status. Criticism is widespread that American medicine is swiftly degenerating into a hurried and depersonalized form of production-line service. A department store is said to take better care of its merchandise than a hospital does of its patients. Medical mistakes kill anywhere from 44,000 to 98,000 hospitalized patients in the United States a year, says a recent report from the Institute of Medicine, which calls the errors stunning and demands major changes in the nation's health care system to protect patients.[4] At the same time, medical costs are sky-high, and the popular symbol of medicine has become the dollar sign, equating medicine with business. A number of patients try to get out of their financial burden by filing bankruptcy or by suing for malpractice.

The scene has markedly changed since the time when Robert Louis Stevenson wrote his eulogy of the doctor, which said: "There are men and classes of men that stand above the common herd; the soldier, the sailor, and the shepherd not infrequently; . . . the physician almost as a rule. He is the flower (such as it is) of our civilization."[5] The patient no longer believes, as he did at that time, that the physician can do no wrong. As a consequence, while once a relative rarity, malpractice suits are now common throughout the United States. According to the American Medical Association, one-fourth of all U.S. physicians will be sued for malpractice before the end of their careers.

Factors that stimulate claims, with or without regard to the issue of negligence, are severity of injury and indirect influences of an economic, psychological, or sociological nature. Such influences include interpersonal problems between provider and patient leading to a breakdown in rapport during the course of therapy; frustration with the manner in which specific complaints about ongoing or proposed modes of treatment, including complications, are handled or not handled; unrealistic expectations by patients regarding the outcomes of medical treatment, based in part on misinformation and in part on problems of communication between patient and physician (including problems related to obtaining consent for surgery); and a growing national trend toward suit-consciousness, health care consumerism, and other sociological stimuli to litigation. Those most likely to be sued are the anesthesiologists, orthopedists, surgeons, and obstetricians. The bond between them and their patients tends to be thin, and their errors tend to be self-evident.

At the other end of the spectrum has been the psychiatrist, the talking doctor, who stands in contrast to the surgeon, the cutting doctor. For a long time, almost anything seemed acceptable in talking. Dr. David Viscott in *The Making of a Psychiatrist* said that it was a standing joke in medical school that it did not matter whether a psychiatrist was a quack, because psychiatrists did so little it was unlikely that they could do any harm. It was not, he said, until you were out practicing psychiatry for a while that you really knew how bad psychiatrists could get.[6] In a review of the book, Thomas Lask of the *New York Times* quipped that he would not go so far as to say that one has to be out of his mind to go to a psychiatrist for help, but it evidently makes it easier.[7]

In the past most litigation involving psychiatrists resulted from physical and not psychic damage to the patient. Nowadays, and to some extent in the past, litigation involving psychiatrists allege physical or psychic damage resulting from faulty diagnosis, improper certification in commitment proceedings, failure to exercise adequate suicidal precaution, breach of confidentiality, revival of memory of abuse, failure to report a patient who poses a danger, improper administration of medication or of electroshock treatment, and sexual relations with patients.

Unless injury to the patient is physical or there has been obvious misconduct, as in the cases later discussed, the patient is in a difficult position to associate the harm with the therapy and, even if the patient does establish causality, to establish negligence. And a cause of action based on breach of contract would also be difficult to sustain since the psychiatrist, when treatment commences, makes a point of promising nothing. An extralegal consideration of undoubted importance dissuading a lawsuit is the reluctance to reveal one's personal life in a courtroom. Moreover, researchers who seek to study psychiatric malpractice may be denied access to the necessary data. To illustrate, investigators seeking to identify the factors associated with suicides at a mental institution are likely to find that necessary records are labeled confidential or have been lost and that relevant personnel are unavailable.

Until the 1980s, the number of lawsuits against psychiatrists was miniscule compared with suits against other physicians (psychiatrists comprise about 6 percent of all physicians). A nationwide study by the National Association of Insurance Commissioners found that of 71,778 malpractice claims filed against all physicians between 1974 and 1978, only 217 (0.3 percent) were against psychiatrists, but in 1985 an insurance underwriter reported that "the number of lawsuits filed against mental health practitioners has skyrocketed in recent years."[8] From 1985 through 1998, more than $13.3 million was paid out in psychotherapy-related claims against psychiatrists, according to a report from the Physician Insurers Association of America, which analyzed data from twenty large malpractice insurers nationwide. Overall, psychiatry ranked twentieth in number of claims reported and twenty-third in the amount of money paid out for claims among the twenty-eight specialties surveyed.

One explanation for the increase in malpractice complaints is that restrictions have made it more difficult to hospitalize patients, and those who are hospitalized tend to be discharged more rapidly, so psychiatrists are dealing with sicker people on an outpatient basis. Another explanation for the increase in malpractice complaints is that many insurance plans or managed care providers engage psychiatrists only for medication management and then contract with nonphysicians for psychotherapy. Dr. Paul Appelbaum said, "To the extent that you're seeing people for medication, your risk is increased both because you don't know these patients as well and are not as able to make good judgments about them, and also because there is less coordination of care when there are two caregivers."[9]

Recent years have seen growing attention in the legal and psychiatric literature to the nature of psychotherapy, and to "mal-psychotherapy." The number of books and journal articles on the subject is now considerable. The thought at one time that talk therapy could do no harm has been abandoned. The very concept of therapy would suggest that the therapist exerts some kind of influence or impact, benign or malignant, on the patient. In this connection, Dr. Abraham Kardiner wrote in *My Analysis with Freud*, "Freud was always infuriated whenever I would say to him that you could not do harm with psychoanalysis. He said, 'When you say that, you also say that it cannot do any good. Because if you cannot do any harm, how can you do good?' "[10] Others say the chief danger is wasting the patient's time and money, diverting him from effective treatment; and that may be malpractice. Philip Rieff in his 1966 book *The Triumph of the Therapeutic* claimed that the real danger to humanity in our time is not socialism but therapy.[11]

A fundamental purpose of professional tort liability is to provide a remedy for a wrong, and also to provide something of a certification service for the public. There is a popular saying: "For a wrong, there ought to be a remedy," but is everything permissible in the name of psychotherapy? A therapist when in New York had a spare room, and his father (a retired railroad engineer) said to him, "I can do what you are doing, let me use that room, let me have the patients for whom you don't have the time."[12] The therapist son would have none of that, but on moving to California, and seeing what passed there for therapy, he mused that his father would not by any stretch of the imagination have engaged in such shenanigans.

Yet what is standard of care in psychotherapy? Therapists differ on what is important, and what is of no moment. For example: How often should a patient be seen? For how long? Can sessions of two to three hours several times a week be justified? Should the patient lie on a couch? Should the patient be seen individually or in a group? Should medication be used? Should therapy be split between a therapist who provides medication and another who provides psychotherapy? Should a patient who is suicidal be asked to promise that he will call for help rather than act out suicidal thoughts or impulses? Should inquiry about trauma be made before transference has developed? Should an interpretation be made without corroboration by external information? Should a patient keep a diary during the course of therapy? Should there be any physical touching of a patient? What, if anything, should the therapist reveal to the patient about himself? Is it necessary for the therapist to know about the cultural background of the patient? Should the therapist consult with the patient's family? What should be said about confidentiality? Should a therapist testify on behalf of a patient? How to react to a changing marketplace? Is record keeping essential for psychotherapy? To what extent, if any, does the therapist interfere or help in the patient's daily life? Is therapy case-specific and so very little can be said about a standard of care?

An extraordinary and unprecedented number of psychotherapeutic techniques have emerged in recent decades. Actually, it is not surprising—the human organism can get out of balance in innumerable ways, and there are innumerable ways to regain one's equilibrium. But questions arise: Is the treatment of choice largely a matter of fashion? Which techniques help? Which present dangers? For depression, one might ask, should it be psychotherapy, electroshock, pills, plastic surgery, comedy films, jogging, a new relationship, or a job? Dr. Stephen Appelbaum, when with the Menninger Foundation, crisscrossed the United States to take a firsthand look at various therapies, including primal scream, est, Silva Mind-Control, Rolfing, transcendental meditation, biofeedback, bioenergetics, macrobiotic dieting, and Alexander technique—about twenty new forms of treatment. He found much that was constructive, but he also saw much that dismayed him. He observed, "An unfortunate fact of our time is that poorly trained and untalented people do all kinds of things purporting to be therapeutic, and do so under the imprimatur of glittering titles and institutional affiliations."[13]

The development of guidelines that has occurred is part of a movement towards *evidence-based* practice, but there are many different models of it. One is to base practice upon evidence of change. Another is the *empirically supported treatments* movement, which focuses on the degree of evidence for specific treatments for specific disorders. These models adopt a medical model perspective on psychological dysfunction and its remediation, and is focused on symptom removal. On the other hand, many approaches to psychotherapy do not hold that effectiveness in psychotherapy is homologous to effectiveness of a drug. For one thing, a therapy could be said to be efficacious if it provides a certain kind of opportunity or experience to make a variety of personal changes, none of which are connected in a linear or mechanistic way with what the therapist does. The effectiveness of the therapy is in terms of how it allows individuals to explore their lives and find more meaningful ways of engaging in their existence.

Focus in Tort Cases

Faulty performance or no, in tort law in considerable measure the tail (damages) often wags the dog (the other rules). The extent of injury—or insurance coverage— may compromise the element of fault. Given insurance coverage, some theory more or less is developed to provide an avenue of recovery. As a practical matter, there is a link, more or less, between tort claims and insurance coverage. Thus, the availability of insurance coverage for pastoral counseling encourages suits against pastoral counselors.

Even a single suit, given publicity, triggers litigation in the area. It is what is known as a vicious circle: a lawsuit occurs, it is given publicity, insurance companies advertise the risk (to promote insurance), the insurable become targets of litigation, more litigation ensues, premiums mount, more litigation, and more of the same. In short, one event builds on the other.[14]

On top of that, there is the increasing public demand for accountability—an aspect of the movement called *consumerism*. The phenomenon is growing in the field of medicine, including psychiatry.[15] The development of third-party payment, the pressure of insurance reimbursement for psychotherapy, and federal and state supervision of mental health programs has sharpened the issue. Pushed by the scrutiny that must come with public funding, those in the mental health field are being asked to demonstrate (through extensive forms) what it is that is being treated, what kind of treatment is being offered, what the outcome of the treatment is, and who is doing the treatment.[16] Recent legislation mandates specific physician disclosure standards prior to treatment, pretreatment peer review and review, and record keeping systems.[17] Legislation or judicial decisions also regulate the administration of "intrusive therapies."[18]

Recent legislation also seeks to make every physician something of a supervisor over other physicians, though they are not in his employ (the development is on the horizon for other professions as well). A number of states have enacted mandatory reporting statutes requiring a physician to report a colleague's professional misconduct, subject to being charged with misconduct for having failed to report witnessed acts.[19] Several states make it unlawful to withhold information from licensing boards about doctors with debilitating problems and make those who knew or should have known liable for the actions of their colleagues. These reporting statutes provide immunity from suit for the complaining doctor—the fear of a defamation suit has been a concern—but it is doubtful whether these statutes, like peer review, have proven to be of much consequence. Surveys indicate that while 38 percent of physicians could identify colleagues who were experiencing debilitation problems, very few say they would discuss this with the individual involved or report the problem to the appropriate authority. And so there is increasing reliance on the malpractice action to weed out incompetency (though the competent physician is apparently sued no less frequently than the incompetent).

Most insurance carriers have placed psychiatrists in the same *risk rating* category as general practitioners, even though the loss ratio of psychiatrists is not as high. The exclusions in a professional liability policy usually provide that the policy does not apply to such risks as injury arising out of the performance of a criminal act, sexual relations with a patient, injury caused by a person while under the influence of intoxicants or narcotics, liability assumed by the insured under an agreement guaranteeing the result of any treatment, electroshock therapy (unless specifically included in the policy at an additional premium), and liability of the insured as the proprietor or executive officer of a hospital or sanitarium.[20]

A plaintiff is more likely to be successful in litigation when a hospital is a party defendant. As a matter of trial tactics, it is generally not advisable to name a nurse or aide as a party defendant, even if primarily responsible for the harm, as juries still equate nurses with Florence Nightingale. A physician still cuts a somewhat appealing figure and juries hesitate to find him liable, but an institution is amorphous. Hence, the hospital is invariably sued alone or with the physician whenever there has been hospitalization. In an earlier day, charitable or governmental immunity protected nonprofit hospitals from liability, but now that the immunity defense has fallen by the wayside, a public or private hospital is liable for its wrongful acts or omissions to act.

Any comment on tort liability must necessarily be tinged with the observation that the law of torts has come to perform a significant function of providing social security. This role was thrust upon it as the result of changes in the social and economic environment, especially the rise of liability insurance. Tort liability originally served as an incentive to procure liability insurance, but now that liability insurance is so very common, it influences the pattern of tort liability. The function of tort law in the larger scheme of social security is open to debate but beyond the scope of this work.

Vulnerable Psychiatrists

The thrust of malpractice litigation into psychiatry appears to be directed at those practitioners who treat the more seriously mentally ill within an institutional setting. The institutional psychiatrist is vulnerable when he uses involuntary commitment procedures to hospitalize a potentially dangerous patient, and he faces a similar hazard when he chooses to discharge that patient. His vulnerability increases when he utilizes electrotherapy or the psychotropic drugs. He is less in danger when he simply sits and listens, only occasionally responding with a supportive or insightful comment. Whenever he acts in a manner that cannot be concretized in relatively simple and understandable cause-and-effect terms, as, for instance, the effect of a drug in producing a noxious, compensable side effect, the psychiatrist need not be overly concerned about malpractice insurance.

The state hospital psychiatrist, often foreign-born and foreign-educated, requires the broadest insurance protection, because he struggles with an enormous caseload consisting of the most severe psychoses in an understaffed and inadequately financed institution. The psychiatrist in private practice, on the other hand, has chosen to treat, in the comfortable isolation of his office, those patients with less serious mental illnesses, despite the fact that he may be better trained. The economic and therapeutic rewards of private practice far outweigh those offered by a state hospital system. His patients are communicative and manageable, and he rarely has to make the decisions or utilize the therapeutic modalities that later form the basis for a malpractice action.

The private practice psychiatrist encounters litigation for negligent psychotherapy primarily when he assumes a role forbidden to him by society. It is even possible for such a role to have therapeutic consequences, as in the case of Dr. John Rosen, who struck some schizophrenic patients in order to make them more communicative and accessible, a form of therapeutic behavior that will, upon occasion, resolve an acute psychosis.[21] Yet doctors are not supposed to strike patients, and such a corporeal role cannot be accepted by the court or society.

Overall, the fact that relatively few instances in which psychotherapy has been deemed by a court to be negligent is remarkable, considering the number of individuals who have been treated by psychotherapy. As Dr. Kardiner observed, if communication can be therapeutic, driving sick people sane, then the negative is also possible. That psychiatrists powerfully influence the lifestyles, values, and attitudes of their patients would seem beyond doubt (for example, the number of divorces or changes in employment of persons in therapy are disproportionate to the average). That such influence could be contrived to work for the benefit of the psychiatrist and to the detriment of the patient is quite another matter and most difficult to establish in a court of law.

Revival of Memory Cases

Recent years have witnessed the development of the revival of memory of childhood sexual abuse—which has been the subject of intense controversy. Patients have come out of therapy convinced that their parents or stepparents had sexually abused them when they were children, and they blame their lifelong difficulties on the abuse. In bringing suit against their parents, they claim delayed discovery that would suspend the statute of limitations because they had psychologically dissociated and buried their memories of childhood sexual abuse. Approximately half of the states rushed to extend the statute of limitations in the 1980s and 1990s.

Many patients later retracted these allegations, but the damage had already been done; families were divided, and parents were defamed and stigmatized. Finding that professional organizations and licensing boards were of little or no assistance, consumers of mental health services organized. Pamela Freyd, an educational psychologist accused with her husband of unspecified abuse of her estranged daughter, led the way in forming the False Memory Syndrome (FMS) Foundation in 1992. Hundreds of parents joined. With an advisory board of scientists and scholars, the FMS Foundation gained almost immediate credibility in the media.

In 1994, Gary Ramona in California made history when, as a parent, he sued his daughter's therapists for inducing false memories of incest and was awarded $500,000. The court held that the therapists owed a duty of care not only to the patient but also to the patient's parents. The litigation helped transform legal and popular attitudes toward recovered memories from broad acceptance to serious doubt. It was a turning point in the recovered memory debate. The experts testifying on behalf of Ramona unfolded a tale of "suggestive mischief" played by "inept therapists" that had led not to true memories but to sad fantasies woven into the "obsessional intrusions" of a depressed and bulimic girl.[22]

Shortly thereafter, in 1995 in Minnesota, multimillion-dollar jury decisions were returned in false memory cases brought by former patients and their parents against the therapists. For the first time, awards for malpsychotherapy paralleled those for malsurgery. Lawsuits against psychiatrist Diane Humenansky resulted in awards of $2.46 and $2.5 million, and then several settlements in other cases. Treatment in the cases involved the diagnosis of multiple personality disorder, otherwise called dissociative identity disorder. Dr. Humenansky used hypnosis, guided imagery, and sodium amytal to help her patients "recover memories," some of which involved belief in a satanic ritual abuse cult.[23] In 1997, as a result of the lawsuits, the Minnesota Board of Medical Practice ordered the suspension of Dr. Humenansky's license for an indefinite period of time.

Then, too, in other much publicized litigation, Dr. Bennett Braun, founding president of the International Society for the Study of Multiple Personality and Dissociation, was sued by eleven former patients who retracted memories of recovered abuse, one of the cases resulting in a settlement of a spectacular $10.6 million.[24] In addition, he lost his academic appointments and he agreed to a two-year suspension of his medical license in a settlement with the Illinois Department of Professional Regulation.[25]

Therapists who allegedly uncover dissociative identity disorder have claimed that its genesis is childhood abuse, so in every case of dissociative identity disorder, they have said, an allegation of child abuse is warranted. In a 1988 article in *Psychiatric Annals*, Daniel Hardy, a psychiatrist who also holds a law degree, wrote, "The psychiatrist or therapist must be alert to the potential danger of a malpractice suit arising from failure to diagnose multiple personality disorder."[26] As it turned out, just the opposite has happened, to wit, diagnosing or uncovering dissociative identity disorder may be regarded as malpractice, which follows the proposition that dissociative identity disorder is treatment-created or sometimes the result of self-hypnosis. Dr. Paul McHugh, then director of the Department of Psychiatry and Behavioral Science at Johns Hopkins, wrote, "[Dissociative identity disorder] is an iatrogenic behavior syndrome, promoted by suggestion and maintained by clinical attention." He noted that multiple identities disappear when the therapist does not ask about them, take notes about them, or otherwise take an interest in them.[27] Clinics specializing in the treatment of dissociative identity disorder have closed their doors.

In a position statement issued in March 2000 by the Board of Trustees of the American Psychiatric Association, four recommendations are made:

> (1) Regardless of issues of childhood abuse, all patients should received a complete psychiatric evaluation. Psychiatrists should maintain an empathic, nonjudgmental, neutral stance toward re-

ported memories of sexual abuse. As in the treatment of all patients, care must be taken to avoid prejudging the cause of the patient's difficulties or the veracity of the patient's reports. A strong prior belief that physical or sexual abuse or other factors are or are not the cause of the patient's problems is likely to interfere with appropriate assessment and treatment.

(2) When no corroborating evidence is available to confirm or refute reports of new memories of childhood abuse, treatment may focus on assisting patients in coming to their own conclusions about the accuracy of their memories or in adapting to uncertainty regarding what actually occurred. The therapeutic goal is to help patients understand the impact of the memories/abuse experience on their lives and to reduce the impact of these experiences.

(3) When asked to provide expert opinion involving memories of abuse, psychiatrists should refrain from making public statements about the historical accuracy of individual patients' reports of new memories based on observations made in psychotherapy.

(4) Further research and education regarding memory and childhood abuse are required to enhance psychiatrists' ability, on the basis of empirical evidence, to assist patients struggling with these profoundly difficult issues.[28]

With the growing legal backlash against therapies that try to elicit suppressed recollections, insurers are excluding revival of memory from coverage. For lawyers, the dinner bell sounded. With the news of the large judgments, law firms recently have been holding conferences exploring the potential of suing psychotherapists. Apart from undue familiarity with patients, nothing has done more to discredit psychotherapy than revival of memory of childhood sexual abuse. In the conclusion of a study of revival of memory cases, psychologist Terence Campbell wrote, "The incompetence of legions of psychotherapists amount to a public health hazard, and decisive action is warranted as a result."[29] The tide has turned against revival of memory therapy (but many families have not recovered, and they remain angry about it).[30]

Psychotherapy versus Chemotherapy

As we point out in the discussion on torts, the determination whether in a specific case a defendant will be held liable is a matter of policy and involves the consideration of a number of factors, including the foreseeability of harm to the plaintiff, the degree of certainty that the plaintiff suffered injury, the closeness of the connection between the defendant's conduct and the injury suffered, the moral blame attached to the defendant's conduct, and the policy of compensating injured persons and of preventing future harm. Causation is very much a matter of practical politics, and for that reason the issue does not lend itself to a ready and easy solution.

Psychotherapy is no longer the dominant form of treatment in psychiatry. The influence of psychoanalysis has diminished as advances have been made in biological psychiatry. But more than in any other specialty of medicine, psychiatrists devotedly and cultishly follow certain leaders, conceptual systems, and therapeutic rituals. One criterion that a court may apply in determining whether a professional person is negligent is the obligation to keep abreast of progress in the profession.

If psychiatry purports to deal with human conflict, it is, indeed, a specialty that is itself torn by internecine conflict. Generally speaking, psychiatrists can be categorized into two groups: directive-organic and analytic-psychological. The directive-organic group is medically oriented, utilizing such physical therapies as electroshock and drugs, and approaching their patients with firm suggestion and environmental manipulation. The analytic-psychological group prefers to do only psychotherapy, seeing patients several times weekly. It expresses an abhorrence for the physical therapies. It views drugs as a chemical straitjacket and electroshock as the ultimate form of barbarism.[31]

The tendency of the courts not to pass judgment on the appropriate therapy or the efficacy of different forms of therapy is reflected in Judge Benjamin Cardozo's observation that the law treats medicine with diffidence and respect. Thus, the courts refuse to consider which "of two equally reputable methods of psychiatric treatment"—psychoanalysis as against a physiological approach—would prove most efficacious in a particular case.[32] In *Youngberg v. Romeo,*[33] which involved the training, or *habilitation,* of a mentally retarded individual at a state institution, the U.S. Supreme Court noted, "It is not appropriate for the courts to specify which of several professionally acceptable choices should have been made." It went on to say, "[L]iability may be imposed only when the decision by the professional is such a substantial departure from accepted professional judgement, practice, or standards as to demonstrate that the person responsible actually did not base the decision on such a judgment."

In 1982, Dr. Rafael Osheroff ignited a controversy when he initiated a lawsuit against Chestnut Lodge, a private psychiatric hospital in suburban Maryland. Although the case was settled without court adjudication, it generated widespread discussion on the growing controversy between psychotherapy versus pharmacotherapy and whether the courts would play a role in that controversy.[34] The central issue in the case was whether Chestnut Lodge committed malpractice in relying exclusively on psychotherapy. After the case was settled and even before, when it was pending, Dr. Osheroff waged a public campaign, talking to reporters and peppering professional journals with letters and phone calls about his case. Soon the entire profession was talking about *Osheroff v. Chestnut Lodge.* He discussed his treatment before a large audience at the 1989 annual meeting of the American Psychiatric Association in San Francisco, where it was the subject of a three-hour panel discussion featuring Osheroff and six psychiatrists, including an official from Chestnut Lodge, and it was debated at that annual meeting of the American Psychiatric Association and in the pages of the *American Journal of Psychiatry* by Dr. Gerald L. Klerman and Dr. Alan A. Stone.[35]

The treatment of Dr. Osheroff during his seven-month stay at Chestnut Lodge was intensive psychotherapy. In accordance with the practice at Chestnut Lodge, he received no medication. He showed no improvement; instead, he showed distinct deterioration. For months he spent nearly every waking moment—sometimes sixteen hours—trudging an estimated eighteen miles a day up and down the hall of a locked ward in the hospital. The soles of his feet blistered, ulcerated, and turned black. He lost forty pounds and stopped bathing and shaving. He could not sit still long enough to eat with a knife and fork—instead, he would snatch food off a plastic tray as he paced. He repeatedly asked for medication, but his hospital psychiatrist told him to forget drugs, that they would only obscure his real problem—a narcissistic personality disorder rooted in his relationship with his mother. Prior to his hospitalization at Chestnut Lodge, he was given medication for depression by a psychiatrist, to no avail.[36]

His family, appalled by his deterioration, moved him from Chestnut Lodge to Silver Hill, a private hospital in Connecticut, where with chemotherapy, he showed substantial improvement and was discharged after a three-month stay. At Silver Hill, Osheroff made a point of noting, he was addressed as "Dr. Osheroff," not "Ray," as he was called at Chestnut Lodge. (Physicians tend to regard the honorific "Dr." as part of their name, and while addressing a physician without it may assist in a regressive technique, they regard that as insulting.) In his lawsuit against Chestnut Lodge, Osheroff claimed that the hospital and the two psychiatrists responsible for his treatment committed malpractice by misdiagnosing his biologically based depression and treating it with intensive psychotherapy alone, when effective and widely prescribed medication was available. He also alleged that the Lodge failed to obtain his informed consent about the probable duration and method of treatment. The Lodge contended that Osheroff was actually suffering from a narcissistic personality disorder for which drugs are not the appropriate therapy. The Lodge's treatment, it contended, was endorsed by a respectable minority of psychiatrists and therefore was not malpractice. "Breakdown is breakthrough," it is oft-said. One of the few things on which everyone agreed is that when Osheroff signed himself in at the Lodge, he appeared to be suicidally depressed.

Klerman, who was scheduled to be one of the experts on behalf of Osheroff in the litigation, argued that a patient has a right to "effective treatment," and he said, "there was no scientific evidence for the value of psychodynamically oriented intensive individual psychotherapy." He called the Lodge's treatment "criminal" and "cruel and negligent." In response, Stone said that the term *effective treatment* is used as a way to promulgate ideas about using uniform scientific standards of treatment in the psychiatric field and about a consensus regarding efficacious treatment. Klerman postulated that efficacious treatment should be measured solely by the results of controlled clinical trials, and because psychopharmacology has more supportive studies than psychotherapy, it is the more effective mode of treatment. Klerman challenged the *respectable minority* doctrine, which holds that if a minority of respected and qualified physicians approve of and practice a standard of care, that would constitute a sufficient defense to a malpractice claim.[37]

The tradition of using psychoanalysis on patients with major mental illnesses rooted itself firmly in the Washington-Baltimore area thanks to Adolf Meyer, an early member of the American Psychoanalytic Association and a large presence in the local Washington-Baltimore society. It was there that two private clinics—Chestnut Lodge in Rockville, Maryland (founded in 1910 by Ernest Luther Ballard), and the Sheppard and Enoch Pratt Hospital in Towson, Maryland (opened in 1891 as the Sheppard Asylum)—became the flagship hospitals for applying psychoanalysis to gravely ill patients. In 1922, Harry Stack Sullivan, perhaps the most famous figure in the psychoanalytic treatment of psychoses, arrived at the Sheppard.

Following the *Osheroff* litigation, Chestnut Lodge and other institutions turned to the use of drugs for nearly all of their patients. One member of the Chestnut Lodge staff commented, "The days of drug-free treatment at the Lodge are a thing of the past, yet pressures towards conformity rob our field of the opportunity to use individual clinical judgment, particularly with refractory cases, such as the

Lodge specializes in treating."[38] In 2001, as a result of money woes, Chestnut Lodge closed its doors.

Dr. Daniel Casey of the U.S. Veterans Hospital in Portland, Oregon, and a prominent researcher in psychopharmacology, had this to say about psychopharmacology as standard of care:

> The principle forms of treating mental illnesses should be primarily through psychopharmacology. However, if someone's life is a mess and the needed changes do not occur once the psychopharmacological treatments have provided their full benefits, then psychotherapy aimed at improving the functioning lifestyle seems reasonable. However, this does not necessarily require a medical degree or psychoanalytic training. The central issue is whether psychological approaches could be of meaningful value in helping a person gain greater function in their life after medicines have also been given their best chance at helping the patient.
>
> I would consider it malpractice to fail to offer lithium to a case of bipolar disorder. Some patients will not take medicine during an episode of bipolar illness and then one's options are considerably more limited. However, to fail to offer at any time or to fail to continue to offer on a timely schedule access to lithium (or other effective anti-bipolar drugs) would not meet the current standards of practice.[39]

In view of the various approaches in psychiatry to therapy, is it suitable, as Klerman suggested, that courts pass judgment on the appropriate therapy or the efficacy of different forms of treatment? In some instances, the courts or legislatures step in and impose a standard of care. The duty to report a patient who poses a danger and child abuse reporting statutes are impositions of a duty to warn and protect. The informed consent doctrine imposes a duty to advise patients of the risks of treatment.

Yet another notable example of a duty of care imposed by a court is *Helling v. Carey*.[40] In this case, the undisputed expert testimony was that the standard of care of ophthalmology did not require pressure tests for glaucoma in patients under forty years of age in cases of similar circumstances to that of the plaintiff. The court rejected the professional norms and determined that an ophthalmologist's failure to perform a simple, noninvasive test that would have prevented the patient's blindness was negligence. The decision changed the practice of ophthalmology. Ophthalmologists now routinely give glaucoma tests to patients in young adult age groups. In any event, *Helling* does not translate well to psychiatry. In psychiatry, there are no tests comparable to an eye pressure test.[41]

Electroshock Therapy: An Improper Treatment?

In every type of case, the lawyer becomes something of a specialist on the particular matter in issue. He draws books from the library and reads whatever he can about the subject. To be sure, he is a dilettante, but on the issue in dispute he stands ready to do battle with the experts. It is with a slow dismay that he realizes that psychiatrists themselves do not know exactly what happens when a person is given electroshock (also known as electroconvulsive therapy, or ECT). All they have are unverified theories and the knowledge that it gets results.[42]

Electroshock is an approved method of treatment, although it is not a preferred method by all clinicians. In the 1950s, with the development of less risky means of preventing spinal fractures, ECT had become "the treatment of choice," as Dr. Lothar Kalinowsky put it, for manic-depressive illness and major depression.[43] It was found to be more effective than other therapies, and it acted swiftly. In the 1950s and 1960s many psychiatrists devoted a considerable amount of their practice to "buzzing" patients. These psychiatrists were held in low regard and were frequently referred to as "shockiatrists," despite the fact that ECT was an established treatment.[44]

The year 1959 was a kind of golden year for psychiatry, when neither Kalinowsky nor anyone else knew that the antipsychiatric movement was about to bring ECT to an end, at least for a period of time.[45] Quite a number of specialists as well as many patients contended that it was barbarous, unscientific, and dangerous and ought to be outlawed. Before the advent of phenothiazine tranquilizing drugs, ECT was used as a punishment for violating institutional rules in mental hospitals and prisons. While the evidence on this is mostly anecdotal, it suggests that the practice was widespread. In Ken Kesey's popular novel *One Flew Over the Cuckoo's Nest*, Big Nurse's first effort to transform the hero, McMurphy, into a good patient was by means of ECT.[46] In 1950 the *Journal of the American Psychiatric Association* published an article by Dr. Mervyn Shoor and Dr. Freeman Adams on ECT as a management technique. They wrote, "Our goals were not curative. . . . We had in mind the management of chronic disturbed psychotic patients, free of restraint, seclusion, and sedation." They selected patients for ECT on the basis of need for control.[47]

In the 1960s, I often listened to Dr. Karl Menninger, renowned dean of American psychiatry, rail against electroshock. Each year at graduation exercises at the Menninger School of Psychiatry he condemned its use. Years later, in 1980, I asked him what he then thought of the widely controversial views about ECT. He responded:

> I spent many years of my younger professional life fighting electroshock therapy. It came to be very widely used by some and also very disapproved of by others. Patients usually develop an indescribable fear of it. They sometimes improve after it, especially in cases of depression. Some are made worse. I remember a case in which I was called as a consultant after a very fine university professor had failed to respond to all the [other] treatments in the books, including hard work and long and expectant idle waiting. They had, however, scrupulously avoided giving her shock therapy. I said I was not an advocate of it but occasionally it seemed to do a lot of good. They gave her one or two shocks and she recovered pronto! Everybody (well, *some* people) thought I was a wizard, including her.
>
> It probably has definite and considerable value in treating depression, but I do not know if we feel very certain about the criteria for its elective use. I do feel certain that it has been greatly abused, overused, oversold, and overinflicted on the patients and it not infrequently injures memory. Because it is a machine effect and so easily produced and so impressive whether or not successful, on the whole I think it is a dangerous modality for psychiatry.[48]

Over the years countless patients have voiced complaints about ECT. Some patients perceive ECT as a terrifying experience (at least initially), some regard it as an abusive invasion of personal autonomy, some experience a sense of shame because of the social stigma they associate with ECT, and some report extreme distress from persistent memory deficits.[49] Here is a complaint: "Electroshock convulsions resulted in my brain being 'taught' to have convulsions. In other words, I am now epileptic. This side effect is not super-common but has been documented since the 1940s."[50]

In early days of ECT, mortality was a significant problem. The commonly quoted overall mortality rate in the first few decades was 0.1 percent, or 1 per 1,000. Over the years, safer methods of administration have been developed, including the use of short-acting anesthetics, muscle relaxants, and adequate oxygenation. Present mortality is very low. In the least favorable recent series reported, there were 2.9 deaths per 10,000 patients. Overall, the risk is not different from that associated with the use of short-acting barbiturate anesthetics. Nonetheless, ECT remains controversial. Its opponents play up its risks, and to this day, they call ECT a "gruesome treatment."[51] Its advocates play down the risks. Complications may still arise from ECT.

The psychiatrist may be liable if he fails to make a reasonable disclosure to the patient of the significant facts and the more probable consequences and difficulties inherent in the treatment, including the risk of fractures. Depending on the circumstances, severity of the need, and urgency, the psychiatrist is obliged to communicate with and advise the spouse or other family members who are available and competent to advise or speak for the patient.[52]

ECT involves at least three considerable dangers (reflected in the premium for insurance policies covering ECT, which usually carry a 25 percent surcharge). Fractures and dislocations are a hazard, although over the years new methods have been developed to diminish the risk. Apnea or cessation of breathing is a danger that must be guarded against by artificial respiration.[53] Following the treatment the patient will have memory impairment and find himself in a severe state of confusion that may result in loss of self-control.

The most numerous cases in litigation involve fractures resulting from the convulsion induced during the treatment, but these cases are of an earlier time. Next most frequent are cases in which the patient is left unattended during the posttreatment period and injures himself in some way. Another series of cases involve the psychiatrist's failure to disclose the possible hazards of the treatment, and in some cases his affirmative statements that no harm could possibly result.[54]

The doctrine of *res ipsa loquitur*, justifying a presumption of negligence, does not apply to injuries resulting from electroshock treatment. The *res ipsa* doctrine, although invested with an esoteric aura, means nothing more than that certain events bespeak negligence. In a commonsense view, the event implicates the defendant: "The thing speaks for itself." The aura surrounding the phrase, though, prompted Lord Shaw of the House of Lords to say, "If that phrase had not been in Latin nobody would have called it a principle."[55]

In the seminal case on the *res ipsa* doctrine, a barrel of flour falling from a warehouse onto a passerby in the street was deemed more consistent with negligence on the part of the warehouseman than any other explanation. The phrase, found in Cicero, was used in the case by Chief Baron Pollock, an English gentleman

---

CONSENT TO ELECTROSHOCK THERAPY

Date _____   Time _____

1. I (We) authorize Dr. _____ and assistants of his choice, to administer electroshock treatment, and relaxant drugs and other medication to __(Name of Patient)__ and to continue such treatment at such intervals as he and his assistants may deem advisable.

2. I understand that this treatment consists of passing a controlled electric current between two electrodes applied to the patient's temples. In some instances, the patient may be given medication prior to treatment to reduce tension and produce muscular relaxation. I understand that the patient will not feel the electric current and will feel no pain. When the electric current is administered, the patient becomes unconscious and has strong convulsive muscular contractions which may last from 35 to 50 seconds. The patient gradually regains consciousness and his confusion clears within 15 to 60 minutes. The patient may experience headache and nausea.

3. I understand that the treatments may cause temporary confusion and memory impairment. I also understand that certain risks and complications are involved in the treatment. The most common risk is fracture and dislocation of the limbs and vertebrae. I acknowledge that these and other risks and complications of this procedure have been explained to me.

4. In addition to the foregoing, the strict care which will be required immediately following treatment and during convalescence has been fully explained to me.

5. The alternative methods of treatment have been explained and no guarantee or assurance has been given by anyone as to the results that may be obtained.

Signed _____

Signed _____

Witness _____

---

with a classical education.[56] When applicable, *res ipsa* means simply that rather than the plaintiff proving defendant negligent, the defendant is forced to produce evidence that he was not. Much the best observation was made by the Mississippi Supreme Court when it said in a classic case, "We can imagine no reason why, with ordinary care, human toes could not be left out of chewing tobacco, and if toes are found in chewing tobacco, it seems to us that somebody has been very careless."[57]

In the cases involving fractures during ECT, the courts have noted that since their occurrence is not dependent on the lack of care in administering the treatment, the doctrine has no bearing on the injury. Fractures occur during treatment even when it is properly administered, therefore the injury cannot in and of itself denote negligence. Fractures are part of the "calculated risk of the treatment."[58] The plaintiff must show that the treatment was not administered in consonance with the usual electroshock method employed by the usual skilled practitioner.

In a leading case on negligent ECT, the plaintiff suffered a compression fracture of his ninth thoracic vertebra during the first treatment. He complained of pain in his back after the treatment. Successive shock treatments nevertheless were administered and the injury was aggravated. The psychiatrist failed at any time to take x-rays. The plaintiff was allowed to use as evidence the *Standards of Electroshock Treatment* prepared by the American Psychiatric Association. Among the standards is one that states, "If the patient should complain of pain or impairment of function, he should receive a physical examination, including x-rays, to ascertain whether he suffered accidental damage." The court held that the defendant psychiatrist could be held to the published standards and was negligent in not taking an x-ray.[59]

In cases centering on the problem of posttreatment observation, someone, usually one on the hospital staff, has failed to keep watch over the patient who is in a state of confusion and in some way causes injury to himself. In some cases he falls out of bed; in others he falls down a flight of stairs. Generally deciding in favor of the plaintiff, the courts take the view that failing to observe the patient in his confused state constitutes negligence. The psychiatrist is held liable when he fails to direct that the patient be attended,[60] and the hospital is held liable when it fails to exercise reasonable safeguards.[61]

The most difficult cases concern the alleged lack of consent on the part of the patient, or an inadequate consent due to a failure on the part of the psychiatrist to disclose fully the nature and hazards of the treatment.[62] It is usually argued that the very fact that electroshock is recommended, at least the initial treatments, indicates that the patient, on account of his agitation or depression, is not in a condition either to consent or not consent. In one noted case, the court began its opinion with the stringent statement concerning disclosure and consent as generally applied to physicians: "[A patient] must have full and frank disclosure by a physician of all pertinent facts relative to his illness and treatment prescribed or recommended; otherwise any consent obtained from the patient for administration of such treatment is ineffectual." But having said that, the court then went on to say that complete and full disclosure when dealing with a mental patient may not always be the rule. In cases where, as the court put it, the patient is overwhelmed with anxiety, the physician may not be required to make a complete disclosure. In this particular case the defendant psychiatrist not only failed to inform the patient of the dangers of electroshock but in fact told him no harm could result, so as to reassure and calm him.[63]

Undertaking ECT does not fall within the obligation of a plaintiff in a personal injury case to minimize his damages, although ECT may alleviate the plaintiff's suffering. As the Louisiana Court of Appeals put it, "[A] plaintiff's refusal to submit to electroshock therapy is [not] unreasonable."[64] In the case of an involuntarily committed patient, ECT (like psychosurgery) is deemed an intrusive therapy that will not be imposed against the patient's will.[65]

It is highly unusual for a medical treatment to become the subject of local legislation, but just such an event occurred in California in regard ECT. The California legislature in 1973 sought to interdict entirely the use of ECT (along with lobotomy and psychotropic drugs). The law was challenged in court and enjoined as an unlawful restriction on medical practice.[66] The legislature revised the law to set consent and reporting requirements and to limit the use of ECT in patients under the age of twelve. Other states also restricted the use of ECT.[67] It has become statutorily regulated with strict procedures for its application on incarcerated or committed individuals. However, even in the many states that by law permit the use of ECT, the departments of mental health in many states do not allow it, and as a result, it is not available in state-run hospitals or in many of the smaller community hospitals that serve the uninsured, members of minority groups, and the more severely ill. Thus, ECT is not done in state hospitals in Michigan, but patients may be referred to the private sector for it.[68] Liability insurance premiums for the use of ECT remains high, so that is a disincentive to its use.

Following passage of the legislation in California, the American Psychiatric Association in 1975 established a Task Force on Electroconvulsive Therapy. The task force surveyed members of the association, reviewed the published accounts, and held public hearings in order to get a picture of the then contemporary ECT practice. Their report supported the use of ECT for patients with major depressive disorders, particularly for those whom psychotropic drugs had not helped.[69] ECT is supported as well for patients with mania or who are suicidal, as ECT is quick acting, unlike medication, which takes a long time to take effect. Its use is also supported for the treatment of patients who are catatonic, schizophrenic, or who are in a state of delirium (independent of the cause of the delirium). Its use is also supported in the treatment of women during the early trimester of pregnancy (avoiding the side effects of medication). There is growing use in the treatment of children, as it calls for a low threshold of electricity and they are physically able to undergo ETC.

The controversies over ECT, however, have taken a toll. The availability of ECT is uneven and sparse, although making a comeback. Henry Ford Hospital, the major hospital in Detroit, reinstituted it in 2000. ECT is now an ambulatory treatment, but insurers tend not to cover ECT unless administered in a hospital, so the patient is unnecessarily hospitalized. As a result of the outcries against ECT, the FDA has put a cap on the amount of electricity, but practitioners often exceed it in order for it to be effective. Risk factors are brain lesions, cardiovascular problems, or unstable heart.

The name *electroshock* is frightening but is no longer the fearsome treatment pictured in films. The term is a hangover from the time when the procedure was indeed frightening because it was used without general anesthesia and was often abused. It has been suggested that it now be called a "stimulation" procedure.[70] Anesthesia, controlled oxygenation, and muscle relaxation make the procedure so safe that the risks are less than those that accompany the use of some psychotropic drugs, and for elderly people, systemically ill individuals, and pregnant women, ECT is now a safer treatment for mental illness than any alternative.[71] Dr. Keith Russell Ablow had this to say:

> Unlike medications, ECT is not profitable to industry. If it were, there might be a flurry of industry-supported research to document its effectiveness and reduce its stigma. Psychiatrists would get the same hard-sell educational materials on ECT as we do on antidepressants. Maybe even some pens, pads of paper and briefcases with little lightning bolts or some-

thing, just like the ones we get with drug logos. But it's the power company that is paid for electrical current, not a pharmaceutical manufacturer.[72]

In recent years ECT has been making a comeback.[73] Too much electricity kills (as in that used to carry out the death penalty), but a little electricity may be curative. Researchers recommend that ECT should be considered more frequently as the treatment of choice for depressed patients with delusions, patients at high risk for suicide, older patients who cannot tolerate tricyclic antidepressants and whose history shows them to be poorly responsive, severely depressed patients without delusions, and those with limited insurance coverage.[74] In an address at the American Psychiatric Association Institute on Hospital and Community Psychiatry, Dr. John Nardini observed:

> I am sure that most of you in the field have known many patients who certainly would have been dead long since had they not had the benefit of shock treatment. Furthermore, prolonged hospitalization and the economic distress to the individual and his family would have been so much more extreme without that benefit. It is a mystery to me how shock treatment has come to be so ill-regarded. The antipathy for shock exists in various ways and at various levels and it has resulted in the deprivation of prompt and effective treatment for many individuals. One of the things that has made me feel earlier intervention of shock treatment is indicated is, of course, the high index of suicide and suicidal potential. I have known many patients who would have been alive for many years thereafter had they had shock treatment instead of other approaches.[75]

"That many people have negative things to say about electroshock is not surprising," says Dr. Max Fink, a longtime advocate of ECT. He says, "Most people have negative things to say about their doctors and how they failed to cure them. All humans die; every one of us is a medical failure; and, blaming the doctor or his treatment is fair game." And he says:

> What is surprising about electroshock is its remarkable efficacy and extraordinary safety. It is antidepressant, antipsychotic, antimanic, and anticatatonic; a breadth of action not matched by any other treatment for mental disorders. And, now that we have been through 65 years of experiments, it has become remarkably safe; in patients with systemic disorders, it is the safer option when compared to the risks of medicines. The increased use of ECT, now estimated at 100,000 patients in the U.S. annually, is due to one fact—the repeated failure of medicines to help these patients, and the success of ECT when medicines fail. It is for pharmacotherapy failures that ECT has been resurrected. However, many hospitals owned by insurance schemes do not have facilities for electroshock. From their point of view, the need for pre-ECT medical evaluations, the charges by anesthesiologists, the paucity of trained psychiatrists, and the hospital rules that often require in-patient care, all make the initial cost too high for them to encourage its use. The return of electroshock is not due to any managed care effect.[76]

During the 1990s, though a time of resurgence of the use of ECT, there has been little litigation involving ECT.[77] Indeed, a suit for malpractice for suicide was brought when ECT was *not* given. In an unreported wrongful death action, the psychiatrist was sued because thirteen years earlier the patient had been helped by him with ECT. The widow claimed that the patient, her husband, had gone to him again for ECT but had received medication without success. The court held for the psychiatrist, apparently on the theory that the court would not mandate a course of therapy when the treatment given meets standard of care.

What about the right of a voluntary patient in a state hospital to opt for ECT? In this situation, the California Court of Appeals said, "Where informed consent is adequately insured, there is no justification for infringing upon the patient's right to privacy in selecting and consenting to the treatment. The state has varied interests which are served by the regulation of ECT, but these interests are not served where the patient and his physician are the best judges of the patient's health, safety and welfare."[78]

Professional Guidelines on Treatments

The American Psychiatric Association, through its American Psychiatric Press, in 1989 published the monumental 3,000-page, four-volume *Treatment of Psychiatric Disorders* (prepared by the Task Force on Treatment of Psychiatric Disorders). The prepublication infighting spilled a lot of professional blood. Those opposing a so-called official treatment manual believed it would spur malpractice suits against psychiatrists. They said it would provide contentious or dissatisfied patients and their attorneys with ammunition in the form of an allegedly authoritative checklist of standards against which treatment would be measured in a courtroom.[79] A clinician providing therapy other than that mentioned in the official treatment manual would have difficulty in justifying his actions. When expert witnesses at trial are in disagreement (as is often the case), practice standards play a particularly important, if not determinative, role in the outcome of the case.[80]

The treatment efforts of psychiatrists are indeed graded by the manual not only for malpractice or professional competency questions but also for reimbursement. Because payment for health care today comes mainly by way of a third-party payer and is distributed among a variety of health service providers, evaluation and regulation of practice are increasingly practiced by the payers. The informed consent doctrine requires practitioners to inform patients of the various treatment alternatives, but the reimbursement policy influences what will be treated, how it will be treated, and who will do the treating. In making such an assessment, the third-party payer looks to authoritative guidelines. The treatment manual was generated, in large measure, to satisfy the health care payer.

Several psychiatrists launched a petition drive aimed at compelling the APA to cancel publication of the work. Clinical experience encourages therapists to use their own intuitive impression when selecting and applying treatment methods. They eschew the appropriateness of standardized treatments, insisting that they should be able to use their creative thinking and professional judgment. In the end, the APA issued a disclaimer, saying that the book is not official policy, but rather an "approved" task force report. In the disclaimer, the APA states that the work contains information on evolving knowledge, does not encompass all approaches, is not intended to impose rigid methods, and leaves final assessment up to the practitioner.[81] The term *guidelines* is used rather than *standards*, to suggest flexibility in treatment.[82] It is nonetheless argued by attorneys in the courtroom as state of the art, and in clinical circles psychiatrists are warned, "When we depart from the APA guidelines, we become vulnerable to a lawsuit."[83]

The issue of negligence is rarely raised, however, where anachronistic therapeutic modes are applied to psychiatric disorders, notwithstanding the availability of newer and more effective therapies. In this area, the issue of informed consent may well be applicable. It would appear that a psychiatric patient should be told what treatment modalities are available for his particular disorder and how they work, and then be given some approximation of what they may require in time and money. In some instances, his cognitive capacities may be so impaired by psychosis that the information will have to be imparted to a legally responsible member of the family. For example, if a therapist opts to treat a major psychosis like acute schizophrenia with psychotherapy alone, because of some strong antidrug convictions, he is entitled to do so. At the same time, he should inform the family what the current consensus of psychiatric literature has to say about results, undesirable consequences, and so forth, when various treatment modes are compared. Similarly, if a patient consults a therapist because of acute anxiety related to some stressful life event, he should have the information that will enable him to choose between the intensive long-term psychotherapies and the brief methods.

Increasingly, psychiatry has been called upon to define its methods and results to the consuming public. In addition to the courts, the leaders of major labor unions and the health insurers have looked at the results of the psychiatric therapies with understandable concern about the return on the insurance dollar. Beyond a doubt, it would be extremely difficult within the definition of *malpractice* to prove negligence when the efficacies of utilized psychiatric treatment modes have never been fully established and a significant segment of the psychiatric community is espousing their use, albeit solely on an impressionistic basis. This difficulty in establishing negligence would particularly characterize the talking therapies where the influence of doctor on patient, whether pernicious or therapeutic, would be virtually impossible to concretize to a jury. The continuation of a form of treatment over years, however, in the face of deterioration or the absence of improvement may prove to be a more easily demonstrable matter.

When a patient does not improve or his status deteriorates, as in the case of Osheroff, it should occasion referral for consultation and a reevaluation of diagnosis, psychodynamics, and therapeutic technique. The consultant should probably have a conceptual orientation somewhat at variance with the referring psychiatrist to avoid a validation and simple mirroring of his views. Such consultative help will not only be useful to the patient but to the psychiatrist as well, should a malpractice defense ever be necessary.

Managed Care

A current phenomenon that affects the standard of care in psychiatric treatment and choice of treatment is the role of managed care. It is no secret that the overall purpose of managed care is to reduce the cost of medical care. This can be in direct contradiction to providing the most appropriate psychiatric care that is available to the patient. By determining treatment choices based on economic incentives, HMOs have succeeded in establishing new standards of care, often to the detriment of patient care.

This situation has perhaps affected psychiatry more than other specialities. Since the mid 1980s, mental health expenditures have skyrocketed to 10 percent of overall health costs. In reaction, it is now quite common for employers to contract with HMOs to administer mental health benefits with control over the choice of mental health care provider, treatment, and length of therapy. Patients enrolled in managed care organizations may not have access to new, effective but expensive drugs or information about them from their physicians, who may be implicitly prohibited from discussing expensive therapies. The managed care physician has divided loyalties: to the patient, who deserves good care, and to the organization, which may demand that corners be cut at every opportunity. Under capitation plans, the less the physician does, the more he or she earns. The result of managed care is widely said to be a complete separation between economic concerns and therapeutic standards.

A backlash has occurred. Physicians now seek to form unions to safeguard their interests (under the law, only physicians who are employees may form a union). The Clinton administration endorsed a consumer's medical bill of rights, which included the repeal of gag clauses that prevented doctors from disclosing financial incentives of treatment decisions and included an appeal process if needed care is denied. The proposal was not adopted on the federal level.

Until recently, the argument that HMOs do not make medical decisions but only insurance decisions provided them with some medical malpractice protection. In scores of lawsuits around the country, HMOs have asserted that they have no legal liability for negligence or medical malpractice because they are administering employee benefit plans. Under the 1974 Employee Retirement Income Security Act (ERISA), a person in an employer-sponsored health plan may recover the benefits in question and can get an injunction clarifying the right to future benefits, but courts have repeatedly held that the law does not allow compensation for lost wages, death or disability, pain and suffering, or other harm that a patient may suffer as a result of the improper denial of claims. But things are changing.

In mid-1997, Texas became the first state to allow medical malpractice suits against HMOs. Missouri achieved a similar result by making it clear that HMOs practice medicine. Approximately twenty other states are considering similar laws, including New Jersey, Rhode Island, Connecticut, Washington, New York, and California. Proposals have also been made at the federal level. Some courts have ruled that recipients of health care may bring an action against HMOs on the grounds of "bad faith," just as they may against insurers on that ground. The Illinois Supreme Court held that a patient's HMO may be held vicariously liable for negligence of its independent-contractor physicians under agency law. A few states—New York for example—have enacted a bill of rights for managed care patients that states that a managed care organization must provide the number of consumer grievances it has received each year and the number of grievances decided in favor of the consumer.

New Restrictions on Bringing a Malpractice Claim

Restrictions on bringing a medical malpractice claim have multiplied, notwithstanding the development of HMOs restricting care. The medical profession has been successful in persuading various state legislatures to alleviate the medical malpractice crisis. Lobbyists placed much of the blame for the crisis on the law of negligence, and various modifications of the law were rushed through the legislatures of almost every state.

The legislation varies considerably. Caps have been imposed on awards for pain and suffering and limitations on expert testimony. Many states now require submitting the case to a screening board before filing an action, others require submission to arbitration, and others impose restrictions on the contingent fee. Many commentators say the reform has deformed tort law. The restrictions are under challenge. Trial lawyers have leveled a wide array of constitutional salvos against the "doctors' legislation."

In some measure, the counterattack has been successful. Several state supreme courts have held that the right to recover damages for injury is a fundamental right, thereby requiring strict scrutiny of equal protection review. The restrictions also are called an "unconstitutional limitation on access to the courts." The Missouri Supreme Court declared its state's mediation plan unconstitutional on grounds that it violates the right to seek immediate redress in the courts. Constitutional guarantees of substantive due process ensure that legislation or other governmental actions will not deprive any citizen of "life, liberty, or property without due process of law." Laws that diminish tort rights are subject to challenge as constituting a taking of the injured person's property, the right to sue, without due process of law. Many state constitutions contain a prohibition against special legislation.

Then, too, there is an end-run that may be made around the restrictions. To avoid the cap on compensatory damages, allegations are made that would allow punitive damages. Several states allow punitive damages awards in medical malpractice upon a showing of gross negligence.

The National Practitioner Data Bank

As part of the Health Care Quality Improvement Act of 1986, which included provisions granting limited immunity to persons or organizations participating in peer review activities, Congress established the National Practitioner Data Bank (NPDB).[84] It became operational in 1990. Under it, state medical and dental licensing boards are required to report to the Data Bank certain disciplinary actions taken on grounds related to the professional competence or professional conduct of the licensed professional. Denial of privileges to a hospital must be reported to the Data Bank, and also judgments and settlements of lawsuits must be reported. Hospitals must query the Data Bank at least every two years for each member of their medical staff; state licensure boards are not required to make a query of the Data Bank but may do so. The general public does not have access to the information in the Data Bank, although consumer organizations have lobbied for access. Attorneys for plaintiffs in malpractice suits can access the Data Bank only if the plaintiff can prove that the defendant health care entity failed to make a query on the practitioner defendant. Neither malpractice insurers nor third-party payers are given access to the Data Bank, but apparently these entities are requiring physicians to request and turn over their own Data Bank records as a condition of receiving coverage or reimbursement.

Physicians may request their own records from the Data Bank and are to receive a copy from the Data Bank of each report at the time it is made. They may dispute any report made against them (but the space is limited to six hundred letters). They may circumvent any report to the Data Bank by using their P.C. (professional corporation) as the named party in any litigation or in settling the case. Attorneys for plaintiffs want to posture a case so that it will be settled, and realizing that a practitioner will be reluctant to settle if it will be reported to the Data Bank, they only name the hospital as party defendant in cases where a mishap occurred in a hospital. Insurance companies draft the information that goes to the Data Bank, and they tend to spin it in favor of the physician. The federal General Accounting Office has issued a report that is critical of the accuracy of the information contained in the Data Bank, including the information that is provided by state medical boards.[85]

Notes

1. J. Freiberg, "The Song Is Ended but the Malady Lingers On: Legal Regulation of Psychotherapy," *St. Louis U. L. J.* 22 (1978): 519. See also R. D. Glenn, "Standard of Care in Administering Nontraditional Psychotherapy: Problems in Law and Medicine," *U.C.D. L. Rev.* 7 (1974): 56; T. E. Shea, "Legal Standard of Care for Psychiatrists and Psychologists," *West. State U. L. Rev.* 6 (1978): 71. Liability without fault (strict liability) has been urged in the case of psychiatric care. B. R. Furrow, *Malpractice in Psychotherapy* (Lexington, Mass.: Lexington Books, 1980).

2. W. Sutton with E. Linn, *Where the Money Was* (New York: Viking Press, 1976).

3. C. T. Onions (ed.), *The Shorter Oxford English Dictionary* (Oxford: Clarendon Press, 3d ed. 1965). Approximately one-third of the states have statutes of limitations specifically applicable to malpractice actions, usually providing a shorter period of time (generally two years) in which the action must be instituted. (The statutes of limitations usually provide a three-year period for a negligence action and one year for intentional torts.)

4. For a critique of the report, see S. B. Nuland, "The Hazards of Hospitalization," *Wall Street Journal*, Dec. 2, 1999, p. 22. For patient safety, the traditional approaches include credentialing of health care professionals, morbidity and mortality conferences, peer review when incidents occur and are reported, tort liability, and criminal liability. The focus is generally on injuries, meaning little attention is paid to near misses. Mary R. Anderlik of the University of Houston Law Center writes, "At the center of attention are events of professional negligence, i.e., incidents of sub-standard or below average performance by a professional resulting in patient injury. A system intended to compensate for negligent injury may be a poor proxy for periodic competency testing for health care professionals or a structure of sanctions and rewards linked to the development and dissemination of best practices by organizations. The threat of liability for negligence may promote mediocrity rather than innovation to improve safety." M. R. Anderlik, "Introduction to Patient Safety," *Health Law News* (University of Houston Health Law and Policy Institute), Mar. 2000, p. 3.

5. P. Theroux (ed.), *The Book of Eulogies* (New York: Scribner, 1997), p. 281.

6. D. S. Viscott, *The Making of a Psychiatrist* (New York: Arbor House, 1972).

7. T. Lask, "The Making of a Psychiatrist" (review), *New York Times*, Dec. 27, 1972, p. 37. Attorney Donald Dawidoff was one of the first to argue for a cause of action against a psychiatrist not only for malpractice in improperly rendering electroshock or drug therapy but also for faulty or negligent rendering of psychoanalysis and psychotherapy. See D. J. Dawidoff, *The Malpractice of Psychiatrists* (Springfield, Ill.: Thomas, 1973). Dawidoff's own history with psychiatry is sadly depicted by his son in N. Dawidoff, "My Father's Troubles," *New Yorker,* June 12, 2000, p. 58.

8. Quoted in J. L. Kelley, *Psychiatric Malpractice* (New Brunswick, N.J.: Rutgers University Press, 1996). In 1996 according to the Civil Justice Survey of State Courts, the latest compilation from the U.S. Department of Justice Bureau of Justice Standards, a total of 10,278 tort cases in the nation's seventy-five largest (by population) counties were decided by a trial. Some 1,201 (11.7 percent) involved medical malpractice. About 85 percent of the total, and

93 percent of the medical malpractice cases, were jury trials. The median medical malpractice award (compensatory and punitive) was $285,576, second highest of any category of tort cases listed. Only asbestos litigation was more expensive than medical malpractice. Cases won against medical doctors averaged almost $400,000 (for both surgeons and nonsurgeons); dentist and "other professional" awards were substantially lower. Psychiatrists and other mental health professionals were not listed separately, nor were physician-related awards separated from hospital or clinic-related ones. The median for all tort cases was $30,500. Awards over a million dollars were common in successful cases brought against surgeons (about 27 percent) and nonsurgeon M.D.s (21 percent), but rare in other tort categories (0–7 percent). The award amounts do not reflect the probability that the plaintiff will win in the first place. Plaintiffs won in 23 percent of medical malpractice trials, a much larger proportion than in other categories (48 percent overall; 41 percent for nonmedical professionals, 58 percent for automobile cases, and 57 percent for intentional torts). Punitive damages were award in only about one percent of successful medical malpractice cases, a number well below the average for all torts (3.3 percent). See, in general, R. Bonnie, "Professional Liability and the Quality of Mental Health Care," *Law, Medicine & Health Care* 16 (1988): 299; P. F. Slawson, "Psychiatric Malpractice: Ten Years' Loss Experience," *Med. & Law* 8 (1989): 415; id., "Psychiatric Malpractice: A Regional Incidence Case Study," *Am. J. Psychiatry* 126 (1970): 1302; Notes, "Medical Malpractice: The Liability of Psychiatrists", *Notre Dame Law.* 48 (1973): 693; "Psychiatric Malpractice: A Survey", *Washburn L. J.* 11 (1972): 461.

9. Quoted in J. Frieden, "Psychotherapy Problems Top Malpractice Complaints," *Clinical Psychiatry News,* Feb. 2000, p. 1.

10. A. Kardiner, *My Analysis with Freud* (New York: Norton, 1977), p. 69. On deterioration in therapy, see R. B. Stuart, *Trick or Treatment: How and When Psychotherapy Fails* (Champaign, Ill.: Research Press, 1970); D. Tennov, *Psychotherapy: The Hazardous Cure* (New York: Doubleday, 1976); H. H. Strupp, "The Performance of Psychiatrists and Psychologists in a Therapeutic Interview," *J. Clin. Psychol.* 14 (1958): 219; D. Hartley, H. B. Roback, & S. I. Abramowitz, "Deterioration Effects in Encounter Groups," *Am. Psychologist* 31 (1976): 241. A central belief that dominated psychoanalysis was the idea that diseases or illnesses could be deciphered, that they were laden with symbolic messages like short stories by an author, and the most frequent culprit, the experts explained, was a "refrigerator mother." E. Dolnick, *Madness on the Couch: Blaming the Victim in the Heyday of Psychoanalysis* (New York: Simon & Schuster, 1998). Psychoanalysis was given wide application. L. Stone, "The Widening Scope of Indications for Psychoanalysis," *J. Am. Psa. Assn.* 2 (1954): 567. In the 1960s, in standard practice, psychotherapy tended to excuse or tolerate self-indulgent, aggressive, and impulsive behavior, in most cases explaining it away as a defense against anxiety. In the 1970s it was seen that this worked against the recovery of patients, and a more demanding psychotherapy developed, in which patients were expected to bring their behavior under control before help could be found for their emotional distress. Dr. Paul R. McHugh, University Distinguished Service Professor of psychiatry at the Johns Hopkins University School of Medicine and formerly psychiatrist-in-chief at the Johns Hopkins Hospital in Baltimore, excoriates those psychotherapists who to this day sit by as patients make up their own rules for living or disregard consequences and moral meanings. He also maintains that those who have manic depression and schizophrenia are not simply expressing deep-seated psychological conflicts, as Freudianism had taught, but have medical diseases treatable by medications. P. R. McHugh, "Romancing Depression," *Commentary* 112 (Dec. 2001): 38.

Controversy surrounds the question whether treatment of mental illness deserves parity in insurance coverage with the treatment of other medical conditions. In principle, yes, but in practice? John F. Kihlstrom, professor of psychology at the University of California, Berkeley, writes: "[P]arity has to be earned by a mental-health industry whose practices are not yet on a par with the rest of the health care industry. Parity in mental-health services will be achieved, and parity in payments deserved, when mental illness is rigorously diagnosed on the basis of underlying pathology, as in the rest of medicine; when proposed new therapies are based on established scientific principles; when specific treatments have demonstrated to be effective for specific illnesses; and when practitioners routinely choose the most cost-effective alternatives." J. F. Kihlstrom, "Mental-Health Goals" (ltr.), *New York Times,* Dec. 15, 2001, p. 26. See also A. A. Stone, "The New Paradox of Psychiatric Malpractice," *New Eng. J. Med.* 311 (1984): 1384.

11. P. Rieff, *The Triumph of the Therapeutic* (Harmondsworth: Penguin, 1973). See also B. Richards, *Images of Freud: Cultural Responses to Psychoanalysis* (New York: St. Martin's Press, 1989); P. Rieff, *Freud: The Mind of the Moralist* (London: Gollancz, 1959).

12. Comments by Dr. Harold Greenwald in panel moderated by Ralph Slovenko on "Health and the Celebration of Life" at the 55th annual meeting of the American Orthopsychiatric Association in San Francisco, Mar. 30, 1978.

13. S. A. Appelbaum, *Out in Inner Space: A Psychoanalyst Explores the New Therapies* (Garden City, N.Y.: Doubleday, 1979), p. 66. In searching for a cure for his mentally ill brother, the writer Jay Neugeboren traveled the country looking at a variety of treatment programs, and it brought him up against a heated controversy: therapy versus drugs, which matters more? J. Neugeboren, *Transforming Madness* (New York: Morrow, 1999), reviewed in T. Parks, "In the Locked Ward," *New York Review of Books*, Feb. 24, 2000, p. 14. In *Selling Serenity: Life among the Recovery Stars* (Boca Raton, Fla.: Upton Books, 1999), Andrew Meacham calls into question addiction treatment programs. In a blurb of the book, Dr. Thomas Szasz says, "It is a superb account of Americans' irrepressible faith in humbug, now masquerading as a combination of medicine and religion, therapy and virtue."

A parody of regression therapy is the unorthodox New Age treatment called *rebirthing therapy*, which is supposed to overcome "reactive attachment disorder" in which children resist forming loving relationships and become unmanageable and violent. Wrapped in a flannel blanket meant to represent the womb, the child is pushed against with pillows and urged to fight their way out and become "reborn." In a nationally publicized incident in Colorado, a child died of asphyxiation. Colorado does not require therapists to be licensed, although they must register with state. C. Caldwell, "Death by Therapy," *Weekly Standard*, May 28, 2001, p. 20; A. Cannon, "From Mumbo Jumbo to a Child's Death," *U.S. News & World Report*, Sept. 18, 2000, p. 36. See chapter 12, on regulation of psychotherapy.

14. In a Texas case, a minister advised the wife to seek separation from the husband, due to their marital problems. She followed this advice. The husband, later, in a state of rage, shot her, seriously injuring her. The couple later reconciled and then jointly sued the minister for his counsel and advice. They prevailed. The case sent clergy scurrying to insurance companies. Correspondence from Robert M. Plunk, vice president of Preferred Risk Mutual. Following the Texas case, a number of alienation of affection suits were filed against ministers, and there have been other types of cases. United Press International news report, "Ministers Taking Out 'Peace of Mind' Policy," *Chicago Sun-Times*, Oct. 19, 1980, p. 30; "Suing Clergymen for Malpractice," *Time*, Jan. 12, 1981, p. 75. A new crop of insurance policies were spawned to guarantee that, when doling out advice, men of God have more than God on their side. See Associated Press news release, "Malpractice Insurers Are Finding a New Market among Ministers," *New York Times*, May 18, 1980, p. 49; Editorial, "Suing the Clergy," *Detroit News*, May 15, 1980, p. 22.

15. A. R. Somers, "Accountability, Public Policy, and Psychiatry," *Am. J. Psychiatry* 134 (1977): 959. See also T. G. Gutheil, *The Psychiatrist in Court: A Survival Guide* (Washington, D.C.: American Psychiatric Press, 1998).

16. Congress has been asking: Does psychotherapy work? Does it work well enough to be paid for out of public funds? B. S. Herrington, "Congress Asks: Does Therapy Work?" *Psychiatric News*, Mar. 21, 1980, p. 1; "Therapy Efficacy Test Bill Finally Introduced," *Psychiatric News*, Sept. 19, 1980, p. 3. In a study some years ago, University of Minnesota Psychology Professor William Schofield surveyed a randomized sample of 377 psychologists, psychiatrists, and psychiatric social workers, and uncovered what he called the YAVIS Syndrome, an overwhelming preference for patients who are "young, attractive, verbal, intelligent, and successful." They are, on balance, healthier in the first place—a ready-made success package. In effect, the psychiatric profession has abandoned the psychotic or seriously disturbed individual. See E. Ames, "What Your Shrink Really Thinks of You," *New York*, Apr. 7, 1980, p. 40.

17. R. Slovenko, "On the Need for Recordkeeping in the Practice of Psychiatry," *J. Psychiatry & Law* 7 (1980): 399.

18. E. L. Hodgson, "Restrictions on Unorthodox Health Treatment in California: A Legal and Economic Analysis," *U.C.L.A. L. Rev.* 24 (1977): 647; M. J. Karson, "Regulating Medical Psychotherapists in Illinois: A Question of Balance," *John Marshall J. Practice & Procedure* 11 (1978): 601; R. Plotkin, "Limiting the Therapeutic Orgy: Mental Patients' Right to Refuse Treat-

ment," *Nw. U. L. Rev.* 72 (1977): 461; J. E. Smith, "Electroconvulsive Therapy: The Patient's Right to Consent in Utah," *J. Contemp. L.* 5 (1979): 233.

19. Michigan law provides that the duty of a physician to report an impaired physician does not apply to a physician who is in a "bona fide health professional–patient relationship" with the impaired physician. MCL sec. 333.16223.

20. What about the discharge of a tort judgment in bankruptcy? In Kawaauhau v. Geiger, 523 U.S. 57 (1998), the U.S. Supreme Court held that debts arising from recklessly or negligently inflicted injuries do not fall within the willful and malicious injury exception to discharge under bankruptcy law. The decision affirmed the Eighth Circuit's opinion, and is contrary to earlier holdings of the Sixth and Tenth Circuits. Relying on the words of the bankruptcy law and other statutory indications, the U.S. Supreme Court held that a typical malpractice judgment is not a debt for "willful and malicious injury." The high court's opinion relied on a doctrine learned by first-year law students in their course on torts: Garratt v. Dailey, 279 P.2d 1091 (Wash. 1955), to wit, intended acts that cause injury are distinguishable from acts done with intent to cause injury or with knowledge to a substantial certainty that injury will occur.

21. Hammer v. Rosen, 7 N.Y.2d 376, 198 N.Y.S.2d 65 (1960).

22. The case is recounted in M. Johnson, *Spectral Evidence* (Boston: Houghton Mifflin, 1997). See also R. Ofshe & E. Watters, *Making Monsters: False Memories, Psychotherapy, and Sexual Hysteria* (New York: Scribner, 1994). In 1995, Christopher Barden, an attorney and psychologist, began circulating to federal and state legislatures a proposal for a new law, the "Truth and Responsibility in Mental Health Practices Act." A key sentence states: "No tax or tax exempt moneys may be used for any form of health care treatment, including any form of psychotherapy, that has not been proven safe and effective by rigorous, valid and reliable scientific investigations and accepted as safe and effective by a substantial majority of the relevant scientific community." The words *tax exempt* would exclude coverage of such therapies not only by public programs but also by private insurers, since the insured write off the cost of health insurance. The law would also include requirements for informed consent. In 1997, in response to the lobbying efforts of Tom Rutherford, whose daughter had a revival of memory in therapy of childhood sexual abuse, the Indiana state legislature passed a law requiring that mental health providers obtain informed consent from any prospective patient that would inform the patient of the "risks and relative benefits of proposed treatments and alternative treatments." Barden's proposal was signed not just by him but by a number of respected psychologists and psychiatrists. The argument is made that any psychotherapeutic technique which cannot be scientifically proven to be effective constitutes an experimental and dangerous procedure, mandating informed consent for experimentation.

Law professor Alan Scheflin and Dr. David Spiegel write, "Strange as it may sound, psychiatrists today are probably safer from legal liability for authorizing psychosurgery that, despite its highly controversial history in medicine and law, is now making a comeback, than they are from simply talking with a patient about memories of the past." A. W. Scheflin & D. Spiegel, "From Courtroom to Couch: Working with Repressed Memory and Avoiding Lawsuits," in D. A. Tomb (ed.), *Diagnostic Dilemmas* (Philadelphia: Saunders, 1998), p. 847. Dr. Paul Fink, a former president of the American Psychiatric Association, organized a "Leadership Council" consisting of a group of therapists, lawyers, etc., who promote the validity of repressed memories, recovered memory therapy, dissociative memories, and multiple personality disorders. It was organized in reaction to recovered memory therapists being sued by former patients who have recanted these memories. The group included Dr. Richard Kluft, Dr. David Speigel, Professor Alan Scheflin, and Dr. Bessel Van der Kolk. See chapter 11, on duty of therapists to third parties.

23. Dr. Humenansky's legal defense was paid for by her American Psychiatric Association insurance with Legion Insurance and Professional Risk Retention Group. They turned around and sued Dr. Humenansky's defense lawyers for legal malpractice, and lost. According to reports, the insurance firms employed five experts for the trial, two of whom were paid over $100,000 for their services.

24. The reason in settling was that there was a substantial body of evidence that continued to grow, that was persuasive, and that would have resulted in a very severe verdict against Dr. Braun, probably exceeding his policy limits. In addition to losing his practice,

academic appointments, and earnings, Dr. Braun agreed to a two-year suspension of his medical license in a settlement with the Illinois Department of Professional Regulation.

25. See J. Cannell, J. I. Hudson & H. G. Pope, "Standards for Informed Consent in Recovered Memory Therapy," *J. Am. Acad. Psychiatry & Law* 29(2001): 138; M. J. Grinfeld, "Recovered Memory Lawsuit Sparks Litigation," *Psychiatric Times*, Dec. 1999, p. 1. See J. Acocella, *Creating Hysteria* (San Francisco: Jossey-Bass, 1999).

26. D. W. Hardy, "Multiple Personality: Failure to Diagnose and the Potential for Malpractice Liability," *Psych. Annals* 18 (1988): 543.

27. P. McHugh, "Psychiatric Misadventures," *Am. Scholar*, Autumn 1992, p. 497.

28. "APA Stakes Out Positions on Controversial Therapies," *Psychiatric News*, Apr. 21, 2000, p. 45.

29. T. W. Campbell, *Smoke and Mirrors: The Devastating Effect of False Sexual Abuse Claims* (New York: Insight Books, 1998). In *Therapy's Delusions* (New York: Scribner, 1999), Ethan Watters and Richard Ofshe claim that, over the years, talk therapy has masqueraded as a scientific discipline and has cost patients time, money, and their mental well-being.

30. That attitudes about revival of memory therapy have changed is indicated by the award given in June 2001 by the American Psychological Society to Dr. Elizabeth Loftus, who for over a decade was criticized for her work debunking revival of memory. The award states: "As a result of her pioneering scientific work as well as her activity within the legal system, society is gradually coming to realize that such memories, compelling though they may seem when related by a witness, are often a product of recent reconstructive memory processes rather than of past objective reality." See also J. Mont, "Recovered Memories and the Psychologists [Who] Create Them: A Study of the Repressed Memory Controversy," *Det. C. L. Rev.* 1997: 164.

31. See T. M. Luhrman, *Of Two Minds: The Growing Disorder in American Psychiatry* (New York: Knopf, 2000).

32. United States v. Klein, 325 F.2d 283, 286 (2d Cir. 1963). In this case Judge Kaufman commented about disagreements among psychiatrists on treatment: "Mental disorders being what they are, it is not surprising that eminent psychiatrists differ as to methods of treatment. Here, [one psychiatrist] believed that [the accused] would respond to a psychoanalytic form of therapy; [the government psychiatrist] favored a more physiological approach. Courts of law, unschooled in the intricacies of what may be the most perplexing of medical sciences, are ill equipped to choose among such divergent but responsible views." For an aching back (a common ailment), Lisa Gubernick consulted eight different specialists—an osteopath, chiropractor, acupuncturist, psychiatrist, homeopath, physiatrist, neurologist, and a celebrity doctor—and got eight different diagnoses and recommended treatments. L. Gubernick, "'Have I Got a Cure for You!'" *Wall Street Journal*, Oct. 6, 2000, p. W-1. See M. Kowalski, "Applying the 'Two Schools of Thought' Doctrine to the Repressed Memory Controversy," *J. Legal Med.* 19 (1998): 503. See also the discussion of the two schools, or respectable minority, doctrine in chapter 3.

33. 457 U.S. 307 (1982).

34. A challenge to procedures followed by the Maryland Health Claims Arbitration office appears in Osheroff v. Chestnut Lodge, 62 Md. App. 519, 490 A.2d 720 (Md. App. 1985). See R. Reisner, C. Slobogin, & A. Rai (eds.), *Law and the Mental Health System* (St. Paul, Minn.: West, 1999), pp. 148–56.

35. G. L. Klerman, "Implications of *Osheroff v. Chestnut Lodge*," *Am. J. Psychiatry* 147 (1990): 409; A. A. Stone, "Law, Science, and Psychiatric Malpractice: A Response to Klerman's Indictment of Psychoanalytic Psychiatry," *Am. J. Psychiatry* 147 (1990): 419. See also J. L. Kelley, *Psychiatric Malpractice* (New Brunswick, N.J.: Rutgers University Press, 1996); J. G. Malcolm, *Treatment Choices and Informed Consent: Current Controversies in Psychiatric Malpractice* (Springfield, Ill.: Thomas, 1988). Stone later wrote, "Psychoanalysis is losing favor as part of psychotherapeutic treatment as the Freudian paradigm is replaced by scientific advancements." A. A. Stone, "The Decline and Fall of Psychoanalysis—and What It Means to Physicians," *TEN* 3 (2001): 48.

There is an extensive literature on psychopharmacology vs. psychotherapy in the treatment of mental illness. See, e.g., E. Frattaroli, *Healing the Soul in the Age of the Brain* (New York: Viking, 2001); J. A. Hobson & J. A. Leonard, *Out of Its Mind* (Cambridge: Perseus, 2001); T. M. Luhrman, *Of Two Minds: The Growing Disorder in American Psychiatry* (New York:

Knopf, 2000); R. R. Slavney & P. R. McHugh, *Psychiatric Polarities* (Baltimore: Johns Hopkins University Press, 1987); E. S. Valenstein, *Blaming the Brain: The Truth about Drugs and Mental Health* (New York: Free Press, 1998); see also J. Acocella, "Three Cheers for Psychotherapy," *New Yorker,* May 8, 2000, p. 112; L. Luborsky, B. Singer, & L. Luborsky, "Comparative Studies of Psychotherapies," *Arch. Gen. Psychiatry* 32 (1975): 995.

36. S. G. Boodman, "A Horrible Place and a Wonderful Place," *Washington Post Magazine,* Oct. 8, 1989, p. 18.

37. Subsequently, Stone expressed disillusionment with psychoanalysis (but not psychotherapy), and he wrote that "the social and intellectual history of psychoanalysis involves opening our eyes to sordid facts and gaining new understanding." A. A. Stone, Book Review, *Am. J. Psychiatry* 155 (1998): 851. See also A. A. Stone, "Where Will Psychoanalysis Survive?" *Harvard Magazine,* Jan./Feb. 1997, p. 34. Psychologist Carol Tavris says, "No one knows why medication helps some people but has no effect on others. No one knows why psychotherapy helps some people and has no effect on others. And when medication or therapy do work, no one knows why they do." C. Tavris, "The Know-Nothing Healers," *Times Literary Supplement,* Oct. 27, 2000, p. 10. Some find a therapeutic element to the martial arts that helps children with attention deficit disorder cope. S. Saulny, "Using Martial Arts for Attention Disorders," *New York Times,* Dec. 2, 2000, p. 16.

38. Personal communication (Apr. 24, 1990). Edward Dolnick wrote, "The medical community had followed the case closely—they saw it as 'psychiatry on trial'—and no one missed the message. Chestnut Lodge had long represented the state of art in psychotherapy; now this haven of healing had been declared a danger to its patients. For decades, 'talk therapy' had dominated psychiatry and held its rivals in open contempt, but its day was gone. From all sides—from those studying schizophrenia, autism, obsessive-compulsive disorder, and now depression—came the message that in the future psychotherapy would play a considerably diminished role. The more serious the illness, the less likely that anyone would treat it by talk alone." E. Dolnick, *Madness on the Couch* (New York: Simon & Schuster, 1998), p. 278. Dr. Thomas Szasz, the well-known critic of the medical model of mental illness, as well as an adamant opponent of the use of "coercive" efforts to keep an individual from committing suicide, agreed to pay $650,000 to the widow of one of his patients, a physician who had manic-depressive illness and killed himself. The complaint filed against Szasz alleged that he instructed and advised his patient to stop taking lithium in June 1990; in December of the same year, the physician hanged himself with battery cables. The complaint further alleged that Szasz had failed to render "psychiatric medical care and treatment in conformity with the customary and accepted sound standards of medical care," "failed to properly diagnose and treat," "failed to provide proper therapy to treat manic depression," and "failed to keep adequate and proper medical records." Szasz's attorney maintained that the patient had stopped taking lithium of his own accord and Szasz himself did not concede he had committed malpractice though settling the case. Klein v. Szasz, State of New York, Onondaga Cy, Index No. 92-660, RJI No. 33-92-640; discussed in K. R. Jamison, *Night Falls Fast: Understanding Suicide* (New York: Knopf, 1999), pp. 253–55. For Szasz's critiques, see T. Szasz, *Pharmacracy: Medicine and Politics in America* (Westport, Conn.: Praeger, 2001); id., "A Moral View on Suicide," in D. Jacobs & H. N. Brown (eds.), *Suicide: Understanding and Responding* (Madison, Conn.: International Universities Press, 1978), pp. 437–47.

39. Personal communication (Nov. 1, 1994). Before the advent of medication, therapy was limited to talk therapy, lobotomy, or electroshock. Freud had cautioned that psychoanalysis had nothing to offer in the treatment of psychosis. Until useful medicines came along, he suggested, the best course was to focus on neurotic rather than psychotic individuals, on the worried well rather than the profoundly sick. "Psychoanalysis," Freud observed in 1909, "meets the optimum of favorable conditions where its practice is not needed, i.e., among the healthy." E. L. Freud (ed.), *The Letters of Sigmund Freud* (New York: Basic Books, 1975), p. 278.

40. 83 Wash.2d 514, 519 P.2d 981 (1974), noted in chapter 3.

41. A. Gawande, "No Mistake: The Future of Medical Care: Machines That Act Like Doctors, and Doctors Who Act Like Machines," *New Yorker,* Mar. 30, 1998, p. 74.

42. There was at one time a psychoanalytic theory that ECT was a punishment that assuaged guilt, and thus was curative of depression. The best-selling 1946 autobiographical novel by Mary Jane Ward, *The Snake Pit,* and the famous 1948 film based on it, told of the

experiences of a woman in a crowded mental hospital where therapy for schizophrenia included being wrapped in wet, cold sheets, boiled in a bathtub, and given electroshock treatment. The "snake pit" of the title referred to the medieval practice of lowering the mentally ill into snake pits in the belief that a fright that would unhinge a sane person would cure an insane one. See G. J. Alexander & A. W. Scheflin (eds.), *Law and Mental Disorder* (Durham: Carolina Academic Press, 1998), pp. 981–1001.

43. L. B. Kalinowsky, "Convulsive Shock Treatment," in S. Arieti (ed.), *American Handbook of Psychiatry* (New York: Basic Books, 1959), vol. 2, p. 1510.

44. See D. S. Viscott, *The Making of a Psychiatrist* (New York: Harbor House, 1972); see also R. Cancro, "Functional Psychoses and the Conceptualization of Mental Illness," in R. W. Menninger & J. C. Nemiah, *American Psychiatry after World War II* (Washington, D.C.: American Psychiatric Press, 2000).

45. E. Shorter, *A History of Psychiatry* (New York: Wiley, 1997).

46. In a fictional story Chinese-born writer Ha Jin, a young, gay man in China, is sent to a mental hospital where a doctor confides that homosexuality is not a disease and cannot be cured, but still he says, "Electrotherapy is prescribed by the book—a standard treatment required by the Department of Public Health. I have no choice but to follow the regulations." H. Jin, *The Bridegroom* (New York: Pantheon, 2000).

47. M. Shoor & F. H. Adams, "The Intensive Electric Shock Therapy of Chronic Disturbed Psychotic Patients," *Am. J. Psychiatry* 107 (1950): 279.

48. Letter of Jan. 17, 1980, quoted with permission.

49. It is well-known that ECT may be responsible for retrogressive amnesia, but what has not been clearly defined is the effect of ECT on autobiographical versus interpersonal memories. Reporting on research, Dr. Frank J. Ayd Jr. points out that bilateral ECT causes more marked amnesia for events and details than right unilateral ECT, especially for impersonal memories. The results indicate that the amnesic effects of ECT are greatest and most persistent for knowledge about the world, compared with distinctly remote events and for less salient events. Bilateral ECT produces more profound amnesic effects than right unilateral ECT, particularly for memory of impersonal events. F. J. Ayd, "Reading and Reflections," *Psychiatric Times*, Aug. 2001, p. 5. Leonard Roy Frank of San Francisco edited and published a book, *The History of Shock Treatment* (1978), that is highly critical of ECT. The periodical *Madness Network News*, also published in San Francisco, takes aim at ECT.

In a sexual abuse malpractice claim, McNall v. Summers, 25 Cal. App.4th 1300, 30 Cal. Rptr.2d 914 (1994), the trial judge commented on the expert testimony of Dr. Maria Lymberis, a psychiatrist: "Dr. Lymberis said that women do not like orgasm because it's the same to them as electroshock therapy. And, still, when I go home and I am listening to the radio and I get Dr. Toni Grant or some of these on, there are women calling in all the time wondering how they can achieve orgasm. And here's a woman who says that women to do not want it because it's just the most horrible experience that they could possibly have next to electroshock therapy." Dr. Dmitri Dosrtzev, embryologist at Wayne State University School of Medicine, points out that not infrequently women who suffer having an orgasm compare it to ECT. Personal communication (Nov. 11, 1999).

50. Personal communication (Oct. 29, 1999). The saga of Nobel Prize–winning mathematician John Forbes Nash Jr. has been dramatized in book and film. With psychoanalysis and medication failing, Nash was brought to the Carrier Clinic, a private mental hospital in New Jersey that had a reputation for the aggressive use of medication and electroshock (unlike institutions at the time such as McLean, Austin Riggs, or Chestnut Lodge, whose psychoanalytical orientation and long-term approaches based on the talking cure were regarded, especially by academics, as more humane and appropriate). From the outset, Nash's wife and sister drew the line at electroshock. "We debated electroshock," they recalled, "but we didn't want to mess with his memory." Nash apparently did not get electroshock but insulin therapy. S. Nasar, *A Beautiful Mind: A Biography of John Forbes Nash, Jr.* (New York: Simon & Schuster, 1998), p. 306. See also J. Didion, "Varieties of Madness," *New York Review of Books*, Apr. 23, 1998, p. 17; C. C. Mann, "Mathematics and Madness," *Wall Street Journal*, June 19, 1998, p. W-9; A. O. Scott, "From Math to Madness, and Back," *New York Times*, Dec. 21, 2001, p. WK-1. In the film version of *A Beautiful Mind* (2001), director Ron Howard suggested that the cure for Nash's paranoid schizophrenia was love.

51. See P. R. Breggin, *Electroshock: Its Brain-Disabling Effects* (New York: Springer, 1979);

id., *Toxic Psychiatry* (New York: St. Martin's Press, 1991), pp. 184–215; J. Horgan, *The Undiscovered Mind: How the Human Brain Defies Replication, Medication and Explanation* (New York: Free Press, 1999).

52. Mitchell v. Robinson, 334 S.W.2d 11 (Mo. 1960).

53. Whether psychiatrists are qualified to give anesthesia for ECT is controversial. See T. Pearlman, M. Loper, & L. Tillery, "Should Psychiatrists Administer Anesthesia for ECT?" *Am. J. Psychiatry* 147 (1990): 1553.

54. See S. Taub, "Electroconvulsive Therapy, Malpractice, and Informed Consent," *J. Psychiatry & Law* 15 (1987): 7.

55. Ballard v. North British R. Co., [1923] Sess. Cas. H.L. 43, 56.

56. Byrne v. Boadle, 2 H. & C. 722, 159 Eng. Rep. 299 (1863).

57. Pillars v. R.J. Reynolds Tobacco Co., 117 Miss. 490, 78 So. 365 (1918). See D. B. Dobbs, *The Law of Torts* (St. Paul, Minn.: West, 2000), pp. 370–81.

58. Farber v. Oklon, 40 Cal.2d 503, 253 P.2d 520 (1953); Quinley v. Cocke, 183 Tenn. 428, 192 S.W.2d 992 (1946); Foxluger v. State, 23 Misc.2d 933, 203 N.Y.S.2d 985 (Sup. Ct. 1960); Johnson v. Rodis, 151 F.Supp. 345 (D.C. 1957), *rev'd on other grounds*, 251 F.2d 917 (D.C. Cir. 1958).

59. Stone v. Proctor, 259 N.C. 633, 131 S.E.2d 297 (1963); *Standards for Electroshock Treatment* (Washington, D.C.: American Psychiatric Assn., 1953).

60. Brown v. Moore, 247 F.2d 711 (3d Cir. 1957).

61. Quick v. Benedictine Sisters Hosp. Assn., 257 Minn. 470, 102 N.W.2d 36 (1960); Adams v. Ricks, 91 Ga. 494, 86 S.E.2d 329 (1955).

62. In Wilson v. Lehman, 379 S.W.2d 478 (Ky. 1964), the court held that where there is no evidence of any false representations, a patient's consent to electroshock treatment will be presumed from his voluntary submission to it.

63. Woods v. Brumlop, 71 N.M. 221, 377 P.2d 520 (1962).

64. Dohmann v. Richard, 282 So.2d 789 (La. App. 1973); discussed in volume 1, chapter 22, on duty to minimize damages.

65. See the discussion in chapter 2, on the right to refuse treatment.

66. Aden v. Younger, 57 Cal. App.3d 662, 129 Cal. Rptr. 535 (1976); Northern California Psychiatric Society v. City of Berkeley, 223 Cal. Rptr. 609 (1986).

67. C. Sanger, "Regulation of Electroconvulsive Therapy," *Mich. L. Rev.* 75 (1976): 363.

68. In obtaining an informed consent, some states require that the patient be told that the risks of ECT are (1) confusion, (2) impairment of memory, and (3) fracture of bones. It is difficult enough to get a patient or family to consent but mentioning the risk of fracture frightens them away. See the standard form that appears in this chapter.

69. Task Force Report, *Electroconvulsive Therapy* (Washington, D.C.: American Psychiatric Association, 1978).

70. L. Cammer, *Up from Depression* (New York: Simon & Schuster, 1969). In response, Joe Kennedy Adams, Ph.D., wrote: "Dr. Leonard Cammer, one of electric shock treatment's most outspoken advocates, has tried to allay public fear concerning its use. He believes the 'shock' scares a lot of people and calls the procedure 'electric-stimulation treatment.' I don't believe the word 'shock' in this case scares people nearly enough, and propose that this technique be called 'electric shock torture.'" J. K. Adams, "You're in for the Shock of Your Life," in S. Hirsch (ed.), *Madness Network News Reader* (San Francisco: Glide, 1974), p. 84. See also C. H. Kellner & D. Ramsey, "Please No More 'ECT'" (ltr.), *Am. J. Psychiatry* 147 (1990): 1092.

71. M. Fink, *Electroshock: Restoring the Mind* (New York: Oxford University Press, 1999); D. Smith, "Shock and Disbelief," *Atlantic*, Feb. 2001, p. 79.

72. K. R. Ablow, *To Wrestle with Demons* (Washington, D.C.: American Psychiatric Press, 1992), p. 31.

73. G. Borzo, "Electroconvulsive Therapy Undergoes Renaissance," *Clinical Psychiatry News*, Sept. 2000, p. 11. Psychosurgery, too, is making a comeback in the treatment of obsessive-compulsive disorder when not responsive to medication or other treatment. For its use in the treatment of chronic fatigue, see T. M. Burton, "Surgery on the Skull for Chronic Fatigue? Doctors Are Trying It," *Wall Street Journal*, Nov. 11, 1999, p. 1.

74. The National Institute of Mental Health stated in a report: "Given a diagnosis for which the efficacy of ECT has been established, the immediate risk of suicide (when not

manageable by other means) is a clear indication for the consideration of ECT. Acute manic episode—especially when characterized by clouded sensorium, dehydration, extreme psychomotor agitation, high risk for serious medical complications or death through exhaustion, and nonresponse to pharmacological interventions—are also clear indications for ECT. The severe and unremitting nature of the patient's emotional suffering, or extreme incapacitation, are also important considerations." "Electroconvulsive Therapy," Consensus Development Conference Statement, 1985, vol. 5, no. 11. See also J. Markowitz, R. Brown, J. Sweeney, & J. J. Mann, "Reduced Length and Cost of Hospital Stay for Major Depression in Patients Treated with ECT," *Am. J. Psychiatry* 144 (1987): 1025; S. Squire, "Shock Therapy's Return to Respectability," *New York Times Magazine*, Nov. 22, 1987, p. 78; G. Stone, "When Prozac Fails . . . Electroshock Works," *New York*, Nov. 14, 1994, p. 55.

A consumer-oriented mental health organization, however, insists that the NIMH report presents an incomplete picture of ECT and overlooks serious problems. The executive director of the National Mental Heath Consumers' Self-Help Clearinghouse said that the report's positive recommendations on ECT "really concern us," since "even aspirin doesn't deserve such an enthusiastic level of endorsement." He worries that the report's support for ECT will deter people from being "cautious when they seek ECT treatment or evaluate whether it is right for them or their loved ones." "Consumer Group Criticizes Unpublished ECT Report," *Psychiatric News*, Nov. 5, 1999, p. 1.

75. Quoted in *Roche Report: Frontiers of Psychiatry*, Mar. 1, 1980, p. 1.

76. Personal communication (Nov. 9, 1999). See M. Fink, *Electroshock: Restoring the Mind* (New York: Oxford University Press, 1999); see also M. Fink, "Treating Depression" (ltr.) *New York Times*, Oct. 8, 1999, p. 30. Dr. Fink has a Web site dedicated "to helping both psychiatrists and patients better understand electroconvulsive therapy and how best to take advantage of its benefits." The Web site address is *www.electroshock.org*.

77. In Shafran v. St. Vincent's Hospital, 694 N.Y.S.2d 642 (N.Y. App. 1999), the patient experienced status epilepticus that lasted for several hours, she lapsed into a coma for approximately ten days, and she sustained permanent injuries including bilateral deafness, memory loss, and seizure disorder. These injuries persisted until she died six years later. At trial the jury returned a verdict in favor of the defendants, but the appellate court reversed, remanding the case for a new trial, on the ground that the trial judge had improperly excluded defense experts. In McNall v. Summers, 25 Cal. App.4th 1300, 30 Cal. Rptr.2d 914 (1994), the trial court ruled that the three-year statute of limitations for commencing suit had run on a claim that ECT was negligently administered. The appellate court reversed, remanding for a new trial, on the ground that memory loss suspended the running of the prescriptive period. In Andre v. Mecta Corp., 186 A.D.2d 1, 587 N.Y.S.2d 334 (1992), the patient brought a products liability claim against the manufacturer of the ECT machine, claiming inadequacy of warnings about memory loss. The court held that the manufacturer is not liable to a patient for any failure to warn the hospital or its staff of the side effects of the treatment with the machine. The court noted that the side effect of memory loss was well-known to the hospital staff and even appears as one of the "rare or uncommon side effects" in the printed consent form signed by the patient.

78. Aden v. Younger, 57 Cal App.3d 662, 129 Cal. Rptr. 535 (1976); see M. Shapiro, "Legislating the Control of Behavior Control: Autotomy and the Coercive Use of Organic Therapies," *S. Cal. L. Rev.* 47 (1974): 237. For the well-being of a fetus or of a newborn during breast-feeding, ECT is safer than medication in the treatment of a mother suffering depression or mood disorder. Dr. Fink contends that the depression of Andrea Yates, who in that condition drowned her five children, could likely have been lifted by ECT, but Texas law so severely restricts it as to be unavailable in public facilities. M. Fink, "Compassion for Andrea Yates" (ltr.), *New York Times*, Mar. 14, 2002, p. 30.

79. D. Goleman, "Psychiatry: First Guide to Therapy Is Fiercely Opposed," *New York Times*, Sept. 23, 1986, p. C-1.

80. To illustrate, in James v. Woolley, 523 So.2d 110(Ala. 1988), the Alabama Supreme Court upheld a finding of negligence in the choice of a vaginal delivery rather than a cesarean section by relying, in part, on the physician's failure to comply with the American College of Obstetrics and Gynecologists' guidelines recommending a cesarean delivery for infants estimated to weigh more than four kilograms. In Pollard v. Goldsmith, 572 P.2d 1201(Ariz. App.), the Arizona Court of Appeals found evidence of a violation of the standard of care in failing

to follow the guidelines set by the American College of Surgeons' Prophylaxis Against Tetanus and Wound Management, which require that patients with wounds indicating an overwhelming possibility of tetanus be given human immune globulin. D. W. Shuman, "The Standard of Care in Medical Malpractice Claims, Clinical Practice Guidelines, and Managed Care: Towards a Therapeutic Harmony?" *Cal. West. L. Rev.* 34 (1997): 99.

81. The American Psychiatric Press advertises the second edition of *Treatments of Psychiatric Disorder* as "the treatment companion to DSM-IV. It is a compendium of state-of-the-art treatments of all major psychiatric disorders." In the editor's words, it offers "useful approaches" rather than "rigid guidelines."

82. Guidelines are meant to improve medical care by codifying what panels of experts deem to be best practice in a given field, but the problem is that many physicians are unaware of any number of guidelines, and those who read them often fail or refuse to follow their recommendations. M. D. Cabana et al., "Why Don't Physicians Follow Clinical Practice Guidelines? A Framework for Improvement," *JAMA*, Oct. 20, 1999, p. 1458; M. Sherman, "Study Finds Lapses on Medical Guidelines," *New York Times*, Nov. 2, 1999, p. D-10.

The term *practice parameters*, as used by the American Medical Association, encompasses (1) standards, which are generally accepted principles for patient management; (2) guidelines, which are recommendations for patient management that may identify a particular management strategy or a range of strategies; and (3) other patient management strategies, such as practice options and practice advisories. As a rule, a practice parameter may be introduced as evidence of the standard of care in malpractice litigation, provided that it is relevant to the clinical issues involved and meets certain indicia of reliability. E. B. Hirshfeld, "Should Practice Parameters Be the Standard of Care in Malpractice Litigation?" *JAMA* 266 (Nov. 27, 1991): 2886. See also J. M. Finder, "The Future of Practice Guidelines: Should They Constitute Conclusive Evidence of the Standard of Care?" *Health Matrix: J. Law-Medicine* 10 (2000): 67.

83. Comments of Dr. R. N. Bhavsar, Director of Education at Northville State Hospital, Northville, Mich., at conference on Mar. 19, 1998.

84. 42 U.S.C.A., §§11101–11152.

85. "National Practitioner Data Bank: Major Improvements Are Needed to Enhance Data Bank's Reliability" (GAO-01-130, Nov. 30, 2000). See also J. Aske, "Disciplinary Actions: Report to National Practitioner Data Bank Constitutes Defamation," *Am. J.L. & Med.* 27 (2001): 127; M. Kadzielski, "The National Practitioner Data Bank: Big Brother or Paper Tiger?" *HealthSpan* (July/Aug. 1992), p. 8; J. Lovitky, "The National Practitioner Data Bank: Coping with the Uncertainties," *J. Health L.* 33 (2000): 355; J. Reichert, "Researchers Question Reliability of National Practitioner Data Bank," *Trial* 35 (Nov. 1999): 102.

5

Admission or Apology in Liability Prevention

Admissions play a role as proof of fault in all types of cases, but they have special importance in cases of malpractice (professional negligence). Unlike in ordinary negligence cases, expert testimony is required as a matter of law to prove a case of malpractice. An admission obviates that requirement.[1] A party is in no position to complain that when making the statement, he was not under oath or subject to cross-examination. After all, it is that person's own statement. According to the familiar phrase, "Anything that you say may be used against you."[2]

When, if ever, then, should a physician make an admission of wrongdoing, or of an error, or to express sorrow? Should the physician always send a bill, since failure to do so might indicate culpability? Should the physician ever say to a patient, "I'm sorry?" Good manners are essential for social life, but given the risk of litigation, one must be wary. A Tokyo office worker, reminiscing about living for a while in New York, said that Japanese friends in that city had advised her not to apologize too readily to Americans when confrontations arose. In the United States, they warned, saying "sorry" could be taken as an admission of wrongdoing, inviting legal action. The Japanese are a people who apologize profusely.[3]

A Miami attorney, Samuel J. Powers Jr., had this to say in an address to a medical association:

Some things that happen in your practice have a severe emotional impact on you. It's only natural to sympathize with a patient. Some physicians, emotionally overwrought under such conditions make statements to the effect that they're sorry this or that happened, as though they hoped to lessen its impact on the patient or on his relatives, but all they are really doing is digging their own graves. People nowadays are conscious of the fertility of this field of malpractice suits—and they remember those statements when you go to trial.[4]

To be courteous is to let down one's guard and invite disaster. The word *sorry* in conjunction with other language or circumstances may constitute an admission.[5] From experience, one physician writes, "In today's legal climate, doctors grieve, and apologize, at their own peril."[6] In an Oklahoma case, the doctor diagnosed the patient's condition as a tumor, but when he operated, he found that she was pregnant. The doctor then told the woman and her husband, "I'm sorry, I should have done more tests on you." The only witnesses at the trial were the plaintiff and her husband, who testified as to this statement, and the doctor, the defendant, who was only asked his qualifications. The Oklahoma Supreme Court ruled that the remark was sufficient to make a prima facie case of malpractice, and it remanded the case to be tried before a jury.[7]

Was the doctor's statement an admission of negligence? Apart from this statement, and the harm done, there was no evidence to show that the doctor's conduct was unskillful and not in accord with the work of physicians of good standing. Suppose an attorney loses a case and says to his client, "I'm sorry. I lost your case. I should have done more research." Will this statement alone be sufficient to take the case against the attorney to the jury even though the attorney may have in reality done much more than the average attorney in the community might have done?[8] Bob Eaton, then the chairman and CEO of Chrysler Corporation, observed,

There's a disconnect between what we were taught in civics class and the way the adult world really works. And the word for that disconnect is cynicism. . . . [Y]ou can't say "I'm sorry" anymore. If your tree falls on your neighbor's house, you can't say "I'm sorry." That's admitting guilt. Better let your lawyer handle it with his lawyer. If a company makes a mistake and ships a defective product, it can't simply say "I'm sorry," and then make it right. Instead, it's forced to treat its friends and customers as potential litigants. . . . There's something wrong with a system that robs you of the catharsis and the simple civility of saying, "I'm sorry. What can I do to make it right?" There's something wrong when being intellectually honest makes you dead meat for people who aren't.[9]

Afraid of what might be said, lawyers advise doctors not to go to the funeral of a patient. Physicians at funerals are heard to say, "We did the best we could." But how good was that? Does it in fact measure up to the standard of care?

The statement, "I'm sorry," should not be sufficient to establish fault, says one commentator in a law review article, "for this is what every decent human would say when the desired result was not accomplished even though he performed at his highest capability which might be far above that of his colleagues in his community . . . On the other hand, one should not have to spell out everything which the law requires in order to hold the defendant doctor negligent."[10]

Two leading authorities on the law of evidence, Stephen Saltzburg and Kenneth Redden, are not very reassuring in a lengthy comment in their manual on the Federal Rules of Evidence about the effect of an apology.[11] Massachusetts in 1986 enacted legislation that excludes an expression of sorrow as an admission. It provides: "Statements, writings or benevolent gestures expressing sympathy or a general sense of benevolence relating to the pain, suffering or death of a person involved in an accident and made to such a person or to the family of such a person shall be inadmissible as evidence of an admission of liability in a civil action."[12] The legislature in Texas in 1999 and California in 2001 enacted legislation patterned after that in Massachusetts, and the highest courts of Vermont and Georgia made a similar change via judicial opinions in 1992. Thomas Gutheil and Paul Appelbaum urge regional professional societies to promote the enactment of similar legislation in other states.[13] In any event, the legislation and judicial opinions ensure freedom only to say one is sorry, but not of other types of admissions. Thus, if someone says, "I'm sorry, this is all my fault, I was yelling at my wife on my cell phone and wasn't looking," everything after "I'm sorry," is admissible in evidence as an admission.

Are physicians between a rock and a whirlpool? On the one hand, admissions or even an apology may be used against the physician as evidence in a malpractice suit, while on the other hand, the physician is told that the physician-patient relationship is improved by leveling with the patient, which thereby lessens the risk of a malpractice suit. Time beyond count, we hear doctors or others advising doctors: "People sue when they are angry, so say you are sorry."[14] "A warm relationship with a patient is the best defense against malpractice. You don't have a warm relationship when you regard the patient as an adversary."[15]

In yet another suggestion, Joan Vogel and Richard Delgado in a law review article urge the enactment in law of an affirmative duty on the physician to disclose medical mistakes or malpractice. They say that if the primary physician and other members of the treatment team conceal malpractice, the patient may believe that his pain, debilitation, or loss of function is merely unfortunate results of the operation or procedure. A duty to disclose malpractice is necessary, they say, because the medical profession does not regulate itself effectively, discourages the reporting of malpractice to patients, and erects formal and informal barriers to a patient's access to information. This proposed duty to disclose malpractice is consistent, they say, with current trends in tort law, such as the development of the doctrines of informed consent, collective responsibility, duty to warn, and duty to supervise. It would remedy a serious imbalance in the physician-patient relationship as well as enable some victims of malpractice to obtain relief who would otherwise be unable to do so. It would give tangible expression, they say, to the moral imperative that professionals who injure their clients must inform them of the injury.[16]

Of course, physicians who misrepresent the nature, outcome, or prognosis of a completed procedure, or who either by silence or reassurance willfully conceal the state of the patient's condition, may be liable for fraud.[17] Physicians have an obligation to tell the truth about a patient's condition, even if that would reveal one's own or a prior physician's negligence.[18] In such cases, unless disclosure is made, the statute of limitations will be tolled as to fraud, and if other physicians are involved, conspiracy as well. Therefore, writes Dr. Robert M. Wettstein, a patient with tardive dyskinesia who comes to the physician for diagnosis or treatment should be told he has TD, regardless of whether he inquires specifically about it or whether it is a consequence of present or past negligence. Dr. Wettstein says, "The physician should not deny, if the patient asks, and arguably should volunteer if the patient does not ask, that the TD is a result of negligence, if the clinician believes this to be the case."[19]

C. G. Schoenfeld, the late book editor of the *Journal of Psychiatry & Law,* said that he filed a negligence suit against a hospital "only because it wouldn't say it was sorry." His mother was dropped by nurses in transferring her from a stretcher to a bed, fractured her hip, and died from complications following the injury. The jury awarded him $176,000. He said, "If they had just faced up to what they did and sat down with me and said, 'We're sorry,' I would never have sued. They did the one thing that you never do to a man who has suffered the terrible loss of a loved one—they insulted my intelligence with tortured explanations."[20]

A television documentary, *Diagnosis: Malpractice,* began with a patient saying, "I was forced to sue. No one came to me and said, 'we're sorry, we made a mistake.'"[21] The viewpoint is frequently heard that patients often sue physicians or hospitals not so much for the original mistake as for the lack of openness and honesty and for the wish to see the physician called to accountability. In a study, when patients were asked whether "once the original accident had occurred, could anything have been done which would have meant you did not feel the need to take legal action?" 41 percent (not 100 percent) of the respondents replied "yes," and gave as the most important reason, "explanation and apology."[22]

In litigation, however, the expression of genuine sympathy could lead to some form of utterance that, in the hands of a skillful lawyer, might be turned into an admission of wrongdoing. Is it possible to express sympathy and concern without it being turned into an admission of liability? Is it like walking a tightrope?

Should one attempt it, or should one, like a motorist involved in an accident, adopt bludgeoning tactics and blame the other party? Are good manners incompatible with the law, or with insurance coverage? Insurers are often blamed for much of the lack of courtesy because, as a rule, most liability insurance policies will have a provision saying that after an accident, one must not make any admission of liability. The following clause is typical: "The insured shall not, except at his own cost, voluntarily admit his liability, or offer or promise any payment, assume any obligation, or incur any expense other than for first aid to others at the time of the accident." Premiums, if not coverage, will be affected.

Liability insurance companies consider an admission by the insured party that he has done something wrong as failure of cooperation, voiding insurance coverage. Insurers insert cooperation clauses into insurance policies in an attempt to prevent any collusion and to eliminate any connivance between the insured and a third-party claimant. An admission of liability would detrimentally affect the insurer's ability to conduct an effective defense against the claim. Therefore, before a physician should ever state to a patient that he did something wrong, he needs to be aware of what effect such a statement might have on his insurance coverage. Thus, in a pragmatic sense, there are definite reasons why a physician should refrain from stating that something is or is not his fault unless he has cleared it with his insurance company.[23]

Consider what others do. When a street criminal commits a crime, he remains silent or says, "I didn't do it." When large companies are charged with violating the law, its spokesmen turn to gobbledygook, or they have no comment: "The charges are so ridiculous that they are unworthy of comment." Or they pass the buck: "Under normal conditions, our product is accident-proof, but we can't guarantee it when the consumer doesn't follow the instructions."

Lawyers and negotiators do not make admissions, but they do not lie; they dissemble. A law professor says, "In representing a client, lawyers can be dishonest—they can twist and bend—because everyone knows that's what they do."[24] "Just remember that lying can get you into a lot of trouble if not done properly," advises a lawyer. That was in a cartoon, but many would say it is true to life.[25]

Lawyers understand the importance of never admitting to anything—it's the lawyer's commandment. It is most important, at least from a legal perspective, to say nothing and, particularly, to admit no guilt or responsibility whatsoever. In a discussion on automobile accidents, a commentator on national television advised: "Don't apologize. Don't say anything about it."[26] That is typical lawyer advice. "If you start explaining or apologizing to the victim," says a lawyer specializing in insurance cases, "you will be giving him crucial evidence for a suit against you."[27]

There is a classical parable (about the *M'raglim*) that describes the process of becoming lost. One does not suddenly find himself in the depths of a dark, trackless forest, but instead, one deviates from the familiar, broad roadway a step at a time. Gradually and imperceptibly, one strays farther and farther from the road until one ends up lost in the forest.

A woman whose husband was negligently killed by a third party confessed her feelings to a friend, "The freedom is wonderful. I'm enjoying life now as never before. I'm glad he's dead." Being completely honest about one's feelings may be healthy, confession may be good for the soul, but in a wrongful death action, the value of the case is jeopardized by introduction of this evidence.[28]

The compulsion to confess—or boast, if you will—has resulted in crucial evidence in criminal as well as in civil cases. "People love to spill their guts, and they hang themselves."[29] Ernesto Miranda, whose name is given to the warning that police must give a suspect before questioning, was in the end convicted on the basis of statements he made to a girlfriend about the crime.[30] James Earl Ray boasted while imprisoned in London of participating in a conspiracy to kill civil rights leader Martin Luther King Jr. A London policeman, who overheard Ray make the comments after his arrest, was the lead-off witness in the hearings.[31]

Many times a physician ends up with a result that is not satisfactory and there is always a question as to what caused the detrimental outcome. While it is important for the physician to be open and honest with the patient about the patient's problem or condition, it is not necessary, however, for the physician to tell a patient what might constitute legal fault for any adverse development. Apart from other considerations, there is a very real risk that such an opinion will later be proven to be wrong. In many cases, a physician thinks he is responsible for a problem (or, probably more often, he feels some other physician or entity is responsible for the problem) when later, after all the evidence has been gathered, it becomes clear that someone else is responsible. During or immediately following treatment it is usually premature for physicians to attribute fault when indicating to a patient what has happened. For example, if a sponge has been left in after surgery, the patient should be told about this problem (the patient will likely find out about it anyway), but the doctor need not make a determination as to who is to blame for it. It might have been a nurse's fault, or a doctor's fault, or both.

As a result, physicians ought not to admit fault, regardless of what may have occurred. This may not comport with the ideal of physician-patient rapport, but it is appropriate, given the complexities of the legal ramifications of the relationships. While a physician has a duty to say, for example, the ureter was injured during surgery, he does not have an obligation to tell the patient whether that injury was the result of his negligence. To be sure, a physician provokes a lawsuit when he is dismissive of a patient or lacks empathy, but it is one thing to say, "I'm sorry this turned out badly," and quite another to admit negligence.

As a matter of practice, the physician usually does not say, "Sorry, I gave you the wrong medicine," but, rather, "I'm going to change your prescription." Because the physician seldom admits either a mistake or malpractice, it makes it more precious for the lawyer to latch onto any statement where, in front of third persons, in court, or in his own hospital records, the doctor confesses he goofed. The situation is a *tabula in naufragio*. Hospital or other medical records as well as depositions are an important source of admissions. That is why the plaintiff's attorney goes over the records or deposition with a fine-tooth comb and why doctors and other personnel must be careful about what is noted. Nowadays many law firms have nurses or other medical personnel on their full-time staff just to study and advise on material in medical records.

The altering of records—or other conduct of that ilk—is commonly regarded as an admission. The courts often speak of a "presumption" against the spoliator. By resorting to wrongful devices the individual is said to give ground for the belief that he thinks his case is weak and not to be won by fair means.[32] Accordingly, a party's false statement about the matter in litigation, whether before suit or on the stand; his fabrication of false documents; his destruction or concealment of relevant documents or objects; his undue pressure, by bribery or intimidation or other means, to influence a witness to testify for him or to avoid testifying; his attempt to corrupt the jury; his hiding or transferring property in anticipation of judgment—all of these are instances of admission by conduct.[33]

Statements made by the physician to his attorney are protected by the attorney-client privilege, but what about statements made by the physician to an investigator of his own insurer? Are these communications privileged? In law, there is no insurer-insured privilege like that of the attorney-client privilege. Is the insurer's investigator to be considered an agent of the attorney, even though the investigator is not in the employ of the attorney, thus entitling communications to be the work product of the attorney? By and large, the courts say that the statements are in preparation for trial within the meaning of the work product rule and, therefore, the plaintiff must show prejudice, hardship, or injustice, and good cause in order to obtain a production order. As this can usually be shown, these statements are subject to discovery.[34]

Some physicians, when sued, call the suing party or attorney, telling them it is all a misunderstanding and asking them to drop the lawsuit. Caught up in the emotional side of litigation, they fail to see how the legal system works, and they make statements often to their detriment.

Some lawyers representing a complainant will, as part of the investigation of the case, consult with the treating doctor to get his side of the story. Doctors often decry the abuse of the legal process, including the filing of a suit without interviewing them, but when that is done, it may inure to the disadvantage of the doctors. What he says (except in the course of a settlement negotiation) can be used against him.[35] Many lawyers, it must be noted, consider it unethical to get the doctor's side of the story without the doctor having legal assistance, for that would be an underhanded way of getting admissions.[36]

One lawyer who defends the practice of consulting with the treating doctor but telling him that he may wish to have his lawyer present says: "Invariably there are two sides to every story. Should I wait until filing a complaint to find out just what are the basic facts? I say to the doctor, 'We want to have your version. We want to truly find out what happened.'" If the doctor replies, "I'm not going to talk to you," the lawyer at trial (if put into evidence) may argue to the jury, "We tried to talk with the doctor, we asked for an explanation, but he wouldn't talk to us."[37]

What about utterances not intended for the outside world, as in an internal report or where one makes entries in a secret diary, or in process notes, or where one is overheard talking to oneself? Are they admissible in evidence?

Organizations of every type, be it a hospital or a television company, have to be able to take a look back at their own work when questions arise so that they can correct mistakes, but members of the organization will likely not be candid about their failures if they know those reports might later be used against them or the organization. Legally, however, internal investigative reports are generally not shielded from discovery.[38] Most jurisdictions do not recognize a "self-critical analysis" privilege. Thus, to take an example, the evaluation and recommendation portion of a report prepared by a chemical company's employees concerning a tank car derailment that gave rise to a lawsuit was not exempt from discovery.[39] Peer review reports, however, are privileged.

In a complaint against a physician, the patient has a right to discover process notes as well as the records of the physician. Process notes (or information in a computer) may be analogized to a diary. Notes in a diary may be used not withstanding the ordinary expectation of privacy. A seizure of a diary does not violate the Fourth Amendment's prohibition of "unreasonable searches and seizures." John W. Hinckley Jr.'s diary was used as evidence against him.[40] In a child custody case, a diary in which the father recorded his feelings about the child was used against him.[41] As stated in the Advisory Committee's Notes to the Federal Rules of Evidence, "[A] party's books or records are usable against him, without regard to any intent to disclose to third persons."[42]

Even statements made in prayer may be used as evidence. A case that went to the British Columbia Court of Appeals involved an accused who, in his cell, slid off his chair, fell to his knees, raised his hands and prayed, "Oh, God, let me get away with it just this once." The room was equipped with a video camera and concealed microphone. The supplication was offered as evidence. Though he was speaking to God, the appellate court allowed the introduction of the evidence as an admission. A dissent would have excluded the statement on the grounds that it was made in complete privacy.[43]

Given the negative consequences in law of an apology or admission, the crucial question becomes: Does the apology or admission so enhance the physician-patient relationship that litigation is put out of mind? Is it really helpful to therapy to be apologetic or to admit mistakes? Or does it just get the doctor into more difficulty? And what does it do to the magic in the art of healing?

And do we say "I'm sorry" because we truly feel remorse for a wrongdoing we have done, or is it merely a way to ease our conscience between now and the next time we hurt someone? Some neurotic individuals, whether they cause harm or not, are always saying they are sorry. Psychiatrists recognize it as masochism.[44] On the other hand, some people are so ill-mannered that they do not apologize or admit wrongdoing whatever the circumstances.

Actually, the failure to admit error or to express sorrow is only one form of irritation that may prompt a lawsuit. Apart from psychoanalysts, physicians tend not to be mindful about the time that patients spend waiting in the office. Like airlines overbooking and infuriating passengers, physicians schedule several patients for the same time. Patients consider it unprofessional, if not unethical, and they become angry, ready to sue on any pretext.[45] There is always the hope of hitting the jackpot in the litigation lottery.

One might suggest that if there is a positive transference, the patient will recognize that the physician is only human, and makes mistakes, but if there is a negative transference, the admission or apology will just fuel the discord. In Erich Segal's *Love Story*, love means not having to say you're sorry.[46] But what a thin line separates love from hate. People will slap you on the back one day and feel like slapping your face the next. A taxi driver says, "Lovers come in my cab and leave as enemies."[47] But be that as it may, patients know that the real defendant in a malpractice suit, the one who will be paying the judgment, is not the doctor, beloved or not, but the insurance company.

At a recent annual meeting of the Association of American Trial Lawyers, an organization of lawyers who represent plaintiffs, word got around that physicians were urging colleagues to confess errors to their patients. The trial lawyers exclaimed, "That's wonderful!"

Notes

1. Illustration may be noted of the physician's statement justifying the case going to the jury without the necessity of expert testimony. "Oops, I cut in the wrong place," was the evidence used against a surgeon in Orozco v. Henry Ford Hosp., 408 Mich. 248, 290 N.W.2d 263 (1980). In Hill v. McCartney, 590 N.W.2d 52 (Iowa App. 1998), a dentist's statement that he "did something freaky" was held to be enough of an admission to stand as patient's expert testimony for trial. In Sheffield v. Runner, 163 Cal. App.2d 48, 328 P.2d 828, 830 (1958), where the patient died in her home from pneumonia, the doctor said, "I should have put her in the hospital." In Wickoff v. James, 159 Cal. App.2d 664, 324 P.2d 661 (1958), where the patient's intestine was torn during a sigmoidoscopic examination, the doctor said, "Boy, I sure made a mess out of things." In Pappa v. Bonner, 268 Ala. 185, 105 So.2d 87 (1958), involving damage to a young child's central nervous system, the doctor admitted the child was not given proper postoperative care. In Lashley v. Koerber, 26 Cal.2d 83, 156 P.2d 441 (1945), the physician admitted that he should have x-rayed and said that it was his own fault. In Stickman v. Synhorst, 243 Iowa 872, 52 N.W.2d 504, 506 (1952), involving catastrophic hemorrhage, the doctor said, "I don't know whether I can perform that operation [on another person] after the mess I made out of you." In Wooten v. Curry, 50 Tenn. App. 549, 362 S.W.2d 820 (1961), noted in *NACCA L. J.* 28 (1961–62): 163, a malpractice action for failure to make a postoperative examination to prevent a patient's vagina from closing following a hysterectomy, the doctor said he was sorry it happened and could probably have avoided it if he had made the proper postoperative examination. See D. W. Louisell & H. Williams, *Medical Malpractice* (Albany, N.Y.: Matthew Bender, 1969), vol. 1, sec. 11.28.90; T. F. Lambert, "Law in the Future," *Trial*, Aug. 1983, p. 62. But cf. Locke v. Pachtman, 446 Mich. 216, 521 N.W.2d 786 (1994).

2. F. W. Cleary (ed.), *McCormick on Evidence* (St. Paul, Minn.: West, 3d ed. 1984), p. 774.

3. C. Haberman, "Japan, Land of a Million Mea Culpa's," *New York Times*, Oct. 4, 1986, p. 4.

4. "'Witless Pedantry' Is Blamed in 90% of Malpractice Suits," *Medical Tribune*, Dec. 7, 1962, p. 12.

5. Giangrasso v. Schimmel, 190 Neb. 228, 207 N.W.2d 517 (1973). In Peterson v. Richards, 73 Utah 459, 272 P. 229 (1928), the doctor said that he was sorry about the condition of the patient's hand. The patient's fingers were in some manner injured in the hospital. In a malpractice action, the doctor's statements were used against him as an admission. In Wojcik v. Hutzel Hospital, Circuit Court for Wayne County, Michigan, case no. 84-420-030, the doctor said to the patient in the presence of several witnesses that "different doctors perform this surgery in different ways" and that he was "sorry."

6. A. J. Dajer, "Physicians and Fate" (ltr.), *New York Times*, Apr. 24, 2001, p. D-3.

7. Greenwood v. Harris, 362, P.2d 85 (Okla. 1961).

8. That query was posed in Note, *Okla. L. Rev.* 15 (1962): 476. Following a collision, a motorist says, "Thank God I've got insurance." It is debatable whether it is an admission of fault. See Wilbur v. Tourangeau, 71 A.2d 565 (Vt. 1950); A. H. Travers, "An Essay on the Determination of Relevancy under the Federal Rules of Evidence," *Ariz. St. L. J.* 1977: 327. In some cases the physician admits his error, says he will not send a bill, and indeed, announces that he will pay for the second or subsequent corrective surgery. Barrette v. Hight, 353 Mass. 268, 230 N.E.2d 808 (1967). Under Rule 409 of the Federal Rules of Evidence, evidence of furnishing or offering or promising to pay medical, hospital, or similar expenses occasioned by an injury is not admissible to prove liability for the injury. The rule is designed to encourage people to help others when a problem arises for which one party may feel some responsibility, even if not legal responsibility.

9. B. Eaton, "No Joking Matter" ("My Turn" column), *Newsweek*, Sept. 23, 1996, p. 20.

10. Note, *Okla. L. Rev.* 15 (1962): 476.

11. S. A. Saltzburg & K. R. Redden, *Federal Rules of Evidence Manual* (Charlottesville: Michie, 3d ed. 1982), p. 199.

12. Mass. Gen. Laws, ch. 233, sec. 23 D.

13. T. G. Gutheil & P. S. Appelbaum, *Clinical Handbook of Psychiatry and the Law* (Philadelphia: Lippincott Williams & Wilkins, 3d ed. 2000), p. 179.

14. Communication by Dr. Bruno Bettelheim (July 26, 1983).

15. Comment by Dr. Gene L. Usdin in 1986 Distinguished Lectureship, "The Stress and Gratification of a Physician," at Tulane University School of Medicine. Admissions or apologies are recommended in S. S. Kraman & G. Hamm, "Risk Management: Extreme Honesty May Be the Best Policy," *Annals of Internal Medicine* 131 (1999): 963; S. Keeva, "Does Law Mean Never Having to Say You're Sorry?" *ABAJ*, Dec. 1999, p. 64; D. W. Shuman, "The Role of Apology in Tort Law," *Judicature* 83 (2000): 180; A. W. Wu, T. A. Kavanaugh, S. J. McPhee, B. Lo, & G. P. Micco, "To Tell the Truth," *J. Gen. Internal Medicine* 12 (1997): 770; D. Grady, "Doctors Urged to Admit Mistakes," *New York Times*, Dec. 9, 1997, p. B-15. Dr. Barry Farber, a professor of psychology at Columbia Teachers College, who has studied self-disclosure by therapists, says it can be helpful to therapy when therapists apologize for their mistakes. Quoted in E. Goode, "Therapists Redraw Line on Self-Disclosure," *New York Times*, Jan. 1, 2002, p. D-5. It is significant to note that many of the proponents of extreme honesty are on the staff of VA hospitals, where there is a single employer and a single insurer (the U.S. government), quite unlike the private domain, where staff is independent of the hospital and insurers are varied, each at odds with the other. The Department of Veterans Affairs imposes a policy of full disclosure to patients who have been injured because of accidents or medical negligence, and fair compensation for injuries.

16. J. Vogel & R. Delgado, "To Tell the Truth: Physicians' Duty to Disclose Medical Mistakes," *U. C. L. A. L. Rev.* 28 (1980): 52. In November 1999, the Institute of Medicine issued a report, "To Err Is Human: Building a Safer Health System," which estimated that between 44,000 and 98,000 people die each year nationwide as a result of avoidable errors that occurred in hospitals (not to mention injuries in hospitals or injuries and deaths outside the hospital due to medical errors). The report defines *errors* as "the failure of a planned action to be completed as intended," or "the use of a wrong plan to achieve a goal, compromising safety." The report emphasizes that "safety does not reside in a person, device or department, but emerges from the interactions of components of a system." In response to the report, Pres-

ident Clinton in December 1999 directed the Quality Interagency Coordination Task Force to evaluate the recommendations of the report. R. Pear, "Clinton Orders Steps to Reduce Medical Mistakes," *New York Times,* Feb. 22, 2000, p. 1.

The Bill of Rights of Patients provides that a patient has a right to know (1) what was done, (2) how it was done, and (3) why it was done. See, e.g., Mich. Stat., sec. 20201. The National Patient Safety Foundation urges all health care professionals and institutions to embrace the principle of dealing honestly with patients. Its statement of principle provides: "When a health care injury occurs, the patient and the family or representative are entitled to a prompt explanation of how the injury occurred and its short-term and long-term effects. When an error contributed to the injury, the patient and the family or representative should receive a truthful and compassionate explanation about the error and the remedies available to the patient. They should be informed that the factors involved in the injury will be investigated so that steps can be taken to reduce the likelihood of similar injury to other patients." The American Medical Association and the American Hospital Association, however, have vehemently opposed mandatory reporting of errors. They contend that if doctors and hospital employees fear being sued, they will be reluctant to discuss the lessons that could be learned from their mistakes.

There have been efforts by consumers of health care to open the National Practitioner Data Bank to the public. The NPDB, established in 1990 by the U.S. Department of Health and Human Services, contains information on malpractice payments made by physicians as well as disciplinary actions taken by local and state medical boards and hospitals. Currently, only HMOs, hospitals, and health care organizations have access to the NPDB. S. Barlas, "Pressure to Make Data Bank Public," *Psychiatric Times,* May 2000, p. 56. See chapter 7, on informed consent.

17. See, e.g., Baum v. Turel, 206 F.Supp. 490 (D.C. N.Y. 1962).

18. T. K. LeBlang, "Disclosure of Injury and Illness: Responsibilities in the Physician-Patient Relationship," *Law, Medicine & Health Care* 9 (1981): 4.

19. R. M. Wettstein, "Tardive Dyskinesia and Malpractice," *Behav. Sci. & Law* 1 (1983): 91. In a subsequent communication, Dr. Wettstein said, "I don't think I definitely have formed my opinion at this point about a doctor telling a patient he was negligent in prescribing medication and can see good arguments for either side." Communication from Dr. Robert M. Wettstein (July 15, 1987).

20. After the verdict was announced, the jurors called Schoenfeld into the deliberation room to talk about how they reached the decision. A juror suggested to Schoenfeld that he finance a hospital fund in his mother's memory for patients who cannot afford private nurses. Schoenfeld seized on the idea and said he would organize the fund with a substantial portion of the $176,000. C. Lachman, "He Wins 176G Suit & Will Give It Away," *New York Post,* Nov. 25, 1981, p. 9.

21. ABC, Dec. 27, 1986.

22. C. Vincent, M. Young, & A. Phillips, "Why Do People Sue Doctors? A Study of Patients and Relatives Taking Legal Action," *Lancet* 343 (1994): 1611. History is replete with illustrations. Armenians strike out against the Turks, we are told, because Turkey never said it was sorry about its genocide of Armenians. One Armenian writes:

> So long as the Turkish nation denies what happened to the Armenians 70 years ago, terrorists will strike. I regret this, but as a first-generation descendant of survivors of the massacres, I can understand the bitterness Armenians worldwide feel toward the blatant denial of history. If the Turks displayed a modicum of intellectual honesty, and laid the cards on the table, Armenians could become reconciled to the events of World War I, and the terrorism would stop.

B. Odian, "A Turkish Admission Would Halt Terrorism" (ltr.), *New York Times,* June 11, 1987, p. 26.

In 1970, on May 4, four Kent State students were killed and nine others wounded by Ohio National Guardsmen who were on campus to quell violent antiwar demonstrations. For years, at Kent State, the situation was not diffused. Yearly, on the May 4 anniversary, people on campus become tense and wary. Prage Golding, who became president of Kent State in 1977, said that the May 4 preoccupation at the university can be attributed partly to the fact that no one accepted the blame or apologized for the killings. "Without admitting liability, the state of Ohio should have told the families of the dead and wounded that it was sorry about what happened," said President Golding. "Politically, there are times when you have to say something the lawyers might not want you to." Quoted in R. Alsop, "Kent State: Symbol or Footnote?" *Wall Street Journal*, Apr. 28, 1978, p. 16.

23. Insurance carriers caution the physician against making any statement that might be misconstrued as an admission. Orally and in policy sales literature, they caution and admonish: "Admit nothing, deny everything." And they urge doctors not to brag or comment to patients about professional liability coverage. "First Aid for Malpractice Cases," *Medical World News*, June 7, 1963, p. 127. Insurance carriers are known to insist on meticulous enforcement of cooperation clauses or to defend only on the basis of reservation of rights. Such enforcement dare not offend public policy, however, by chilling or choking off discovery of facts and apparently may not be operative at all until a claim is filed against the insured. Many of the damaging admissions have occurred before the physician-patient relationship has been terminated, prior to the filing of a claim.

In preparation for trial, discovery may be made by a request for admission or by depositions or interrogatories. A party may serve on another party a written request for the admission of the truth of any matter, not privileged, that is relevant to the subject matter involved in the pending action, including the existence, description, nature, custody, condition, and location of books, documents, or other tangible things and the identity and location of persons having knowledge of a discoverable matter. Michigan Court Rule 2.302. A default judgment may be entered against a defendant who fails to answer interrogatories. Wood v. Detroit Automobile Inter-Exchange, 412 Mich. 573, 321 N.W.2d 653 (1982). The court may refuse to allow the disobedient party to support or oppose designated claims or defenses. Michigan Court Rule 2.313(B)(2b). Reasonable expenses including attorney fees may be assessed against an opponent who improperly denies a request. Michigan Court Rule 2.323(B)(2). In responding to a request for admissions, the party is not permitted to say he does not know, but he may say that following inquiry he is unable to make a statement. Quite often, by the time a compliance order is obtained, it is time for trial and nothing happens.

24. Comment by Professor James J. White, "Effective Negotiation Techniques for Lawyers," Institute of Continuing Legal Education, Southfield, Mich., June 10, 1987.

25. "Pepper and Salt," *Wall Street Journal*, Sept. 4, 1986, p. 23. In the congressional hearings on the Iran-Contra affair, Secretary of State Schultz testified without a lawyer at his side, prompting cartoonist Ohman of the *Oregonian* to say, "I guess that means he's telling the truth."

26. T. Coleman, "Money Matters," NBC, Oct 15, 1982.

27. Comment by Alan J. Schnurman of New York, quoted in K. Johnson, "You Can Get Sued, Even at Home," *New York Times*, Jan. 10, 1982, p. F-15.

28. *Detroit Free Press*, Apr. 26, 1978, p. C-3. San Francisco attorney Richard Brown says that families don't realize when they pour out their souls to an insurance adjuster or company employee that their words might later be used against them. Brown handled a Delta-crash case in which a distraught family member remarked to a sympathetic adjuster that the victim, a married man, had been having an extramarital affair. "They threw it back at us in settlement talks and really took us by surprise," says Brown. Quoted in B. Bean, "Damage Control," *Wall Street Journal*, Nov. 7, 1986, p. 1.

29. Comment by attorney William E. Wisner, "Handling the Personal Injury Case," Institute of Continuing Legal Education, June 18, 1987, in Southfield, Mich.

30. Miranda v. Arizona, 384 U.S. 436 (1966).

31. *Wall Street Journal*, Nov. 10, 1978, p. 1.

32. In the *Rubiayat* of Omar Khayyam, it is said:

> The Moving Finger writes; and having writ
> Moves on; nor thy Piety nor Wit
> Shall lure it back to cancel half a Line;
> Nor all thy Tears wash out of a Word of it.

Trans. E. Fitzgerald (Boston: Houghton Mifflin, 1886).

33. F. W. Cleary (ed.), *McCormick on Evidence* (St. Paul, Minn.: West, 3d ed. 1984).

34. Chadbourne v. Superior Court, 36 Cal. Rptr. 468, 388 P.2d 700 (1964); Newton v. Yates, 170 Ind. App. 486, 353 N.E.2d 485 (1976); LaCroix v. Grand Trunk R. Co., 368 Mich. 321,

118 N.W. 302 (1962); Taylor Construction Co. v. Saginaw Circuit Judge, 372 Mich. 376, 126 N.W.2d 57 (1963); Powers v. City of Troy, 28 Mich. App. 24 (1970); Peters v. Gaggos, 72 Mich. App. 138, 249 N.W.2d 327 (1976); Schmitt v. Emery, 211 Minn. 547, 2 N.W.2d 413 (1942); Note, "Agents Reports and the Attorney-Client Privilege," *U. Chi. L. Rev.* 21 (1954): 752; Annot., "Insured-Insurer Communications as Privileged," 55 A.L.R.4th 336 (1987).

35. Federal Rules of Evidence, Rule 408.

36. The American Bar Association Code of Professional Responsibility and Code of Judicial Conduct provides in Disciplinary Rule 7-103, on communicating with one of adverse interest: "During the course of his representation of a client, a lawyer shall not: (1) Communicate or cause another to communicate on the subject of the representation with a party he knows to be represented by a lawyer in that matter unless he has the prior consent of the lawyer representing such other party or authorized by law to do so. (2) Give advice to secure council, if the interests of such person are or have a reasonable possibility of being in conflict with the interests of his client."

Informal Opinion No. 908 of the Standing Committee on Professional Ethics of the American Bar Association (Feb. 24, 1996) provides that it is not unethical behavior for a potential plaintiff's attorney to interview a potential defendant so long as the latter knows that the statement is being taken by the lawyer in his status as attorney for the plaintiff. Once a complaint has been filed, a lawyer is prohibited from giving the other party any advice other than the advice to secure a lawyer. W. T. Grant Co. v. Haines, 531 F.2d 671 (2d Cir. 1976).

Professor Harry Cohen of the University of Alabama School of Law, founder and editor of the *Journal of the Legal Profession*, observed,

> I believe that if there is any doubt that a person could be a defendant, the lawyer who interviews him without more, could be guilty of breach of the new A. B. A. Model Code Section 4.3 dealing with a lawyer contacting another who is not explicit about a situation where there is no "adverse party." However, I believe that where it is reasonable to assume that a doctor (or other person) could be a defendant, the lawyer must be very careful when implying that the lawyer is disinterested in the matter. The cases generally say that the lawyer must not approach one whom the lawyer believes will be an adverse party without telling that person that he or she should hire a lawyer and cautioning them that they should not say anything against their own interests. This is especially true where the person's ignorant or unaware of their involvement in the situation. See Lyons v. Paul 321 S.W.2d 944 (Tex. Ct. Civ. App. 1959). It is true that the cases deal with parties to suits but as I read them and the ethics opinions they seem to deal with all adverse parties. In the doctor cases, I believe that a caution to the doctor before his lawyer talks to him or her would cause the doctor to call his lawyer. The lawyer who would talk to the doctor to get his side of the story without a strong cautionary statement could well be in breach of 4.3.

Communication from Professor Harry Cohen (July 6, 1987).

37. Texas attorney Wayne Fisher in 1986 ABA Program on Medical Malpractice for Attorneys, Physicians and Risk Managers.

38. J. Friendly, "Decision in CBS Cases Raises New Concerns," *New York Times,* Apr. 30, 1983, p. 48. Here are interrogatories put to defendant(s) that they are obliged to answer: "Please state whether or not any committees or hearings were held by Defendant Hospital with respect to the care and treatment of Plaintiff during confinement to said Hospital, and if so, please state what action, if any, was taken by Defendant Hospital, or on its behalf, in the regular course of business or in preparation for litigation, concerning any matters relating to the occurrence complained of in this action? Were any statements obtained by Defendant Hospital or on its behalf from any person concerning any matter relating to Plaintiff's decedent's condition?"

39. Peterson v. Chesapeake & Ohio Ry. Co., 112 F. R. D. 360 (W.D.Mich. 1986).

40. S. Taylor, "Hinckley Lawyers Urge Federal Judge to Bar Use of Some Evidence," *New York Times,* Oct. 28, 1981, p. 11. In the correctional institution where he was held for psychiatric examinations, Hinckley wrote daily in a diary labeled "The Diary of a Person We Know." The guards routinely read the diary and other papers, except for correspondence with lawyers, while Hinckley was out of his cell. Hinckley's lawyers sought to suppress the material

because it contained "Mr. Hinckley's most private (if not secret) thoughts about his legal situation." They argued that under the Fourth Amendment, Hinckley "has a reasonable expectation that his handwritten papers would not be read by prison guards." S. Taylor, "Hinckley's Notes Discussed in Secret," *New York Times*, Oct. 22, 1981, p. 15.

41. See volume 1, chapter 7, on elusive evidence.

42. Advisory Committee's Notes to Rule 801(C), Federal Rules of Evidence.

43. United Press International news report, *New Orleans Times-Picayune*, Sept. 11, 1980, p. 3.

44. L. H. Farber, "I'm Sorry, Dear," in L. H. Farber (ed.), *The Ways of the Will* (New York: Basic Books, 1966); reprinted in L. H. Farber, *Lying, Despair, Jealousy, Envy, Sex, Suicide, Drugs and the Good Life* (New York: Harper & Row, 1976), p. 123. Russell Baker writes amusingly about apologies in "Never Say Sorry," *New York Times Magazine*, Jan. 10, 1982, p. 19.

45. G. Kolata, "Remedy for Waiting: A Special Report," *New York Times*, Jan. 4, 2001, p. 1.

46. E. Segal, *Love Story* (New York: Harper & Row, 1970).

47. M. Rose, "Taxi Passengers Are No Bargain," *New York Times*, June 26, 1987, p. 27.

6

Breach of Confidentiality

Just as claims are made over geographical territory, individuals by natural impulse make claims controlling information about themselves. Ethologists call the geographical claim a *territorial imperative,* and a set of facts, which are of several varieties, a territorial-like *information preserve.* This preserve includes the content of an individual's mind or biographical facts about the individual. There is also, akin to the information preserve, as ethologists put it, a *conversational preserve.* Control over these preserves is threatened by a summons to talk, by being overheard, or by queries that are seen as intrusive or untactful. They are protected in law, more or less, by various procedural and substantive principles.

The legal duty of professional confidentiality or secrecy refers to the obligation not to release information about a client or patient without his permission, except when divulgence is required by law. The concept of privileged communication, which is discussed in volume 1, chapter 4, involves the right to withhold information in a legal proceeding—testimonial privilege statutes establish when a therapist must or must not testify concerning patient information in a judicial or administrative proceeding. Outside a judicial proceeding, the duty of professional confidentiality is in essence a restriction on the volunteering of information.

A professional person is bound, legally as well as ethically, to hold in confidence all information that is revealed to him or discovered as a result of his relationship with his client or patient. To a considerable degree the law regulates the extent to which information confided by a patient is actually nondisclosable. Reporting laws, such as those for child abuse or the duty to warn the potential victim of a dangerous patient, require therapists to make disclosures of patient information.[1] That notwithstanding, the management of confidentiality on a daily basis is much more a matter of professional ethics than of legal requirements.[2]

The usual case of breach of confidentiality by psychiatrists outside the judicial process occurs in response to a request for information that they believe to be warranted either on moral or legal grounds. Nonetheless, the disclosure may be improper and may result in an adverse judgment based on defamation, invasion of privacy, or breach of confidentiality. Only an action for defamation is subject to the defense of truth. A breach of secrecy, even if the statement is true, may result in a claim in tort for invasion of privacy or in contract for breach of a fiduciary duty. These actions, of course, are not limited to physicians or psychiatrists. They also include lawyers and other professionals who enjoy a confidential relationship. A number of states provide that the willful betrayal of a professional secret constitutes unprofessional conduct, justifying, in addition to sanctions in tort or contract law, suspension or revocation of the right to practice. Few actions have been brought under these statutes, however. In some countries, breach of professional confidence constitutes a criminal offense.

The professional's duty to keep information confidential did not arise full-blown and has never been an absolute principle. When Hippocrates urged medical secrecy, he and his followers were in a minority; medical secrecy apparently was not the rule in his day. In the time of the Roman Empire and in the Middle Ages, physicians disclosed all manner of things about patients. As the role of a physician approached that of a priest, the concept of confessional secrecy spread through Catholic countries during the sixteenth century to include the physician. The spirit of the French Revolution and its concern with individual liberty stirred interest in this area and inspired a provision in the French Penal Code of 1810. In the nineteenth century, the idea of absolute medical secrecy, as well as other absolutes, gained ground. In the twentieth century, there has been a return to the view that medical secrecy is relative, which was, in effect, the view of Hippocrates.[3]

The ethical and legal prohibitions are designed not to deter each and every breach of confidentiality but those deemed unjustified. According to the Hippocratic oath, still administered at most medical schools at graduation, the physician pledges that "whatsoever I shall see or hear in the course of my profession as well as outside my profession in my intercourse with men, if it be what should not be published abroad, I will never divulge, holding such things to be holy secrets."[4] The oath, however, helps the physician little in deciding when, and to whom, he should reveal what he has seen or heard with regard to a patient, because the proscription gives no criteria for determining that which ought to be spoken. An oath, like any ritual text, serves not in a literal but symbolic meaning. Its essential point is that, as a general principle, the physician will preserve the confidence of his patient, but there may be exceptions.

The most significant contribution to ethical history subsequent to Hippocrates was made by Thomas Percival of England, a physician, philosopher, and writer, who in 1803 published his Code of Medical Ethics, which bears his name. It is clear from the records and the preface to the American Medical Association's first-adopted Code of Ethics, in 1847, that it was based on Percival's Code. Through the years, while there have been revisions to reflect the temper of the time and the desire to express basic concepts with clarity, the language and concepts of the original Code adopted in 1847 have generally remained the same. The version adopted in 1957 states in pertinent part: "A physician may not reveal the confidence entrusted to him in the course of his medical attendance or the deficiencies he may observe in the character of his patients, unless he is required to do so by law, or unless it becomes necessary in order to protect the welfare of the individual or of the community."[5] This principle of the AMA (adopted by the American Psychiatric Association) carries the comment: "Sometimes a physician must determine whether his duty to society requires him to employ knowledge, obtained through confidences entrusted to him as a physician, to protect a healthy person against a communicable disease to which he is about to be exposed. In such instance, the physician should act as he would desire another to act toward one of his own family in like circumstances."[6]

Principles of medical ethics are not laws but standards. In the discharge of his professional obligations, the physician must look to the nature of his profession and the place it holds in society. For the general welfare of society, lawmakers in approximately a dozen situations demand that the physician under penalty come forward and make known information about a patient. Statutes in most states require the physician to report contagious and infectious diseases, to file certificates of birth, and to certify causes of death on certificates of death or stillbirth along with such medical data as can be furnished. The physician has the same duty as any other citizen to render aid and assistance in enforcing the criminal laws. It is generally a criminal offense for any individual who knows of treasonous activities to fail to notify the proper authorities, but there is no duty to report other offenses. Several states have statutes that require physicians who treat persons suffering an injury such as gun and knife wounds that may have been received in an unlawful manner to report the facts to the police. The various states have statutes that require reporting of parents who are thought to physically abuse their children. In various states, under the *Tarasoff* doctrine, a therapist has a duty to warn others that a patient may pose a danger.[7]

Legislation requires physicians to report or allow the inspection of their records if they prescribe, administer, or dispense any scheduled drugs, including barbiturates and amphetamines. Various states require physicians to report to the commissioner of the state department of health the full name, address, and date of birth of every person who, in the opinion of the physician, is dependent upon controlled drugs. Another section of the law immunizes physicians from civil or criminal liability for such reporting and provides that their reports will not be admissible as evidence in trials against the drug abuser and that they shall be held confidential by the commissioner.[8]

In *City of New York v. Bleuler Psychotherapy Center*,[9] a New York state court ordered a psychotherapy center to provide the medical records of a former patient, Andrew Goldstein, who killed Kendra Webdale by pushing her from a subway platform into the path of an oncoming train. The Department of Mental Health (DMH) had subpoenaed the records, but the center declined to produce them. The court in ordering the center to produce the records cited the New York Mental Hygiene Law, which provides that a court can order the release of documents if it finds "that the interest of justice significantly outweigh the need for confidentiality." The director of the DMH stated that its responsibilities include reviewing local services and facilities for persons with mental disabilities in the city and determining whether (1) there are any gaps in the system, (2) more services are needed, (3) the quality of services is adequate, and (4) other types of services are necessary. Consequently, the court ruled that the DMH needed the records in order to determine whether Goldstein's treating mental health providers acted properly in the past and to see what steps can be taken to minimize the occurrence of similar incidents. The court noted that the disclosure would be to an agency that has a statutorily mandated responsibility to investigate, and furthermore, the court noted, the agency must keep the information confidential.

Obviously, there is no liability for invasion of the right of privacy or defamation when one does what the law requires. It is the promiscuous nontestimonial disclosure of information that leads to liability. Thus, in one case, a complainant was allowed recovery against her physician on a theory of breach of contractual relation because of disclosure made to her husband concerning her diagnosis and statements made by her while in psychotherapy.[10] Likewise, the protection of society does not include warning a prospective wife that her prospective husband (patient) is a psychopathic personality and has a poor character.[11] Further, invasion of privacy by unwarranted disclosure of information resulting in the patient's loss of employment has been recognized and given redress.[12]

Given that work constitutes a major part of one's life, it is not surprising to find psychiatrists discussing their patients during their leisure time. Many of us prefer shop talk to small talk. In some cases, the psychiatrist may be attempting to deal with his own anxieties about a patient or to obtain free supervision and support. When the patient is a VIP, a Very Important Person, the psychiatrist in revealing the patient's identity may be bragging or trying to gain prestige, but this is the patient who is probably most harmed by nothing more than a disclosure that he is seeing a psychiatrist. As it is, it is difficult to get a VIP to undertake treatment in a community where he is well-known. The press has a so-called gentlemen's agreement not to publish a politician's sex life and drinking habits unless it hits a police blotter, but it will disclose his history of medical or psychiatric treatment. One notable exception was that of Richard Nixon, who before becoming president was seen over an extensive period of time by Dr. Arnold Hutschnecker, a specialist in psychosomatic medicine—a fact that was referred to openly in British newspapers, although not so openly in the United States.

The Group for the Advancement of Psychiatry in its report *The VIP with Psychiatric Impairment,* pointed out that one prominent psychiatrist in Washington, D.C., in his long experience has never been able to maintain a member of Congress in psychotherapy for more than a few months. The VIP fears that disclosure about his treatment would jeopardize his status and position. The disclosure of Senator Thomas Eagleton's history as a mental patient and the type of treatment (electroshock) resulted in his being dropped as the Democratic vice-presidential candidate and set back George McGovern's campaign for the presidency. In all these cases, omission of identifying material in discussing patients would lessen the hazard of invasion of privacy.[13]

Writing about a Patient

The prominent physician-author William Carlos Williams in 1926 wrote about a patient without concealing his identity. He should have known better. The patient brought a lawsuit against Dr. Williams that was settled for $5,000, an amount that equaled his annual salary, and he never made that mistake again.[14] In writing about a patient, the nonpsychiatric physician usually has no difficulty, because the configuration of the body can be discussed without anyone recognizing the patient. Psychiatrists, on the other hand, are obliged to disguise their clinical data, even though it is detrimental to the scientific value of the material, in order to avoid the recognition of the patient. Freud in his "Notes upon a Case of Obsessional Neurosis" (1909) pointed out that the case history was not easy to compose, not only because of the inevitable compression, but also because of the need for greater discretion in print. His powers of presentation were taxed, as the patient was well known in Vienna. Freud said, "How bungling are our attempts to reproduce an analysis; how pitifully we tear to pieces these great works of art Nature has created in the mental sphere."[15] In his opening remarks, Freud explained how it is that intimate secrets could be more easily mentioned than the trivial details of personality by which a person could be readily identified, and yet it is just these details that play an essential part in tracing the individual steps in an analysis.

Freud published six case histories, now classic in psychoanalytic literature. The first of these, a case of hysteria, was turned down by the editor of the first journal to whom he sent it, apparently on the ground that it was a breach of discretion. In the fourth study, the actual name of the subject was used, but in this case, Freud had never seen him. He based his study almost entirely on an autobiographical book. In this study, Freud apparently was unconcerned about public reprimand or a defamation suit, notwithstanding the fact that the subject, Dr. Daniel Paul Schreber, had paranoia—the most litigious type of personality—and was the presiding judge in a division of an Appeals Court in Saxony and a member of a distinguished family. Freud's other case histories are referred to as "The Case of Dora," "The Little Hans Case," "The Man with the Rats," "The Wolf-Man," and "A Case of Female Homosexuality." As a precautionary measure, psychiatric journals usually advise contributors of articles that where case presentations are submitted, it is the author's responsibility to disguise the identity of the patient.

About Freud himself, Drs. Ernest Jones and Max Schur, with permission, each published some information of his private life, but the Freud Archives promises to keep secret material on his boyhood until fifty years hence. Public figures are held to have lost, to some extent at least, their right of privacy. Hence, there is no liability when they are given additional publicity as to matters within the scope of the public interest they had aroused.

Dr. Martin Orne was criticized in 1991 when it was revealed that he had allowed a biographer of Pulitzer Prize–winning poet Anne Sexton access to audiotapes of his therapy sessions with her in the 1960s. Sexton, who committed suicide in 1974, wrote confessional poetry, much of which was drawn from her troubled life that included more than twenty hospitalizations, ten suicide attempts, and extramarital affairs. When she entered therapy with Dr. Orne, who was then on the faculty at Harvard, she was a Boston housewife. He encouraged her to write poetry as part of her therapy and taped their sessions to help her remember their content and advance her treatment. Sexton wrote a poem to him in 1962, in which she said, "But you, my doctor, my enthusiast, were better than Christ; you promised me another world to tell me who I was."[16] Dr. Orne released the tapes only after five years of prodding by the biographer, Diane Wood Middlebrook, and with the blessing of Sexton's daughter and literary executor, Linda Gray Sexton. He was heavily criticized by mental health professionals, who believed that his action set a dangerous precedent and violated widely adopted guidelines that confidential medical records not be made public without the patient's explicit permission. He was even attacked in a *New York Times* editorial, which accused him of betraying Sexton and dishonoring his profession. He responded in an opinion piece in that newspaper: "Sharing her most intimate thoughts and feelings for the benefit of others was not only her expressed and enacted desire, but the purpose for which she lived."[17]

Frederick Wiseman's 1967 film *Titicut Follies*, containing scenes at Massachusetts Correctional Institution at Bridgewater where "insane persons" charged with crime and "defective delinquents" were committed, was enjoined from exhibition in a proceeding brought by the state under its "obligation to protect the right of privacy of those committed to its custody." The decision was significant in that it protected the privacy of inmates at a correctional institution, who traditionally have been considered not to have any rights. The film depicted many inmates in situations that would be degrading to one of ordinary mentality and sensitivity. Although to a casual observer most of the inmates portrayed make little or no specific individual impression, others were shown in close-up pictures, sufficiently clearly exhibited (in some instances naked) to enable acquaintances to identify them. Wiseman contended that no asserted right of privacy may be protected from the publication of the film because the conditions at Bridgewater are matters of continuing public concern. Indeed, it was concern over conditions at Bridgewater that led various public officials a few years earlier to consider showing a documentary film in the hope that it might arouse public interest and lead to improvement. Arguably, the privacy argument was used by the state to prevent exposure of its own malfeasance and nonfeasance. The court said, however, that a presentation to the public of conditions at an institution would not necessitate the inclusion of some episodes shown in the film, nor would it justify, without valid written consents and releases, the depiction of identifiable inmates naked or in other embarrassing situations.[18] Needless to say, the court's ruling made *Titicut Follies* a prized item on the film-society circuit and guaranteed Wiseman's fame; and though the ban is no longer in force, Wiseman is still known as the person who documented, in gruesome detail, the conditions at a facility for the criminally insane.

Ownership and Access to Records

The question often arises as to the ownership of the records of the patient and the right to use or inspect them. A physician or hospital may not grant or deny access to records purely on the basis of an alleged personal property right in them, but confidentiality is a consideration. In the absence of a court order or authorization by the patient, the physician or hospital as custodian may be liable for an invasion of privacy by disclosure of confidential information. On the other hand, when the patient has signed a consent for their inspection the physician or hospital may not deny an insurance company or other third party access to its records.

Oddly enough, while a court demand for information worries psychiatrists most, the demand that affects them most frequently comes from a third party who has some legal or moral right to information. Confidentiality about the patient and accountability of the therapist are entwined, and to some extent at odds. The crucial questions are: What disclosure is necessary, and is that disclosure unfair? Is the alleged privacy of the patient a fig leaf covering the naked self-interest of the therapist? Dr. Herbert Modlin of the Menninger Foundation wrote, "We should differentiate the privacy of the patient and the privacy of the doctor. Occasionally it might be that our secrets—not the patient's—are threatened by exposure."[19] There is no black box in the treating room as there is in an airplane, and physicians have a code of silence about their colleagues that makes the police blue code relatively garrulous. The most frequent type of demand today is from insurance companies who pay for a good part of psychiatric treatment. They use certain ploys, such as the blanket consent form, and withhold payment unless the information is supplied. They also know the patient cannot go to court for redress without jeopardizing his privacy even more.[20]

Those who support the position that the physician or hospital should have the absolute right to deny access to records argue that the patient, except in rare instances, lacks the understanding, competency, or knowledge to evaluate a record properly or even know what is in it. However, as in the case of the testimonial privilege, when there is waiver of the privilege, the physician or hospital cannot refuse.[21]

Medical records of the physician in private practice are considered his property but, like hospital records, are subject to a limited property right on the part of the patient with respect to the information they contain. Access to records allows a patient to question procedures (and to obtain information about his health that may worry him). In cases of physical illness, the courts have held that an x-ray film, for example, belongs to the physician (even though the cost is paid by the patient), without a specific agreement to the contrary. The physician must provide the information contained in the x-ray or other medical record, however, if requested to do so by the patient. Having a limited property right, the patient can demand disclosure not only to himself but also, for example, to an insurance company.

Psychiatrists would argue that a different principle is needed for psychotherapy. The nonphysiological part of a psychiatric record, unlike an x-ray, is not hard data and might reasonably be said to be the entire work product of the therapist. There is also the pragmatic consideration that psychiatric records can readily be destroyed or may be prepared in a way unintelligible to others. Before malpractice suits became a matter of concern, many therapists, particularly those who were not engaged in research or teaching, kept no or few records of their sessions, except date of appointment, and would rely entirely upon their memory. Some record keeping is now prudent, at least until the time set by the statute of limitations has run on a suit for malpractice. In practice, psychiatrists refuse a patient's request to see his own treatment record on the ground that it would be detrimental to his health. Moreover, the patient has no right to demand that records concerning him be destroyed.

One person whose sexual history was taken when he was a young man by the Kinsey Institute for Sex Research later became a U.S. senator, and not wanting to take any chance of revelation, he wanted his record. The institute refused to return or expunge it. Wardell B. Pomeroy, a colleague of Kinsey, wrote in his book on the institute, "It was Kinsey's guarantee of absolute confidence to those who gave histories that made the research possible. . . . He was acutely conscious of his responsibilities in this respect, and he drilled it into everyone who came to work for him. Everyone had to understand the supreme importance of respecting confidences."

Pomeroy added, "I believe that there was something more to this than Kinsey's basic rocklike integrity. I think he liked secrets, that their possession gave him a sense of power. And there was no question that the histories did give him a unique potential power. They included political, social, and business leaders of the first rank, and with his intimate knowledge of their lives Kinsey could have figuratively blown up the United States socially and politically."[22]

Until the latter part of the nineteenth century, hospital and medical records were used almost exclusively for purposes of treatment, teaching, and research. In the twentieth century new uses developed for them—and the old privacy is gone. In former times, a physician and his patient met in complete privacy in office or home, but now there are other people in the picture—specialists and hospitals, technicians and machines, insurance carriers, employers, and unions. Increasingly team care has replaced individual practice; government is a third party, providing for all or part of the expense.

Various public or private agencies, such as the police, colleges, credit rating organizations, civil service, and employers, as well as insurance companies, request information or recommendations. The request may come from the patient himself with regard to such matters as a college application or employment. Parents or other members of the family may exert pressure for confidential material. Some psychiatrists, when a release has been given by the patient, provide information if it is considered to be for the good of the patient.

The release of information regarding psychiatric treatment of a patient to an insurance company is an issue of increasing importance. If insurance companies are to provide coverage for psychiatric illness, they must be able to obtain sufficient information to assess fairly the costs of their programs. Psychiatrists, however, generally feel that the insurer should accept their work and not expect the same detailed information regarding psychical disorders as in the case of physical disorders. Some employees, rather than have their employers informed that they are seeking psychiatric help, forego company insurance and pay themselves, or else they forego seeing a psychiatrist. In a position statement, the American Psychiatric Association Task Force on Confidentiality as It Relates to Third Parties urged framers of national health care proposals to recognize the imperative need for safeguarding the confidentiality of medical records in any national health care system.[23]

Right of privacy, too, may conflict with adequacy of treatment. Quality control of care and treatment means review of individual patients and therapists. In *Wyatt v. Stickney*,[24] Judge Johnson in setting out minimum standards for public institutions ordered individualized treatment plans. For review, data must be submitted to the mental health board. Civil libertarians expressed concern that the data would go beyond the board and they contested the identification of patients. Michigan and New York for a time used a code system to conceal the names of patients and therapists, but the system has been dropped. The disturbing consideration is the use of the records for purposes unrelated to treatment. For example, any federal agency can exercise the legal authority given the government to examine records of patients in Veterans Administration hospitals; it is done not only for purposes of treatment or for determination of disability payments, but also even when the patient makes application for any type of federal employment.

The social or behavioral science researcher can present a reasonable claim for information, but he has no legal right to it. For example, a researcher engaged in a study of suicide may wish to examine the records of every patient who has attempted suicide; he relies on the voluntary cooperation of the hospital, and he sometimes obtains it. Much social science research is modeled on a dyadic relationship between the researcher and subject, and the researcher seeks personal information about the respondent, his family, friends, and associates. Kinsey's research is an example of this professional model for social research.

For research in bureaucratic settings, the information that is collected is aggregate information rather than personal in the way that it is collected and in the sense that the researcher is interested in aggregates rather than particular individuals. Nevertheless, such information may have profoundly personal consequences if an individual's name comes to light or if sources of information are revealed. Moreover, revelations of information may have important consequences for the bureaucracy or organization itself. This model of research is more like journalistic or investigative activities than professional-client relations.

The impact on privacy resulting from the easy access to information contained in computer data banks has evoked much concern. Present technology will permit, within a very small space, the consolidation and storage of data equivalent to a 300-page book on every person in the country. Actually, though, data inside a computer may be safer than data in old-fashioned records. It provides selective access to information because it may be arranged into groups: (1) information without particular medical significance, such as name, address, occupation, and marital status; (2) medical information, but not of a secret nature, such as height and weight, blood group, immunizations, and refraction; and (3) other types of information, based on the interaction between the physician and patient, which would be available only to someone with the correct code number, namely, the patient's personal doctor or the patient, who could then decide whether to allow anyone else to have the information.[25]

Americans with Disabilities Act

Under the Americans with Disabilities Act, an employer may ask an individual for documentation when an employee requests reasonable accommodation for a disability. The employer is entitled to know that the employee has a covered disability for which reasonable accommodation is needed. In response to a request for reasonable accommodation, the employer cannot ask for documentation that is unrelated to determining the existence of a disability and the need for an accommodation. This means that in most situations an employer cannot request an employee's complete medical records because they are likely to contain information unrelated to the disability at issue and the need for accommodation.

An employer may require that the documentation about the disability and the functional limitations come from an appropriate health care or rehabilitation professional. The appropriate professional in any particular situation will depend on the disability and the type of functional limitation it imposes. Appropriate professionals include, but are not limited to, physicians (including psychiatrists), psychologists, nurses, physical therapists, occupational therapists, speech therapists, vocational rehabilitation specialists, and licensed mental health professionals. The individual can be asked to sign a limited release allowing the employer to submit a list of specific questions to the health care or vocational professional. The employer is obliged to maintain the confidentiality of all medical information collected during this process, regardless of where the information comes from.

Disclosure to Avoid Harm

It sometimes happens that strict confidentiality may jeopardize the patient or society. There may be danger, for example, of the patient committing suicide. There may be danger in the patient continuing work, as in the case of an airplane pilot who should be grounded because of severe mental disorder, but who, fearful of losing his job, does not tell his employer. Although the law imposes no duty to come to the aid of third persons, the psychiatrist may properly act in such emergencies. He may reveal a confidence when it becomes necessary in order to protect the welfare of the patient or the community. In such situations, the revelation is made only to avert catastrophe. As he is acting in his role as healer, a psychiatrist is not likely to be liable in damages for invasion of privacy. Thus, in one case, a physician who revealed to the patient's spouse that the patient had a venereal disease was not held liable.[26]

The general public and persons in therapy alike will not lose trust in the psychiatrist as a keeper of secrets if in cases of emergency he does not adhere to strict and absolute confidentiality. Sooner or later, the patient usually realizes that the psychiatrist has acted in his best interest (which is not the case when an opposing party in litigation compels a psychiatrist to testify). However, situations of real emergencies necessitating disclosure are rare.

In furnishing psychiatric information, the physician's traditional function has been to treat the sick, not to prepare historical reports or explanatory documents. What happens when psychiatric information is furnished? In all areas, could not the recipient of the information do as well, or even better, if he applied his usual method of decision making, uncontaminated by psychiatric data that he understands poorly? The practice of supplying a label (e.g., schizophrenic) may be especially misleading. Dr. Marc Hollender suggested that the general expectation that requests will be answered by the psychiatrist stems, in part, from the general practice of medicine. He pointed out that too little attention has been paid to the social significance of data applied to how a person feels, thinks, and lives, on the one hand, and to how his body functions, on the other. He added: "It may be that psychiatrists have had too great a need to prove their usefulness as members of society. As possessors of special and secret data (much like the possessor of choice bits of gossip), they can gain recognition, and perhaps even power, if they are willing to share their possessions with others who can use them. In my opinion, they have even been seduced to claim that they have the ability to foretell the future in a way that no one else can."[27]

Dr. Arnold Hutschnecker suggested that mental health certificates should be required for political leaders, similar to the Wasserman test demanded by states before marriage. He contended that psychological and axiological (value) tests now exist that would pinpoint psychopathology so that mentally unstable individuals would be prevented from attaining jobs of political importance. He cited the mentally disturbed Secretary of Defense James Forrestal and John Foster Dulles, with his constant brinkmanship, to name only two. More sensibly, he said, testing should be required at a student level, before a person has acquired a position of power.[28]

While strict confidentiality may jeopardize the patient or society, it is always debatable whether a disclosure can be construed as a benefit either to the patient or society. This thorny problem received wide publicity when two employees of the National Security Agency, Vernon F. Mitchell and William H. Martin, defected to the Soviet Union. A psychiatrist who had seen Mitchell turned over his records and testified before a secret session of the House Un-American Activities Committee. He expressed his belief that a patient who defects and causes a threat to national security loses his right to confidentiality because the rights of the government far exceed the rights of the individual. The psychiatrist then disclosed the defector's problems of family, religion, and sex. For this, he was taken to task by a number of general practitioners and psychiatrists. The Medical and Chirurgical Faculty of the State of Maryland, where the psychiatrist practiced, investigated the possible breach of medical ethics but ruled in his favor, concluding that the interest of the nation transcends that of the individual. The faculty said that the psychiatrist acted in an ethical and cooperative manner with public authorities and had given the testimony in secret session to the committee. The public release was through this committee rather than through the psychiatrist.[29]

The Secret Service from time to time has asked psychiatric hospitals and clinics to report patients who have made verbal or written threats against the president. At one time FBI Director Hoover urged all physicians to report to the bureau any facts relating to espionage, sabotage, or subversive activity coming to their attention. Psychiatrists generally criticized the American Medical Association for cooperating with the bureau and for going even further by urging its members to help catch even a petty thief. Guttmacher attacked this suggestion with wry humor: "It is not too fantastic to predict that before long the physician's inner examining room may resemble a rural post office with its walls plastered with the mugs of wanted felons."[30]

The duty to warn or protect, otherwise known as the *Tarasoff* duty, is discussed at length in chapter 11, on duty to third persons.

Examination at Request of Court or Employer

Psychiatrists are not bound by a confidential relationship when they are carrying out an examination at the request of a third party, such as a court, employer, or university. The psychiatrist in these cases is in an examining rather than a treating role. The individual sometimes cooperates, however, believing that there will be respect for confidentiality as in the usual physician-patient relationship. It seems clear that the individual is entitled to confidentiality when the psychiatrist appears to be acting in a treating role and fails to advise otherwise.

It is contrary to medical ethics, as well as against the law, for the police or the district attorney to exploit the relationship of physician and patient in order to obtain a confession from the accused. While some consider this naive, psychiatrists carrying out an examination pursuant to court order should caution the accused that communications are not privileged, notwithstanding the possible resultant loss of valuable information. The statutes of many states provide that communications to a psychiatrist in the course of a court-ordered psychiatric examination are without privilege only on issues involving the person's mental condition; that is, the psychiatrist may testify to the accused's insanity at the time of the offense or at the time of the trial, but he may not report, for example, on the validity of an alibi.

In *Leyra v. Denno*,[31] the accused had been allowed little sleep and was suffering from a sinus condition when the police brought in a psychiatrist, who was identified as a general practitioner. The questioning by the psychiatrist, who was skilled in hypnosis, was a subtle blend of threats and promises of leniency. Working in a room that was wired, the psychiatrist, "by subtle and suggestive questions, simply continued the police effort" to obtain a confession from the accused. The Supreme Court ruled the confession inadmissible in evidence, equating the procedure with mental coercion. In another case, *Oaks v. Colorado*,[32] it was held that a psychiatrist could not testify about the criminal activity of the defendant, whom he examined for the state before charges had been brought, on the ground that he had obtained the information under the guise of a psychiatric examination.

Presentence Reports

The confidentiality of a presentence-investigation report of a probation department, diagnostic center, or court probation clinic is a matter that has been receiving considerable attention. These reports to the court often have great influence on the type and length of sentence given. The issue here is not the right of a criminal defendant to have information withheld from the court, but rather the right of the court to withhold information from the defendant or his attorney. The controversy involves the extent to which due process requires disclosure of the contents of the report to the defendant. According to one view, a presentence-investigation report should be treated not as a public document but as a confidential compilation of information for the sole use of the sentencing judge. It is considered that strict adherence to confidentiality has made it possible for the probation officer to give the court a much more accurate picture of the defendant than would be possible if it were known that the contents of the report were going to be divulged to the defendant or others. As one court said, "To strip a presentence-investigation report of its confidentiality would be to divest it of its importance and value to the sentencing judge, because there might be lacking the frankness and completeness of disclosures made in confidence."[33]

There is a growing body of opinion, however, that supports the view that the defendant and his attorney should be given an opportunity to examine the presentence report. Defense attorneys contend that the right to see a presentence report is a basic and fundamental right, the denial of which will allow hearsay evidence to go unchallenged, thus depriving the defendant of cross-examination and confrontation of witnesses. Three organizations—the American Bar Association in its Standards Relating to Sentencing Alternatives and Procedures, the American Law Institute in its Model Penal Code, and the National Council on Crime and Delinquency in its Model Sentencing Act—have recommended that the report be disclosed to the defense. Making the report available to the defense provides certain safeguards to the defendant, primarily giving him an opportunity to explain matters in the report that may not have been explained as fully as he feels they should have been. Many years ago, in 1944, an Advisory Committee of the Supreme Court recommended full disclosure of the presentence report, but the recommendation was rejected. More recently, though, either by statute or judicial decision, some states have provided that the defense must be given a summary of the presentence report, and others have ruled that the defendant is entitled to full disclosure.[34]

Rule 32(c) of the Federal Rules of Criminal Procedure gives the court full discretion to disclose information contained in the presentence report when the court believes it is necessary to do so. The rule also provides that a presentence report shall not be submitted to the court or its contents disclosed to anyone else, unless the defendant has pleaded guilty or has been found guilty. The policy behind the rule is to avoid prejudice on the part of the court. If the purpose of the report is not for sentencing but is to provide the court with information to assist it in passing upon the advisability of reducing bail, the report is permissible, even though it contains certain presentence factors.[35] As probation and diagnostic services develop, the issue of the extent to which a presentence-investigation report ought to be preserved as a confidential document will assume increased importance.

Confidentiality in Corrections

Psychotherapy and group counseling have been introduced in correctional institutions and agencies. Confidentiality is of utmost importance when dealing with individuals distrustful of others. There is a difference of opinion, however, as to whether a prison psychiatrist is duty bound to report knowledge of new crimes being planned by the patient.[36] The viewpoint supporting confidentiality defends it thus: "It is not the role of the psychiatrist to uncover such information under the guise of therapy, if he expects to expose it to the warden. . . . [D]isclosure under these circumstances is a sort of 'psychic entrapment.' The physician ought to either warn his patient beforehand of the reservations he has concerning confidentiality or, having committed himself to secrecy, he should maintain it."[37] The physician who commits himself to secrecy, however, leaves himself vulnerable to blackmail subsequently by the inmate.

Testing in Schools

The use of psychological testing in schools gives rise to a similar issue. For sundry reasons, parents may exert pressure upon school authorities for disclosure of confidential material. There has been an upsurge of litigation challenging various testing procedures and placements, seeking parental participation in placement procedures and even money damages for inappropriate placement of students. There is usually contained in a student's records a comprehensive dossier of official test scores, extracurricular activities, teacher appraisals of student attitudes and social behavior, and sometimes reports or letters from psychiatrists and special guidance agencies. In a recent New York case, the mother of a girl who was prohibited from attending her junior high school graduation as punishment for "bad citizenship" sought access to the records to determine the nature of her daughter's offense. The State Education Commissioner ruled in favor of the mother, saying, "No one has a greater right to such information than the parent."[38]

Do test results belong in the category of secrets, to be seen only by professional eyes? Or is their proper function best served when they become common knowledge in the school and its community? In some towns, names and scores are listed in the local newspaper, much like the results of an athletic contest. How should a school administrator, teacher, or guidance worker respond when a mother wants to know, for example, her son's IQ? Should the school send aptitude test profiles home with the children? One cartoonist depicted a mother calling the family physician, "It's about Benny, doctor. He's just come from school with an IQ of 104! Should I put him right to bed?"

Arguments against parental access to records stress that the information is not in terms that parents can absorb and use and that teachers and guidance workers, fearing parental displeasure, will be less than candid in making reports. While parents may have the right to know whatever the school knows about the abilities, performance, and problems of their children, mere access to records would simply give the illusion of information and at the same time would undoubtedly discourage teachers and others from entering subjective judgments in a student's record. In current practice, psychiatric reports and personality test results are not made available to the student or parent; they may, however, discuss these matters directly with the teacher, psychiatrist, or psychologist. The right of parents to know about the abilities and performances of their children refers to knowledge in terms they can understand and absorb.[39]

Psychiatrist as Double Agent

When a psychiatrist is hired by an institution or agency, his allegiance is diffused between the institution and the patient. This is a relatively new position for the physician who, not so long ago, had a strictly personal relationship with his patient. The physician represented no temporal authority but was the intermediary between the forces of nature or God and the individual. He had a priestlike function. Rarely did he have to choose between serving the private and the common good.

Szasz calls the psychiatrist who is hired by a third party a double agent. Writing about the college psychiatrist, Szasz says that in the case of a homosexual student, the psychiatrist serves as a disguised medical policeman.[40] Before publishing this accusation, Szasz presented it at the 1967 annual meeting of the American Orthopsychiatric Association, at which time numerous college psychiatrists came up to the podium to deny that confidences were being divulged to the authorities, except when necessary to prevent a suicide.

Actually, it is in the criminal-law and the military settings that the psychiatrist is a double agent. The college psychiatrist may make isolated divulgences, but in the context of criminal proceedings (both pretrial and posttrial) the psychiatrist is required in every case to make a report to the authorities. In order to make an adequate report, he invites the confidence of the accused, which cannot be directly divulged but will surely affect the report. Thus, a person charged with writing a bad check, who confides to the psychiatrist that he has brutally killed someone, will surely not be recommended for probation on the bad check charge.

In the military, as in nonmilitary criminal-law administration, there is routine reporting in evaluating offenders as well as persons who apply for discharge as conscientious objectors. Georges Clemenceau said that "military justice is to justice as military music is to music."[41] The analogy can be seen in psychiatry as well.

Some university health services quite appropriately notify the student body that exceptions to confidentiality will be made when a student's mental condition is such that immediate action must be taken to protect the student or others from serious consequence of his illness and also when a student is referred for evaluation and an opinion or recommendation is requested. In the first situation, immediate voluntary or involuntary hospitalization may be arranged, and the college administration and parents may be notified as quickly as possible. In cases of the second type, called *administrative referrals*, the student is informed initially that a report will be made to the referring individual or agency, but the actual content of the interview remains confidential.[42]

Thus, the prevailing practice as to notification of parents of minors for treatment of mental disorder is, curiously enough, just the opposite of the procedure generally followed and approved by the law in the case of treatment of minors for physical illness. In psychotherapy, notification is made only in emergencies, whereas in treatment for physical illness, lack of notification in emergencies is legally excused, time being of the essence. With venereal disease and drug use now constituting public health emergencies of the first order, legislation has been enacted in a number of states allowing minors over the age of twelve or fifteen to give consent to medical examination or treatment without parental consent.[43]

As part of its program of health care, a number of large companies have retained psychiatrists to care for the emotional problems of their employees. The Group for the Advancement of Psychiatry in its report on confidentiality said, "If the psychiatrist is administratively tied to the personnel division of a company, the confidential relationship cannot exist, and it behooves him to clarify his position with the employee. We regard failure to do so as a serious abridgement of the physician's ethical responsibility." The report drew special attention to the psychiatrist working for public mental health hospitals, prisons, and law-enforcement agencies.[44]

Actually, there is nothing new about psychiatrists working for public health hospitals. In the early part of the nineteenth century the states, beginning with Massachusetts in 1830 when it passed a law authorizing the establishment of a lunatic institution, took over responsibility for the care of the mentally ill; between 1840 and 1850 most of the other states did the same. It will be recalled that the first association of psychiatrists was known as the Association of Medical Superintendents of American Institutions for the Insane. During recent decades, however, psychiatrists by and large have abandoned the mental hospital for private practice.

In the 1960s and 1970s, psychiatry was extended beyond the insulated doctor-patient relationship, and the psychiatrist once again found himself not acting in intimate privacy with his patient. His relationship with the patient, in some cases, has become a matter of public concern. He finds himself in a two-faced position that strains his patient's confidence and demands of him the skill and judgment to satisfy interests other than his patient's while maintaining his professional conscience and integrity intact. The administration of his art and practice is shared partially with other essential parties. The legal profession has encased him in a situation that sets him up as a manipulator of his patient's life—both present and future—despite the fact that confidentiality does not grow well in an environment polluted with deceit. The psychiatrist has contributions to make beyond his traditional role, but in such situations it is necessary that he recognize and clarify, to all parties concerned, the precise nature of each of these situations.[45]

Notes

1. J. C. Beck (ed.), *Confidentiality and the Duty to Protect: Foreseeable Harm in the Practice of Psychiatry* (Washington, D.C.: American Psychiatric Press, 1990); A. R. Felthous, *The Psychotherapist's Duty to Warn or Protect* (Springfield, Ill.: Thomas, 1989); R. W. Pettis, "*Tarasoff* and the Dangerous Driver: A Look at the Driving Cases," *Bull. Am. Acad. Psychiatry & Law* 20 (1992): 427; R. W. Pettis & T. G. Gutheil, "Misapplication of the *Tarasoff* Duty to Driving Cases: A Call for the Reframing of the Theory," *Bull. Am. Acad. Psychiatry & Law* 21

(1993): 263. See also A. Felthous, "The Duty to Warn or Protect to Prevent Automobile Accidents," in R. I. Simon, *Review of Clinical Psychiatry and the Law* (Washington, D.C.: American Psychiatric Press, 1990), vol. 1, pp. 221–38. The *Tarasoff* doctrine is discussed in chapter 11.

Almost all states require physicians to make a report when a patient is injured by a gun, knife, or other deadly weapon. In Colorado, for example, physicians must report to the police any injuries caused by a firearm, knife, or other sharp instrument or "any other injury which the physician has reason to believe involves a criminal act, including injuries which the physician has reason to believe involves a criminal act, including injuries resulting from domestic violence." Colo. Stat., sec. 12-36-135.

A number of states (California, Kentucky, Michigan, New Mexico, New Hampshire, Rhode Island, and Colorado) have mandatory reporting laws that specifically address domestic violence as well as child abuse and elder abuse. See, e.g., Calif. Welfare & Institutions Code, sec. 15630 (reporting of known or suspected elder abuse). See G. J. Alexander, "Big Mother: The State's Use of Mental Health Experts in Dependency Cases," *Pacific L.J.* 24 (1993): 1465. Complete documentation of domestic-violence-related injuries must be noted in the victim's medical record, which could later be used as evidence in prosecuting the batterer. Opponents of the mandatory reporting of spousal abuse perpetuate the stereotypes of battered women as being helpless and childlike. The portrayal of victims as helpless is evident in the legislative intent of some of these state statutes. For instance, the legislative findings and purpose of the New Mexico reporting statute indicate that the "legislature recognized that many adults in the state are unable to manage their own affairs or protect themselves from exploitation, abuse or neglect." See J. T. R. Jones, "Kentucky Tort Liability for Failure to Report Family Violence," *No. Ky. U.L. Rev.* 26 (1999): 43; M. M. McFarlane, "Mandatory Reporting of Domestic Violence: An Inappropriate Response for New York Health Care Professionals," *Buff. Public Interest L.J.* 17 (1998/1999): 1.

Mandated reporters are not deemed agents of the state and therefore are not obliged to give a Miranda warning. People v. Salinas, 131 Cal. App.3d 925, 182 Cal. Rptr. 683 (1982).

2. See R. Slovenko, *Psychotherapy and Confidentiality* (Springfield, Ill.: Thomas, 1998); D. I. Joseph & J. Onek, "Confidentiality in Psychiatry," in S. Bloch, P. Chodoff, & S. A. Green (eds.), *Psychiatric Ethics* (Oxford: Oxford University Press, 3d ed. 1999), pp. 105–40. See also E. W. Grabois, "The Liability of Psychotherapists for Breach of Confidentiality," *J. Law & Health* 12 (1997–98): 39. Randy Cohen, who writes the weekly column "The Ethicist" answering questions on ethics for the *New York Times Magazine*, says that among professionals, physicians write most frequently and they inquire about confidentiality. Lawyers write only to criticize his responses, and politicians, he says, never write. Needless to say, he will never hear from a head of state. For a collection of his writings, see R. Cohen, *The Good, the Bad, and the Difference* (New York: Doubleday, 2002).

3. S. S. Gilder, "How Safe Is a Secret?" *Medical Counterpoint*, May 1970, p. 54.

4. L. Edelstein, *The Hippocratic Oath: Text, Translation and Interpretation* (Baltimore: Johns Hopkins Press, 1943).

5. See M. Coady & S. Block (eds.), *Codes of Ethics and the Professions* (Melbourne: Melbourne University Press, 1996).

6. See American Psychiatric Association, *Guidelines on Confidentiality* (Washington, D.C.: American Psychiatric Press, 1987); S. Block, P. Chodoff, & S. A. Green (eds.), *Psychiatric Ethics* (New York: Oxford University Press, 3d ed. 1999), p. 519.

7. In Garner v. Stone, No. 97A-320250-1 (Ga. DeKalb Cy. Super. Ct., 1999), a jury found that in this case the therapist's duty to protect a patient's confidence outweighed the duty to warn others. The therapist, a psychologist, issued a warning to the police chief that the patient, a police officer, was "burned out and should not be on the street carrying a gun." The day the therapist issued the warning, the patient began therapy with a psychiatrist, who found him fit for duty and posing no threat. Suppose an individual is on trial in a death penalty case. May or should a therapist testify that his patient confessed the crime to him, which would exonerate the individual charged with the offense? It is arguable that under *Tarasoff*, there is a duty to report, though the state (rather than the patient) is not going to kill the individual. The issue is discussed in Symposium, "The Wrong Man Is about to Be Executed for a Crime He Did Not Commit," *Loy. L.A. L. Rev.* 29 (1996): 1543–1798.

Health care providers are not required to report an impaired health care professional if the information was learned through a treatment relationship. See Mich. Comp. Laws, sec.

333.16223. See chapter 11, on duty of therapists to third parties. See also R. Slovenko, *Psychotherapy and Confidentiality* (Springfield, Ill.: Thomas, 1998).

8. Years ago psychiatrist John Felber brought a class-action suit in federal court against the state of Connecticut on behalf of all physicians in the state, contending that the law infringed upon physicians' rights to privacy and confidentiality with patients and violated physicians' rights of due process of law. In addition, he contended the law fails to provide a definition of the term *drug-dependent*, it conflicts with the state's privileged-communications law, and it constitutes "an unreasonable exercise of police power." Ruling against him, the court said that there is no constitutional basis for privilege or confidentiality between physician and patient and that the matter rests entirely in the power of the legislature to enact laws related to these matters. While some matters of privacy have received constitutional protection in Supreme Court decisions, this court ruled that the physician-patient relationship is not so protected. Felber v. Foote, 321 F.Supp. 85 (D.C. Conn. 1970).

The constitutionality of the reporting provisions of the New York law was upheld in Roe v. Ingraham, 357 F.Supp. 1217 (S.D. N.Y. 1973). Dr. Thomas Szasz criticized the reporting requirement as "another giant step forward in the transformation of the American physician from doctor into detective, from protector of the patient into spy for the state." He suggested that if the state wants to register "addicts" and "habitual drug users," it could order them to register themselves. "Of course," Szasz says, "many might wisely refrain from such self-denunciation . . . so our lawmakers chose what must have seemed to them a more 'efficient' way of getting these 'patients' registered: namely, by ordering their physicians to denounce them to the authorities." Ltr., *New York Times*, Mar. 24, 1973, p. 32.

9. 695 N.Y.S.2d 903 (N.Y. Sup. Ct. 1999).

10. Furness v. Fitchett, [1958] N.Z.L.R. 396. One of the early cases awarding relief based upon the invasion of privacy, although not characterized as such, involved a doctor who brought in a lay assistant to help him in a childbirth situation. The doctor had made no disclosure that the assistant was not a doctor. DeMay v. Roberts, 46 Mich. 160, 9 N.W. 146 (1881). See S. D. Warren & S. Brandeis, "The Right to Privacy," *Harv. L. Rev.* 4 (1890): 193; W. L. Prosser, "Privacy," *Calif. L. Rev.* 48 (1960): 383.

11. Berry v. Moench, 8 Utah2d 191, 331 P.2d 814 (1958).

12. Carr v. Watkins, 227 Md. 578, 177 A.2d 841 (1962) . See also R. B. Little & E. A. Strecker, "Moot Questions in Psychiatric Ethics," *Am. J. Psychiatry* 113 (1956): 455.

13. See G. Annas, "Candidates Deserve Medical Privacy," *New York Times*, Feb. 1, 2000, p. 25.

14. Dr. Williams recounts the incident in *The Autobiography of William Carlos Williams*. See H. Markel, "Patients Are Discovering 'My Doctor, the Author,'" *New York Times*, Aug. 22, 2000, p. D-7.

15. In *The Standard Edition of the Complete Psychological Works of Sigmund Freud* (London: Hogarth Press, 1955).

16. D. W. Middlebrook, *Anne Sexton: A Biography* (New York: Houghton Mifflin, 1991). See also M. Kakutani, "A Poet's Life through a Sexual Lens," *New York Times*, Aug. 13, 1991, p. C-16. See J. Berg, "Grave Secrets: Legal and Ethical Analysis of Postmortem Confidentiality," *Conn. L. Rev.* 34 (2001): 81; S. Carton, "The Poet, the Biographer, and the Shrink: Psychiatrist-Patient Confidentiality and the Anne Sexton Biography," *U. Miami Ent. & Sports L. Rev.* 10 (1993): 117.

17. M. T. Orne, "The Sexton Tapes," *New York Times*, July 23, 1991, p. 27. See also P. Chodoff, "The Anne Sexton Biography: The Limits of Confidentiality," *J. Am. Acad. Psychoanal.* 20 (1992): 639.

18. Commonwealth v. Wiseman, 356 Mass. 251, 249 N.E.2d 610 (1969); noted in *Colum. L. Rev.* 70 (1970): 259; *Harv. L. Rev.* 83 (1970): 1722. In subsequent legislation, Massachusetts specifically stated that patients are to be protected "from commercial exploitation of any kind. No patient shall be photographed, interviewed, or exposed to public view without either his express written consent or that of his legal guardian." Mass. Gen. Laws, ch. 19, sec. 29(f).

19. H. C. Modlin, "How Private is Privacy?" *Psychiatry Digest*, Feb. 1969, p. 13.

20. Correspondence from Dr. Maurice Grossman, chairman of American Psychiatric Association Task Force on Confidentiality (Sept. 17, 1984).

21. Clarkson Memorial Hosp. v. Reserve Life Ins. Co., 350 F.2d 1006 (8th Cir. 1965); Wallace v. University Hosp., 170 N.E.2d 261 (Ohio App. 1970). In Gaertner v. State, 385 Mich.

49, 187 N.W.2d 429 (1971), the plaintiff, as guardian of a mentally incompetent minor, sought access to medical records regarding the treatment of his ward when an inpatient in several state institutions. The state attorney general asserted that there is a statutory duty to keep such records confidential and also argued that access to the records could not be allowed because the hospital physicians might lose their medical licenses through prosecution for violation of various statutory provisions. Pointing out that the privilege of confidentiality was designed for the protection of the patient, the court held that, since a mentally incompetent ward cannot act for himself, the law would allow his guardian to waive the privilege for his benefit and ruled that the lawful representative should have access to all the patient's hospital records. See generally *Brit. Med. J.*, Feb. 26, 1972, p. 577.

22. W. A. Pomeroy, *Dr. Kinsey and the Institute for Sex Research* (New York: Harper & Row, 1972; reprint, New Haven, Conn.: Yale University Press, 1982).

23. See M. Grossman, "Insurance Reports as a Threat to Confidentiality," *Am. J. Psychiatry* 128 (1971): 64. North Carolina psychiatrist Pamela Wright-Etter and Kevin Etter refused to turn over psychotherapy notes to Blue Cross/Blue Shield without their patients' explicit consent. The Blues claimed that the generic consent-release form signed by their patients sufficed for them to turn over the records, which the Blues wanted to examine after a patient filed a complaint with the company about fees the psychiatrists charged for a particular service. The psychiatrists disagreed about the consent-form requirement, insisting on relinquishing records only where patients gave their explicit, contemporaneous consent following a specific request. And since not all patients gave their explicit consent—in fact, most refused to do so—the Blues would not reimburse the psychiatrists for some of the psychotherapy sessions, with several of the reimbursement denials made retroactively. The decision not to turn over the records cost the psychiatrists thousands of dollars in reimbursements, and led to a decision not to participate in other health insurance companies' provider panels, and their ultimate decision to close their medical practice. The American Psychiatric Association Assembly presented them with the 2001 Profile of Courage Award. J. Arehart-Treichel, "Standing Up to Insurers Wins Psychiatrists APA Award," *Psychiatric News*, Dec. 7, 2001, p. 5.

24. 344 F.Supp. 373, 387 (M.D.Ala. 1972).

25. See D. Brin, *The Transparent Society* (Reading, Mass.: Addison-Wesley, 1998); A. Etzioni, *The Limits of Privacy* (New York: Basic Books, 1999); C. J. Sykes, *The End of Privacy* (New York: St. Martin's Press, 1999); A. F. Westin (project director), *Databanks in a Free Society* (New York: Quadrangle, 1973).

In accordance with the mandate of the "administrative simplification" provisions of the Health Insurance Portability and Accountability Act of 1996, 42 U.S.C. §201 *et seq.*, the Department of Health and Human Services (HHS) published final privacy regulations on December 28, 2000. Although they were issued in December 2000, most covered entities are not required to be compliant until April 14, 2003, the effective date. According to the preamble to the final privacy rule, the need for federal privacy protection originated from the rapid growth in the electronic exchange of information, recent advances in scientific technology, advances in genetic sciences, information, and increased efforts to market health care to consumers. The HHS Office of Civil Rights noted that gaps in existing state laws often allow health care providers and others to distribute personal health information without notice or consent in cases that have nothing to do with medical treatment or reimbursement.

The privacy regulations as written are anything but simple. In HHS's view, the privacy regulations seek to strike a balance between the need to protect privacy with the benefits of free flow of information. The *covered entities* under the regulations are defined as health plans, health care clearinghouses, and health care providers who transmit certain health care information electronically. A provider who submits only paper copy claim forms and does not transmit any other information electronically is not a covered entity and thus does not fall within the ambit of the regulations.

Protected health information is defined as "individually identifiable health information" that is transmitted electronically, maintained electronically, or transmitted or maintained in any other form or medium. Individuals have the right to inspect and obtain a copy of their own protected health information, but individuals do not have the right to access psychotherapy notes. HHS has specifically excluded the following from the definition of psychotherapy notes: medication prescription and monitoring, counseling session start and stop times, the modalities and frequency of treatment furnished, and results of clinical tests. Also, any summary of the following are excluded from the definition: diagnosis, functional status, treatment plan, symptoms, prognosis, and progress to date. If psychotherapy notes are not separated from the medical record, they do not fall within the definition of *psychotherapy notes,* and the patient will have a right of access. With the exception of psychotherapy notes, a patient has the right to request amendments to protected health information; for example, a patient may request that errors in the record be corrected.

The covered entities are required to provide notice to individuals on how medical information about the patient will be used and disclosed and how the patient can gain access. As a separate requirement, covered entities must obtain consent and authorization to use and disclose protected health information. A privacy notice may be combined in a single document with an authorization but not in a single document with a consent. Typically the terms *consent* and *authorization* are often used synonymously, but in the regulations these terms are considered different. A covered entity must obtain an authorization for use and disclosure of protected health information for purposes other than treatment, payment, and health care operations (TPO).

There are a few situations in which a covered entity is required to obtain a consent but not an authorization to use or disclose psychotherapy notes in connection with TPO. Specifically, access without authorization is limited to (1) the person who created the psychotherapy notes for treatment purposes; (2) for uses or disclosures in conducting training programs in which students, trainees, or practitioners in mental health learn under supervision to practice or improve their skills in group, joint, family, or individual counseling; and (3) for use by the covered entity to defend a legal action or other proceeding brought by the patient. 45 CFR, sec. 164.508(a)(2).

According to HHS, although authorization is generally required in most situations for use and disclosure of psychotherapy notes in connection with TPO, authorization will rarely be necessary because psychotherapy notes usually do not include information that entities would typically need for purposes of TPO. 65 Fed. Reg. at sec. 82.515. This, however, does not square with the modern health care age of managed care utilization review that routinely demands a great deal of information before payment is made for psychiatric care.

In addition, HHS has carved out other exceptions that allow a covered entity to use or disclose psychotherapy notes without a specific authorization: (1) when required by the Secretary of HHS to investigate compliance, (2) when required to do so by law, (3) when required by a health oversight agency in order to oversee the originator of the notes, (4) to coroners regarding a deceased individual, and (5) when needed to avert a serious and imminent threat to health or safety. 45 CFR, sec. 164.508(a)(2). It is important for mental health providers to execute valid authorizations, given that authorization is required in many instances for uses and disclosures in connection with psychotherapy notes. In order for an authorization to be valid, at a minimum all of the core elements set forth in the rule must be contained in the authorization. 45 CFR, sec. 164.508(c).

In response to the concern expressed by the scientific community that useful research activities could be impeded due to the impractical and expensive requirements under the regulations, some research accommodations were included in the final rule. A covered entity may use or disclose protected health information without authorization by the research participant if the covered entity obtains documentation that an alteration or waiver of the research participant's authorization for use or disclosure of information for research purposes has been approved by an Institutional Review Board (IRB) or a privacy board. Authorization is also not needed if the covered entity obtained representations from the entity, and that access to the information is necessary for research. Moreover, a covered entity may always use or disclose for research purposes health information that has been deidentified without falling out of compliance with the regulations. 45 CFR, secs. 164.502(d), 164.514(a–c).

Pursuant to the final rule, all state laws that are contrary to the rule are preempted unless one of the four listed conditions is met. 45 CFR, sec. 160.203. A state law would not be preempted if HHS determined that the state law was serving a compelling need related to health safety and welfare, or if the state law provides for the reporting of disease or injury. 45 CFR, sec. 164.502(a–d).

26. A.B. v. C.D., 7 Fed. 72 (1905), Simonsen v. Swenson, 104 Neb. 244, 177 N.W.831 (1920). Dr. Karl A. Menninger observed:

It is true that the physician has a loyalty to his patient and a responsibility for treating the professional relationship with respect and honor. But the doctor also has other responsibilities. He has a responsibility to society, to the hospital, to the rest of the medical profession, and to science. No patient has a right to exploit the confidential relationship offered by the physician to make the physician a *particeps criminis*. The physician cannot condone moral and legal irresponsibility on the part of the patient. For example, a patient comes to a VA Hospital with certain psychiatric symptoms, and in the course of his history he confesses that he has been receiving compensation for self-inflicted gunshot wounds, which he had claimed were received in combat. The psychiatrist who receives this information has no right to withhold from the clinical records the fact that the patient has been defrauding the government, even though this confession was made in confidence. Another instance that recently came to my knowledge was one in which a patient was accepted in a VA Hospital for treatment for which he was completely ineligible. Because certain individuals were sympathetic and felt that he needed the hospitalization (and considered that the information concerning his ineligibility was given to them in confidence and could not be betrayed), they joined in concealing this information from the Registrar over a period of nearly two years. In effect, this was conspiracy to defraud the government and did irreparable harm to the patient, even though those in charge of him really felt that they were doing the best thing. If a patient tells a doctor in confidence that he has brought a time bomb into the hospital and hidden it under the bed of one of the other patients, it is a strange doctor indeed who would feel that this professional confidence should not be violated.

K. A. Menninger, *A Manual for Psychiatric Case Study* (New York: Grune & Stratton, 1962), pp. 36–37.

27. M. H. Hollender, "The Psychiatrist and the Release of Patient Information," *Am. J. Psychiatry* 116 (1960): 828. Following the passage of the Civil Rights Act of 1964, the number of employers utilizing objective personnel tests markedly increased. While ostensibly neutral, these tests disqualified a disproportionate number of nonwhites, prompting the Supreme Court to proscribe their use unless the employer could prove that they measured aptitudes and skills related to job performance. Griggs v. Duke Power Co., 401 U.S. 424 (1971); discussed in H. N. Bernhardt, "Griggs v. Duke Power Co.: The Implications for Private and Public Employers," *Texas L. Rev.* 50 (1972): 901.

28. In another proposal, Dr. Leopold Bellak, clinical professor of psychiatry at Albert Einstein College of Medicine, suggested that candidates for president and vice president be tested for organic brain problems such as lesions and tumors that could interfere with memory, problem solving, attention span, and the ability to think abstractly. T. Andersen, "Psychiatrist Wants Brain Tests for Presidential Candidates," *Gannett Westchester Newspapers*, Aug. 30, 1984, p. 3. Dr. Abraham L. Halpern responded, "I can see much harm and no good that can come from routine psychological testing of candidates for President and Vice-President. . . . [S]uch testing is not likely to uncover significant mental impairments or characterological deficits not already discernible by the public." A. L. Halpern, "Democracy Beats Mental Tests" (ltr.), *Gannett Westchester Newspapers*, Sept. 7, 1984, p. 13. See M. J. Halberstam, "Who's Medically Fit for the White House?" *New York Times Magazine*, Oct. 22, 1972, p. 39; A. A. Hutschnecker, "The Lessons of Eagleton," *New York Times*, Oct. 30, 1972, p. 31. W. Gaylin, "What's Normal?" *New York Times Magazine*, Apr. 11, 1973, p. 14.

29. *Washington Post*, Sept. 22, 1960, p. 1; Dec. 22, 1960, p. 1.

30. M. Guttmacher, *The Mind of the Murderer* (New York: Grove Press, 1960), p. 215.

31. 347 U.S. 556 (1954).

32. 371 P.2d 443 (Colo. 1962).

33. Morgan v. State, 142 So.2d 308 (Fla. App. 1962); see J. B. Parsons, "The Pre-Sentence Investigation Report Must Be Preserved as a Confidential Document," *Fed. Prob.* 28 (1964): 3; P. Roche, "The Position for Confidentiality of the Presentence Investigation Report," *Albany L. Rev.* 29 (1965): 206.

34. California and New Jersey provide that when the conviction has been for serious crime, the report must be fully disclosed and counsel must be given an opportunity to rebut its content. Virginia provides that the report must be presented in open court, with the de-

fendant being apprised of its content and having an absolute right to cross-examine the person who prepared it. Connecticut provides that the defendant shall be furnished the report, but the court's discretion determines the limits of the defense's rights to interrogate the investigator. Maryland, Michigan, Minnesota, and North Carolina provide that the substance of the report must be disclosed, but provision is made to safeguard from disclosure the sources of information it contains (the rule suggested in both the ALI's Model Penal Code and the ABA's Project on Minimum Standards for Criminal Justice). See R. H. Kuh, "For a Meaningful Right to Counsel on Sentencing," *A.B.A.J.* 7 (1971): 1096.

35. E. N. Bartin, "Looking at the Law," *Fed. Prob.* 28 (1964): 61.

36. A. MacCormick, "A Criminologist Looks at Privilege," *Am. J. Psychiatry* 115 (1959): 1068.

37. N. Fenton, "Group Counseling: A Method for the Treatment of Prisoners and for a New Staff Orientation in the Correctional Institution," In R. Slovenko (ed.), *Crime, Law and Corrections* (Springfield, Ill.: Thomas, 1996), p. 605.

38. *New York Times*, Mar. 5, 1972, p. 9; See W. Creech, "Psychological Testing and Constitutional Rights," *Duke L.J.* 1966: 332; J. H. Ricks, "On Telling Parents about Test Results," *Test Service Bull.* no. 54 (New York: Psychological Corp., Dec. 1959); C. W. Sherrer & R. A. Roston, "Some Legal and Psychological Concerns about Personality Testing in the Public Schools," *Fed. Bar. J.* 30 (1971): 111.

39. State Boards of Education usually set out a policy protecting psychiatric reports and personality test results from disclosure. For example, the Michigan State Board of Education provides:

> (1) Specific responses to personality tests, projective and nonprojective, shall be adequately safeguarded from becoming accessible to the public. An interpretation summary of test results may be made available by such qualified personnel only to individuals directly concerned with the educational welfare of the pupil. However, specific responses and interpretation summaries may become part of published research findings and reports where the identities of the individuals tested are properly safeguarded.
>
> (2) A transfer of individual personality-test interpretation summaries to other school districts or agencies shall not be made without the permission of the parent or guardian expressed in writing and filed with the sending district.

40. T. S. Szasz, "The Psychiatrist as Double Agent," *Transaction*, Oct. 1967, pp. 6–24.

41. R. Sherrill, *Military Justice Is to Justice as Military Music Is to Music* (New York: Harper & Row, 1970).

42. In typical fashion, universities advise in the campus paper about their health service thus: "The students' contacts with our services are strictly confidential. Absolutely no one in the university is notified of a student's visit, nor does it appear on any student's record. An exception would be if one of the deans or other administrative officials referred a student or faculty member to the clinic in order that it might render an opinion concerning that person. One other exception would be where the clinic feels the student is so upset, for instance, that he should leave school; then the clinic might notify the parents, but almost never over the student's objections." Parents, however, assume that a college will notify them if their son or daughter becomes seriously ill or gets into disciplinary, academic, or other acute trouble. It may be an understandable assumption, since parents are often paying the tuition bills—but it is usually quite wrong. M. Clayton, "Privacy vs. Protection," *Christian Science Monitor*, Feb. 12, 2002, p. 16. A lawsuit filed against the Massachusetts Institute of Technology by parents who claim they should have been notified of their daughter's worsening mental health before her committing suicide has pushed many universities to intervene and to inform parents about students when a threat to health or another crisis exists. See D. Sontag, "Who Was Responsible for Elizabeth Shin?" *New York Times Magazine*, Apr. 28, 2002, p. 57.

43. At least forty-three states have passed laws to permit physicians to diagnose and treat venereal disease in minors on their own consent. Twenty-five states have extended, to at least certain minors, the right to treatment in such matters as contraception and other pregnancy-related conditions, drug addiction, and sometimes the full range of medical ser-

vices. The majority of these states, however, limit the broad range of services to what are called emancipated minors—usually those eighteen or over, or married, or living away from home and supporting themselves.

44. Group for the Advancement of Psychiatry, *Confidentiality and Privileged Communication in the Practice of Psychiatry*, Report No. 45, p. 106.

45. For additional and extended discussion of confidentiality issues, see R. Slovenko, *Psychotherapy and Confidentiality* (Springfield, Ill.: Thomas, 1998).

7

Informed
Consent

From early childhood we learn to fear two classes of people:
police, because they carry guns, and physicians, because they intrude our bodies
and they give shots. The police are controlled by the law on search and seizure and
physicians by the law on consent.

As a legal matter, liability arising out of medical treatment where consent is
lacking can rest on one of two theories: battery or negligence. Typically, an action
based on battery occurs where the physician obtains the consent of the patient for
the performance of a particular procedure but thereafter performs a different procedure for which consent was not obtained. Without authorization for a procedure,
the physician may be held liable in battery even though it is skillfully performed
and is successful.[1]

On the other hand, when consent is given for a procedure but injury results
due to an undisclosed risk, the theory in such a case is usually negligence. Again
it is of no moment that the treatment was skillfully performed. Two landmark cases
decided in 1960 within days of each other announced the doctrine of informed
consent.[2] Under the doctrine the patient's mere consent to a procedure became
no longer an adequate authorization for treatment. Instead, the consent must be
an informed consent—to wit, the physician must inform the patient of the nature
and purpose of the proposed procedure, the likelihood of success, the hazards of

the procedure, and any alternative forms of treatment. In other words, the duty became not merely to obtain consent, but also to make disclosures.[3]

Throughout history physicians obtained the consent of a patient to a treatment, and information about the treatment was provided, but information was not given that might unduly alarm the patient. The assumption among physicians was that patients did not really want to know what was wrong with them (it would only cause needless anxiety) or that they could not possibly understand. The Hippocratic tradition of benevolent paternalism is now widely regarded as in conflict with the autonomy of patients and their right to be fully informed in making decisions. Physicians are now expected to be facilitators of patient decision making rather than the decision makers. It is no longer assumed that the patient shares the physician's values about anything. Stirred by wider consumer protection and rights movements, patients learned to abandon the role of a child accepting treatment from a paternalistic physician; they began to assume the guise of adults. The doctrine of informed consent is seen as a bulwark against the medical profession's paternalistic domination of patients.[4]

Professor Alexander Capron has argued that the doctrine can serve six salutary functions. It can (1) protect individual autonomy, (2) protect the patient's status as a human being, (3) avoid fraud or duress, (4) encourage physicians to carefully consider their decisions, (5) foster rational decision making by the patient, and (6) involve the public generally in medicine.[5] The doctrine is now reflected in consent forms that health care institutions require all patients to sign upon admission and before various procedures are performed, and it has provided the starting point for federal regulations on human experimentation.

In psychotherapy or psychoanalysis, the spelling out of possible risks of therapy tends to be suggestive and so, Freud recommended, preliminary discussions should be kept to a minimum (but in the course of therapy Freud often made suggestions).[6] In any event, psychotherapy is marked by surprises, so what can be told, or should be told? Psychoanalytic psychotherapy is a voyage very much like sailing—where one goes depends on the wind, and that is unpredictable. Should a therapist inform a patient that a risk of therapy may be divorce or erotic feelings toward the therapist? Moreover, unlike surgery, psychotherapy is not a one-time event but a process, and the patient presumably can withdraw at any time during therapy. In recent years the revival of memory of child sexual abuse has prompted proposals to enact legislation that would require a psychotherapist to obtain an elaborate informed consent before embarking on "any treatment method not proven safe and effective."[7]

The doctrine of informed consent is tied to the doctrine of assumption of risk. Informed consent, in effect, is an assumption of the announced risks of therapy. What about an assumption of the risk of malpractice? Exculpatory clauses are closely scrutinized and are not given effect when there is a special legal relationship or overriding public interest as in the case of medical treatment. As a matter of law, a consent form, signed in advance, that absolves a physician or hospital from liability for negligence is not valid as a release. In a California case,[8] the patient was admitted to the hospital on condition that he execute a release absolving the hospital "from any and all liability for the negligent or wrongful acts or omissions of its employees." The California Supreme Court held that although one may, generally speaking, voluntarily assume a risk, a release is not valid when one is compelled to assume a risk to obtain essential medical treatment. In this situation, the court said, the releasing party does not really acquiesce voluntarily in the contractual shifting of the risk, nor does he receive an adequate consideration for the transfer of the risk.

Determining whether a consent for medical care is valid calls for consideration of three elements: (1) competency, (2) disclosure, and (3) voluntariness. While there is consensus about these elements, the tests in determining them are far less settled. For competency, Dr. Paul Appelbaum and Dr. Thomas Grisso proposed several cognitive abilities. The first is the ability to communicate and sustain a choice—if the patient cannot make a preference known or if he repeatedly changes his mind, his decision-making capacity is impaired. The second is the ability to understand relevant information. The third is the ability to appreciate the situation and its consequences. The fourth and final ability, as proposed by Appelbaum and Grisso, is that required to manipulate information rationally. A patient whose logic is faulty is unlikely to have sound judgment. The appointment of a guardian is called for when the patient is deemed incompetent.[9]

The disclosure required of alternative treatments are those generally acknowledged within the professional community as feasible, their risks and consequences, and their probability of success. Some courts have held that alternatives should be disclosed even if the alternative is more hazardous or if the physician is not capable of performing it or evaluating its risk.[10] The courts may, however, limit the disclosure requirement by concluding that some alternatives are not legitimate treatment options.[11]

The field of psychiatry is broadly divided into three fields or combinations thereof: psychotherapy, pharmacological therapy, and behavior therapy. The field is marked by an almost chaotic character of divisions that proclaim one approach as authentic and describe others as moribund. Within psychotherapy, a proliferation of approaches came about in the 1960s: gestalt, transactional analysis, bioenergetics, and so forth. As therapies proliferated, so did psychotherapists, and now it is a bewildering maze.[12]

Impact of the Health Care System

In practice, consent is transfigured by the health care system. As is well known, health care is a function of the interplay between the individual patient, the caregiver, the system that organizes the services, the purchasers and payors who preselect the care, and the private and public agencies that provide oversight and compliance with the system.

Health care is now mostly *managed care.* Under it, various alternative forms of treatment, as a practical matter, may be unavailable. Managed care organizations have been accused of withholding necessary services through several mechanisms, including restriction of access to specialists, limitations on covered medications, denial of coverage for new forms of technology, administrative review of physicians' decisions, and capitation plans under which the physician is paid more to do less.[13] A gag clause included in one health plan (but no longer) prevented or discouraged physicians from telling their patients about different kinds of treatments.[14] Under managed care, diagnosis, informed consent, and treatment are to be done in the allotted ten or fifteen minutes for an office appointment.

Elements of an Informed Consent Action

A patient suing under the theory of informed consent is obliged to allege and prove (1) defendant physician failed to inform him adequately of a material risk before securing his consent to the proposed treatment, (2) if he had been informed of the risks he would not have consented to the treatment, and (3) the adverse consequences that were not made known did in fact occur and he was injured as a result of undergoing the treatment. As informed consent is a negligence—not intentional—tort action, proof of damages is necessary. A complaint of battery, on the other hand, may be based solely on an insult to bodily integrity.

The concept of informed consent provides a cause of action in cases of unsuccessful or poor outcome even though consent to the procedure has been given and even though negligence in treatment cannot be established. The Oklahoma Supreme Court put it thus, "this requirement, labeled 'informed consent,' is, legally speaking, as essential as a physician's care and skill in the *performance* of the therapy" (emphasis by court).[15] Moreover, as a legal strategy, a plaintiff by expanding the issues in litigation can expand the scope of discovery or the opportunity to employ experts.

Initially the lack of an informed consent—like lack of consent to a procedure—was deemed a battery, but gradually the various state courts held it constituted negligence (malpractice). The medical profession in Texas persuaded the state legislature to enact legislation to that effect.[16] One by one, the various states by court decision or statute have deemed lack of an informed consent to constitute negligence, not battery, but a number of recent decisions have again called it battery.[17] Under negligence any judgment would fall under the practitioner's liability policy. On the other hand, insurance policies do not afford protection against judgments for intentional wrongs like battery. Moreover, judgments attributable to intentional wrongs are also not discharged in bankruptcy.[18] Punitive damages are usually awarded in the case of an intentional tort.

Viewing the failure to provide information for an informed consent as a negligence case, negligence rules would seem to apply. That means not only that there would be insurance coverage but also that the standard for disclosure would be the standard prevailing in the relevant medical community. It being an action in malpractice, the complainant would have to present expert testimony about the risks or alternatives of the treatment. A traditional professional standard would focus on what physicians usually tell patients about a procedure under the same or similar circumstances—a matter of medical judgment—but many jurisdictions have changed the test from what the reasonable physician would disclose to what the reasonable patient would like to know.[19]

Tardive Dyskinesia

The timing of information about the risk of tardive dyskinesia in the use of neuroleptic medication is controversial, as that side effect is not a result of acute treatment, and many clinicians feel that discussion about a possibly permanent side effect at the initiation of treatment could deter initiation of a needed intervention. Dr. Jerrold G. Bernstein advised in his widely used book on drug therapy, "Since tardive dyskinesia does not occur early in the course of antipsychotic treatment, it is probably not appropriate to discuss this complication at the outset of treatment;

discussion of this potential complication can be reserved until later in the treatment, after the patient recovers from the acute manifestations of psychosis, and the physician has decided on a course of treatment which may involved a more prolonged period of administration of the neuroleptic."[20] Likewise, Dr. Frank J. Ayd advised that in the initial stages of neuroleptic therapy, especially when it is reasonable to assume that neuroleptic administration will be of short duration, the risk of TD need not be stressed because all the available data (with the exception of one report) on the time of onset substantiate that it rarely appears until after three months of neuroleptic therapy, the risk increasing steadily thereafter.[21] However, since patients may change physicians, it is important to have the patient's neuroleptic drug history. Many chronic patients are transient and may have been taking neuroleptics for some time that were prescribed by a number of physicians. In determining causation, the law is interested more in the straw that broke the camel's back than in all the straws already piled on its back. Arguably, it may be said that the last straw was not the proximate cause, but that is a jury question.

Informed Consent as Ploy

How often is the doctrine of informed consent used as a ploy in litigation to rationalize a desired outcome? Most of the time? A great deal of the time? Some of the time? A survey of cases would indicate that the answer is most or a great deal of the time. So, as far as the law is concerned, what is the significance of research on informed consent that has been funded by millions of dollars—yes, millions of dollars—by various foundations? The publication of articles and books on the topic continues without end in sight.[22]

Social scientists tend to take the law at face value, but as far as the law is concerned, the doctrine of informed consent is very much a ploy, so research on it might just as well be on abracadabra. As historian A. J. P. Taylor said of one research project, "It is 90 percent true and 100 percent useless." In the literature, the tactical use of the concept in litigation is rarely mentioned. Its significance as an ethical concern is another matter.

As a legal matter, as we have noted, the liability arising out of a treatment where consent is lacking can rest on one of two theories: battery or negligence. Typically, an action based on battery occurs where the physician performs a particular treatment for which consent was not obtained. An example is the case where a surgeon removed a fibroid tumor in circumstances where the patient had consented to an abdominal examination under anesthesia, but had specifically requested "no operation." "The wrong complained of," the court said in the oft-cited decision in *Schloendorff v. Society of New York Hospital*,[23] "is not merely negligence. It is trespass."

When consent is given for a particular treatment but injury results due to an undisclosed risk, the theory in such a case is usually negligence. An example is where vertebrae were broken during electroshock treatment. The latter type of case falls under the doctrine of informed consent that developed since the 1970s. In either case, the elements of consent include the competence of the patient and the voluntariness of the consent. Information about the risk is the additional element under the doctrine of informed consent.

Trying to measure up to the terms of informed consent, and seeking to avoid liability, medical practitioners encumber their practices with forms as they go through the ritual of providing information. Taking the informed consent doctrine literally, and seeking to avoid liability, the medical practitioner resorts to wordy ritualistic disclosures (which patients rarely read or understand).

The concept of informed consent was essentially developed at law to provide another cause of action in cases of poor outcome when negligence in treatment could not be established. In a case of lack of informed consent, as in a case alleging battery, the fact that the treatment was properly performed is immaterial. And it is always a can of worms whether the elements of informed consent are satisfied.[24]

At other times the doctrine of informed consent is used as a way to bar or express condemnation of a procedure. To this end it has been used against electroshock therapy or psychosurgery. The psychosurgery case in 1973 at Detroit's Lafayette Clinic is illustrative. At a conference at the clinic, chaired by Dr. Elliot Luby and myself, the subject of the experiment, Louis Smith (then known as John Doe), was interviewed in the presence of a group of approximately thirty persons, including psychiatrists, a judge, and some staff members of the clinic. While some expressed doubt about the merit of the experiment, they all agreed that there was a valid consent. Smith had above average intelligence with the ability to communicate better than most university students. He was at the time an inmate at the Ionia state facility for sex offenders, but with repeal of Michigan's sexual psychopath law, he would be released in a few months, irrespective of the experiment. Smith sought the experiment, he said, in order to control outbursts of aggression.[25]

Without consulting Smith, Michigan Legal Services lawyer Gabe Kaimowitz, representing himself and certain individual members of the Medical Committee for Human Rights, filed a taxpayers' suit to halt the state-funded experiment. A panel of three judges in Wayne County Circuit Court listened to three weeks of testimony. In a 41-page opinion, Judge Horace Gilmore, writing the opinion, ruled that an involuntarily confined individual cannot give a legitimate consent as he is living in "an inherently coercive atmosphere." The court would allow a prisoner to consent only to low-risk, high-benefit procedures. Nothing was said about Smith's pending discharge.[26]

Several years later, upon Judge Gilmore's retirement from the bench, he said in an interview in the *Detroit News*, "I could control your violent behavior, too, by just removing all of your brain. What they wanted to do just wasn't right."[27] It was clear that he opposed psychosurgery to control violence. The doctrine of consent gave a rationale for the decision to bar it. It served as a ploy.

Product Advertising

Prescription drugs (with the exception of oral contraceptives) have long been recognized as an exception to the rule in product liability law that generally mandates that the manufacturer of a product directly warn foreseeable users of known dangers inherent in the product's use. Under the traditional *learned intermediary* doctrine the physician and not the manufacturer of a prescription drug has the duty to inform the patient of the drug's risks and benefits, on the theory that the physician is in the best position to evaluate the patient's needs. Nowadays, however, direct advertising to consumers by pharmaceutical companies arguably negates the learned intermediary doctrine.[28] By advertising in the media, the companies seek to persuade the public to use their product or to alert them to a new development.[29]

Concerning one's health, people tend to be more emotional than rational and they often urge their physician to carry out a procedure or prescribe a medication. A patient, for example, may want an antibiotic simply for a sore throat and will be angry unless given it. Physicians aim to please and are often in a quandary as to whether they should disabuse patients of a treatment they seek. It is said that, at the very least, direct-to-consumer pharmaceutical advertising has injected an element of skepticism into psychotherapy. The therapist must evaluate that the patient's narrative is indeed the patient's narrative and not ad copy.

Pharmaceutical makers are not required to submit commercials to the Food and Drug Administration, although many do so voluntarily. The director of the FDA's drug marketing division reports that probably the most common problem is a lack of balance—the presentation of the risk information is not commensurate with the benefits information.[30]

Then, too, medical information is found on the Internet. Some physicians now say that one-third of their patients get health information online, and they complain of the added time these patients often require because of their online-inspired questions and preconceptions. Patients turning to the Internet come to their physician's office with printouts from Web sites detailing the latest drug or medical technology. Physicians must wade through stacks of downloaded data full of irrelevant information and bizarre cures, and must defend their expert opinions against tales derived from the Internet. Also, patients put additional demands on physicians' time with questions sent by e-mail. Physicians who do not respond are likely to lose those patients to physicians who are more accommodating.[31]

The Placebo Prescription

What about a placebo? A *placebo*, Latin for "I shall please," is typically a sham treatment that a physician uses merely to please or placate anxious or persistent patients. The placebo looks like an active drug but, unknown to the patient, it has no pharmacological properties of its own. Until fairly recently, nearly all of medicine was based on placebo because physicians had little effective medicine to offer. Placebos are "lies that heal," as Dr. Anne Harrington, a historian of science at Harvard University, puts it.[32] Much of this sort of improvement can be attributed to spontaneous remission of an illness or to the fact that some people would have gotten better anyway. Of course, the ethics of informed consent would require a physician to tell the patient what he was giving him, but that would undercut the placebo effect.[33] In a wry comment, philosophy professor Gerald Dworkin says, "If placebos are to be prescribed and the patient's confidence enhanced, we need to have a range of names for these inert substances. I suggest the following: Prevaricaine, Fibusef, Deceptement."[34]

Psychiatry, like the rest of medicine, is no stranger to placebo cures and to the efficacy of strongly held belief systems in relieving all sorts of distress. One in three adults in the United States uses complementary therapies, like chiropractic, acupuncture, homeopathy, herbs, and folk remedies. More than half the country's medical schools now offer courses in alternative medical practices, and patients are looking for physicians familiar with complementary as well as mainstream medicine. In many cases the wisdom of it may be questionable. The late Carl Sagan warned against pacifying a public that is poorly schooled in scientific principles.

Those suffering real illnesses need to know how to tell an effective remedy from a gimmick that catches the public imagination.[35]

Assurances about Treatment

The doctrine of informed consent calls for information about expected outcome, which, in some cases, may seem like an assurance. At times, assurances are made to alleviate anxiety or encourage the undertaking of treatment. Suppose the patient says to the physician, "You've told me about risks, but what I want to know is, how will it come out?" In the event of what is considered an assurance, there may result a contractual action for breach of warranty. One court put it thus: "Generally, a physician undertakes only to utilize his best skill and judgment. When he negligently fails to do so he may have committed a tort. However, a physician may, by express contract, agree to effect a cure or warrant that a particular result will be obtained. In such instances an action in contract may lie against a physician."[36]

Thus, a plastic surgeon was held liable for breach of contract by telling a patient that he would give her "a nose like Hedy Lamarr's."[37] In another case the court held that the statement that electroconvulsive therapy is "perfectly safe" might properly be found to be a warranty, and hence summary judgment was not granted.[38] The prescriptive period in a contract action is usually five years, while a tort action is usually barred after one year for intentional wrongdoing, two years for malpractice, and three years for ordinary negligence. Various states have enacted legislation that requires "an agreement, promise, contract, or warranty of cure relating to medical care or treatment" to be in a signed writing.[39]

Disclosure of Risks of Nontreatment

In the event a patient refuses treatment, it is to be noted there comes into play the concept of *informed refusal*, according to which the physician is obliged to inform the patient of the significant risks of inaction. Thus, in *Truman v. Thomas*,[40] where a patient declined to take a pap test, the physician was held liable for failing to warn her of the risks involved in declining to take it. The patient died from cancer of the cervix. Had the patient undergone a pap smear at the time recommended, the cervical tumor probably would have been discovered in time to save her life. She had said she could not afford the cost of the test—the physician offered to defer payment but she wanted to pay cash, and on another occasion she said "she just didn't feel like it."

To be material, a risk must be one that is not commonly appreciated. In *Truman*, there was no evidence to suggest that the patient was less than competent. The physician claimed that the risk of not undergoing a pap smear would be known to a reasonable person. He also argued that a patient who rejects a physician's advice has the burden of inquiring as to the consequences of this decision. The court said it was for the jury to decide whether it was reasonable for the physician to assume that the patient appreciated the potentially fatal consequences of her conduct.

The question has been asked: Should a physician, to avoid *Truman*-type liability, conjure up horrors as vividly as possible in order to persuade the patient? Must the physician do a hard sell in order to avoid the application of the *Truman* rule, manipulating information in order to get the patient to do what the physician thinks is best therapeutically? Assuredly, that practice would work against patient autonomy, the goal of informed consent.

Disclosure of Physician's Conflict of Interest

Beginning in the early 1900s, plaintiffs began to seek an expansion of the disclosure obligations of physicians beyond providing information about a proposed treatment. In one group of cases, patients have contended that physicians have an obligation to disclose any personal interests that may affect their professional judgment. Patients have alleged that the physician denied necessary care as a result of a managed care incentive compensation system and that the physician had an obligation to disclose it. In another group of cases, patients have claimed that physicians were obligated to inform them about risks arising out of the personal characteristics of the physician.

The courts have held that the concept of informed consent is broad enough to encompass a physician's research or financial interest, as it might affect the physician's professional judgment. The California Supreme Court put it thus: "[W]e hold that a physician who is seeking a patient's consent for a medical procedure must, in order to satisfy his fiduciary duty and to obtain the patient's informed consent, disclose personal interests unrelated to the patient's health, whether research or economic, that may affect his medical judgment."[41] Under managed care the physician is burdened with a conflict of obligations: an obligation to the patient, and an obligation to the health plan. Presumably, the financial arrangements between the health plan and the physician should be disclosed.[42] Under managed care plans, the less the physician does, the more money he makes.

What about the ethics of gifts by pharmaceutical companies to physicians, or the trips and dinners provided by the companies? After all, as was said in the classic satirical novel *Don Quixote* (1605–1615) by Miguel de Cervantes Saavedra (1547–1616) "gifts break rocks." They have an influence, at least unconsciously. Observant patients may see the various objects in the physician's office—pens, clocks, books, stationery, briefcases—all emblazoned with the name of a pharmaceutical company. One patient asked the physician, "Are you in the pocket of the company?" Yet another observed, "My psychopharmacologist has a Lucite Prozac clock, Prozac pen set and Prozac stationery in his office."[43]

Disclosure of Skill or Status Risks

Most risks that must be disclosed relate to the therapy or procedure, but some courts have required disclosure of risks relating to the physician and the physician's capacity to perform. Like an accordion, the doctrine of informed consent can be contracted or expanded to fit the needs of the moment. The experience and success rate of the physician are relevant, not to the decision to accept treatment, but to the decision to accept it at the hands of a particular physician. In 1986 the Federal Government established a National Practitioner Data Bank listing malpractice decisions and disciplinary actions, but contrary to expectations, the data is not available to patients. Hospitals, licensing agencies, and other medical groups are given access to the data, and, to protect patients, they are expected to use it in the providing of health care.[44] Under Medical Practice Acts physicians have an obligation to report an impaired colleague.

Increasingly nowadays various publications list the best doctors of various specialties in a community. A nearly full-page advertisement in the *New York Times* said about a medical guidebook: "Don't leave one of the most important decisions in your life to chance. With this guide in hand, you're on your way to finding the very best doctor where you live and work."[45] Needless to say, it omits many fine doctors and includes many who are merely well-known. The medical profession itself is increasingly studying and sometimes publishing outcome records. In a respected treatise on health law, it is stated: "Informed consent doctrine can encompass the requirement that a physician disclose differential success rates, forcing physicians to present their 'batting averages.'"[46]

Patients normally expect that physicians acting within the ambit of their professional work will exercise the skill, knowledge, and care normally possessed and exercised by other members of their profession of the same school of practice in the relevant medical community. Similarly, physicians implicitly undertake to meet at least such a standard of care. As long as the physician measures up to the standard of care in carrying out a treatment, what more is relevant? If more is required, what would (or should) physicians reveal about themselves to a patient? What compromises their ability to treat a patient? Must they disclose that they have just had a quarrel with their spouse? Must they disclose that they engage in high-risk adventures (like mountain climbing) that may result in injury and make them unavailable to continue therapy for possibly a lengthy time? That they have a heart condition? Or that they engage in forensic consultations and may have to interrupt therapy from time to time? More seriously, must a physician reveal that he has AIDS or has a history of alcoholism? Does it present a risk to patients? Where is the line to be drawn between a patient's right to know and a physician's right to privacy about his own health?

In a New Jersey case, the hospital informed patients that the physician, a plastic surgeon, had AIDS. The physician was also a patient at the hospital. He brought suit against the hospital, claiming invasion of privacy and breach of confidentiality. As a result of the disclosure, his practice declined. He argued: (1) the risk of transmission of HIV from surgeon to patient is too remote to require informed consent, and (2) the law of informed consent does not require disclosure of the condition of the physician. The court ruled that the hospital had not only the right but the duty to disclose.[47] It said: "It is axiomatic that physicians performing invasive procedures should not knowingly place a patient at risk because of the physician's physical condition."[48] While recognizing that the risk of transmission of the virus from a provider to patient is low, the court saw other risks, such as the risk of extended uncertainty and testing for a patient exposed to a surgical accident involving a surgeon with AIDS.[49]

The Maryland Supreme Court has also held that a physician who has tested HIV-positive must disclose that fact to the patient before performing an invasive procedure.[50] Arguably, the risk of AIDS may be the basis for an emotional distress claim.[51] The courts that require a physical injury resulting from the tort as a basis for emotional harm recovery may dismiss the case on the ground that no physical injury (or manifestation or objective symptom) has been shown. In such a jurisdiction, the patient exposed to carcinogens may possibly be able to show some actual physical changes at the cellular level, even though those changes are not presently causing any symptoms. In that event, the court could conceivably regard the fear of future harm as parasitic to a claim for physical harm.[52]

A physician's failure to disclose his chronic alcohol abuse was held in a Louisiana case, *Hidding v. Williams*,[53] to have vitiated the patient's consent to surgery. There was a poor outcome, but the report of the case does not indicate that the physician was under the influence of alcohol at the time of surgery, or that his hands trembled, or that the care fell below acceptable standards. Nonetheless the Louisiana Court of Appeals said: "Because this condition creates a material risk associated with the surgeon's ability to perform, which if disclosed would have obliged the patient to have elected another course of treatment, the fact-finder's conclusion that non-disclosure is a violation of the informed consent doctrine is entirely correct."[54]

During the course of the trial a member of a medical review panel, asked whether a doctor suffering from alcohol or drug dependency has an affirmative obligation to relay this to the patient, answered: "I certainly think that if a physician or anybody in a position of life and death over someone knows that they're suffering from this condition, they should at least let this person know that they have these problems."[55]

In contrast, the Arizona Court of Appeals declined to allow evidence as to alcoholism of an anesthesiologist as a separate claim of negligence, absent a showing that he was intoxicated or impaired at the time of the surgery.[56] The plaintiff argued that alcoholism necessarily diminishes a physician's capacity to render the proper standard of care. The plaintiff cited legislation regulating the medical profession wherein unprofessional conduct is defined to include habitual intemperance in the use of alcohol. The court recognized that an alcoholic doctor might present a danger to the public if allowed to continue to practice medicine, but that, it said, is a matter for the medical board in deciding whether to revoke a license to practice. In a tort case, on the other hand, the court said, the issue is whether the physician exercised the proper standard of care in treating a particular patient at a particular time.[57]

What about a physician in his senior years who is aware that his skills are diminishing? His success rate is dropping. Should or must he disclose to his patients that he is beginning to suffer the inevitable results of aging? Or that his success rate is declining and is a certain percentage? Institutional peer review is designed to restrict a physician's practice to those procedures he is competent to perform. Hospitals, too, are supposed to screen their staff to reduce the level of risk to their patients, defining risk by a competency/quality definition.

In a Wisconsin case,[58] the plaintiff sued her physician for failure to inform her that he had very little experience in performing an operation on an aneurysm. As result of the physician's inexperience, the plaintiff alleged she was rendered a quadriplegic. It was discovered that the physician had never performed surgery on a large basilar bifurcation aneurysm such as the plaintiff's. The Wisconsin Supreme Court stated that the duty to disclose information that is "material" to a patient's decision must be decided on a case-by-case basis.[59] A bright-line rule that a physician must always give his qualifications to every patient would be impossible, the court said. The court held that in this particular case, the plaintiff introduced enough evidence that had a reasonable patient in her position been made aware that the physician lacked experience with this surgery, it likely would not have been undergone with him. "A reasonable person in the plaintiff's position would have considered such information material in making an intelligent and informed decision about the surgery."[60]

The Washington Court of Appeals has held that a surgeon's duty to obtain informed consent did not require him to disclose his lack of experience in performing a particular surgical procedure.[61] In this case, the plaintiff needed to have her gallbladder removed. The plaintiff's physician had never performed a gallbladder removal at the time he obtained the plaintiff's consent. The surgery was delayed, however, and during the delay, the physician performed a gallbladder removal on two patients. During the plaintiff's surgery, the physician misidentified and damaged her bile duct and, as a result, she suffered numerous complications after the surgery.

The Washington Court of Appeals stated that the duty to disclose material facts include only those facts that relate to the proposed treatment. The court declined to follow the recent number of cases applying a broader construction of *material fact*. Applying the traditional approach, the court held that a physician's lack of experience in performing a surgical procedure is not a material fact for purposes of finding liability predicated on failure to secure an informed consent.[62]

The consensus that a physician does not have to disclose his experience or qualifications to a patient apparently has a major exception. In a situation involving high-risk treatment, such as brain surgery, a patient's right to know the doctor's experience becomes more important than a physician's right to privacy.[63] Although this rule is not a bright-line rule, it does set forth a guideline that physicians should follow. In routine, low-risk procedures, a physician does not have a duty to disclose that they are not experienced with the particular procedure. Yet, in situations where experience may determine life or death, the issue of the doctor's experience is critical. Quite likely, in these high-risk situations, the physician has a duty to disclose the fact that he has not performed the procedure or has less experience than someone else who could perform the procedure. The physician should ask himself, "Would I want to know this information if I were the patient?" If the answer is "yes," it seems logical that the physician should disclose the information. The diplomas and citations on the walls of the physician's office as well as the age of the physician would, in some measure, indicate the experience and competency of the physician. Often, hospital patients are unaware that they are being treated by a medical student or resident rather than a fully trained physician.

According to a report of the National Conference of State Legislatures, at least eleven states have enacted laws to make physician profiles available to the public. Physicians have managed to keep similar laws from being passed in eight other states. In 1996, Massachusetts became the first state to publish physician malpractice histories and hospital disciplinary records on the Internet. Under the Physician Profile Act, the state now provides information on a physician's number of malpractice suits and settlements, warnings by the medical board, and hospital disciplinary measures. The Ohio State Medical Board Web site currently lists about 32,000 physicians' ages, educations, medical specialities, official reprimands, and license suspensions and revocations. Proposed legislation would add the following physician information to the site: malpractice settlements and awards, felony and some misdemeanor convictions, and any restrictions on hospital admitting privileges.[64] Of course, information about a physician or hospital may be useless if the patient does not have the freedom to choose a physician or hospital.

Causation Complexities

In litigation, it must be shown that if the physician had made proper disclosure, a reasonable patient would have declined treatment. The patient must prove causation, namely, that a reasonable patient would not have consented to treatment had the information been disclosed.[65] A cause of action predicated on the lack of informed consent requires that the patient's injury be the direct and proximate cause of the treatment. This element of proof is difficult when an injury is not immediately identifiable as the direct consequence of the treatment. In a casebook on law and the mental health system, this point is illustrated by the following hypothetical fact situation:

> A patient feels that she is not advancing in her job as her intellectual potential might dictate due to excessive passivity and an inability to direct subordinates. On the therapist's recommendation, the patient agrees to undergo assertiveness training, but is not informed that such training may alter personal relationships. The training is successful to the extent that the patient has become more assertive and better able to cope in the work place; however, her husband is unable to adjust to her new and more assertive personality and tensions in the marriage cause it to break up. Theoretically, the patient could assert that she would not have consented to the therapy had she been informed of the risks. In this situation the patient faces the significant difficulty of proving both that the psychotherapy in fact led to the personality change and that this was the proximate cause of the failure of her marriage.[66]

The patient must also prove that the omitted risk materialized and constituted the injury that could have been avoided by an alternative treatment or no treatment. Certainly, an alcoholic surgeon may have an impairment that might seriously affect performance, and thus the success rate. As law professor Barry Furrow put it: "The statistical probability that an alcoholic may be impaired more often than a non-alcoholic physician of the same skill and training suggests patients face enhanced risks."[67]

In *Hidding*, the Louisiana Court of Appeals held that failure to disclose a history of alcohol abuse violated the informed consent requirement and constituted fault, but what about the question of causation, since alcoholism may not always impair a physician's performance? Is a plaintiff entitled to argue that he would have escaped injury if the defendant had not treated him at all? Is the defendant entitled to argue that the plaintiff may get an award only if he received treatment inferior to that provided by other physicians?[68]

In these and in other situations, the law on torts is used to accomplish the task of hospital supervision or of medical boards in regulating the practice of medicine. The Public Citizen Health Research Group has noted that fewer than one-third of the 10,289 physicians disciplined nationwide were kept from practicing medicine, even temporarily. A spokesman for Public Citizen said: "Consumers should be able to find out if their doctors have a black mark on their records."[69] Yet, worthy as this goal may be, it may undercut programs of treatment of impaired physicians.[70]

Contributory Negligence of Patient

What about contributory negligence of a patient in failing to request or obtain information? Is informed consent one-way or two-way? What are the responsibilities, if any, of the patient in obtaining information?[71] Might not the patient pose questions when details about a proposed treatment are unclear? Customarily, patients are asked whether they have any questions about the treatment, or what they might expect of the treatment. If patients were to have a duty, would it be objective or subjective? Who is the reasonably prudent patient? One unsophisticated man beginning psychotherapy thought that he would lie down on a couch and a hot towel would be put around his head.

Ordinarily, contributory negligence is a defense to an action based on negligence, whereas it is not responsive to an action in battery or other intentional wrongdoing. When an individual is attacked intentionally, it is no defense that the individual did not get out of the way. Contrary to theory, however, although the action based on lack of informed consent is negligence, the courts impose no duty on a patient to ask questions or otherwise obtain information about a proposed treatment. Almost without exception the courts are uniform in so holding. Hawaii said that it is "unfair and illogical" to impose an affirmative duty on a patient to make an inquiry or otherwise affirmatively act with respect to informed consent.[72] Dr. Jerome Groopman of Harvard Medical School observes that patients who think that a physician possesses a near-divine capacity for healing cause problems for the physician—the patient may assume that the physician knows everything, and the patient, or the family, does not offer information that can be vital to a correct diagnosis or treatment.[73]

That view is sustained by the jurisprudence. In *Brown v. Dibbell*,[74] the Wisconsin Court of Appeals observed that the informed consent doctrine speaks "solely in terms of the *doctor*'s duty to disclose and discuss information related to treatment and risks" (emphasis by court). The court said:

> [The doctrine] does not intimate, let alone place upon a patient an affirmative duty to investigate, question, or seek quantification of the information provided by the doctor. Rather, the entire gravamen of the informed consent [doctrine] is that a patient is not in a position to know treatment options and risks and, standing alone and unaided is unable to make an informed choice. The doctor, who possesses medical knowledge and skills, has the affirmative burden both to comprehend what a reasonable patient in a similar situation would want to know and to provide the relevant information. Moreover, while every individual has a duty of ordinary care for their own person, the underpinning of the contributory negligence defense, we perceive defining the dimensions of a patient's duty in an informed consent case to be a virtually impossible task. What degree of knowledge or insight can be demanded of one whom the law recognizes as unqualified to make decisions involving the complexities of medical science without assistance? The concept that a patient can be contributorily negligent, for example, by not asking enough or precisely proper questions, seems contrary to the [doctrinal] scheme and the reason for placing the burden on the doctor.[75]

Some years ago the Washington Supreme Court, quoting from a decision from North Dakota, said:

> On the question of contributory negligence, in such cases as the one at bar, it is the law that "It is not a part of the duties of a patient to distrust his physician, or to set his judgment against that of the expert whom he has employed to treat him, or to appeal to other physicians to ascertain if the physician is performing his duty properly. The very relation assumes trust and confidence on the part of the patient in the capacity and skill of the physician; and it would indeed require an unusual state of facts to render a person who is possessed of no medical skill guilty of contributory negligence because he accepts the word of his physician and trusts in the efficacy of the treatment prescribed by him. A patient has the right to rely on the professional skill of his physician, without calling others in to determine whether he really possesses such skill or not. The patient is not bound to call in other physicians, unless he becomes fully aware that the physician has not been, and is not giving proper treatment."[76]

In *Dibbell*, on appeal from the Wisconsin Court of Appeals, the Wisconsin Supreme Court took a unique tack. It agreed with the defendant that a doctor's duty to inform a patient does not obviate a patient's duty to exercise ordinary care for his own health and well-being; rather, a doctor and a patient have a joint responsibility to ensure that informed consent is obtained.[77] The Wisconsin Supreme Court said,

> [P]atients have a duty to exercise ordinary care for their own health and well-being; that contributory negligence may, under certain circumstances, be a defense in an informed consent action because the action is based on negligence. We thus recognize that a patient bringing an informed consent action is not exempt from the duty to exercise ordinary care for his or her own health and well-being. We also agree, however, with the court of appeals that the very patient-doctor relation assumes trust and confidence on the part of the patient and that would require an unusual set of facts to render a patient guilty of contributory negligence when the patient relies on the doctor.[78]

The court concluded that the trial court in this case should have given the jury an instruction on contributory negligence tailored to the patient's duty to exercise ordinary care in providing complete and accurate information to her doctors in response to their questions concerning personal, family, and medical history.[79] In a footnote, the court cautioned, "We do not address whether a patient's duty to exercise ordinary care requires the patient to volunteer information or to spontaneously advise the doctor of material personal, family or medical histories that the patient reasonably knows should be disclosed."[80]

Would a physician welcome numerous inquiries by a patient? Would it be an annoyance not easily tolerated? Dr. Ira Ockene of the University of Massachusetts Medical Center commented, "Every so often an appropriately assertive patient and family ask all the right questions, and on such occasions I have commented to the house staff that if all patients and families were similar the practice of medicine would grind to a halt."[81] Time pressures do not permit it. "This inadequacy of time allotment has been exacerbated by managed care and by the pressures of modern medicine, but existed long before HMO's ever darkened the horizon."[82]

Exceptions to Informed Consent Doctrine

As a defense, a physician may claim one of several exceptions to the informed consent doctrine: emergency, therapeutic privilege, or waiver. As these are affirmative defenses, the physician bears the burden of proof.[83]

Emergency. In an emergency, a physician may render treatment without the patient's expressed consent. The rationale for the exception is that the patient's consent is implied in an emergency, inasmuch as a reasonable person would consent to treatment in an emergency if able to do so. The term *emergency*, however, is not self-defining. At one extreme, an emergency may be said to exist when the patient is injured to the extent of being unconscious. At the other extreme, an emergency is found to exist merely when "suffering or pain would be alleviated" by treatment.[84] Closely related to the emergency exception is the exception for incompetent patients, who in varying circumstances may be treated without their consent.

Therapeutic Privilege. Under what is known as therapeutic privilege a physician may withhold information for therapeutic reasons. The therapeutic privilege is justified where disclosure would complicate or hinder treatment or pose psychological harm to the patient. Few cases turn on its application. Its parameters are uncertain, and it is difficult to justify in operational terms. It cannot be used with third-party authorizers such as guardians.[85] The doctrine appears to be on the wane. At the same time, it is recognized that a patient has no duty to know or inquire.

Waiver. The exception of waiver comes into play when the patient specifically requests not to be informed about the risks but only wants the physician's final judgment. "Whatever you think best, doctor," is the attitude of many patients. Waiver may be conceptualized as the opposite of therapeutic privilege. In waiver the patient gives up the right to autonomy; in therapeutic privilege the physician deprives the patient of that right in the interest of the patient's health.[86]

Autonomy is often surrendered to illness. Do patients want decisional autonomy? A number of commentators have noted that patients want to be informed but do not actually want to make their own health care decisions. In the book *The Practice of Autonomy: Patients, Doctors, and Medical Decisions*,[87] law professor Carl Schneider examines the law of bioethics by looking at the lives of patients. He argues that bioethics has reached a point of paradox: Bioethicists increasingly seem to think patients have a duty to make their own medical decisions, but it is increasingly clear, he says, that many patients do not want to do so. He also notes significant evidence that "the more severe a patient's illness, the less likely the patient is to want to make medical decisions." He writes:

> To appreciate the . . . reason patients might reject the leading role in their medical decisions, we should recall the syllogism that lies silent at the

heart of the autonomist paradigm: People want to make all decisions that shape their lives. Few decisions matter more than medicine's life-or-death, sickness-or-health, fit-or-fall choices. Therefore patients want to make their own medical decisions. This syllogism is flawed because some patients conclude they will reach wiser decisions by deferring to the expertise and judgement of someone else. But the syllogism errs in other ways, ways suggested by what Talcott Parsons called the "sick role, with how people feel when they are ill." The autonomy paradigm rests on assumptions about the natural desire of all people to control themselves and their surroundings. These assumptions are overstated even for the population at large. But sick people differ from healthy people, for they often feel frightened, discouraged, dull-witted, abstracted, uninterested, and weary. These feelings, I suggest, may inhibit them from making medical decisions.[88]

In a debate in bioethics circles it is argued that a patient may not waive the right to information on the theory that the doctrine of informed consent is designed to enhance the autonomy of the patient. Therefore, it is argued, a right to waive information would involve a right to avoid one's responsibility to act as an autonomous moral agent.[89] As a practical matter, however, a patient cannot be forced to listen to the risks of a treatment, or be required to read an informed consent form or listen to a video that is used for risk disclosure. The other side of the debate is typified by the position of John Stuart Mill, the renowned proponent of liberty, who would not preclude individuals from acting in ways that would result even in their certain deaths.[90]

What about genetic testing, about which nowadays there is much publicity? Patients need a great deal of education to be able to assess the need for and the consequences of genetic testing. Some patients want to know if they have an increased risk of a disease, but it may be unethical to test for a disease that is not curable, as it would only arouse anxiety. Then there are implications for the patient's family. In the case of a familial gene, there is a good chance that members of the family have the same problem. Informing them may shatter their world, too. And the patient must decide whether to falsify on the myriad forms and applications that ask for divulgence of certain conditions: life and medical insurance policies, job applications, and so on.[91]

Are people ready to confront information derived from genetic testing? The desire of Adam and Eve to become "as gods" precipitated their exile from the Garden of Eden. God gave them a beautiful garden but forbade them to eat of the fruit of knowledge. God knew that they were not developed enough to deal with the knowledge that would be revealed by the fruit. The emphasis on "No," combined with the availability of the forbidden, however, was, in legal terms, a *pernicious temptation*, unfenced and unguarded, provocative by its very obviousness. Likewise, the snakelike configuration of DNA in humans creates a temptation to experiment that could lead to dire or unexpected results. The writer Richard Powers puts it thus: "Humanity's eternal and well-grounded fear is that our wisdom will fail to pace our expertise. Its eternal hope is that our expertise will somehow scare our wisdom into rising to the occasion. With such knowledge, the Bible warns, comes much grief."[92]

Conclusion

The doctrine of informed consent is commonly regarded as a can of worms—the physician can never be sure what information about what risk must be disclosed. The decisions by the courts tend to favor the patient when an untoward consequence results from treatment, even though the treatment measures up to standard of care.

We have come a long way. The Hippocratic oath makes no mention of an obligation of a physician to speak with a patient. Indeed, the only reference to the issue in the Hippocratic corpus advises against conversation:

> Perform ... [these duties] calmly and adroitly, concealing most things from the patient while you are attending to him. Give necessary orders with cheerfulness and serenity, turning his attention away from what is being done to him; sometimes reprove sharply and emphatically, and sometimes comfort with solicitude and attention, revealing nothing of the patient's future or present condition. For many patients through this cause have taken a turn for the worse, I mean by the declaration I have mentioned of what is present, or by a forecast of what is to come.[93]

In ancient Greece the participation of the patient in decision making was considered undesirable, since the physician's primary task was to inspire confidence. In medieval times, discussions between physician and patient were viewed solely as an opportunity for the physician to offer comfort and hope. Medical writing of the time emphasized the need for the physician to be manipulative and even deceitful. In his 1803 work *Medical Ethics,* the English physician Thomas Percival cautioned physicians against providing patients with any negative information:

> A physician should not ... make gloomy prognostications. ... For the physician should be the minister of hope and comfort to the sick; that by such cordials to the drooping spirit, he may smooth the bed of death; revive expiring life; and counteract the depressing influence of those maladies, which rob the philosopher of fortitude and the Christian of consolation.[94]

Nearly half a century later in 1847, the American Medical Association's first code of ethics included Percival's mandate of communicating hope, admonishing the physician to adhere to his "sacred duty ... to avoid all things which have a tendency to discourage the patient and to depress his spirits." Moreover, the AMA explicitly advised against allowing the patient any voice in diagnosis and treatment, indicating that physicians "should ... unite tenderness with firmness, and condescension with authority, [so] as to improve the minds of their patients with gratitude, respect, and confidence."[95] Today, that would likely result in litigation.

Notes

1. The oft-cited case of Mohr v. Williams, 95 Minn. 261, 104 N.W. 12 (1905), is but one of many cases in which the plaintiff's consent was not to the act actually performed. In Bang v. Miller Hospital, 88 N.W.2d 186 (Minn. 1958), it was held to be a jury question whether consent for removal of a prostate gland included consent to cut the plaintiff's spermatic cords.

See A. McCoid, "A Reappraisal of Liability for Unauthorized Medical Treatment," *Minn. L. Rev.* 41 (1957): 381.

2. See Natanson v. Kline, 186 Kan. 393, 350 P.2d 1093 (1960); Mitchell v. Robinson, 334 S.W.2d 11 (Mo. 1960). The term *informed consent* first appeared in Salgo v. Leland Stanford Jr. Univ. Bd. Of Trustees, 154 Cal. App.2d 560, 317 P.2d 170 (1957). See R. R. Faden & T. L. Beauchamp, *A History and Theory of Informed Consent* (New York: Oxford University Press, 1986).

3. In the case of psychotherapy, where there is no bodily contact, there is by definition no cause of action in battery (though there may be a cause of action for intentional infliction of mental distress). The form of trespass to the person known as *battery* involves some physical contact with the complainant. There being no touching in the talking therapies, there is no battery. The question of defense—consent or whatever—arises only when the plaintiff has proved that a presumptive tort has been committed. With the advent of the doctrine of informed consent, an action lies in negligence (malpractice) where the lack of informed consent is the wrongdoing and the poor outcome is the harm for which damages are assessed. See R. Slovenko, "Psychotherapy and Informed Consent: A Search in Judicial Regulation," in W. E. Barton & C. J. Sanborn (eds.), *Law and the Mental Health Professions* (New York: International Universities Press, 1978), pp. 51–70. An action in malpractice requires expert testimony. Jaskoviak v. Gruver, 638 N.W.2d 1 (N.D. 2002).

4. The principle of self-determination includes the right to a death choice, which manifest itself as refusal of life-sustaining or life-saving treatment. Jehovah's Witnesses refuse blood transfusions out of obedience to scripture, which they believe is divinely inspired. Thus, when a Witness admitted in a hospital emergency room after suffering a life-threatening trauma injury explained that his refusal of blood was "between me and Jehovah. . . . I'm willing to take my chances. My faith is that strong. . . . I wish to live, but with no blood transfusions. Now get that straight." The court upheld his refusal. In re Osborne, 294 A.2d 372 (D.C. 1972). The patient was managed successfully without blood.

5. A. Capron, "Informed Consent in Catastrophic Disease Research and Treatment," *U. Pa. L. Rev.* 123 (1974): 340. Slaveholders generally intervened in the health affairs of their slaves, particularly in the case of life-threatening illnesses. While some slaveholders sought the consent of their slaves for certain treatments, others did not. Concealing ailments from the owners was one way that slaves could maintain a degree of control over their bodies.

6. Freud advised against "lengthy preliminary discussions before the beginning of the analytic treatment," but he did recommend that patients should be told of the difficulties and sacrifice that analytic treatment involves so the patient would be deprived "of any right to say later on that he had been inveigled into a treatment whose extent and implications he did not realize." He stated that questions as to the probable duration of a treatment are almost unanswerable since psychoanalysis is always a matter of long periods of time—"of half a year, or whole years—of longer periods than the patient expects." J. Strachey (ed.), *Standard Edition of the Complete Psychological Works of Sigmund Freud* (London: Hogarth Press, 1958), vol. 12, pp. 129–30.

7. Allen Feld, director of continuing education for the False Memory Syndrome Foundation and a retired member of the faculty of the School of Social Work at Marywood University, writes: "The therapist should explain in lay language his or her theoretical orientation and approach to helping, as well as prior experiences with this therapeutic approach and a summary of published outcome studies. It is reasonable for society to expect a therapist to be familiar with the research that supports his or her chosen theoretical orientation and that describes its effectiveness when used with the patient's problems. This process also allows an opportunity to discuss what the therapist perceives to be the risks, side-effect or anxieties that may be common in therapy in general and known to be associated with the chosen therapeutic approach. This is also a suitable time for a therapist to make the patient aware of the emergency procedures available should they become necessary." A. Feld, "More Thoughts on Informed Consent," *FMS Foundation Newsletter,* July/Aug. 2000, vol. 9, no. 4, p. 6. See J. Cannell, J. I. Hudson & H. G. Pope, "Standards for Informed Consent in Recovered Memory," *J. Am. Acad. Psychiatry & Law* 29 (20001): 138. See also R. Slovenko, "'I'm Not a Detective' in 'Revival of Memory,'" in C. H. Cwik & J. L. North (eds.), *Scientific Evidence Review* (Chicago: American Bar Association, 1998), monograph no. 3; P. J. Fink, "The Attack on Psychotherapy," *Clinical Psychiatry News,* Nov. 1998, p. 23. See the discussion in chapter 12, on regulation of psychotherapy.

8. Tunkl v. Regents of University of California, 60 Cal.2d 92, 32 Cal. Rptr. 33, 383 P.2d 441 (1963).

9. P. S. Appelbaum & T. Grisso, "Assessing Patients' Capacities to Consent to Treatment," *New Eng. J. Med.* 319 (1988): 1635. See also J. W. Berg, P. S. Appelbaum, C. W. Lidz, & L. S. Parker, *Informed Consent: Legal Theory and Clinical Practice* (New York: Oxford University Press, 2001); T. G. Gutheil & H. Bursztjn, "Clinicians' Guidelines for Assessing and Presenting Subtle Forms of Patient Incompetence in Legal Settings," *Am. J. Psychiatry* 143 (1986): 1020; R. Macklin, "Some Problems in Gaining Informed Consent for Psychiatric Patients," *Emory L. J.* 31 (1982): 345. Clinicians have long known that sick persons, although appearing to have normal mental capacity, may have difficulty thinking clearly when presented with complex clinical choices. It has been observed that very sick patients might reason in a manner similar to children younger than ten years of age. E. J. Cassell, A. C. Leon, & S. G. Kaufman, "Preliminary Evidence of Impaired Thinking in Sick Patients," *Annals Int. Med.* 134 (June 19, 2001): 1120; L. Tarkan, "Debating Patients' Capacity to Decide," *New York Times,* Oct. 2, 2001, p. D-5. In practice, differing levels of competency are considered depending upon the decision. What happens frequently is when the risk of a treatment is low and the benefit is high and the patient refuses treatment, a somewhat knowledgeable patient may be found incompetent so that consent may be sought from a substitute decision maker and treatment administered despite the patient's refusal. L. Roth, A. Meisel, & C. W. Lidz, "Tests of Competency to Consent to Treatment," *Am. J. Psychiatry* 134 (1977): 279. In Grimes v. Kennedy Krieger Institute, 366 Md. 29, 782 A.2d 807 (2001), the Maryland Court of Appeals questioned whether parents may consent to their child's participating in any nontherapeutic study that is not designed to benefit the child. The opinion has far-reaching consequences and raises questions about a parent's right to consent to medical research.

10. See Gemme v. Goldberg. 626 A.2d 318 (Conn. App. 1993); Holt v. Nelson, 523 P.2d 211 (Wash. App. 1974).

11. Lienhard v. State, 431 N.W.2d 861 (Minn. 1988).

12. See P. R. McHugh, "Psychiatric Misadventures," *American Scholar* 61 (1992): 497; "Psychotherapy Awry," *American Scholar* 63 (1994): 17.

13. See T. H. Boyd, "Cost Containment and the Physician's Fiduciary Duty to the Patient," *DePaul L. Rev.* 39 (1989): 131; D. Orenticher, "Paying Physicians More to Do Less: Financial Incentives to Limit Care," *U. Richmond L. Rev.* 30 (1996): 151; see also R. W. Dworkin, "Why Doctors Are Down," *Commentary,* May 2001, p. 43.

14. The health plan that had a gag rule on treatment alternatives received extensive negative publicity, and it was discredited. The Congress and various states banned it.

15. Scott v. Bradford, 606 P.2d 554, 556–57 (Okla. 1979).

16. Texas Rev. Civil Stat., tit. 71, art. 4950i; see W. J. Curran, "Informed Consent, Texas Style: Disclosure and Non-Disclosure by Regulation," *New Eng. J. Med.,* Mar. 1, 1979: 482.

17. See Hernandez v. Schittek, 305 Ill. App.3d 925, 713 N.E.2d 203 (1999); Dingle v. Belin, 358 Md. 354, 749 A.2d 157 (1999); Duttry v. Patterson, 741 A.2d 199 (Pa. 1999). In Rubino v. Defretias, 638 F.Supp. 182 (D.Ariz. 1986), the court held that the state statute abrogating battery as a basis of an informed consent action is unconstitutional on the ground that the Arizona constitution established a fundamental right to bring an action against a physician based on the common-law theory of battery.

18. Negligence and intentionally torturous behavior are as a factual matter points along a continuum, but legally there is a bright line, with dramatically different consequences. Section 523(a)(6) of the Bankruptcy Code exempts from discharge any debt "for willful and malicious injury by the debtor to another entity or to the property of another entity." A typical malpractice judgement is not a debt for willful and malicious injury.

19. The prudent physician standard is followed in Culberston v. Mermitz, 602 N.E.2d 98 (Ind. 1992). Apart from fault (failure to provide information), the plaintiff patient must also establish causation, to wit, that if he had been informed on the risks he would not have consented to the treatments.

20. J. G. Bernstein, *Handbook of Drug Therapy in Psychiatry* (St. Louis: Mosby, 3d ed. 1995), p. 28.

21. F. J. Ayd, "Ethical and legal Dilemmas Posted by Tardive Dyskinesia," *Int'l Drug Therapy Newsletter* 12 (1977): 29; see R. Slovenko, "Update on Legal Issues Associated with Tardive Dyskinesia," *J. Clin. Psychiatry* 61 (2000): 45 (supp. 4).

22. See "Empirical Research on Informed Consent: An Annotated Bibliography," *Hastings Center Report Special Supplement,* Jan.–Feb. 1999; see also E. R. Saks & S. H. Behnke, "Competency to Decide on Treatment and Research: MacArthur and Beyond," *J. Contemp. Legal Issues* 10 (1999): 103.

23. 105 N.E. 92 (N.Y. 1914).

24. In Australia, a physician was found negligent for not warning a patient of a 1:14,000 risk of sympathetic ophthalmia when operating to restore vision in an affected eye but causing impaired vision in the previously unaffected eye. Rogers v. Whitaker, [1992] 175 CLR 479. Even a speculative risk has been deemed the basis for a successful claim of negligence. In Chapel v. Hart, [1998] 156 A.L.R. 517, a claim of negligence was upheld when an ear, nose, and throat surgeon failed to warn of a risk that was so rare as to be deemed by the court to be speculative in an operation that the court unanimously agreed was performed in a competent and technically satisfactory manner. In his book *The Silent World of Doctor and Patient* (New York: Viking, 1984), Dr. Jay Katz of Yale University called the doctrine "a fairy tale."

25. For this experiment, the principal physician-investigator, whom I had not known previously, asked that I chair an informed consent review committee, which was a separate entity from the medical committee set up to oversee the soundness of the experimental design. As I was dependent on the clinic for teaching and research opportunities, the appointment of two independent outsiders to the committee—a priest (a man of God) and an accountant (a man of commerce)—were welcome additions. A few days after the initial meeting of the consent committee, I advised the principal investigator that litigation was pending in Mississippi in connection with psychosurgery performed on young delinquents apparently without consent. I was told that "we will make sure that there is informed consent available from our patient."

I met individually with Louis Smith on six occasions, each session lasting approximately an hour. In addition, he was interviewed in my seminar on law and psychiatry. On this occasion the group consisted of approximately thirty persons, including some psychiatrists, a judge, and a few staff members from Lafayette Clinic, in particular the principal investigator. Following the interview, after Louis Smith left the seminar room, the atmosphere suggested that those present were highly critical of the value of the experiment. I have never been an advocate of psychosurgery to control behavior. As is customary, the subject or patient did not hear the discussion of his case.

No one can be sure of another's motive, or even of one's own motives. Some of the group believed his desire "to do something useful, to atone for my guilt" was a motivating force in his volunteering for the experiment. A few others felt that he was volunteering as a means to obtain release. But there was near unanimity of opinion that his prime motivation was fear—fear that he would explode in the free world as he had done seventeen years earlier, when he had strangled a nurse and performed necrophilia. He insisted that he would seek psychosurgery if it were "the only means of helping my physical problem," even if there were other ways to obtain release. He had little faith in his ability to control himself. In a conversation with the director of the State Department of Mental Health I was told the subject had been informed that he would be released in a few months, irrespective of the experiment.

Louis Smith was told of the risks, even of the risk of death. There was, actually, a page-one headline in a local paper, "Surgery May Cure—or Kill—Rapist" (*Detroit Free Press,* Jan. 7, 1973). He was given no promises. To summarize my interviews, I asked him to write his answers to the following questions, which he did:

Q. Would you seek psychosurgery if you were not confined in an institution?

A. Yes, if after testing showed that it would be of help.

Q. Do you believe that psychosurgery is the way to obtain your release from the institution?

A. No, but it would be a step in obtaining my release. It is like any other therapies or program to help a person to function again.

Q. Would you seek psychosurgery if there were other ways to obtain your release?

A. Yes, if psychosurgery were the only means of helping my physical problem after a period of testing.

Q. Would you want legal representation to explore whether or not there are ways to obtain your release without psychosurgery?

A. No, because I feel that [the principal investigator and the director of the State Department of Mental Health] will release me when I have shown I am a capable person.

Q. Are you in favor of newspaper and other publicity surrounding your case?

A. It makes no difference, because if the [principal investigator] thinks that by me stating me views in public will be of help to him and the clinic, so be it.

Smith protested the intervention by Michigan Legal Services lawyer Gabe Kaimowitz, saying to me: "I was in the institution for 17 years and no one showed any concern. Now Kaimowitz speaks out for my 'rights' without even talking to me. The doctors came to the institution, gave me a chance, treated me like a man. I have great faith in [the principal investigator]. He'll check out the best treatment. He'll do the best. I did wrong, and perhaps by this experiment something will be learned to help others. I killed a woman. I can't function as I am. I need some kind of treatment."

Shortly after Kaimowitz filed suit, I received a phone call from Charles Halpern of the Mental Health Law Project in Washington, D.C. At the time I was chairman of the Committee on Legal Approaches to Mental Health of the American Orthopsychiatric Association, which subsequently cosponsored the Mental Health Law Project. Halpern said that he wanted to join forces with Kaimowitz, but Kaimowitz, for reasons known only to him, chose to go it alone.

As I told Halpern, I felt that the experiment could not be tainted due to lack of consent. But, I added, the subject had a great deal of faith in the investigator, the first person in his seventeen years of confinement to show any interest in him, and a strong relationship had developed between them. The development of such a relationship, de facto though not de jure, causes consent not to be really informed. As the informed consent concept has developed at law, "sufficient information must be disclosed to the patient so that he can arrive at an intelligent opinion," but by whom is the information to be given? The crucial factor is not the amount of information, or even the contents, but rather *who* provides it.

Obtaining a statement of alternatives from one experimenter or physician is not the same as obtaining opinions from different parties with whom a relationship has developed. Smith was advised of the alternatives by the principal investigator. Not until that relationship was diluted by other health professionals did his view change. (The United Store Workers Union says that it has been able to reduce the amount of surgery performed on its members by having a second doctor review each recommended operation before it is performed).

De facto, it is neither age nor confinement that puts consent in question. Indeed, Smith, not being under pain or stress, made a more valid consent than does the ordinary ill person who calls upon a doctor. The expectations of a patient and the great dependence on a doctor affect mightily the rationality of decision making. When in distress or pain, one regresses to a childlike state. To put it another way, the child in everyone tends to dominate the personality when one is in great stress or pain. We cannot yet quantitate stress to measure the legality of a consent.

Actually, the consent given by Smith was not before the court. On the first day of trial, the director of the Department of Mental Health withdrew authorization of the experiment because of adverse public reaction to news reports about it. The court, however, stated that the issues raised were of sufficient public importance to be decided in a declaratory decree. No one, except the state attorney general, wanted to let go of the case. All of the participating attorneys contended the trial should be continued in order to establish the rights of institutionalized persons.

A panel of three judges listened to three weeks of testimony. As there were no factual issues to be resolved, the proceedings took on the air of a seminar. In a 41-page opinion drawing heavily from the briefs submitted by the petitioners, the court concluded that an involuntarily confined individual cannot give a legitimate consent as he is living in "an inherently coercive atmosphere." (The court would allow a prisoner to consent only to low-risk, high- benefits procedures.) The decision did not foreclose "the performance of psychosurgery on such persons once the procedure has advanced to a level where its benefits clearly outweigh its risks." Given the current state of knowledge about how the brain works, the court judged that presently the benefits do not outweigh the risk.

Historically, as we have noted, the informed consent doctrine evolved to facilitate proof of cases and the payment of compensation to injured persons, but in the psychosurgery case, the concept was used not to facilitate proof of the complainant's case but to bar a modality of practice. In any event, to take *informed consent* literally is to miss the point. The use of subterfuge, if you will, is as ancient as history itself. Over two thousand years ago the Talmud did away with capital punishment, but it could not do so directly, for the world was unprepared for it. And so the sages of the Talmud devised regulations that had the quality of religious sanction that made it impossible to carry it out. In the case of psychosurgery, there was no rationalization available to the court in its quest to ban psychosurgery in prisons, with the possible exception of the Eighth Amendment prohibition against cruel and unusual punishment.

Informed consent is thus a spurious issue. To apply the time-honored test of consent literally is to expend energy needlessly. Review committees, as they presently look over consent forms, are one example of the waste of time. A more realistic approach would be to provide a subject or patient with different opinions—from different persons over a span of time in which relationships can develop.

Moreover, the information which is disclosed does not now include aftercare. An experimenter sometimes promises a subject that he will receive good care in the event of a poor or harmful outcome. Is he able to make good on that promise? To my knowledge there has been no systematic study of the subjects of failed experiments. Society, having high stakes in research, must pay the cost of unpredictable results. At a minimum there should be a no-fault clinical research insurance plan to provide care for anyone harmed. A guardian *ad experimentem* might be appointed.

26. Kaimowitz v. Department of Mental Health, Cir. Ct. Wayne County, Mich., 2 Prison L. Rptr. 433 (July 10, 1973). For a discussion of the case, see S. I. Shuman, *Psychosurgery and the Medical Control of Violence* (Detroit: Wayne State University Press, 1977). See also J. Pressman, *Last Resort: Psychosurgery and the Limits of Medicine* (Cambridge: Cambridge University Press, 1998).

27. D. Josar, "Judge of 40 Years Never Tires of Career," *Detroit News*, Dec. 29, 1996, p. E-1.

28. See Perez v. Wyeth Laboratories, 734 A.2d 1245 (N.J. 1999); J. O. Castagnera & R. R. Gerner, "The Gradual Enfeeblement of the Learned Intermediary Rule and the Argument in Favor of Abandoning It Entirely," *Tort & Ins. L.J.* 36 (2000): 119; W. J. Thomas, "Direct-to-Consumer Advertising: Catalyst for a Change in the Therapeutic Model in Psychotherapy?" *Conn. L. Rev.* 32 (1999): 209. General warnings like "see your doctor" do not give the consumer a sufficient caveat on the risks of a drug. J. D. Hanson & D. A. Kysar, "Taking Behaviorism Seriously: Some Evidence of Market Manipulation," *Harv. L. Rev.* 112 (1999): 1420.

29. "Pharmaceutical companies are increasingly souping up their advertising for prescription drugs in a style more commonly associated with products sold from open shelves in drugstores and supermarkets." M. Freudenheim, "Influencing Doctor's Orders: Ads Help Sales of Prescription Drugs, but at What Cost?" *New York Times*, Nov. 17, 1998, p. C-1. See also H. W. Jenkins, "Ads That Make Us Well," *Wall Street Journal*, Apr. 11, 2001, p. 19.

30. See G. Winter, "Search for an Easy Solution Fuels an Industry Rooted in Gullibility," *New York Times*, Oct. 29, 2000, p. 1.

31. "Doctors are being pressured," says Dr. Raymond Woosley, chairman of the pharmacology department at Georgetown University. "People are saying, 'I will go to another doctor if I don't get it from you.'" Quoted in S. G. Stolberg, "Want a New Drug? Plenty To Choose From on T.V.," *New York Times*, Jan. 23, 2000, p. WK-5. A 28-page special section, "Health & Medicine," *Wall Street Journal*, Oct. 19, 1998, discusses the impact of health care information available to consumers. One study suggests that only 20 percent of patients who went to a physician asking for a particular prescription did not receive it. W. J. Thomas, "Direct-to-Consumer Pharmaceutical Advertising: Catalyst for a Change in the Therapeutic Model in Psychotherapy?" *Conn. L. Rev.* 32 (2000): 209, 226; see also D. J. Carr & B. H. Bowers, "Recent Developments in Learned Intermediary Doctrine," *The Brief/American Bar Association* 31 (Winter 2002): 5. With panic spreading about anthrax and other ills, physicians reported that they have had to fend off requests for unnecessary medication from patients fearful that any itch or sniffle is a symptom of anthrax. Medicating the worried well is unsound medicine and bad public policy, these physicians said, but what of patients who refuse to be reassured and are so overwrought that they cannot function? See J. Gross, "Doctors Asked to

Treat the Worried-Well," *New York Times,* Oct. 17, 2001, p. B-1. For a defense by a physician of product advertising as leading to a more informed patient, see R. Dolinar, "Doctors Don't Practice Medication by TV Ad" (ltr.), *Wall Street Journal,* Mar. 26, 2002, p. 23.

32. Quoted in S. Blakeslee, "Placebos Prove So Powerful Even Experts Are Surprised," *New York Times,* Oct. 13, 1998, p. D-8.

33. See T. S. Jost, "The Globalization of Health Law: The Case of Permissibility of Placebo-Based Research," *Am. J. Law & Med.* 26 (2000): 175; M. Talbot, "The Placebo Prescription," *New York Times Magazine,* Jan. 9, 2000, p. 34.

34. G. Dworkin, "The Placebo Prescription" (ltr.), *New York Times Magazine,* Jan. 30, 2000, sec. 6, p. 8.

35. An estimated 15 million adults in the U.S. are coupling prescription drugs with herbal remedies or high-dose vitamins—inviting unpredictable interactions. Physicians and patients often do not broach the subject of alternative medicine or herbal supplements, and that could be dangerous. M. Chase, "Patients Need to Keep Their Doctors Informed about Herbal Therapies," *Wall Street Journal,* Nov. 16, 1998, p. B-1. A special issue of the *Journal of the American Medical Association* that was devoted to alternative medicine had its genesis in letters from physicians asking the *Journal* for information on some of the treatments their patients were asking about. D. Grady, "To Aid Doctors, A.M.A. Journal Devotes Entire Issue of Alternative Medicine," *New York Times,* Nov. 11, 1998, p. 21; G. Kolata, "The Herbal Potions that Make Science Sick," *New York Times,* Nov. 15, 1998, p. WK-4.

36. Kozan v. Comstock, 270 F.2d 839, 845 (5th Cir. 1959). See also Clevenger v. Haling, 394 N.E.2d 1119 (Mass. 1979); Guilmet v. Campbell, 385 Mich. 57, 188 N.W.2d 601 (1971); see A. J. Mioler, "The Contractual Liability of Physicians and Surgeons," *Wash. U.L.Q.* 1953: 413; K. Tierney, "Contractual Aspects of Malpractice," *Wayne L. Rev.* 19 (1973): 1457. The Northeastern Health Alliance advertises: "Stop smoking in just 2½ hours. Money back guarantee. Many times more effective than drugs or traditional hypnosis." Advertisement in *Baltimore Sun,* Nov. 15, 1998, p. 5.

37. Sullivan v. O'Connor, 363 Mass. 579, 296 N.E.2d 183 (1973). In a lawsuit that was settled, Julie Andrews claimed that doctors assured her that surgery to remove noncancerous throat nodules would eliminate her vocal problems, but instead she was left with "profound vocal difficulties, including severe hoarseness." Associated Press news release, Sept. 12, 2000.

38. Johnson v. Rodis, 251 F.2d 917 (D.C. 1958).

39. See, e.g., Mich. Comp. Laws 566.132. Quite often a consent form includes a paragraph that no guarantees are made, such as: "I understand that the practice of medicine and surgery is not an exact science and that diagnosis and treatment may involve risks of injury, or even death. I acknowledge that no guarantees have been made to me as to the result of examination or treatment in this hospital."

It may be said that linking payment to outcome creates better incentives for providers, and reassures patients. Lawyers may be paid on a contingency fee basis. The medical profession, however, has shown virtually no interest in such arrangements. Indeed, the American Medical Association flatly condemns outcome-based payments as unethical. The AMA's Code of Medical Ethics 6.01 (1994) provides, "A physician's fee should not be made contingent on the successful outcome of medical treatment. Such arrangements are unethical because they imply that successful outcomes from treatments are guaranteed, thus creating unrealistic expectations of medicine and false promises to consumers." See D. A. Hyman, "Medicine in the New Millennium: A Self-Help Guide for the Perplexed," *Am. J. Law & Med.* 26 (2000): 143.

40. 27 Cal.3d 285, 611 P.2d 902, 165 Cal. Rptr. 308 (1980).

41. Moore v. Regents of the University of California, 51 Cal.3d 120, 131–32, 793 P.2d 479, 485, 271 Cal. Rptr. 146, 152 (1990). But cf. Neade v. Portes, 739 N.E.2d 496 (Ill. 2000). See K. Eichwald & G. Kolata, "When Physicians Double as Businessmen," *New York Times,* Nov. 30, 1999, p. 1; S.G. Stolberg, "Financial Ties in Biomedicine Get Close Look," *New York Times,* Feb. 20, 2000, p. 1. To avoid a conflict of interest, Dr. George Nicklin of the NYU School of Medicine says that he does not own any drug stocks. Address at the annual meeting of the American Academy of Psychoanalysis, "Spirituality and Money," on May 13, 2000, in Chicago.

42. R. D. Alarcon, "Culture and Ethics of Managed Care in the United States," in A. Okasha, J. Arboleda-Florez, & N. Sartorius (eds.), *Ethics, Culture and Psychiatry* (Washington, D.C.: American Psychiatric Press, 2000); E. H. Moreim, "Economic Disclosure and Economic Advocacy: New Duties in the Medical Standard of Care," *J. Legal Med.* 12 (1991): 275.

43. L. Slater, *Prozac Diary* (New York: Random House, 1998), p. 5. Dr. Bruce Leff of John Hopkins University puts it this way, "There is no free lunch." B. Leff, "When Doctors Go for Drug Makers' Gold" (ltr.), *New York Times,* Dec. 30, 2000, p. 30. See also C. Adams, "Doctors on the Run Can 'Dine 'n' Dash' in Style in New Orleans," *Wall Street Journal,* May 14, 2000, p. 1; S. G. Stolberg & J. Gerth, "High-Tech Stealth Being Used to Sway Doctor Prescriptions," *New York Times,* Nov. 16, 2000, p. 1; A. Zuger, "Fever Pitch: Getting Doctors to Prescribe Is Big Business," *New York Times,* Jan. 11, 1999, p. 1. The American Medical Association Council on Ethical and Judicial Affairs developed guidelines entitled "Gifts to Physicians from Industry" which addresses entertainment, gifts, and subsidized Continuing Medical Education (CME) conferences. In sum and substance, if the subsidized gift or activity is of modest value and serves to enhance the educational aspect of a meeting or CME event, it is ethical. One psychiatrist surmises, "Riding the ski train to Winter Park, with a 30-minute presentation given on the train followed by six hours of free skiing, may not pass the AMA's guidelines." C. Zilber, "Pharmaceutical Industry Gifts and Integrity," *Colorado Psychiatry Soc. Newsletter,* Sept. 2000, p. 3. See also Randy Cohen's ethicist column on "Conference Call," *New York Times Magazine,* Sept. 24, 2000, p. 28.

In the light of several highly publicized research-related deaths and injuries, there has come into question the concept of risk in medical trials, leading to a sudden upsurge in lawsuits. Recently some thirteen leading medical journals worldwide warned that money was corrupting medical research, as drug companies increasingly rely on nonacademic research groups to conduct trials, rather than (presumably more independent) scientists connected to universities and hospitals. In the face of all evidence to the contrary, lay people believe that medical research personnel are acting in their best interests. Even when they have been explicitly informed to the contrary, they still believe they are getting the treatment that is best for them, not best for science. Studies show patients believe they will receive a therapeutic benefit from research. The underestimate the risks and overestimate the benefits of medical research. P. Waldmeir, "The Guinea Pigs Demand Justice," *Financial Times,* Oct. 18, 2001, p. 12. Dr. Paul Appelbaum coined the expression *therapeutic misconception* to describe the patient's mistaken belief that every aspect of the research project to which the patient is invited to enroll will benefit him directly. P. Appelbaum et al., "False Hopes and Best Data: Consent to Research and the Therapeutic Misconception," *Hastings Center Report,* Apr. 1987, p. 20. On conflicts of interest in clinical research, see Symposium, *Widener Law Symposium J.* 8 (2001): 1–152.

44. M. Fretag, "Tracing Doctors Who Err," *New York Times,* Nov. 5, 1989, p. E-4. See also F. X. Rockett & R. L. Ruecker, "The Place for Public Documents: On File or Online?" *New York Times,* Mar. 19, 2002, p. D-6.

45. Advertisement of Castle Connoly Guide, "How to Find the Best Doctors," *New York Times,* Oct. 10, 1998, p. 13. See also Survey, "Detroit's Top Docs," *Hour,* Oct. 2000, p. 79.

46. B. R. Furrow et al., *Health Law* (St. Paul, Minn.: West, 2d ed. 2000), p. 317.

47. Behringer Estate v. Princeton Medical Center, 249 N.J. Super. 597, 592 A.2d 1251 (1992).

48. 592 A.2d at 1277–78.

49. 592 A.2d at 1280.

50. Faya v. Almaraz, 329 Md. 435, 620 A.2d 327 (1993).

51. See Marchia v. Long Island R.R. Co., 31 F.3d 1197 (2d Cir. 1994).

52. See Buckley v. Metro-North Commuter R.R., 79 F.3d 1337 (2d Cir. 1996).

53. 578 So.2d 1192 (La. App. 1991).

54. 578 So.2d at 1196.

55. 578 So.2d at 1197. A treatise on health law states: "[T]he fact that alcohol abuse might on some occasions create risks for patients does seem at first glance to mandate disclosure. Disclosure creates the risk that a patient will refuse the physician's care because of the status or the addiction, rather than looking at the particular case and the risks posed. The physician will then be stigmatized on the basis of personal information not previously known, and now used against him. On the other hand, alcoholism might be argued as most similar to other risks that a physician might present to a patient, such as a surgeon's wound infection rates or a loss of ability with age. The principle of informed consent, requiring disclosure of all risks material to a patient's decision, appears elastic enough to include these addiction risks." B. R. Furrow et al., *Health Law* (St. Paul, Minn.: West, 2d ed. 2000), pp. 321–22.

56. Ornelas v. Fry, 151 Ariz. 324, 727 P.2d 8199 (1986).

57. In Reaves v. Bergsrud, 982 P.2d 497 (N.M. App. 1999), the New Mexico Court of Appeals cited the Arizona decision in holding that absent proof that a physician's mental impairment contributed to the plaintiffs injuries, the physician's condition is irrelevant. In this case, during discovery, the plaintiff learned that the physician had bipolar disorder and that his medical license had been temporarily suspended some years earlier when he inappropriately quit his psychiatric care and medication. The physician refused to answer the plaintiff's interrogatories regarding his condition and treatment. The plaintiff did not allege that the physician's mental health was the cause of postoperative problems. In fact, she conceded that "she did not claim that the defendant was impaired during the time of treatment of her." Therefore, the court concluded that the physician's mental status at the time of the plaintiff's treatment was irrelevant to the proceedings. Moreover, the court held that the physician-patient privilege applied, barring discovery of the physician's mental health treatment. However, where relevant, discovery of a litigant's medical history, be it that of a plaintiff or defendant, has been allowed under the patient-litigant exception to testimonial privilege (see the discussion in volume 1, chapter 4, on testimonial privilege). For another holding in accord with the Arizona and New Mexico decisions, see Shamburger v. Behrens, 380 N.W.2d 659 (S.D. 1986).

58. Johnson v. Kokemoor, 545 N.W.2d 495 (Wis. 1996).

59. 545 N.W.2d at 504.

60. 545 N.W.2d at 506. In Duttry v. Patterson, 741 A.2d 199 (Pa. 1999), the Pennsylvania Superior Court said, "We are not implying that surgeons must inform all their patients about their education background and experience, but where such information is sought, the patient deems it very relevant and truthful answers must be given in order to obtain valid consent." See A. D. Twerski & N. B. Cohen, "The Second Revolution in Informed Consent: Comparing Physicians to Each Other," Nw. U.L. Rev. 94 (1999): 1.

61. Whiteside v. Lukson, 947 P.2d 1263 (Wash. App. 1996).

62. 947 P.2d at 1265. A similar holding was handed down in Duttry v. Patterson, 771 A.2d 1255 (Pa. 2001). In this case, the defendant surgeon, prior to surgery for esophageal cancer, allegedly informed the plaintiff that he performed esophageal operations once a month. The plaintiff sued under an informed consent theory, but was denied the opportunity to provide evidence that the defendant had limited surgical experience. The Pennsylvania Supreme Court held that evidence regarding the defendant's prior surgical experience was properly excluded because informed consent concerns a lack of information about the nature of the operation itself, not about the physician's personal capacities. The court noted, "We realize that some of our sister states have expanded the concepts of the doctrine of informed consent so that they require a physician to inform the patient not only of the risks of the procedure itself, but of personal attributes, interests, and experience of the physician." The court considered that the doctrine of informed consent should not be the legal panacea for all damages arising out of any type of malfeasance by a physician or for expanding the doctrine into a catchall theory of recovery, since other causes of action provide avenues for redress to the injured patient. For example, it is conceivable that a physician's lack of expertise in performing an operation would support a plaintiff's case in negligence, or the patient may have a cause of action for misrepresentation when the physician allegedly provides inaccurate information regarding his experience in performing a procedure. 771 A.2d at 1259.

63. See Johnson v. Kokemoor, supra note 58.

64. Representative Tom Bliley, R-Va., chairman of the House Commerce Committee, has introduced legislation to give the public access to the federal databank that tracks records on health care providers. The proposal is modeled after the Massachusetts law that provides patients with profiles of all physicians licensed in the state, including disciplinary actions and malpractice payments. D. Pace, "Bill Seeks to Publicize Malpractice Payments" (Associated Press news release), Detroit News, Aug. 29, 2000, p. 3.

James B. Stewart, author of Blind Eye: How the Medical Establishment Let a Doctor Get Away with Murder (New York: Simon & Schuster, 2000), urged the House Commerce Committee to put the database on the Internet and also add criminal convictions to the reports of malpractice awards and license suspensions. F. Barringer, "Seeking Access to Data on Doctors," New York Times, Sept. 18, 2000, p. 18. See also "Controversy over Plans to Post Malpractice Data on the Internet," Psychiatric Times, Apr. 2000, p. 61; "Congress Considers Public Access to Physician Malpractice Data," Psychiatric News, Apr. 21, 2000, p. 8. Various state bureau of health services list licensing actions regarding health care providers (information listed includes the provider's name, profession, license number, date of birth, address, the nature of the complaint, the licensing action taken and the effective date of the action). Public Citizen (1600 20th St., N.W., Washington, D.C., 20009) has published a three-volume set listing 13,012 "questionable doctors."

65. Cases dealing with informed consent present a special problem in regard to causation. How crucial is testimony by the plaintiff patient in order to hurdle the issue if he testified that he would have not undergone the medical procedure if the defendant physician had informed him of the risk? In Hamilton v. Hardy, 37 Colo. App. 375, 549 P.2d 1099 (1976), the plaintiff patient's failure to testify what she would have done if the physician had informed her of the risk of abnormal blood clotting associated with birth control pills did not defeat her claim. The court said the test is what a reasonable person would have decided if adequately informed. Is that sufficient proof of what the plaintiff would have done? Is the plaintiff's testimony on the issue enough? The courts are reluctant to permit a jury to believe the plaintiff's testimony, and they require that the plaintiff go further and show that a reasonable person would also have refused it. However, in Scott v. Bradford, 606 P.2d 554 (Okla. 1979), the Oklahoma Supreme Court said that a patient need only testify that he would not have undergone the treatment if he had known of the risk. The jury would determine whether the testimony was credible.

66. R. Reisner, C. Slobogin, & A. Rai, *Law and the Mental Health System* (St. Paul, Minn.: West, 1999), p. 255.

67. "Quality Control in Health Care: Developments in the Law of Medical Malpractice," *J. Law, Medicine & Ethics* 21 (1993): 173, 178.

68. In a concurring opinion in *Hidding*, Judge Grisbaum wrote (578 So.2d at 1198):

I agree with the majority and the trial court's analysis . . . that a doctor's failure to inform his patient that he suffers from an alcohol or any other related substance abuse problem constitutes de facto a breach of the "intent" of the informed consent statute. However, it appears that the majority and the trial court went to great lengths in elaborating upon the fact that (1) in this case there was the existence of a material risk which was unknown to the patient and that (2) there was a failure to disclose that risk on the part of the physician and that (3) no doubt this want of disclosure would have led a reasonable patient in the plaintiff's position to reject the medical procedure or at least choose a different course of treatment. However, neither the majority nor the trial court addressed the last and most vital inquiry, which is necessary to prove a breach of the Uniform Consent Statute and that is the question of injury. Both the majority and the trial court seem to imply that, if there is a breach of the informed consent statute and a resulting injury, then (automatically) liability attaches. In other words, a cause-in-fact relationship between failure to disclose and injury appears unnecessary. On this conclusion, I disagree. After reviewing this record in its entirely, I am convinced there was a reasonable factual basis to conclude that [the physician], at the time of the operation in question, was a practicing alcoholic. From this factual scenario, I suggest the gut question proposed is simply this: whether a professed and practicing alcoholic can operate upon any patient without breaching his standard of care. In other words, if there is a resulting injury and the doctor performing the operation is a practicing alcoholic and this alcoholism is not disclosed to the patient prior to the surgery, do we have liability? Given this factual scenario and considering the record in its entirety, I say, "Yes." Ergo, this question must be viewed on a case-by-case basis.

69. C. Stevens, "Bad Doctors Keep Eluding State's Discipline," *Detroit News*, Oct. 20, 1993, p. 1.

70. R. Lowes, "Remedial Education for Physicians," *Medical World News*, Nov. 1993, p. 20.

71. In regard a lawsuit filed against Lenox Hill Hospital by a woman alleging that its mishandling of a lab test led her to have an unnecessary abortion, Dr. Bertrand Bell, distinguished university professor at Albert Einstein College of Medicine at Yeshiva University, writes, "Perhaps the situation would have been different if all patients had the option of routinely reviewing laboratory, X-ray and pathology reports. These reports are frequently not

definitive, and a patient's interpretations can be useful—sometimes critical." Ltr., "Read Your Own Chart," *New York Times,* Oct. 5, 1998, p. 22.

72. See Keomaka v. Zakaib, 8 Haw. App. 518, 532, 811 P.2d 478, 486 (1991).

73. Quoted in G. Niebuhr, "Believer and Skeptic See Spirituality in Medicine," *New York Times,* Nov. 18, 2000, p. 19.

74. 220 Wis.2d 200, 582 N.W.2d 134, 137 (Wis. App. 1998).

75. 582 N.W.2d at 137–38.

76. Kelly v. Carroll, 36 Wash.2d 482, 501, 219 P.2d 79, 90 (1950), quoting from Halverson v. Zimmerman, 60 N.D. 113, 125, 232 N.W. 754, 759 (1930).

77. Brown v. Dibbell, 227 Wis.2d 28, 595 N.W.2d 358 (1999).

78. 595 N.W.2d at 367.

79. 595 N.W.2d at 369.

80. 595 N.W.2d at 369 n. 13. See C. V. Ford, *Lies! Lies!! Lies!!: The Psychology of Deceit* (Washington, D.C.: American Psychiatric Press, 1996); L. Pankratz, *Patients Who Deceive* (Springfield, Ill.: Thomas, 1998). Patients who have a substance use disorder often attempt to hide or legitimize their substance use as part of drug-seeking behavior when they are trying to procure psychoactive pharmaceuticals from health care professionals. Some substance-abusing patients are quite creative and ingenious in their efforts to obtain prescriptions (e.g., faking painful medical illnesses in order to obtain pain medications). See S. D. Wiley, "Deception and Detection in Psychiatric Disorders," *Psychiatric Clinics of North America* 21 (1998): 869.

81. I. S. Ockene, "Why Hospitals Are Getting Dangerous" (ltr.) *Wall Street Journal,* Dec. 9, 1999, p. 27.

82. Ibid. In a consumer guide to hospital stays, *Take This Book to the Hospital with You: A Consumer Guide to Surviving Your Hospital Stay* (New York: St. Martin's Press, 1997), Charles B. Inlander, president of the People's Medical Society of Allentown, Pennsylvania, suggests that patients ask lots of questions. See A. Tang, "Staying on Guard for Medical Errors," *New York Times,* Dec. 5, 1999, p. BU-11.

83. See A. Meisel, "The 'Exceptions' to the Informed Consent Doctrine: Striking a Balance between Competing Values in Medical Decision Making," *Wis. L. Rev.* 1979: 413.

84. Sullivan v. Montgomery, 155 Misc. 448, 279 N.Y.S. 575 (City Ct. 1935).

85. For criticism of therapeutic privilege, see E. G. Patterson, "The Therapeutic Justification of Withholding Medical Information: What You Don't Know Can't Hurt You, or Can It?" *Neb. L. Rev.* 64 (1985): 721; M. Somerville, "Therapeutic Privilege: Variation on the Theme of Informed Consent," *Law, Med. & Health Care* 12 (1984): 4.

86. E. A. Plaut, "The Ethics of Informed Consent: An Overview," *Psychiatry. J. Univ. Ottawa* 14 (1989): 435.

87. New York: Oxford University Press, 1998.

88. P. 48.

89. D. E. Ost, "The 'Right' Not to Know," *J. Med. & Philosophy* 9 (1984): 301.

90. M. Strasser, "Mill and the Right to Remain Uninformed," *J. Med. & Philosophy* 11 (1986): 265.

91. S. C. Gwynne, "Living with Lethal Genes: Some Advice," *Time,* Oct. 12, 1998, p. 89. See Comment, "Father and Mother Know Best: Defining the Liability of Physicians for Inadequate Genetic Counseling," *Yale L.J.* 87 (1978): 1488. See also the debate in G. Laurie, "In Defense of Ignorance: Genetic Information and the Right Not to Know," *European J. Health Law* 6 (1999): 199; M. C. Bottis, "Comment on a View Favoring Ignorance of Genetic Information: Confidentiality, Autonomy, Beneficence and the Right Not to Know," *European J. Health Law* 7 (2000): 173.

92. "Too Many Breakthroughs," *New York Times,* Nov. 19, 1998, p. 31.

93. Hippocrates, *Decorum* 2:297–99, trans. W. H. S. Jones (Cambridge, Mass.: Harvard University Press, 1979).

94. T. Percival, *Medical Ethics* (1803), ed. C. D. Leake (Huntington, N.Y.: Robert E. Krieger, 1975), pp. 31–32.

95. Codes of Ethics of American Medical Association, ch. 1, art. 1, sec. 4 (1847).

8

The Boundary Violation of Undue Familiarity

Boundary violations in psychotherapy involve transgressions that may be sexual or nonsexual in nature. Of these transgressions, the most publicized is the sexual exploitation of a patient, or *undue familiarity* in the language of the American Psychiatric Association. In a boundary violation, one cannot as a rule assess the immediate impact to discern whether harm has occurred, but for the boundary violation of undue familiarity, the inevitability of harm or causality is alleged and assumed.[1]

Questions arise: What is the appropriate recourse—a disciplinary proceeding, a malpractice action, or a criminal prosecution? What fits the offense? Is the psychotherapist unfairly singled out? Special moral principles, we know, apply to people because of the role that they occupy. This is called *role-specific morality*.

Sexual relations between a psychotherapist and patient is compared to incest or rape, upon the observation that the patient's ostensible consent is a result of the phenomenon of transference, or the power imbalance that exists between therapist and patient. Dr. Judd Marmor, a former president of the APA, stated: "[S]uch behavior between a patient and therapist has all the elements of incest at an unconscious level and represents an equivalent dereliction of moral responsibilities."[2] Psychiatrist Nanette Gartrell observed, "These patients end up with the same emotional problems you see in incest victims."[3] Laura Brown, a clinical psychologist, testified at a trial:

> The reason sexual involvement with a patient is so harmful is due to the "parent-child" relationship symbolized by the transference. Were a therapist to be sexual with a client it would be replicating at a symbolic level the situation in which a parent would be sexual with a child. The kinds of harm that can flow from those sorts of violations of trust are very similar.[4]

In a number of speeches and publications, sex therapists William Masters and Virginia Johnson urged that when sexual seduction of a patient can be firmly established by due process, regardless of whether the seduction was initiated by the patient or the therapist, the therapist should be prosecuted for rape.[5]

Sexual relations between psychotherapist and patient is a topic that captures the headlines and is sensationalized. Books and journal articles about the issue, written by both patients and therapists, have proliferated in recent years.[6] A review of four books by therapists, all published in the early months of 1990, appeared in an essay aptly titled "Disturbances in the Field."[7]

In a commentary typical of the genre, a writer of a law review article stated: "Therapist-patient sexual exploitation is a significant social problem. . . . The consequences to victims, who are primarily women, are devastating."[8] Another stated: "The worst misfortune which can befall a vulnerable female psychiatric patient is to superimpose upon her already fragile condition a lascivious psychiatrist and compulsive lecher as a healer."[9] The symptoms usually suffered by patients as a result of the sexual intimacy are said, but not proven at trial, to include a worsening of previously existing psychiatric symptoms, increased difficulty in personal relationships, feelings of guilt, emptiness, and suppressed rage, an inability to trust, and an increased risk of suicide.[10] Some reports have suggested that as many as 1 percent of the patients who become sexually involved with their therapist commit suicide.[11] The studies are not clear on how the patients were located, or whether subsequence is mistaken as consequence. The Latin expression for that kind of reasoning: *post hoc, ergo propter hoc*—after this, therefore because of this.

The reports in the literature have become the basis for legislation or for the justification of large awards in litigation with the number of lawsuits dramatically increasing.[12] In recent years, some twenty-five states have passed legislation making sexual contact between psychotherapist and patient a criminal act (Alaska, Arizona, California, Colorado, Connecticut, Delaware, District of Columbia, Florida, Georgia, Idaho, Iowa, Kansas, Maine, Michigan, Minnesota, Mississippi, New Hampshire, New Mexico, North Dakota, Ohio, South Dakota, Texas, Utah, Washington, Wisconsin). These laws declare that consent is no defense.[13] No less than three states (California, Minnesota, Wisconsin) have enacted statutes requiring a therapist to report a former therapist accused by a patient of sexual exploitation to the appropriate licensing authority, or to inform and enable the patient to report the sexual conduct.[14]

The statutes have been challenged, to no avail, on the ground that they are vague. Colorado's statute defines *sexual contact* as:

> [K]nowingly touching . . . the victim's intimate parts by the actor, or . . . the actor's intimate parts by the victim, or . . . knowingly touching . . . the clothing covering the immediate area of the victim's or actor's intimate

parts if that sexual contact can reasonably be construed as being for the purpose of sexual arousal, gratification, or abuse.[15]

In upholding the constitutionality of the statutory definition, the Colorado Supreme Court noted that the trial court had instructed the jury that the state had to prove beyond a reasonable doubt that the sexual contact was "for the purpose of sexual arousal, gratification, or abuse."[16]

The Minnesota Supreme Court used the same reasoning in upholding the constitutionality of a similar statutory definition of *sexual contact*.[17] However, shortly thereafter, the Minnesota legislature amended its statute to provide a detailed definition, and to include the "touching of the clothing covering the immediate area of the intimate parts."[18] The statutes of Florida and Maine prohibit the specific sexual acts of intercourse, fellatio, cunnilingus, and sodomy, rather than any contact for sexual gratification.[19]

A civil cause of action for sexual exploitation likewise arises regardless of any actual consent of the patient or former patient, and regardless of whether such acts occurred during any treatment, consultation, assessment, interview, or examination. The legislatures of no less than four states have specifically made sexual contact with a patient malpractice per se.[20] The following is an example of language from a complaint: The defendant "mishandled the transference by not terminating treatment when the plaintiff took her clothes off in front of the defendant"; as a result of the ensuing sexual acts the plaintiff suffered "physical pain and suffering, emotional pain and suffering, shame, attempted suicide, and expenses for recovery and rehabilitation."[21]

Assuredly, intimacy with patients does them no good, and it will disillusion them. Frieda Fromm-Reichmann, who was married briefly to her analyst, Erich Fromm, advised therapists, "Don't have sex with your patient. You'll always disappoint them." However, should it be *automatically* assumed that it does *great* harm, as though the patient had actually suffered rape or incest? Should it be *automatically* assumed that the patient is without the capacity to consent? Transference of feelings from the past to the present is not the same as present reality. Transference jargon has beclouded common sense and has gotten juries and judges to accept the existence of transference dementia.

Transference—the unconscious assignment to others of feelings and attitudes that were originally associated with important figures in one's early life—is a universal phenomenon occurring in every aspect of one's daily life. In psychoanalytic or insight-oriented psychotherapy, the therapist utilizes this phenomenon as a therapeutic tool to help the patient understand emotional problems and their origins. The transference may be negative (hostile) or positive (affectionate).[22] Questions arise, such as: When does transference begin and how can we know it? Does transference interfere with the capacity to make intimate or important personal decisions? When does transference end? Does it end with treatment? If not, how soon after treatment, if ever?

As a rule, intimacy with a patient does not occur with hospitalized or incompetent psychotic patients, but rather with well-functioning or borderline individuals. In psychiatric parlance, a *borderline individual* is one who is unstable in a variety of areas, including interpersonal relationships, behavior, mood, and self-image.[23] In the vast majority of cases, the patient is not caught up in a psychotic transference. Does the patient, as a result of the sexual relations, suffer a broken marriage, a suicide attempt, or severe deterioration of social function? Why are the patients not hospitalized after such an episode? Indeed, the APA's malpractice insurance policy, like most other policies, does not cover undue familiarity, thereby depriving these patients, who have allegedly suffered great harm, of a source of compensation for their suffering.

In the usual tort case, the plaintiff has the burden of establishing fault, causation, and the extent of damages. In undue familiarity cases, however, the courts today tend to *assume* great harm and a causal nexus linking the defendant's conduct to the injury. In no other area of tort law is professional misconduct or incompetence, standing alone, sufficient to impose liability. Only in the sexual misconduct cases have the courts, for the most part, adopted a per se rule that liability is established even in the absence of proof of actual injury. For instance, in a Washington case,[24] a therapist defended a sexual misconduct suit on the grounds that the patient had not been damaged by the affair. The court replied: "The most elementary conceptions of justice and public policy require that the wrongdoer shall bear the risk of the uncertainty [of actual damages] which his own wrong has created."[25] Only exceptionally is proof of damages required.[26]

In the usual case, the jury, shocked by the reprehensible behavior, punishes the therapist by awarding compensatory damages. If the jurisdiction allows punitive damages, they are added for good measure. The large jury awards establish a basis for substantial settlements in later cases, and for blackmailing. "Pay up, or I'll sue." Insurance carriers have come to consider these cases as indefensible, and most now specifically exclude coverage. Justice James Heiple of the Illinois Supreme Court entered a dissent to lawsuits based on sexual relations with a patient:

> This is not a proper claim for malpractice. It should not be recognized in law. There is no suggestion that the plaintiff in this case was a minor, was mentally retarded or was under any other legal disability. She knew what she was doing and did it.
>
> At the moment the sexual relationship began, the treatment relationship ended. From that time forward, the plaintiff and the defendant were engaged in a frolic, a mutually agreeable detour from any recognized or accepted treatment regimen. To hold the defendant legally liable under such conditions is to countenance a legal form of extortion or blackmail. The law should not permit it. The complaint should be dismissed. Even if such a claim were to be recognized, the attempt to fit this type of claim into a negligence or willful and wanton format is wholly misplaced. There is no allegation that the parties fell off a bed or injured any part of the plaintiff's anatomy. The plaintiff, having willingly engaged in a frolic, now seeks to use the legal system as a toll for a shakedown.[27]

Ordinarily, it is incumbent upon the complainant to establish an exacerbation of symptoms as a result of the behavior of the defendant. However, this burden of proof is notably absent in undue familiarity cases. In reality, the post-traumatic stress disorder claimed by the complainant may only be a secondary gain syndrome, which occurs when patients' symptoms increase when they become aware that they will be awarded damages for the symptoms.[28] One of the more amusing examples in the literature is the Pope and Bouhoutsos elaboration of the "therapist-patient sex syndrome." In their 1986 book, Pope and Bouhoutsos noted that patients most likely to develop this syndrome (a configuration of symptoms constituting a condition) may be those with borderline and histrionic personality disorders. They also noted that the syndrome itself resembles the borderline and histrionic personality disorder.[29] Hence, this is a syndrome that resembles the way the sufferers were before they developed the syndrome and, in fact, is characterized by the sufferers' premorbid condition. In relation to any other issue, this train of logic would simply be laughable.

Litigation alleging sexual misconduct by a therapist is actually of fairly recent origin. Until the 1970s, such events rarely led to litigation. The landmark cases are *Zipkin v. Freeman*,[30] a decision by the Missouri Supreme Court in 1968, and *Roy v. Hartogs*,[31] a much-publicized New York case from the mid-1970s. The impetus to sue can be attributed to the decreased stigma associated with being a psychotherapy patient, the realization that patients who report undue familiarity are probably not fantasizing, and, certainly, media reports of high damage awards and the theory of the case.

In *Zipkin* a court, for the first time, conceptualized the therapist-patient sexual intimacy in psychodynamic terms of transference and the therapist's handling of that transference. Writing for the majority of the Missouri Supreme Court, Judge Seiler wrote: "[The defendant] mishandled the transference phenomenon, which is a reaction the psychiatrists anticipate and which must be handled properly."[32] In discussing therapist-patient sexual intimacy in terms of the therapist's responsibility to handle the transference appropriately, the opinion indicated that even less extreme expressions of the therapist's attraction to the patient (e.g., swimming, dancing) may constitute malpractice. The jury awarded the plaintiff $17,000. The court, however, reduced the award to $5,000. That was in 1968, when the dollar had much more value than today.

Zipkin did not specifically turn on allegations of sexual contact, although a sexual relationship was at least implied by the testimony, which included allegations of nude swimming parties. The doctor's misconduct consisted of misusing the therapeutic relationship to induce the plaintiff to attend social events with him, to leave her husband and move into a farm owned by the doctor, and to take property from her husband. The plaintiff testified that she fell in love with the defendant, put her faith and trust in him, and did or said anything he told her was good for her. Experts testified that the defendant's "treatment" of the plaintiff was a distortion of the transference phenomenon that caused the plaintiff serious, and perhaps permanent, emotional harm.[33]

Prior to *Zipkin*, most of the reported cases were brought by husbands who claimed damages as a result of their wives' sexual relationship with a therapist. In most jurisdictions, these types of cases were barred by so-called heart-balm statutes that did away with civil liability for alienation of affections, seduction, and criminal conversation. In a California case, the California Court of Appeals held that the therapist owed no duty of care to the patient's husband, and the husband was also held not to be a direct victim despite his attendance at some therapy sessions.[34]

In *Hartogs*, Julie Roy charged Dr. Renatus Hartogs with "inducing" her to have sexual intercourse as a part of her prescribed therapy. The case, decided in 1976, was chronicled in a book, *Betrayal*, coauthored by the plaintiff and Lucy Freeman.[35] A television film followed. In the film, the doctor orders the timid woman around his office, screams at her, talks incessantly of "curing" her, and sits behind a large, imposing desk to conduct the noncouch sessions. The advertisements for the film proclaimed, "The true story of a vulnerable woman who turns to a psychiatrist for help. . . . Instead, he lures her into a sexual relationship!" The book carries the subcaption, "The true story of the first woman to successfully sue her psychiatrist for using sex in the guise of therapy."[36] As it turned out, neither in this case nor in later cases would it be necessary to allege that sex was engaged in under the guise of therapy. It is irrelevant whether or not the therapist tells the patient at the outset that a sexual relationship is proper therapy, with the patient consenting.

The trial court was convinced by the argument of plaintiff's counsel, which may be paraphrased as follows: Transference deprives patients of the ability to exercise independent judgment. It negates any free will. It accomplishes the same result as hypnosis or drugs. Therefore, the legislation abolishing the common-law cause of action for seduction should not apply in the case of a psychotherapist.[37]

After a protracted trial, the jury awarded Julie Roy $250,000 in compensatory damages and $100,000 in punitive damages. However, Judge Myers, the trial judge, reduced by $200,000 the jury's compensatory verdict, leaving $50,000 for damages in that category. He allowed the $100,000 in punitive damages to stand. The judge stated that the plaintiff had not proved that "permanent emotional damage" resulted from Dr. Hartogs's "treatment." In a 23-page opinion, Judge Myers wrote:

> The court has observed this plaintiff during the trial, which lasted almost two weeks. She certainly did not appear to be psychotic. She was well poised and well groomed. She spoke coherently and related her case with precision, clarity, excellent memory, and without inhibition. I could not discern the slightest sign of abnormal behavior during the entire trial even under what must have been harrowing cross-examination.[38]

At the same time, Judge Myers described Dr. Hartogs's behavior as "heinous and atrocious."[39] He stated: "When one considers how vital it is both for society at large and, more particularly, for the medical profession that such conduct, as presented here, be eradicated . . . it cannot be held as a matter of law that the jury's assessment of $100,000 was excessive."[40] He concluded, "A patient must not be fair game for a lecherous doctor."[41]

Dr. Hartogs appealed Judge Myers's decision and later, in September 1975, filed for bankruptcy. In January 1976, the Appellate Term of the Supreme Court of New York cut the compensatory damages from $50,000 to $25,000 and eliminated the punitive damages. The majority opinion stated:

> Plaintiff's condition was of long standing, and began years before she became defendant's patient. There is no evidence to support a permanent worsening of the condition by defendant's acts; nor is there proof demonstrating a permanent impairment of her ability to work in a position comparable to that she had before or during the period she was defendant's patient. Given the fact that she may recover only for the aggravation of her condition by defendant . . . we conclude that an award of more than $25,000 would be excessive.[42]

The court further ruled that Dr. Hartogs's conduct, while inexcusable, did not warrant punitive damages.[43] In a concurring opinion, Presiding Justice Markowitz commented: "The subject matter of this case was highly sensational forcing the participants to operate in a charged atmosphere rather than the calm almost cloistered climate of the routine civil courtroom."[44]

Justice Riccobono dissented from any award of damages. He pointed out that although the plaintiff was suffering from a number of emotional problems, her competency was never placed in issue, stating, "Is it not fair to infer, therefore, that she was capable of giving a knowing and meaningful consent?"[45] He added, "The relief sought by this plaintiff constitutes the closest approach to a conventional action for seduction, and hence must be treated as such."[46] While New York and most other jurisdictions have abolished actions for seduction, for the psychotherapist, and the psychotherapist alone, "malpractice" replaces "seduction" and the action continues.[47]

Justice Riccobono's dissent has received no attention. Since 1976, sexual misconduct has represented 15 percent of all lawsuits against psychiatrists and has accounted for one-third or more of the payout for psychiatric malpractice claims. Judgments in the six-digit range have not been uncommon.[48] In a California case,[49] the parties agreed to a $2.5 million settlement to avoid an appeal, after an initial $4.7 million award, all compensatory, no punitive damages, was returned by a jury. In a Virginia case,[50] the jury awarded $650,000 in compensatory damages. A claim for punitive damages was dropped because of doubts as to whether defendant's insurance policy would cover or indemnify against punitive damages. Today, as a result of these jury verdicts, merely filing a complaint against a psychotherapist alleging sexual misconduct usually results, on average, in a settlement of $110,000. To avoid the peril of the jury, or a hearing before a medical board, and to avoid publicity, most cases are settled. One might ask, why gamble when the law provides a sure win? A few years ago Joel Klein, then general counsel for the APA, observed:

> Probably the biggest single problem, and the one that's most difficult to address, is the issue of sex between therapist and patient. Insurance companies generally are so concerned about the explosive nature of this problem and the risks involved—sympathetic juries, large damages, punitive damages—that they now refuse to cover it. Very few cases actually go to trial, since most are settled, usually at a high figure, perhaps higher than one would expect. In malpractice terms, the best data we have suggests that during the years when insurance companies were covering this risk, probably a third or more of the payout for malpractice claims was for sex cases.[51]

In a Pennsylvania case,[52] the jury returned a verdict for the plaintiff in the amount of $665,000: $275,000 for compensatory damages exclusive of costs for future psychiatric care, $90,000 for future psychiatric care, and $300,000 for punitive damages. The court disallowed the $90,000 awarded for future psychiatric treatment, as "the plaintiff did not demonstrate that it was probable she would undergo future psychiatric care . . . and could not trust another doctor."[53] In this case, the plaintiff sought treatment from the defendant when she was suffering from a condition called "harried housewife syndrome."[54] She testified that the defendant "became a God" to her and that she "was dependent on him."[55] In various cases, a clinic is also held responsible for "negligent supervision."[56]

In the usual case, the analysis is cursory.[57] The fact of sexual intimacy alone clouds the issue of injury. There is a principle in our jurisprudence that injury must be individually established, not presumed based on the class of alleged misconduct. Lawyers say that a classification is no substitute for personalized accounts. In general, however, in therapist sexual relations cases, the court does not closely inquire whether this patient's relations with men have actually worsened, or whether *her* emotional problems have been resolved but for the therapist's undue familiarity, or even whether there were lost wages or medical bills. The undue familiarity may very well have caused emotional harm, but if so, one would expect the plaintiff, as in other cases alleging emotional distress, to exhibit or prove it. Women who have been raped experience a rape trauma syndrome. Do women who are sexually involved with a therapist as a result of the transference phenomenon experience a similar syndrome? The answer is "no." The exception is so rare that it warrants comment in the professional journals.[58]

All of the reported cases have involved sexual relations between a male doctor and a female patient. It has been said that this is another example of the exploitation of women. In actuality, there have been instances of sexual relations between female doctors and male patients. Surveys show that anywhere from 6 to 10 percent of male therapists and 3 to 8 percent of female therapists acknowledge being sexually involved with patients during treatment. However, regardless of the harm, a man even in these litigious times does not think of suing a woman for having had sex with him. The news of a man filing such a suit would be as odd as that of a man biting a dog. To what psychological aberration can we ascribe this failure to file suit? Is it because a man who brings suit on this account would be treated with derision, or are men better able to handle such sexual episodes than women? Does transference turn women but not men into helpless waifs?[59]

In past years, a therapist in a gesture of empathy might put his hand on the shoulder of a depressed, weeping mother who had recently lost her son. However, in today's litigious climate he shrinks from doing so, fearing, as one therapist stated, "the witch hunt against consciously or unconsciously experienced sexual intent toward an innocent patient."[60] One of the consequences of the current climate is that depersonalization has taken place between therapists and patients. Therapists sit defensively behind their desks, careful not to spontaneously smile, conduct themselves in a very prim and proper manner, and dispense their psychotherapeutic or medication products to consumers—no longer fellow human beings experiencing emotional pain. When Dr. Elissa Benedek, in her capacity as president of the APA, stated that as soon as a therapist experiences an emotion of sexuality towards a patient, the therapist must immediately transfer the patient to another therapist, it was apparent that the leadership in psychiatry had gone overboard.[61]

Some suggest that sexual relations with a former patient is never permissible.[62] Others suggest a waiting period following termination of therapy, during which time even social contact would be precluded.[63] In 1988, the APA amended its ethics code to read: "Sexual involvement with one's former patient generally exploits emotions deriving from treatment and therefore almost always is unethical."[64] Dr. Ruth Tiffany Barnhouse entered a protest: "To claim that former patients are forever out of bounds is to say that the wounds cannot be healed and that maturation does not occur. It infantilizes patients by preserving indefinitely the therapist's superior status as one who is more powerful, more mature, and still symbolically in the parental role."[65]

Legislation in California and Minnesota prohibits sexual contact with a former patient for two years.[66] The ban is allegedly warranted in order to deal with the risks of impaired decision making, fraud, and exploitation of a fiduciary relationship. Furthermore, even after years of marriage to a therapist, the patient under the theory might, when seeking a divorce, also claim damages for emotional distress—a cause of action arguably not barred by a statute of limitations because the damages were not earlier recognizable.[67] What about freedom of association? Are people who fall in love able to exercise any better judgment about the qualities of their companion? The decision-making ability of former patients is said to be impaired by residual transference.

One survey of psychologists, conducted in California, found the perceived harm of sexual relations with a patient during the course of therapy to range from great to none at all. Positive effects were reported in some cases. The 704 psychologists who responded said that 559 of their patients reported having sexual relations with the previous therapist. Female patients were involved with a male therapist in 92 percent of the cases. One-half of the sexual contacts with male patients involved male therapists. When the therapist initiated sexual intimacies, the respondents felt that the patient was adversely affected in 82 percent of the cases. When the patient initiated sexual intimacies, respondents thought the patient was adversely affected in 39 percent of the cases. The patients had negative feelings about the relationship in 29 percent of the cases. Sixteen percent reported positive effects.[68]

Actually, anyone, male or female, unable to handle sex will be traumatized by it, whether the partner is a doctor, lawyer, or movie star. Every person in love is exposed, extended, and fragile; damage may arise from any broken relationship.[69] Judging from the reports, however, the consequences of sexual involvement with a therapist are even more dire than those arising from a rape in the streets. It boggles, or ought to boggle, the imagination.

What about causal connection? Mere simultaneity between an event and an illness does not demonstrate any causal connection between the two events. Indeed, without statistical studies with reasonable confidence limits, one might well conclude that the temporal relationship is simply the result of chance.

Suppose a woman is all at once a patient in psychotherapy, a churchgoer, a law student, and a litigant in a divorce proceeding. The illustration is not far-fetched. How does a sexual affair with her therapist compare with one involving her priest, her lawyer, or her law professor? Is she less or more vulnerable in one situation than another?

The lecherous professor is a standard figure at most colleges. In this setting, there is usually a quid pro quo—sexual favors in return for a passing grade.[70] The outrage over these incidents is miniscule, compared to that visited upon the psychotherapist, though the quid pro quo is absent from the psychotherapy situation.

In the case of clergy members, transference often borders on the delusional. The *Minneapolis Star Tribune* sent a questionnaire to Minnesota clergy inquiring about their sexual activities and drug use. While there has been growing concern about the behavior of clergy, the survey was roundly condemned. "You can just smell the sensationalist stories coming," wrote the editor of the *Catholic Bulletin*.[71] Some feared that "the survey [would] undermine the confidence people have in their priests and ministers, whatever the numbers reveal."[72] Yet, surveys about psychotherapists are done almost as a matter of course.

In a Michigan case, *Teadt v. Lutheran Church*,[73] a parishioner sued a minister and the church, alleging breach of fiduciary duty, intentional infliction of emotional distress, vicarious liability, and negligent hiring, supervision, and retention, all arising out of a sexual relationship between the parishioner and minister. The Michigan Court of Appeals rejected all of these theories. The court ruled that breach of fiduciary duty was not cognizable as an action against a minister, as no financial transactions were involved, and it ruled that the parishioner failed to allege extreme and outrageous conduct required to serve as a basis for a claim of intentional infliction of emotional distress.

Malpractice litigation involving attorneys or other professionals for sexual intimacy, apart from job-related sexual harassment suits, is virtually nonexistent. While the psychotherapist is sanctioned by his peers and subjected to legal liability, the lawyer and others are not, even though existing rules of professional conduct would seem to forbid it.[74] The State Bar of California proposed an amendment to the Rules of Professional Conduct that would prohibit a lawyer from demanding sexual relations as a condition of representation if "the lawyer's ability to perform legal services would be impaired."[75] The Los Angeles County Bar Association claimed that a blanket prohibition would infringe upon lawyers' free association and privacy rights under the U.S. Constitution.[76] One lawyer said that the only people she meets are clients and lawyers, and she is not about to engage in sexual relations with another lawyer.

An Illinois appellate court found a divorce lawyer who had sexual relations with his client breached no fiduciary duty, despite allegations that the client was "psychologically coerced or seduced" into having relations with him.[77] Deciding a case of first impression in Illinois, the appellate court refused to create a "new species of legal malpractice" that "inherent in every attorney-client contract there is a duty to refrain from intimate personal relationships.[78] According to the court, the breach of duty actionable in malpractice must be a breach "more clearly linked to the attorney's legal representation."[79] The lawyers' conduct may have been unethical, but that is a question best left to disciplinary agencies, the court concluded.[80]

The transference phenomenon is construed as unique to the psychotherapist-patient relationship, and as validation of emotional injury when sexual relations occur. In *Simmons v. United States*,[81] the Ninth Circuit Court of Appeals explained:

> We note that courts do not routinely impose liability upon physicians in general for sexual contact with patients. . . . The crucial factor in the therapist-patient relationship which leads to the imposition of legal liability for conduct which arguably is no more exploitative of a patient than sexual involvement of a lawyer with a client, a priest or minister with a parishioner, or a gynecologist with a patient is that lawyers, ministers and gynecologists do not offer a course of treatment and counseling predicated upon handling the transference phenomenon.[82]

As one who in this context would single out psychotherapists, Dr. Spencer Eth says:

> I would distinguish sexual relations with a therapist from sexual activity with other classes of individuals such as attorneys, professors or employers. Although all of these relationships are asymmetric, only the psycho-

therapeutic relationship emphasizes self-disclosure and transference. In that context the capacity for free choice is significantly diminished and the potential for exploitation significantly enhanced.[83]

The ethical provision of the American Psychiatric Association states:

The requirement that the physician conduct himself/herself with propriety in his/her profession and in all the actions of his/her life is especially important in the case of the psychiatrist because the patient tends to model his/her behavior after that of his/her psychiatrist by identification. Further, the necessary intensity of the treatment relationship may tend to active sexual and other needs and fantasies on the part of both patient and psychiatrist, while weakening the objectivity necessary for control. Additionally, the inherent inequality in the doctor-patient relationship may lead to exploitation of the patient. Sexual activity with a current or former patient is unethical.[84]

To be sure, transference feelings are particularly intense in the psychoanalytic situation. However, most cases of sexual intimacy do not occur with patients in psychoanalysis, but with patients in other forms of therapy where the transference is less intense and quite like that which occurs in other human situations. Under managed care, the prevailing practice in psychiatry is chemotherapy, where the role of transference, it is quipped, is about the same as that with a druggist in a supermarket.

All human relationships are tinged with transference. Nearly everything we do can be traced to earlier experiences. Every relationship is a mixture of a real relationship and transference phenomenon. Additionally, every relationship is asymmetrical, but in courtroom arguments transference becomes something mysterious and powerful. Dr. Martin Bauermeister says, "The suggestion that another human being by coming in clinical contact with us is incapacitated to make decisions about sexual relations is suspect of hubris and of a gross overestimation of our power over other people."[85]

From what I have seen or heard, the patients in the majority of litigated cases became sexually involved with the therapist in the hope of developing a long-term relationship. When the relationship failed to develop, joy turned to rage. The patient once again felt rejected. In these litigious times, such a patient retains a lawyer, for revenge as much as for compensation. It is the termination of the relationship, not the sexual relations, that causes the outrage.[86] In every reported case, the patient apparently sued only when the therapist terminated the relationship. In *Hartogs*,[87] Julie Roy turned to the legal process when, after making increasing demands for more time with Dr. Hartogs, he abruptly ended the relationship and refused to see her any longer. In *The Mourning Bride*, William Congreve wrote: "Heaven has no rage like love to hatred turned, nor hell a fury like a woman scorned."[88]

In many cases, the patients have a history of drug abuse, delinquent behavior, broken homes, and sexual promiscuity. They are manipulative, often outwitting the therapist. In rape cases, the sexual history of the victim is generally inadmissible in assessing credibility.[89] Should the same policy be followed in undue familiarity cases? During the Middle Ages, exorcists knew about the danger of becoming possessed themselves after being closeted alone for long periods of time with demoniacally possessed young women who, as a sign of their bewitchment, often acted seductively. Evidence that the Devil also had taken possession of the priests was naturally based on their later developing sexual feelings toward these women while trying to rid them of their demons.[90]

In sexual misconduct cases before medical boards or at a trial, the defense typically claims that a psychiatric disorder led the complainant to make false accusations. Typically, evidence of the sexual history of the complainant at a trial is inadmissible in assessing credibility.[91] At board hearings, however, where the rules of evidence do not apply, a New York study reports that physicians there are allowed to make "reasonable connections" between the complainant's psychiatric history and her discounted credibility. South Carolina reports experts testifying on the classification of patients as a "borderline personality." Massachusetts reports the introduction of psychiatric evidence that patients were suffering from the types of mental instabilities that would cause them to lie about their experiences with their physicians.[92]

The assumption that women, whether or not in psychotherapy, are helpless victims in sexual relationships bespeaks of ignorance in worldly matters. One of the great themes of literature is the power that women have exercised over men who have fallen for them. As stated in a cover story, "America's Decadent Puritans," in London's *Economist*: "The decadence lies in too readily blaming others for problems, rather than accepting responsibility oneself."[93] Yet, Dr. Thomas Gutheil's suggestion that patients play an observable role in therapist-patient sexual relations brought forth a flurry of letters in protest.[94]

Might the patient be, ever so slightly, to blame? The doctrine of comparative negligence, adopted in most states, allows the court to apportion fault between plaintiff and defendant. Yet, it is rare that any fault is attributed to the patient. In the case of incest where the participants are both adults, they are both culpable under the law. One jury in an undue familiarity case found the patient to be 15 percent at fault and reduced the award accordingly.[95]

It is observed that "a professional relationship is essentially a fiduciary one and that even women who engage willingly in sex with the fiduciary have the right to consider themselves victims,"[96] but such dictum applies, in practice, only in the case of psychotherapy. The theory of a fiduciary duty usually involves financial transactions (as in the relationship between a bank and client).[97] Sexual relations with a therapist, however, has been called "the ultimate betrayal."[98]

In a theory of malpractice, a tort of negligence rather than a breach of a fiduciary duty, the fault is placed entirely on the therapist. Steven Bisbing, a psychologist and lawyer who is with the program in psychiatry and law at Georgetown University Medical Center, states: "Both ethically and legally, patient-therapist sex is always the therapist's fault."[99] Dr. Larry Strasburger claims that "responsibility is always with the therapist. If the patient is a masochist and asks to be beaten, the therapist has a duty not to beat the patient."[100]

The theory in a malpractice action is that the psychotherapist, by virtue of his training, is supposed to be able to handle the transference. To accept this as an explanation, however, one must believe that the therapist is diabolically clever and manipulative while reducing the patient to a mere dupe. For one thing, transference usually has little or nothing to do with the behavior. Secondly, the law does not distinguish the transference in intense five-times-a-week psychoanalysis from once-a-month psychotherapy.[101] In many instances, the therapist is the innocent and vulnerable one, especially where the patients are young, attractive, sexy, and malicious. Resistance in therapy takes many forms. One of them is to seduce the therapist out of his professional distance and objective attachment. Often, both therapist and patient are emotionally deprived, and they short-circuit therapeutic work to gratify their immediate emotional needs. Various religions forbid a man and a woman who are not married to be alone together in a closed space—the risk of a sexual encounter was recognized, especially when the get-togethers are frequent.

Having already been held liable to his patient for damages for mental distress, Dr. Hartogs also lost his bid to have his insurer pay the award or repay him for the cost of his defense. A malpractice insurance contract does not cover intentional torts or acts that are not necessarily related to the rendering of professional services. The court ruled that since the psychiatrist's "therapy" was undertaken for his own personal satisfaction, his actions did not, as between the psychiatrist and his insurer, constitute malpractice within the meaning of the policy.[102] Hence, there was no coverage. The court further held that, in any event, public policy precluded the court from allowing the psychiatrist to recover such expenses. To allow recovery would be "to indemnify immorality and to pay the expenses of prurience."[103]

In later cases, however, a number of courts ruled that since sexual familiarity occurs with some frequency in the course of psychotherapy, it is a risk of the practice, not an intentional tort but malpractice, and therefore comes within malpractice insurance coverage.[104] These courts have ruled that sexual activity is a departure from the standard of care, no different than an improper administration of medication, and therefore, covered by the malpractice insurance policy.[105] In a Michigan case, *Vigilant Insurance Co. v. Kambly*,[106] the court upheld coverage for sexual familiarity under the malpractice insurance policy on the rationale that the victim should not be penalized for the acts of the insured—the coverage is as much protection for the victim as it is for the doctor. The court stated, "Coverage does not allow the wrongdoer unjustly to benefit from his wrong. . . . It is not the insured who will benefit, but the innocent victim who will be provided compensation for her injuries. . . . In this instance, there is great public interest in protecting the interests of the insured party."[107]

In 1985, however, the APA excluded coverage for undue familiarity from its member malpractice insurance program. The policy still provides cost of legal defense up to $100,000 when sexual involvement is denied. Most members of the APA board of trustees thought that dropping coverage for unethical sexual behavior would help deter its occurrence. A women's committee took a strong stand, to no avail, in favor of retaining insurance coverage "to compensate victims for their distress."[108] The exclusion reads: "This insurance does not apply to injury due to or caused by any sexual activity by the insured. . . . 'Sexual activity' is defined to include the physical touching of any person intended as sexual stimulation." Were the concern primarily about the great harm presumably sustained by patients, one should logically desire a source of compensation for them. Deterrence sounds fine, but other unethical or harmful conduct is not excluded from coverage.[109] To get around the undue familiarity exclusion, attorneys are alleging other theories as a cause of action (e.g., abandonment, breach of fiduciary duty).[110] Tort liability rules do (or should) appreciably depend on the principle of compensatory justice.[111]

In reality, deterrence is not the motive for excluding coverage. With cases multiplying like locusts, the main concerns involve the drain on the APA's liability insurance program and the image of the profession. The insurance program had gone through hard economic times and could not afford to compensate all of these claimants.[112] The program's London reinsurers were willing to continue providing full coverage for sexual misconduct cases only if premiums were raised to a level that would have made malpractice insurance unaffordable for the majority of APA members.[113] With all of the publicity, the reputation of the profession was at stake, including fears of an erosion of public trust in psychiatry. Even Ann Landers, a longtime champion of psychiatry, expressed second thoughts about the ethics of psychiatrists.[114]

Every profession has concern about its image. It is so important that, as Sir Francis Bacon once said: "I hold every man a debtor to his profession."[115] When Judge Brigieta Volopichova entered a topless glamour contest in Czechoslovakia, her colleagues were furious, demanding that she be removed from the bench. She brought the judicial profession into disrepute, but to justify a disciplinary hearing, the demand was said to be necessary to protect society: "Young men will be committing crime in the hope of being tried by her. . . . She may cause the crime rate to rise."[116]

Psychiatry as a profession is especially sensitive about its image. Over a century ago, Sigmund Freud cautioned his followers not to become romantically involved with their patients. Despite his warning, a number of them married former patients or conducted lengthy affairs with them. He warned about the peril to the profession, and he taught his followers that once sexual contact between therapist and patient begins, the therapeutic relationship is destroyed. He believed that no kind of erotic contact, not even an "innocent" kiss, should be initiated in the therapeutic relationship. Freud feared that sexual contact might confuse the patient and lead to the "danger" of further erotic intimacy.[117]

Sexual contact with a patient or client, whether or not there is actual harm, jeopardizes the professional relationship and tends to make it a waste of time. When sexual relations begin, therapy ends. In their book *The Imperial Animal*,[118] anthropologists Lionel Tiger and Robin Fox point out that people are limited in the type of bond or pattern of relationship that is possible with another person. One kind of relationship seems to preclude another. Thus, the nurturing relationship cannot coexist with a sexual relationship, hence the incest taboo. When people in a professional relationship enter into a love or courtship relationship, they usually imperil the professional one. One type of relationship is replaced by another or none at all. It is quite another thing to say, however, that harm to the therapy relationship is always accompanied by great harm to the patient.

To be sure, the numerous publications about undue familiarity are not taken by lawyers with a pinch of low-sodium seasoning. They rely on them for litigation purposes, and for large awards. The use by psychotherapists of such terms as *incest, rape, permanent injury, suicidal ideation,* or the myriad diagnostic entities that have been applied to patients who have had sexual relations with their therapist have made psychotherapists vulnerable to civil and criminal condemnation in the courts. Surely, there is an injunction in the Hippocratic oath against seducing a patient, and another in the profession's code of ethics. For violations of such injunctions, let therapists suffer the sanctions of the appropriate medical and licensing authorities. However, the therapist alone should not be singled out for condemnation in a tort or criminal action. In so doing, the psychotherapist is denied the equal protection of the laws without reasonable justification.[119] Criminalization plays into the image of a psychiatrist as sex-mad, weirdo, or not like others. As a rule of law the psychotherapist is denied a defense of consent, whereas, for other fiduciaries, consent is a question of fact.

The repeal of laws on seduction and alienation of affections does not apply to the psychotherapist. Under the rubric of malpractice, the psychotherapist is excepted because of "misuse of transference." Jorgenson and Randles write: "The nature of the psychotherapist-patient relationship grants great power to the psychotherapist."[120] Presumably, through the relationship, the psychotherapist can exercise more magic than a magician. Moreover, on a theory of breach of fiduciary duty, the therapist is held liable, though transference is not involved, when he engages in a sexual relationship with a friend or spouse of the patient.[121] In any event, the condemnation must mirror the offense, and compensation must reflect actual, rather than presumed, harm.

Victim groups want to criminalize the behavior of the therapist, as has been done in a number of states. But these groups fail to appreciate the impact of such criminalization. The trauma of a criminal or even civil process is rarely taken into account. Sanctions imposed by a medical or licensing authority, on the other hand, constructively punish the perpetrator without harming the victim.[122] Rightly or wrongly, however, medical or licensing authorities are perceived as ineffective in disciplining their errant members. Others say that legislation criminalizing sexual contact between therapist and patient is needed in view of the many unlicensed therapists who are not accountable to any authority.[123]

In any event, prosecutions of therapists under the criminal statutes have rarely occurred. The statutes are not used by prosecutors to put therapists behind bars, rather more likely to pressure therapists to resign or take leave from their profession. It would be an end run around a medical board proceeding. It would be less time-consuming, but does it provide a fairer result? Furthermore, given that consent is no defense, entrapment by a police agent would also be unavailing as a defense.

A therapist may be forced to defend his conduct in a number of arenas: (1) a civil action brought by the patient on a variety of tort theories, (2) a criminal action brought by the prosecutor, or (3) a disciplinary action brought before the state licensing agency. Would patients threaten to file a criminal complaint or a complaint with the medical board or licensing agency as a means of extortion? Just an allegation of sexual misconduct results in emergency suspension of a license. In 1939, when New York repealed its law on alienation of affections, seduction, and criminal conversation, it explained in the preamble that it was doing so because of the

> grave abuses, causing extreme annoyance, embarrassment, humiliation and pecuniary damage to many persons wholly innocent and free of any wrongdoing, who were merely the victims of circumstances, and such remedies having been exercised by unscrupulous persons for their unjust enrichment, and such remedies . . . in many cases having resulted in the perpetration of frauds, it is hereby declared as the public policy of the state that the best interests of the people of the state will be served by the abolition of such remedies.[124]

Today, the action for seduction or criminal conversation is viable against psychotherapists under the rubric of malpractice, or as sexual misconduct under the criminal statutes. Calling sexual relations with a therapist incest or rape is hyperbole. Either all love is incestuous and the meaning of incest becomes so broad that it is useless, or we have to draw a line between true incest of parent-child and the therapeutic situation. The word *transference* in Greek means "metaphor." It is time to wake up to reality.

Notes

1. There have been numerous complaints against psychotherapists for many kinds of boundary violations and sanctions against them after investigation. The fundamental ethical issues revolve around providing competent treatment without exploitation. Competent treatment can be provided best when the therapist maintains a clear professional relationship with the patient, not influenced by intrusions that would weaken objectivity. Also, a patient enters treatment with the expectation that the therapist is obligated to do what is in the patient's best interest and not what is in the therapist's best interest.

Dr. Jeremy Lazarus of the American Psychiatric Association's Ethics Committee gives examples of common boundary violations that have led to ethics complaints: (1) a patient gives the therapist an expensive gift, (2) a patient takes the therapist out to lunch, (3) a patient gives the therapist insider information about a stock deal, (4) a famous patient invites the therapist to a high-society party, (5) a social relationship turns into a professional relationship and the social relationship continues, (6) a patient gives the therapist an expensive piece of medical equipment that will benefit the therapist's patients but also will provide additional revenue for the therapist, (7) the therapist asks the patient for personal advice in an area in which he or she is an expert, (8) the therapist gives a patient a gift or reduced fee after the patient refers a friend, (9) the therapist solicits funding for the therapist's research project from a wealthy patient, (10) the therapist routinely hugs or holds the patient, (11) the therapist regularly reveals personal information about the therapist to a patient, (12) a grateful patient arranges groups of people to whom the therapist can talk about his innovative treatment, (13) the therapist writes the introduction for a book the patient is about to publish, (14) the patient wants to introduce the patient's child to the therapist's child for the purpose of a social relationship, (15) the patient, a restaurant owner, offers the therapist a special, free meal at his restaurant, (16) the therapist attends important social functions of the patient, (17) the therapist meets a patient for treatment sessions outside of the usual place of practice without therapeutic justification, (18) the therapist is in a book discussion group with the patient, (19) the therapist asks his spouse to have the family auto serviced by the patient, an excellent auto mechanic, (20) the therapist consciously or unconsciously lives out his fantasies through his patients, (21) the therapist gives his patient a ride home. J. Lazarus, "More on Boundary Violations," *Psychiatric News*, Nov. 5, 1993, p. 4. See R. S. Epstein, *Keeping Boundaries* (Washington, D.C.: American Psychiatric Press, 1994); G. O. Gabbard, "Boundary Violations," in S. Bloch, P. Chodoff, & S. A. Green (eds.), *Psychiatric Ethics* (Oxford: Oxford University Press, 3d ed. 1999), pp. 141–60.

Marilyn Monroe became a member of the household of Dr. Ralph Greenson, her psychoanalyst—a totally antianalytic approach to therapy that was highly criticized by psychiatric colleagues when it became known years later. Eleven years after her suicide, Dr. Greenson defended his unorthodox therapeutic procedure in the *Medical Tribune* (Oct. 24, 1973), saying, "It was controversial, I know that. Nevertheless, I have practiced for some thirty-five years, and I did what I thought best, particularly after other methods of treatment apparently hadn't touched her one iota." But by making her a quasi member of his household, he transgressed one of the rules of analysis stated in his own textbook, *The Technique and Practice of Psychoanalysis* (New York: International Universities Press, 1967). In the book *The Last Days of Marilyn Monroe* (New York: William Morrow, 1998), the author Donald H. Wolfe suggests that Dr. Greenson was faced with the dilemma of justifying himself before colleagues, while at the same time not revealing the depth of his knowledge concerning the circumstances of Marilyn Monroe's death, for in doing so he would have to reveal his identity as an agent of the Communist International (pp. 383–84).

The unorthodox approach by Michigan psychiatrist Reuven Bar-Levav led to his death at the hands of one of his patients. He violated every boundary rule that therapists are supposed to practice. He took groups of patients on trips, he had lunch or dinner with them, and he also had sex with at least one patient and was accused of assaulting her. His style was often confrontational. He entered the lives of his patients. A number of psychiatrists in the community wrote to him over the years, urging him to practice psychotherapy according to well-developed and well-established rules. Granted, following the rules does not ensure a cure, but it may prevent many therapists from going off the deep end. He was completely impervious to criticism and reason. He was his own authority and therefore learned nothing from others. He was a clever psychopath (in the view of many psychiatrists) who probably did some good, which has largely been exaggerated by former patients, as their well-being depends on their maintaining a positive transference. They do not know or do not care to know that transference is a distortion. D. Zeman, "Therapy's Deadly Dividing Line," *Detroit Free Press*, Sept. 30, 1999, p. 1. See M. T. Singer & J. Lalich, *"Crazy" Therapies* (San Francisco: Jossey-Bass, 1996).

The debate continues on what constitutes a boundary violation and what is the effect of a violation on treatment. See, e.g., J. Kroll, "Boundary Violations: A Culture-Bound Syndrome," *J. Am. Acad. Psychiatry & Law* 29 (2001): 274. Dr. Glen O. Gabbard, who has written extensively on boundary violations, concludes, "Except for sexual contact with patients and financial dealings with patients other than the fee, professional boundaries in psychotherapy are fluid and largely a matter of clinical judgment and context." G. O. Gabbard, "Commentary: Boundaries, Cultures, and Psychotherapy," *J. Am. Acad. Psychiatry & Law* 29 (2001): 284. Dr. William H. Reid writes, "I don't always like the phrase 'boundary violations.' It is often misunderstood (or poorly defined), and can be used to lump a broad variety of behaviors that may be imprudent or improper into an amorphous category of assumed immorality. Many boundary violations are destructive, and some reprehensible; but not all are unethical or even countertherapeutic per se." W. H. Reid, *A Clinician's Guide to Legal Issues in Psychotherapy* (Phoenix: Zeig, Tucker & Co., 1999), p. 80. On a therapist testifying on behalf of a patient, see R. Slovenko, *Psychotherapy and Confidentiality* (Springfield, Ill.: Thomas, 1998), pp. 521–44; L. H. Strasburger, T. G. Gutheil, & A. Brodsky, "On Wearing Two Hats: Role Conflict in Serving as Both Psychotherapist and Expert Witness," *Am. J. Psychiatry* 154 (1997): 448. Self-disclosure (such as offering feedback on the therapist's own emotional reactions to what the patient is saying) is recommended by therapists interviewed in E. Goode, "Therapists Redraw Line on Self-Disclosure," *New York Times*, Jan. 1, 2002, p. D-5.

Throughout his career, Freud violated three of his major rules for the conduct of psychoanalysis: (1) maintaining confidentiality, (2) avoiding giving advice, and (3) sharing personal information or emotional reactions with the patient. Anna, his youngest daughter, entered analysis with him at the age of twenty-three (she never married and remained tied to him). D. J. Lynn & G. E. Vaillant, "Anonymity, Neutrality, and Confidentiality in the Actual Methods of Sigmund Freud: A Review of 43 Cases, 1907–1939," *Am. J. Psychiatry* 155 (1998): 163.

2. See K. Pope, "Research and Laws Regarding Therapist-Patient Sexual Involvement: Implications for Therapists," *Am. J. Psychotherapy* 49 (1986): 564. Psychoanalyst Richard Chessick says, "It is well known that sexual activity between a patient and a therapist represents a crossing of the incest barrier." "Malignant Eroticized Countertransference," *Am. Acad. Psychoanalysis* 25 (1997): 219; reprinted in R. Chessick, *Psychoanalytic Clinical Practice: Selected Papers* (London: Free Association Book, 2000).

3. See D. Goleman, "New Focus on Presenting Patient-Therapist Sex," *New York Times*, Dec. 20, 1990, p. B-21.

4. Simmons v. United States, 805 F.2d 1363, 1365 (9th Cir. 1986).

5. W. Masters & V. Johnson, "Principles of the New Sex Therapy," *Am. J. Psychiatry* 133 (1976): 548. See also G. C. Hankins, M. I. Vera, G. W. Barnard, & M. J. Herkov, "Patient-Therapist Sexual Involvement: A Review of Clinical and Research Data," *Bull. Am. Acad. Psychiatry & Law* 22 (1994): 109, 113.

6. See S. Baur, *The Intimate Hour* (New York: Houghton Mifflin, 1997); J. D. Bloom, C. C. Nadelson, & M. T. Notman (eds.), *Physician Sexual Misconduct* (Washington, D.C.: American Psychiatric Press, 1999); S. B. Bisbing, L. M. Jorgenson, & P. K. Sutherland, *Sexual Abuse by*

Professionals: A Legal Guide (Charlottesville, Va.: Michie, 1995); R. S. Epstein, *Keeping Boundaries* (Washington, D.C.: American Psychiatric Press, 1994); G. O. Gabbard (ed.) *Sexual Exploitation in Professional Relationships* (Washington, D.C.: American Psychiatric Press, 1989); J. C. Gonsiork (ed.), *Breach of Trust: Sexual Exploitation by Health Care Professionals and Clergy* (Thousand Oaks, Cal.: Sage, 1995); H. S. Strean, *Therapists Who Have Sex with Their Patients: Treatment and Recovery* (New York: Brunner/Mazel, 1993); P. Trumpi, *Doctors Who Rape: Malpractice and Misogyny* (Rochester, Vt.: Schenkman, 1997). For a bibliography, see H. Lerman, *Sexual Intimacies between Psychotherapists and Patients, an Annotated Bibliography of Mental Health, Legal and Public Media Literature Including Relevant Legal Cases* (Fullerton, Cal.: Dept. of Counseling, California State University, 1984).

7. J. Bolker, "Disturbances in the Field," *Readings: A Journal of Reviews and Commentary in Mental Health* 5 (1990): 8. At the time of the 1985 annual meeting of the American Psychiatric Association, an extensive three-part series embarrassing to the profession appeared in the *Dallas Times-Herald*. S. Smith & B. Laker, "Sex & Therapists," *Dallas Times-Herald*, May 20–22, 1985.

8. L. Morin, "Civil Remedies for Therapist-Patient Sexual Exploitation," *Golden Gate U. L. Rev.* 19 (1989): 401, 432.

9. T. Lambert, "Tom on Torts," *Assn. of Trial Law. of Am. L. Rep.* 25 (1982): 98, 99. A full-page drawing depicting the therapist as a wolf accompanies the article by J. Epstein, "The Exploitative Psychotherapist as a Defendant," *Trial*, July 1989, p. 52. See also M. Beck, "Sex and Psychotherapy: Doctors Sleeping with Patients—A Growing Crisis of Ethical Abuse" (cover story), *Newsweek*, Apr. 13, 1992, pp. 52–58; E. Goode, "The Ultimate Betrayal," *U.S. News & World Report*, Mar. 12, 1990, p. 63.

10. K. Pope, "Therapist-Patient Sex Syndrome: A Guide for Attorneys and Subsequent Therapists to Assessing Damage," in G. O. Gabbard (ed.), *Sexual Exploitation in Professional Relationships* (Washington, D.C.: American Psychiatric Press, 1989), pp. 39–55. One study reports a wide range of uncomfortable and sometimes life-threatening feelings or symptoms experienced by "survivors of sexual exploitation" by medical and mental health professionals and clergy but without explanation notes a few exceptions (e.g., a lesbian who did not feel damaged by her first—and apparently only—sexual relationship with a man). Its data showed that the clients abused in medical contexts experienced the greatest harm, whatever the brevity of the relationship. E. Disch & N. Avery, "Sex in the Consulting Room, the Examining Room, and the Sacristy: Survivors of Sexual Abuse by Professionals," *Am. J. Orthopsychiatry* 71 (2001): 204.

11. S. Smith, "The Seduction of the Female Patient," and S. W. Twemlow & G. O. Gabbard, "The Love-Sick Therapist," in G. O. Gabbard (ed.), *Sexual Exploitation in Professional Relationships* (Washington, D.C.: American Psychiatric Press, 1989), pp. 57–87; K. Pope & J. Bouhoutsos, *Sexual Intimacy Between Therapists and Patients* (New York: Praeger, 1986).

12. N. Gartrell et al., "Sexual Abuse of Patients by Therapists: Strategies for Offender Management and Rehabilitation," in R. D. Miller (ed.), *Legal Implications of Hospital Policies and Practices* (San Francisco: Jossey-Bass, 1989); N. Gartrell et al., "Management and Rehabilitation of Sexuality Exploitive Therapists," *Hosp. & Community Psychiatry* 39 (1988): 1070.

13. See L. H. Strasburger, "There Oughta Be a Law: Criminalization of Psychotherapist-Patient Sex as a Social Policy Dilemma," in J. D. Bloom, C. C. Nadelson, & M. T. Notman (eds.), *Physician Sexual Misconduct* (Washington, D.C.: American Psychiatric Press, 1999), pp. 13–36; K. C. Haspel, L. M. Jorgenson, J. P. Wincze, & J. P. Parsons, "Legislative Intervention Regarding Therapist Sexual Misconduct: An Overview," *Prof. Psychol. Res. Pract.* 28 (1997): 63; L. Jorgenson, R. Randles, & L. Strasburger, "The Furor over Psychotherapist-Patient Sexual Contact: New Solutions to an Old Problem," *Wm. & Mary L. Rev.* 32 (1991): 645; S. Diesenhouse, "Therapists Start to Address Damage Done by Therapists," *New York Times*, Aug. 20, 1989, p. E-5. In State v. Leiding, 112 N.M. 143, 812 P.2d 797 (1991), the New Mexico Court of Appeals held that in the absence of a specific criminal statute on sexual relations in therapy, it is not a crime whatever the effect of the transference phenomenon on consent. In this case the prosecutor maintained that every instance of sexual contact between a therapist and patient constitutes unlawful sexual penetration. Testifying for the prosecution, Dr. Martin Orne contended that transference can be so intense in therapy that the patient will not be able to withhold consent. The court, however, concluded that in order for there to be criminal sexual penetration under the statute, the victim must be so mentally impaired as to be unable to understand the nature of consequences of the act. The court noted that the therapist may

THE BOUNDARY VIOLATION OF UNDUE FAMILIARITY

well be subject to other sanctions or remedies: loss of license to practice, civil liability for damages for malpractice, and criminal fraud. Not all malpractice is a crime.

14. L. Strasburger, L. Jorgenson, & R. Randles, "Mandatory Reporting of Sexually Exploitative Psychotherapists," *Bull. Am. Acad. Psychiatry & Law* 18 (1990): 379. Of 1,423 psychiatrists responding to a national survey, 65 percent reported treating patients who had been sexually involved with previous therapists, but the surveyed psychiatrists reported it in only 8 percent of cases. The majority favored mandatory reporting of such incidents. N. Gartrell et al., "Reporting Practices of Psychiatrists Who Knew of Sexual Misconduct by Colleagues," *Am. J. Orthopsychiatry* 57 (1987): 287.

15. Colo. Rev. Stat., sec. 18-3-401(4) (1986).

16. People v. West, 724 P.2d 623, at 625 (Colo. 1986).

17. State v. Tibbets, 281 N.W.2d 499 (Minn. 1979); State v. Bicknese, 285 N.W.2d 684 (Minn. 1979).

18. Minn. Stat. Ann., sec. 609.341 (11) (IV) (West Supp. 1992), discussed in Jorgenson, Randles, & Strasburger, supra note 13.

19. Fla. Stat. Ann., sec. 491.0112 (West 1991); Me. Rev. Stat. Ann., tit. 17A, secs. 251(1)(C), 253(2)(1) (West Supp. 1991).

20. Cal. Civ. Code, sec. 43.93(b) (West Supp. 1992); Ill. Ann. Stat., ch. 70, par. 802 (Smith-Hurd 1989); Minn. Stat. Ann., sec. 148A.02 (West 1989); Wis. Stat. Ann., sec. 895.70(2) (West Supp. 1991).

21. Sigmund Freud said of the transference experiences of the patient on the couch: "What are transferences? They are new editions or facsimiles of the impulses and phantasies . . . aroused . . . during the progress of the analysis . . . they replace some earlier person by the person of the physician . . . a whole series of psychological experiences are revived, not as belonging to the past, but as applying to the person of the physician at the present moment." S. Freud, "Fragment of an Analysis of a Case of Hysteria" (1905), *Standard Edition* (London: Hogarth, 1953), p. 16. Over the years Freud enlarged this aspect of transference to make it central to the analytic situation as a process of the patient's living out his infantile relationships via the "transference neurosis." S. Freud, "Remembering, Repeating and Working-Through" (1914), *Standard Edition.*

22. Bahry v. Laucher, Washtenaw County, Michigan, No. 89-5191-NM (1990).

23. While a single profile of a victim of sexual misconduct may be impossible, some of the commonalities that the literature and clinical experience have demonstrated to be found repeatedly in this population include dynamics of vulnerability, aspects of borderline personality disorder, previous sexual abuse, and various bonding mechanisms. T. Gutheil, "Patients Involved in Sexual Misconduct with Therapists: Is a Victim Profile Possible?" *Psychiatric Annals*, Nov. 1991, p. 661.

24. Omer v. Edgren, 38 Wash. App. 376, 685 P.2d 635 (1984).

25. Ibid. at 638, citing Wenzler & Ward Plumbing & Heating Co. v. Sellen, 330 P.2d 1068, 1069 (Wash. 1958), and quoting Bigelo v. RKO Radio Pictures, Inc., 327 U.S. 251 (1946). See also Corgan v. Muehling, 167 Ill. App.3d 1093, 118 Ill. Dec. 698, 522 N.E.2d 153 (1988).

26. In Carmichael v. Carmichael, 597 A.2d 1326, 1329 (D.C. App. 1991) (quoting Washington v. Washington Hosp. Ctr., 579 A.2d 177, 181 (D.C. App. (1990)), the District of Columbia Court of Appeals held that the patient failed to present sufficient evidence that any malpractice had caused her harm, noting that she did not present expert testimony showing "a causal relationship between [the malpractice] and [her] injury." The court found that the expert testimony that her symptoms were of the sort commonly associated with transference abuse was "simply insufficient." Id. at 1330. The court pointed out that this witness was never asked if in his opinion the patient's injuries were caused to a reasonable medical certainty by the therapist's malpractice. Id. Furthermore, the testimony that the patient's symptoms were consistent with malpractice was held to be "not enough." On this basis, the judgment on the malpractice claim was reversed. Id. at 1330-31. In Iwanski v. Gomes, 611 N.W.2d 607 (Neb. 2000), the court found that the complainant had not supported her claim, beyond her assertion, that transference had played a role in her sexual involvement with her physician.

27. Dissenting opinion of J. Heiple, Corgan v. Muehling, 143 Ill.2d 296, 574 N.E.2d 602 at 611-12 (1991). In this case the treatment began in March 1979 and continued until October 1980, and during this period of time, the plaintiff and the defendant repeatedly engaged in "mutually agreeable sexual intercourse. The plaintiff now claims that this sexual relationship disturbed her psychological well-being, and she would like the defendant to pay her damages

of $3.75 million." 574 N.E.2d at 611. See L. I. Sederer & M. Libby, "False Allegations of Sexual Misconduct: Clinical and Institutional Consideration," *Psychiatr. Serv.* 46 (1995): 160.

28. This was claimed by the defense in the 1989 malpractice case brought by a Denver woman, Ms. Roberts-Henry, against her former psychiatrist, Dr. Jason Richter, the subject of a ninety-minute *Frontline* documentary on PBS. The documentary was reviewed in W. Goodman, "When a Psychiatrist Becomes a Lover," *New York Times,* Nov. 12, 1991, p. C-18. Dr. Richter, immediately after terminating psychotherapy, began a sexual affair with the patient. A subsequent psychiatrist, Dr. Martha Gay, helped the patient to complain, and was *attacked by* Dr. Richter's defense attorneys. Drs. Gay and Richter were both insured by the American Psychiatric Association's insurance company, but Dr. Gay complained that Dr. Richter's attorneys were too aggressive, risking harming her and her patient, and that the case manager's handling of herself, Dr. Richter, and their lawyers contained a conflict of interest. The jury found Dr. Richter 82 percent responsible for the patient's injuries. L. Hartman, "Doctor-Patient Sex and Frontline," *Psychiatric News,* Dec. 6, 1991, p. 1; "APA Responds to Ethical Issues in 'Frontline' Telecast," *Psychiatric News,* Dec. 6, 1991, p. 1.

29. See K. Pope & J. Bouhoutsos, supra note 11.

30. 436 S.W.2d 753 (Mo. 1968).

31. 366 N.Y.S.2d 297 (N.Y. Civ. Ct. 1975), *reversed,* 381 N.Y.S.2d 587 (N.Y. App. Term. 1976).

32. 436 S.W.2d at 761.

33. Ibid. at 759–60.

34. Smith v. Pust, 23 Cal. Rptr.2d 364 (Cal. App. 1993).

35. J. Roy & L. Freeman, *Betrayal* (New York: Stein & Day, 1976).

36. Ibid. Ironically, a bit earlier Freeman collaborated with Hartogs on a book *The Two Assassins* (New York: Crowell, 1965), a psychological study of Lee Harvey Oswald and Jack Ruby. Hartogs had examined Oswald when Oswald was thirteen and charged with truancy.

37. 366 N.Y.S.2d at 299.

38. Ibid.

39. Ibid.

40. Ibid.

41. Ibid.

42. 381 N.Y.S.2d at 589 (citation omitted).

43. Ibid.

44. Ibid.

45. Ibid. at 591.

46. Ibid. at 592.

47. In Cotton v. Kambly, 300 N.W.2d 627 (Mich. App. 1980), the plaintiff filed suit claiming that the defendant induced her to engage in sexual intercourse with him as part of her therapy. The defendant argued that the plaintiff's allegations were akin to claims for alienation of affection, criminal conversation, or seduction. Since these causes of action had been abolished by statute, the defendant contended that the plaintiff failed to state an actionable claim. The court disagreed, however, and held that plaintiff had sufficiently pleaded a claim for malpractice. The court reasoned that the essence of her claim was the doctor's departure from proper standards of medical practice. Thus, "while the facts alleged by plaintiff might also state a cause of action for common law seduction, we do not find that seduction was the gist of her malpractice claim." Id. at 628–29.

48. R. Simon, *Clinical Psychiatry and the Law* (Washington, D.C.: American Psychiatric Press, 2d ed. 1991), pp. 411–13.

49. Walker v. Parzen, Cal. Super. Ct., July 7, 1981, referenced in *Am. L. Rep.* 24 (1981): 295.

50. Combs v. Silverman, No. LE596 (Va. Cir. Ct. Feb. 5, 1982).

51. J. Talbot, "The Professional Liability Crisis: An Interview with Joel Klein," *Hosp. & Community Psychiatry* 37 (1986): 1012.

52. Greenberg v. McCabe, 453 F.Supp. 765 (E.D.Pa. 1978).

53. Ibid. at 773.

54. Ibid. at 770.

55. Ibid. at 771.

56. See, e.g., Nelson v. Gillette, 571 N.W.2d 332 (N.D. 1997).

57. See, e.g., L. L. v. Medical Protective Co., 362 N.W.2d 174 (Wis. Ct. App. 1984).

58. R. Goldstein, "Pseudo-Rape Trauma Syndrome," *Newsletter Am. Acad. Psychiatry & Law,* 15 (Sept. 1990): 58–59.

59. G. V. Laury, "When Women Sexually Abuse Psychiatric Patients under Their Care," *J. Sex Education & Therapy* 18 (1992): 111.

60. Personal communication from psychiatrist Theodore Pearlman (Oct. 30, 1990). While touching a patient is considered a boundary violation in psychotherapy, the healing power of touch has a long history. The scriptures tell of healing by the laying on of hands. In popular custom, parents kiss away a child's boo-boo. After the Oklahoma City bombing, volunteer therapists gave massages to exhausted rescue workers, numbed survivors, and overworked pathologists. The state medical examiner observed that the massage therapists were accomplishing more in fifteen minutes than psychologists (or practitioners who call themselves "debriefers") could in an hour or two. G. H. Colt, "The Magic of Touch" (cover story), *Life,* Aug. 1997, p. 52. Touching is regarded as alternative medicine. See B. A. Brennan, *Hands of Light: A Guide to Healing through the Human Energy Field* (New York: Bantam Doubleday, 1988). See also A. Montagu, *Touching: The Human Significance of Skin* (New York: Harper & Row, 3d ed. 1986). It turns out that hormones, body chemicals, and even genes agree that hugging is good for you. T. Field, *Touch* (Cambridge: MIT Press, 2001), reviewed in *Economist,* Jan. 26, 2002, p. 74.

61. E. Benedek, Editorial, *Psychiatric News,* Aug. 17, 1990, p. 3. When the patient is referred, will the patient be told the reason for the referral? How will the patient feel? Rejected? In certain cases, consultation with another therapist would be appropriate.

62. C. C. Kleinman, "Crossing the Border: Sexual Relationships between Therapist and Patients," address at the Carrier Foundation Medical Foundation Education Symposium, Belle Mead, N.J., Nov. 13, 1991.

63. P. Appelbaum & L. Jorgenson, "Psychotherapist-Patient Sexual Contact after Termination of Treatment: An Analysis and a Proposal," *Am. J. Psychiatry* 148 (1991): 1466. Iowa's statute covers sexual activity with a patient occurring within one year of the termination of therapy. Iowa Code, sec. 709.15 (Supp. 1992). Some laws cover instances in which it can be proven that therapy was "terminated primarily for the purpose of engaging in sexual contact." "Patient-Therapist Sex, Civil Commitment Getting State's Legislative Attention," *Psychiatric News,* Dec. 20, 1991, p. 4.

64. American Psychiatric Association, *Principles of Medical Ethics with Annotations Especially Applicable to Psychiatry* (Washington, D.C.: American Psychiatric Press, 1989). See R. J. Maurer, "Ohio Psychotherapist Civil Liability for Sexual Relations with Former Patients," *U. Toledo L. Rev.* 26 (1995): 547.

65. R. T. Barnhouse, "Sex with Former Patients" (ltr.), *Clinical Psychiatry News,* Oct. 1992, p. 4. Colorado's statute prohibits sexual activity only when there is an ongoing professional relationship. Ferguson v. People, 824 P.2d 803 (Colo. 1992). Florida's statute prohibits a sexual relationship between a therapist and patient after the professional relationship is terminated where "the professional relationship is terminated primarily for the purpose of engaging in sexual conduct." Shapiro v. State, 696 So.2d 1321 (Fla. App. 1997).

66. Cal. Bus. & Prof. Code, sec. 43.93 (West Supp. 1992); Minn. Stat. Ann., sec. 148A (West 1989).

67. L. Jorgenson & R. Randles, "Time Out: The Statute of Limitations and Fiduciary Theory in Psychotherapist Sexual Misconduct Cases," *Okla. L. Rev.* 44 (1991): 181. See also D. DeRose, "Adult Incest Survivors and the Statute of Limitations: The Delayed Discovery Rule and Long Term Damages," *Santa Clara L. Rev.* 25 (1985): 191; S. Torry, "Divorce-Malpractice Suit Won by Heiress," *Washington Post,* Oct. 22, 1989, p. B-1; C. Allen, "Power to Make Therapists Jittery," *Insight,* Dec. 4, 1989, p. 49.

68. J. Bouhoutsos et al., "Sexual Intimacy between Psychotherapist and Patients," *Prof. Psychol. Res. & Prac.* 14 (1983): 185.

69. P. Rutter, *Sex in the Forbidden Zone: When Men in Power—Therapists, Doctors, Clergy, Teachers, and Others—Betray Women's Trust* (New York: St. Martin's Press, 1989).

70. "One in Six Graduate Women Report Sex with Professors," *New York Times,* Jan. 28, 1986, p. C-3. Philip Roth's novel *The Dying Animal* (Boston: Houghton Mifflin, 2001) depicts a sexual affair between a student and a senior professor who is also a TV celebrity. His course attracts a number of young women, but he does not make a pass until the course is over and grades have been given. He invites the students to a party at his apartment, where by the end of the evening one of them is sure to share his bed. After all, he says, "many of these girls

have been having sex since they were fourteen" and it is no big deal to them. See D. Lodge, "Sick with Desire," *New York Review of Books*, July 5, 2001, p. 28. In a cartoon by David Sipress in the *New Yorker* (Sept. 3, 2001), a man sitting at a desk lined with books says, "I've been invited to address a conference of professors of twentieth-century American literature who are sleeping with their students."

71. Quoted in "Catholic Asks for Turnabout on Sex Poll," *St. Petersburg Times*, Mar. 9, 1991, p. E-3.

72. Ibid.

73. 237 Mich. App. 567, 603 N.W.2d 816 (1999).

74. M. Freedman, "The Professional Responsibility of the Law Professor: Three Neglected Questions," *Vand. L. Rev.* 39 (1986): 275; J. Hall, "Sex, Clients, and the Criminal Defense Lawyer," *Champion*, Sept./Oct. 1990, p. 29.

75. C. Allen, "Writing Briefs, Making Whoopee," *Insight*, Mar. 4, 1991, p. 58.

76. R. Schmitt, "Stated Simply, It'll Be Hands off for Those Long Arms of the Law," *Wall Street Journal*, Nov. 13, 1990, p. B-1.

77. Suppressed v. Suppressed, 565 N.E.2d 1091, 1092 (Ill. Ct. App. 1990).

78. Ibid. at 104.

79. Ibid.

80. Ibid. at 105.

81. 805 F.3d 1363 (9th Cir. 1986).

82. Ibid. at 1366.

83. Personal communication (Jan. 20, 1987).

84. *The Principles of Medical Ethics with Annotations Especially Applicable to Psychiatry*, American Psychiatric Association, 1993, sec. 2, anno. 1.

85. "Consent for Sex?" *Psychiatric News*, May 5, 1989, p. 44. A century ago it was considered that even extended eye contact with any predatory male would be sufficient to lead a woman astray. As a consequence, it was suggested that women should neither travel alone nor stare at strangers. In one prosecution, the prosecuting attorney asked the expert witness: "Do you advise nervous women never to travel alone since a man, simply through mental suggestion. . . ." The expert replied: "Simply through mental suggestion . . . no, but from a steady gaze, yes." R. Harris, *Murders and Madness* (New York: Oxford University Press, 1989), p. 189.

86. Psychotherapist Carl Goldberg says that the wrong is a breach of a "psychological contract." C. Goldberg, *Therapeutic Partnership: Ethical Concerns in Psychotherapy* (New York: Springer, 1977). In one case known to me, a psychiatrist upon the death of his wife notified all of his patients that he would not be seeing them for a month. One patient, a middle-aged woman who was seen in therapy tri-weekly, responded, "I see that you are in grief. Come and stay with me." He declined, but a few days later, she called urging him to come and stay with her. He agreed, while informing her that in doing so he would no longer be her psychiatrist. After several months of staying with her, he moved out. She was incensed, apparently expecting marriage or a long-term relationship. She filed a complaint. He lost his license and membership in the American Psychiatric Association, and she got $110,000. To be sure, he might have sought counseling to help deal with his grief, but was justice done?

87. 366 N.Y.S.2d 297 (N.Y. Civ. Ct. 1975), *reversed*, 381 N.Y.S.2d 587 (N.Y. App. Term 1976).

88. London: Lowndes, 1788.

89. Federal Rules of Evidence, Rule 412.

90. See A. Huxley, *The Devils of Loudun* (London: Chatto & Windus, 1952); see also A. M. Ludwig, *How Do We Know Who We Are?* (New York: Oxford University Press, 1997).

91. Department of Professional Regulation v. Wise, 575 So.2d 713 (Fla. Ct. App. 1991); C. Gentry, "Court Veils Sexual History," *St. Petersburg Times*, Feb. 16, 1991, p. B12.

92. A. L. Hyams, "Expert Psychiatric Evidence in Sexual Misconduct Cases before State Medical Boards," *Am. J. Law & Medicine* 18 (1992): 171.

93. "American's Decadent Puritans," *Economist*, July 28, 1990, p. 11.

94. T. Gutheil, "Borderline Personality Disorder, Boundary Violations, and Patient-Therapist Sex: Medicolegal Pitfalls," *Am. J. Psychiatry* 146 (1989): 1356, 1518–19; 147 (1990): 129–30, 963, 1258–59, 1391.

95. Kulick v. Gates, No. 41624 (Mass. Super. Ct. May 21, 1985), referenced in *Am. L. Rep.* 28 (1985): 471.

96. Ibid.

97. See Treadt v. Lutheran Church, 237 Mich. App. 567, 603 N.W.2d 816 (1999).

98. E. Goode, "The Ultimate Betrayal," *U.S. News & World Report*, Mar. 12, 1990, p. 63.

99. D. Goleman, supra note 3, at p. 87.

100. Comment at meeting of the American Academy of Psychiatry and Law in Orlando, Fla. (Oct. 18, 1991).

101. C. Clements, "The Transference: What's Love Got to Do with It," *Psychiatric Annals* 17 (1997): 556.

102. Hartogs v. Employers' Mut. Liab. Ins. Co., 391 N.Y.S.2d 962 (N.Y. Spec. Term 1977).

103. Ibid. at 965. The courts generally hold that a medical malpractice insurance policy does not cover a therapist's sexual contact with a patient. See, e.g., Smith v. St. Paul Fire & Marine Ins. Co., 353 N.W.2d 130, 132 (Minn. 1984); Standlee v. St. Paul Fire & Marine Ins. Co., 693 P.2d 1101 (Idaho Ct. App. 1984); Hirst v. St. Paul Fire & Marine Ins. Co., 683 P.2d 440 (Idaho Ct. App. 1984). See S. Gunnells, "Patient-Therapist Sexual Relations: Professional Services Rendered? A Case Comment on *Doe v. Swift*," *Law & Psychol. Rev.* 14 (1990): 87.

104. St. Paul Fire & Marine Ins. Co. v. Mitchell, 164 Ga. App. 215, 296 S.E.2d 126 (1982). In two subsequent cases decided on the same day, the Minnesota Supreme Court ruled that a malpractice insurance carrier may be held liable for a therapist's sexual involvement with a patient. In St. Paul Fire & Marine Ins. Co. v. Love, 459 N.W.2d 698 (Minn. 1990), the Minnesota Supreme Court stated:

> In determining whether the patient's claim results from professional services provided or which should have been provided, we believe the focus must be on the therapist's entire conduct. The question then becomes whether the sexual aspect of the conduct is inextricably related to the professional services provided or withheld. If the linkage is absent or slight, the patient's claim cannot be said to result from professional services provided or withheld.

459 N.W.2d at 701. The court concluded:

> When . . . the transference phenomenon pervades the therapeutic alliance, we believe the sexual conduct between therapist and patient arising from the phenomenon may be viewed as the consequence of a failure to provide proper treatment of the transference. In other words, the patient's claim results from the providing of improper professional services or the withholding of proper services.

459 N.W.2d at 702.

In the other case, St. Paul Fire & Marine Ins. Co. v. D. H. L., 459 N.W.2d 704 (Minn. 1990), a marriage and family therapist, while counseling a patient for sexual addiction and marital problems, had a sexual relationship with the patient. As in the *Love* case, St. Paul refused to defend the therapist in a suit brought by the patient, arguing the policy was limited to "claims that result from professional services that you provided or should have provided." 459 N.W.2d at 705.

Agreeing with St. Paul, the trial court found no coverage. The Minnesota Supreme Court remanded to determine whether transference was involved in the sexual conduct. If transference was involved, there would be coverage. How will the court divine whether the sexual behavior was the result of transference? The Minnesota Supreme Court decided that it would resort to expert testimony to resolve the issue. 459 N.W.2d at 706. However, what expert can sufficiently distinguish between transference and reality.

105. Cotton v. Kambly, 300 N.W.2d 627 (Mich. Ct. App. 1980).

106. 319 N.W.2d 382 (Mich. Ct. App. 1982).

107. Ibid. at 385 (citation omitted).

108. "APA Moves to Discourage Sexual Misconduct in Therapy," *Psychiatric News,* Jan. 4, 1985, p. 17.

109. B. Northrup, "Treating the Mind & Psychotherapy Faces a Stubborn Problem: Abuses by Therapists," *Wall Street Journal*, Oct. 29, 1986, p. A-1. In order to protect clients, three states (Alaska, South Dakota, and Ohio) require attorneys who do not have legal malpractice insurance or carry a certain level of insurance to notify their clients in writing of that fact. A number of other states are considering adopting that requirement.

110. See A. A. Stone & D. C. MacCourt, "Insurance Coverage for Undue Familiarity: Law, Policy, and Economic Reality," in J. D. Bloom, C. C. Nadelson, & M. T. Notman (eds.), *Physician Sexual Misconduct* (Washington, D.C.: American Psychiatric Association, 1999), pp. 37–88; L. Jorgenson, S. B. Bisbing, & P. K. Sutherland, "Therapist-Patient Sexual Exploitation and Insurance Liability," *Tort & Ins. L. J.* 27 (1992): 595; R. Slovenko, "Liability Insurance Coverage in Cases of Psychotherapy Sexual Abuse," *J. Psychiatry & Law* 21 (1993): 277.

There is division of opinion whether a clinic where the therapist is on the staff may be held liable for the therapist's sexual abuse of a patient. One of two broad approaches is used: direct and vicarious. Under direct liability, the clinic is held responsible for its own negligence in hiring, retaining, or supervising the therapist. Under vicarious liability, otherwise known as *respondeat superior,* it is not necessary to prove fault on the part of the clinic. Vicarious liability may be imputed to the clinic even though the therapist is not acting in the course of his employment. In Andrews v. United States, 732 F.2d 366 (4th Cir. 1984), the court held that the employer was not liable for the acts of a physician's assistant who "seduced" a patient because the physician's assistant was not furthering the employer's business by seducing the patient. In Marston v. Minneapolis Clinic, 329 N.W.2d 306 (Minn. 1982), the court, applying a *but for* test, held the clinic liable for its employee's sexual misconduct. The court ruled that the jury could weigh the facts and determine that the sexual contact would not have occurred but for the psychologist's employment with the clinic. In the conclusion of a vigorous and lengthy dissent in Doe v. Samaritan Counseling Center, 791 P.2d 344 (Alaska 1990), which held a clinic responsible for the sexual abuse of a patient by a therapist, Justice Moore wrote:

> The motivation for the court's holding is not difficult to find. Therapist-patient sex is a serious problem in the psychotherapeutic community. However, imposing vicarious liability on mental health employers for the sexual misconduct of their employees is not an appropriate response to the problem. . . . [I]mposing vicarious liability would create incentives to invade the privacy of the therapist-patient relationship that is essential to the psychotherapeutic enterprise. . . . [P]erhaps most important, spreading the cost of therapist-patient sex to the consumers of mental health services is unfair.

111. G. Schwartz, "The Ethics and the Economics of Tort Liability Insurance," *Cornell L. Rev.* 75 (1990): 313.

112. A. A. Stone, "No Good Deed Goes Unpunished: The Case of Martha Gay, M.D.," *Psychiatric Times,* Mar. 1990, p. 24; see also S. Diesenhouse, "Therapists Start to Address Damage Done by Therapists," *New York Times,* Aug. 20, 1989, p. E-5.

113. Letter of Oct. 24, 1994, from Dr. Alan I. Levenson, CEO of Psychiatrists' Purchasing Group, to Newsletter, Louisiana Psychiatric Medical Association.

114. Interview with Ann Landers, reprinted in *Time,* Aug. 21, 1989, p. 62. Dr. Jules Masserman, one of the preeminent psychiatrists of the twentieth century, was accused of drugging a female patient with sodium amobarbital in order to have sexual relations with her in his office. B. Noel, *You Must Be Dreaming* (New York: Poseidon Press, 1992). In response, Dr. Alan Stone commented, "The APA had been terribly battered by two decades of revelations about sexual abuse of patients. Now the finger of accusation had pointed at a former president." A. A. Stone, Book Review, *Psychiatric Times,* Apr. 1993, p. 32.

115. F. Bacon, preface to *Maxims of the Law,* quoted in J. Bartlett, *Familiar Quotations* (10th ed. 1919).

116. Reuters news release, Aug. 9, 1990.

117. Freud made these comments in response to the practice of Dr. Sandor Ferenczi of embracing his patients. In nearly thirty years of practice, it never became erotic intimacy, and he claimed that his technique helped his patients. From all reports, they did improve. Freud was mainly concerned about the reputation of the profession. E. Jones, *The Life and Work of Sigmund Freud* (New York: Basic Books, 1953), vol. 3, p. 163.

118. L. Tiger & R. Fox, *The Imperial Animal* (New York: Holt, Rinehart & Winston, 1971).

119. Of equal protection of the laws, see Williamson v. Lee Optical, 348 U.S. 483, 489 (1955); Briggs v. Kerrigan, 431 F.2d 967, 969 (1st Cir. 1970); Doe v. Director of Dept of Social Servs., 468 N.W.2d 862, 870 (Mich. Ct. App. 1991), *reversed,* 487 N.W.2d 166 (Mich. 1992).

120. L. Jorgenson & R. Randles, supra note 67, at p. 189.

121. Figueiredo-Torres v. Nickel, 584 A.2d 69 (Md. 1991); Rowe v. Bennett, 514 A.2d 802

(Me. 1986); Mazza v. Huffaker, 300 S.E.2d 833 (N.C. App. 1983); Jackenthal v. Kirsch, New York County Sup. Ct., Nov. 1, 1995, No. 18423/90; Doe v. Wood, 10 PNLR 50 (1995). In Barbra Streisand's film *The Prince of Tides*, the analyst became involved with the patient's brother following the consultation process. B. Streisand, "Physicians, Heal Thyselves," *Newsweek*, June 29, 1992, p. 14. A malpractice action by a spouse of the patient against the therapist for sexual involvement with the patient-spouse has generally not been successful. In effect, the therapist is held not to have a duty in this regard to the spouse of the patient. In Homer v. Long, 599 A.2d 1193 (Md. App. 1992), the court held that the spouse failed to state a cause of action primarily because the damages suffered (the adultery or the breakup of the marriage) constituted "alienation of affections," a cause of action that had been abolished in the state. The court further stated that the therapist owed no duty to the spouse "even if, as here, the spouse is the one who initially employed the therapist and is paying the therapist's fees."

122. As the rules of evidence do not strictly apply in board proceedings, evidence may be discovered that could not easily be obtained within the confines of a judicial proceeding. The Michigan Public Health Code, specifically section 333.16221, sets forth the authority of the Department of Consumer and Industry Services to investigate activities related to the practice of a health professional. This section of the code also lists numerous specific violations which are grounds for proceeding with disciplinary action. Sexual contact with a patient can be ground for a personal disqualification, that being lack of good moral character. The sanctions permitted for lack of good moral character include probation, limitation, denial, suspension, revocation, restitution, community services, or fine. MCL 333.16226.

123. M. Borruso, "Sexual Abuse by Psychotherapists: The Call for a Uniform Criminal Statute," *Am. J. L. & Med.* 17 (1991): 289.

124. Annot., "Constitutionality, Construction, and Application of Statutes Abolishing Civil Actions for Alienation of Affections, Criminal Conversation, Seduction, and Breach of Promise to Marry," 158 A.L.R. 617–18 (1945) (discussing New York Civil Practice Act, art. 2A, sec. 61-a).

9

Failure
to Treat
and
Related
Issues

In general, nonfeasance does not result in liability unless there is a duty to act. With some exception, there is no duty to render assistance to another who is in peril, no matter how easily aid might be furnished, and regardless of whether the failure to act is inadvertent or intentional. The expert swimmer, with a boat and a rope at hand, who sees another drowning, is not required to do anything at all about it, but may sit on the dock and watch the person drown. Thus, under this principle, a physician is under no duty to answer the call of a stranger who is dying and might be saved.[1]

Deeply rooted in the law of torts is the distinction between *nonfeasance* and *misfeasance,* but during the last century liability for nonfeasance has been imposed in a limited group of relations, in which public sentiment and views of social policy have led the courts to find a duty of affirmative action. A special relation between the parties has afforded a justification for the creation of a duty. Notably, upon the formation of a physician-patient relation, there comes about a duty on the physician to care for the patient. A carrier is required to take reasonable affirmative steps to aid a passenger in peril, and an innkeeper to aid his guests. It also is recognized that if the defendant's own negligence has been responsible for the plaintiff's situation, a relation has arisen that imposes a duty to make a reasonable effort to give assistance and avoid any further harm. Moreover, when a duty of care is voluntarily undertaken, as when one comes to the rescue of another, the rescuer assumes a duty to use proper care in the performance of the task. Just when the duty is undertaken, when it ends, and what conduct is required, are nowhere clearly defined, and perhaps cannot be.

Once therapy is undertaken, the physician-patient relationship continues until (1) it is terminated by mutual consent, (2) it is ended by the patient, (3) the services are no longer needed, or (4) the physician withdraws after giving the patient reasonable notice. As a matter of good practice, if not law, a physician who wishes to terminate a patient in need of further care should at least offer to refer the patient to another therapist. A physician who abandons a patient who later harms himself or another could be held liable for malpractice.

As hereinafter discussed, an action for failure to treat may arise out of the inpatient or outpatient setting.

Institutionalized Patients

In the case of an individual who has been institutionalized, the right to treatment is generally claimed on the basis of provisions of the commitment statute that premise involuntary commitment on the patient's need for care and treatment. While not common, it has been held that an involuntarily committed patient may recover damages for inordinate length of confinement resulting from a lack of proper psychiatric care. The claim may be based on a violation of an individual's constitutional right to freedom. In *O'Connor v. Donaldson*,[2] it will be recalled, the U.S. Supreme Court ruled that "a State cannot constitutionally confine without more [i.e., without treatment] a nondangerous individual who is capable of surviving safely in freedom by himself or with the help of willing and responsible family members or friends." Put another way: under *Donaldson*, the mentally ill have no right to treatment, no more than anyone else, and they may not be kept in an institution without treatment (whatever that is) when they are not gravely disabled or dangerous on account of mental illness. Donaldson was awarded both compensatory and punitive damages.

In another much-discussed case, *Whitree v. State*,[3] the state of New York was held liable for confining and failing to treat a patient who had been committed because of incompetence to stand trial.[4] The patient was confined for over fourteen years; he was a patient only in the sense that he was "patient." Had he received the maximum sentence for the theft alleged, he would have been in jail for three years. His expert testified that with proper care his competence to stand trial could have been restored within three to six months after admission. His diagnosis at commitment was chronic alcoholism with paranoid features, whereas upon discharge he was found to be "a schizoid personality with paranoid features, but not in such a state of idiocy, imbecility, or insanity as to be incapable of understanding or contributing to his defense." The court commented that the hospital record "was about as inadequate a record as we have ever examined."

Earlier, in the right to treatment case of *Rouse v. Cameron*,[5] Judge Bazelon had intimated that failure to supply treatment may "raise a question of due process of law," may "violate the equal protection clause," or may "be so inhumane as to be 'cruel and unusual punishment.'" The remedy afforded in *Rouse* was discharge from the hospital on a writ of habeas corpus; the remedy afforded in *Whitree* was money damage.

The standard of care applied by the court in *Whitree* is the general rule applicable in malpractice cases: careful treatment "consonant with medical standards." The court concluded that careful examination was totally lacking and that no competent professional judgment had been made. Clearly, the total absence of diagnostic investigation is inconsistent with any standard of rehabilitative care. The decision was indicative of the public concern over the inadequacies of state mental institutions and the treatment furnished there.

Failure to Seek Hospitalization

An aspect of failure to treat is failure to seek hospitalization of a patient in need of hospitalization, particularly in the case of a suicidal patient. On the one hand, negligent certification can lead to liability in torts of malpractice (negligence), defamation, or assault and battery.[6] On the other hand, although it does not often occur, a therapist may be held responsible in not seeking the hospitalization of a patient or not providing other treatment.[7]

An illustration is a Wisconsin case, *Shuster v. Altenberg*.[8] A patient who was diagnosed as manic depressive and was taking medication, within an hour of seeing her therapist, drove into a tree at sixty miles per hour, killing herself and leaving her seventeen-year-old daughter a paraplegic. The complaint alleged that the therapist, a psychiatrist, was negligent in his management and care of the patient "in failing to recognize or take appropriate actions in the face of her psychotic condition, including failure to seek her commitment, to modify her medication, to alert and warn the patient or her family of her condition or its dangerous implications." The patient was taking medications that carry warnings not to drive while under their influence.

For the purposes of addressing the legal sufficiency of the complaint, the Wisconsin Supreme Court categorized the allegations as follows: (1) negligent diagnosis and treatment, (2) failure to warn the patient's family of her condition and its dangerous implications, and (3) failure to seek the commitment of the patient. Generally, once a court determines that a claim has been stated as to one particular theory, it will not proceed to determine what additional theories are valid, but in this case the court, upon the request of both parties and in the interest of judicial economy, ruled on all three theories, finding them all legally sufficient. For one, the court said, a therapist may be held liable in negligence for failure to warn of the side effects of a medication if the side effects were such that a patient should have been cautioned against driving, because it was foreseeable that an accident could result, causing harm to the patient or third parties if the patient drove while using the medication. For another, the court said, if it is ultimately proven that it would have been foreseeable to a psychiatrist, exercising due care, that by failing to warn a third person or by failing to take action to institute detention or commitment proceedings someone would be harmed, negligence will be established. The pleadings established grounds upon which a jury could find negligence and could further find such negligence to have constituted the cause-in-fact of the injury.[9] In an article oft-quoted by the courts, Victor Schwartz, then a law professor, wrote:

First, it seems clear that liability could be imposed upon a psychiatrist for a gross error in judgment with respect to whether a patient should be confined. Giving full ambit to psychological justifications for not confining patients unless absolutely necessary, suicidal symptoms may be so apparent that confinement would be ordered by a psychiatrist of ordinary skill. For example, if an individual has made serious suicidal attempts, has been deeply depressed, has suffered loss of sleep, appetite, and in effect is almost unable to function in society, but his psychiatrist has declined to have him placed in a hospital, the psychiatrist might be held liable for the individual's subsequent suicide.[10]

Yet, suicide prediction is notoriously unreliable, with suicide prediction resulting in numerous false positives, that is, prediction that individuals will commit suicide when in fact they would not. The courts recognize that the widespread use of civil commitment to prevent suicide would result in numerous patients who are not suicide risks being subjected to a loss of freedom.[11] In the commitment and release context, the courts tend to indulge professional judgment in the assessment of risks versus benefits, since aberrant behavior such as suicide and homicide occurs only infrequently and is not amenable to reliable prediction.[12]

In a Florida case, Linda Kay Paddock went to a wooded area, took a butane cigarette lighter from her purse, and set her blouse on fire. She suffered serious burns over most of her body but she survived, and she brought a malpractice action against her psychiatrist, Dr. Chowallur Chacko, claiming that he should have had her hospitalized before she burned herself. She saw Dr. Chacko just once before setting herself on fire. The psychiatric testimony at trial was extensive, taking 793 pages of transcript. Her experts testified that she was suicidal and that Dr. Chacko should have sought her hospitalization. After deliberating for thirteen hours, the jury concluded that Dr. Chacko had been negligent, and that his negligence had caused Paddock's injuries. The jury further concluded that Paddock had not been contributorily negligent. They awarded Paddock $2.15 million, twice the largest malpractice award in Orange County, Florida.

The Florida Court of Appeals reversed the judgment, saying that there is no legal duty to commit a patient to a hospital involuntarily, at least not in Florida. Such an obligation, the court said, would "create an intolerable burden on psychiatrists and the practice of psychiatry."[13] The court commented, "The science of psychiatry represents the penultimate grey area. Numerous cases underscore the inability of psychiatric experts to predict, with any degree of precision, an individual's propensity to do violence to himself or others. . . . A substantial body of literature suggests that the psychiatric field cannot even agree on appropriate diagnosis, much less recommend a course of treatment."[14]

Premature Discharge

Premature discharge is another aspect of failure to treat. The psychiatrist and hospital are caught between the Scylla of tardy discharge of a patient and the Charybdis of premature discharge. The former may constitute malpractice or false imprisonment; the latter may result in the patient's assault upon a third person or suicide. The psychiatrist and hospital are clearly in a quandary in determining when to release a patient who has been involuntarily committed because of possible dangerousness. Liability is imposed if a patient who causes harm was negligently released. The intervening criminal act of the patient does not per se break the chain of causal connection so as to insulate the psychiatrist or hospital from liability. A negligent party may be held liable for harm caused by the reasonably foreseeable criminal acts of third persons, in this case, the acts of the patient.

Thus, in one case, an injured party obtained a substantial judgment against a private sanatorium and a psychiatrist for premature release of a patient with aggressive tendencies. The patient, having attacked his wife, had been committed to a state mental hospital and shortly thereafter transferred to a private sanatorium, where he stayed for four months. Both his confinements were uneventful, and the patient, according to the hospital, appeared to have recovered. Shortly after discharge, however, during a conference with the plaintiff, who was the patient's wife's attorney, the patient leaped across the desk, grabbed the attorney's head, and actually bit off a substantial part of his nose, apparently to spite his face.[15]

Insurance or managed care limitations may pose obstacles to treatment resulting in a failure to treat. A physician may have an obligation to assist patients in obtaining payment of health care. At a minimum, a physician must be aware of reimbursement constraints, so that he can promptly advise the patient. A physician may be obliged to engage in bureaucratic infighting, when a utilization review process has rejected his recommendation.[16] The courts have held external utilization review bodies liable for negligent review if a patient suffers harm through denial of care, but that depends on an adequate presentation by the physician.[17]

The following communication was sent by Dr. Dean Robinson of Louisiana to an insurance company, with copies to the state insurance commissioner and the attorney general, and it resulted in a successful resolution to an appeal, with the claim paid in full:

> The following is in response to your letter of reconsideration dated . . . regarding Ms. . . . . In this letter you state that your retrospective review of her hospitalization concluded that her admission was "medically unnecessary."
>
> I have reviewed the medical records, and this case has also been submitted to our in-hospital utilization review committee. All of the medical personnel who have looked at this case are in agreement that this patient clearly meets the criteria for inpatient treatment due to her well-documented suicide risk.
>
> Since the information substantiating her need for hospital treatment is so well established in the chart, we are concerned that your refusal to honor your obligation to pay for her treatment constitutes either a serious breach of professional standards, or is simply an act of bad faith. Since you have also refused to provide us with utilization review criteria employed to justify this decision, as well as refused to provide the name of the physician involved with the retrospective review, we have no choice but to refer this matter to the Louisiana State Insurance Commissioner and to the office of the Attorney General. Recent revisions in the Louisiana Medical Practice Statutes require that any physician who makes judgments regarding medical necessity must have a license to practice in this state. Your failure to provide documentation of this licensure implies that you are potentially in knowing violation of this statute.
>
> In addition, we will file official complaints with the appropriate legislative and licensure authorities in Texas and Arkansas.

This matter can be resolved quickly if you wish by simply honoring your obligation to provide decent service to your beneficiary. Or you can continue to attempt to justify your actions before the appropriate regulatory bodies. Please contact this office if you wish to provide additional clarification of your position.[18]

The Emergency-Room Situation

The emergency-room situation provides a wide area of litigation. Even a private hospital may be held liable for refusing to care for an individual in an emergency situation, on the theory that the public is led to believe that it can come to it in the case of emergency. Frequently, emergency rooms are understaffed, lack facilities, and turn away persons in need of attention. As a general practice, the police tend to take emergency cases to public rather than to private hospitals.

Withdrawing from Providing Treatment

Once there is a professional relationship, which establishes a duty of care, the right to withdraw is contingent upon giving the patient reasonable notice so that he may secure other services. The condition of the patient, the size of the community, and the availability of other services are factors that determine the reasonableness of a withdrawal notice. In undertaking a service, a special agreement may be made that the engagement is limited to a particular treatment or procedure.

In the wake of litigation imposing liability on a psychiatrist on the ground of abandonment, the American Psychiatric Association's Managed Care Help Line received numerous calls about terminating relationships with patients. As a result it provided a sample letter to patients that states:

> This is to inform you that I believe it is necessary to terminate our professional relationship. [Psychiatrist may, but is not required to, specify reason.]
>
> I have been serving as your psychiatrist since [specify date] and am currently treating you for [indicate diagnosis] with a program of [specify treatment mode, including any drugs].
>
> In my view, you [would/would not] benefit from continued treatment.
>
> If you wish to continue to receive treatment, you are, of course, free to contact one of the following [psychiatrists/facilities], [who/which] may be willing to accept you as a patient: [indicate specific referrals here]. If you find that none of these choices is acceptable, please contact me; I will make every effort to suggest additional alternatives. If you do decide to obtain treatment from one of these psychiatrists or facilities, or from any other psychiatrist or facility of your choice, I will be happy to forward your clinical records to your new doctor on your written authorization.
>
> Finally, be assured that I will be available to treat you until [specify date]. (The following factors, among others, may be used to determine what is "reasonable" in a particular situation: condition of the patient, length of the psychiatrist-patient relationship, availability of other psychiatric services in the community, reason for termination, and amount of money owed, if any.)

The APA Office of Healthcare Systems and Financing also advised: "Although 30 days notice is generally considered appropriate, in a rural or other underserved area it may be necessary to provide longer notice. When terminating a relationship with a patient it is also necessary to give proper instructions concerning any medication the patient is taking (e.g., if stopping medication abruptly could cause injury)."[19] The office also advised that it is never appropriate to sever a treatment relationship when a patient is in an emergency situation, unless the patient agrees to see another clinician or is hospitalized.[20]

Faulty Diagnosis

A physician who makes a diagnostic mistake or error in judgment does not incur liability, whatever the harm, provided the error is one that other similarly trained physicians would have made under comparable circumstances, and provided that all necessary diagnostic means were utilized. A mistaken or missed diagnosis does not in itself constitute fault or malpractice. A physician is not a warrantor of cures. The patient must establish that a wrong diagnosis resulting in inappropriate treatment was caused by the physician's failure to exercise ordinary diligence and skill and that it led to untoward consequences. Whenever doubt exists in the physician's mind and the differential diagnosis includes potentially serious conditions, a record that notes that the doubt was considered is persuasive exculpatory evidence. Good faith or honesty alone does not excuse a faulty diagnosis.

The faulty diagnosis upon which suit is premised in psychiatric malpractice usually involves interpreting as psychological a problem that is essentially physical in origin. James Thurber tells about a man who was seeing double, and he went to a psychiatrist, who decided that the man's problem lay in his inability to make up his mind as to which one of two girls he was in love with. The distracted fellow then called on an ophthalmologist who cleared up the condition with eye drops.

Organic (bodily caused) syndromes can mimic functional (mind caused) disorders in their symptomatology. The emotional responses may be identical. Thus, neurological disorders such as brain tumors, various forms of epilepsy, general paresis (the late stages of syphilis), traumatic brain damage (concussion, subdural hematoma), multiple sclerosis, and the diseases of aging (arteriosclerosis) often produce neurotic or psychotic symptoms. Endocrine disorders such as pituitary disorders, hyperthyroidism, and hypothyroidism may produce neurotic and psychotic symptoms. Numerous general medical conditions such as colitis and vitamin deficiency may masquerade as a psychic disorder. It is often charged that physicians tend to overlook the dynamic factors of disorders, while psychiatrists, notwithstanding their medical training, tend to overlook organic factors. The philosophy that history-taking or a physical examination might interfere with transference or might be considered a seduction has at times had tragic results.

Generally, there is no duty to ask for a consultation. However, the fact that psychiatrists are medically trained does not obviate the need to obtain a consultation in certain cases. An example is the negligent diagnosis of a veteran suffering from organic brain damage who was diagnosed at a Veterans Administration Hospital as psychosomatic and was so advised and released without having received proper treatment. The patient, wounded in combat, had experienced blackouts, unaccountable falls, and severe head pains. The court held the hospital liable in negligence because of the presence of manifest neurological symptoms indicative of organic brain damage, which were either overlooked or not understood. The court found the hospital negligent both in the manner of its examination and in failing to make necessary diagnostic tests.[21]

Let us assume negligent failure to properly diagnose with the result of inappropriate treatment. Then there are questions of (1) proximate causation and (2) resultant damages. The defense always is that *even if* proper diagnosis had been made and resultant treatment undertaken, the treatment would have been futile, impossible, or both. The failure to diagnose cancer is the most common of misdiagnosis-type cases. In the cancer case, one can expect to hear that the failure to diagnose cancer, even if true and tantamount to malpractice, would not have made any difference. In other words, "So what?"

This brings us to an evidentiary question: What amount of proof is necessary to show the loss of a chance, and does it have any real value if it is proven? *What* caused a loss is a separate question from what the *nature* and *extent* of the loss are. The *lost chance* doctrine could create an injustice. Health care providers could find themselves defending cases simply because a patient fails to improve or where serious disease processes are not arrested because another course of action could possibly bring a better result.[22] A patient who has been in psychotherapy for over twelve years claims that it was a waste of time and that it resulted in the loss of her child-bearing years. Assuming the therapist was negligent in not obtaining a consultation, or in not using medication, the necessary proof that would sustain a theory of lost chance is a controversial issue.

Assume that an individual was negligently detained and was delayed in boarding the *Titanic*. The wrongful detention would turn out to have saved the individual's life. Some commentators who have considered the "doomed steamer" example have concluded, on a visceral level, that the threat to the ship was simply too remote and contingent to be introduced into a loss valuation. Law professor William Prosser wrote that "if such factors as these are to be considered as reducing value, they must be in operation when the defendant causes harm, and so imminent that reasonable men would take them into account."[23]

In Poland during the time of martial law, as the story goes, a soldier shoots a man on a Warsaw street one evening at ten minutes before eleven o'clock. "But curfew doesn't start until eleven," a bystander protests. "Yes," says the soldier, "but I know where that man lived. He never would have made it on time."

Protecting Patients from Injury

What of injury inflicted by an assaultive patient on another patient? Patients in institutions are entitled to such reasonable care and attention as will insure the safety of themselves and others in light of their known mental and physical conditions.[24] This duty of care not only includes prevention of improper direct acts by hospital personnel but also protection from all conditions that may create danger of injury to the patient. Depending on the circumstances, injury to one patient at the hands of another may be a breach of the duty of reasonable care and may lead to liability on the part of the hospital or the psychiatrist.[25] The administrative personnel have general responsibility for overall operation of the hospital, supplies, facilities, supervision, and hiring of staff.

Thus, a patient in one case brought an action against the hospital for a physical beating received at the hands of a fellow patient, who was suffering from delirium tremens. The hospital was aware of his violent nature and posted a female nurse in his room as a guard. The hospital was found negligent, however, for having breached its duty to provide safe conditions, because one female nurse was deemed insufficient protection for the other patients.[26]

Overcrowding or understaffing in an institution is no defense. In an action brought by a patient in a state mental hospital for injuries suffered from an attack by a fellow patient, the court recognized that the hospital was 38 percent over-crowded and that sufficient funds were not available to employ an adequate staff; but it was held that the state was negligent in not having an adequate number of personnel to provide their patients with the safety that was due them. Insufficiency of attendants in a mental institution is an act of negligence.[27]

To hold either a hospital or a psychiatrist liable, it must be shown that they were in fact negligent and that this negligence was the proximate cause of the injuries sustained. Neither is an insurer of a patient's well-being, but each is held only to a duty of reasonable care to protect against foreseeable occurrences. Thus, the hospital was found not liable in a case where a patient, while in a work party of seventeen patients supervised by only one attendant, was struck by a fellow patient and suffered the loss of one of his eyes. The court found that the hospital had no knowledge of the violent character of the assailant and that the act had occurred so suddenly that even additional attendants would have been unable to prevent the injury.[28]

An issue that occasionally arises in these cases is contributory negligence. As a general principle, a plaintiff's contributory negligence bars his recovery in an action based on the negligence of the defendant, even though the plaintiff's negligence may be much less serious than that of the defendant. However, the defense of contributory negligence may be untenable when the plaintiff's mental condition places him beyond the sphere of responsibility for his acts.[29]

Notes

1. W. P. Keeton (ed.), *Prosser and Keeton on the Law of Torts* (St. Paul, Minn.: West, 5th ed. 1994), pp. 375–82.

2. 422 U.S. 563 (1975); discussed in chapter 2, on right to treatment.

3. 56 Misc.2d 693, 290 N.Y.S.2d 486 (Ct. Cl. 1968), noted in *Harv. L. Rev.* 82 (1969): 1771.

4. The award, in the amount of $300,000, included compensation for moral and mental degradation, physical injuries, pain and suffering, and loss of earnings during the period.

5. 383 F.2d 451 (D.C. Cir. 1966).

6. In O'Rourke v. O'Rourke, 50 So.2d 832 (La. App. 1951), the plaintiff sued the medical officer who had issued a certificate of commitment without making an examination as re-quired by law. The court held that the medical officer, by so issuing a certificate, was liable for resultant damages. Anyone who maliciously and without probable cause initiates com-mitment proceedings may be liable. Strahan v. Fussell, 218 La. 682, 50 So.2d 805 (1951); Dauphine v. Herbert, 37 So.2d 829 (La. App. 1948); Pickles v. Anton, 49 N.D. 47, 189 N.W. 684 (1922); Lindsay v. Woods, 27 S.W.2d 263 (Tex. Civ. App. 1930).

Furthermore, a physician who makes a negligent examination as well as one who makes no examination which causes a competent person to be committed to an institution is liable. Bacon v. Bacon, 76 Miss. 458, 24 So. 968 (1899); Ayres v. Russell, 50 Hun. 282, 3 N.Y.S. 338 (1888). But see Williams v. LeBar, 141 Pa. 149, 21 Atl. 525 (1891); herein was a mere error in judgment. Hospital authorities who interfere with the efforts of a committed person to obtain a writ of habeas corpus may be held liable for damages. Hoff v. State, 279 N.Y. 490, 18 N.E.2d 671 (1939).

In Maben v. Rankin, 55 Cal.2d 139, 10 Cal. Rptr. 353, 358 P.2d 681 (1961), a husband requested a psychiatrist to hospitalize his wife and provide treatment. On grounds of the patient's symptoms and the husband's story, the psychiatrist administered a sedative and admitted the wife to a sanatorium of which he was part owner. Subsequently suing the psychiatrist and hospital, she alleged that she was not mentally ill but had been upset only because of her husband's questionable conduct in marital matters. The court awarded her damages for false imprisonment and assault and battery.

A similar holding awarding damages is Stowers v. Ardmore Acres Hospital, 19 Mich. App. 115, 172 N.W.2d 497 (1969), *aff'd,* 386 Mich. 119, 191 N.W.2d 355 (1971), where the court said that the husband's consent is irrelevant, for he cannot force medical care upon his wife. The Michigan Supreme Court in the course of its decision said: "Psychiatry is a relatively new professional discipline and, as with all disciplines, there is a great deal of controversy within the profession as to precisely what methods of treatment should be used. Psychiatrists have a great deal of power over their patients. In the case of a person confined to an institution, this power is virtually unlimited. All professions (including the legal profession) contain unscrupulous individuals who use their position to injure others. The law must provide protection against the torts committed by these individuals." 191 N.W.2d at 363. See A. McCoid, "A Reappraisal of Liability for Unauthorized Medical Treatment," *Minn. L. Rev.* 41 (1957): 381; W. Kelly, "The Physician, the Patient, and the Consent," *Kan. L. Rev.* 8 (1960): 405.

7. In Kockelman v. Segal, 61 Cal. App.4th 491, 71 Cal. Rptr. 552 (1998), a wrongful death action, the surviving wife alleged that the defendant psychiatrist and clinic were negligent in treating her husband for his chronic depression and that this negligence was a proximate cause of her husband's suicide. The trial court granted summary judgement in favor of the defendants, finding as a matter of law that there was no duty owed to the decedent because he was being treated as an outpatient rather than in a hospital setting. The court of appeals reversed, concluding that this is not the law. The court said, "Whether [the psychiatrist] acted within the duty of care in the circumstances of this case involves factual determinations which must be resolved by the opinions and specialized knowledge of experts in the field. . . . [T]he trial court erred in ruling that [the decedent's] status as an outpatient decided the issue of duty as a matter of law." 71 Cal. Rptr. at 561. See also Bellah v. Greenson, 81 Cal. App.3d 614, 146 Cal. Rptr. 535 (1978).

In Cole v. Taylor, 301 N.W.2d 766 (Iowa 1981), the Iowa Supreme Court held that as a matter of public policy, a patient may not recover in tort on a claim that the psychiatrist, in his professional capacity, should have prevented the patient from committing murder. The *Tarasoff* duty runs to the victim, not to the patient. A slayer may not acquire property as result of slaying. 20 Pa. C.S.A. §8802 ("Slayer's Act"). However, on a theory of malpractice, if the patient commits suicide rather than homicide, a wrongful death action would likely be entertained.

8. 424 N.W.2d 159 (Wis. 1978).

9. See also Freese v. Lemmon, 210 N.W.2d 576 (Iowa 1973); Duvall v. Goldin, 139 Mich. App. 342, 362 N.W.2d 275 (1984); Kaiser v. Suburban Transportation System, 65 Wash.2d 461, 401 P.2d 350 (1965); Annot., 43 A.L.R.4th 153 (1986).

10. V. Schwartz, "Civil Liability for Causing Suicide: A Synthesis of Law and Psychiatry," *Vand. L. Rev.* 24 (1971): 217; cited in Adams v. Carter County Memorial Hosp., 548 S.W.2d 307 (Tenn. 1977).

11. It was so stated in Johnson v. United States, 409 F.Supp. 1283 (M.D.Fla. 1976).

12. Schrempf v. State, 66 N.Y.2d 289, 496 N.Y.S.2d 973, 487 N.E.2d 883 (1985). The standard of care is evaluated in terms of the therapist's speciality. Stepakoff v. Kantar, 393 Mass. 836, 473 N.E.2d 1131 (1985).

13. Paddock v. Chacko, 522 S.E.2d 410 (Fla. App. 1988). The case is discussed at length in J. L. Kelley, *Psychiatric Malpractice* (New Brunswick, N.J.: Rutgers University Press, 1996).

14. 522 So.2d at 413.

15. Vassalo v. Halcyon Rest Hosp., cited in *Medical World News,* Oct. 14, 1966. See also Merchants National Bank & Trust Co. v. United States, 272 F.Supp. 409 (D.C. No. Dak. 1967)—Veterans Administration hospital doctors ignored indications of the seriousness of a mental patient's illness and placed the patient at a ranch, from which the patient departed and killed his wife. See Underwood v. United States, 356 F.2d 92 (5th Cir. 1966). This case involved the negligent release of a mentally ill airman who had been hospitalized and had been known to have attacked his estranged former wife; the air force then assigned him to duty where he had access to firearms with which he shot and killed his former wife. See Higgins v. State, 43 Misc.2d 793, 252 N.Y.S.2d 163 (1964)—negligence was found in allowing a state hospital pa-

tient to leave the hospital grounds without permission, and such negligence was deemed the proximate cause of injuries sustained by a young boy, who was beaten by the patient.

On the other hand, no liability is imposed for an honest error in judgment in releasing a patient into the community. Thus, in a New York case, the state was not held culpable for the violent actions of a state mental hospital patient on leave, inasmuch as qualified physicians of the institution had judged the patient to be sufficiently controlled to be able to go home for a specified period. Orman v. Nell York, 37 App. Div.2d 674, 322 N.Y.S.2d 914 (Sup. Ct. 1971).

16. Wickline v. State, 192 Cal. App.3d 1630, 239 Cal. Rptr. 810 (1986).

17. Wilson v. Blue Cross of Southern California, 271 Cal. Rptr. 876, 222 Cal. App.3d 660 (1990).

18. The form letter is suggsted in the *Newsletter of Louisiana Psychiatric Medical Society*, Fall/Winter 1999, p. 17.

19. American Psychiatric Association, 1400 K St., NW, Washington, D.C. 20005 (tel.: (202) 682-6070).

20. Abandonment of a patient who thereupon harms another may give rise to a cause of action by the patient against the therapist. In a case that caused concern in the psychiatric community, a lawsuit was filed against Dr. Myron Liptzin by the patient, a law student at the University of North Carolina, who killed two people on the streets of Chapel Hill eight months after Dr. Liptzin last saw him. The student, Wendell Williamson, was found not guilty by reason of insanity in the criminal proceeding against him, and then he sued Dr. Liptzin, of the University of North Carolina student health clinic, claiming that he had not taken his psychosis seriously enough. Experts pointed to flaws in Dr. Liptzin's treamtent—including failure to obtain and read the full record of the patient's prior hospitalization and misdiagnosis. Dr. Liptzin had said the patient had a delusional disorder, rather than schizophrenia, and he allowed the patient to leave treatment without a specific follow-up appointment. In rebuttal, Dr. Liptzin noted that the lack of specific referral was in keeping with the standard of care provided by a student health service, and he seemed to suggest that he chose a less stigmatizing diagnosis because he did not want to damage his patient's career prospects and that his treatment would have been the same regardless of the diagnosis. The jury, after three days of deliberation, returned a $500,000 verdict against Dr. Liptzin. North Carolina follows a rule of contributory negligence under which a plaintiff who is in any way negligent cannot be compensated, but the jury exculpated Williamson of any fault. The North Carolina Court of Appeals reversed, holding that the "defendant's alleged negligence was not the proximate cause of plaintiff's injuries." Williamson v. Liptzin, 539 S.E.2d 313 (N.C. App. 2000). The North Carolina Supreme Court declined to hear the plaintiff's appeal of the ruling. Williamson v. Liptzin, 548 S.E.2d 734 (N.C. 2001). See P. S. Appelbaum, "Can a Psychiatrist Be Held Responsible When a Patient Commits Murder?" *Psychiat. Serv.* 53 (Jan. 2002): 27; R. Slovenko, "The Verdict Against Myron Liptzin—Who Sets the Standard of Care?" *Psychiatric Times*, Sept. 1999, pp. 20–21. See also Cole v. Taylor, supra note 7.

21. Hungerford v. United States, 307 F.2d 99 (9th Cir. 1962), *overruled on other grounds*, Ramirez v. United States, 567 F.2d 854 (9th Cir. 1967). In another case, a psychiatric resident's emergency-room diagnosis of viral sore throat and "hysterical reactions" (when the patient actually had a rare staphylococcal infection that ultimately caused his death) led to a $200,000 settlement against the hospital. As well as maintaining that the psychiatric resident was not competent to examine the patient, the plaintiffs (patient's wife and three children) alleged that he had been negligent in diagnosing the breathing difficulties as hysterical in origin and in not calling for a consultation since the symptoms were out of his field of expertise or knowledge. It was alleged that he should have kept the patient under observation at the hospital, where a tracheotomy could have been performed. The hospital claimed that the patient had a disease that was very rare in adults, that all patients with sore throats cannot be hospitalized, and that no consultation was required in view of the known symptoms. Weinshenk v. Kaiser Foundation Hosp., Cal. Super. Ct., Alameda Cy., Docket No. 40027, 1971.

22. In Delaney v. Cade, 255 Kan. 199, 873 P.2d 175 (1994), the Kansas Supreme Court, while recognizing a cause of action for the lost chance for a better recovery due to malpractice, expressed a caveat: "In adopting and applying the loss of chance theory to medical malpractice cases, it must always be kept in mind that the practice of medicine and the furnishing of appropriate health care is not an exact science. In many, if not most, instances there is more than one acceptable approach to treatment, and the fact that one doctor selects one

method as opposed to another does not in and of itself mean that one method is better than or preferable to another. For every treatment there are undoubtedly other doctors who might have performed or used a different one. Courts should use extreme caution in second-guessing the methods used by medical care providers, particularly in an area as nebulous as the loss of a chance for a better or more satisfactory recovery." 873 P.2d at 187. See R. B. Stuart, *Trick or Treatment: How and When Psychotherapy Fails* (Champaign, Ill.: Research Press, 1970).

23. W. Prosser, *Handbook of the Law of Torts* (St. Paul, Minn.: West, 4th ed. 1971), p. 321; discussed in J. H. King, "Causation, Valuation, and Chance in Personal Injury Torts Involving Preexisting Conditions and Future Consequences," *Yale L.J.* 90 (1981): 1353.

24. Wood v. Samaritan Institution, 26 Cal.2d 847, 161 P.2d 556 (1945); G. Garcetti & J. M. Suarez, "The Liability of Psychiatric Hospitals for the Act of Their Patients," *Am. J. Psychiatry* 124 (1968): 961.

25. A Texas appellate court held that a patient who was assaulted at a hospital operated by the Texas Department of Mental Health and Mental Retardation may sue the department for violating the patient bill of rights promulgated under the Texas Health and Safety Code. Texas Dept. of Mental Health & Mental Retardation, 2000 WL 550822 (Tex. App. 2000).

26. Univ. of Louisville v. Hammock, 127 Ky. 564, 106 S.W. 219 (1907). See Annot., 48 A.L.R.3d 1288 (1972).

27. Luke v. State, 253 App. Div. 783, 1 N.Y.S.2d 19 (1937). See also Rossing v. State, 47 N.Y.S.2d 262 (Ct. Cl. 1944); Gould v. State, 181 Misc. 884, 46 N.Y.S.2d 313 (Ct. Cl. 1944).

28. DiFiore v. State, 275 App. Div. 885, 88 N.Y.S.2d 815 (1949).

29. Gould v. State, 181 Misc. 884, 46 N.Y.S.2d 313 (Ct. Cl. 1944); DeMartini v. Alexander Sanitarium, 192 Cal. App.2d 442, 13 Cal. Rptr. 564 (Ct. App. 1961).

10
Suicide

Suicide or attempted suicide is appallingly common. Since the 1950s the suicide rate in the United States has tripled. About 30,000 people a year commit suicide; another 750,000 attempt it, including 500,000 whose suicidal attempts are severe enough to bring them to an emergency room. One in five high school students say they seriously considered suicide within the year. More than 90 percent of all suicides involve mental illness or the abuse of alcohol, drugs, or an alcohol-drug combination. According to the Center for Disease Control, between 1981 and 1998, 19,312 people in Michigan took their lives by self-inflicted injury (homicides and killings by police killed 17,945).[1]

The majority of people who commit suicide are profoundly depressed. It is redundant but necessary to say—when living hurts too much, when hope is lost, suicide is taken as a way out. Most people at high risk for suicide, however, remain undiagnosed and untreated, though there are effective ways to treat the psychiatric illnesses most commonly associated with suicide.[2] The reasons for suicide vary, but a number of common risk factors have been identified.

In many cases, it is a happenstance whether an individual carries out a suicide or homicide, or both. Danger to self is often the flip side of danger to others. (In times gone by, attempted suicide or suicide were regarded as criminal, just as attempted murder or murder, it being a happenstance that occurs, and a suicided person was buried apart from others.) Introject formations may be so tormenting that the individual may seek release from them by suicide or homicide.[3] *Introjection*, of course, is the unconscious mental process whereby loved or hated external objects are symbolically absorbed within oneself. It is the converse of projection. In severe depression, the individual may unconsciously direct unacceptable hatred or aggression toward oneself or others. The indescribable pain of depression (often as a result of rage turned inward) may prompt suicide. In certain times and places, exorcism would be used to get rid of the introject, or as commonly said, the devil.[4]

The rate of suicide attempts in individuals with comorbid panic disorder tends to be higher than the rate of suicide attempts in individuals with depression alone. The association is strong between suicide attempts and panic disorder. Panic disorder's debilitating symptoms can lead to major depression, as might be expected when being constantly plagued by recurrent, unexpected panic attacks where there is intense apprehension, fearfulness, or terror, often associated with feelings of impending doom. The idea of suicide to end the pain becomes attractive.[5]

Suicide may also reveal a guilty conscience, from which death is the only escape.[6] There occurs the phenomenon of splitting, by which suicide is fantasized as a means of getting rid of the bad part of the self rather than to die. Then, too, as usually portrayed in opera, suicide may be provoked by a beloved's rejection.

Among youths the strongest risk factors are depression, substance abuse, homosexuality, and suicide contagion. Homosexual youths are two to three times more likely to attempt suicide than other young people, and annually they comprise up to 30 percent of completed youth suicides. Whatever the cause, be it discrimination or sexual conflict, internalized self-loathing is common.[7] Suicide has notably increased among youths with significant conformity problems, which supports the concept of contagion: when they closely identify with those who have committed suicide, and when faced with seemingly impossible problems, suicide may appear an attractive solution.[8]

Out of hate for their parents, youngsters may want to kill them, one or both, but instead they commit suicide. The hostility toward the parents is directed toward the self. The suicide is a symbolic killing of the parent. In lieu of taking their own lives, they often become very depressed as a result of the inner-directed hate.

According to reports, more youngsters than ever are depressed—suicide rates for children and teens have tripled since the 1970s. Nearly one out of ten youngsters who develop major depression before puberty goes on to commit suicide. Youngsters who develop depression are three to four times more likely than peers to have drug and alcohol problems by their mid-twenties. Their parents are more likely to be divorced or in conflict. Studies routinely document that children of divorce have a significantly higher suicide rate than children from intact families. There is often a family history of mental illness, giving rise to a genetic explanation for the depression.[9]

In this day of genetic research, it is said that there are genes not only for mental illness but also for impulsivity, aggression, and violence that may lead to heavy risk. Researchers today set out organic causes of suicide along with the social ones. Neurological damage to the fetus caused by alcohol or cocaine use may predispose children to mood disorders that lead to suicide; lack of maternal attention may deprive them of early developmental stability; diet may work adversely on their brains.[10]

Malpractice Suits

Suicide is reportedly the leading cause of malpractice suits filed against mental health professionals—about 20 percent of the total. That number has little to do with the merit of most litigation involving suicide, as it is often based on a mistaken belief that the therapist could have predicted, and intervened to prevent, the suicide. The therapist is often made the scapegoat.

The psychiatrist or hospital is required to use reasonable care and skill to detect a patient's tendency to commit suicide or otherwise injure himself. The most common allegations in a complaint for malpractice following a patient's suicide are: (1) failure to predict or diagnose the suicide; (2) failure to control, supervise, or restrain; (3) failure to medicate properly; (4) failure to observe the patient continuously (twenty-four hours) or on a frequent enough basis (e.g., every fifteen minutes); (5) failure to take an adequate history; (6) inadequate supervision and failure to remove belt or other dangerous objects; and (7) failure to place the patient in a secure room. Failure to detect suicidal tendency, however, is not malpractice "where there is no proof that generally accepted medical standards required the psychiatrist to conclude that the patient was likely to commit suicide."[11] The psychiatrist or hospital is not an insurer of the safety of the patient or others. There must be something to give notice that special care is required.

No one is required to guard against or take measures to avert that which, under the circumstances, would not be reasonably anticipated as likely to happen. It is said, though, that some 50 to 70 percent of patients who subsequently kill themselves communicate their intent in advance, yet for one reason or another, there is a failure to respond to these clues to suicide. Dr. Robert Simon observes, "The evaluation of suicidal risk is one of the most complex, difficult and challenging clinical tasks in psychiatry. Patient suicides are all too common in the practices of mental health clinicians. It is even more common in the practice of primary care physicians.[12] Thus it is extremely important for the practitioner to understand how to conduct a competent suicide-risk assessment."[13] Dr. David S. Viscott puts it this way:

In the practice of psychiatry there are, to put it mildly, many uncertainties. I treated some patients who were so manipulative I would worry before they arrived at the beginning of every session whether they would show up or if they'd killed themselves. You just can't hospitalize everyone who *might* be suicidal. You often can help a patient a great deal more by showing him he can overcome his fears himself *without* hospitalization, but I learned you should never withhold protection in a hospital setting if you believe a patient needs it. Most patients who say they are suicidal won't kill themselves, and yet those patients who *do* kill themselves generally tell someone about their plans or make a cry for help at least once. It's then that they need help the most. When patients really want to kill themselves they usually do it right, by jumping out of windows, by taking massive overdoses of drugs or poison when no one is home, or by swimming miles out from shore on a lonely beach to the point of exhaustion. When a patient who really is suicidal calls for help and you miss the clues and let him go back on the street, the chances, even then, are that he will not kill himself right away. Every patient who presents himself as suicidal needs to be closely followed the first time, just to ensure yourself another chance to pick up clues you might have missed.[14]

Suicide is the number one cause of premature death among manic-depressive and schizophrenic individuals. Approximately 15 percent of suicides are people diagnosed as manic depressive or schizophrenic.[15] Among individuals in the general population the suicide rate is approximately 1 percent.[16] Studies have found that a person who buys a handgun is fifty-seven times more likely than a member of the general population to commit suicide within a week of purchasing the weapon and that suicide is the leading cause of death among gun buyers in the first year after the weapon was purchased.

No-Suicide Pact

In recent years the *no-suicide pact* (or *contract for safety*) has made its way into clinical practice as a way to remove the threat of a suicide. Patients are asked to promise (in writing) that they will not engage in suicidal behavior for a set period of time and that they will call for help rather than act out suicidal thoughts or impulses. This approach is designed to solidify the therapeutic alliance, but it may falsely reassure the clinician, and it may take the place of adequate suicide assessment.[17] The no-suicide pact was originally conceived as an inpatient management technique, but it subsequently has been used in other settings and situations, often, unfortunately, with scant effort to evaluate efficacy. There is no indication that suicide is less likely in the case of a no-suicide pact or that it serves a preventive function.[18] Indeed, the pact may have a negative impact on a patient. Several people close to Marilyn Monroe, because of their concern for her, got her to agree to a no-suicide pact, whereby if she ever seriously thought of killing herself, she would call them. Suicidal individuals have been heard to object to an obligation put on them under the pact. As they say, "Don't lean on me." "The only time you can really rely on a suicide prevention contract is when the patient refuses to sign one," says Dr. Robert Simon. In that case, he says, at least the practitioner will not be mislead into a false sense of security.[19]

Determinative Factors in Litigation

Determinative factors in litigation are knowledge or notice that the patient is likely to harm himself and subsequent failure to take reasonable and permissible precautionary measures. If the evidence shows that the patient has had a suicidal proclivity of which the psychiatrist knew or should have been aware, a case of malpractice may be made out against him or the hospital. This is a form of faulty diagnosis that results in faulty prognosis. As the courts put it, a psychiatrist or hospital has a responsibility to protect a patient from self-inflicted injuries if the possibility of such acts is reasonably predictable. In order for there to be contributory negligence, or an independent intervening cause, which would bar a claim, the patient must be capable of exercising the care of a reasonable person.[20] With the shift in tort law from a concept of contributory negligence, which bars a claim of a plaintiff entirely, to that of comparative negligence, which only lessens that claim, there is a tendency to consider the patient's own behavior resulting in suicide.[21] The issues of foreseeability of self-inflicted injuries and the ability to exercise reasonable care are both questions for the jury.[22]

If the psychiatrist or hospital has been put on guard as to a patient's suicidal tendency and as to the probable method of carrying it out, as in the case where suicides or dangerous escapes have been attempted in a particular way in the past, the duty to protect and prevent is increased correspondingly. Among allegations that are asserted are the following: (1) the psychiatrist did not give proper attention to the patient's history, (2) the psychiatrist failed to give appropriate orders to the hospital staff, or (3) the hospital staff failed to carry out the orders.[23] In the managed care era, the heightened risk of patient suicide arises from premature discharge.

Documentation is important. Indeed, it is said: "What protects you [the psychiatrist] from liability is *not* that you have made the 'right' decision, but your documentation of a process—the process by which you have assessed and responded to the likelihood that your patient would commit suicide. Your documentation should answer three basic questions: What did I do? Why did I do it? On what basis did I reject alternative ways of responding?"[24]

Unlike a hospital, a household tends to be informally organized, unable to watch over a family member who is suicidal, so they bring the individual to a hospital, expecting it to provide the necessary care and attention. Hence, the liability rate of a psychiatrist or hospital is greater in the case of an inpatient suicide than that of an outpatient suicide, where there is less control over a patient, but there may be a duty to seek commitment of a patient.[25] The issue is discussed in chapter 9, on failure to treat.

Physician-Induced Suicide

Suicide-inducing characteristics of the psychiatrist or what may be called iatrogenic or physician-induced suicide has rarely been alleged in a legal action, notwithstanding the psychiatric literature on suicide as a possible response to therapist behavior or to countertransference attitude. Harry Stack Sullivan pioneered the concept that the therapist influences simply by observing. In law, however, suicide-inducing characteristics are too subtle and difficult to establish.[26]

The question is: Can psychotherapy precipitate or contribute to a suicide? The answer is: yes.[27] To put it starkly, Jim Jones in Guyana sent hundreds of his followers to their death. Here, the issue is not one of control or supervision as in the case of a hospitalized patient, where security is expected, but rather whether the therapist by malignant intervention triggered or precipitated the suicide. Suppose, for example, the therapist dwells on homosexuality in a way that upsets the patient, and he is unable to deal with it and becomes increasingly depressed. Other examples in the outpatient setting where it might be said that the suicide is the fault of the therapist is where the patient is abandoned, or a confidence is breached causing the patient great humiliation. Clearly, returning a gun to a suicidal patient would be hard to explain to a jury.

Failure to Provide a Particular Treatment

What about not providing a particular treatment, such as medication or electroconvulsive therapy? Though the patient is suicidal, some psychiatrists, psychologists, and social workers contend that there is no need for chemicals or ECT, and, if anything, these methods are counterproductive; they would suggest a glass of wine instead. Others take an opposite opinion.

A psychiatrist who testifies against a psychologist whose patient has committed suicide may say that the suicide could have been averted by the use of medication or other somatic therapy that a psychologist or social worker, by the limitation of their license, would be unable to perform. Dr. Stanley Lesse, psychiatrist and editor of the *American Journal of Psychotherapy*, wrote:

> Those who treat severe depressions should have the broadest possible knowledge of the limitations of various psychotherapeutic techniques. Similarly, they should have an intimate knowledge of the benefits and limitations of the antidepressant drugs. . . . Finally, the therapist who does not have facilities for emergency hospitalization at his disposal, should this become necessary, should not treat severely depressed patients, let alone suicidal patients.[28]

Likewise, says Dr. Mortimer Ostow: "A patient with psychotic or suicidal depression should not be treated by a psychologist, even under supervision."[29] One might say that on the day that Sylvia Plath committed suicide by putting her head in an oven, she might, if she had had ECT, still be alive.[30]

Until fairly recently, medical psychoanalysts themselves avoided psychiatric drug therapy. Even now those who use it consider it a kind of second-class treatment. Many psychoanalysts, however, continue to withhold drug therapy entirely on the general principle that it might interfere with the treatment and that it involves the psychoanalyst in direct interference with the patient's life. Others contend that where drug therapy is indicated, withholding it constitutes a far greater interference and can be challenged from an ethical, if not from a legal point of view.[31]

Those analysts or nonmedical therapists who do not do drug therapy set up a combined treatment in which they provide the psychotherapy and call upon a drug therapist to offer that treatment simultaneously. Although in many instances this is the best arrangement that can be made for a given patient, some consider it bad practice. Ostow claims that it is bad practice because to administer drug therapy properly, one needs the data obtained in psychotherapy. Second, Ostow says, in order to understand what the patient has to say, one must be able to distinguish between the contribution made by the patient and that made by the medication.[32] Others say division of treatment is poor practice because it splits the transference.

The practice of writing prescriptions for a patient, sight unseen, is a violation of the medical code, even though done at the request of a psychologist or social worker or other member of a treatment team. In many large state hospitals, as an operational or practical matter, it may not be possible for the doctor to regularly see all patients, or to see them adequately, so he writes a prescription or order and it is carried out over a long period of time by nurses or other aides. As a consequence, patients in hospitals have protested and have claimed a right to refuse treatment. Under the Michigan Medical Practices Act (as others), a physician should not prescribe medication for a patient whom he has not personally seen, nor should the medication be administered nor its effect monitored by someone who is not a physician.[33] In these circumstances, malpractice is readily assessed by showing breach of the statutory standard of care.

Police Suicide

Police officers, we all know, are exposed daily to potential assaults and murder on the streets, yet there is another danger lurking within their own ranks: suicide. In thinking of epidemics, we think of diseases such as AIDS that ravage an entire society, but epidemics can also occur within specific groups of people. Police work is an occupation replete with psychological stress and trauma, danger, and availability of firearms. Under such conditions, an increased risk of suicide can be expected.

Indeed, police officers kill themselves more than they are killed by others. In the Detroit area several police were reported to have committed suicide in recent months.[34] Major epidemiological studies have shown that the police suicide rate is over three times that of the general population, and rates appear to have increased since the early 1990s. Moreover, many police suicides are purposely misclassified on death certificates as accidents or undetermined deaths. Suicide has an insurance dimension that could foreclose benefits for the family. Also, out of a desire to protect family members and also the department from the stigma of suicide, fellow officers at the scene of the suicide withhold information from medical examiners. Thus, the actual number of police suicides may be substantially higher than what is officially reported.

Police suicide can devastate the morale of entire agencies and leave individual officers with intense feelings of guilt, remorse, and disillusionment; many feel they should have done something to prevent the suicide. To dissuade suicide, police departments often view it as a disgraceful rather than heroic police death and do not afford police families the support after a suicide that they would ordinarily receive in the case of death of an officer.

There is an interaction of personality and environment, but there is controversy as to whether personality or occupational elements most influence police suicide. Occupational influences include psychological stress, interpersonal and work relations, availability of firearms, alcohol use, and retirement.[35]

Police officers generally choose police work because, like physicians, they want to help people. The police motto is "to protect and to serve." Psychiatrists generally consider the desire to help people as being partially determined by a need to sublimate one's dependency needs by taking care of others.

Police officers are often found to be immature and have a need to sublimate conflicts with authority by becoming the authority (police officers are often characterized as bullies), and they are often macho (with need to prove their masculinity and adequacy). By and large, police officers walk a very narrow line between power and authority. There is an inverse relationship between authority and power—power is used when there is a failure of authority. In the words of one police officer complaining of burnout to Dr. Gerald Shiener, consultant to the Detroit Police Department, "It seems like no one has any respect for the uniform anymore." Another stressed out police officer described police work as the "human garbage collectors for the city." Another said, "We protect the rich from the poor."[36]

A spate of police suicides in France set off uncommon news coverage and embarrassed the government. A prominent Paris lawyer commented that the police in France are scorned by the public and badly treated by their superiors, so it is no wonder they feel bad. To a number of young people, *les flics* (as the police are known in France) are walking emblems of the state, who are fun to taunt, insult, and, when possible, bombard with bottles and stones. Some days, police officers say, they feel surrounded by hostility. They feel they get no support or understanding from their superiors. During the days of the Soviet Union, police suicide was a very infrequent event. The police had unchallenged authority.

What about professional help for the police? Approximately 80 percent of suicides have communicated their intent by speaking of their plans or of "when I won't be around anymore." Psychiatrists find a pattern of early suicide predictors among these individuals; they become overly aggressive; they stay after work to drink with other police officers, and they use alcohol to treat sleep problems; they buy a better and more powerful pistol; they put their family in the background, in favor of their drinking buddies; they cause damage to people's property; they kill animals; and they withdraw, watching progressively more violent films.

There is a relationship between suicide and the reluctance of police officers to see a psychiatrist. Police officers tend not to be introspective, and they often internalize their frustrations and negative emotions. On psychological testing, an increased risk of suicide has been found in persons with high hostility scores. Police officers are expected to use as little force as possible and to always be pleasant regardless of what others did or said to them. Even though their authority is challenged, they are expected to contain their rage. Suggestions for police suicide prevention include intervention programs and suicide awareness training. Organizational support and confidential psychological services that officers feel they can trust are important in reducing suicide. Training in suicide awareness may also help officers to understand their own feelings and to cope with emotional adversities. The first and most important step is to recognize that the problem exists. Police suicide is a fact that cannot be ignored.[37] In recent years, most police departments have instituted mandatory counseling for all officers who have shot someone, as a way of helping these officers cope with the stresses that arise from such an act. By and large, police officers tend to feel that seeing a "shrink" would stereotype them as weak or crazy.

Certifying the Cause of Death

Insurance coverage for accidental death or injury usually includes exclusionary language for self-inflicted injuries that occur within a certain period of time but, by and large, the courts have tempered the exclusion by reading into it an intent requirement. A *suicide* is defined in the Random House Dictionary as "a person who *intentionally* takes his or her own life" (emphasis added). Mental illness may undercut intent as in the test of criminal responsibility.[38] Social and judicial attitudes regarding suicide have gradually turned away from assessing guilt and toward protecting suicidal persons and their beneficiaries.[39]

In the absence of policy language providing that the exclusion applies whether the insured was "sane or insane," the courts have allowed recovery when the deceased was not able "to form a conscious intention to kill himself and to carry out that act, realizing its physical and moral consequences." This standard calls for psychiatric testimony that addresses the mental state of the insured at the time of his death. In a minority of jurisdictions, courts construing policies that contain the additional exclusionary language that it applied whether the death by the insured's own hand occurred while "sane or insane" have held that the language does not apply when the insured was so mentally disordered as not to understand that his act would result in death or that the act was committed under an insane impulse.[40]

Penal statutes against suicide or a suicide attempt have been repealed, or they are unenforced. Relatives of those who commit suicide, feeling not only bereaved but stigmatized, often try to persuade the certifying authority against the certification of suicide on the death certificate. The death certificate is prima facie evidence of the cause of death.

To be sure, there is a broad borderline area between clear-cut suicide and other modes of death that are equivocal, and there is tremendous variability in the information about the personality and behavior of the deceased. Unless there is a suicide note, it is not easy to evaluate the intention of a dead person—did the person die of natural causes, by accident, by suicide, or was he murdered?[41] It is often difficult, for example, to decide whether a death in an automobile collision was accident or suicide. Those with a drug addiction are disturbed persons on the edge of deliberate suicide, but there is the possibility of accident in the course of the barbiturate habit. Individuals who enact masturbation fantasies of being tied up and abused, with partial hanging as part of the fantasy, may accidentally be asphyxiated.[42] Those who engage in repeated acts of self-injury do not wish to kill themselves but use their self-injury to relieve pain, while suicidal persons seek to terminate unendurable pain by ending their lives.[43]

One of the important roles of the coroner or medical examiner is to classify the manner of death among the categories of natural, accident, suicide, or homicide. Is the coroner or medical examiner up to the task? Most coroners are elected (many are funeral directors); few pathologists are medical examiners. In more than 80 percent of cases, manner of death is readily and unambiguously assigned to one of these four categories on the basis of scent investigation, witness interviews, autopsy findings, and toxicology results. In some cases, however, manner of death is not so readily established and will be listed as pending until further investigation, analysis, or consultation is completed.

Manner of death determinations have important legal implications in homicide prosecutions, denial of life insurance coverage as we have noted under a suicide or self-inflicted injury exclusion, establishment of liability for accidental deaths, and other contexts. Manner of death determinations may also have important emotional implications for survivors of the decedent and may affect the reputational interests of the decedent and those associated with the decedent.

During the latter half of the twentieth century, coroners and medical examiners began to turn to psychiatrists, psychologists, and criminologists for assisting in determining manner of death in equivocal cases, resulting in the development of the approaches known as *psychological autopsy, psychiatric autopsy,* and *behavioral reconstruction.* Apparently, however, no coroner or medical examiner office has a psychiatrist on its staff. The *Daubert* ruling on scientific evidence has apparently not been held to apply to psychological testimony on manner of death.[44]

Summary

In a study of suicide in a state hospital setting, Dr. M. J. Kahne found that 25 percent of the psychiatrists whom he interviewed had experienced a consummated suicide by a patient in treatment. These psychiatrists, however, did not differ in any significant respect as to personality, sex, marital status, or countertransference attitudes from their more fortunate colleagues. In looking over this 25 percent, which numbered 79 psychiatrists, Kahne found that the foreign-born or foreign-educated psychiatrist was more likely to have a patient suicide. Language and cultural barriers are impediments to good psychiatric care. The most vulnerable psychiatrists also tended to have the largest caseloads and received a minimum of advisory and consultative support.[45]

Dr. Seymour Halleck suggests that the detriments of authorizing malpractice litigation for suicide may outweigh any social benefit. Speaking as a teacher at a medical school, Halleck noted, "I usually work with residents and I don't want them to get sued. So we do a lot of things which I don't think are in the best interest of the patient."[46] In that vein, law practitioners Joel Klein and Stephen Glover said that liability "may well affect psychiatric behavior in perverse ways." They wrote:

> To avoid liability, psychiatrists are likely to become extremely cautious. They will increase their supervision of inpatients, and rely more extensively on chemical and physical restraints. They may also seek to delay the release of inpatients and hospitalize outpatients. Yet, for many of these patients, the risk of suicide may actually be quite low, and the therapeutic benefits of increased freedom substantial. These individuals, and society as a whole, will suffer as a result of the increased caution. Indeed, the liability rule could conceivably encourage psychiatric conduct that leads to more suicide. Cautious psychiatrists may decide not to provide any treatment at all to potentially suicidal patients.[47]

Halleck, however, does not call for complete immunity from liability, recognizing that there are times that therapists are "grossly negligent" with suicidal patients.[48] Psychiatrists can do nothing about suicidal people who are not under their care, but presumably it is a different matter when such people are under their care. The following case illustration points out the considerations in suicide litigation.

Suicide in Malpractice Litigation: Case Illustration

An action was brought by a widow for the death of her husband, Louis R. Genovese, who committed suicide by jumping from a window of the Veterans Administration hospital in New Orleans after having cut the window screen with a pocket knife in his possession. There were no threats of suicide or previous attempts. She alleged that failure to detect the suicidal intent of the deceased and remove him to the psychiatric ward to take other measures for his security constituted negligence on the part of the hospital and its agents.

Genovese at an earlier time was admitted to the hospital complaining of "vague abdominal pains, intermittent shortness of breath, swelling of the feet and ankles, dizzy spells, orthopnea, and stiffness of the fingers." His medical history shows that he suffered from ulcerative colitis and he had undergone surgery for this condition two years earlier. Various examinations and clinical tests were made. Dr. George Adcock examined the patient and wrote the following order: "Consult psychiatry in the A.M. 48-year-old white male postoperative colectomy for ulcerative colitis. Has lost all interest in caring for self and exhibits marked intermittent periods of hostility and feelings of persecution. Would you evaluate? Thanks." The consultation was not obtained, however, as the patient left the hospital three days later against medical advice.

Approximately four months later the patient was again admitted to the hospital, complaining of mild pain and discharge from his rectal stump. Various tests were made in contemplation of possible additional surgery. A routine psychiatric consultation was ordered by Dr. Mohammad Atik and Dr. Richard S. Cohen, with the notation: "Psychiatric consult. Patient-ulcerative colitis. Past history psychosis. Please evaluate." The request was received by Dr. Richard Stone, staff psychiatrist, but the consultation was not made prior to the patient's death. Five days after the consult request, however, the patient was presented by a senior medical student to Dr. Henry Colomb, psychiatrist and professor of psychiatry at L.S.U. Medical School, in connection with a demonstration form of clinical teaching. Student notes made as a result of this demonstration showed, "Patient presented this A.M. to Dr. Colomb. Diagnosis of anxiety with some degree of depression was arrived at." Three days later the patient jumped to his death.

Numerous members of the Veterans Administration hospital staff and other physicians who had occasion to examine or observe the patient testified that there had been no indication that would justify placing the patient in a neuropsychiatric ward. Expert witnesses were called by the plaintiff and the defendant.

Dr. William Sorum, a psychiatrist, testified as an expert of behalf of the plaintiff. His testimony follows:

DIRECT EXAMINATION BY PLAINTIFF ATTORNEY
Q. Have you had experience in determining the presence of suicidal intent in hospitalized patients?
A. Yes. Every psychiatrist has.
Q. Have you treated such patients?
A. Yes.
[The doctor's qualifications are set out to qualify him.]
Q. Dr. Sorum, is suicidal intent discoverable in a patient?
A. I think to a greater or lesser degree you can. You can usually find leads that you look for in a patient if they truly have suicidal intent, but of course in some patients it would be what we consider obscure. I mean, there is no such thing as saying this one will and this one won't; it's an individual thing that you have to look for with the aid of guideposts which are set up by the patient as a rule.
Q. But there are factors and leads that are discoverable in patients with that intent, are there not, Doctor?
A. Yes, they are often discoverable, at least in retrospect; a lot of leads can be found after it is all over. There are a lot of suicides that take place in general hospitals. At Charity Hospital we used to have similar incidents to this every year, just by people jumping out of windows, in surgical wards and in other wards besides that.
Q. Is the medical profession becoming more aware of this problem?
A. Yes, it is. I believe it is considered around the fourth leading cause of deaths. . . .

Q. Is there a movement on to increase security measures to prevent this, Doctor?

A. Well, yes, and for other reasons. There is no doubt that the presence of psychiatric wards in general hospitals is increasing, and in the private hospitals I am associated with, there is general agreement for the need for increasing security measures. For example, when a patient displays a certain behavior pattern whereby we would suspect the possibility of something like that, the patient is transferred to the psychiatric ward if at all possible.

Q. And by transferring this patient to a psychiatric ward, what security measures would actually be put in force, Doctor?

A. Well, he would come under closer control and increased supervision, for one thing, and he would be kept from just wandering through the hospital corridors or anything like that, and objects are taken from him that he could use to hurt himself or somebody else. . . .

BY THE COURT

. . . I want to know what you would look for in a patient to make [the determination that he has suicidal tendencies].

A. Well, first, what he has been saying about it, if anything, if he has ever talked about committing suicide, or had any past history of any attempt at suicide, or any recent signs of change in his behavior pattern, if he appeared to be vague, or impulsive in his actions, whether he has been showing any depression, or loss of weight, or loss of appetite, some of the cardinal signs of anorexia, waking up early in the morning, expressions of hopelessness, any changes in personal habits, and things of that sort. . . . The general appearance of the patient is of course an important indication as to whether or not he has any emotional problems or any mental illness that needs attention. . . . You have to correlate all of your findings. . . .

BY PLAINTIFF ATTORNEY

Q. Dr. Sorum, aren't there several places in this record where there are entries denoting anxiety reaction on the part of the patient?

A. This is one here. . . .

Q. Doctor, doesn't this student admit-note give the history of the patient, and doesn't it list as an impression "anxiety reaction"? Doesn't it say that, Doctor?

A. Yes. . . .

Q. This is the consultation sheet, isn't it, Doctor?

A. Yes, sir.

Q. Now, isn't there a diagnosis of anxiety reaction appearing on the clinical record signed by Dr. Adcock? I am referring to the narrative summary, signed by Dr. Adcock, stating, "Initial impression was anxiety reaction, possible underlying psychosis"?

A. Yes, that's what it says. . . .

Q. Would anxiety that was present to the degree that a physician would make a note of it in the medical record indicate that it was to a greater degree than, let's say, most of us would be considered to possibly have?

A. Yes, I would say so. . . .

BY THE COURT

Q. Does it sound like a man who was about to commit suicide, from your experience?

A. Well, just from reading these entries, it would sound like somebody who was disturbed and depressed. Losing all interest in self is a sign of depression. It would appear, just from that, that here was a person who could have been unconsciously asking for help. You can't say that one or any of these things would be an indication that a man was about to take his life, but it does show that he was very disturbed and upset; and of course it is significant that a behavior pattern of that nature would interfere with his care, and that probably should be taken into consideration in all respects.

BY PLAINTIFF ATTORNEY

. . .

Q. I show you an entry. "Patient has lost all interest in caring for self," and again that is dated May 24, and it is signed by Dr. Adcock. What does that indicate to you, Doctor?

A. That is often a sign of depression and would suggest some deterioration in his character, perhaps. . . .

Q. The diagnosis is, "Probable manic-depressive psychosis," and it's signed by Dr. Toups.

What does that mean, Doctor, *probable manic-depressive psychosis?*

A. Well, that's a diagnosis that usually indicates mood swings, instability, and temperament which approaches a very pathologic trend. It's more beyond the average swing, I would say.

Q. I show you another entry, Doctor, and it is dated October 6, 1962, and was signed by Dr. M. Belanger, "Very quiet and withdrawn." Now, the fact that a patient is withdrawn, does this perhaps indicate one of the signposts you previously discussed?

A. It may or may not indicate the presence of depression in a patient. I mean, you couldn't make a decision on that from just that entry.

Q. But would that be part of a cumulative effect?

A. Yes. . . .

Q. Dr. Sorum, taking the cumulative effects of the various entries that we have covered, does the medical record of Mr. Genovese indicate to you that he had suicidal tendencies, and if that is so agreed, that the patient's security should have been indicated?

A. Well, this is certainly in retrospect, but certainly he had suicidal tendencies, because he did take his own life. Now, what you are asking me is to tell you from the record whether they should have been aware of his disturbed condition during his different admissions to the hospital, and whether during his last admission he showed signs that should have put them on guard to the extent that security measures would have been taken; is that what you are asking me?

Q. Yes, sir.

A. I note that a psychiatric consult was ordered, according to this record, so we can certainly assume this man was depressed. It is also evident from the record that he was largely uncooperative and that he was quite careless with his person and apparently was hostile at points, and also withdrawn, so I think that we can say, judging from this entire history of his treatment and his behavior pattern in the hospital, that he was disturbed grossly.

Of course, when you attempt to predict what a patient may or may not do, it is difficult. Some persons can enter a hospital for treatment and display many of the symptoms and be quite harmless to themselves or others, and of course the reverse could also be true; but taking this record in its entirety, I think you can safely say that this was a situation that warranted, as you say, security measures.

Q. Doctor, from this record that you have reviewed, would you consider his death by suicide probable or not?

A. I think you would have to consider it possible, yes.

Q. Would you say it was a distinct possibility?

A. As a possibility, yes. Of course, I feel that I would be in a much better position to answer your questions had I been there and seen and talked to this patient. There's no better way to learn a person, to really find out about his attitudes and temperament and his condition than being right there and studying him firsthand. That's the best way to evaluate a patient. There's no better substitute than personal contact with the patient. . . .

Q. . . . the position of the hospital record indicates that there was no psychiatric consult held; isn't that right, Doctor?

A. Yes, there was no formal consultation, at least, not from what I can observe here. . . .

Q. Doctor, would the ordinary standard of care indicate that if a formal psychiatric consultation was held that there would be a formal report or some report in the record, that there was a formal psychiatric consultation?

A. Well, I'm not familiar with the procedural aspect of the VA hospital—

Q. Doctor, what would a delay of some eight days between the time of a request for a psychiatric consult and the psychiatric consultation itself, what would that indicate to you? Wouldn't that be undue delay?

A. Well, again I don't know what the situation is in the VA hospital, what problems they may have, or the procedure, but we often have consultations that are delayed for various reasons, so that's something I wouldn't be qualified to answer.

Q. Considering the record of this individual, his medical record, with which you are familiar, would you say an eight-day delay was an undue delay, Doctor?

A. It's really hard to answer that question, since, as I said, I am unfamiliar with the conditions there. On the surface one would wonder about that, but again that is a qualified statement. I don't know what the situation was.

Q. Well, would it be more desirable to have it sooner, Doctor?

A. Yes, you could say that, certainly, the sooner the better. I guess in retrospect, we can say that easily. . . .

Q. Would an entry by a physician in the medical record, that he was awaiting the results of the psychiatric consult, would that express his concern over the delay?

A. Perhaps.

Q. Dr. Sorum, in view of the medical record that was present at the time, in view of the pending delay of the psychiatric consultation, would the ordinary standard of care indicate that you should take, or that the physician should take, some minimum security measures, such as removing knives?

A. I would say this: in a really depressed patient, it might be a good idea if he appears to be that depressed. It all would depend on his behavior pattern at the time.

Q. Would it include removing the availability of easy access to windows in a high building?

A. Well, of course, that's one of the chief ways that this happens in general hospitals. . . . I would say that's one of the chief things you have to look for. In fact, that's one of the two most acute situations you have to watch for, that and a gun.

CROSS-EXAMINATION BY DEFENSE ATTORNEY

Q. Doctor, whom do you consider to be experts in the field of suicide in the United States?

A. Dr. Shneidman, Dr. Farberow, and others. Those two men in particular are well-known authorities in the field, and they have written books on the subject.

Q. Are you familiar with the books, *Clues to Suicide,* and *The Cry for Help?*

A. Yes, sir, I am, and if I had known that Dr. Shneidman was going to be here, I would have brought one down for him to autograph. . . .

Q. Doctor, as far as you know from your own knowledge of the medical record in this case, the notations that were made by the various doctors were not made by psychiatrists, but by medical doctors; isn't that correct?

A. I don't believe there were any notations by psychiatrists. . . .

Q. Doctor, isn't it true that approximately eight out of ten people who commit suicide have given definite prior warnings of their suicidal intentions, namely either having attempted suicide or threatened to commit suicide?

A. I am sure it's something like that. I mean, that's the one big thing. Of course, you have people who do talk about it and threaten to do it and who do not do it, so there's just no 100 percent answer to that. I will say that usually people who have committed suicide have given some leads. The difficulty is ascertaining what the leads are and whether they are sufficient to justify a psychiatric consultation or psychiatric care.

Q. So, in other words, Doctor, would you say that prior attempts at suicide or threats to commit suicide, that those cases would be considered the more probable suicidal risks; isn't that true?

A. Yes, those are the best signs. Of course, there are other signs—pressure, depression, that sort of thing, but as I say, those are good signs and should be watched for. . . .

Q. Now, Doctor, you used the word *retrospectively* in your direct examination in connection with this man's suicidal intentions.

A. Yes, that's right, and he must have had them, because he did end his life. It's easy to look back retrospectively after something has already happened.

Q. In other words, that was after the fact the man did commit suicide. I think we can all agree now that he had plenty of signs, such as depression and signs of waking at an early hour, and trailing feces, and things of that sort. Also you can say retrospectively that he was probably thinking in terms of being unable to get a job afterwards, and being put on charity, and things of that sort; but again that's conjecture, just my opinion.

I also think you testified, if I understood you correctly, that depression in and of itself is not evidence of a person who is going to commit suicide. Is that correct, Doctor?

A. There are many depressed people who do not commit suicide to every one that does; but there is no doubt that this is becoming an increasing problem that does come up over and over again.

BY THE COURT

Q. Are there more suicides per capita now than there were, say, twenty-five years ago?

A. I believe so, but Dr. Shneidman can probably give you later facts on that.

Q. Life is more complicated, now, isn't it?

A. Much more, yes sir.

    . . .

Q. Do you think, based on what you have seen in this hospital chart, that there should have been an indication that a treating physician should have transferred him to a neuropsychiatric ward to prevent him from doing just this sort of thing?

A. Well, I don't know how crowded this ward might have been at the time that they would have transferred him to it, and I don't know what the setup and the rules are at the VA hospital, although I know it is a good hospital. I can say that I think now they should have transferred him, but what I would have thought then, before this happened, since I wasn't at the hospital and am not familiar with their procedures there, I just couldn't say. I hadn't seen the man. My thought now is that he either should have been transferred or proper precautions taken to prevent this sort of thing. I wish they had, but it may actually have been that they didn't have sufficient psychiatric help to take care of the situation. I just don't know. When you're sitting in this vantage point, you can look back and second-guess what could have been done to prevent this, but as to just what action I would have advocated prior to this suicide, I couldn't say at this time. . . .

REDIRECT EXAMINATION BY PLAINTIFF ATTORNEY

Q. Doctor, forgetting the problem of whether or not this hospital had enough psychiatric help available to provide for the consultation requested, wouldn't it have been favorable and desirable to have this consultation earlier than eight days in any event?

A. I would think it would be desirable.

Q. Would not the ordinary standard of care in the community dictate that this patient should have had a psychiatric consultation earlier than eight days?

A. Yes, I would think so. . . .

Q. And concerning these signs which are noted in this record, would not the ordinary standard of care dictate that pending a psychiatric work-up, weapons for example, would be removed from the patient?

A. Weapons?

Q. A penknife.

A. Oh, I would think so. However, we have used a lot of open-ward care with certain types of patients, even if they have depression. I mean, sometimes we take what would be considered, I suppose, calculated risks, and I have at times ordered people to be allowed to retain certain things in their possession because it gives them a sense of identity, of being themselves.

BY THE COURT

Q. Razors?

A. Yes, sir, exactly. Of course, sometimes that doesn't work out so well. Even psychiatrists are not infallible. . . .

Dr. Edwin S. Shneidman, codirector and founder of the Suicide Prevention Center in Los Angeles, testified as an expert on behalf of the defendant. His testimony follows:

DIRECT EXAMINATION BY DEFENSE ATTORNEY

Q. Dr. Shneidman, will you give us your full name and present position, please?

A. My name is Edwin S. Shneidman, and I will indicate my three main positions.

I am codirector and founder of the Suicide Prevention Center, which is a unit supported by a seven-year grant of which I am the principal recipient, with Dr. Norman Farberow, from the National Institute of Mental Health of the United States Public Health Service; secondly, I am coprincipal investigator for the Veterans Administration Central Research Unit, for the study of unpredicted deaths.

These two facilities work hand and hand in their overall study of suicide and its cause.

Third, I am currently clinical professor of psychiatry and psychology of the University of Southern California School of Medicine.

Those are my three main positions.

In addition I serve as consultant to the State Hospitals in California, and on their editorial boards, and so on. . . .

Q. Have you published any books or any other professional articles in the field of suicide and suicide prevention?

A. Yes, sir, specifically in the field of suicide. I have coauthored with Dr. Farberow two texts, one called, *Clues to Suicide*, and the other is called, *The Cry for Help*, both published by McGraw-Hill, the first in 1957, and the second in 1961. . . .

BY DEFENSE ATTORNEY

. . . Your Honor . . . we tender him at this time as an expert witness in the field of suicides.

THE COURT

All right. [Plaintiff attorney] may cross-examine.

CROSS-EXAMINATION BY PLAINTIFF ATTORNEY

Q. Doctor, I take it from your testimony here today that you are not a psychiatrist?

A. That's true, sir.

Q. You have had no medical training?

A. That's right.

Q. In other words, you are not a doctor of medicine?

A. That's true.

Q. Is Dr. Farberow a physician?

A. No, we are both clinical psychologists, and we are practitioners, and we do research in the field of psychology. . . .

Q. Have you ever testified as an expert witness before in court?

A. Yes, sir.

Q. For the Veterans Administration?

A. No, sir, but Dr. Farberow has done that. . . .

BY THE COURT

Q. Doctor, I am just a little interested in this subject from perhaps another viewpoint. I am a former legislator, and this question of people practicing medicine who have not obtained a medical license has been brought up a number of times.

Do the physicians in California where you practice consider that you are practicing medicine?

A. Oh, no, sir. I am not practicing medicine. . . .

Q. . . . Do you have to be licensed to do what you are doing by the State of California?

A. Yes, sir. I am licensed. Would you like to see the license?

Q. No, I am just trying to find out if there is any comparison in the status of a psychologist in California as compared to Louisiana, and particularly where a question of medical treatment is concerned. . . .

A. As a matter of fact, Your Honor, I am not licensed; I am certified.

Q. Certified?

A. Certified by the American Board of Medical Examiners. Here's the certification. No person in California can call himself a psychologist without that certificate. It's awarded as a result of examinations.

BY THE COURT

I think the Doctor's qualifications are acceptable. . . . You may proceed.

BY DEFENSE ATTORNEY

Q. Doctor, will you tell us about your position in the Veterans Administration in the Central Research Unit for the Study of Unpredicted Deaths and at the Suicide Prevention Center?

A. Yes, sir. First, there are two separate units actually, and I will deal with them separately, if you don't mind; and I will deal with them, if I may, historically.

For a number of years we in the VA family have been interested in this problem of suicide and its many and varied causes, and as a result of work already done in that field, we had completed a book and perhaps a dozen or so articles, and that's the way it began. Then as a result of joint discussions on the subject, it was decided to establish a central research unit which was to serve Veterans Administration Hospitals throughout the country, and all records of all individuals who committed suicide, while wards of the VA hospitals in patient status, were to be sent to this central research unit in Los Angeles. The next folder to the suicide folder in the case was to be sent along also as a nonsuicide control folder, so that we would have at this repository a clinical correspondence folder very much like the present one, and likewise a folder that had been next to the suicide folder, which as I said, was labeled a nonsuicide control folder. The purpose was to analyze and compare the two folders, the suicide and the nonsuicide, in an effort to ascertain the motivating factors which might have brought about the suicide in question, and to try and ascertain the signs or indications or any possible tip-offs that a person might be contemplating taking his own life.

In a sense, our main responsibility might be labeled as a searching for clues to attempted suicides and as trying to ascertain, from a comparison of these two records, the type of behavior patterns that should be looked for in patients, particularly with regard to any symptoms of despair or despondency and things of that sort. There are many clues to be looked for in connection with a patient's mental behavior or pattern while being treated in a hospital, so that could be called the primary purpose of this study and of the records in individual cases.

By the Court

Q. Can this study be applied to the problem of preventing suicides, as well as finding out what may have caused the suicide after it has happened?

A. Oh, yes, Your Honor, that's what we are actually trying to do in this study of these records. We hope, by going through them and analyzing them and comparing them, to take a case of suicide, for example, out of the realm of unpredicted deaths into the realm of predictable suicides, the results of which might through proper application prevent suicide in many cases; it might keep them from reaching fruition.

Of course, our biggest problems, as you might expect, are sudden unexpected deaths, where there have been no indications that they were going to take place; and that's why we get in these records and go over them minutely, looking for clues that might well serve as signposts in the future dealing with patients. That's our principal mission, as I said, at the Central Research Unit, and as a result of our studies along that line, we have published three medical bulletins. . . . I have copies of all these here, if they would be of any interest to you. . . .

By Defense Attorney

Q. Doctor, could you tell us a little bit more about these suicidal folders and the nonsuicidal control folders, what you do with them and what you try to find out from them in your work at the Central Research Unit?

A. Yes. These suicide and nonsuicide folders are sent in to the VA from hospitals throughout the country. I get the folders as a matter of routine at the center in Los Angeles in due time. Now, those are the suicide folders. The other folders are simply folders of veterans, some dead and some alive, who did not commit suicide. . . . We have a procedure which we have initiated which we have labeled "Psychological autopsy."

... [We] discuss the case, and then each of us will indicate whether we think the case was a suicide or a control folder, where no suicide occurred. . . .

THE COURT

Q. Do the majority of you agree or disagree in advance of finding out what actually happened?

A. Well, at the beginning we found that we were in disagreement more often than not, I guess you would say; but after a couple of years, it got so we independently found that we were agreeing more than at the beginning. Through the benefit of the discussions, we found that we were refining the clues, the distilled notions, we call them, and it got to be a rare event when we couldn't agree from the facts as presented in the record on a diagnosis of the particular psychological autopsy. After a couple of years, it got so we would have a pretty good notion of what was going on, and we rarely disagreed after that. . . .

BY DEFENSE ATTORNEY

Q. Doctor, do you receive many calls at the Suicide Prevention Center from people, for one reason or another, who are in some kind of emotional condition where suicide could be considered a possibility?

A. Yes, we are listed in the telephone book, and we receive calls from around the community every day and every night. We are always receiving calls from people who are in distress in the local community. . . .

Q. Doctor, would you tell us about suicides in Veterans Administration hospitals in comparison with other hospitals and hospital systems?

A. Yes. . . . Of all the statistics on deaths in Veterans Administration hospitals, suicides account for 0.3 of 1 percent of all deaths. Now, this is not very different from other suicidal death statistics in other hospital systems. In fact, it's lower than some others. For example, state-hospital systems have a slightly higher suicidal rate than the Veterans Administration hospitals. . . .

Q. Dr. Shneidman, how many clinical folders have you reviewed approximately in this type of system you are talking about, the control cases and the suicide cases?

A. If you would permit me to say it loosely, I will say hundreds. That would not be an exact answer, of course; but I don't know how many—a great many.

Q. Doctor, at my request did you examine the clinical folder of the patient, Louis R. Genovese?

A. Yes, sir, I did.

Q. After having reviewed that folder, Doctor, would you tell us your judgment in the light of having examined and studied many other folders of veterans who did and did not commit suicide?

A. I am sure the Court will not, nor anyone else in the courtroom, misunderstand my remark when I begin saying that it was an extremely interesting folder, I mean, in the sense that it's a cryptic folder and a kind of mysterious folder in a way, at least to me, who looked at it.

For one thing, I knew that it was a folder of suicide, so I was not obliged to make a blind analysis in this case without knowing the outcome. I knew he had committed suicide.

If I can deal with an analysis rather than a technicality, in a suicide, it can be thought of as a kind of internal debate, a debate within the individual. It's when the forces of life and the forces of death are in concert. We call this a *debate*, internal ambivalence. Rarely do we find a case where the individual is unambivalent about taking his own life.

Now, the evidence of internal debate in this case is not actually visible in the record. There are certain symptoms, but nevertheless I want to say that I would have called this a control case; in other words, I would have classified this as a nonsuicide control case.

If I may use the word *perturbation*, which is just a general English word meaning "the state of being upset," the evidences of perturbation are there; but hospital patients generally are perturbed.

There are evidences here of anxiety, but anxiety is a normal concomitant of hospitalization. Those are some of the reasons why I say that if I had made a blind diagnosis of this case, without knowing the result, I would have said this would have been in the category of a nonsuicide.

BY THE COURT

Q. If you had used the blind autopsy that you spoke of, you would have held that this was not a suicide?

A. Yes, sir, I would have. Of course, I know now that the man did commit suicide, so I would have been wrong; but from all the evidence set forth in these records, I would have felt otherwise.

Q. You would have put this death in the nonsuicide category?

A. Yes, I certainly would, Your Honor. I would have put this case in the nonsuicide group.

Now, if I may elaborate a bit on some of these symptoms which are noted in the record and their possible significance, I would like to do so.

Q. Go right ahead.

A. These are things which can have significance, but sometimes only for the person who is doing the performing, so to speak, and if I am getting out of order in this discussion, you will please so rule me.

Q. You may proceed.

A. . . . I take the position theoretically that most people who kill themselves—and incidentally suicide, we must understand, is an occurrence that is comparatively infrequent.

Just for the record, I will say that suicide across the board is about the tenth leading cause of death, so you would have to say that it occurs relatively infrequently. Now, of course, in some age groups and some occupations that will vary. In fact, in some occupations it would be listed as the third cause of death possibly, and in others maybe eleventh, depending on the many factors necessarily involved; but as I say, in general, suicides are listed as about the tenth leading cause of death.

Also, in hospital care one must treat the entire patient. It's something like a fire, a conflagration. I think one ought to be alert to fires; but you don't turn the hospital upside down in terms of fire prevention.

There is something else I might point out in connection with any determination that is made as to whether to put a psychiatric label on a patient; relatives and friends do not generally take kindly to placing the patient in a psychiatric ward, so something like that has to be considered very seriously before such action is taken. The presence of anxiety or depression in a patient is something that has to be assessed as to the total picture.

BY THE COURT
Q. Do people consider that a disease or illness of this sort has a stigma attached to it?
A. Oh, yes sir. . . . We are ever mindful of the terrific taboo on suicidal deaths. It is factual, I believe, that in our society there are only two kinds of death that are understandable and expected, and those are natural deaths and deaths due to accidents. Other deaths, particularly suicides, fall into another category, and suicides are the worst kind of thing because they leave such a question mark, particularly from the viewpoint of family and friends. The question involves possible emotional problems, possible physical impairment, or both, and it is, regardless of how we would have it, a stigma in our society today. No one wants to go through with anything like that. . . . Well, this patient did not communicate in anything like a discernible way his own private suicidal intentions; that is, in theory persons who are bent on self-destruction will generally let other people know about it, either in clearly stated language, such as, "I am going to kill myself," and "I am going to commit suicide." Or, they will let people know this in a somewhat coded, or elliptical, or guarded language. If I should say in this court, for example, "This is the last time in my life I will ever be in New Orleans."

Physicians and psychiatrists and psychologists in this courtroom would not from the mere uttering of that sentence arrive at any meaning such as that I was contemplating suicide, unless there were other substantiating clues or signs that they had previously observed, whether it be depression or despondency or other type of irregular mental disturbance. . . . You have to have something to go on more than just a statement. You have to notice irregularities or recall clues of various kinds in a patient's behavior pattern before the groundwork is laid for any such assumption. An example of that would be if a patient shows a tendency to give away things, like, "Here, have my box of cigars," or "Take my watch"—things of that sort. Those are all clues that we have to look for in any patient, regardless of whether they are in a psychiatric ward or not.

The only clues of any significance that I have noted in this record with respect to that sort of thing, were those stated by the widow, and they are very cryptic. One would have needed literally the wisdom of Solomon and the genius and intuition of Freud to have caught them in this case.

Now, whether these clues were given by the individual deliberately, or whether those things just happened, we don't know. We know that in some cases a patient who ultimately ends up taking his life will give guarded signs of his intention. They may even give these unconsciously, but in other cases there have unfortunately been absolutely no signposts to indicate that something was going to happen of that nature. It just happens all of a sudden, and that's it.

Sometimes a person will write something which obviously gives away, so to speak, his suicidal intent, for example, something to the effect that no one is to see it until after he is dead, and he may leave it in a place where it can obviously be found. This happens all the time.

I have looked in vain in this record for such signals. I was not impressed by the patient's sleep record, for example. Sometimes that is a signal, the way a patient will display sleeplessness in various ways, such as sitting on the side of his bed or walking through the corridors during the night, or making a disturbance of some sort during the early morning hours, displaying evidence of insomnia in some fashion, but none of that is listed in this record.

I used the word *code* a few moments ago. One of the things we are continually trying to do in connection with a patient's behavior pattern is what we call *to break the code*, which means simply to unravel all the clues we do uncover, or that the patient voluntarily discloses, or perhaps accidentally, so we are principally engaged in watching for typical clues in persons who are under observation.

By the Court

Q. What are some examples of some of these typical clues?

A. Well, Your Honor, like someone going on vacation, and Mr. Jones, for example, might say, "I won't be here when you come back," or something like that. Now, of course, you can't take a simple statement like that, as I said before, and arrive at a definite diagnosis of his condition, but that is one of the clues we do take into consideration in evaluating a patient's behavior, both emotional and physical; and if there are enough clues, we can arrive at an evaluation and then determine what is the next step to be taken.

In summary, behavioral clues are clues of behavior such as would give rise to the indication in any way that a person may be contemplating suicide, and as I said, these clues would include giving away things, making arrangements of one sort or another which could be interpreted as some kind of signal, or remarks made in conversation to those about him, which may or may not be couched in language that would alert someone to his intentions.

A typical suicide is a person who has made some kind of threats or, of course, attempts on his life, so as to put the universe on the alert so that they will come around to treating his pain or anguish or loneliness, or putting him in this state of perhaps despondency and anxiety.

Now, we do have cases that present a clinical story of a person shooting himself or throwing himself out of a window, and that being the first overt suicidal act on his part that has been indicated. That would come more under the nature of an impulsive category, and there would be hardly any clues or signals given in advance of the act.

Q. Do you think that some of these acts or signals, as you call them, result from a desire to arouse sympathy?

A. Well, that could be in some cases, Your Honor, but in the case where a person does end his life, it is a very profound and deep thing which is done rather than a desire to arouse sympathy, I would think. It may start out as what we would call a cry for help, or something of that nature; and if there is no help, then perhaps it gets into another category where there is no turning back, at least in the mind of the potential suicide.

BY DEFENSE ATTORNEY

Q. Dr. Shneidman . . . In general hospitals what is the appropriate use of a neuropsychiatric ward in the prevention of suicide?

A. To give him sanctuary, that is, to put him at a place where he can't hurt himself.

Q. . . . When is a neuropsychiatric ward used for a patient in a medical hospital?

A. . . . I would say when a patient shows acute and gross emotional disturbance, when he really becomes a management problem, and I am referring particularly to his impact on other patients. He may not be a problem to himself actually, but he may just be a problem to the others about him, in which case a change would be desirable; but that's a management problem more than it would be an individual one. Now, if he shows signs of delusions, or anxiety, or hallucinations, or something such as that, he would be better cared for in terms of that specialty, so that would be another reason for him to be transferred to the neuropsychiatric ward.

Q. Doctor, in your opinion, from reviewing this clinical record and from reviewing the other clinical information furnished you in regard to this patient, do you think that this patient should have been placed in a neuropsychiatric ward?

A. No, I don't think so. I have voiced that opinion after reviewing all the records I have had available in this case, and it is based on my knowledge and experience in this field. I think there would have been protests all around if this had been done in this case.

BY THE COURT

Q. Protests by whom?

A. By him.

Q. By the patient?

A. Yes, sir.

BY PLAINTIFF ATTORNEY

If the Court please, I am going to object to any further questions along this line. I don't think this man is a medical expert in any sense of the word, from his own admission, nor is he an expert on admissions to hospitals. I have waited a long time to make the objection, but I think we are getting far afield now.

BY THE COURT

Well, I don't think the question of being admitted to the hospital is a medical problem or that it requires the action of a medical doctor. Actually that was my question of the Doctor, because I want to get the whole picture before me. I am going to have to decide this case. The Doctor certainly is a prominent expert in the field of suicides and comparing records, one record with another, and making autopsies about suicides. The objection is overruled. You will have an opportunity to cross-examine him, and I will weigh his testimony in the light of the qualifications that the Doctor has given me. The objection will be overruled because I feel that I must have his entire opinion based on his experience and his training and his qualifications.

BY THE COURT

Q. Doctor, I don't know whether you answered my question or not. I had asked you by whom protest would have been made, in your opinion, had he been moved to the neuropsychiatric ward.

A. I thought I answered that question, Your Honor—by him.

Q. You mean by the patient himself?

A. Yes, sir.

Q. Now in the light of the objection which has been made by [the plaintiff attorney], I would like for you to go into the question of why you feel that you are qualified to answer this question, if you will, Doctor.

A. Yes, sir. Based on my experience as a person who has worked in general medical and surgical hospitals and who has examined hundreds and hundreds and hundreds of these records, about which I have already testified, together with my work in the Suicide Prevention Center in Los Angeles, and the fact that I have made a study of this particular matter for years and years, and that I have authored or coauthored several books on the subject, and my vast experience with the Veterans Administration in connection with these many hospitals and hospital records.

Q. Have you actually worked with MDs in hospitals in connection with your work in this field?

A. Oh, yes, sir, very often. I don't want to sound immodest, but I think Dr. Farberow and I occupy a somewhat unusual position in current American psychology, that is, in the new specialty which is called *suicidology*.

BY DEFENSE ATTORNEY

Q. Now, Doctor, in your examination of the records in this case, did you find indications that, in your opinion, would have called for emergency action?

A. No, sir, I did not.

Q. Doctor, can you say something about the relationship between a condition like depression and suicide?

A. Well, depression has classically been related to suicide, and it is accurate to say that if one were limited to one single symptom, the best answer to suicide would be depression; but now most depressives are not suicidal, and many suicidals are not depressives. It's kind of an overlapping ellipsis . . . the two are not synonymous. They are far from being synonymous.

Q. Would you say something about the relationships between psychotics and suicides?

A. Well, there again the same answer would hold true. Most psychotics, or I would say over 99 percent, do not commit suicide. On the other hand, psychosis and suicide do overlap.

Q. Doctor, after having examined this particular folder in this particular case, in the light of your psychological autopsy that you have described in your testimony and your general background in this field, how would you have assessed this case, as a suicide or nonsuicide?

A. Well, I can only repeat, of course, what I have said before. I would have assessed this case as nonsuicidal.

Q. Will you give us your reasons for that opinion, Doctor?

A. Yes. From my examination of the record, based on my experience in going over many hundreds of similar type folders, you might say, I would have seen his psychological symptoms in the normal range of perturbation for a person who is hospitalized. I would have noted that he had some changes in mood, but I simply would have felt that these were explainable in terms of what was going on in his life.

For me to holler "fire"—and I am not hollering "fire"—but for me to say *suicide* would have meant that I would have had to have some visible clues which weren't apparent from what I could ascertain from these records.

Q. Doctor, do you feel that any special action on the part of the VA staff was called for prior to the time of this veteran's death in relation to suicidal risk?

A. No.

CROSS-EXAMINATION BY PLAINTIFF ATTORNEY

Q. Doctor, for the record, you would say that you never saw Mr. Genovese, wouldn't you?

A. Yes, sir, I never saw him.

Q. Would you give us some of the signposts that you look for in these records, Doctor, some tip-offs that would be likely to be found in these clinical records?

A. Yes, Sir.

BY THE COURT

Do you mean tip-offs in the records when the patients committed suicide?

BY PLAINTIFF ATTORNEY

Yes, Your Honor.

BY THE COURT

Very well.

BY PLAINTIFF ATTORNEY

Q. Would you give us some of the signposts and guides, so to speak, that you would be likely to find in clinical records of patients who take their own lives?

A. Yes, sir. First, we look for a history of a previous suicidal intent, like a cutting of the wrist, an injection or pills, an attempted hanging, and so forth, any history that might be in the record pertaining to that sort of thing.

Q. Well, those things that you just mentioned fit in one category, a previous attempt at suicide, do they not?

A. Yes, sir. I might point out at this time that we consider the most critical sign to be the history of the patient and a continuous, growing concern on the part of others of its generally downward course. I mean, history of eating disturbances, sleeping disturbances, and behaviors of sorts, and that might well include a history of impulsive self-destructive behavior. That history would also include things that wouldn't look like suicide intent, such as accidents, some sorts of mutilation, and getting hurt in different ways. Unless supported by other symptoms, these would seem to be purely accidental for the most part. We try to keep all of those possibilities in constant focus in our diagnosis and treatment of these patients.

Q. How about leaving the hospital against medical advice? . . . Isn't that included in this record, Doctor?

A. Yes, it is.

Q. Isn't that a sort of tip-off of possible suicidal tendencies, Doctor? . . .

A. No, that would be more of a tip-off, I think, to difficulties in caring for him. I would look to see what preceded this, as to what motivated him to leave, and as to what he did when he left. I don't think that in itself would be consistent with suicidal behavior.

Q. Let me phrase that a different way, Doctor. Would you be more likely to expect suicide from a patient who had left the hospital without medical advice than from one who hadn't?

A. As a statistics case, I think so, yes.

Q. Well, any kind of case; isn't that right?

A. Yes, that's right. . . .

Q. And this is not completely unlike a tendency to self-destruction, is it?

A. I must distinguish, if you will permit me, in my own mind between the mere fact of being upset and an indication or tendency of being upset to the point where suicide might be contemplated. Of course, in this case we know that it was a suicidal record.

Q. Doctor, we are not asking you now to tell us whether this was a suicidal record. You have already told us that, and you have already said that you would vote the other way, and that you would have made a mistake on that, because he was a suicide; isn't that right?

A. True.

Q. So we know that already. We are trying now to get for the benefit of the Court all these facts now, so that the Court can weigh all factors, and we are entitled to explore these things with you. Would you agree to that?

A. Absolutely.

Q. I think you want to be fair to these litigants in the determination of this case, do you not, sir?

A. Yes, I do.

Q. Now, getting back to my question, a person who leaves a hospital against medical advice is somebody who is mentally disturbed, at least to some extent; wouldn't that be true?

A. Yes, it would.

Q. Most suicides are mentally disturbed, aren't they, Doctor?

A. Yes. . . .

Q. I believe you stated that it would take Solomon and Freud to find enough clues in this record to be able to anticipate suicide, as far as this patient was concerned.

A. No, I didn't say that. My previous statement was that it would have taken

Solomon and Freud to determine that this was a suicide record. Now, there are indicia of suicide in this sense in practically every record, I mean, as far as finding peculiar behavior patterns on the part of the patient, but you have to get the complete work-up on the patient before trying to analyze what's wrong with him. Until you get all the factors in place, it's more or less an educated guess, as far as the true picture is concerned.

Q. Does it help you, when you're trying to make this educated guess, if you call in a psychiatric consultant and thereby get the benefit of his notes about that?

A. Yes.

Q. Would it be fair to say that that would have helped a great deal in this case?

A. Yes, sir. . . .

Q. Wouldn't a psychiatrist have been in a better position to judge whether this man was a potential suicide if he did a complete psychiatric consultation than you did from this record?

A. It would depend, sir. I don't know how to answer that question. I will have to say in this field I am not an ordinary psychologist. I have had years of experience in this field, as I stated at the beginning. . . . Well, it's a curious thing, but what's going through my mind right now is that it has been my experience that very often psychiatrists who conduct a consult will have to go to the record and look it over to recall what the true situation was. . . .

Q. Doctor, is character change one of the tip-offs you look for?

A. Yes, sir.

Q. Character change is reflected in this record, is it not, Doctor?

A. Yes, sir. . . .

Q. Would a feeling or demonstration of a feeling of hopelessness be one of the things you would look for?

A. Oh, yes.

Q. That's in this record too, isn't it?

A. I'm not sure, sir.

Q. Isn't there an indicium of that in this record? . . . Would an entry which reads, "Has lost all interest in caring for self," be a tip-off, Doctor?

A. Of suicide, sir?

Q. Yes, sir.

A. It could be in the context of other things.

Q. Including such things as character change, depression, loss of sleep, mutilating surgery; is that right, Doctor?

A. Well, obviously I am thinking of, and I think we are both talking about a total picture, a cumulative effect, a gestalt of the many items involved; and in all candor I have to say that I would have had to put this case in the background, just from going over it and considering its many aspects.

Q. Would it be fair to say, Doctor, that most records that you see do have the benefit of psychiatric work-ups? . . . Do you see many records where there is an entry made months before about requesting a psychiatric consult and no consult, and then another entry in a later admission to the hospital requesting a psychiatric consult, and then a delay of eight days is allowed to take place? Do you see any records like that?

A. No, sir. . . .

Q. Do you have any impression that you could give as to whether or not that would be an unusual thing?

A. Oh, it would be on the side, yes.

Q. It's on the long side?

A. Yes, sir.

Q. And if there had been a psychiatric work-up, Doctor, two things might have occurred, would they not? Number one, treatment might have helped this man, and number two, it might have produced some information on which to make a better judgment on whether he was suicidal; isn't that correct? . . .

A. Could I state, sir, that I was impressed by the fact that he was seen by a psychiatrist, who, I was told, was a professor of psychiatry at L.S.U. on the Saturday before; and I can't believe that had that person noted suicidal tendencies, he would not have been alerted to the fact, and he would have done something, noted it in the record or something. That transgresses my imagination.

Now, as to your question, had there been a psychiatric consult, and had the results indicated that the patient was a potential suicide, I am sure then that the psychiatrist would have put down some appropriate entry, and medical steps would have been taken.

. . .

Q. Doctor, being seen by a psychiatrist the Saturday before, as you stated, would not be the same thing as having a psychiatric consult, would it?

A. No, it wouldn't, but I can only repeat what I said before, which was that if the psychiatrist had examined him (and if he was a qualified psychiatrist, which I understand he was), then I can't believe that if he had found trends which would indicate that the man was a potential suicide, that he would not have done something about it. I just can't believe that.

Q. Doctor, considering the state of this record, would you agree, perhaps in the light of several tip-offs that were present, that some minimum security might have been put into effect, such as, for example, removing a knife from the patient?

A. From the record, no, sir.

Q. You don't think that would have been advisable?

A. Not from the record.

Q. Do you mean to say, Doctor, that these signposts and the several tip-offs that we talked about were not significant enough in this record to justify this kind of action in your judgment?

A. That's true, sir; they would not have been.

Q. You mentioned some sort of tip-off, such as giving a box of cigars away, is that right, Doctor?

A. Yes, that is considered one of the tip-offs that we look for, and like telling the nurse goodbye on the floor, things of that sort. Those are all things that we look for, but as I said before, they are not of necessity in themselves indicia that the man, or that anybody, is contemplating taking his life.

Q. Saying goodbye to the nurse, that would be one of the tip-offs?

A. Yes, that's the kind of thing that you would consider to be a tip-off, but not necessarily of itself. There has to be other substantiating evidence if such is the case.

Q. Do you put entries in the hospital record such as telling the nurse goodbye, or anything like that?

A. Yes, ordinarily, that is put in if it has any special significance. Of course, if it's just on somebody leaving the hospital, then it has no significance, so it's not put in. . . . A lot depends on the circumstances of such an incident, of course, whether we place any significance to it. . . .

In a lot of cases like that, the nurse on duty will use her own judgment as to whether to include it in her notes, the same as any of the hospital personnel and physicians. Although that is common phraseology, it can be significant of a diseased mind. We call that sort of thing *suicidal ideation*, talking as though well, he was going away, things like that. Now, once the staff is alerted, then of course that generates a lot more information, because then a closer surveillance is kept on the patient's activities and demeanor, and particularly on anything he might say that would fall into the phraseology. . . .

Q. In a case where there has been no alert made, Doctor, you wouldn't ordinarily find entries such as saying goodbye to the nurse, would you?

A. No, that's true.

Q. Or giving away boxes of cigars?

A. No, you wouldn't find that ordinarily.

Q. But you might find that kind of entry if there had been a complete psychiatric consult, might you not, Doctor?

A. Yes, sir. It wouldn't be in the typical language of a psychiatric consult perhaps, but it might. . . .

Q. Doctor, I think in one of your books or papers, you wrote that in a study made at random of twelve cases, eleven of them were jumps out of windows, isn't that right?

A. Yes, sir.

Q. Don't you think it would be a good idea to build all VA hospitals with similar protections for the patients?

A. I'm not sure about that. I have had debates with myself over that over the years, and I'm not sure of my position.

Q. Patients wouldn't jump if these stops were on all the windows, would they?

A. No, but it's more complicated than that. There are cases where definite harm can result from putting these stops on the windows, just like putting certain persons behind bars, and things like that. You just can't adopt the same method for everybody. At least, that's my thought on it.

Q. Well, Doctor, a suicide in a hospital could not take place without the availability of a method of doing so; isn't that correct?

A. No, that's not correct, sir. We have cases where individuals will get up from a chair and run across a hall and smash their skulls against the other wall.

Q. Well, that type of suicide is rare in hospitals, is it not, Doctor?

A. Oh, very, yes, sir.

Q. You wouldn't take a person whom you think might be a suicidal risk and put him on a window ledge just to find out if he would take a jump, would you?

A. No, not I. . . .

Q. And you wouldn't give him a weapon, would you, sir?

A. No, I wouldn't give him a weapon. Now, are you referring to a knife?

Q. Yes, any weapon.

A. Well, I need to modify that statement, which I stated too quickly. Although I wouldn't give him a weapon, if that means that I wouldn't permit him to eat with a knife and fork or permit him to shave himself, then that would be something else. It would depend upon the state of the patient in his own mind, his own stature.

Now, I certainly wouldn't give him a loaded gun, not would I put him in a room is seclusion. It is the general psychiatric consensus, with which I happen to concur, that isolation of a patient can be injurious. We believe that putting a person in seclusion is not only not the best treatment for a potential suicide but is one of the worst.

Q. Is a psychiatrist likely to be more apt or able to predict traits of a potential suicide than a layman?

A. Oh, yes, sir.

Q. Would he be more likely to detect those traits in a hospital where he had him under observation than in a nonhospital situation?

A. Yes.

Q. The likelihood would increase in both situations; is that right, Doctor?

A. Yes, sir. . . .

A. Well, I am reflecting, and in response to your question, often the first important tips come from nursing personnel, and psychiatric aides, and aides on the ward; that is to say, it doesn't take a psychiatric consultation to see these clues if they are visible enough.

Q. Well, the kind of prompt, suitable treatment that we are talking about, or that you referred to in your text, is treatment by a professional psychiatrist, or someone like you; isn't that true?

A. Yes, sir. If a person is determined to be suicidal or to have suicidal tendencies, there should be prompt treatment.

Q. Would you recommend, or would you not, Doctor, that some security measures be taken for many patients where you may not be ready to make a diagnosis that he is suicidal, but it is suspected? Don't you recommend conservative treatment in that kind of situation?

A. No, sir. My record indicates that I actually recommend the open-door policy, and part of the total treatment is reintegration with the community and reunion with the family.

Q. I don't think I made my question clear.

A. I'm sorry, sir.

Q. Let's assume that you have a patient who had signs that may not be sufficient for you to determine that he is definitely suicidal, but you suspect it. Would you not treat that patient different from a patient, let's say, where you did not suspect it?

A. If I suspected he was suicidal?

Q. Yes.

A. Yes, I would. . . .

Q. Could we use as an analogy a situation where often a physician will treat someone for a disease that may necessarily occur or exist, but where they have a suspicion of it?

A. I'm not sure I follow your reasoning on that question, sir.

Q. I am thinking of a situation for example, if I may enlarge upon the question,

Doctor, of a childhood disease that the child is treated for but which he isn't necessarily going to contract, for instance, tetanus, for which he is given antitoxin.

A. Well, I am one who likes to use analogies, and I know some of the pitfalls of using them. People have pointed this out to me, but giving a shot in relation to tetanus is different, I think, in our society, from putting a person in a neuropsychiatric ward, or in suicide status.

I think it would be possible to put every person who shows any sign of psychiatric impairment in wards and throw a net over the whole ward, indeed, over the whole hospital; but that's something I would not agree with.

Q. What about protection on the windows, instead of a net over the whole hospital, Doctor?

A. I can say in all honesty, and I am speaking in all honesty when I say that I am not sure. For one thing, it's a minor inconvenience to many people in terms of ventilation and this kind of thing, but if it's a question of serving to accomplish its set purpose, that's the big question of course. . . .

BY THE COURT

Q. How many suicides occur a year in VA hospitals?

A. A couple of hundred, sir.

Q. A couple of hundred a year?

A. Yes, sir.

BY PLAINTIFF ATTORNEY

. . .

Q. Would it be fair to say, Doctor, that this record contains most of the symptoms you look for, except threats of suicide and previous attempts?

A. Yes, sir, it contains many of them. . . .

Q. Do most of your control records have . . . repeated requests for a psychiatric consult?

A. Many of them show requests for psychiatric consult. . . .

Q. Doctor, are there any signposts or tip-offs missing here from this record except a previous attempt and threats of suicide?

A. Yes, sir.

Q. What is that, Doctor?

A. The wholeness or the gestalt of it; the fact that no one sensed it was going to happen, none of the hospital staff, no doctors, nobody said, "Suicide." That's what's missing—no relative, nobody. It came as a complete surprise. . . .

REDIRECT EXAMINATION BY DEFENSE ATTORNEY

Q. Doctor, a number of factors were discussed by you on cross-examination as to whether there were suicide signposts.

A. Yes, sir.

Q. Isn't it really a question of degree?

A. Well, I would rather say it would be a qualitative difference, in that each signpost would depend somewhat on the other, and that's why I mentioned a few minutes ago that you have to take the gestalt, or the whole picture, in order to arrive at an opinion.

Q. Now, Doctor, on direct examination you gave an expert opinion. Do you wish to change that opinion now?

A. What opinion is that?

Q. That from your experience, from looking at that clinical folder involving this patient, that you were of the opinion that it was a nonsuicide case.

A. No, sir, I don't wish to change that.

RE-CROSS-EXAMINATION BY PLAINTIFF ATTORNEY

Q. Doctor, in considering all the signposts and all the testimony and the whole record that we discussed, would it be fair to say that it would all add up to the slightest suspicion of suicide?

A. Yes, in this sense, no suspicion to an absolute certainty, but in this sense, one can have some suspicion of suicide about everybody—me, you, everybody—and in that sense I will say yes. As I said at the beginning of my testimony, I don't want to holler fire unless there's something to alert me to it. It's not good practice, either, to call everyone suicidal. So to answer your question, I would not have suspected it in this case. I would have guessed wrong on this case.

Q. You would have guessed wrong.

A. Yes, sir.

Dr. William C. Super, psychiatrist, and Director of Psychiatry at Charity Hospital in New Orleans, testified as an expert on behalf of the defendant. His testimony follows:

DIRECT EXAMINATION BY DEFENSE ATTORNEY

Q. Dr. Super, would you state your full name and occupation, please?

A. Dr. William C. Super. I am a psychiatrist.

Q. Doctor, would you give us a brief history of your background and education and the various Boards to which you belong?

A. I received my medical degree from Tulane University in 1949. I had a year of internship at the Walter Reed General Hospital in 1949 and 1950. I received my psychiatric training at the Menninger Foundation Hospital from 1950 to 1953. I served as chief of the mental installation at Fort Hood, Texas, from 1953 to 1955, and since that time I have been director of psychiatry at Charity Hospital.

I am certified by the American Board of Psychiatry and Neurology; I am a Fellow in the American Psychiatric Association, and I am on the staff of the Tulane and L.S.U. Medical Schools.

Q. Do you have any connection with any other hospitals beside Charity Hospital?

A. I am on the staff of DePaul, and I was formerly on the staff of Touro Infirmary.

Q. Approximately how long have you been director of psychiatry at Charity Hospital?

A. Since 1955.

Q. During that time, Doctor, did you have any occasion to come into contact with patients in which suicide was a possibility?

A. Yes.

Q. Approximately how often, how many patients would you say that would have been?

A. That's difficult to say, but I would estimate that approximately of all the patients I examined, perhaps suicide was a question in at least ten a month, so that I would say probably several thousand patients in which suicide has been a question.

BY DEFENSE ATTORNEY

I tender the Doctor as an expert in the field of suicide.

BY PLAINTIFF ATTORNEY

I have no questions.

BY THE COURT

All right, proceed. Your qualifications are accepted.

BY DEFENSE ATTORNEY

Q. Doctor, I am going to ask you some questions, but I would ask that you don't go into them in great detail but answer them fully, if you please. Are you familiar with the standard of care in the community as regards psychiatric patients in psychiatric wards?

A. Yes.

Q. Would you tell us something about that, please? What is the standard of care; how are they handled?

A. I am familiar in general with the standard of care as we know it, but of course there will be variations in what I have to say with regard to that because different conditions exist in different hospitals and with regard to different patients; but generally there are some facets that I can discuss. Do you want me to refer specifically to depressed patients or suicidal patients?

Q. Well, just take a psychiatric patient in general, just how are they handled in a psychiatric ward? Are they locked up, or what? That's what I want to know.

A. Oh, I see. As I said now, there is a great variation in this. Some of the severely ill psychiatric patients for the most part are placed in closed wards, where they are protected from themselves and from their environment, and this is the case in a general hospital, such as Charity, VA, or Touro, or in specific psychiatric hospitals, such as DePaul, or one of the state mental hospitals.

Some patients, who are less severely ill, are placed in open psychiatric units and are cared for there. Other patients in general hospitals remain on the general hospital wards, medical wards, that is, if their condition is not considered dangerous and if they have come in with physical complaints that are to be treated there.

Then many of course are treated as outpatients, either in clinics run by the State or by private psychiatric offices or doctors.

Q. Doctor, would you tell us briefly how you would handle a psychiatric patient with suicidal intent in contrast with psychiatric patients with no suicidal intent?

A. Well, if suicide is a question and one considers that to be so after an evaluation of the situation, that this patient would be a serious risk, the patient is placed immediately in a closed ward and precautions are taken; and this is certainly so at Charity Hospital, to see that he doesn't injure himself or anyone else. Precautions are instituted immediately, and we even go beyond simply putting the patient in a closed ward. It involves the patient being constantly observed, and with patients of this sort we remove shaving equipment or knives or pens, even spectacles, and also belts, anything with which a patient might harm himself; and we place him at that time in a room in which there is nothing except a bed and a mattress, but no other items, and the room is a safe room. There is no way to get out of it. It has safety screens.

Now, these precautions are taken until such time as the psychiatrists treating him are convinced that he is no longer a suicidal risk or until it is discovered that the initial impression was a mistaken one and that he really wasn't a suicidal risk in the first place.

Q. How do you care for other medical patients with emotional problems?

A. Well, of course that varies a great deal. It depends on the severity of the mental problem; and if it is considered severe enough to recommend that the patient be transferred to the psychiatric unit, then that is done. The patient is transferred. However, sometimes he is transferred to the open unit, in fact, more commonly to that one than the closed one. And then at other times, he is left on the medical ward, where he is of course more easily treated, and it is decided later what disposition is to be made.

Q. What are the signs which indicate to you that a patient has suicidal tendencies or is a suicidal risk?

A. Well, one becomes concerned about the risk of suicide when there are sufficient signs which point in that direction. No one particular item is generally enough to make a diagnosis that a person is a suicidal risk, but given enough items, you are able then to decide whether or not he comes in that category. I think with enough observation of a patient, and after gathering all the information you can about him, including his demeanor and habits and complaints, if any, and so forth, you can be about 95 percent or 99 percent sure whether he is a suicidal risk or not. Of course, first off we try to find out everything we can about the patient, because the more we know, the more we can either corroborate our suspicions that he is a suicidal risk or determine that he is not. For instance, his age, sex, marital status, anything that we can find out about him. Given enough clues and piece them all together, you can come up with a pretty good diagnosis of his mental problem, if there is one. If you arrive at a diagnosis of a manic-depressive type, that will make you quite concerned; and if you have a schizophrenic reaction with depression, you are concerned; and even if you have alcoholism with depression, then one is concerned. Those are some of the diagnoses.

Now, if a person or patient talks in terms of feeling very despondent, saying things to the effect that life isn't worthwhile, or that he doesn't want to go on, or that it's hopeless, or that he has nothing to live for, or if patients talk in terms of what should be done with their belongings and this kind of thing, or if they have a great deal of preoccupation with death, or as to the time they are going to go, then you would have concern. We run into all those symptoms, such as a patient saying he would be better off dead, and things like that. Other things we look for are symptoms of severe insomnia, lack of appetite, weight loss, and so forth.

Q. How about prior attempts at suicide, Doctor?

A. Well, of course, any attempt or prior attempt at suicide, you have to take that into consideration, certainly.

Q. Doctor, is depression synonymous with suicidal risk?

A. No.

Q. What are the different kinds of depression?

A. Well, there are different types of diagnoses in which depression is an important aspect. You have the psychotic depressive reaction, the manic depressive, the neurotic depressive reaction, or just ordinary depressive reaction. You can have obsessive compulsive reaction, with depression, and so forth. In other words, the depression is the primary thing.

Q. What would be the difference between neurotic depression and psychotic depression?

A. Well, psychotic depression presents the type of person that I was referring to, the severe depressive type who is often profoundly changed in that he has suddenly lost appetite, lost weight, and has feelings of persecution, and unworthiness, and uselessness, things of that sort. He may even have delusions of guilt and may even be dangerous to himself or others.

Now, neurotic depression is something that most of us have experienced at times when we feel depressed. That's what the term *neurotic depression* means. It's something denoting anxiety and brings on crying spells usually, but ordinarily it produces hope for the future and the individual wants to go on with life.

Q. There is quite a difference, then, isn't there, Doctor?

A. Yes, there is.

Q. Doctor, is there any way of telling whether a person is a probable suicidal risk?

A. Well, yes, when you take the whole thing. You have got to make a complete study, and learn all you can about him, before you can make such a judgment.

Q. Doctor, at my request, have you examined the complete medical record of the deceased Louis R. Genovese?

A. Yes.

Q. Doctor, based on the hospital records, do you have an opinion as to whether or not the treatment rendered to the deceased was equal to the standard of care in the community?

A. Yes, I will say it was up to the standard of care in the community.

Q. What would be the reason for your opinion, Doctor?

A. Well, it was handled pretty much the way most patients would be with the kind of findings that were apparent in the chart, and I think the hospital staff acted in what would be ordinary medical practice.

Q. Doctor, from your complete survey of this chart, is it your opinion that this man had a psychosis prior to the time he committed suicide?

A. It is my opinion that there is insufficient evidence to indicate that he did have this psychosis. I don't know if he had that psychosis. I don't know that.

Q. Doctor, I show you this clinical record, dated 10/8, and this is a notation by Dr. Cohen, and I ask you to read that, please.

A. Right here?

Q. Yes.

A. "Blood pressure four times a day and record. Psychiatric consult. Patient with ulcerative colitis. Past history psychosis. Please evaluate."

Q. In your opinion, Doctor, did this man have a record of a past history of psychosis?

A. As far as I know, I saw no evidence of such degree of disturbance to warrant such a diagnosis.

Q. And that would be in your field more than Dr. Cohen's, who is a general M.D.; is that right?

A. Yes.

Q. Doctor, I show you from the clinical record a notation on 5/24/62, and I will ask you to read that, please.

A. Consult psychiatry—I can't make this out. "Forty-eight-year-old white male, postoperative. Colectomy for ulcerative colitis. Has lost all interest in caring for self and exhibits marked intermittent periods of hostility and feeling of persecution. Would you evaluate?" That's May 24, 1962.

Q. That's right. Now, Doctor, in your opinion, would that be sufficient in itself to conclude that this man had a psychosis?

A. Well, one would have to consider that there is a possibility, particularly with this phrase about having lost all interest, because that is one of the classic symptoms. If someone has lost interest in caring for himself, that can be a sign of severe depression reaction, or it can be a sign of schizophrenic reaction. Hostility would indicate possibly a serious mental disturbance, and certainly feeling of persecution would point toward a possible paranoid type of psychosis.

Q. Doctor, if the language appears in the record that this man had a possible underlying psychosis, would that in itself connote that this man was an actual psychotic?

A. No.

Q. Would that be more or less to evaluate and to rule out that possibility?

A. Yes.

Q. Doctor, based on the hospital record of the deceased, do you have an opinion as to whether or not this man could have been considered a suicidal risk?

A. Based on the record prior to the suicide, the actual suicide, there was insufficient evidence to indicate that he was a suicidal risk.

Q. Doctor, what are the reasons for your opinion?

A. I thought there was a lack of sufficient evidence.

Q. A lack of sufficient evidence to anticipate an attempt to commit suicide?

A. That's right.

Q. Doctor, do you have an opinion as to whether this man should have been removed to a neuropsychiatric ward?

A. Well, surely he should have been, because he ultimately did commit suicide, but based on the record, there was insufficient data to warrant such a judgment that one would need to remove him to a locked ward.

Q. Doctor, the evidence in the case shows that Dr. Colomb, a noted psychiatrist, examined the deceased some three days prior to his death and did not find that this man was a suicidal risk in all probability. Would your opinion have been the same?

BY PLAINTIFF ATTORNEY

I object to that question, if the Court please. That's a misstatement of fact. There's no evidence in the record to that effect.

BY THE COURT

Well, I will let him answer. He can say whether he would agree or not. He's an expert.

BY DEFENSE ATTORNEY

Q. What is your answer, Doctor?

A. I would agree.

BY THE COURT

Q. What do you base that answer on, Doctor?

A. Well, I know Dr. Colomb, and I respect him and his knowledge and ability; but of course I would make my own evaluation of the patient's condition.

If a psychiatrist says to me that a patient that I am going to get one way or the other is a suicidal risk, or even that he is not a suicidal risk, I am not going to accept that at its face value, because I always make my own evaluation and judgment. After I do that, I either agree totally with what they have said, or I do not.

BY THE COURT

Q. Is this testimony your own independent judgment of the situation, then?

A. Yes, sir.

Q. The fact that Dr. Colomb, the psychiatrist, makes his finding does not have control over what your evaluation is?

A. Certainly not, sir.

BY THE COURT

That's what I thought. I could have almost answered that for you.

BY PLAINTIFF ATTORNEY

Q. If Dr. Colomb interviewed this man and was of the opinion that he was not a suicidal risk, would the hospital be correct in relying on that evaluation, the VA hospital?

A. Well, yes, that's right. Certainly they would be right to rely on his recommendations since he is a qualified psychiatrist.

CROSS-EXAMINATION BY PLAINTIFF ATTORNEY

Q. Doctor, would it have been helpful to you if you had examined this patient while he was still alive, if you had seen him before making your determination?

A. Oh, yes.

Q. The best way to determine whether a patient has suicidal tendencies is to have a psychiatrist to have a full work-up on him, isn't that true?

A. Yes, I would say so. A five-minute interview with a patient is worth several hours of reports from other people. Just to see someone for a few minutes to me is worth so much more.

Q. I suppose it would be more helpful to have a formal psychiatric consult, a full-length one, than have a five-minute interview, too; wouldn't you say that is correct?

A. Yes.

Q. You don't do psychiatric consultations in five minutes, do you, Doctor?

A. No.

Q. Would you agree that with a depressed patient psychiatric consultation is therapeutic in itself?

A. Yes.

Q. If a surgeon—a physician not a psychiatrist—referred a patient to you with the notation that he had a past history of psychosis, would you be more likely to schedule a patient for an early consultation than if you didn't have that notation?

A. Well, simply to take a past history of psychosis in itself does not say too much, because certainly there are patients who are psychotic for years and out in the community. If I had a patient who was psychotic, I would try to ascertain whether it was really an emergency situation. For instance, if the patient was acutely psychotic or had acute paranoid schizophrenia or a manic depressive reaction, then I would certainly try to see him as soon as possible.

Q. Doctor, I realize that there are signals which you can get that are more significant than others, and there has been some reference to that in this case; but is it fair to say that you would consider a reference note of a past history of psychosis as a significant reference, particularly if you did not ever see the patient, which is true in this case?

A. Yes, I would have to take it in the terms in which it was presented, if I didn't see the patient. I would consider it a fairly serious case if that's all I had to go on.

Q. And you would accept the reference at its face value if that's all you knew about the patient; is that right?

A. Yes, I would.

Q. Do you sometimes place patients in psychiatric wards, pending psychiatric work-up, if you can't get to them right away?

A. Well, I do if it's an acute problem such as widely disturbed patients, very paranoid patients, or possibly dangerous or violent depressed patients. In fact, where you had a marked depressed patient, you would more than likely admit him to the closed unit pending a thorough evaluation, because if you didn't, you might be too late.

Q. Is it fair to say, Doctor, that the ordinary standard of care in the community would dictate that a patient who is awaiting a psychiatric consultation, and who has some emotional problem, ought to be watched more closely than the patient who doesn't?

A. No, I don't think so. Simply the fact that one is awaiting consultation doesn't mean the patient would bear more close watching than any other patient. Usually patients who are awaiting psychiatric consultation are no real management problem on a ward. Of course, if they did display any type of violence, or if we considered them dangerous, we would put them in a closed ward.

Q. What about the patient about whom the observation has been made that he has lost all interest in himself? Would that kind of patient bear more watching than one about whom that observation is made?

A. You mean that the physician may be requesting this of the nursing staff?

Q. In terms of total hospital care.

A. Well, he might request this, but I would have to know more about whom the notation was being addressed to. I think normally it is up to the judgment of the physician to decide if the patient needs more observation; but, as I say, I don't think that notation by itself means anything in particular. I don't think that that necessarily implies any emergency. I think rather that that must be for the benefit of the nursing staff or the personnel who had the care of this patient.

Q. Let me put it differently, Doctor. If you had a patient and you had noted that the patient had lost all interest in the care of himself, that he exhibited marked intermittent periods of hostility and feelings of persecution, would you make the suggestion to the staff that he be watched a little more carefully than a patient about whom those entries were not made?

A. I would, yes.

Q. Would you consider, in the ordinary standard of care among physicians and psychiatrists in the community, that there would be something that ought to be done?

A. Well, putting it in the terms that you do, yes.

Q. Is that a signpost to a possible suicide attempt, that a patient has lost interest in caring for himself, or no longer takes care of himself?

A. Yes, that's one of the possible indications, but, as I said before, that in itself is not diagnostic. Any one thing can mean many things. You have to take the whole picture.

Q. Is this one of the things that could be included in that picture, Doctor?

A. Yes.

Q. If a patient appears to be withdrawn or unusual, is that a signpost?

A. It might be, yes. Now, some of these things you are referring to were present in his previous admittance, as I recall, not in the current one.

Q. Well, Doctor, let me say that we are looking at the whole gestalt, as Dr. Shneidman put it, and if we did that, we would take not only the present signposts, but the ones with references to his previous admission; wouldn't that be correct?

A. Not so much the first visit. I think we would be more concerned with the current picture rather than the earlier one. I mean, in the terms of immediate management, one would be concerned with how the patient appeared and acted at the time of his current admission, not when it was present at the previous admission. For instance, if he was depressed about something on the first admission, and it had more or less worked itself out, then he would be over that. In that light, I think these would be comparatively new symptoms that we would be concerned with.

Q. However, these current symptoms that we have been discussing could be regarded as signposts to possible suicide; would that be a correct statement?

A. Yes, but with these depressed conditions, they do get over them, and this patient could have been depressed over something or some condition that existed or developed following his previous visit to the hospital. That's what I mean.

Q. Well, Doctor, I don't want to quibble, but I am just asking if, in evaluating a man's emotional condition, we shouldn't take in his entire history and background to further aid the evaluation?

A. Yes, we always take the history.

Q. And you consider the background of what prior troubles he may have had in evaluating his entire condition, don't you, Doctor?

A. Yes, you do that. What I am getting at is that we are more concerned with current problems as a rule than in something that he might successfully have gotten over.

Q. Would you consider it significant that in the course of a couple of days in the hospital, two doctors don't see anything significant that would call for a psychiatric consultation, and then in the course of two days two other doctors decide that the patient ought to have a consultation? Would you conclude that something had occurred to make them reach that conclusion?

BY DEFENSE ATTORNEY
That's an unfair statement, if the Court please. We object to it.

BY THE COURT
. . . I think you ought to be more specific with that question. Suppose you tell him who did what and ask him what he thinks about it, and for what reason.

BY PLAINTIFF ATTORNEY

Q. What I am getting at, Doctor, is: let's assume that it is a fact, according to the record, that Dr. Valle, who admitted the patient, and Dr. Toups, who examined him the same day, that neither one of them saw any necessity for a psychiatric consultation; and then within the course of two days, Dr. Colomb and I believe Dr. Atik decided that one was necessary. Would you consider that to be significant, that there was some change in the patient that brought that about?

A. It could be that, or it could be that these were different doctors with a different view of the thing, and that they saw things the previous doctors hadn't seen. They might have made a more thorough examination, and they might have simply, in the course of evaluating his illness of ulcerative colitis, determined that he should have a psychiatric work-up or consultation. It's not uncommon to obtain a psychiatric consultation when one is indicated. It doesn't have to be an emergency or anything like that.

Q. Doctor, if you were referred to a patient for a psychiatric consultation with an entry on the referral note of past history of psychosis, would you try to see that patient sooner than within eight days?

A. Well, I try to see any patient as soon as I can.

BY DEFENSE ATTORNEY

If Your Honor please, is he talking about a general situation or this specific patient?

BY THE COURT

I think he's asking a general question.

BY DEFENSE ATTORNEY

All right, thank you.

BY PLAINTIFF ATTORNEY

Q. Would you answer the question, Doctor?

A. Well, generally speaking, I attempt to see them as soon as I can. Now, if I have direct communication with the physician, I will ask him if this is an emergency or can this patient wait, and of course, then my next step depends on what he says. Sometimes, therefore, when it would contain a past history of psychosis, I would be inclined to handle it in a routine manner, to answer your question.

Q. You wouldn't put that patient ahead of one on whom there was no such note on the referral slip?

A. No, not just on that alone. As I said before, I would not be so much interested in a past history of psychosis as I would be in whether he currently was psychotic.

Q. Is character change one of the signposts you would look for in a possible suicide?

A. Well, no, it's not particularly direct in itself. It's not one of the cardinal signs of suicide. More often when you see a person with a character change, it could well be a brain tumor or brain damage of some sort, rather than an indication that the person is going to commit suicide.

Q. What about previous mutilating surgery; is that significant?

A. Previous mutilating surgery?

Q. Yes.

A. Well, you would have to consider that this might tend to make a person depressed in itself, but it is not common enough to be one of the cardinal signs of suicide in general; but it would make you wonder if the person was not depressed as a result of this, yes. Now, certainly just on the face of it, a man who has the kind of surgery that Mr. Genovese had has to be somewhat depressed; anyone is with this.

Q. Would you say, Doctor, that a person who is hospitalized and who is a potential suicide is more likely to be detected than one who is not hospitalized?

A. Not necessarily. Generally speaking, many suicides, successful suicides, communicate their intent to someone, and often this includes physicians who miss the boat and don't pick it up.

Q. What about psychiatrists, aren't they more capable of ascertaining that possible development through these various signposts we have been discussing?

A. Well, psychiatrists ought to be able to pick it up. Certainly they should be more apt to pick up these indications, these potential suicides.

Q. Does psychiatric treatment help depression?

A. Yes. That's one of the things we can cure.

BY THE COURT

Q. Is that done by drugs, or how?

A. The best treatment for a severe depressive is still electroconvulsive therapy, which is shock treatment. That will snap them out of it.

Q. Shock therapy sometimes also has unpleasant side effects, doesn't it?

A. Yes, sir.

Q. Are depressives the most common type of suicide?

A. Yes, sir, depressives commit suicide more often than patients with other categories of illness or disease that we know about.

BY THE COURT

Very well.

The court ruled for the defendant. It found that foreseeability of harm, an essential element to actionable negligence, was not established by the plaintiff. Frederic v. United States, 246 F.Supp. 368 (E.D.La. 1965).

Notes

1. S. A. Webster, "Suicide Attempts Put Financial Burden on Society," *Detroit News,* Nov. 26, 2000, p. 12. The San Francisco Suicide Prevention Hotline and Crisis Center estimates that about thirty people die jumping off the Golden Gate Bridge each year and about twice that number are saved by workers on the bridge. Going west did not prove a salvation. Some of the bridge workers regard suicidal people with contempt—as workplace hazards who tie up traffic, distract them from their jobs, and give the bridge a bad name. M. Williams, "Threaten to Jump From the Golden Gate: You'll Get Tough Love," *Wall Street Journal,* Sept. 10, 2001, p. 1.

One psychiatrist says: "Half of my patients seen every day have attempted suicide, and I am not talking of 'gestures.' One-quarter have tried to kill themselves in the last twelve months. Suicidality is the norm in the practice of psychiatry. So, how to deal with all this, especially in a managed care environment? If I focus on their imminent death, I would usually fail them, as a hospitalization of a few days would yield only another failure." Personal communication (Oct. 18, 2000). See H. Hendin et al., "Therapists' Reactions to Patients' Suicide," *Am. J. Psychiatry* 157 (2000): 2022; reviewed in E. Goode, "Patient Suicide Brings Therapists Lasting Pain," *New York Times,* Jan. 16, 20001, p. D-1.

2. B. Bongar et al. (eds.), *Risk Management with Suicidal Patients* (New York: Guilford Press, 1998). In a number of writings culminating in the book *Fatal Freedom: The Ethics and Politics of Suicide* (Westport, Conn.: Praeger, 1999), the iconoclast Dr. Thomas Szasz objects to the labeling of suicide as a "mental illness" and putting the "cure" under the control of doctors. Criticized in P. S. Links, "An Old Idea Repackaged," *Canadian Med. Assn. J.* 163 (2000): 313.

The phenomenon of suicide terrorism, which came to the fore in the United States on September 11, 2001, may be illuminated by the event that took place in 1978 in Guyana. In the community that he established, Rev. Jim Jones preached that Armageddon was on the horizon. He convinced his followers that to escape it and achieve salvation they had to drink a suicide potion, and also give it to their children, with the result that over nine hundred people died. The cult members accepted Jones as a kind of savior-god, in effect turning over to him the mental functioning involved in reality perception. As a result of a process similar to brainwashing, Jones became able to decide for them what was right or wrong, real or unreal, and how they should live. In an effort to stabilize their personalities, they turned to Jones as an omnipotent parent figure who, they unconsciously wished, might rescue them. Similarly, the suicide bombers are emotionally immature, and mostly they have been selected for years of training. Many of them led very undistinguished and unfulfilled lives. A. J. Eisnitz, "Suicide Terrorists: How Can They Do It?" *Bull. Psa. Assn. of New York* 39, no. 3 (Fall 2001): 5. Dr. Paul McHugh describes terrorists as people who have an "overvalued idea," a passion that leads them to ignore all other considerations such as personal safety, humane feelings, compromise, or temporizing alternatives. Like the Unabomber and Jack Kevorkian, they have overvalued ideas that are inaccessible to argument and persuasion. Their behavior, McHugh contends, will continue unless they are captured or killed. P. R. McHugh, "A Psychiatrist Looks at Terrorism," *Weekly Standard,* Dec. 19, 2001, p. 21. See also J. A. M. Meerloo, *Suicide and Mass Suicide* (New York: E. P. Dutton, 1968).

3. See D. J. West, *Murder Followed by Suicide* (London: Heinemann, 1965); M. F. Abramsky & M. Helfman, "Murder-Suicide," in H. V. Hall (ed.), *Lethal Violence 2000* (Kamuela, Hawaii: Pacific Institute for Study of Conflict and Aggression, 1996); D. Cohen, M. Llorente, & C. Eisdorfer, "Homicide-Suicide in Older Persons," *Am. J. Psychiatry* 155 (1998): 390; P. M. Marzuk, K. Tardiff, & C. S. Hirsch, "The Epidemiology of Murder-Suicide," *JAMA* 267 (1992): 333. The classic sociological study of suicide is E. Durkheim, *Suicide* (New York: Free Press, 1951). The book has stood the test of time. Durkheim talked of alienation, a disconnection of a sort. Another classic, one that is recommended reading in a number of training programs in psychiatry or psychology, is A. Alvarez, *The Savage God: A Study of Suicide* (New York: W. W. Norton, 1971), which states: "Suicide excuses are mostly casual. At best they assuage the guilt of the survivors, soothe the tidy-minded and encourage the sociologists in their endless search for convincing categories and theories. They are like a trivial border incident which triggers off a major war. The real motives which impel a man to take his own life are elsewhere; they belong to the internal world, devious, contradictory, labyrinthine, and mostly out of sight" (p. 97). Kirilov in Dostoyevsky's *The Possessed* said, "All I'm looking for is the reason that people do not kill themselves." He conjectured only two reasons why we do not all kill ourselves: pain and fear of the next world.

4. Introjection is related to the more primitive fantasy of oral incorporation. At one time an oil company advertised, "Put a tiger in your tank."

5. F. J. Ayd & C. Daileader, "The Correlation between Suicide and Panic Disorder," *Psychiatric Times,* Sept. 2000, p. 37.

6. In an early and famous Massachusetts case, John Francis Knapp was tried for the murder of one Joseph White. The prosecution, headed by Daniel Webster, claimed that Knapp aided and abetted one Crowinshield, who actually struck the fatal blows. It was therefore crucial to the prosecution to show Crowinshield's guilt—even though Crowinshield himself had committed suicide before the trial. In his closing argument, Webster discussed the probative value of the suicide on the issue of Crowinshield's guilt. He said, "When suspicions, from without, begin to embarrass him, and the net of circumstances to entangle him, the fatal secret struggles with still greater violence to burst forth. It must be confessed, it will be confessed; there is no refuge from confession but suicide, and suicide is confession." Commonwealth v. Knapp, 7 American State Trials 395, 515–16.

7. G. Remafedi, "Suicide and Sexual Orientation," *Arch. Gen. Psychiatry* 56 (1999): 885.

8. J. Leo, "Could Suicide Be Contagious?" *Time,* Feb. 24, 1986, p. 59. Unless the individual is a celebrity or the mode of suicide is unusual (as in the case of Charles Bishop, who crashed a plane into a high-rise building in Tampa), newspapers usually shun suicide stories out of respect for surviving family members and because they raise the specter of invading privacy. Media coverage also spurs copycats. B. Smith & M. Fechter, "Feeding Frenzy or Good Reporting?" *Tampa Tribune,* Jan. 11, 2002, p. 1. A special section of the *New York Times* on "Education Life" focuses on student suicide, and it lists causes: leaving home, fitting in,

forming relationships, meeting expectations, finding a career, academic pressure, information overload, choices, and broken homes. L. Berger, "The Therapy Generation," *New York Times*, Jan. 13, 2002, sec. 4A, p. 30. One study claims that 60 percent of teenagers have considered suicide. Many of them are living in homes where they are disconnected—physically or emotionally—from one parent or both. M. W. Merrill, "Teen Pilot Represents Thousands of Disconnected Kids," *Tampa Tribune*, Jan. 11, 2002, p. 19.

9. See J. Barron, "Youth Suicides: Are Their Lives Harder to Live?" *New York Times*, Apr. 15, 1987, p. 13; M. Elias, "Kids and Depression: Are Drugs the Answer?" *USA Today*, Nov. 30, 1999, p. 1.

10. See K. R. Jamison, *Night Falls Fast: Understanding Suicide* (New York: Knopf, 1999). See also H. L. P. Resnik (ed.), *Suicidal Behaviors: Diagnosis and Management* (Boston: Little, Brown, 1968).

11. In Fernandez v. Baruch, 52 N.J. 127, 244 A.2d 109 (1968), a disorderly patient was brought to an emergency room after a scuffle in which he was not seriously injured. Because of his peculiar behavior, he was given a brief psychiatric examination and found to be in an acute state of anxiety without psychosis. Tragically, the patient committed suicide in a police car shortly after release from the emergency room. His widow claimed that the examining psychiatrist, whom she sued along with the hospital, should have informed the police that the deceased, although then calm, was suffering from a dangerous mental condition with homicidal-suicidal tendencies and that the psychiatrist should have advised the police of the need to continue the administration of a tranquilizing drug (Thorazine) and of the effects of its discontinuance. The court found that the hospital and the psychiatrist were not negligent under the circumstances, as they had at the time acted with all appropriate care.

See also Johnson v. Grant Hospital, 286 N.E.2d 308 (Ohio App. 1972), where the court noted that a nurse is required in preventing a suicide to exercise both the standard of care of a reasonably prudent person not specially trained as well as the standard of care of one having her special training, and on the question of her behavior as to a reasonably prudent person no expert testimony as to a standard of care is required. See Special Section, "Suicide," *Am. J. Psychiatry* 130 (1973): 450.

12. Some 35 percent of individuals who committed suicide were seen by a primary care physician within a week of the suicide, and 75 percent within a month. Barriers to diagnosis are concern about stigmatizing the patient, uncertainty about how to diagnose and whom to treat, time constraint (average length of visit is seven minutes), discomfort with emotional language, lack of access to psychiatrists, and reimbursement considerations. L. S. Schneider et al. (eds.), *Diagnosis and Treatment of Depression in Late Life* (Washington, D.C.: American Psychiatric Association, 1994), p. 411.

13. R. I. Simon, "The Suicidal Patient" in L. E. Lifson & R. I. Simon (eds.), *The Mental Health Practitioner and the Law* (Cambridge: Harvard University Press, 1998), p. 166. See also B. Bonger, *The Suicidal Patient: Clinical and Legal Standards of Care* (Washington, D.C.: American Psychological Association, 1991); F. Flach (ed.), *Malpractice Risk Management in Psychiatry* (New York: Hatherleigh Press, 1998); D. G. Jacobs (ed.), *The Harvard Medical School Guide to Suicide Assessment and Intervention* (San Francisco: Jossey-Bass, 1999); A. Roy (ed.), *Suicide* (Baltimore, Md.: Williams & Wilkins, 1986); R. G. Goldstein, D. W. Black, A. Nasrallah, & G. Winokur, "The Prediction of Suicide," *Arch. Gen Psychiatry* 48 (1991): 418; H. Hendin, "Psychodynamics of Suicide, with Particular Reference to the Young," *Am. J. Psychiatry* 148 (1991): 1550; R. M. A. Hirschfeld & J. M. Russell, "Assessment and Treatment of Suicidal Patients," *N. Eng. J. Med.* 337 (1997): 910; D. H. Hughes, "Can the Clinician Predict Suicide?" *Psychiatr. Serv.* 46 (1995): 919; J. T. Maltsburger, "Calculated Risk Taking in the Treatment of Suicidal Patients: Ethical and Legal Problems," *Death Stud.* 18 (1994): 439; P. M. Marzuk et al., "The Effect of Access to Lethal Methods of Injury on Suicide Rates," *Arch. Gen Psychiatry* 49 (1992): 451; G. E. Murphy, "Why Women Are Less Likely Than Men to Commit Suicide," *Comp. Psychiatr* 39 (1998): 165; M. Rosenbluth, I. Kleinman, & F. Lowy, "Suicide: The Interaction of Clinical and Ethical Issues," *Psychiatr. Serv.* 46 (1995); 919; G. S. Truant, M. B. O'Reilly, & L. Donaldson, "How Psychiatrists Weigh Risk Factors when Assessing Suicide Risk," *Suicide & Life-Threatening Behav.* 21 (1991): 106; A. D. Weisman & J. W. Worden, "Risk Rescue Rating in Suicide Assessment," *Arch. Gen. Psychiatry* 26 (1972): 553. The trend toward imposing probation conditions intended to shame or humiliate the probationer has led to a number of suicides. A. Horwitz, "Coercion, Pop-Psychology, and Judicial Moralizing: Some

Proposals for Curbing Judicial Abuse of Probation Conditions," *Wash. & Lee L. Rev.* 57 (2000): 75.

14. D. S. Viscott, *The Making of a Psychiatrist* (New York: Arbor House, 1972), p. 175.

15. The borderline personality disorder is also linked to frequent suicidal thoughts, threats, and attempts, or self-hurting, self-mutilating behavior such as cutting or burning. The person with borderline personality experiences chronic feelings of emptiness, sadness, or depression.

16. E. F. Torrey, *Surviving Schizophrenia* (New York: HarperCollins, 3d ed. 1983), p. 271.

17. R. I. Simon, "The Suicide Prevention Contract: Clinical, Legal, and Risk Management Issues," *J. Am. Acad. Psychiatry & Law* 27 (1999): 445.

18. See J. A. Chiles & K. D. Strosahl, *The Suicidal Patient: Principles of Assessment, Treatment, and Case Management* (Washington, D.C.: American Psychiatric Press, 1995).

19. M. C. Miller, D. G. Jacobs, & T. G. Gutheil, "Talisman or Taboo: The Controversy of the Suicide-Prevention Contract," *Harv. Rev. Psychiatry* 6 (1998): 78; R. I. Simon, "The Suicide Prevention Contract: Clinical, Legal, and Risk Management Issues," *J. Am. Acad. Psychiatry & Law* 27 (1999): 445. See also D. A. Lott, "Risk Management with the Suicidal Patient," *Psychiatric Times*, Aug. 2000, p. 9.

20. In Weathers v. Pilkinton, 754 S.W.2d 75 (Tenn. 1988), the Tennessee Supreme Court held that suicide of a patient is an independent intervening cause that will relieve a physician of liability unless the patient "did not have willful and intelligent purpose to accomplish this." It is generally held, however, liability may attach even if the patient "knew and understood the nature of his or her act." Courts impose an affirmative duty on the therapist "to see that the patient does not do harm to himself or others."

In Cowan v. Doering, 215 N.J. Super. 484, 522 A.2d 444 (1987), the New Jersey court said:

> We find no sound reason to adopt the sterile and unrealistic approach that if a disabled plaintiff is not totally incompetent, he is fully legally accountable for his own negligence. In view of the present state of medical knowledge, it is possible and practical to evaluate the degrees of mental acuity and correlate them with legal responsibility. In our view, a patient known to harbor suicidal tendencies whose judgement has been blunted by a mental disability should not have his conduct measured by external standards applicable to a normal adult. Where it is reasonably foreseeable that a patient by reason of his mental or emotional illness may attempt to injure himself, those in charge of his care owe a duty to safeguard him from his self-damaging potential. This duty contemplates the reasonably foreseeable occurrence of self-inflicted injury regardless of whether it is the product of the patient's volitional or negligent act.

For a critique, see P. S. Appelbaum, "Patients' Responsibility for Their Suicidal Behavior," *Psychiat. Serv.* 51 (Jan. 2000): 15; S. H. Behnke, "Suicide, Contributor Negligence, and the Idea of Individual Autonomy," *J. Am. Acad. Psychiatry & Law* 28 (2000): 64. See volume 1, chapter 22, on duty to mitigate damages.

21. In Sheron v. Lutheran Medical Center, 2000, CJ C.A.R. 4416, the Colorado Court of Appeals said, "[A]lthough there is some contrary authority in other jurisdictions, we hold that a patient who is treated by health care providers for suicidal ideations, and who later commits suicide, may be found comparatively negligent or at fault in a subsequent wrongful death action based upon that treatment."

22. Hunt v. King County, 481 P.2d 593 (Wash. 1971). Cases are cited in Annot., "Civil Liability for Death by Suicide," 11 A.L.R.2d 751, 782–92 (1950). See H. J. Zee, "Blindspots in Recognizing Serious Suicidal Intentions," *Bull. Menninger Clinic* 36 (1972): 551.

23. At trial, in the case of an institutionalized patient, the argument that is made is that precautions were inadequate in view of the suicidal tendency, and there are many cases holding hospitals and psychiatrists responsible for the death. Liability for the suicide of a hospitalized patient turns on the foreseeability of suicidal tendency and upon the duty owed by the physician and hospital to provide reasonable precautions to protect the patient from himself. Vistica v. Presbyterian Hosp. & Medical Center, 67 Cal.2d 465, 62 Cal. Rptr. 577, 432 P.2d 193 (1967). See A. Holder, "Liability for Patient's Suicide," *J. Am. Med. Assn.* 215 (1971): 1879; I. Perr, "Liability of Hospital and Psychiatrist in Suicide," *Am. J. Psychiatry* 122 (1965):

631; H. Waltzer, "Malpractice Liability in a Patient's Suicide," *Am. J. Psychotherapy* 34 (1980): 89.

Expert testimony is needed in suicide cases. Payne v. Milwaukee Sanitarium Foundation, 260 N.W.2d 386 (Wis. 1977). Problems of suicide are examined in Surprenant v. State, 46 Misc.2d 190, 259 N.Y.S.2d 306 (Ct. Cl. 1965) (plaintiff was a mentally retarded patient given to temper tantrums during which he would break glass; during a tantrum, the plaintiff drove his hand through a window). See Collins v. State, 23 App. Div.2d 898, 258 N.Y.S.2d 938 (1965) (patient had a history of suicide attempts, yet the mental hospital assigned him to a general ward and he hanged himself). See also Lawrence v. State, 44 Misc.2d 756, 255 N.Y.S.2d 129 (Ct. Cl. 1964) (patient with known suicidal tendencies was placed in a room on the second floor of a state mental hospital without protective gates or bars on the windows and with inadequate supervision; this was constituted actionable negligence which was the proximate cause of the death of the patient, who jumped from a window). See Benjamin v. Havens, 60 Wash.2d 196, 373 P.2d 109 (1962) (psychiatrist was sued for failure to select a suitable hospital and failure to prescribe necessary restraints, and the hospital was sued for failure to supervise or restrain the patient properly). See Tissinger v. Wooley, 77 Ga. 886, 50 S.E.2d 122 (1948) (psychiatrist was sued for selecting a hospital unsuitable for a suicidal patient, and the hospital was sued for not guarding the patient). See Stallman v. Robinson, 364 Mo. 275, 260 S.W.2d 743 (1953) (failure to check safety belt of patient in a closed ward). See also Gregory v. Robinson, 338 S.W.2d 88 (Mo. 1960) (patient pushed his way through the door as the psychiatrist was leaving the closed ward and leaped out of an unbarred window).

Hospitals have been held liable for allowing a patient to commit suicide in sundry ways, as in Daley v. State, 273 App. Div. 552, 78 N.Y.S.2d 584 (1948) (suicide by drowning in a vat of boiling soap); Browner v. Bussell, 50 Ga. App. 840, 179 S.E. 228 (1935) (suicide by slashing wrist and throat); Hunt v. King County, 481 P.2d 593 (Wash. 1971) and in Spivey v. St. Thomas Hosp., 31 Tenn. App. 12, 211 S.W.2d 450 (1947) (suicide by jumping from a window); Broz v. Omaha Maternity and Gen. Hosp. Ass., 96 Neb. 648, 148 N.W. 575 (1914) (suicide by taking poison); Dow v. State, 183 Misc. 674, 50 N.Y.S.2d 342 (1944) (suicide by hanging).

Liability is also imposed where negligently allowed escape terminates in a patient's death, as in Burtman v. State, 188 Misc. 153, 67 N.Y.S.2d 271 (1947) (exposure to inclement weather); Arlington Heights Sanitarium v. Deaderick, 272 S.W. 497 (Tex. Civ. App. 1925) (patient killed by a train); Phillips v. St. Louis & S.F. Ry., 211 Mo. 419, 111 S.W. 109 (1908) (by a streetcar); Hawthorne v. Blythewood, 118 Conn. 617, 174 Atl. 81 (1934) (by drowning).

24. S. H. Behnke & J. T. Hilliard, *The Essentials of Massachusetts Mental Health Law* (New York: Norton, 1998), p. 144.

25. In Bellah v. Greenson, 81 Cal. App.3d 614, 146 Cal. Rptr. 535 (1978), the court pointed out the duty of care owed to a hospitalized patient differs from that of treatment of an outpatient, but there is a duty as well in the outpatient setting "to see that the patient does not do harm to himself or others."

26. V. E. Schwartz, "Civil Liability for Causing Suicide: A Synthesis of Law and Psychiatry," *Vand. L. Rev* 24 (1971): 217; A. A. Stone, "Suicide Precipitated by Psychotherapy," *Am. J. Psychotherapy* 25 (1971): 18. It has been suggested that Freud out of rivalry drove Victor Tausk, one of his most brilliant students, to suicide. Freud arranged for Tausk to go into analysis with Helene Deutsch while she was in analysis with Freud, and he allegedly got at Tausk via Deutsch. P. Roazen, *Brother Animal: The Story of Freud and Tausk* (Middlesex, England: Penguin Press, 1970).

27. The same question has been asked about medication. The development of new-onset suicidal ideation or violent behavior has been linked to medication. See J. Cornwell, *The Power to Harm* (New York: Viking, 1966); C. M. Vale, "The Rise and Fall of Prozac: Products Liability Cases and 'The Prozac' Defense in Criminal Litigation," *St. Louis U. Pub. L. Rev.* 12 (1993): 525.

28. S. Lesse, "Editorial Comment," *Amer. J. Psychotherapy* 19 (1965): 105. See also W. Tomlinson, "President's Column," *News Quarterly of La. Psychiatric Assn.*, Fall 1980, p. 3.

29. Communication from Dr. Mortimer Ostow.

30. R. G. Arnot, "Electroshock Therapy" (ltr.), *Atlantic*, Mar. 1980, p. 31.

31. Communication from Dr. Mortimer Ostow.

32. See M. Ostow (ed.), *The Psychodynamic Approach to Drug Therapy* (New York: Mental Health Materials Center, 1979); M. Ostow, "Is It Useful to Combine Drug Therapy with

Psychotherapy?" *Psychosomatics* 20 (1979): 731. See also M. Clark, "Drugs and Psychiatry: A New Era," *Newsweek*, Nov. 12, 1979, p. 98.

33. Mich. Comp. Law, sec. 333.1801 *et seq.* But see Mich. Stat., sec. 17074(3) (physician's assistant prescribing drugs).

34. Under a law passed in 1976, Congress set up a fund to provide special death benefits to survivors of killed law officers. The law did not specify what types of death result in payments, so the Justice Department spelled out such things as death caused by injuries from bullets, explosives, sharp instruments, blunt objects, chemicals, radiation, bacteria, and climatic conditions. The U.S. Supreme Court declined to consider expanding the benefit (a one-time payment of $100,000) to law officers who commit suicide over job stress, which had been urged in a case involving a Massachusetts law officer's death. Yanco v. United States, 70 U.S.L.W. 3463 (2002).

35. Workers' compensation law does not provide benefits for an injury caused "by the employee's willful intent to injure the employee's self." See, e.g., Iowa Code, sec. 85.16(1). A claimant must show that the job caused the mental injury and the mental injury was caused by stress of a greater magnitude than the day-to-day stress experienced by workers in the same or similar jobs. See Humboldt Community Schools v. Fleming, 603 N.W.2d 759 (Iowa 1999).

36. Personal communication (Oct. 23, 2000).

37. See J. M. Violanti, *Police Suicide: Epidemic in Blue* (Springfield, Ill.: Thomas, 1996); A. E. Kureczka, "Surviving Assaults: After the Physical Battle Ends, the Psychological Battle Begins," *FBI Law Enforcement Bull.* 71 (Jan. 2002): 18.

38. See State Farm Fire & Cas. Co. v. Wicka, 474 N.W.2d 324 (Minn. 1991); Comment, "Mental Incapacity and Liability Insurance Exclusionary Clauses: The Effect of Insanity Upon Intent," *Cal. L. Rev.* 78 (1990): 1027.

39. There is in law a presumption against suicide. Thus, when violent death is shown to have occurred and the evidence is not controlling as to whether it was due to suicide or accident, it is presumed that the death was not by suicide. See, e.g., Dick v. New York Life Ins. Co., 359 U.S. 437 (1959). The reasons: There is the human revulsion against suicide and a social policy that inclines toward the fruition rather than the frustration of plans for family protection through insurance.

40. The California Supreme Court stated, "If the insured did not understand the physical nature and consequences of the act, whether he was sane or insane, then he did not intentionally kill himself." Searle v. Allstate Life Ins. Co., 38 Cal.3d 425, 439 (1985). See G. Schuman, "Suicide and the Life Insurance Contract: Was the Insured Sane or Insane? That Is the Question or Is It?" *Tort & Ins. L.J.* 28 (1993): 745. To determine the manner of death, coroners do not routinely secure psychological data. Only a few self-inflicted gunshot head wound cases are referred for a psychological autopsy, and those are instances where the manner of death was contested by members of the decedent's family. Thus, nearly all cases of self-inflicted gunshots to the head are classified as suicide without the benefit of a psychological autopsy. L. E. Weinberger et al., "Psychological Factors in the Determination of Suicide in Self-Inflicted Gunshot Head Wounds," *J. For. Sci.* 45 (2000): 815.

41. An expert is permitted to testify on cause of death because the testimony would be helpful to the jury, as it may not be able to differentiate between a self-inflicted wound and one inflicted by another. State v. Bradford, 618 N.W.2d 782 (Minn. 2000). The expert need not offer a definitive answer as to the cause of death for the testimony to be admissible. Jahn v. Equine Servs., PSC, 233 F.3d 382 (6th Cir. 2000). See R. I. Simon, "Murder Masquerading as Suicide: Post-Mortem Assessment of Suicide Risk Factors at the Time of Death," *J. For. Sci.* 43 (1998): 1129; R. I. Simon, "You Only Die Once—But Did You Intend It?: Psychiatric Assessment of Suicide Intent in Insurance Litigation," *Tort & Ins. L.J.* 25 (1990): 650; E. F. Wilson, J. H. Davis, J. D. Bloom, P. J. Batten, & S. G. Kamara, "Homicide or Suicide: The Killing of Suicidal Persons by Law Enforcement Officers," *J. For. Sci.* 43 (1998): 46.

42. R. E. Litman, "Psychological-Psychiatric Aspects in Certifying Modes of Death," *J. For. Sci.* 13 (1968): 47.

43. B. S. Yasgur, "Self-Mutilating Patients Generally Aren't Suicidal," *Clinical Psychiatry News*, Aug. 2000, p. 36. Freud postulated a death instinct, a theme taken up by Dr. Karl A. Menninger in his books *Man against Himself* (New York: Harcourt, Brace, 1938) and *Love against Hate* (New York: Harcourt, Brace, 1942). Many people choose slow destruction by

alcohol or drugs or by smoking. See M. Vargas Llosa, "A Languid Sort of Suicide," *New York Times,* Sept. 1, 2000, p. 25.

44. See generally M. Baden, *Unnatural Death: Confessions of a Medical Examiner* (New York: Random House, 1993); W. V. Spitz (ed.), *Medicolegal Investigation of Death: Guidelines for the Application of Pathology to Crime Investigation* (Springfield, Ill.: Thomas, 1993).

45. M. J. Kahne, "Suicide among Patients in Mental Hospitals: A Study of the Psychiatrists Who Conducted Their Therapy," *Psychiatry* 31 (1968): 32.

46. Quoted in J. L. Kelley, *Psychiatric Malpractice* (New Brunswick, N.J.: Rutgers University Press, 1996), p. 67.

47. J. I. Klein & S. I. Glover "Psychiatric Malpractice," *Int'l J. Law & Psychiatry* 6 (1983): 131, 141.

48. Quoted in J. L. Kelley, supra note 46, p. 68. See R. J. Goldberg, "The Assessment of Suicide Risk in the General Hospital," *Gen. Hosp. Psychiatry* 9 (1987): 446; L. L. Havens, "The Anatomy of a Suicide," *N. Eng. J. Med.* 272 (1965): 401.

11

Duty of Therapists to Third Parties

The law is in controversy as to when therapists owe a duty to persons other than their patients. The general principle is elastic, to wit, the risk that may result from one's behavior, as reasonably perceived, determines the duty of care to be obeyed as well as to whom the duty is owed. Third-party liability cases are subject to a variety of doctrinal descriptions. The courts may find as a threshold matter that the party owes no duty to the injured person or that the party's action was not the proximate cause of the injury. Establishing duty is a matter of surviving summary judgment and getting the case before a jury. If a duty is found, then the question is whether there has been a breach of that duty. *Duty* and *breach* are the touchstones of liability.

The issue of duty was highlighted in the most celebrated of all torts cases, *Palsgraf v. Long Island R. R. Co.*[1] A late-arriving passenger rushing to catch the defendant's train was pushed by a train porter as he was about to board and a package was dislodged from his grasp, falling upon the rails. It contained fireworks, it exploded, and the concussion overturned a weight scale a distance away on the platform, injuring Helen Palsgraf, the plaintiff, who was waiting for a train to take her and her young daughter to the beach.

Judge Cardozo, for the majority, held that though there was physical injury, there was no liability because there was no negligence toward the plaintiff. Negligence, he noted, must be founded upon the foreseeability of harm, hence duty, to the person in fact injured. The defendant's conduct was not a wrong toward the plaintiff merely because there was negligence toward someone else. The plaintiff, Judge Cardozo said, must "sue in her own right for a wrong personal to her, and not as the vicarious beneficiary of a breach of duty to another." The train porter's behavior was reasonably foreseeable to cause injury to the passenger but not to Palsgraf standing a distance away on the platform. Given the circumstances, the train porter owed a duty to the passenger boarding the train, but not to Palsgraf.

The fact that the porter's action led to Palsgraf's injury, albeit physical, made no difference. The conduct of the porter involved "no hazard [to Palsgraf that] was apparent to the eye of ordinary vigilance," said Judge Cardozo. His theory, now the prevailing view in various jurisdictions, ended the case. There being no duty as to Palsgraf, there was no need to discuss causation or harm. The young daughter, witnessing the injury to her mother, and suffering emotional distress, was likewise outside the ambit of duty.

In dissent, Judge Andrews rejected Cardozo's theory that a defendant owed a duty of care only to foreseeable plaintiffs. Andrews argued that a person's duty to act reasonably is owed to society at large, not simply to particular persons. All persons injured by negligent conduct were wronged, Andrews argued, not just those as to whom harm was foreseeable. The crucial question for Andrews involved the issue of causation that Cardozo said the court did not have to face. Andrews understood that the law does not impose liability for all injuries that were caused by a defendant's negligence in the sense that they would not have occurred but for that conduct. The injury must have been proximately caused by that conduct. Andrews argued that the term *proximate cause* meant that "because of convenience, of public policy, of a rough sense of justice, the law arbitrarily declines to trace a series of events beyond a certain point." Andrews argued that foreseeability was a more malleable concept than Cardozo believed, and that the question whether the defendant's negligence was a proximate cause of the plaintifff's injury was properly for the jury.

The opinions thus disagreed on two grounds: whether the issue was duty or proximate cause, and whether the issue (whichever it was) should go to the jury. Cardozo thought that Palsgraf was an unforeseeable plaintiff as a matter of law, whereas Andrews did not. Cardozo's view, limiting duty to foreseeable plaintiffs, limits the extent of liability. Cardozo's view was adopted in the *Restatement of Torts.*

In the event a duty of care is owed to the plaintiff, by whatever theory, that of Cardozo or Andrews, then the question arises as to whether the type of harm (or damage) is compensable. In a view that has changed, courts have ruled that emotional distress, without physical injury or physical impact, is not compensable.

The question arises: Can therapy of a patient result in a foreseeable risk of harm to a third party? The answer is "yes." One result of malpsychotherapy may be a patient's acting out in an unlawful manner. Clearly, to take an extreme example, one who hypnotizes a patient and suggests the commission of a crime is a wrongdoer.[2]

In preventing physical injury, mental hospitals, we know, have a duty to protect third parties. They are obliged to exercise reasonable care in preventing escapes and in deciding on releases. In numerous cases, hospitals or staff members have been held liable for breach of this duty. Thus, as one court put it, a state mental hospital "has a duty to protect the community from acts of insane persons under its care."[3]

Hence, in jurisdictions where there is no charitable or governmental immunity, the courts have placed on mental hospitals a duty owed to the general public to exercise reasonable care in escape prevention or release decisions. In these cases, the courts, for the most part, have not distinguished between foreseeable and unforeseeable victims. The cases, for the most part, involved rather obvious diagnostic, administrative, or communication errors.[4]

The courts are mindful of the extent of liability insurance coverage, although this is unmentioned in determining to whom a duty of care is owed. Liability insurance policies are drawn to narrow the scope of liability coverage. There is a miscegenational union of insurance and liability. The courts not only consider the foreseeability of harm, but they also assess the competing public policy considerations for or against imposing liability. As one court expressed it, "Liability must be controlled by workable and just limits."[5]

Jurisdictions on essentially identical facts reach different conclusions in carrying out the formula that the risk as reasonably perceived determines the duty to be obeyed. Apart from hospital discharge cases, a number of jurisdictions (or various courts within a jurisdiction) allow only the patient to sue over negligent treatment, even when that malpractice causes physical injury to others—as occurs when tuberculosis is improperly treated and consequently passed on to family members. In an Illinois case of this sort, the defendant physician raised the specter of potentially unlimited liability to all those infected by his patient, as well as all those whom they infect. The defendant physician also asserted that allowing the patient's immediate family to sue would constitute an artificial distinction between family members and all others whom his patient or his patient's family might infect. The majority of an intermediate appellate court agreed.[6] Justice Charles Freeman, however, dissented and would have extended the duty to the patient's immediate family. He said, "I cannot agree that limiting the right to sue . . . to a patient's immediate family members, i.e., to those with whom he has special relationships, is an artificial and arbitrary distinction."[7]

In this type of situation, on the other hand, many jurisdictions have not limited a cause of action only to the patient. In a case decided by the Pennsylvania Supreme Court, a physician negligently advised a patient exposed to hepatitis that she could be confident she had not contracted the disease and was not contagious if she remained symptom-free for six weeks. However, the correct waiting period is six months. The patient refrained from sexual intercourse for eight weeks after the exposure and then resumed sexual intercourse with the plaintiff. Both patient and plaintiff were later diagnosed with hepatitis. The court held that the plaintiff had a cause of action against the physician.[8]

For negligent infliction of emotional distress (as distinguished from physical injury), many jurisdictions restrict liability in the absence of a preexisting relationship between the plaintiff and the tortfeasor. In a 1980 California case, *Molien v. Kaiser Foundation Hospital*,[9] the California Supreme Court relaxed the rule to permit recovery by plaintiffs who meet a *direct victim* test. The direct victim question is said to be a matter of duty. In all cases, judges decide the question as to whom a duty is owed, whereas causation is usually a jury determination.

In *Molien* a physician incorrectly and negligently informed a patient that she had an infectious type of syphilis, and she was advised to tell her husband. The misdiagnosis allegedly caused her to become "upset and suspicious that [her husband] had engaged in extramarital sexual activities; tension and hostility arose between the two, causing a break-up of their marriage and the initiation of dissolution proceedings." The husband sued the hospital and the diagnosing physician for the emotional distress that he suffered and for the loss of consortium. The California Supreme Court, in holding that the complaint stated a cause of action, said that the husband was a direct victim of the physician's alleged negligent act.

The basic principle underlying *Molien* was reaffirmed by the California Supreme Court in 1992 in *Burgess v. Superior Court*.[10] In *Burgess*, the plaintiff was a pregnant woman who went into labor, and because of the physician's malpractice, delivered a child with brain damage. She filed suit in her own behalf against the physician on a theory of negligent infliction of emotional distress. In upholding a judgment in favor of the plaintiff, the court reviewed the dimensions of the doctrine of negligent infliction of emotional distress, because the use of the direct victim designation has tended to obscure rather than illuminate the relevant inquiry.

In a unique fashion, the court made a distinction between bystander cases and direct victim cases. Bystander liability is premised upon a defendant's violation of a duty not to negligently cause emotional distress to people who observe conduct that causes harm to another. Because in such cases the class of potential plaintiffs could be limitless, resulting in the imposition of liability out of all proportion to the culpability of the defendant, the courts have circumscribed the class of bystanders (nearby family members) to whom a defendant owes a duty to avoid negligently inflicting emotional distress.[11] In contrast, the label "direct victim" was used by the court to distinguish cases in which damages for serious emotional distress are sought as a result of a breach of duty owed the plaintiff that is "assumed by the defendant or imposed on the defendant as a matter of law, or that arises out of a relationship between the two."

Duty to Warn or Protect under *Tarasoff*

Social changes have increased the likelihood that therapists will care for potentially dangerous patients who are not under custodial control. No decision caused more concern in the psychiatric community than the decision by the California Supreme Court in *Tarasoff v. Regents of University of California*.[12] Among psychiatrists, the name of the case has become a household word. Decided in the mid-1970s, it continues to be discussed at numerous psychiatric meetings and in countless publications.[13]

Nonetheless, psychiatrists, by and large, do not realize that it was a case based on the pleadings, that is, to resolve the question whether the law imposes a duty owed to third parties as a result of a danger posed by a patient in an outpatient setting. Duty is essentially a question of whether the law will impose a legal obligation on one party for the benefit of another. While foreseeability of the harm is an important consideration in determining whether a duty exists, the courts must also assess the competing public policy considerations for and against recognizing the asserted duty in any individual case. In the event that the court determines that no duty exists, summary disposition for failure to state a claim is the appropriate remedy.

In *Tarasoff*, the trial court had sustained a demurrer to the complaint. (A *de-*

murrer declares that even if everything stated in the complaint were true, it does not state facts sufficient to constitute a cause of action. It is, in effect, a legal shrugging of the shoulder: "So what?" In modern procedure a motion to dismiss or summary judgment replaces the demurrer, and if denied, the case simply proceeds to trial on the merits.) The California Supreme Court, in reversing the trial court, imposed a duty on psychiatrists or other psychotherapists to protect third parties from potential harm by their patients. In so doing, the court made the therapist a proper party defendant whenever a patient causes injury to another. In the course of discovery, when it is learned that the offender was or is in therapy, the therapist is named as defendant, jointly or singly.

In jurisdictions following *Tarasoff*, it is no longer possible for therapists to get out of the case by summary disposition on the ground that they owe no duty in law to the injured party. Under *Tarasoff*, there is a duty, and it is a matter for the jury to decide on the basis of the facts of the particular case whether reasonable care was exercised. The outcome then becomes, many have said, a lottery. "It must be borne in mind," the U.S. Supreme Court once observed, "negligence cannot be established by direct, precise evidence such as can be used to show that a piece of ground is or is not an acre. Surveyors can measure an acre, but measuring negligence is different."[14]

The *Tarasoff* litigation did not go to trial on the merits, that is, on the basis of the facts involved, it having been settled. The importance of the case is that it imposed a legal duty on therapists to third persons irrespective of the standard of care in treating the patient or whether there was any treatment. When a case may go to a jury, insurers and others tend to settle. *Tarasoff* involved physical injury to a third person.

In *Tarasoff*, Prosenjit Poddar, a 25-year-old graduate student from India at the University of California, had met weekly with Dr. Lawrence Moore, a clinical psychologist at the outpatient department of the university hospital, for a total of eight sessions. He revealed his fantasies of harming, even killing, a young woman who had rejected him. He distrusted Dr. Moore, for he believed that Dr. Moore might betray him.

Dr. Moore, with the concurrence of a colleague at the clinic, concluded that Poddar should be committed for observation under a 72-hour emergency psychiatric detention provision of the California commitment law. He notified the campus police both orally and in writing that Poddar was dangerous and should be committed.[15] The campus police went to Poddar's apartment, brought him to the station for questioning, and they also talked to other people familiar with him. They warned him to stay away from the girl. They concluded that commitment was not necessary. Poddar did not return to the clinic. Two months later, when the young woman, Tatiana Tarasoff, returned from vacation he stabbed her to death. She was 19, immature, unaware of what her sexuality was doing to Poddar.

The chief of the clinic was outraged that Dr. Moore would break confidentiality and report Poddar to the police. He scolded Dr. Moore, "You realize, don't you, that by betraying his trust, you destroyed whatever chance you had of helping him?" "It was past that point," replied Dr. Moore. "And besides, I think he wanted me to break confidentiality. His telling me of his intentions was his way of saying, 'Look, I'm out of control. I'm going to kill this girl unless you stop me. Won't you please stop me.'"

What if the *Tarasoff* case had gone to trial? What would the plaintiff have had to prove at trial? How could the plaintiff establish that the patient divulged a threat to the therapist or otherwise posed a danger if records may be protected from discovery under the therapist-patient privilege?[16] How should the warning have been made and to whom should it have been made? It may have been held that the therapist in fact discharged the duty mandated by the court, since he had notified the campus police, and the victim's brother also had notice of the threat, as the police spoke to Poddar in the brother's presence. Given these facts, it could be said that the therapist discharged his duty of care as outlined by the court.

However, one might ask, was the therapy below standard of care? The *Tarasoff* case might have been litigated, purely and simply, as one of malpsychotherapy, like malchemotherapy, resulting in the patient harming others. One colleague at the clinic had suggested that the treatment of Poddar may have been beyond the ability of Dr. Moore. Was Dr. Moore able to handle the case? Not long before, events in Dr. Moore's life—a suicide attempt by his wife and her attempted murder of their child—had traumatized him. Following the death of Tarasoff, he was dismissed from the clinic (that would not have been admissible at trial as the law of evidence excludes "subsequent remedial repairs").

The case might have been litigated or decided on the basis of negligent treatment rather than on the formulation of a special duty to third persons. That approach was not taken because of the difficulty in establishing standard of care in psychotherapy. The attorney for the Tarasoff family decided not to argue that malpractice in psychotherapy resulted in the killing because of the difficulty or impossibility, he perceived, in establishing standard of care in psychotherapy.[17] When the treatment of the patient is negligent and results in a foreseeable injury to a third person, there is no need to establish a special relationship, as liability would follow under the principle set out in *Palsgraf*. Instead of arguing negligence in treatment, the attorney in *Tarasoff* argued that as a result of the special relationship between physician and patient, there is also a special relationship to those who might be injured by the patient. It was a novel argument. In the circumstances of the case, the defendants contended no duty of care was owed to Tarasoff or her parents and that, in the absence of such a duty, they were free to act in disregard of Tarasoff's life and safety.

The California Supreme Court during the 1970s was a progressive court that wanted to expand theories of law and did so in this case and others, and was followed in other jurisdictions. The argument by the attorney for the Tarasoff family prevailed. The court held that by virtue of the special relationship that a therapist has with a patient, there is a duty of care owed to third parties who might be injured by the patient. It is immaterial whether the treatment of the patient falls below the standard of care or whether there is a causal nexus between the treatment or the lack of it and the injury to the third person. Under the rule of the case, the duty is imposed even when there is no treatment whatever but simply an interview. The court noted:

> Although under the common law, as a general rule, one person owed no duty to control the conduct of another, nor to warn those endangered by such conduct, the courts have carved out an exception to this rule in cases in which the defendant stands in some special relationship to either the person whose conduct needs to be controlled or in a relationship to the foreseeable victim of that conduct.

The court went on to say that the special relationship with the patient also creates a special relationship with a victim of the patient. Declaring the existence of a special relationship, the court could apply the common-law doctrine that a special relationship creates a duty of care. The common law did not impose an obligation to aid or protect another, even if the other is in danger of losing his life, unless that person created the peril or when there is a special relation between the parties (such as carrier-passenger, innkeeper-guest, or physician-patient).[18] Unless there is a special relation between the parties, a duty arises only by virtue of misfeasance done by that party that foreseeably will cause injury to the plaintiff, that is, the risk created by the party that is reasonably to be perceived determines the duty to be obeyed.

Under the *Tarasoff* innovation, a special relation between *A* and *B* creates a special relation with *C* who is hurt by *B* even though *A* is not negligent toward *B*. Under the common law, a special relation between *A* and *B* did not create a special relation between *A* and *C* who may be injured by *B*. *Tarasoff* and its progeny represents an evolution of the law from no duty, a duty to those in a special relation, and now to those who might be harmed by one to whom a duty is owed.[19] The court said:

> Although plaintiffs' pleadings assert no special relation between Tatiana and defendant therapists, they establish as between Poddar and defendant therapists the special relation that arises between a patient and his doctor or psychotherapist. Such a relationship may support affirmative duties for the benefit of third persons. . . . Although the California decisions that recognize this duty have involved cases in which the defendant stood in a special relationship *both* to the victim and to the person whose conduct created the danger, we do not think that the duty should logically be constricted to such situations. (emphasis by court)

Under the ruling, when it is fairly known or knowable that a patient poses a danger, the therapist is obliged to use "reasonable care" to protect potential victims. What care is reasonable, the court ruled, is not limited to the issuance of a warning. The court set out various courses of action; to wit, warning the victim or someone likely to tell the victim of the danger, notifying the police, or taking other steps reasonably necessary under the circumstances. What is reasonable, the court said, can be determined only on a case-by-case basis.[20]

In Louisiana, it has been held that a *Tarasoff*-type lawsuit is not one of malpractice, or professional negligence, but ordinary negligence, inasmuch as the plaintiff is not a patient but a third party; hence, the therapist is not covered under the Medical Malpractice Act that Louisiana enacted to limit liability for physicians who enroll in the plan. The act was enacted in 1975 in response to a perceived medical malpractice insurance crisis. To circumvent its limitations, injured third parties argued that the *Tarasoff*-type case is one of ordinary negligence, and the Louisiana Supreme Court held accordingly. The court ruled, "The Act applies solely to claims 'arising from medical malpractice.'" Inasmuch as the act limits liability in derogation of the general rights of tort victims, any ambiguities in the act must be strictly construed against coverage, the court ruled.[21]

Professor Michael Perlin reported that as of the end of May 1999, *Tarasoff* had been cited in 497 published cases.[22] In *Tarasoff*, there were two dissents that fore-

MICHIGAN

330.1946   Threat of physical violence against third person; duties.
[M.S.A. 14.800(946)]

Sec. 946. (1) If a patient communicates to a mental health professional who is treating the patient a threat of physical violence against a reasonably identifiable third person and the recipient has the apparent intent and ability to carry out that threat in the foreseeable future, the mental health professional has a duty to take action as prescribed in subsection (2). Except as provided in this section, a mental health professional does not have a duty to warn a third person of a threat as described in this subsection or to protect the third person.

(2) A mental health professional has discharged the duty created under subsection (1) if the mental health professional, subsequent to the threat, does 1 or more of the following in a timely manner: (a) Hospitalizes the patient or initiates proceedings to hospitalize the patient under chapter 4 or 4a.

(b) Makes a reasonable attempt to communicate the threat to the third person and communicates the threat to the local police department or county sheriff for the area where the third person resides or for the area where the patient resides, or to the state police.

(c) If the mental health professional has reason to believe that the third person who is threatened is a minor or is incompetent by other than age, takes the steps set forth in subdivision (b) and communicates the threat to the department of social services in the county where the minor resides and to the third person's custodial parent, noncustodial parent, or legal guardian, whoever is appropriate in the best interests of the third person.

(3) If a patient described in subsection (1) is being treated through team treatment in a hospital, and if the individual in charge of the patient's treatment decides to discharge the duty created in subsection (1) by a means described in subsection (2)(b) or (c), the hospital shall designate an individual to communicate the threat to the necessary persons.

(4) A mental health professional who determines in good faith that a particular situation presents a duty under this section and who complies with the duty does not violate section 750. A psychiatrist who determines in good faith that a particular situation presents a duty under this section and who complies with the duty does not violate the physician-patient privilege established under section 2157 of the revised judicature act of 1961, Act No. 236 of the Public Acts of 1961, being section 600.2157 of the Michigan Compiled Laws. A psychologist who determines in good faith that a particular situation presents a duty under this section and who complies with the duty does not violate section 18237 of the public health code, Act No. 368 of the Public Acts of 1978, being section 333.18237 of the Michigan Compiled Laws. A certified social worker, social worker, or social worker technician who determines in good faith that a particular situation presents a duty under this section and who complies with the duty does not violate section 1610 of the occupational code, Act No. 299 of the Public Acts of 1980, being section 339.1610 of the Michigan Compiled Laws. A licensed professional counselor who determines in good faith that a particular situation presents a duty under this section and who complies with the duty does not violate section 18117 of the public health code, Act No. 368 of the Public Acts of 1978, being section 333.18117 of the Michigan Compiled Laws. A marriage and family therapist who determines in good faith that a particular situation presents a duty under this section and who complies with the duty does not violate section 1509 of the occupational code, Act No. 299 of the Public Acts of 1980, being section 339.1509 of the Michigan Compiled Laws. A music therapist who determines in good faith that a particular situation presents a duty under this section and who complies with this duty does not violate section 4.11 of the professional code of ethics of the national association for music therapy, inc., or the clinical relationships section of the code of ethics of the certification board for music therapists.

(5) This section does not affect a duty a mental health professional may have under any other section of law.

cast problems that would arise with the new legal duty. Justice Stanley Mosk's main concern was that therapists would have trouble predicting when a patient might be dangerous. Justice William Clark worried that the divulgence of patient confidentiality would be detrimental to the profession, the patient, and successful treatment. He also expressed concerns about a potential increase in civil commitments. To this day, writings about *Tarasoff* continue unabated.

Identity of Potential Victim in a *Tarasoff*-Type Case. Is the identity of the victim a matter of consequence in a *Tarasoff*-type case? Legally, should identity matter? Should it matter whether danger is to person or property?[23] Logically, what difference should the identity of the victim or type of harm make? Logically, the test would be: Is the threat serious, and is the potential harm imminent and serious? The patient says he plans to poison the water supply, blow up a building, or kill the first person that crosses his path. Is there not a prima facie absurdity to limiting the duty of care to the situation when the victim is identifiable? The scope of harm is potentially greater when the general populace is threatened. The answer, of course, lies not in logic but in law—the legal consequences of the distinction are enormous. If the therapist's duty is to protect society, every victim can sue, but if the duty is owed only to an identifiable victim, only that victim has a cause of action. Under a duty to protect society, one and all in a crowd of people harmed by the patient could maintain a suit against the therapist. The potential of liability could be withering (save the practice of limiting liability to insurance limits).

The potential victim in the *Tarasoff* case was readily identifiable. In the years since *Tarasoff,* the courts in various states have responded either by narrowing its range of applicability to a specific individual or by broadening it to include unidentifiable individuals.[24] The U.S. District Court in Connecticut expanded its range of applicability from an identifiable individual to a "class of victims." In the Connecticut case, a duty was imposed on a psychiatric resident's psychoanalyst for not notifying that resident's medical school that the resident was a pedophile. The court noted that the analyst had available feasible and not unreasonably burdensome mechanisms for control.[25] Apart from *Tarasoff,* legislation mandates that physicians and others report child abuse when there is suspicion of it; the degree of proof is minimal.

In the *Tarasoff* scenario, to safeguard themselves and to make sure of their legal duty, psychiatrists in various states have lobbied for legislation to provide that issuance of a warning alone discharges their duty. A number of states have enacted such legislation (sometimes known as a *Tarasoff limiting statute*) that makes it possible for the psychiatrist to obtain summary disposition by having given a warning. Such legislation encourages psychiatrists to take that route, though it is formalistic and not likely to be helpful. While these statutes do not exclude other options, they do establish warnings as the easy and simple route to take. Ironically, a legal concern for patients and victims has produced a response in which formalism—not clinical judgment—has become the rule of the day.[26]

The Ohio Supreme Court ruled that the *readily identifiable victim* rule is applicable only in the context of failure to warn, but there is a duty to protect when the victim is not identifiable. The court, citing authority, stated,

> Unlike a duty to warn case, in which the therapist needs to know the identity of the victim in order to adequately act, the therapist in a duty to

commit case need only know that the patient is dangerous generally in order to adequately commit him. As a practical matter, the victim's identity is irrelevant to whether the doctor can adequately act—by committing the patient, the therapist is able to protect all possible victims.

The court does not believe that it is wise to limit any duty to commit according to the victim. Arguably, the patient who will kill wildly (rather than specifically identifiable victims) is the one *most* in need of confinement. In negligent release cases, a defendant's duty generally has not been limited to readily identifiable victims, and the court believes a similar rule is appropriate here. Citizens outside of the "readily identifiable" sphere but still within the "foreseeable zone of danger" are potential victims a therapist should consider if he has a duty to them and a means of adequately protecting them.[27]

In 1998, the South Carolina Supreme Court stated: "South Carolina law does not recognize a general duty to warn of the dangerous propensities of others. . . . However, when a defendant has the ability to monitor, supervise, and control an individual's conduct, a special relationship exists between the defendant and the individual, and the defendant may have a common law duty to warn potential victims of the individual's dangerous conduct. . . . This duty to warn arises when the individual has made a specific threat of harm directed at a special individual."[28]

Rejecting *Tarasoff*. In recent years, when confronted with the scenario of a patient posing a danger, appellate courts in Florida, Mississippi, Texas, and Virginia have rejected imposing a duty under *Tarasoff*.[29] The Florida Court of Appeals stated:

If our society has progressed (or regressed) to such a point that there should now be recognized new causes of action where none have existed before, we conclude that it is the better part of judicial wisdom to await the establishment of such causes of action by legislative action after input as to all the variables from competing elements of society. We are unprepared and unwilling as jurists to declare that such a cause of action exists because we now conclude, with the more limited fact- finding resources at our disposal, that there is presently a sufficient societal interest to protect that requires judicial activism.[30]

In *Tarasoff*, Chief Justice Mathew Tobriner wrote, "In this risk-infested society we can hardly tolerate the further exposure to danger that would result from concealed knowledge of the therapist that his patient was lethal." In contrast, in 1999, the Texas Supreme Court said, "Mental-health professionals make disclosures at their peril." The court noted that while those who report child abuse in good faith are immune from civil and criminal liability, mental health professionals are not shielded from civil liability for disclosing threats in good faith.[31]

Consequences of *Tarasoff*. When the *Tarasoff* decision was handed down, many therapists offered fatalistic predictions of harm to the psychotherapeutic relationship. According to a study by Dr. Renee Binder and Dale NcNiel, the impact of *Tarasoff* on the relationship has been minimal. The study examined the effects of *Tarasoff*-like decisions upon the therapist-patient relationship, and also how potential victims fared in light of the decisions. All second-, third-, and fourth-year psychiatric residents (N = 46) in a university-based psychiatric residency program in San Francisco were interviewed about their experiences related to issuing a *Tarasoff* warning. Almost half of the residents (N = 22) reported having issued a *Tarasoff* warning. Most warnings were issued for patients seen in inpatient units and emergency rooms. In almost half the cases, the resident was unable to contact the intended victim but did report the threat to a law-enforcement agency. The most common reaction among those warned was anxiety mixed with thankfulness; most expressed an intent to modify their behavior to increase safety. The second most common reaction was denial that the patient would ever hurt them. The clinicians reported that in most cases issuing the warning had a minimal or positive effect on the psychotherapeutic relationship.[32]

What happens when the police are notified of a threat? It did not safeguard Tatiana Tarasoff. Psychiatrists Richard Balon and Rizwan Mufti of Detroit randomly called three police departments in southeastern Michigan, introduced themselves as physicians, and asked about the disposition of a physician's or psychotherapist's notifications of dangerousness. They were unable to find any procedure for handling these notifications or any established guidelines, and they were unsure if notification was ever registered or acted upon. They pondered, "[O]ne has to question the rationale of mandating the notification of authorities when no guidelines have been established to handle these notifications, as well as when it is possible that no action will be taken."[33]

HIV and AIDS. The treatment of a patient with HIV/AIDS involves issues of guilt, shame, fear of contagion, and association with sexually transmitted disease, and especially for the latter reason, therapy places a burden of responsibility on both patient and therapist to prevent its spread. At the same time, they must be mindful that the stigma associated with it drastically affects an individual's personal and social life, his occupation and means of livelihood. All states require that cases be reported to public health authorities, while only some require that the patient's name be reported. Some states also require reporting cases or names of individuals who test positive for HIV. Over thirty states variously require, allow, or forbid health care workers (including mental health professionals) to warn patients' sexual contacts of the risk of exposure to sexually transmitted diseases, including HIV/AIDS. It would be a bureaucratic nightmare to implement a requirement that a patient's various sexual contacts be notified of the risk of HIV. A public registry of persons infected with HIV, like the registry of sex offenders, would likely face a challenge by the ACLU.[34]

Genetic Disease. The duty of a physician to warn relatives of a patient of the presence of a genetic disease in the family has rarely been addressed, statutory attention to the issue is even more rare, and policy development is embryonic. Theoretically, analogy may be made to the duty to report infectious disease, though infectious diseases are contagious, while genetic diseases are not. In *Olson v. Children's Home Society of California*,[35] the California Court of Appeals held that having knowledge of a genetic condition does not create a duty to disclose it to genetic relatives. In this case, Barbara Olson had the defendant adoption agency, Children's Home Society of California (CHS), arrange for her son's adoption. Thirteen years later she, then married, gave birth to another child. This child died of the genetically transmitted disease combined severe immune deficiency (CSID). She contacted CHS to inquire about the health of the son she had put up for adoption and was informed that he also had CSID but was alive. The plaintiff and her husband filed suit against CHS for the wrongful death of their child, intentional infliction of emotional distress, and fraud. Claiming that CHS had a duty to warn them that their child had a genetic disease, the plaintiffs alleged that—if warned of the danger—they would have either not conceived the child or received medical treatment to save his life. The trial court dismissed the complaint on the ground that the plaintiffs "failed to allege any legal duty." Affirming, the court of appeals rejected the plaintiff wife's argument that there was a special relationship between her and CHS that imposed a duty on CHS to notify her of the 50 percent risk of having another affected male child, stating that "special relationship situations generally involve some kind of dependency or reliance." The court distinguished *Tarasoff* by noting that in that case there was a "nexus between the impending peril and the specific duties undertaken by the defendants in those special relationships."[36]

Is *Tarasoff* applicable in respect to genetic information? The harm, genetic disease, has already been done. At best then, a health care professional can only prevent a relative from losing a chance of therapy or survival if disclosure is made in circumstances when therapy or a cure are available. In that event, does the health care professional have a duty to the genetic relatives of his patients? The New Jersey Supreme Court said, "The foreseeability of injury to members of a family other than one immediately injured by the wrongdoing of another must be viewed in light of the legal relationships among family members. A family is woven of the fibers of life; if one strand is damaged, the whole structure may suffer. The filaments of family life, although individually spun, create a web of interconnected legal interests."[37]

More recently, the New Jersey Superior Court held that a direct duty existed of a health care professional toward the children of a patient who was suffering from retroperitoneal cancer with multiple polyposis of the colon to warn the children of the immediate risk to their own health: "Although an overly broad and general application of the physician's duty to warn might lead to confusion, conflict or unfairness in many types of circumstances, we are confident that the duty to warn of avertible risk from genetic causes, by definition a matter of familial concern, is sufficiently narrow to serve the interests of justice."[38] The relevance of the nature of the information was key to the foundation of the duty. The strongly hereditary influence of multiple polyposis alerted the health care professional to a specific and easily identifiable class of persons who were at increased risk. Moreover, that class of persons was restricted (blood relatives of the patient), so to allow the action did not raise the prospect of opening liability to an unlimited group of potential litigants. Thus the nature of the information delineated the duty and its scope. The trial court in the case had found that genetically transmissible diseases differed from contagious or infectious diseases or threats of harm, because the "harm is already present within the non-patient child, as opposed to being introduced, by a patient who was not warned to stay away. The patient is taking no action to cause the child harm."

The influence of genetic factors in psychiatric disorders is highly variable. The environmental and genetic interactions that influence most psychiatric conditions are likely to differ between individuals and have variable impacts on each individual. Although many genetic conditions are currently untreatable, most psychiatric disorders respond to some form of treatment. Individuals with identified psychiatric genetic disorders may mitigate the effects of the disorder through medical treatment, psychotherapeutic intervention, and lifestyle changes. In addition, much scientific effort has bee invested in gene therapy, with the eventual goal of reversing the effects of the deleterious gene. In an article in *Psychiatric Times*, it is concluded, "As psychiatric genetics enter into the gene identification era, more clinical applications will be discovered. Although the future of psychiatric genetics will be discovered. Although the future of psychiatric genetics will answer many scientific and clinical questions, it will also raise many questions about the legal, ethical and social implications of these answers."[39]

Recovered Memory Cases

In revival of memory of childhood sexual abuse, the harm that is the matter of litigation is allegedly created by the therapist; in *Tarasoff*, on the other hand, the danger is posed by the patient. The controversy surrounding newly recovered memories of childhood sexual abuse revolves around their accuracy, and that involves questions about memory: (1) Can memories of childhood sexual abuse, be it a single incident or chronic abuse, be repressed completely? (2) If so, can those memories be recovered? (3) If recovered, how is their accuracy determined? And (4) to what extent does the present transform the past?[40] The debate on reports and recollections of child sexual abuse goes back to at least 1896, when Freud argued that repression of early childhood seduction (sexual molestation) had etiological significance for adult hysteria. He later recanted, saying that he was wrong about the repression of actual experiences of child sexual abuse and that it was fantasies (of sexual contact with parents or other adults) that drove the hysteria.

In response to the controversy over the concept of repression, the fourth edition of the American Psychiatric Association's *Diagnostic and Statistical Manual of Mental Disorders,* in its discussion of dissociative identity disorder and other dissociative disorders, shifted from the term *repression* to *dissociative amnesia.* The theory is that trauma, especially childhood trauma, creates a brain process leading to a dissociative episode, in which explicit memories of the trauma are lost. Though the name of the mechanism has changed, the approach to the buried memories remains the same. According to theorists and clinicians, the original memories can be retrieved through the use of recovered memory therapy (RMT), especially if the clinician pays attention to the emerging implicit memories that take the form of bodily sensations (often called *body memories*), repetitive memories, flashbacks, and so on.[41] Looking at bodily sensations is another version of the lie detector that is likewise a matter of controversy.[42]

The question arises: Do family members who are hurt by recovered memory therapists have a right to react in the legal setting? They suffer emotional distress. Clearly the patient has a basis for a malpractice action against the therapist; a number of patients who have recanted memories of sexual abuse have reunited with their families and then brought suit against the therapist for malpractice.[43] But what about a claim against a therapist filed by one other than the patient?

Parents conceivably may proceed: (1) on a theory as in *Molien* that the parents are direct victims of the therapist's negligence, or (2) on a theory as in *Tarasoff* that the special relationship with the patient creates a special relationship with the victim who is harmed by the patient.

When adults in therapy claim recovery of repressed memories of childhood sexual abuse, the abuse supposedly is repressed until, with the help of a therapist, it is remembered. Treatment programs use a variety of techniques to help patients recover memories of sexual abuse, many of them guided by the book *The Courage to Heal*, which contains statements such as "If you are unable to remember any specific instances . . . but still have a feeling that something abusive happened to you, it probably did," and "If you think you were abused and your life shows the symptoms, then you were."[44]

The book encourages revenge, anger, and deathbed confrontations. (It is quite possible that therapists who encourage their patients to act out may themselves be acting out vicariously.) The veracity of the patient's recovered memories is apparently never questioned. The book advises, "You are not responsible for proving that you were abused."[45] Various treatment centers advertised, "Remembering incest and childhood abuse is the first step to healing."[46]

A number of therapists arrange for their patients to confront the alleged perpetrator in the therapist's office, with the therapist present to provide support and validation for the survivor. The therapists say that when people hold onto anger, they are at risk for developing a variety of physical illnesses. Some therapists have regular behavioral rehearsals, using an *empty chair* model, whereby the patient yells and screams at the empty chair. Allegedly, the expression of anger and confrontation is empowering.

Psychologist Carol Tavris debunks the approach in these words: "[T]he major side-effect of the ventilationist approach has been to raise the general noise level of our lives, not to lessen our problems. I notice that the people who are most prone to give vent to their rages get angrier, not less angry. I observe a lot of hurt feelings among the recipients of rage."[47] Robert Hughes, astute observer of the culture, writes, "The ether is now jammed with confessional shows in which a parade of citizens and their role-models, from LaToya Jackson to Roseann Barr, rise to denounce the sins of their parents, real or imagined."[48]

Patients, once convinced that they have been abused, are furious at their parents and blame them for their troubles. They take such actions as suing the parents, refusing to let them see their grandchildren, or ruining their reputations by informing friends and acquaintances about the newly discovered memories.[49] In apparently no case of revival of memory has there been any objective or corroborating evidence to support a claim of abuse.[50] What evidence warrants an interpretation by the therapists? Is any needed? The prominent psychoanalyst Dale Boesky commented in an address to a psychoanalytic group: "As the first century of psychoanalysis draws to a close, we confront an ironic paradox. We are elaborating new theoretic models with pluralistic enthusiasm but we are still unable to reach a consensus about how to evaluate whether even a single interpretation is useful or not."[51]

Dr. Paul McHugh, chairman of the Department of Psychiatry (now University Distinguished Service Professor) at John Hopkins University and a leading member of the Scientific and Professional Advisory Board of the False Memory Syndrome Foundation, said, "To treat for repressed memories without any effort at external validation is malpractice pure and simple."[52] Moreover, he added, to refuse to provide information about the patient to clinicians working with the parents raises the question of absence of good faith.[53] In many cases, the memory hurts the psychological well-being not only of the patient but—through false accusations of incest and sexual abuse—other members of the patient's family. Families, distressed and furious, retaliate with lawsuits and a campaign to deal with revival of memory therapists.[54]

National news weeklies *Time* and *Newsweek*, in the same week in November 1993, both had cover stories on hidden memories.[55] The *Time* article stated, "Repressed-memory therapy is harming patients, devastating families and intensifying a backlash against mental-health professionals."[56] Earlier that year, *Insight*, another national news weekly, had a cover story, "Malignant Memories: Therapists as Coaches."[57] Also, at about the same time, the *New Yorker* ran a two-part article, "Remembering Satan."[58]

The American Medical Association has twice warned against the use of memory enhancement techniques in eliciting accounts of childhood sexual abuse. The wording of its last resolution, in August 1993, was especially harsh. It stated: "The AMA considers recovered memories of childhood sexual abuse to be of uncertain authenticity, which should be subject to external verification. The use of recovered memories is fraught with problems of potential misapplication." The American Psychiatric Association has issued similar warnings.[59] In no uncertain terms, McHugh said, "[Recovery of memory] is the biggest story in psychiatry in a decade. It is disaster for orthodox psychotherapists who are doing good work."[60] Professor Richard Ofshe and Ethan Watters describe memory recovery therapy as a new form of "quackery."[61] Psychiatrists have long been called the Rodney Dangerfields of the medical profession—they get no respect, and controversies like that over revival of memory make it even more difficult to include mental health under insurance coverage.

Safe from the backlash, enjoying governmental immunity, were prosecutors who brought charges of sexual abuse against parents or others on the basis of little more than the flimsy evidence of a revived memory. Some feminist prosecutors used the occasion to voice rage against sexual abuse. Then, with the backlash, judicial opinion turned against evidence derived from repressed memory. In 1997, Judge Mansfield of the Texas Court of Criminal Appeals said, "I believe that any testimony relating to so-called 'repressed memory syndrome' is inherently suspect and should not be admissible in Texas courtrooms."[62] Health insurers have been urged to act as regulators of health care providers by not providing reimbursement to therapists who engage in revival of memory of child sexual abuse.[63]

In California, as we earlier noted, in the early 1990s Gary Ramona sued a medical center and a pair of psychotherapists who he claimed created false memories in his daughter of his sexually abusing her as a child.[64] His lawsuit alleging malpractice sought damages for emotional suffering from the breakup of his family, and for harm to his career and reputation. He could theoretically have elected to sue on a theory of defamation, but California law grants a conditional privilege to therapists.[65]

Gary Ramona succeeded in getting his complaint put to the jury. It will be remembered that, as Cardozo put it, the court—not the jury—determines whether a duty of care is owed the plaintiff. The trial court rejected a defense motion for summary judgment. The court held that the therapists owed a duty of care not only to the patient but also to the patient's parents.[66] With the case going to the jury, Ramona was awarded $500,000, but it was consumed by legal expenses. At the time, no attorney would take the case on a contingency fee basis. The jury award was for "pain and suffering"; there were no economic damages—although he lost his managerial job at a wine company, he obtained another position.

The court's holding that a duty of care is owed was by itself a victory for aggrieved parents whatever the outcome at trial. When a defendant is said to owe a duty to the plaintiff, as we have noted, the defendant cannot avoid a trial by summary judgment. It allows litigation, and the possibility of it may discourage irresponsible therapy. Win or lose at trial may be secondary. A legal strategy is to torment one's adversaries until they cease their behavior. Some do, some don't, but most come away largely ruined, financially (if there's no insurance) or emotionally.[67]

Does the decision in *Ramona* open the door to any litigation by a person aggrieved by an interpretation made by a therapist to a patient? In an address at the 1994 annual meeting of the American Psychiatric Association in Toronto, Dr. Judith Herman, author of *Trauma and Recovery*, said about the *Ramona* decision, "The fact that a third party was given standing to speak on malpractice because he was not happy with the treatment of his daughter really opens the door to permit anyone who is dissatisfied with our treatment of any patient to lay claim against us." Of course, the court did not say that the public at large may bring a claim against the therapist. She acknowledged at the time of her address that she did not have access to the transcripts in the case.

Dr. Thomas Gutheil, who testified on behalf of the defense in *Ramona*, asked: "Whose therapy was this anyway? Should the father have been called in to approve each interpretation as it occurred to the therapist? Should the father's consent to the therapy have been sought, even though the patient was not a minor? Should the patient herself have been warned, in some caricature of the warning needed in a forensic context, that her therapy might conceivably be harmful to her father's peace of mind?"[68]

Gutheil posed a hypothetical scenario: "Let's say a young man comes to treatment to work on trouble with relationships. A few years into psychotherapy, without any prompting by the therapist, the patient decides that the problem has been his failure to acknowledge that he is gay. Working this issue through, he feels much better—until he tells his parents, who are homophobic and become outraged at this news. They decide to sue the therapist for implanting foreign ideas or brainwashing or whatever."

The scenario is what law professors call a "parade of horribles" or "slippery slope," in which it is argued (without proof) that one action will unleash a host of unpleasant consequences. In *Ramona*, the therapists operated on the basis of unsupported theories, and they urged the patient to blame someone else for their problems. The trial judge in *Ramona* relied on *Molien*, where the patient was advised to inform her husband that she had syphilis. In a special verdict answering questions put to them, the jury concluded: (1) the defendants were negligent in providing health care to Holly Ramona by implanting or reinforcing false memories that the plaintiff had molested her as a child, (2) the defendants caused the plaintiff to be personally confronted with the accusation that he had molested Holly Ramona, and (3) the plaintiff suffered damages that were caused by the negligence of the defendants. The court found that the therapists assumed a duty of care to the parent when they encouraged the daughter to confront him with accusations of abuse. The jury foreperson explained that the jury felt the therapist "had reinforced the memories by suggestions and by sending her [the patient] to a therapy group for eating disorders that was filled with sex abuse victims."

In an article in the *American Journal of Psychiatry*, Dr. Paul Appelbaum and law professor Rose Zolteck-Jick cautioned that aggrieved third parties would have the power to bring effective treatment to a halt by filing suit or threatening to do so. Appelbaum and Zolteck-Jick concluded that, although concern about therapeutic practices related to memories of childhood abuse may be warranted, allowing nonpatients to sue would be ill-advised, as it would have therapists unclear regarding how to avoid duties to third parties.[69] In the *Harvard Law Review*, law professors Cynthia Grant Bowman and Elizabeth Mertz wrote that the imposition of third-party liability against therapists would compromise the interest of sexual abuse survivors.[70]

A number of courts have heeded their message. The Minnesota Court of Appeals, citing the *Harvard* article, declined "to extend the law to recognize a duty to third-party non-patients when there is no contractual relationship, duty to warn, or duty to control."[71] The Illinois Supreme Court also declined to impose a duty in this type of case.[72] It said:

> A number of considerations relevant to the duty analysis strongly militate against imposition of duty here. . . . Approval of the plaintiff's cause of action . . . would mean that therapists generally, as well as other types of counselors, could be subject to suit by any non-patient third party who is adversely affected by personal decisions perceived to be made by a patient in response to counseling. This result would, we believe, place therapists in a difficult position. . . . Concern about how a course of treatment might affect third parties could easily influence the way in which therapists treat their patients. Under a rule imposing a duty of care to third parties, therapists would feel compelled to consider the possible effects of treatment choices on third parties and would have an incentive to compromise their treatment because of the threatened liability. This would be fundamentally inconsistent with that therapist's obligation to the patient. . . . Hoping to avoid liability to third parties. . . . a therapist might instead find it necessary to deviate from the treatment the therapist would normally provide, to the patient's ultimate detriment. This would exact an intolerably high price from the patient-therapist relationship and would be destructive of that relationship.[73]

In a dissent, Justice Moses Harrison said, "My colleagues expound at length about the need to protect medical providers from liability to some indeterminate class of nonpatient third parties. . . . Plaintiff here was not a chance bystander or random member of the general public. He was a relative of the therapist's patient, he was the alleged cause of the patient's psychological difficulties, and, according to the complaint, the therapist specifically arranged to have him participate in the patient's therapy sessions as part of the patient's treatment program."[74]

Unless such claims are allowed, the third party argued, negligent and harmful treatment may well continue unchecked because the patient is too emotionally altered to recognize the harm that has taken place. In another case, the Iowa Supreme Court rejected this paternalistic approach. The court said, "It assumes that competent adults who voluntarily undergo mental health treatment cannot decide for themselves whether the treatment is beneficial, an assumption we believe is unjustified."[75]

Similarly, in California, in 1999 in *Trear v. Sills*,[76] the California Court of Appeals rendered a decision at variance with *Ramona*. The California Court of Appeals observed, "Out-of-state cases which have allowed such suits to go forward, and commentators who favor tort liability, however, have invariably not come to grips with the impossibility of verification and the conflicts of interest that a duty to a possible abuser creates." In this case, unlike in *Ramona*, the therapist had not seen the parent, but if courts were to hold that therapists only face the possibility of liability upon meeting with a third party, therapists would become reluctant to meet with a parent whose child may be an abuse victim, and this would dampen family therapy. In light of the decision of the court of appeals in *Trear*, the trial court's decision in *Ramona* might have been reversed if it had been appealed.

In 1994, the same year as the decision in *Ramona*, the California Court of Appeals carried out a review of every case decided in California after *Molien*. In *Bro v. Glaser*,[77] the California Court of Appeals noted that plaintiffs in California usually lose the argument that they are direct victims. It said that to be a direct victim, the plaintiff must show (1) a preexisting consensual relationship between the plaintiff and the defendant, and (2) that the defendant's conduct was sufficiently outrageous to trigger, as a matter of public policy, an obligation to compensate the plaintiff.

Again in California, and in the same year, the direct victim issue again arose. In *Underwood v. Croy*,[78] the wife, who had been seeing a therapist, abandoned her husband and two minor children. The husband discovered that the wife and therapist were having an affair and claimed that the affair was the reason the wife walked out. The California Court of Appeals held that the husband and minor children were not direct victims and hence had no cause of action against the therapist. The trial judge had observed:

> The bottom line is that the question of duty, as a matter of law, is an issue of public policy. Our appellate courts may wish to extend public policy to find a duty of care is owed by a marriage counselor to his patient's various relatives when his sexual exploitation of the patient destroys the marriage which he was retained to help preserve. Such is not the law under existing authority.

The Pennsylvania Supreme Court, although earlier ruling that a third party who contracted hepatitis as a result of a negligent diagnosis of the patient had a cause of action against the physician, recently said that a psychiatrist owed no duty to a minor patient's parents that extended beyond the confidential confines of the psychiatrist-patient relationship. The court overturned a lower court verdict in which psychiatrist Judith Cohen and the University of Pittsburgh's Western Psychiatric Institute and Clinic were ordered to pay $272,232 in damages. As time went on in therapy, the patient had memories of her parents sexually abusing her. The allegations were reported, and her father was arrested three times and her mother twice. The court said that a psychiatrist treating a minor for sexual abuse has no duty of care to the child's parents. Justice Ronald Castille, writing for the majority, said, "To hold otherwise would create an unworkable conflict of interest for the treating therapist, . . . which would necessarily hinder effective treatment of the child.''[79]

A Different View. To be sure, there is conflict of authority.[80] In *Hungerford v. Jones*,[81] the New Hampshire Supreme Court in 1998 allowed a cause of action to parents for the malpractice of their adult children's therapist. The defendant, Susan Jones, was a social worker whose only training in diagnosing and treating repressed memories of childhood sexual abuse was her attendance at a weekend seminar. Nonetheless, she took on the treatment of the patient. During the course of the therapy, the defendant led the patient to believe that her anxiety and nightmares were caused by body memories of past abuse. She led the patient into a trance to employ a recovery technique she referred to as "visualization" or "imagery." Through this, the patient claimed to have recalled five specific episodes of sexual assault by her father, the first beginning when she was five years old, with the last ending only two days before her wedding. At the defendant's insistence and direction, she confronted her father, Joel Hungerford. When he denied the allegation of abuse, the defendant directed the patient to file a complaint for aggravated felonious sexual assault with the police. The defendant came to the police station to validate the truth of the allegations, and to encourage prosecution as a means of empowering the patient. Criminal charges were brought against the father but were subsequently dropped when the court determined the recovered memories were inadmissible, for lack of scientific reliability. Thereafter, the father filed suit against the therapist for malpractice in the care of his daughter.

The New Hampshire Supreme Court was certified to address two issues upon appeal of the defendant's motion to dismiss. First, does a mental health care provider owe a duty of care to the parent of an adult patient when that parent is identified as the perpetrator of sexual abuse in the course of the patient's therapy? Second, to what extent is any such duty owed? The court found four elements that need to be met to establish third-party liability: (1) the accused is the patient's parent, (2) the therapist lacks appropriate experience and qualifications, (3) the therapist uses a psychological phenomenon or technique not generally accepted by the mental health community, and (4) the accusations are made public. The court clarified that although it was extending the duty of care to parents in such cases, the court was imposing "no more than what a therapist is already bound to provide—a competent and carefully considered professional judgment." The court said:

> Imposing a duty of care on therapists who elect to publicize accusations of sexual abuse against parents, or who encourage patients to do so, should not unreasonably inhibit sexual abuse diagnosis or therapy. Recognizing such a duty where parents are implicated, however, should result in greater protection for parents and families from unqualified or unaccepted therapeutic diagnoses. While imposition of this duty may impair societal efforts to bring some sexual abusers to justice, we recognize its need due to the increased foreseeability and devastating consequences of publicized false accusations against parents.
>
> Accordingly, in response to the district court's questions, we hold that a therapist owes an accused parent a duty of care in the diagnosis and treatment of an adult patient for sexual abuse where the therapist or the

patient, acting on the encouragement, recommendation or instruction of the therapist, takes public action concerning the accusation. In such instances, the social utility of detecting and punishing sexual abusers and maintaining the breadth of treatment choices for patients is outweighed by the substantial risk of severe harm to falsely accused parents, the family unit and society. The duty of care to the accused parent is breached by the therapist when the publicized misdiagnosis results from (1) use of psychological phenomena or techniques not generally accepted in the mental health community, or (2) lack of professional qualification.[82]

The Wisconsin Supreme Court in 1999 addressed the duty of therapists to third parties and, over a dissent, said that it agreed with the reasoning of the New Hampshire Supreme Court. In *Sawyer v. Midelfort,*[83] parents brought suit against their daughter's longtime therapists, a psychiatrist and an unlicensed social worker, for implanting false memories of abuse. The daughter had confronted her parents with allegations of physical abuse by both parents and childhood sexual abuse by the father. She filed a lawsuit against her parents, alleging that her father had impregnated her at age thirteen and that her mother had arranged for an abortion. That lawsuit died for lack of progress. In the lawsuit by the parents against the therapists, the court noted that it had extended third-party liability in professional malpractice cases against architects, attorneys, and accountants. But, most importantly, the court noted, it had extended a psychiatrist's duties to warn patients of side effects of medications to protect third parties from injury.[84]

The Wisconsin Supreme Court then engaged in a six-prong analysis to determine whether public policy precluded imposing third-party liability. The court determined that (1) the injury sustained by the parents was not too remote from the alleged negligence, (2) the injury was not too wholly out of proportion to the culpability of the negligent tortfeasor, (3) in retrospect it did not appear too highly extraordinary that the negligence should have brought about harm, (4) allowance of recovery would not place too unreasonable a burden on the negligent tortfeasor, (5) allowance of the recovery would not be too likely to open the way for fraudulent claims, and (6) allowance of recovery would not enter a field that has no sensible or just stopping point. However, the court indicated that such an analysis is fact specific.

The court pointed out that the only reason that the parents were able to bring their lawsuit was because they had obtained their daughter's records. The court, in dicta, observed that confidentiality and testimonial privilege may prevent other lawsuits, but, as other courts have noted, when the patient confronts a parent in a therapy session, as occurred in this case, privilege is waived.[85] Moreover, waiver of privilege obtains when a patient is named as a party defendant. Otherwise, in jurisdictions that allow a third-party suit against a therapist for malpsychotherapy, the problem arises: How does the third party obtain evidence of what occurred in therapy, given the privilege that shields confidential communications between therapist and patient? In *Ramona,* the court held that privilege was waived because the patient filed a lawsuit against her father, and the therapist had seen the father on an occasion or two.[86] In *Tarasoff*-type cases, a third party injured by a patient is given access to records to establish that the therapists should have given a warning of the danger posed by the patient.

Psychotherapists have long resisted the notion that they must prove the value of what they do—and they claim confidentiality. They point out that under the laws in the various states they are not free even to identify whether a person is in therapy with them, as this would constitute a violation of the patient's confidentiality.[87] The California Board of Behavioral Science states: "If a therapist is incompetent or grossly negligent in treating a client, the Board can investigate the particulars of that situation. However, it is virtually impossible for the Board to conduct such an investigation without the consent and cooperation of the actual client. The confidentiality of psychotherapeutic communication is protected by law and therapeutic treatment records cannot be obtained without a written release from the client, if the client is an adult."[88] When a patient sues a therapist, the privilege of confidentiality is waived, but when a patient does not waive the privilege, a third party faces obstacles in obtaining information as to what went on in therapy.

An Ideology of Blaming the Parent. The history of psychoanalysis is marked by blaming the parent—a tendency exacerbated during the tumultuous 1960s when trust was not to be placed in anyone over the age of thirty years. Then, patients' troubles were frequently attributed to childhood sexual abuse.[89] In *Trear*,[90] the California Court of Appeals observed, "[B]y the late 1970s and 1980s, there was a resurgence of Freud's initial view that childhood sexual abuse was at the root of many if not most psychological ills." The court went on, "Granting the early-Freudian assumption (as distinct from the later-Freudian assumption) that abuse is widespread and the root cause of most dysfunction, it is simply not outrageous for a therapist to act on that premise." Of course, Freud abandoned his blind faith in the idea that alleged memories of abuse are always what they purport to be. However, he found that from the perspective of therapy, the reality of abuse or seduction was irrelevant. Thus, in therapy, it does not matter whether the mind is reacting to trauma, coping with everyday turmoil, or just imagining.

Under this view, the therapist works not with the past, but with the patient's story of the past. The past is immutable, so why any interest by the therapist in the past? Dr. Herbert Spiegel says:[91]

> If the disease is biological or of recent psychosocial origin, a reductionist search for causation is a useful approach. The focus is on signs and symptoms that can be contained or neutralized by various medications. But if the syndrome is dominated by illness behavior, the patient's personal history is most effective as a narrative used within the context of a psychotherapeutic strategy. The therapeutic goal is to free the patient from a preoccupation with causation from the past and, instead, to focus more attention on meaning and direction for the present and the future.

In the early years of psychoanalysis, therapists said very little, sometimes remaining silent throughout the session, or they would say, "Can you tell me more about that?" In his book *The Unknown Murderer*,[92] Theodor Reik cautioned that psychoanalysis had no contribution to make to evidence of guilt, as psychoanalysis is concerned with mental or inner reality rather than material or outer reality. More and more, however, therapists have turned from listening and exploring with the patient to making interpretations about the cause of symptoms, though without objective evidence in support of those interpretations. Psychotherapy moved from old ideals of neutrality to treatments based on empathy and even advocacy for patients.

Actions against revival of memory therapists could be measured by the harm suffered by the plaintiff, the moral blame attached to the defendant's conduct, and the policy of preventing future harm.[93]

Interference with Family Relations. Another doctrinal approach in law is the old action in tort for "interference with family relations." As a result of the estrangement of a family following revival of memory of childhood sexual abuse, reunification of families, even after a retraction, has not taken place for most families. In any event, the tort for interference with family relations is "rather ragged in form."[94] It developed initially as an offshoot of the action for enticing away a servant and depriving the master of the quasi-proprietary interest in his services. Also, under the early common law, the status of a wife as well as that of minor children was that of more or less valuable as servants of the husband and father, and that action was extended to include the deprivation of their services. The loss of such services was the gist of the action.

In comparatively recent years, there has been a gradual shift of emphasis away from services and toward a recognition of more intangible elements in domestic relations, such as companionship and affection. In a widely publicized case in the late 1970s in Boulder, Colorado, a mother whose 25-year-old son sued her for "parental malpractice" filed her own suit against the son's psychiatrist, Dr. Jeffrey Anker. The doctor had encouraged the son to sue her "for therapeutic reasons." (The demise of family immunity barring suits between family members began with the automobile accident cases, and in these cases the insurance company is the defendant as a practical matter.) The son was described as a "hippie" who was suspended from high school for selling marijuana, who chose to live with friends on a beach in Hawaii, and who refused to find work. In her suit, the mother said the parental malpractice action against her caused her "great grief, sorrow, and even anger" and she claimed that she had been subjected to widespread "ridicule and embarrassment." The case was apparently settled.[95]

Then, too, at one time the law recognized an action for alienation of affections. Thus, in a 1966 case in Washington, an action for alienation of affections was allowed when a pastor counseled a woman to leave her husband who was "full of the devil."[96] That has changed. The courts in various states have held that a husband has no cause of action against a therapist who had a sexual relationship with the wife who was a patient. In a California case, *Smith v. Pust*,[97] the patient's husband was held not to be a direct victim, and the husband was also held not to be a patient notwithstanding his attendance at some therapy sessions.

To Sum Up

The law on duty to third parties has its twists and turns. The law of torts is evolving on the responsibility of psychiatrists not only to their patients but also to third parties reasonably foreseeable as victims of harm caused by their patients. In many circumstances, the duty of the therapist runs not only to the patient but also to others.

Notes

1. 48 N.Y. 339, 162 N.E. 99 (1928). The opinion is reproduced in every torts course book. See G. T. Schwartz, "Cardozo as Tort Lawmaker," *DePaul L. Rev.* 49 (1999): 305; see also A. L Kaufman, *Cardozo* (Cambridge: Harvard University Press, 1998).

2. Under the influence of Jim Jones, members of the People's Temple in Jonestown murdered Congressman Leo J. Ryan and then committed suicide en masse. United States v. Layton, 549 F.2d 903 (N.D.Cal. 1982).

3. Jones v. State of New York, 267 App. Div. 254, 45 N.Y.S.2d 404 (1943). A hospital breaches its duty of care by failing to provide adequate security in view of a patient's known violent tendencies. See Fair v. United States, 234 F.2d 288 (5th Cir. 1956).

4. See, e.g., Merchants National Bank & Trust Co. of Fargo v. United States, 272 F.Supp. 409 (D. N.D. 1967); Homere v. State, 79 Misc.2d 972, 361 N.Y.S.2d 820 (1974).

5. Iancona v. Schrupp, 521 N.W.2d 70 (Minn. App. 1994).

6. Britton v. Soltes, 205 Ill. App.3d 943, 563 N.E.2d 910 (1990). In Ellis v. Peter, 211 A.D.2d 353 (1995), the New York Supreme Court declined to recognize a duty on the part of a health care professional to the spouse of a patient who had contracted tuberculosis (but who had been wrongly diagnosed) because "a physician's duty of care is ordinarily one owed to his or her patient and does not extend to the community at large; the wife may also be considered to be in that class of persons whom the defendant knew or reasonably should have known were relying on him for a duty of care to his patient, but defendant's duty of care will not be so extended, since there is no indication of the point where that duty would end."

7. 563 N.E.2d at 916.

8. DeMarco v. Lynch Homes, 525 Pa. 558, 583 A.2d 422 (1990). In Bradshaw v. Daniel, 854 S.W.2d 865 (Tenn. 1993), one of the first cases involving the risk of exposure to a patient's noncontagious disease, the court had to determine whether the physician had a duty to warn the patient's wife of her risk of exposure to Rocky Mountain Spotted Fever. The physician's patient contracted and subsequently died from the disease, but the physician never advised the patient's wife of the risks of exposure or the cause of her husband's death. The wife died from the disease. The plaintiff's expert testified that the disease was contracted through ticks and the ticks "clustered," so that people hiking together would be exposed to the disease vector, the ticks. The expert also testified that if untreated, the disease has a 40 percent mortality rate, but if treated quickly there is only a 4 percent mortality rate. The court held that the "existence of the physician-patient relationship [was] sufficient to impose upon the physician" a duty to warn identifiable third persons against risks from a patient's illness. The court stated that the case was "analogous to the *Tarasoff* line of cases adopting a duty to warn of danger and the contagious disease cases adopting comparable duty to warn." Here, as in *Tarasoff,* the court found that "there was a foreseeable risk of harm to an identifiable third party." 854 S.W.2d at 872. The *Bradshaw* case is discussed in C. M. Parker, "Camping Trips and Family Trees: Must Tennessee Physicians Warn Their Patients' Relatives of Genetic Risks?" *Tenn. L. Rev.* 65 (1998): 585. The *Tarasoff* case is herein discussed.

9. 27 Cal.3d 916, 616 P.2d 813, 167 Cal. Rptr. 831 (1980).

10. 2 Cal.4th 1064, 9 Cal. Rptr.2d 615, 831 P.2d 1197 (1992).

11. See Thing v. LaChusa, 48 Cal. Rptr.3d 644, 257 Cal. Rptr. 865, 771 P.2d 814 (1989).

12. The case was actually heard twice. *Tarasoff I,* 118 Cal. Rptr. 129, 529 P.2d 553 (1974), *vacated, Tarasoff II,* 17 Cal.3d 425, 121 Cal. Rptr. 14, 551 P.2d 334 (1976).

13. See J. C. Beck (ed.), *The Potentially Violent Patient and the* Tarasoff *Decision in Psychiatric Practice* (Washington, D.C.: American Psychiatric Press, 1985); A. R. Felthous, "The Clinician's Duty to Protect Third Parties," *Psychiatric Clin. North America,* (Philadelphia: Saunders, 1999), vol. 22, no. 1, pp. 49–60; D. Truscott, "The Psychotherapist's Duty to Protect: An Annotated Bibliography," *J. Psychiatry & Law* 21 (1993): 221.

14. Schulz v. Pennsylvania Railroad Co., 350 U.S. 523, 525 (1956).

15. Dr. Moore wrote: "At times he appears to be quite rational, at other times he appears to be quite psychotic. . . . [C]urrently, the appropriate diagnosis for him is paranoid schizophrenic reaction, acute and severe. He is at this point a danger to the welfare of other people and himself. That is, he has been threatening to kill an unnamed girl who he feels has betrayed him and has violated his honor. He has told a friend of his . . . that he intends to go to San Francisco to buy a gun and that he plans to kill the girl. He has been somewhat more cryptic with me, but he has alluded strongly to the compulsion to 'get even with,' and 'hurt' the girl."

16. See discussion in volume 1, chapter 4, on testimonial privilege.

17. Personal communication (Nov. 15, 1977).

18. See, e.g., Osterlind v. Hill, 263 Mass. 73, 160 N.E. 301 (1928). See M. A. Menlowe & A. M Smith, *The Duty to Rescue: The Jurisprudence of Aid* (United Kingdom: Dartmouth Publishing, 1993). See the discussion in chapter 9, on failure to treat.

19. Compare the American Law Institute, *Restatement (Second) Torts,* sec. 315, which provides: "There is no duty to control the conduct of a third person as to prevent him from causing physical harm to another unless (a) a special relationship exists between the actor and the third person which imposes a duty upon the actor to control the third person's conduct, or (b) a special relationship exists between the actor and the other which gives to the other the right to protection."

20. In a Maryland case, Shaw v. Glickman, 45 Md. App. 718, 145 A.2d 625 (1980), the plaintiff, a dentist, was in group therapy conducted by the defendant psychiatrist and his wife, a psychiatric nurse. In the group were Mr. and Mrs. Billian. Unknown to Mr. Billian, an amorous relationship developed between Mrs. Billian and the dentist. One of the group therapists, upon learning of the extramarital affair, disclosed it to Mr. Billian in an individual therapy session. Some days later, Mr. Billian broke into the dentist's home, and finding his wife in bed with him, shot him. The dentist filed an action for damages, naming as defendants both Mr. Billian and the psychiatric team that had been conducting the group therapy sessions. The complaint charged that the defendant therapists had failed to warn him of Mr. Billian's unstable and violent condition and the foreseeable and immediate danger that it presented to the plaintiff. The Maryland Court of Appeals held that, unlike in *Tarasoff,* there was no threat revealed to the group therapists by Mr. Billian to kill or injure the dentist, and there was no confiding of any animosity or hatred toward the dentist. Although Mr. Billian was known by the therapists to tote a gun, the court held that that fact does not give rise to the inference that Mr. Billian did so for the purpose of harming the dentist. Anyhow, we must say, the dentist ought to have known of the danger. As the court put it, Mr. Billian invoked "the old Solon law and [shot] his wife's lover."

21. Hutchinson v. Patel, 637 So.2d 415 (La. 1994). See A. L. Almason, "Personal Liability Implications of the Duty to Warn are Hard Pills to Swallow: From *Tarasoff* to *Hutchinson v. Patel* and Beyond," *J. Contemp. Health Law & Policy* 13 (1997): 471; P. D. Liuzza, "*Hutchinson v. Patel,* Louisiana Supreme Court's First Response to *Tarasoff* Duty to Warn: Broadens Recovery but Narrows Liability," *Loy. L. Rev.* 40 (1995): 1011.

22. M. L. Perlin, "*Tarasoff* at the Millennium: New Directions, New Defendants, New Dangers, New Dilemmas," *Psychiatric Times,* Nov. 1999, p. 20. See also S. A. Anfang & P. S. Appelbaum, "Twenty Years after *Tarasoff:* Reviewing the Duty to Protect," *Harv. Rev. Psychiatry* 4 (1996): 67; V. Merton, "Confidentiality and Lawyers," *Emory L.J.* 31 (1982): 263.

23. In a Vermont case, the court held the duty to protect included a situation where the patient set fire to the family barn, located 130 feet from their home. At the time the patient was a voluntary outpatient under the care of a counselor in a community mental health clinic. He told the counselor that he "wanted to get back at his father." Peck v. Counseling Service of Addison County, 146 Vt. 61, 499 A.2d 422 (1985). Query: What would the therapist have had to do if the patient had threatened to damage his father's car or kill his father's dog? In *Peck,* the therapist allegedly honestly believed that the patient would not burn his father's barn, but the law of negligence does not have a good faith exception; such an exception would likely spawn falsification of what the therapist in fact believed. The decision was based on a finding that the therapist should have had better procedures which might have enabled him to make a better assessment of the risk.

24. See Jablonski v. United States, 712 F.2d 391 (9th Cir. 1983); Brady v. Hopper, 570 F.Supp. 1333 (D.C. Colo. 1983); Hamman v. County of Maricopa, 161 Ariz. 58, 775 P.2d 1122 (1989); Eckhardt v. Kirts, 179 Ill. App.3d 863, 534 N.E.2d 1339 (1989). The various statutes enacted as of 1989 and a model statute proposed by the American Psychiatric Association are discussed in P. S. Appelbaum, H. Zonana, R. Bonnie, & L. H. Rot, "Statutory Approaches to Limiting Psychiatrists' Liability for Their Patients' Violent Acts," *Am. J. Psychiatry* 146 (1989): 821. A recent issue of *Behavioral Sciences & the Law,* 19 (2001): 321–449, is on the clinician's duty to warn or protect.

The immediacy of the risk has been a consideration in establishing a duty to warn or protect. In a Louisiana case, Viviano v. Stewart, 645 So.2d 1301 (La App. 1994), the patient, Billy Viviano, sued his psychiatrist, Dr. Dudley Stewart, for breach of confidentiality in notifying Federal Judge Veronica Wicker that Viviano threatened to kill her. The plaintiff argued that the danger, if any, was not "imminent" and therefore the breach of confidentiality was not justified. The jury decided in favor of the defendant following four weeks of trial. The decision was finally upheld by the Louisiana Supreme Court, after nine years of legal wrangling. Following the *Viviano* litigation, in December 1994, the word *imminent* was removed from the APA ethics guidelines, thereby allowing a disclosure in less than imminent circumstances. The qualification "imminent" was originally included in order to narrow the situation calling for a breach of confidentiality but, as illustrated by the *Viviano* case, it put a difficult burden on the therapist to establish an imminent danger. See R. Slovenko, *Psychotherapy and Confidentiality* (Springfield, Ill.: Thomas, 1998), pp. 270–341.

25. Almonte v. New York Medical College, 851 F.Supp. 34 (D.Conn. 1994); discussed in F. Bruni, "Jury Finds Psychiatrist Negligent in Case of Pedophile Patient," *New York Times*, Oct. 9, 1998, p. 27; L. McCullough, "A Training Analyst's Dilemma: The Limits of Confidentiality," *Psychiatric News*, Sept. 4, 1998, p. 2. The court compared Doe v. British Universities North American Club, 786 F.Supp. 1286 (D.Conn. 1992), finding no duty to warn about a counselor's sexual orientation because sexual molestation is not a foreseeable risk of homosexuality. 851 F.Supp. at 41.

26. R. Slovenko, "The Tarasoff Progeny," in R. I. Simon (ed.), *Review of Clinical Psychiatry and the Law* (Washington, D.C.: American Psychiatric Press, 1990), vol. 1, ch. 8, p. 177. See also P. S. Appelbaum, H. Zonana, R. Bonnie, & L. H. Roth, "Statutory Approaches to Limiting Psychiatrists' Liability for Their Patients' Violent Acts," *Am. J. Psychiatry* 46 (1989): 821.

27. Estates of Morgan v. Fairfield Family Counseling Center, 77 Ohio St.3d 284, 673 N.E.2d 1311, 1331 (1997).

28. Bishop v. So. Car. Dept. of Mental Health, 331 S. C. 79, 502 S.E.3d 78 (1998). See also Valentine v. On Target, 353 Md. 544, 727 A.2d 947 (Md. 1999).

29. Green v. Ross, 691 So.2d 542 (Fla. App. 1997); Boynton v. Burglass, 590 So.2d 446 (Fla. App. 1999); Thapar v. Zezulka, 42 Tex. 824, 994 S.W.2d 635 (1999); Nasser v. Parker, 455 S.E.2d 502 (Va. 1995). A federal district court in Mississippi stated, "While Tarasoff may be the law in California, plaintiff has cited no authority showing that this decision represents the law in Mississippi." Evans v. United States, 833 F.Supp. 124 (S.D. 1995). The Hawaii Supreme Court limited *Tarasoff* to cases involving potential victims of violent assault, thereby declining to extend it to risks of self-inflicted harm or property damage. Lee v. Corregedore, 925 P.2d 324 (Haw. 1996). See A. R. Felthous & C. Kachigian, "The Fin de Millenaire Duty to Warn or Protect," *J. for. Sci.* 46 (2001): 1103. Compare Pate v. Threlkel, 661 So.2d 278 (Fla. 1995), noted hereinafter in regard to genetic disease.

30. Green v. Ross, 691 So.2d 542 (Fla. App. 1997).

31. The Texas Supreme Court declined to adopt a duty to warn, reasoning that the confidentiality statute governing mental health professionals in Texas makes it unwise to recognize such a duty. The court found that the Texas Legislature had chosen to guard a patient's communication with a mental health professional. In 1979, three years after *Tarasoff* was decided in California, the Texas legislature enacted a statute that classifies communications between mental health professionals and their patients as confidential and prohibits mental health professionals from disclosing them to third parties unless an exception applies. No exception in the statute provides for disclosure to third parties threatened by the patient. Thapar v. Zezulka, 42 Tex. 824, 994 S.W.2d 635 (1999).

Without immunity, mental health professionals are faced with a dilemma. If they do report, they may face a wrongful death suit in the event of a killing of a third person, as in *Tarasoff*, and, on the other hand, if they do not report, they may face a suit for breach of confidentiality. In a case in Georgia featured in the *New York Times*, a psychologist warned the police captain that a patient, a police officer, threatened to harm him. The officer was adversely affected by the report and he sued the psychologist. The jury awarded him $280,000, which was settled with the insurance company for $230,000. D. T. Max, "The Cop and the Therapist," *New York Times Magazine*, Dec. 3, 2000, p. 94.

32. R. L. Binder & D. E. McNiel, "Application of the Tarasoff Ruling and Its Effect on the Victim and the Therapist Relationship," *Psychiatric Services* 47 (1996): 1212. See also L. Wulsin, H. Bursztajn, & T. G. Gutheil, "Unexpected Clinical Benefits of the *Tarasoff* Decision: The Therapeutic Alliance and the 'Duty to Warn,'" *Am. J. Psychiatry* 140 (1983): 601. Dr. Paul R. McHugh of the Johns Hopkins Department of Psychiatry and Behavioral Sciences observed,

"I have had no problem with the *Tarasoff* ruling. The whole idea after all is to bring realism into psychiatry and psychotherapy." Personal communication (Jan. 15, 2002).

33. R. Balon & R. Mufti, "*Tarasoff* Ruling and Reporting to the Authorities" (ltr.) *Am. J. Psychiatry* 154 (1997): 1321.

34. One of the first cases on whether health care providers are required to warn third parties of potential risks of HIV/AIDS infection was Reisner v. Regents of University of California, 31 Cal. App.4th 1195, 37 Cal. Reptr.2d 518 (1995). In this case the patient, a twelve-year-old girl, had received a transfusion contaminated with HIV antibodies during surgery. Her physician, the defendant, continued to treat her but did not inform her or her family about the contaminated blood, the danger of contracting AIDS, or precautionary measures to prevent the spread of the disease. Years later the patient began dating Daniel, and they became intimate not knowing the risks. Shortly thereafter, the patient died and Daniel discovered he was HIV-positive. He sued, claiming negligence, arguing that the physician owed him a duty of care. The physician contended that the *Tarasoff* duty did not apply in this situation because the third party was both unknown and unidentifiable. The court disagreed and stated that the physician had a duty to warn his patient, her parents, or "others [who were] likely to apprise [plaintiff] of danger." The court concluded that "a timely warning to the [patient] would have prevented Daniel's injury" and that the injury to Daniel was foreseeable. Accordingly, the court held that the physician did owe a duty to Daniel and "[o]nce the physician warns the patient of the risk to others and advises the patient how to prevent the spread of the disease, the physician has fulfilled his duty—and no more (but no less) is required." The court noted the possibility that the duty could extend beyond Daniel. The court left open the possibility that someone who contracted HIV from Daniel could state a claim against the defendant. However, the court stated that "the doctor's liability to fourth and fifth persons would by its nature be limited by traditional causation principles." 31 Cal. App.4th at 1204.

In Lemon v. Stewart, 111 Md. App. 511, 682 A.2d 1177 (1996), the Maryland Court of Appeals was faced with a similar issue. Specifically, the court had to determine (1) when a patient is diagnosed with HIV or AIDS, does the patient's physician have a duty to inform the patient's family members? and (2) do the family members of the patient have a cause of action against the physician for breaching the duty? In this case the patient tested positive for HIV, but he was discharged from the hospital without being told of his HIV status. A year later the patient was readmitted to the hospital and was informed that he was HIV-positive. The plaintiffs suing the physician and hospital were relatives of or otherwise had personal contact with the patient. They claimed that if the physician had informed the patient, the health authorities, or them when the patient first tested positive for HIV, they would have taken more precautionary measures to protect themselves. The court held that the "defendants had no duty to inform the [plaintiffs] of the [patient's] HIV status and that [they] have no cause of action against the defendants based on their failure to inform [the patient], each other or the Health Department." The court reasoned that since none of the plaintiffs had been sexual or needle-sharing partners with the patient, they were not foreseeable potential victims of any breach of duty to the patient. The court stated that "[t]o recognize a common law duty on the part of the health care providers to inform persons such as [plaintiffs] would not only be thoroughly impractical but would constitute a wholly unwarranted invasion of the patient's privacy." The plaintiffs, therefore, had failed two parts of the *Tarasoff* test— foreseeable harm and reasonably identifiable victims. 111 Md. App. at 524.

Michigan's partner-notification statute calls upon the health care provider to contact the appropriate local health department for assistance with partner notification. Specifically, the statute states that the physician "shall" refer the individual to the local health department if both of the following conditions are met: "(a) The test results indicate that the individual is HIV infected; and (b) [The physician who] administered the test determines that the individual needs assistance with partner notification." M.C.L., sec. 333.5114(a). The statute leaves some discretion to the health care provider. The provider may deem that the individual does not need assistance with partner notification and therefore, the health department need not be notified. For example, there would be no need to notify the health department if a married man in a monogamous relationship contracted HIV from a blood transfusion. The provider could deem that there is no need for partner notification as long as the married man planned to tell his wife. The problem arises when an individual has contracted HIV and shared needles or had many sexual partners, but agrees to try to notify all the potentially affected individuals. It becomes a judgment call on the part of the physician as to whether that individual needs assistance with partner notification. See S. P. Clifton, W. S. Wheeler, & S. H. Patton, "HIV-Related Laws in Michigan Public Health Code: A Primer for the General Practitioner," *Mich. B.J.* 73 (1994): 156.

Reports are not uncommon of individuals with HIV deliberately infecting others. It is their way of expressing their rage or acting out their psychopathic tendencies. The lack of health care and the high cost of medication fuel the anger. In China, on the streets of Tianjin, one of the country's biggest cities, hundreds of infected individuals threatened to attack passers-by with blood-filled syringes. Many were arrested. R. McGregor, "Chinese AIDS Sufferers Attack Passers-by," *Financial Times*, Jan. 19–20, 2002, p. 2.

How does partner notification affect mental health care providers? A duty may arise if the provider is treating an HIV-infected patient who refuses to reveal his HIV status to sexual partners and continues to engage in unprotected sex with these partners. In this situation there would be a third party who would be exposed to a potentially dangerous situation, and depending on the state law, the mental health professional may have a duty to warn sexual partners. In a study conducted with regard to HIV-infected patients who refuse to reveal their HIV status to an uninformed sexual partner, it was found that there was not a high likelihood that the mental health professional would breach confidentiality. Although the mental health professionals realized the dangerousness of the situation, only about one-third were likely to notify the uninformed sex partner. The study noted that many mental health care professionals felt that their responsibility differed from that of physicians (which is wrong in most cases) and that many of the respondents did not know the current law on the duty to protect in their state. S. J. Simone & S. M. Fulero, "Psychologists' Perceptions of Their Duty to Protect Uninformed Sex Partners of HIV-Positive Clients," *Behav. Sci. & Law* 19 (2001): 423. In these cases, it may prove difficult for the plaintiff—the third party—to prove causation, i.e., the plaintiff has to prove that the warning would have actually prevented the transmission; in other words, the transmission occurred after the warning should have taken place. See generally B. Bernstein, "Solving the Physician's Dilemma: An HIV Partner-Notification Plan," *Stan. L. & Pol'y Rev.* 6, no. 2 (1995): 127; F. Buckner & M. Firestone, "'Where the Public Peril Begins': 25 Years after *Tarasoff*," *J. Legal Med.* 21 (2000): 187; L. O. Gostin & J. G. Hodge, "Piercing the Veil of Secrecy in HIV/AIDS and Other Sexually Transmitted Diseases: Theories of Privacy and Disclosure in Partner Notification," *Duke J. Gender Law & Policy* 5 (1998): 9; L. S. Gruman, "AIDS and the Physician's Duty to Warn," *Med. & Law* 10 (1991): 415, 455.

35. 252 Cal. Rptr. 11 (Cal. App. 1988).

36. 252 Cal. Rptr. at 13. In Pate v. Threlkel, 661 So.2d 278 (Fla. 1995), the Florida Supreme Court was asked to decide whether a physician has a legal duty to warn a patient's children of the genetically transferable nature of the condition for which the physician is treating the patient. Though Florida had rejected *Tarasoff*, the Florida Supreme Court in *Pate* held that the physician's alleged duty to warn extended to the children of the patient even though the children were not in the role of patient. The duty, the court said, would be satisfied by warning the patient. There were two reasons for this: (1) confidentiality prohibited the physician from revealing confidential communications in most instances absent the patient's consent, and (2) to require the physician to seek out and warn various members of the patient's family would often be difficult or impractical and would place too heavy a burden upon the physician. 661 So.2d at 282. For a discussion of the issue, see E. W. Clayton, "What Should the Law Say about Disclosure of Genetic Information to Relatives?" *J. Health Care Law & Policy* 1 (1998): 373; L. J. Deftos, "Genomic Torts: The Law of the Future—the Duty of Physicians to Disclose the Presence of a Genetic Disease to the Relatives of Their Patients with the Disease," *U. San Francisco L. Rev.* 32 (1997): 105; M. R. King, "Physician Duty to Warn a Patient's Offspring of Hereditary Genetic Defects: Balancing the Patient's Right to Confidentiality against the Family Member's Right to Know—Can or Should *Tarasoff* Apply," *Quinnipiac Health L.* 4 (2000): 1; C. M. Parker, "Camping Trips and Family Trees: Must Tennessee Physicians Warn Their Patients' Relatives of Genetic Risks?" *Tenn. L. Rev.* 65 (1998): 585; N. A. Stepanuk, "Genetic Information and Third Party Access to Information: New Jersey's Pioneering Legislation as a Model for Federal Privacy Protection of Genetic Information," *Catholic U. L. Rev.* 47 (1998): 1105.

37. Schroeder v. Perkel, 87 N.J. Super. 53, 432 A.2d 834 (1981). See generally A. Brownrigg, "Mother Still Knows Best: Cancer-Related Gene Mutations, Familial Privacy, and a Physician's Duty to Warn," *Fordham Urb. L. J.* 26 (1999): 247; F. Buckner & M. Firestone, "'Where the

Public Peril Begins': 25 Years after *Tarasoff*," *J. Legal Med.* 21 (2000): 187; J. W. Burnett, "A Physician's Duty to Warn a Patient's Relatives of a Patient's Genetically Inheritable Disease," *Houston L. Rev.* 36 (1999): 559; J. Petrila, "Genetic Risk: The New Frontier for the Duty to Warn," *Behav. Sci. & Law* 19 (2001): 405; S. M. Suter, "Whose Genes Are These Anyway?: Familial Conflicts Over Access to Genetic Information," *Mich. L. Rev.* 91 (1993): 1854.

38. Safer v. Estate of Pack, 291 N.J. Super. 619, 677 A.2d 1188 (1996).

39. D. W. Tsuang, S. V. Faraone, & M. T. Tsuang, "Clinical Uses and Ethical Implications of Psychiatric Genetic Counseling," *Psychiatric Times*, Oct. 2001, p. 32. See also G. T. Laurie, "Protecting and Promoting Privacy in an Uncertain World: Further Defences of Ignorance and the Right Not to Know," *European J. Health Law* 7 (2000): 185.

40. See N. M. Bradburn, L. J. Rips, & S. K. Shevell, "Answering Autobiographical Questions: The Impact of Memory and Inference on Surveys," *Science* 236 (Apr. 10, 1987): 157; J. F. Kihlstrom, "The Cognitive Unconscious," *Science* 237 (Sept. 18, 1987): 1445; L. M. Williams, "Recall of Childhood Trauma: A Prospective Study of Women's Memories of Child Sexual Abuse," *J. Consulting & Clin. Psychology* 62 (1994): 1167; response, E. F. Loftus, M. Garry, & J. Feldman, "Forgetting Sexual Trauma: What Does It Mean When 38% Forget?" *J. Consulting & Clin. Psychology* 62 (1994): 1177.

41. See J. R. Noblitt & P. S. Perskin, *Cult and Ritual Abuse* (Westport, Conn.: Praeger, 2000); K. S. Pope & L. S. Brown, *Recovered Memories of Abuse* (Washington, D.C.: American Psychological Association, 1996).

42. For a critical view of recovered memory therapy, see H. I. Lief & J. M. Fetkewicz, "Casualties of Recovered Memory Therapy: The Impact of False Allegations of Incest on Accused Fathers," in R. C. Friedman & J. I. Downey (eds.), *Review of Psychiatry* (Washington, D.C.: American Psychiatric Association, vol. 18, no. 5, ch. 5, pp. 115–41.

43. Joyce-Couch v. DeSilva, 77 Ohio App.3d 278, 602 N.E.2d 286 (1991); see H. I. Lief & J. Fetkewicz, "Retractors of False Memories: The Evolution of Pseudomemories," *J. Psychiatry & Law* 23 (1995): 411.

44. E. Bass & L. Davis, *Courage to Heal: A Guide for Women Survivors of Child Sexual Abuse* (New York: Harper & Row, 1988), p. 81. This sentence became so notorious that in the third edition (HarperPerennial, 1994) the sentence was modified to read, "If you genuinely think you were abused and your life shows the symptoms, there's a strong likelihood that you were" (p. 23).

45. Third ed., p. 332.

46. Variations of the theme is commonplace in psychotherapy. Psychoanalyst Michael Miletic, for example, reports a hockey player able to play again when in the course of therapy, a repressed memory is unblocked. Through a lot of work, he said, what was reconstructed was that the act of standing at the blue line with a puck and with a forward potentially charging at him brought back traumatic memories of when he was beaten as a youngster by his father. R. Lipsyte, "Outside the Norm: The Psychology of Athletes, " *New York Times*, Feb. 6, 2000, p. S-1. That notion is exemplified in Alfred Hitchcock's 1945 film *Spellbound*, starring Gregory Peck and Ingrid Bergman. Freud at one time believed this, but it is an oversimplification and ignores the role of narrative and suggestion in psychotherapy. Did the psychoanalyst get any objective evidence that the father beat the player? The question is rhetorical.

47. C. Tavris, *Anger: The Misunderstood Emotion* (New York: Simon & Schuster, rev. ed. 1989), p. 129.

48. R. Hughes, *Culture of Complaint* (New York: Oxford University Press, 1993), p. 7.

49. R. Slovenko, "The 'Revival of Memory' of Childhood Sexual Abuse: Is the Tolling of Statute of Limitations Justified?" *J. Psychiatry & Law* 21 (1993): 7; H. Wakefield & R. Underwager, "Recovered Memories of Alleged Sexual Abuse: Lawsuits against Parents," *Behavioral Science & Law* 10 (1992): 483. Leading forensic psychiatrists have written: "On clinical grounds and in the patient's interests, such issues are best resolved in the therapeutic context: working through the past experience, dealing with the troubling symptoms, and going on with one's life. Litigation, however, precludes such an approach by shifting the venue to an adversarial setting that may well prevent, for example, such constructive approaches as working with the family in therapy together." T. G. Gutheil, H. Bursztajn, A. Brodsky, & L. H. Strasburger, "Preventing 'Critigenic' Harms: Minimizing Emotional Injury from Civil Litigation," *J. Psychiatry & Law* 28 (2000): 5. See D. F. Brown, A. W. Scheflin, & D. C. Hammond, *Memory, Trauma Treatment, and the Law* (New York: W. W. Norton, 1998); R. Moore, *The Creation of Reality*

in Psychoanalysis (Mahwah, N.J.: Analytic Press, 1999); R. Ofshe & E. Watters, *Making Monsters: False Memories, Psychotherapy, and Sexual Hysteria* (New York: Scribner's, 1994); R. I. Simon & D. W. Shuman (eds.), *Predicting the Past: The Retrospective Assessment of Mental States in Civil and Criminal Litigation* (Washington, D.C.: American Psychiatric Press, 2000).

50. See A. Piper, H. G. Pope, & J. J. Borowiecki, "Custer's Last Stand: Brown, Scheflin, and Whitfield's Latest Attempt to Salvage 'Dissociative Amnesia,'" *J. Psychiatry & Law* 28 (2000): 149.

51. D. Boesky, "Correspondence Criteria and Clinical Evidence in Psychoanalysis," address on Jan. 13, 2000, at a meeting of the Michigan Psychoanalytic Society in Southfield, Mich. To what extent, if any, must there be historical truth as the basis for an interpretation? Clinicians say that they are concerned with clinical utility. They lift resistance to memories that are used in treatment if they have efficacy, regardless of their historical accuracy; but at least historical accuracy is essential in a courtroom. It is also important when third parties will be affected, as they are in the case of allegations of sexual abuse. See R. Slovenko, *Psychotherapy and Confidentiality* (Springfield, Ill.: Thomas, 1998), pp. 523–44; D. P. Spence, *Narrative Truth and Historical Truth: Meaning and Interpretation in Psychoanalysis* (New York: Norton, 1982). In a series of cartoon case histories by Sarah Boxer, a reporter for the *New York Times,* the psychoanalyst is "more Freudian than Freud, willing to build an interpretation on the slimmest evidence." S. Boxer, *In the Floyd Archives: A Psycho-Bestiary* (New York: Pantheon, 2001), p. vii.

52. P. R. McHugh, "To Treat," *FMS Foundation Newsletter,* Oct. 1, 1993, p. 1. Of the distinction between *narrative* and *historical* truth in psychotherapy, McHugh and colleague Dr. Phillip R. Slavney write:

> Although not necessarily grasping all the truth on each iteration, when practiced correctly the life-story approach is not the writing of fiction. . . . [I]n the realm of psychiatry what is depicted in the life story and employed in psychotherapy must be what corresponds to some biographical material that can be referenced, displayed, and critically reassessed by any interested party. It is crucial to make this point because the process of therapy is an attempt to persuade a vulnerable person to see his or her life in a particular fashion—one in which he or she has overlooked opportunities to take charge—and truth is important.
>
> Most patients begin psychotherapy ready to accept what the therapist will offer. Why else have they come? If a story with little or no foundation is composed and urged on the patient in psychotherapy (and if all attempts by the patient to reject the story are considered "resistance"), then it is possible to build up any story and any set of new assumptions. Forcing an interpretation on a patient is not an acceptable technique and has great danger. Here fiction of the most destructive kind can be written and imposed as fact on patients.
>
> The recent outbreak among a sizable group of patients in psychotherapy of false memories—"memories" of infantile sexual abuse and wild ideas of satanic cults and alien abduction—depended on the recurring error that stories could be composed backward simply from the symptoms and then forced on the patient. Patients with severe depression were told that their depression represented the effects of sexual trauma suffered when they were infants and young children, repeated and continuing abuses they had forgotten or "repressed" because they were so devastating. These stories were composed with little effort to consider either alternative diagnoses for the patients' depressions or stories that might better explain their presenting complaints. Even less effort was expended to confirm the presumed, past and forgotten, provocative traumas. "Narrative truth" seemed to rule without any effort at establishing "historical truth."

P. R. McHugh & P. R. Slavney, *Perspectives of Psychiatry* (Baltimore: Johns Hopkins University Press, 2d ed. 1998), pp. 278–79.

Historical truth, however, may be unbearable, so people resort to denials or lies, or they block memory. That may be therapeutic, such as in the case of Dr. Herbert Spiegel, who hypnotized a soldier who was overwhelmed with guilt for not saving a comrade. By hypnosis he became convinced that his comrade was dead and that it would have been futile to try to save him. Reported by Professor Alan Scheflin in an address "Psychotherapy under Siege," at the annual meeting of the Association of American Law Schools on Jan. 5, 2002, in New Orleans. Joseph Goebbels at a mass meeting in Berlin on December 5, 1942 said, "Historical truth may be discovered by professors of history later; we are serving historical necessity." E. K. Bramsted, *Goebbels and National Socialist Propaganda 1925–1945* (Lansing: Michigan State University Press, 1965), p. vi. The belief in Santa Claus brings joy to children, needless to say. The implanting of false *good* memories is suggested as a valuable therapeutic technique in L. Sher, "Memory Creation and the Treatment of Psychiatric Disorders," *Medical Hypotheses* 54 (2000): 628.

53. P. McHugh, "Procedures in the Diagnosis of Incest in Recovered Memory Cases," *FMS Foundation Newsletter,* May 3, 1993, p. 3.

54. The False Memory Syndrome Foundation was formed in 1992, and within a year it had a membership of over 4,600. Over 12,000 families have contacted it. The foundation disseminates information about the nature of memory and about how to deal with revival of memory therapists. See T. W. Campbell, *Smoke and Mirrors: The Devastating Effect of False Sexual Abuse Claims* (New York: Plenum, 1998); S. Taub (ed.), *Recovered Memories of Child Sexual Abuse* (Springfield, Ill.: Thomas, 1999); H. I. Lief & J. M. Fetkewicz, "Casualties of Recovered Memory Therapy: The Impact of False Allegations of Incest on Accused Fathers," in R. C. Friedman & J. I. Downey (eds.), *Review of Psychiatry* (Washington, D.C.: American Psychiatric Press), vol. 18, no. 5, ch. 5, pp. 115–41; J. M. Whitesell, "Ridicule or Recourse: Parents Falsely Accused of Past Sexual Abuse Fight Back," *J. Law & Health* 11 (1996–97): 303.

55. Nov. 29, 1993.

56. L. Jaroff & J. McDowell, "Lies of the Mind," *Time,* Nov. 29, 1993, p. 52.

57. May 24, 1993.

58. The two-part article appears in expanded form in L. Wright, *Remembering Satan* (New York: Knopf, 1994); reviewed in M. Kakutani, "A Family is Destroyed by a Sexual Chimera," *New York Times,* Apr. 29, 1994, p. B-7.

59. "APA Stakes Out Positions on Controversial Therapies," *Psychiatric News,* Apr. 21, 2000, p. 45; cited in chapter 4, on psychiatric malpractice.

60. Quoted in S. Salter, "Recalling Abuse in the Mind's Eye," *San Francisco Chronicle,* Apr. 4, 1993, p. 9. See P. R. McHugh, "The Contemporary Witch-Craze: Remembered Sexual Abuse," *Hopkins Medical News,* Spring 1994, p. 56. For a defense of recovered memory, see D. F. Brown, A. Scheflin, & D. C. Hammond, *Memory, Trauma Treatment, and the Law* (New York: W. W. Norton, 1998). A special issue of the *Journal of Psychiatry & Law,* 27 (1999): 367–705, edited by Daniel F. Brown and Alan W. Scheflin, focuses on the interrelationship between factitious behavior, dissociative disorders, and the law. See also D. Brown, A. W. Scheflin, & C. L. Whitfield, "Recovered Memories: The Current Weight of the Evidence in Science and in the Courts," *J. Psychiatry & Law* 27 (1999): 5. For a response, see A. Piper, H. G. Pope, & J. J. Borowiecki, "Custer's Last Stand: Brown, Scheflin, and Whitfield's Latest Attempt to Salvage 'Dissociative Amnesia,'" *J. Psychiatry & Law* 28 (2000): 149.

61. R. Ofshe & E. Watters, *Making Monsters: False Memories, Psychotherapy, and Sexual Hysteria* (New York: Scribner, 1994). See also E. Watters & R. Ofshe, *Therapy's Delusions* (New York: Scribner, 1999).

62. Schultz v. State, 957 S.W.2d 52 at 77 (Tex. Cr. App. 1997) (concurring opinion). See M. Kowalski, "Applying the 'Two Schools of Thought' Doctrine to the Repressed Memory Controversy," *J. Legal Med.* 19 (1998): 503.

63. In response, some insurers now exclude coverage for revival of memory therapy, which raises the question of its definition—the exclusion in the policy is not defined. To be sure, all therapy involves memory, but *revival of memory* is distinguished from *continuous memory.* Some define *revival of memory therapy* as the "persistent encouragement to recall past events." Others define it as an extreme focus on recovering memories of abuse, "pressure to remember," "stockpile memory," or the "pursuit of memory work in a persistently suggestive manner." Retractors of recovered memory report that the search for memories became the cornerstone of therapy, while the therapist played an increasingly dominant role in the life of the patient. See F. H. Frankel, "Adult Reconstruction of Childhood Events in the Multiple Personality Literature," *Am. J. Psychiatry* 150 (1993): 954.

64. Ramona v. Isabella, Rose & Western Medical Center, No. Civ. 61898 (Supp. Ct. Napa County, 1994); discussed in M. Johnston, *Spectral Evidence* (New York: Houghton Mifflin, 1997). See also J. Acocella, *Creating Hysteria* (San Francisco: Jossey-Bass, 1999).

65. California Civil Code, sec. 47.

66. In a decision handed down in 1994, the trial judge said:

This lawsuit is a compelling one, and it's a compelling one because it not only has the novelty of new and current legal issues, but also because it has a salient emotionalism to it. . . . [T]he most interesting and compelling and difficult [issue] in this case . . . is the question of whether a father may maintain a lawsuit against the therapists or other health care providers of his daughter alleging that he was damaged by their negligent treatment of her. . . . I have found that a duty did exist to him by reason of the circumstances of the case under [California] Supreme Court law. . . . What's going on in a lawsuit of this sort is the conflict of policies. On the one hand, the defendants argue if you allow non-patients to sue health care providers, it will have a terrible, chilling effect upon the ability of any health care provider to do what his or patient needs to provide the kinds of care that his or her patient needs to receive. How, they ask, is a health care provider to know what to do when presented with a patient who recalls or thinks he or she is recalling the sorts of things that are presented by this lawsuit. That's a big concern. That's an argument that has significant social implications attendant to it.

Of equal significance, however, and with equal social implications, is the question of what is somebody, who for the sake of this point we will presume to be factually innocent of having engaged in misconduct with respect to his daughter, to do if confronted with the unfounded and incorrect accusation of having molested her which results in his loss of everything?

It's as unpalatable to some to have health care providers put in the impossible situation of dealing with a patient presenting real problems but knowing that the health care providers might be subjected to liability as it is to others to have a falsely accused parent to lose everything and have no recourse in court.

Those are the kinds of policy issues that the courts are called upon to resolve, because in the area of tort law, and this a tort action, there's very little statutory law. There's very little law created by the legislature that creates norms. . . . And the purposes of tort law are twofold: to provide redress for people who are injured in some way or another; and to mediate, to control, to direct the conduct of other people. . . .

[I]n this case the rules are, from my point of view, fairly clear. They were made clear by the [California] Supreme Court in *Molien v. Kaiser Foundation Hospital,* in which [it was held that the husband] had a cause of action and could sue Kaiser Hospital for the emotional distress he suffered as a result of the negligent treatment of his wife, or the negligent diagnosis—misdiagnosis of syphilis.

The defense lawyers have argued vigorously, and with good reason, that in the ten or twelve years since the *Molien* case was decided, the Supreme Court has been narrowing its application. There's no question but that it has. That case, at the time it was presented to the Supreme Court, had the same kind of conflicts attending to it, the same kind of important policy issues that are present in this case.

The defense lawyers have argued that I should view the *Molien* case as being history; that the Supreme Court has whittled away at it so far that it no longer exists. . . . I think that the *Molien* case is still the law, because the Supreme Court has had numerous opportunities and has been asked on numerous occasions to simply say it is no longer the law. . . . [E]ven as recently as late last year the Supreme Court was asked to do that, and they stressed that the reason Mr. Molien had a cause of action was because of the instruction to his wife to go home and tell him about the diagnosis of her.

Well, think how similar that is to the allegation that the plaintiff is seeking to prove in this case, which is that not only did somebody tell the patient, go home and tell your father, but in fact, the father was summoned to the meeting and the confrontation and presentation of the charge occurred.

67. *Ramona* alerted lawyers to the possibility that psychotherapy negligence suits were winnable. Lawsuits resulting in multimillion-dollar awards followed, and publicity escalated and led to ever more lawsuits. See E. F. Loftus, ''Therapeutic Recollection of Childhood Abuse:

857

When May a Memory Not be a Memory?" *Champion*, Mar. 1994, p. 5; Editorial, "No Standards," *Wall Street Journal*, May 10, 1994, p. 18.

68. T. G. Gutheil, "True Recollections of a False Memory Case," *Psychiatric Times*, July 1994, p. 28. In a *Murphy Brown* television program, the husband is told by his therapist that his wife is the cause of all of his problems and he is urged not to be passive but to act aggressively. He takes out his anger on his wife. The wife complains to the therapist, "Where do you get off telling my husband that I'm the cause of all his problems?"

69. P. Appelbaum & R. Zolteck-Jick, "Psychotherapists' Duties to Third Parties: Ramona and Beyond," *Am. J. Psychiatry* 153 (1996): 457.

70. C. G. Bowman & E. Mertz, "A Dangerous Direction: Legal Intervention in Sexual Abuse Survivor Therapy," *Harv. L. Rev.* 109 (1996): 549.

71. Strom v. C. C., 1997 Minn. App. Lexis 327.

72. Doe v. McKay, 183 Ill.2d 272, 700 N.E.2d 1018 (1998).

73. 700 N.E.2d at 1023.

74. 700 N.E.2d at 1026. For yes, third-party nonpatients should be able to sue therapists, see J. J. Finer, "Therapists' Liability to the Falsely Accused for Inducing Illusory Memories of Childhood Sexual Abuse: Current Remedies and a Proposed Statute," *J. L. & Health* 11 (1996–97): 45; S. F. Rock, "A Claim for Third Party Standing in Malpractice Cases Involving Repressed Memory Syndromes," *Wm. & Mary L. Rev.* 37 (1995): 337; R. Slovenko, "The Duty of Therapists to Third Parties," *J. Psychiatry & Law* 23 (1995): 383.

75. J. A. H. v. Wadle & Associates, 589 N.W.2d 256 (Iowa 1999).

76. 69 Cal. App.4th 1341, 82 Cal Rptr.2d 281 (1999).

77. 27 Cal. Rptr.2d 894, 22 Cal. App.4th 1398 (1994).

78. 30 Cal. Rptr.2d 504 (Ct. App. 1994) (unpublished opinion).

79. Althaus v. Cohen & University of Pittsburgh Western Psychiatric Institute & Clinic, Nos. 70 & 71 W.D. Appeal Docket 1998, J-32-1999. Compare DeMarco v. Lynch Homes, cited supra note 8.

80. The cases are noted in A. Lipton, "Recovered Memories in the Courts," in S. Taub (ed.), *Recovered Memories of Child Sexual Abuse* (Springfield, Ill.: Thomas, 1999).

81. 143 N.H. 208, 722 A.2d 478 (1998).

82. 722 A.2d at 482.

83. 227 Wis.2d 124, 595 N.W.2d 423 (1999).

84. See Schuster v. Altenberg, 114 Wis.2d 233, 424 N.W.2d 159 (1988).

85. See Truman v. Genesis Associates, 935 F.Supp. 1375 (E.D.Pa. 1996).

86. See volume 1, chapter 4, on testimonial privilege.

87. See, e.g., K. S. Pope & L. S. Brown, *Recovered Memories of Abuse* (Washington, D.C.: American Psychological Association, 1996), p. 203.

88. Quoted in *FMS Foundation Newsletter*, May 3, 1994, p. 7.

89. N. G. Hale, *The Rise and Crisis of Psychoanalysis in the United States: Freud and the Americans* (New York: Oxford University Press, 1995).

90. Supra note 76.

91. H. Spiegel, "Silver Lining in the Clouds of War: A Five-Decade Retrospective," in R. W. Menninger & J. C. Nemiah (eds.), *American Psychiatry after World War II* (Washington, D.C.: American Psychiatric Press, 2000). See also A. Rossiter, "The Professional is Political: An Interpretation of the Problem of the Past in Solution-Focused Therapy," *Am. J. Orthopsychiatry* 70 (2000): 150. See chapter 4, on psychiatric malpractice.

92. *The Unknown Murderer* (New York: International Universities Press, 1995).

93. Bastian v. County of San Luis Obispo, 199 Cal. App.3d 520 (1988).

94. W. P. Keeton (ed.), *Prosser and Keeton on the Law of Torts* (St. Paul, Minn.: West, 5th ed. 1984), p. 915.

95. Associated Press news release, "Sued Mom Turns Law on Psychiatrist," May 17, 1979.

96. Carrieri v. Bush, 69 Wash.2d 536, 419 P.2d 132 (1966).

97. 23 Cal. Rptr.2d 264 (Cal. App. 1993).

12

Regulation of the Practice of Psychotherapy

Psychotherapy as now generally defined is the noninvasive treatment of emotional states understood to be pathological or maladaptive. It may be used independently of or in addition to somatic procedures and psychopharmacology. The tradition of an interpersonal, physically noninvasive psychotherapy, however, has long roots. An important psychological element has always been present in all medicine—therapies explicitly addressed to the mind were a novelty or reflection, in part, of the decline in religion. The sacrament of the confession within the Catholic Church may be seen as the practice of psychotherapy. The Gospels present the image of Christ as physician.

Psychotherapy, in the broad sense of the term, thus existed long before there was a name for it. If it is defined as any procedure or process that changes or influences an individual, then its roots reach back to the dawn of man. The word *psychotherapy*, however, has a medical origin. Its first use is attributed to J. C. Reil in a paper published in 1803, "Rhapsodies in the Application of Psychic Methods in the Treatment of Mental Disturbances."[1]

Since then, the term has acquired a vague and general meaning. It has been used to describe everything from the mystical healing rites of the priest-physicians of ancient Greece, drum-beating and *vaudou* practices of certain modern Caribbean and Brazilian Negro peoples, classes in rhythmic dancing in a modern psychiatric hospital, forced labor in an old prison asylum, and lectures on ideas of healthy living, to the more subtle and sophisticated psychoanalytic techniques.[2] Dr. Thomas Szasz has pointed out that if psychoanalysis had not been discovered by physicians working with hysterical patients, the nature of the analytic process would have been formulated differently.[3] Breuer and Freud were physicians and Anna O. took the patient role, and so the psychoanalytic situation was defined as a therapeutic one.

Freud himself was actually embittered by the opposition to psychoanalysis on the part of the medical profession in Vienna, and he, with his early followers, banded together against the hostile medical world. He argued with great passion that psychoanalysts should be broadly trained in the arts and humanities. He welcomed suitable people from all professions, realizing that the discoveries he had made and the theoretical basis established in respect to them had a general and extremely wide bearing. He had no desire to see the potentialities of psychoanalysis limited by regarding it as nothing more than a branch of medical practice. In retrospect, Freud felt that he wasted his youth in the physiological laboratory although he achieved discipline through it.[4]

Following the death of Freud, the medical profession laid claim to the practice of psychotherapy and to the use of the term. While psychiatrists, with more conviction than proof, insist that a degree in medicine is essential to the rendering of any form of psychotherapy, psychologists and others point out that in the vast majority of instances emotional disturbances are entirely beyond the perimeter of traditional medical concerns. The opposition of the medical profession in the United States to the lay use of psychotherapy can in part be attributed to the struggle of the medical profession to secure the respect and recognition for its members who had expert knowledge and training in the field, and in part to the notion of the unity of mind and body (psychosomatic medicine).[5] In the United States, lay psychoanalysis did not come on the scene, with some exceptions (notably, Erik Erikson), until the 1990s.[6]

The official position of the American Medical Association, American Psychiatric Association, and American Psychoanalytic Association, which was jointly set out in 1954 in a "resolution on the Relations of Medicine and Psychology," is that "psychotherapy is a form of medical treatment and does not form the basis for a separate profession." This statement says:

> For centuries the Western world has placed on the medical profession responsibility for the diagnosis and treatment of illness. Medical practice acts have been designed to protect the public from unqualified practitioners and to define the special responsibilities assumed by those who practice the healing art, for much harm may be done by unqualified persons, however good their intentions may be. To do justice to the patient requires the capacity to make a diagnosis and to prescribe appropriate treatment. Diagnosis often requires the ability to compare and contrast various diseases and disorders that have similar symptoms but different causes. Diagnosis is a continuing process, for the character of the illness changes with its treatment or with the passage of time, and that treatment which is appropriate may change accordingly. . . .
>
> Psychiatry is the medical specialty concerned with illness that has chiefly mental symptoms. The psychiatrist is also concerned with mental

causes of physical illness, for we have come to recognize that physical symptoms may have mental causes, just as mental symptoms may have physical causes. The psychiatrist, with or without consultation with other physicians, must select from the many different methods of treatment at his disposal those methods that he considers appropriate to the particular patient. His treatment may be medicinal or surgical, physical (as electroshock) or psychological. The systematic application of the methods of psychological medicine to the treatment of illness, particularly as these methods involve gaining an understanding of the emotional state of the patient and aiding him to understand himself, is called psychotherapy. This special form of medical treatment may be highly developed, but it remains simply one of the possible methods of treatment to be selected for use according to medical criteria when it is indicated. Psychotherapy is a form of medical treatment and does not form the basis for a separate profession.

Other professional groups such as psychologists, teachers, ministers, lawyers, social workers, and vocational counselors, of course, use psychological understanding in carrying out their professional functions. Members of these professional groups are not thereby practicing medicine. The application of psychological methods to the treatment of illness is a medical function. Any physician may utilize the skills of others in his professional work, but he remains responsible, legally and morally, for the diagnosis and for the treatment of his patient.

The medical profession fully endorses the appropriate utilization of the skills of psychologists, social workers, and other professional personnel in contributing roles in settings directly supervised by physicians. It further recognizes that these professions are entirely independent and autonomous when medical questions are not involved; but when members of these professions contribute to the diagnosis and treatment of illness, their professional contributions must be coordinated under medical responsibility.

The law department of the American Medical Association has always considered psychotherapy to be a part of the practice of medicine and has never attempted to further specify grades of psychotherapy. It is of the opinion that the term *psychotherapy* covers activities ranging from marriage counseling to electroshock.[7] News magazines also cover psychiatry in its section on medicine. Likewise, the Association of American Law Schools (AALS) in its directory puts courses in psychiatry and law under the heading "Law and Medicine." However, at the 1972 annual meeting of the AALS, the Law and Medicine Section voted to exclude from its scope matters related to law and psychiatry and to organize a separate section on law and psychiatry. In 1969, *Time* magazine ceased to include psychiatric news items under its section on medicine and inaugurated a new section called "Behavior."

Does any distinction exist between psychotherapy and such clearly nonmedical processes as advice, conversation, and reassurance? In its broader sense, psychotherapy is clearly not a medical discipline; it is obviously the common professional function also of the clergy, teachers, social workers, and psychologists. A question arises, however, if a more cogent definition is used, such as "Psychotherapy is a planned technique of altering the maladaptive behavior of an individual (or group) toward more effective adaptation. The essential ingredient of psychotherapy is the utilization of the therapist's personality interacting with the patient's personality."[8]

Szasz, although he always identifies himself as an M.D. and apparently has never urged that his department of psychiatry separate from the medical school, argues in support of nonmedical psychotherapists. He contends that attempts to distinguish between the aforementioned processes are based on the institutional treatment of a process that can only be understood in instrumental terms. Any instrumental definition is bound to include so many diverse processes that not only is it impossible to restrict psychotherapy to medicine, but it is equally impossible to limit it to any other one profession.[9]

The supporters of nonmedical psychotherapy point out that the ever-increasing demand for psychotherapists (at low cost) is far from being met. There is a wide gulf, it is said, between supply and demand. There is one psychiatrist for approximately every ten thousand persons in the United States. Over the last decade the number of United States medical graduates choosing psychiatric training has declined by about 50 percent (many of the residency training slots are filled by international medical graduates who are supported by federal funding).[10] There is social class and also geographical imbalance in the distribution of psychiatrists. They are disproportionately distributed among the middle and upper classes, leaving large segments of the population without any. More than half practice in fifteen of the largest cities in the United States, and ten states have fewer than fifty each. At one time, one psychiatrist in ten had formal psychoanalytic training, but the number is far less today.

The Joint Commission on Mental Illness and Health in its final report of 1961 recommended that nonmedical mental health workers with proper training and experience be permitted to do general, short-term psychotherapy, and that "deep psychotherapy" be practiced only by those with special training, experience, and competence.[11] The latter group would include those professional persons who lack a medical education but have an aptitude for, adequate training, and demonstrable competence in such techniques of psychotherapy. The training and education required to qualify as a nonmedical psychotherapist has been subject to a great deal of disagreement.[12]

This is not to say that the training and education of the medical psychotherapist is beyond reproach. The qualification of the psychiatrist in doing psychotherapy has been challenged. Psychologists in Illinois at one time sought enactment of legislation that would have precluded psychiatrists from engaging in psychotherapy; they contended that the psychiatric residency program does not provide adequate training in the dynamics of human behavior and in the practice of psychotherapy. Increasingly, psychiatric residency programs devote less attention to psychotherapy and focus on medication. At one time, as it is said, psychiatry was mind without a brain; now it is brain without a mind.

Of course, of all medical disciplines, psychiatry most focuses on psychotherapy. One prominent psychiatrist (who shall remain anonymous) suggests that any restrictive legislation on psychotherapy be aimed primarily at the general medical practitioner. In many medical schools, the only training a student acquires about psychological problems amounts to about forty hours of class lectures over a four-year period. Quite often, the general medical practitioner or other physician is unable to handle adequately a patient in a psychotherapeutic situation. Be that as it may, the general practitioner is at the forefront in dispensing psychiatric medication.

The explanation for many cures lies in various circumstances, particularly the transference relationship, described by Freud. Patients frequently use the term *father-confessor* to describe the functions of the medical practitioner to whom they confide their troubles. The successful physician is almost always a father or God-like figure. Some physicians object to the socialization of medicine because you cannot make a father-figure from a subordinate official of the civil service. However, even young interns serving on the staffs of city hospitals seem to function very well as father figures.

Medical treatment throughout the ages has consisted, in important part, of the placebo effect; rational therapy based on scientific knowledge of chemistry and physiology is fairly recent. *Placebo,* in Latin, means "I shall please." Even with specific knowledge about drugs today, the psychological factors underlying placebo continue to play an important role. A limited view of placebo is that it consists of inert or inactive drugs, but a broader view would include any drug or procedure that has a placebo effect. Most placebo responses are involuntary responses. If the physician believes in the efficacy of a drug or procedure, his belief increases the likelihood of a placebo response, so placebos are usually an interactive process or component given deliberately to produce a pleasant or soothing effect.

Physicians have been prescribing placebos for hundreds of years, but curiously the role of placebos has increased in the age of technology. It is estimated that there is nothing organically wrong with 70 percent of the patients who come to a medical center, but if a sugar pill helps them to feel better, say physicians, isn't it really medicine? Prominent psychiatrist Jerome Frank years ago suggested in a classic book that the placebo effect might be the primary factor underlying all psychiatric remedies.[13] The latest research supports Dr. Frank's finding: psychiatrists, psychologists and other scientific healers are really exploiting the power of human belief, just as shamans and witch doctors do.[14] Can they do it as effectively? In a 1933 lecture, Freud remarked, "I do not think our successes can compete with those of Lourdes. There are so many more people who believe in the miracles of the Blessed Virgin than in the existence of the unconscious."[15]

Regulation of Professions

The regulation of professions may be formal or informal. Institutional policies and customs (that is, hospitals, mental health centers, HMOs, insurance) may allocate the functions and responsibilities of the various categories of mental health professionals. Private clinics set out rules for their staff, professional or otherwise, regarding the treatment of patients (e.g., how much time is to be spent with a patient or the type of medication to be used). In some instances, the functions or responsibilities are mandated by law (for example, psychiatrists are the only category of mental health professionals who are legally authorized to prescribe medication or administer electroshock). Increasingly, the policies and laws that bestow a privilege or monopoly to one or another of the mental health professionals have been the subject of challenge by competing professional groups.

In a very practical sense, insurance coverage of health care or malpractice insurance regulates the scope of the practitioner's activity. The practitioner will not likely carry out a treatment not covered by health insurance or by malpractice insurance. Litigation or the threat of it has proven to be a prime regulator of psychotherapy. It has dampened, for example, the practice of revival of memory of childhood abuse. Thus, a psychiatrist at the risk of litigation would not treat a patient for a sore throat, as that would not be covered by liability coverage for the treatment of mental illness. After a few years out of medical school, the psychiatrist becomes inept at treating physical disorders and he becomes almost on a par with nonmedical therapists, treating only mental disorders.

The regulation and control of certain professions through the use of legislation is not a modern phenomenon. The forerunner of such legislation existed as common law. The medieval guilds, whose organization was at first informal, exercised control over their membership and were entirely self-regulatory. Ultimately, this self-regulation came to be sanctioned by the church and state. Although ecclesiastical control of medical licensure seems strange today, it was logical enough at the time because, until the Renaissance, physicians were usually clergymen. Episcopal authority in effect provided a national system. By the end of the Middle Ages, ideas about state examination had reached northern Europe, and the medical groups all sought official authority to carry out these procedures for their respective personnel.[16]

In the United States, the possibilities of using licensing legislation as an administrative device for the control of the professions were not recognized until a late date. Since 1870, when licensing legislation was first used on a state level, it has become an increasingly important regulatory device, particularly since the 1940s, when laws were enacted ostensibly to protect the public, but in actuality, to protect turf. At the present time, licensing or certification of practitioners of the various professions is quite common and readily accepted. There is legislation, for example, regulating architects, dentists, physicians, psychologists, social workers, and, to some degree, marriage counselors.

Such legislation has not always been so readily acceptable. Considering the history of the country, it is not surprising that at one time the validity of any and all licensing was contested. (One state, Georgia, actually passed a law forbidding the authorities to interfere with quacks.) The most frequent contention was that in a democracy a person possessed an inalienable right to pursue his chosen profession or to meet with and seek assistance from whomever he should choose. It was contended that interference with such a right was a violation of the Fourth Amendment of the Constitution. It was also claimed that it violated freedom of speech guaranteed under the First Amendment. Clergymen pointed out that Jesus spread the word although he was not ordained. It is safe to say that today, however, any regulatory provision that is based on a social need and is not arbitrary or unreasonable will be upheld in the courts.[17]

Although some professions were controlled by legislation long before others, the history of the professions and the legislation controlling them show a remarkable parallel. At first, each profession was an informal organization that had evolved around the specialized skills common to its members. Each group would attempt to limit its membership to those who had attained such skills and applied them in an ethical manner. As soon as conditions permitted, each group urged legislation that would test those who wish to be admitted to the profession. Initially, a *grandfather clause*, a provision for the automatic registration of those who had been engaged in practice for a specified time, was usually included in such legislation.

Gradually, the educational requirements were raised and the entrance examination became increasingly difficult.[18]

All licensing or certification legislation is based on two sometimes contradictory ideas. Such legislation seems to be initiated by the group on the inside that wishes to eliminate competition, but its passage is always urged on the ground that the public must be protected from unfair practices. The profession's public prestige and status is enhanced while the number of persons able to perform these services is limited. Licensing results in an increased cost of the services but is considered economically justified if the burden of higher prices is less than the social cost that would arise from damages to the public health or safety that would occur in the absence of licensing.[19] Regardless of the justification, such acts aim at regulation by general formal denial of a right, which is then made individually available by an administrative act of approval, certification, consent, or permit.[20]

Licensure and certification acts are the two types of legislation most often used to regulate the professions. A licensing act defines the function of the profession and prohibits practice by anyone who is not licensed under the act.[21] A certification act (sometimes called *title licensing*) does not define the function of the profession; it only prohibits the use of a title by those who do not meet the requirements of the act.[22] Thus, a licensing law covers the particular practice, no matter what the person calls himself, while a certification statute covers the particular practice only when the person wishes to identify himself by the use of a certain title. The actual words used in the laws do not necessarily indicate the nature of the law; several of the licensing laws are really certification laws in that the use of the title is the controlling factor.

Both types of acts have advantages and disadvantages. There seems to be little doubt that licensing provides the greater protection for the public. If properly enforced, it can control quackery, whereas certification in itself cannot.[23] A prerequisite for enactment of a licensing act, however, is a definition of the function that is to be regulated. In the case of psychotherapy, there is no general agreement on a definition. The same problem arose in regard to psychology. In 1955, because of the interprofessional climate at the time and the difficulty in legally defining the practice of psychology, the American Psychological Association recommended that legislation take the form of certification.

Regulation by means of a certification statute, however, may easily be circumvented. Since the certification statute does not prohibit the function or practice of any particular profession, all that a charlatan has to do is change his title. As sometimes expressed, "the rat goes to a new sewer." Thus, if the certification statute prohibited the use of the title "marriage counselor," a quack could simply change his title to "family counselor" and continue with the same work he was doing previously. David Mace, then past president and executive director of the American Association of Family and Marriage Counselors (AAFMC), however, argued that certification can be effective, because it would be very difficult for a quack to attract clients when he used an unfamiliar title.[24] New York law, for example, protects only the titles "psychologist" and "social worker." There are no legal restrictions on the use of such titles as "counselor," "psychotherapist," "group therapist," and "psychoanalyst" as long as the person does not hold himself out to be licensed.[25] The New York classified telephone directory lists, among others, metaphysicians, astrologers, and yoga instructors.

Edward J. Rydman, as executive director of the American Association of Family and Marriage Counselors, expressed the opinion that without appropriate guidelines provided by the state, the public has little or no means of determining who is or who is not qualified to do counseling and psychotherapy. The AAFMC continues to favor, as the best solution to the problem of state licensing of marriage counselors, a broad framework of legislation for the proper control of all counseling service offered to the public in the fields of mental health and family regulations, minimum standards in each field to be established by appropriate authorities within the respective professional groups concerned.[26]

Without a workable legal definition of the function of a profession, a licensing statute would appear to be one of certification. It may be noted that many statutes that were first passed certifying psychologists have been repealed and replaced by licensing statutes.[27] Unless a regulatory statute is drawn in terms that are so definite and clear that a person can reasonably ascertain whether he is within the areas of conduct proscribed by the statute, the statute will be considered a denial of due process of law and consequently void.[28] However, the Missouri Supreme Court has held that a statute making the practice of medicine without a license a misdemeanor is not invalid, although the term *practice of medicine* is not given a legislative definition.[29] The court held that the test is whether the language conveys a sufficiently definite warning as to the proscribed conduct as measured by common understanding and practice.

In some parts of the United States and in a number of European countries individuals with a degree in philosophy advertise (without violating the law) that they are available for philosophical consultation, discussing such issues as the meaning of life, the definition of virtue, and so on. From a movement that began in Germany in the 1980s, a small but growing number of philosophers in the United States have opened private practices as "philosopher practitioners," offering a therapy based on the idea that solutions to many personal, moral, and ethical problems can be found not in psychotherapy or Prozac but in philosophical disclosure. They are the modern-day version of Socrates.[30] A philosopher says, "Physicians [would] do well to send patients more often to the library than to the pharmacy, since philosophy has traditionally provided us with soothing and inspirational homilies."[31] Philosophy, after all, is about getting your bearings in life. New York is the first state to consider licensing philosophers. At the turn of the twentieth century, the American Philosophical Association, then founded, was a split from the American Psychological Association.

Psychotherapy has become so complex and fragmented that no single approach can be understood as primary. With the rise of psychopharmacological treatments, many of the forms of psychotherapy have been adapted as supportive psychotherapy both within and beyond the clinical setting. Psychotherapy today is extraordinarily diverse and holds an important position within both medical and nonmedical aspects of culture. Indeed, it seems today that just about everyone—school teachers, housewives, ministers, lawyers, and so on—is playing therapist. With training or without, are they helpful, or harmful? In one study, eight college-educated housewives were given part-time training over a two-year period to provide psychotherapy; their performance was judged comparable to that of more highly trained therapists.[32]

Housewives, however, do not constitute a profession. Indispensable to any would-be profession is a body of esoteric knowledge, mastery of which is the necessary qualification for practice of the profession. In classical sociological theory, professional knowledge becomes social by dint of the professionalization process. Dedication entitles professionals to claim immunity to crass motives or self-interest. It is commonly quipped that professionals *practice* while others *work*— but actually, the idea of *practice* is an expectation of a dedication to improving one's skills. To *profess* was, in its earliest use, the public declaration of one's religion, and it signified a commitment to a particular way of life. Prostitution is frequently called the "oldest profession," but it is not an honored one.[33]

Through the years the concept of a *learned profession* has been distinguished from that of a trade or business.[34] The traditional concept of professionalism posits that the complexity of professional knowledge and service means that professionals should not be subject to lay control, whether exercised through bureaucratic or market mechanisms. As a corollary to this proposition, licensure by the state should be sufficient to shield professionals from attempts at control by others. The codes of ethics of the profession highlight the fiduciary feature of professional life. They stress the trust that their members should provide those seeking their help. They take a vow of service, so for many years the antitrust or antimonopoly laws were not applied to them.

From 1890, when the Sherman antitrust act was enacted, until 1975, the courts held that the learned professions were exempt from the antitrust laws. Few antitrust claims were asserted against professionals of any sort until the mid-1970s. Then, in 1975, the U.S. Supreme Court held that a Virginia state bar rule requiring lawyers to charge minimum prices for specified services was not immune from anti-trust challenge.[35] The Court rejected the lawyers' claim that "professional ethics" protected their mandatory minimum fees against a price-fixing challenge. The Court, however, noted that the "public service aspect, and other features of the professions, may require that a particular practice, which could properly be viewed as a violation of the Sherman Act in another context, be treated differently."[36] With that decision, the Court ended the exemption of the learned professions from the antitrust laws.[37]

The entrepreneurial aspect of professionalism prompted George Bernard Shaw's claim that "all professions are conspiracies against the laity."[38] By 1975 it was not uncommon to refer to health care as an industry. Soon to go as self-serving would be the traditional restriction of medical societies and other professional organizations against the dissemination of price information and advertising. In 1982, by a decision in favor of the Federal Trade Commission (FTC), the Supreme Court inaugurated the era of advertising by physicians and other professionals. The FTC had filed suit against the American Medical Association, holding that it was in restraint of trade because of its code of ethics prohibiting advertising. The FTC did, however, allow the AMA to adopt guidelines prohibiting unsubstantiated, false, and deceptive representations by its members.[39]

Categories of Mental Health Professionals

The mental health profession is actually made up of a variety of distinct professions. It includes psychiatry, psychoanalysis, psychology, social work, and marriage and family counseling. These fields and others are discussed in this chapter. By and large, the public is unaware of their differences. Therapies range from widely accepted, scientifically based treatments to those that are the creation of an individual and often have less grounding in scientific validation or professional acceptance. There is ongoing debate whether it is the personality of the provider or professional training (or medication) that plays the most significant role in therapy.

Psychiatry. The title "psychiatrist" is not as such the subject of regulatory legislation as of usage. In Greek, *psyche* means "soul" and *iatros* means "healer." It is commonly assumed that psychiatrists are also physicians, who are the subject of regulation. The *American Psychiatric Glossary* defines a *psychiatrist* as "[a] licensed physician who specializes in the diagnosis, treatment, and prevention of mental and emotional disorders."[40]

As a matter of custom, it is rare to find a non-M.D. psychotherapist who uses the title "psychiatrist." When the problem arises, it is usually in the case of the foreign medical school graduate who is without a medical license. While there is no legal protection of the titles "analyst," "psychoanalyst," or "psychotherapist," as shall be noted, there is some measure of protection for the term "psychiatrist" under medical practice acts in that it is commonly accepted as a medical specialty, and a non-M.D. using the title would likely be ordered to cease and desist.

Psychiatry is singled out in legislation on commitment procedures and sometimes on school personnel. Apart from these special areas, the assumption is that the profession shares with the rest of medicine with regard to regulatory statutes. In the regulation of physicians, most states by the turn of the twentieth century had passed laws and established state boards of medical examiners. Many of the early laws were permissive, merely prohibiting unlicensed persons from using the title "doctor of medicine," and did not extend to practice. They were more concerned with protecting the title than with protecting the public health. Between 1910 and 1930, following the Flexner Report on medical education and the establishment of the AMA's Council on Medical Education, the licensing laws assumed their present general form and content. That is, unlicensed persons were specifically prohibited from practicing medicine or the healing arts, but the scope of the prohibition was disputed. The statutory definition usually contained language to the effect that any person who advertises or announces to the public a readiness to heal, refers to himself as a doctor, or prescribes for or treats a person's suffering is practicing medicine or a healing art.

There have developed within the medical profession optional subdivisions in the form of specialties that deal with distinctive portions of the body, such as dermatology; and specialties dealing with forms of treatment, such as surgery. These specialties are recognized by certifying boards within the profession itself. In this manner, the American Board of Psychiatry and Neurology is, like other medical specialty boards, a voluntary, nonprofit, nongovernmental organization, established under the sponsorship of the American Medical Association. Training programs are accredited on request and their graduates are examined by the board if they so desire.

A psychiatrist may thus opt to take the examination given by the American Board of Psychiatry and Neurology and thereby represent himself as a board-certified psychiatrist. Approximately half of the membership of the American Psychiatric Association, which now totals some forty thousand, are certified by the American Board of Psychiatry and Neurology. In other words, about half of the nation's psychiatrists practice without certification. The certification examination, however, while it measures something about the psychiatrist's understanding of theory and history and his diagnostic ability, tells practically nothing about his ability to relate to other people or to treat them. An effort, although limited, is made during the examination to get a feel for the way the candidate interacts with patients.

Many general practitioners who work in mental hospitals call themselves psychiatrists although they have had no formal training in psychiatry. While there is no legal requirement of certification or licensure, board certification is required by many private hospitals as a condition to use of its facilities. In the law of torts, one who holds himself out as a specialist in a specific area of practice is held to a higher standard of knowledge and skill.

With the development of medication, insurance and managed care limitations, and competition with nonmedical mental health professionals, psychiatrists are less engaged in psychotherapy or psychoanalysis. Until the 1960s psychiatric training was predominantly psychoanalytic. Psychiatrists were taught to look for the (unconscious) cause of the patient's difficulties—the theory being that interpreting these hidden meanings would take care of the difficulties. Then in the 1960s there came a proliferation of psychotherapy approaches: Gestalt, transactional analysis, bioenergetics, and so on. As therapies proliferated, so did psychotherapists.

The growth of managed care has also affected the market for mental health services. Psychiatrists have found themselves at a competitive disadvantage because, on a per-unit-of-service basis, their fees are generally higher than those of other mental health professionals and, as a group, they are more reluctant to embrace managed care principles. Moreover, managed care systems tend to compartmentalize the roles of various mental health professionals. Thus, psychiatrists are often restricted to providing medical management or pharmacotherapy for patients, whereas psychologists, social workers, and other caregivers who are perceived as less expensive are used to provide verbal therapies. The vast majority of articles in the *American Journal of Psychiatry* are now on pharmacotherapy, not on psychodynamics (the cover of the journal now has drawings of the brain). Training programs in psychiatry provide less and less attention to psychotherapy. The psychiatrist is now called the "hydraulic doctor"—one who raises and lowers the dosage. Biopsychiatrists believe that all serious emotional problems have a physiological cause and can (and should) be treated with medication, perhaps also with psychotherapy as supportive therapy.[41]

Psychoanalysis. Psychoanalysis is the "talk therapy" devised by Sigmund Freud. It is based on free association, dream interpretation, and interpretation of resistance and transference manifestations. In fifty-minute sessions three to five times a week for a number of years, the analysand lies on a couch with the analyst sitting behind and who from time to time may make an interpretation. For decades it has been the butt of jokes, cartoons, and movie spoofs, much to the detriment of its reputation.

It is commonly thought that a person who goes to a psychoanalyst several times a week for several years must be very sick. In actuality, it takes a rather healthy person to withstand the requirement of frequent free association without coming apart. So why do such people undertake the rigors, demands, and expense of psychoanalysis? Because, as Socrates would say, self-knowledge is a source of strength and wisdom. Many prominent individuals such as Judge David Bazelon have acknowledged that they were in analysis.[42] In some places it is considered fashionable to be in analysis. Auditors at the Internal Revenue Service are often perplexed that the taxpayer looks healthy yet claims large medical deductions.

It is commonly believed that the field of psychoanalysis is governed by licensing or certification laws, as is the case with psychiatry, but in fact it is not. There are, moreover, no official accrediting agencies for psychoanalysis. The American Psychoanalytic Association approves training institutes, while a newer group, the American Academy of Psychoanalysis, which proclaims a "constructive coexistence," does not technically approve training institutes but admits individual members deemed qualified and de facto accepts graduates of a number of institutes. The association, at one time, tried to develop a subspecialty certifying board within the American Board of Psychiatry and Neurology, but this was defeated initially within the association and then by the American Boards when the academy protested. This issue crops up periodically as a possibility.

The association's position has been that only those who are trained in its approved institutes are qualified psychoanalysts. The academy's position has been that qualified persons wherever trained should be permitted, if they so desire, to join both organizations. As things stood, a number of analysts trained in association-approved institutes were also members of the academy, but the association excluded those not trained at its approved institutes. Some of the leading training centers that were not recognized by the association included the American Institute of Psychoanalysis, the William Alanson White Institute of Psychiatry, the Psychoanalytic Institute of the New York Medical College, and the psychoanalytic training program of the Tulane University School of Medicine, Department of Psychiatry and Neurology.

The Tulane program was an offshoot of Columbia University. As a result of the efforts of the late Dr. Sandor Rado and other psychoanalysts from the New York Psychoanalytic Institute, who were convinced that psychoanalysis was and should continue to be a medical discipline, the Psychoanalytic Clinic for Training and Research was established in 1944 as part of the Department of Psychiatry of the College of Physicians and Surgeons at Columbia, where the faculty developed a graduate psychoanalytic curriculum, which was approved by the association. Shortly after World War II, in 1949, a group of Columbia-trained psychoanalysts headed by Dr. Robert G. Heath and including Drs. Harold I. Lief, Irwin Marcus, Russell Monroe, and Norman Rucker arrived at Tulane and, in setting up its department of psychiatry, which to this day is combined with neurology, integrated psychoanalytic training into its residency program.

The development of the Tulane program (of which I am a graduate) was viewed initially as a threat to the existence of nonuniversity-affiliated training institutes. Communications were sent to the president of Tulane that urged against the development. Some members of the Tulane group were ostracized by the association. Heath was at first granted and then refused admission in an extraordinary session; Monroe's application was not approved because he was participating in an unapproved training institute. A few years later Marcus and Rucker, when they left Tulane, became members of the association, playing a leading role in that organization. Lief, who later became director of the Division of Family Study of the University of Pennsylvania Department of Psychiatry, never applied to the association for membership, but in 1999, the association invited him to join, and he accepted (without having to pay dues).

The excommunicated and other members at Tulane along with a number of members of the association regarded as analytic pioneers, such as Franz Alexander, Jules Masserman, Sandor Rado, and Clara Thompson formed the academy, which reached a membership of 706 in 1974 (declining to 639 in 1999). The membership consists of Fellows who are physicians and now also nonphysicians and another category, called *scientific associates*. The scientific associates, who may or may not be physicians, are invited and represent approximately 15 percent of the membership. The scientific associates include nonpsychoanalytically trained psychiatrists, many of whom are chairs of departments, and a number of behavioral scientists. The association, which has over double the academy's membership, consists of psychiatrists and a number of psychologists, all psychoanalytically trained in its approved institutes.

Since the development of the Tulane program, a number of psychoanalytic programs have come under the aegis of universities and medical schools. Apart from the program at New York Medical College, a number of the training institutes of the association itself have close ties with medical schools and universities, such as at Case Western Reserve, New York Downstate Medical Center, Pittsburgh, and from the early date, at Columbia. Such relationships tend to arrest the isolation of psychoanalysis from the mainstream of medical thought. They tend to explore the connection between behavior and biology.

Psychoanalysis, as well as psychiatry generally, but less so, is characterized by (1) fewer patient referrals, (2) lower fees per visit, (3) shorter inpatient and outpatient time to treat a patient, and (4) alternatives including social workers, psychologists, and B.A.-level or below mental health professionals. Enrollment in psychoanalytic training institutes, which peaked at 1,194 trainees in 1980, dropped to 909 by 1989.[43] In 1988, in response to the restraint of trade suit by psychologists, a settlement agreement overturned the American Psychoanalytic Association's long-standing policy of restricting analytic training to candidates with medical degrees, opening the field to lay analysis. In 1995, the Michigan Psychoanalytic Institute, so bereft of candidates, opened its doors to attorneys to become psychoanalysts. A frequent topic at meetings of psychoanalytic institutes is, "Does Psychoanalysis Have a Future?"

Psychoanalysis at one time was considered the gold standard of psychotherapy, and it was used in the treatment of neurosis, personality disorders, psychosomatic disorders, sexual disorders, sexual dysfunction, and also to enhance creativity or productivity. Many of these areas have been taken over by medication or cognitive or behavior therapy. The reasons are several. The climate of opinion about psychoanalysis has changed, resulting in the declining prestige of psychoanalysis. It was not always effective, and now there is a changing economic climate, calling for proof of efficacy. Except for electroshock and psychosurgery, psychoanalysis was the only available treatment, but that too has changed.

In the years following World War II the Menninger Foundation in Topeka, Kansas, was the world-renowned institution for the training of psychoanalysts and psychiatrists and the treatment of patients by psychoanalysis and psychoanalytic psychotherapy, but in the latter part of the twentieth century, due mainly to cuts in managed care and an increased use of drugs instead of therapy to treat mental illness, it considered moving to Houston to become a partner with the Baylor College of Medicine and Methodist Health Care System (the proposal did not materialize).

At the 2001 annual meeting of the American Academy of Psychoanalysis members voted to expand the academy's name to the American Academy of Psycho-analysis and Dynamic Psychiatry. The new level of support for the name change was explained: "We are finding a growing interest in our programs among psychiatrists who are informed by dynamic teaching but not formally trained and certified as analysts. We recognize too, that more and more, many of these psychiatrists are making essential contributions to our intellectual activities and our organizational leadership. Finally, we see how much we need to make the Academy more welcoming to the many young psychiatrists who are interested in dynamic psychiatry but are intimidated by the Academy, or who feel our name does not reflect their identity. They misread us, imagining the membership to be comprised exclusively of fully trained and certified psychoanalysts." One member dissented to the name change thus: "I want to remind you of the law of unintended consequences. I think we are giving a message to the public that we are done with psychoanalysis. I am not one of the people who thinks psychoanalysis is dead. I think we are in a bad way but things are going to improve. I think if we sell out now, we are not going to be able to buy our way back in when the stock goes back up again."

Though psychoanalysis may be on the wane as a treatment modality, most of its concepts permeate treatment programs and in developmental and social uses. It continues to be at the center of debates in humanistic fields, including literary studies. "To us he is no more a person / Now but a whole climate of opinion," wrote poet W. H. Auden upon learning of Sigmund Freud's death.[44] Freud's theories left their mark on many endeavors outside psychiatry, and nowhere more so than in the United States (or Argentina). The terms we use, like *neurotic* and *hysteric*, are part of the common language that is heard on the streets, in soap operas, and in the movies. Dr. Richard Restak writes, "Lacking familiarity with psychiatry and psychoanalysis, a visitor from Mars could make little sense of much of contemporary America. He would fail to understand the cartoons of Jules Feiffer, the movies of Woody Allen, the novels of D. M. Thomas or Philip Roth. His grasp of U.S. politics, education, and criminal justice would be incomplete."[45] As a result of the influence of psychoanalysis, particularly around mid-twentieth century, 80 percent of undergraduate college students in the United States studied psychology, either as a major or minor.

Psychology. In 1954 the American Psychoanalytic Association and the American Psychiatric Association jointly condemned the practice of psychotherapy by any but trained physicians, but nevertheless the number of psychotherapists who were not physicians, mostly psychologists, continued to grow rapidly—many of them were graduates of new clinical psychology programs set up with funding from the NIMH or the Veterans Administration.

As of a number of years, the American Board of Examiners in Professional Psychology offers a Diplomate in Clinical Psychology. Minimal requirements are five years of post-Ph.D. experience and successful completion of oral and written examinations. Most states regulate the practice of psychology, some by licensure and some by certification by state boards. In still other states, nonstatutory certification is provided by the state psychological association. The practice of psychology is defined in one regulatory statute as follows:

> [The] rendering or offering to render to individuals, groups, organizations, or the public any psychological service, while representing oneself to be a

psychologist involving the application of principles, methods, and procedures of understanding, predicting, and influencing behavior, such as the principle pertaining to learning, perception, motivation, thinking, emotions, and interpersonal relationships; and the methods and procedures of interviewing, counseling, psychotherapy, and hypnosis; of constructing, administering, and interpreting tests of mental abilities, aptitudes, interests, attitudes, personality characteristics, emotions, and motivation.[46]

A number of state statutes license or certify psychologists according to level or specialty. However, the Committee on Legislation of the American Psychological Association does not favor legislation that permits differentiation of specialists within psychology, regardless of whether these specialties are defined by the functions carried out or by the locale where the work is done. It is believed that these matters are best dealt with by intraprofessional controls.[47] The American Psychological Association, by 1999, represented 159,000 clinicians, researchers, and educators. In 1975 there were an estimated 15,000 clinical psychologists; a decade later there were more than twice that number.

Many acts regulating the practice of psychology include a correlating section that specifically states that nothing in the statute shall be construed as permitting a psychologist, certified or licensed under the statute, to administer or prescribe drugs or in any manner to engage in the practice of medicine. The American Psychological Association Committee on Legislation contends that since psychologists do not represent themselves as being anything other than psychologists, a disclaimer clause on the right to practice other professions is inappropriate. The same might be argued regarding any possible enactment regulating the practice of psychotherapy, but it does allay other professions' fears of encroachment.

While psychologists over the years have generally berated the use of pharmacological treatment, increased competition among caregivers has prompted some psychologists as well as nurse clinicians to seek prescription privileges. They have argued that the knowledge and experience base needed to provide competent pharmacological treatment can be obtained without a medical school education or psychiatric residency training.[48] The American Medical Association, the American Psychiatric Association, and other professional associations have voiced strong opposition, but thus far, psychologists have obtained prescribing privileges only in New Mexico. A number of states, however, do permit prescribing by nurse clinicians, albeit within a limited formulary and with medical oversight. In 1999, the Florida Psychological Association failed in an effort to obtain legislative approval to change the name of psychologists to "psychological physicians." In previous years, it unsuccessfully sought to limit psychological testing to their profession and also to obtain prescribing privileges and independent hospital privileges.[49] Quite often, when medication is considered necessary, psychologists refer the patient to a primary care physician for it (rather than to a psychiatrist to avoid the perceived stigma of seeing a psychiatrist).

Arguing that medical training is not essential to the practice of psychoanalysis, psychologists brought antitrust litigation that forced the American Psychoanalytic Association to allow them (and social workers) into their association. They also challenged insurance practices that excluded them (and other nonmedical mental health professionals) and won the right to compete with physicians as psychotherapy providers.[50]

Social Work. The practice of social work as a certified social worker is defined in regulatory legislation as engaging, under such title, in social casework, social group work, community organization, administration of a social work program, social work education, social work research, or any combination of these in accordance with social work principles and methods. The New York legislation states that "the practice of social work is for the purpose of helping individuals, families, groups, and communities to prevent or to resolve problems caused by social or emotional stress."[51] The Academy of Certified Social Workers issues certificates to qualified social workers who have completed at least two years of supervised experience beyond the M.S.W. (Master of Social Work) requirement. The M.S.W. is the usual degree requirement representing at least two years of graduate course study, one of which normally consists of supervised field experience. Schools of social work offer bachelor's (B.S.W.), master's (M.S.W.), and doctoral (D.S.W.) degrees. The Council on Social Work sets national standards for social work accreditation. State licensing and certification requirements vary.

In the early part of the twentieth century the Boston Psychopathic Childrens' Clinic, the Juvenile Psychopathic Institute in Chicago, and the Henry Phipps Psychiatric Clinic in Baltimore introduced social workers to assist people to get help that E. E. Southard, a psychiatrist, and Mary C. Jarrett, a social worker, described in its broadest sense to mean restoration of capacity for normal living or provision for the greatest possible comfort. The social worker was originally called a "friendly visitor." It was World War I and the impact on existing treatment facilities of the returning psychiatric casualties—the shell-shocked veterans—that gave impetus to formal training for increased numbers of practitioners of what henceforth was to be known as *psychiatric social work*—that is, social work practiced in collaboration with psychiatry.

Psychiatric social work has grown in prominence with the increasing acceptance of both managed care and community-based public sector service and in political strength as the number of its practitioners increase. According to the Bureau of Labor Statistics, the United States now employs over 170,000 social workers in one capacity or another. Social workers provide a large share of the psychotherapy for poor patients. Programs for drug addicts rely heavily on social workers. The growing effort to move mental patients out of long-term hospitalization in state institutions depends on social workers to supervise outpatient cases in the community. In 1975, according to the National Association of Social Workers, 25,000 were engaged in therapy; a decade later 60,000 were.[52]

Marriage and Family Counseling. The field of marriage and family counselors has shown the most explosive growth of all. While before 1964 no state recognized them, and today apparently no more than nine do, there are by some estimates at least 28,000 marriage and family counselors in practice, and perhaps far more. Their exact number is not known, because in most states there is no such license, although they are generally free to practice nevertheless.

Many charlatans now practicing in the mental health field do so under the aegis of the title "marriage counselor" or "family counselor." Some years ago, to test the competency of marriage counseling, investigators, either alone or accompanied by their pretended wives, who visited marriage counselors chosen at random in six cities, found that most of the counselors' performances fell below commonsense standards, and that the so-called credentials displayed on their office walls were fraudulent.[53]

Qualified marriage counselors have sought to improve counseling techniques by training more competent practitioners. In the 1930s they set up the American Association of Marriage and Family Counselors, which has established educational criteria and qualification standards. In past years, proposed state legislation outlining qualifications and licensing procedures for counselors has come and gone, usually disappearing in some committee. But the AAFMC is a national accrediting body for the specialty of marriage counseling, an organization composed of interprofessional membership, divided somewhat equally among psychologists, social workers, psychiatrists, family-life educators, and pastoral counselors. The basic membership requirement is that the person have a doctorate and a few years' experience in one of these fields. An exception to the requirement of a doctorate is made in the field of social work, where an M.S.W. plus experience is accepted. The organization also requires a minimum of two years of specialization in marriage counseling with at least one of the years at an internship center.

Professional Licensed Counseling. About two decades ago various states provided for the licensing of "professional counselors." In its legislation on professional counselors, Michigan provides that the *practice of counseling* means:

> the rendering to individuals, groups, families, organizations, or the general public a service involving the application of clinical counseling principles, methods, or procedures for the purpose of achieving social, personal, career, and emotional development and with the goal of promoting and enhancing healthy self actualizing and satisfying lifestyles whether the services are rendered in an educational, business, health, private practice, or human services setting. The practice of counseling does not include the practice of psychology except for those preventive techniques, counseling techniques, or behavior modification techniques for which the licensed professional counselor or limited licensed counselor has been specifically trained. The practice of counseling does not include the practice of medicine such as prescribing drugs or administering electroconvulsive therapy. A counselor shall not hold himself or herself out as a psychologist. . . . A counselor shall not hold himself or herself out as a marriage and family counselor providing marriage counseling.

Licensure as a professional counselor requires a master's or doctoral degree in counseling or student personnel work from an approved program and at least two years of counseling experience under the supervision of a licensed professional counselor.[54]

In the battle over turf, psychologists were more opposed to the legislation than were psychiatrists. Like the psychologists, professional counselors are precluded from prescribing medication and thus are more in competition with psychologists. Professional counselors joined with psychiatrists in persuading legislatures not to grant prescribing privileges to psychologists—that would have given psychologists an advantage over the counselors.

Encounter and Other Groups. There is no legislation or requirement of professional standards for leaders of encounter or sensitivity training groups. They have
a variety of backgrounds, no common fund of knowledge or experience, and no
common set of professional ethics. The issue of control was raised when the New
York weekly paper the *Village Voice* refused to advertise groups whose claims implied therapy. The paper said that advertising therapy was against professional
standards and, in general, unethical. The sponsors of encounters argued that they
did not conduct therapy or aim at changing the psychological state of participants
in a fundamental way. Encounter groups propose by intensive group experiences
to reduce a person's alienation from other persons, from nature, and from genuine
emotion.

There is always the hazard of a psychotic breakdown when a person moves
from a structured into an unstructured society. The emphasis in encounter or sensitivity groups is on impulse or primary process behavior. Kurt W. Back in *Beyond
Words: The Story of Sensitivity Training and the Encounter Movement* and Jane
Howard in *Please Touch* point out the almost casual acceptance by encounter-
group leaders of possible breakdowns and other effects commonly considered as
detrimental. Fritz Perls in his book on Gestalt therapy states, "Sir, if you want to
go crazy, commit suicide, improve, get turned on, or get an experience that would
change your life, that is up to you. You came here out of your own free will."[55]
Some encounter-group leaders believe that breakdown or disintegration of personality is essential to a redevelopment of personality. Breakdown is a breakthrough.

Some sensitivity groups, which are not of an intensive nature, are coming more
and more to approximate religious retreats, yoga centers, halfway houses, and sin-
gles' weekends at mountain and beach resorts. Apart from sensitivity groups, the
Manhattan telephone directory lists over sixty entries of sundry groups, including
a number of Anonymous-titled organizations (the label was first used in 1937 by
Alcoholics Anonymous) such as Overeating Anonymous, Gamblers Anonymous,
Neurotics Anonymous, and Parents Anonymous. Also in the parental field is the
7,000-member Parents Without Partners organization. Many of these organizations
have developed into big businesses. Smoke Watchers, a franchise operation, now
has branches throughout the country. In many of these groups, psychiatrists are
looked upon with disdain (though some members are in psychiatric treatment
concurrently with their group meetings).

The cultural phenomenon of the increasing number of groups in recent years
reflects the fact that many of the old sources of intimacy and emotional support—
notably the family—have been dispersed. The license and freedom of the group
atmosphere also contribute to its appeal. The open expression of feelings discouraged in an increasingly impersonal world are encouraged in the intimacy of the
group. The group thus contributes to alleviating human distress, but its commercial
aspects tend to vulgarize the encounter.[56]

Pastoral Counseling. As elsewhere, many persons in the United States, before the
decline of religion, turned to members of the clergy for counseling and guidance.
Surveys show that American young people today put the profession of the clergy
near the bottom of the list of occupations they would like to enter. With contemporary psychiatry or psychology now the standard, pastoral counseling is widely
regarded as inept. A survey of 1,045 pastors reveals that 24 percent had not received

any training in counseling. Although 64 percent reported taking one or more courses in pastoral care, pastoral psychology, or pastoral counseling, only 10 percent reported any kind of clinical training involving actual counseling experience under supervision. Furthermore, only 24 percent reported having any counseling or therapy experiences of their own.[57]

Many religious denominations have now established training programs in pastoral counseling and psychology in their seminaries. In the early 1960s, the Menninger Foundation established a pastoral counseling program for clergy, exposing them to the basic principles of psychiatry. A generation before this Rev. Anton Boisen of Elgin State Hospital founded the Council on Clinical Training with active programs for ministers. In recent years, there has been an upsurge of strong fundamentalist religious beliefs to which more and more people are attaching themselves. Freud, though, very much like Marx, believed that religion is an opiate.

Over the past half-century, the number of mental health personnel increased by almost the number of decline of clergy. Churches are turned into restaurants or psychotherapy centers. In considerable measure, psychiatry has replaced religion in America, although polls indicate that most Americans consider themselves religious to some degree, if not particularly devout or observant.[58] The public hears far more about human behavior from psychologists and psychiatrists than from clergy. U.S. Supreme Court Justice Antonin Scalia expressed his bewilderment, "When is it, one must wonder, that the psychotherapist came to play such an indispensable role in the maintenance of the citizenry's mental health?"[59]

Scientology. Scientology, which has gathered much publicity, called itself the "largest mental health organization in the world." When faced with the threat of regulation, it soon claimed to be a religion or church. It condemns psychiatric treatment and aims to supplant psychiatry. It investigates the professional and personal activities of psychiatrists, pickets mental hospitals, and demonstrates at annual meetings of the American Psychiatric Association. It proclaims its "applied religious philosophy" as the way to "step into the exciting world of the totally free."[60]

Scientology's philosophy is part sci-fi, part self-help. Founder L. Ron Hubbard wrote that people are spirits who were banished to Earth 75 million years ago by an evil galactic ruler and need to be cleared of problems and ailments that they have picked up in previous lives by going through a series of auditing sessions with a trained counselor. Scientology is best known for celebrity members such as John Travolta and Tom Cruise.

The U.S. District Court for the District of Columbia ruled that Scientologists may use, sell, or distribute their controversial E-meters "only for use in bona fide religious counseling." The E-meter, a device for measuring electrical skin resistance, is used during auditing, a hypnosis-like procedure in which a counselor unveils a person's engrams for the purpose of "improving health, intelligence, skill, and appearance." Judge Gesell condemned the medical value of the device but denied a request from the Food and Drug Administration that Scientology be entirely prohibited from using it. Judge Gesell restricted the use of the E-meter under limitations within the "church of Scientology." In a previous ruling in the case, a jury sided with the government in condemning the E-meters, but that decision was later reversed by an appeals court on grounds that the Founding Church of Scientology has not been shown not to be a bona fide religion and that the auditing practices of Scientology and the accounts of it are religious doctrine. The appellate court then ordered a new trial, which Judge Gesell heard without a jury.

In addition to restricting the use of the E-meter to religious counseling, Judge Gesell ordered that the device bear a "prominent, clearly visible notice warning that any person using it for auditing or counseling of any kind is prohibited by law to represent that there is any medical or scientific basis [in it] [or] that the device is useful in the diagnosis treatment, or prevention of any disease." The warning must also note that the device has been condemned by the court "for misrepresentation and misbranding" under the food and drug laws and can be used only as part of a religious activity.[61]

Orgone Therapy. Judge Gesell's judgment is reminiscent of the case of psychoanalyst Wilhelm Reich (1897–1951), who was put out of business, not by any organization of physicians or psychologists, but by the Food and Drug Administration. Reich had developed a sex-based method, known as the *orgone theory*, designed to improve orgastic potency, which he elaborates on in his famous and influential book, *The Function of the Orgasm*, first published in 1942.[62] Reich believed sexual energy to be visible and measurable (by means of complicated instruments that he invented) and to function by entirely different laws from those known to physical science. From his earliest clinical observations to his orgone experiments, Reich believed that the prospects for human freedom and happiness depend on our ability to fully affirm our sexual, animal nature. His claims for the *orgone*, as he called his discovery, became increasingly extravagant, culminating in his conviction that it was the only hope of mankind. He got a two-year federal prison sentence for selling his notorious but harmless "orgone box" across state lines. The box, a closetlike container made of sheet metal and Celotex, was said to gather orgone energy from the cosmos and transmit it, with beneficial psychological effects, to anyone who sat inside.

Sex Therapy. Sex therapy is probably the most successful of all the psychological therapies. It deals only with sexual problems so it cannot be regarded as a mainstream psychotherapy. The boom time for sex therapy began in the early 1970s, following the work of researchers Dr. William H. Masters and Virginia Johnson of the Reproductive Biology Research Foundation in St. Louis, Missouri. Pioneers in psychiatry like Havelock Ellis, Krafft-Ebing,[63] and Freud focused broadly on human sexuality, but the research by Masters and Johnson has been more specifically on physiological responses to sexual stimulation and a treatment method to deal with specific sexual complaints. They were accused of mechanizing and dehumanizing sex, of ignoring love and psychology, and of prostituting the most intimate expression to exercises in technique. Even more controversial were some of the methods they developed to treat heretofore incurable cases of male sexual inadequacy through the use of "surrogate wives"—otherwise known as "in-bed therapists." They said that "there is no such thing as an uninvolved partner in any marriage in which there is some form of sexual inadequacy";[64] hence, a marital unit was seen together, but a surrogate was used in cases of partnerless men. Stemming from one of these cases was an alienation-of-affection suit brought by one George E. Calvert against Dr. Masters and several "John Doe" defendants, alleging that without his knowledge or consent his wife was persuaded by Dr. Masters to serve as a surrogate partner, being paid $500 for the first time and $250 for each subsequent sexual service. An out-of-court settlement was reached.

The issue of treatment of symptoms versus treatment of underlying causes of a disorder finds expression in the controversy over techniques employed in sex clinics. Critics argue that sexual expression is not separate but a part of the person, that sexual physiology reflects the psychological but has little to offer in itself, and that sexual problems, unless they are caused by simple ignorance, which is rare, are likely to require long psychological, and not always successful, treatment. In a critical essay, Dr. Natalie Shainess wrote that Xaviera Hollander, the Dutch madam, may find irony in the fact that while she was fighting deportation proceedings in the United States, Masters and Johnson were receiving prizes, honors, and awards. They have been placed on the board of almost every organization even remotely dealing with sex and are on the advisory boards of professional journals. Shainess quoted Hollander who, in her best-seller *The Happy Hooker,* wrote of her services to her clients: "My method is basically the same principle as Masters and Johnson's, only they charge thousands and it's called therapy. I charge fifty dollars and it's called prostitution."[65]

In the wake of Masters and Johnson, numerous sex clinics of the same type as theirs sprung up around the country. The use of surrogate sexual partners, because of the lawsuit and adverse publicity, was discontinued at the St. Louis clinic. Masters and Johnson emphasized, however, the need to understand first the fundamental mechanics of sex. (Some observers say that Americans seem to be the only people in the world who feel a need for instructions on how to copulate.) Masters and Johnson reported an overall success rate of 80 percent in the varieties of sexual disorders that they treated. Their style of therapy was *behavior therapy,* or *conditioning therapy* as it was once called.

The opinion that the effects of behavior therapy are superficial and do not remove the basic neurosis, and that relapse and symptom substitution are to be expected, presupposes as dogma the psychoanalytic view of neurosis and its treatment method. Traditional psychotherapy may have overemphasized the subjective antecedents of behavior. Behavior therapists deny recurrence of symptoms, relapse, and symptom substitution. They suggest that changes in thoughts and feelings may be effected by changing the way that one acts, rather than vice versa. In behavior therapy, unadaptive habits are weakened and eliminated; adaptive habits are initiated and strengthened.

Anyone can call himself a *sexologist,* or expert in human sexuality. A malpractice lawsuit by an injured client is not likely because, apart from the difficulty of establishing causation, it would probably involve embarrassing testimony of impotency. As that deterrent is thus not available, a licensing law to regulate the practice has been recommended by a number of persons in the field, notably Masters and Johnson. The popular Dr. Ruth Westheimer, a.k.a. "Dr. Ruth," offers sex advice in a syndicated column and on radio and television.[66] Nowadays, to deal with their sex problems, more people turn to Viagra rather than to psychotherapy.

Eastern Mental Disciplines. Not too long ago there was much news of the ancient Hindu mental discipline, yoga, which initially in the United States was primarily the refuge of alienated young people. Yoga has an 8,000-year history, but it is new in the Western world and has attracted wide interest. Some 100,000 Americans regularly receive Hindu literature from India. A number of gurus have come to the

United States to teach the discipline. There are now approximately a thousand yoga centers in the country, whereas a half-century ago there were fewer than ten. Lending a new respectability to the practice, doctors and researchers at universities and hospitals have investigated it as a treatment for certain diseases and as a means of therapy for drug addicts, prisoners, and mental patients. In yoga, Hindus say they seek unity with God by first controlling their bodies and minds. Through breathing, posture, and mental concentration exercises, control is sought over every organ of the body, thereby providing deep rest and relaxation.[67]

In another movement, young people have frequently been seen dressed in orange robes, such as certain swamis wear in India, standing on street corners fingering beads and chanting "Hare Krishna, Hare Krishna." *Sankirtana* (congregational chanting) is carried to the people in public parks, schools, on television, in the theater, and on the streets. By chanting and engagement in the service of Krishna, anyone who takes part supposedly will experience the state of *samadhi* (absorption in God's consciousness). The International Society for Krishna Consciousness was formed in 1966 by His Divine Grace A. C. Bhaktivedanta Swami Prabhupada, who came from India on "the order of his spiritual master to preach love of God to the people of the West."[68]

Counseling by Lay Persons. Some efforts have been made to utilize lay persons in counseling work. One pilot program trained "mental-health counselors."[69] The assumption underlying this experiment was that in general, short-term psychotherapy can effectively be done by nonmedical mental health workers. The group chosen to be trained consisted of middle-aged women, experienced in child rearing and family living, who were looking for constructive activity outside the home. On the whole, their efforts achieved good results, but they suffered from the inability to raise the expectations of their patients. The magic element, it was found, is diminished when the therapist does not stand out as different, apart from the great mass of people. North Dakota has experimented with bartenders and beauticians as licensed therapists and counselors.

Comments. Just as a country's artistic and social institutions usually reflect its particular outlook on life, the kind of psychotherapy practiced there often expresses its characteristic philosophy. The increasing Westernization of so-called underdeveloped countries may make their own therapies decreasingly effective. Contrariwise, some Eastern practices now in vogue among certain elements in the United States are not sustained by the dominant culture and can hardly be expected to be effective for the general population or to endure. A cartoon depicts a wealthy businessman, with briefcase, sitting in a chauffeured limousine chanting, "Krishna, Krishna, Hare Hare." Such out-of-the-ordinariness provokes laughter.

Various programs are indicative of the growing awareness that the treatment for many mental illnesses must meet the cultural expectations of the patient and that virtually every culture has given rise to healers who are as effective in dealing with mental problems among their own people as are psychiatrists in Western society. The National Institute of Mental Health, in one of its projects to improve the delivery of psychiatric services, employed some Navajo Indian medicine men on a reservation in Arizona to teach young Indians the elaborate ancient chants that often cure the mental ailments of Navajos.

In Africa, a stronghold of the witchcraft theory of disease and disorder, Dr.

Thomas A. Lambo, a Nigerian who graduated from Britain's Royal College of Surgeons and for many years the only native formally educated psychiatrist in Africa, has tried to suit the cure to the patient by prescribing (with apparent success) animal sacrifices, rituals, and dances. Dr. Lambo, later named director-general of the World Health Organization, said that the most common anxieties he had to deal with are women's fear of not being able to bear children and men's fear that enemies are trying to kill them by witchcraft. So, treating them with therapies that fall within their experience rather than with Western methods, he has integrated indigenous magic with modified urban.

Psychiatrists may dislike such jocular sobriquets as "faith-healer," "head-shrinker," or "medicine man," but there may be more truth than metaphorical cleverness in the terms. (A *headshrinker* is a witchdoctor whose knowledge of the occult constitutes a powerful magic that justifies the reestablishment of infantile dependency.) Among others, it is the thesis of Dr. E. Fuller Torrey, then of the NIMH's International Activities Branch, that "witchdoctors and psychiatrists perform essentially the same function in their respective cultures."[70] He made a study of indigenous psychotherapists in several parts of the world and learned from the so-called witchdoctors that he, as a psychiatrist, was using the same mechanisms for curing his patients as they were and getting about the same results. (In many cultures, however, the therapist can collect his fee only if the patient gets well.) In the Western scientific world, psychiatrists plaster their office with diplomas (often in Latin), while a witchdoctor achieves the same effect by rattling a sacred gourd.

Torrey cites four basic components of curing used by psychotherapists all over the world. The first is naming the affliction (a step that removes the frightening element of the unknown); the second is the effect of their own personal qualities (successful healers have accurate empathy, nonpossessive warmth, and genuineness); the third is the patient's expectation (the great importance of patients' expectations is clearly seen in the use of placebos, the pilgrimage, and the building used for the healing); the fourth comprises the techniques of therapy (some cultures favor one technique over others, but the same techniques are used all over the world).[71]

Administration of Regulatory Acts

Most regulatory legislation provides for boards to administer the provisions of the acts; the size of the boards varies among the states. Most boards are composed of representatives of groups with direct interest in the areas being regulated, a natural result of the requirement that members of the board must be licensed or be qualified to be licensed under the provisions of the act. Quite frequently, these statutes provide that members of the board shall be selected by the governor from a list supplied him by the local state society of the particular profession.[72]

The board's authority usually includes the power to create rules and regulations relative to professional qualifications and the ways and means of testing these qualifications. The California Psychology Licensing Law provides that the examination may be "for knowledge in whatever theoretical or applied fields of psychology as it deems appropriate."[73] The Louisiana Psychology Certification Act simply states that "the examination shall be of such form and content as determined by the board."[74]

There is some question, however, as to whether such broad discretion can be granted the board. The Florida Supreme Court ruled unconstitutional its statute regulating psychology, saying that there was a failure to fix the standards to be applied, which, in effect, delegated the application of the statute without sufficient limitations to the discretion of the board.[75] On the other hand, other courts seem prepared to sustain a delegation of power that is quite wide in scope. The Illinois Supreme Court held that its Medical Practice Act was not invalid in directing the administrative board to do certain things, such as the issuance of a license to practice after the passing of an examination by the applicant to the satisfaction of the department, without furnishing a standard for its guidance.[76]

A common and controversial provision in most licensing acts is one that exempts certain fields and persons from coverage under the act. There is strong indication that the present laws on the practice of psychology cover only the applied activities of psychologists rather than their teaching and research activities. The Committee on Legislation of the American Psychological Association contends that to require the nonpracticing, salaried psychologist of state and federal agencies, research laboratories, or academic institutions to be certified or licensed is contrary to the generally stated purposes of legislation, since there would be little need to protect the public from teaching and research activities.[77] However, it is becoming increasingly common for psychologists employed for a salary by various institutions also to provide direct services of an applied nature to the public, often for a fee.

In the statutes regulating the control of psychology, it is common to find that licensing is not required of all or some of the following groups: (1) teachers and counselors in recognized public and private educational institutions; (2) clergy and other employees of religious organizations; (3) practitioners of medicine; (4) social welfare workers; (5) students of psychology, psychological interns, other persons preparing for licensing, and persons working as assistants to a licensed individual; and (6) persons using psychological techniques in the course of employment by government institutions, as employment-office workers for business and industrial organizations, or as employment-agency workers engaged in employment evaluation for job seekers.

Specific provisions allow out-of-state physicians who are called in for consultation by a physician an exemption from the provisions of the acts. It is also quite common to allow an out-of-state physician a limited number of days of practice in the state without complying with the regulations.[78] Provisions quite similar to these are also found in the acts governing the practice of psychology.

The provisions of a state statute do not apply to persons serving in the armed services. The federal government has control over its military forces, and the states in which these forces operate cannot interfere with their activities. Officials of the federal Public Health Services of the Veterans Administration also are not subject to state licensing provisions as a condition to the performance of their public function. However, the VA requires licensure in some states.

It has also been held that regulators cannot discipline the director of a health insurer for denying treatment to a patient whose physician had said that it was medically necessary. The various states have tried to make medical directors at health maintenance organizations and other managed care groups subject to the same licensing and disciplinary oversight as other physicians. About half of the states require HMO medical directors who make decisions about whether to pay for treatments to be licensed physicians. A federal judge has ruled that a decision on coverage is not the practice of medicine and that coverage determinations is preempted by federal law. A 1974 federal law that governs employee benefit plans bars state officials from disciplining managed care medical directors for decisions about whether to pay for treatments.[79]

Suspension or Revocation of Licensure. The grounds on which a practitioner's license may be forfeited or suspended are usually borrowed from the canons of ethics of the particular profession or from the preexisting principles of case law.[80] The grounds vary from state to state, but a few are common to all: commission of crime; unprofessional and dishonorable conduct; certain kinds of personal incapacity, such as excessive use of intoxicants or addiction to drugs; and judgment of insanity by a court.[81] Only a handful of states specify incompetence as a basis for disciplinary action.[82]

Normally the board that is entrusted with the power to examine applicants and issue licenses or certificates is also given the power to conduct hearings and suspend, revoke, or deny licenses. Generally, it is also entitled to seek judicial action in order to enforce its rules. The full requirements of notice and hearing by the board may be and often are dispensed with if a criminal trial and conviction precedes the board's proceeding. In New York, a felony conviction is per se a ground of revocation; no further hearing is necessary. Most states, however, merely provide that the conviction of certain crimes shall be a ground for revocation.

The board does not go on a fishing expedition; it awaits a formal complaint. The burden of proof in these hearings rests upon the party initiating the board action. The board is not bound by the strict rules of evidence and is usually quite liberal in what it allows as evidence. Rules of evidence need not be applied in board hearings, but its decisions may not be "arbitrary and capricious."[83] The statutes usually grant the board the power to subpoena witnesses, records, and papers, and to administer oaths in taking testimony. Most statutes provide for a review by the judiciary.

Under most statutes, even when cause has been established, suspension or revocation of a license is not mandatory on the board. The statutes provide that a license may be revoked or invalidated. Throughout the country, a license is virtually a blank check; once a license is granted it is virtually permanent, subject only to the payment of a periodic fee. Self-regulation tends to provide not regulation, but protectionism. In 1961, the board of trustees of the American Medical Association, alarmed by the growing problems of discipline within the medical profession with the resultant increasing public apprehension and lack of confidence, appointed a Medical Disciplinary Committee, which concluded: "Medicine's efforts have largely ceased with the discharge of the licensing function. All too seldom are licensed physicians called to task by boards, societies, or colleagues. The Committee would suggest that greater emphasis be given to ensuring competence and observance of law and ethics after licensure."[84]

The AMA committee suggested a reappraisal of the primary function of state medical boards. There has been, however, little change in emphasis or in the development of a more comprehensive approach to the disciplinary problem. State medical licensing boards do not generally pursue their disciplinary functions. Even if a repeated offender is expelled from his medical society and removed from his hospital staff, he can still legally practice medicine as long as he continues to be licensed. Currently the only remedy, if any, apparently is the malpractice suit.

Other Legislation Controlling the Practice of Psychotherapy. The medical practice acts, which define *medical practice* and require practitioners to possess a physician's license, usually apply expressly to the treatment of both mental and physical afflictions and therefore may include psychotherapy within their scope.[85] A few of the physicians' licensure acts, however, do not appear to regulate the practice of psychotherapy at all. For example, the Oklahoma act regards a person as practicing medicine when he treats disease, injury, or deformity of persons by any drugs, surgery, and manual or mechanical treatment.[86] The South Dakota statute defines the practice of medicine as prescribing any drug, medicine, apparatus, or other agency for the cure, relief, or palliation of any ailment or disease.[87] North Carolina and Minnesota specifically omit persons who endeavor to prevent or cure disease or suffering by mental or spiritual means.[88] Tennessee and Ohio define the practice of medicine as treatment of physical ailments or physical injuries.[89]

Opinions of a number of state legal officers have stated that the practice of psychotherapy is not restricted to physicians. In 1959, the New York State Education Department, which is responsible for administering the laws governing all professions in New York, ruled that the use of the title "psychotherapist" was not restricted to physicians by the Medical Practices Act. This ruling was arrived at following extensive hearings, at which representatives of the several professions active in the mental health field were heard. Earlier, in 1956, the attorney general of Michigan rendered an opinion on the question of whether the practice of "psychotherapeutics" by psychologists constituted the practice of medicine within the meaning of the state's Medical Practices Act. It was concluded, "Therapy as such is not prohibited by the Medical Practices Act, which covers only therapy medical in nature." Psychologists and others are not in violation of this act unless they "purport or attempt to cure any physical ailment by the laying on of hands, by magnetic suggestion, or other form of medical or surgical treatment." In 1967, after considerable study of the issue of nonmedical psychotherapy, the attorney general of California reversed his own previous opinion and ruled that psychologists could perform psychotherapy.

Technically speaking, however, in those jurisdictions where the practice of medicine expressly or by implication includes the care of mental afflictions, it is possible that a non-M.D. psychotherapist, when he treats the emotionally distressed, impinges upon the practice of medicine. The courts, however, are unlikely to say that a non-M.D. psychotherapist who treats cases of extreme mental disturbance is illegally practicing medicine.

The California Psychology Licensing Law provides that any person who holds himself out to the public by any title or description incorporating the words *psychology, psychological, psychologist, psychometry, or psychometrist, psychotherapy, psychotherapist, psychoanalysis,* or *psychoanalyst* is representing himself to be a psychologist.[90] The statute defines *psychotherapy* as "the use of psychological methods in a professional relationship to assist a person or persons to acquire greater human effectiveness or to modify feelings, conditions, attitudes, and behavior which are emotionally, intellectually, or socially ineffectual or maladjustive." The California attorney general expressed the opinion that marriage-, family-, or child-counselors might use some psychotherapeutic measure in connection with their work, and while the use of the term *psychotherapist* by a counselor is not proscribed by any statutory provision, the misuse of the term might bring one within the prohibitions in the Psychology Licensing Law and become the basis for disciplinary action.[91]

Informal Regulation of Psychotherapy. Informal or indirect control may have greater impact or at least is as important in influencing a practice as is formal or direct control by licensing or certification. Indeed, explicit regulation of practice is exceedingly difficult. Some have despaired to the extent that support is given only to certification laws that regulate the use of a title rather than to licensing laws that would attempt to regulate a practice.

Indirect controls include taxation, insurance, institutional employment opportunities, tort liability for malpractice, and telephone listings. In particular, tax and insurance considerations may determine whether a practice will prosper or perish. Scientology found it expedient to call itself a church, thereby obtaining benefits accorded religious bodies.

Under the Internal Revenue Code, payments to a psychiatrist, psychologist, or Christian Science practitioner, among others, qualify as a medical tax deduction. Payments are allowed as a deduction under the code for "diagnosis, cure, mitigation, treatment, or prevention of disease or for the purpose of affecting any structure or function of the body."[92] In checking with one Internal Revenue Service office, I was told that payments to social workers do not qualify because "they [social workers] turn you off rather than on with their attitudes."

Insurance plans usually cover only limited inpatient treatment. Many policies specifically exclude "mental illness or emotional or personality disorder except as an inpatient in a general hospital not specializing in the treatment of mental illness." Even insurers that offer contracts that cover the diagnosis and treatment of mental and nervous disorders in a number of instances have refused to reimburse patients for psychologists' services unless these services were under medical referral or supervision. Medicare, Medicaid, and Workers' Compensation present a similar picture. A Social Security amendment that would have enabled licensed psychologists to provide mental health care to Medicare recipients without a physician's prior approval and outside a physician's plan of treatment was turned down in 1972 by the Senate. One senator noted that patients would be better off with physicians who can prescribe drugs on a one-stop basis, since psychologists are not allowed to prescribe drugs. Most states now accept qualified psychologists as independent providers of services.

Institutional employment opportunity is another factor influencing a practice and the development of training and education programs. Here may be noted the decision of the Veterans Administration after World War II to employ large numbers of clinical psychologists, thus creating a market demand. It resulted in pressure for the development of the so-called School of Professional Psychology. Distribution of training grants from the NIMH, while providing important support for psychology as well as social work, has been directed primarily toward the training of psychiatrists.

The acceptance of the psychologist by the courts as an expert witness on the diagnosis and treatment of mental disorders on a par with psychiatrists has generated support for the professional autonomy of psychologists.[93] More recent developments in the area of right to treatment can be interpreted as sanctioning increased utilization and independence for psychologists and other qualified mental health professionals. In the private or quasi-public sector is the question of role of the non-M.D. in the hospital. Some general hospitals have granted staff privileges to psychologists. At present, psychologists are not formally members of the Joint Commission on Accreditation of Healthcare Organization's Council on psychiatric facilities, although it is on the JCAHO's Council on facilities for the mentally retarded.

Regulatory statutes affect malpractice law to the extent that violations may be admissible as evidence of negligence, but even apart from such statutes, negligence may be established and as a result may deter a practice. The threat of suit for malpractice is probably the most effective regulator of the practice of medicine. In like fashion, the risk of a malpractice suit would tend to control the activities of persons who present themselves as psychotherapists. Thus, a marriage counselor would hesitate to conduct psychotherapy with a suicidal person if he could be held responsible for the suicide.

Another important type of control is the telephone directory. Probably the principal way that a professional representation is made known to the public is the listing in the telephone directory. Indeed, listing is so vital to one in business that negligent omission in publishing a name has given rise to legal actions for damages in six figures. The telephone company offers or approves the various headings that appear in its directory, one consideration being the amount of advertising that will appear under the heading, but thereafter apparently exercises little supervision over names published under a particular heading. Telephone companies usually have no policy on checking the credentials of professional listings in directories. In response to my inquiry, one telephone business office simplistically advised: "Normally our customers are honest. The subscriber knows what listing he should be under, and he is not going to mislead because it is to his benefit to be under the right heading. A person who is a plumber would not want to be listed as a physician." In some states, an advertising agency publishes the directory, the telephone company having no voice in the matter other than that the subscriber be a customer.

The New York Telephone Company, after prodding by the state attorney general's office, agreed to start checking the professional qualifications and licenses of persons listed as physicians or psychologists in telephone books throughout the state. The phone company's action came after a partial survey by the attorney general's Bureau of Consumer Fraud and Protection disclosed that nearly 10 percent of the listings under those titles in Manhattan, Brooklyn, and Nassau were of unlicensed persons. The attorney general acted following complaints from the state's Psychological Association and Medical Society that the phone company had refused to determine whether applicants for listing under the two categories were duly licensed to practice as required by law. The Psychological Association, in its complaint, said that "upwards of fifty persons who are not licensed as psychologists are listed in the current Yellow Pages across the state under that heading." The Medical Society's complaint also charged that a cursory examination of the white and yellow pages of directories under the heading "Physicians" had revealed the names of "chiropractors, family counselors, and other unlicensed persons."[94]

Establishing Statutory Control for Psychotherapy. Concerned about the variance of the legal status of psychotherapists among the different states, the American

Orthopsychiatric Association in 1967 formed a committee to formulate a model statute for the practice of psychotherapy, regardless of professional discipline.[95] Initially, the committee addressed itself to defining the underlying objectives of such a statute. This entailed exploration of the existing situation that such action was intended to ameliorate. Most of the substantive advice given the committee focused on the disadvantages of the proposed model statute, stimulating the committee to consider the possible undesirable consequences of a legislative approach.

As a result of these efforts, the committee concluded that psychotherapy, as a function of several different professions, did not require statutory control. As a separate and distinct profession, psychotherapists did not impress the committee, at that time, as being sufficient in numbers or organizational maturity to warrant legislation. It was the committee's opinion that legislation controlling the profession of psychotherapists (distinguished from psychotherapy practiced as one of the functions of another profession, e.g., medicine, psychology, social work, etc.) would be premature. It seemed untimely to run the risk of legislatively freezing the current situation just as nontraditional mental health workers are becoming more active. The traditional professions do not appear to require additional protection; therefore the possibility of inhibiting innovation should be avoided. The extent to which the public is hurt by quackery advertised under the rubric of psychotherapy appeared to be minimal. Although the shortage of data as to who helps and who harms people presents difficulties, the committee nevertheless concluded that there was scant evidence of the title "psychotherapist" being abused.

However, in 1972, following a six-month investigation into the practices of unlicensed mental health therapists, New York Attorney General Louis J. Lefkowitz reported evidence of widespread quackery, sexual misconduct, and the deception of clients through the use of phony academic credentials and titles. A public hearing was held to expose these practices by unlicensed therapists and others purporting to practice as psychotherapists, psychoanalysts, hypnotists, and marriage counselors. The findings, as charged by investigators, include the following:

1. Clients are misled by bogus degrees and titles used and displayed by therapists. Investigators visiting the therapists found more than a dozen degrees, achievement awards, and honorary titles on the walls. One honorary degree from the London Institute for Applied Research is advertised for sale in the magazine for Diner's Club members. (A Viennese diploma is more impressive.)

2. A "great deal of sexual interplay" is routinely imposed on women clients in the name of therapy by male practitioners. According to the investigators, there exists a pattern among male therapists and young female patients whereby the therapist informs the patient that in order for her to work out her problems, she should engage in sexual activities with him. The patients are charged for this stud treatment; otherwise it could not be rationalized as treatment.

3. Hard-sell techniques, similar to the representations made by some dance-lesson studios, are used to entice patients into paying for training as therapists themselves.

4. Patients are encouraged to immerse themselves in the therapy by forsaking friends and contacts outside the therapy group, a situation often resulting in broken marriages and neglected medical and psychiatric problems.

5. The parents of several young psychotherapy clients have offered to pay the therapist to "release" their children from the programs.[96]

Four months later a bill was introduced in the New York Assembly seeking to define the practice of psychological testing and to limit work in the field to persons working under the supervision of a licensed psychologist, physician, registered nurse, or social worker. Strong opposition to the bill was mounted by mental health workers outside the established associations who charged that the proposal would grant a monopoly of the mental health field to a few professionals with advanced degrees, would stifle innovation in the treatment of mental problems, and would put both mental care and career opportunities in the field beyond the reach of poor people.[97] An editorial in the *New York Times*, pointing to the "irreparable harm that has undoubtedly been done to many troubled people whose need for help was compounded by incompetence or outright exploitation," endorsed the bill, but at the same time noted that "unhappy experiences with overly academic and theoretical licensing criteria in education ought to serve as a caution in the mental health field, with its divergent practical and clinical missions and problems."[98] The bill was rejected.[99]

In the latter part of the twentieth century, out of the controversy over repressed memories of child sexual abuse came proposals, as noted in chapter 4, for a new law, the Truth and Responsibility in Mental Health Practices Act. Indiana has enacted a new law on therapeutic practices and informed consent and several other states are reexamining their laws. In his report on mental health, Surgeon General David Satcher said that the public should be able to expect therapy that is safe and effective. The report recommended the implementation of specific treatment methods, referred to as "evidence based practices," that have proven to be effective in the treatment of mental illness.[100] Continuing education programs have been established, but one may wonder what they have accomplished apart from creating a market for speakers. Licensing boards tend to accept credentials at face value in the admission of an applicant to a profession and are more preoccupied with disciplinary matters.

In the 1980s, as noted, adults began suing their parents and others for sexual abuse that had allegedly occurred decades before but had been remembered only recently, usually in the course of psychotherapy. The 1980s saw a wave of shocking allegations that young children were being sexually abused in bizarre and hideous ways. The testimony of children—often coached by well-meaning but badly trained therapists and pushed by zealous prosecutors—sent a number of innocent people to jail, as depicted in the film *The Jaundiced Eye* (the film's title comes from a poem by Alexander Pope, suggesting that those who are determined to see the world in a certain way will find all the evidence they need to support their views).[101]

Finding that professional organizations and licensing boards were of little or no assistance in dealing with malpsychotherapy, as we have noted in chapter 4, on malpractice, educational psychologist Dr. Pamela Freyd in 1992 brought about the False Memory Syndrome Foundation. The inability of the states' disciplinary process to control highly unconventional therapies was earlier highlighted by the widely publicized case involving the suicide of Paul Lozano, a Harvard medical student, who was treated by a Harvard psychiatrist, Dr. Margaret Bean-Bayog. The therapy, which Dr. Bean-Bayog herself acknowledged as "somewhat unconventional," involved her playing the role of a "nonabusive mom." The nature of the therapy came to light when Lozano consulted another psychiatrist, who complained to the Massachusetts Board of Registration in Medicine, but no action was taken.[102] A wrongful death lawsuit brought about suspension of the doctor's license.

A series of successful lawsuits by retractors and parents against therapists using recovered memory therapy also had a number of consequences. Studies of memory were stimulated.[103] The late Dr. Martin Orne, who helped found the FMS Foundation, showed that adults under hypnosis are not literally reliving their early childhoods but presenting them through the prisms of adulthood.[104] In 1993, and again in 2000, the American Psychiatric Association cautioned its members that memories obtained by recovered memory techniques are often not true and that memories obtained under hypnosis may be unreliable. The legal liability associated with recovered memory therapy and hypnosis prompted insurance malpractice carriers to exclude or otherwise limit coverage involving the use of hypnosis in therapy.[105] A number of psychiatric clinics specializing in the treatment of dissociative disorders have closed.

In the popular novel *False Memory*, Dean Koontz wrote, "A therapist without finesse can easily, unwittingly implant false memories. Any hypnotized subject is vulnerable. And if the therapist has an agenda and isn't ethical . . ."[106] Koontz's psychiatrist is an utterly evil character with no sympathetic qualities whatsoever. Koontz clearly wished to portray him as a modern Satan (and he signals that at the outset by naming him Dr. Ahriman, the name of the Zoroastrian devil). He is the most frightening villain in any of Koontz's novels. But the problem is not utterly evil characters; they are found out—much more difficult are the legions of well-intentioned therapists who unwittingly create the environments that foster false memories or other inept psychotherapy. In response to my inquiry, Koontz said:

> Indeed, there is need to set standards for those who want to use the title "psychotherapist." But there should also be meaningful peer review and discipline for those erring practitioners who then meet the standards. Of course, the peer review and policing in the medical profession is all but an abject failure, so I'm not sure there is an easy solution. My feeling is that society needs to be weaned away from the dependency and blind trust in "experts" of all kinds, and that the average person needs to be better educated and then encouraged to trust more in his commonsense.[107]

In 1910 Freud published a paper attacking what he called "wild analysis." He expressed concern that use of psychoanalytic theories by those untrained in psychoanalysis would cause harm. Coincidentally, also in 1910, there appeared the report by Abraham Flexner calling for standards in medical education in order to deal with the pervasive quackery in the practice of medicine. As recently as the end of the nineteenth century, medical education in the United States was in a deplorable state. Hundreds of medical schools were little more than academically anemic apprenticeships. A revolution in medical education resulted from the Flexner report. Medical schools were overhauled, many were closed and the curriculum became science-based. Several contemporary observers have made the analogy between medical education at the end of the nineteenth century and professional education of psychotherapists today. Considering the current scene, Freud's "On 'Wild' Analysis" proved prescient. There are increasing calls for another Flexner report to deal with standards in psychotherapy.[108]

And what about cyberpsych practice on the Internet? In an address at the 2002 annual meeting of the Association of American Law Schools titled "The Illusory Regulation of Psychology: The Teletherapy Example," Professor George J. Alexander of the Santa Clara Law School observed, "Aside from prohibiting unlicensed persons from claiming to be psychologists, all but two states prohibit unlicensed persons from practicing psychology. Despite this fact, the practice of cyberpsych is a booming industry on the internet. There is a dearth of enforcement of state regulation of interstate practice, and effective enforcement is unlikely in the future."[109]

Conclusion

The legal regulation of psychotherapy revolves around the controversy about the medical model and its appropriateness as an approach to the problems of mental illness. Developments in the neurosciences are increasingly expected to inform about the appropriate type of treatment in a given case.[110] In any event, if psychotherapy is indeed a form of education and not part of any medical system, then the legal regulation of psychotherapy becomes similar to the legal regulation of education.[111] In a sense, the process of psychotherapy is to impose order out of chaos. In the course of therapy, the poet Anne Sexton said that the analyst "gives pattern and meaning to what the person sees as only incoherent experience."[112] The task of psychotherapy is to offer the individual a more satisfactory life story or help the individual to move on in the story he already has. Mostly, people enter therapy when they are stuck in a certain chapter of their life and do not know what they want to do next or do not like what they see ahead. The dreams of one in psychoanalysis are often a symbol of a journey. A successful therapeutic experience helps reestablish the narrative flow, reawaken a sense of meaning in one's life, and restore personal control.[113]

Unfortunately, even the best of therapy does not always succeed. In spite of (or because of) therapy, Anne Sexton committed suicide.

Notes

1. J. S. Handler, "Psychotherapy and Medical Responsibility," *Arch. Gen. Psychiatry* 1 (1959): 464.

2. L. S. Kubie, "The General Nature of Non-Technical Psychotherapy," L. S. Kubie, *Practical and Theoretical Aspects of Psychoanalysis* (New York: International Universities Press, 1950), p. 21.

3. T. S. Szasz, "Psychoanalytic Treatment as Education," *Arch. Gen. Psychiatry* 9 (1963): 46.

4. See K. R. Eissler, *Medical Orthodoxy and the Future of Psychoanalysis* (New York: International Universities Press, 1965); E. Jones, *The Life and Work of Sigmund Freud* (New York: Basic Books, 1957).

5. Ibid. Edward Shorter, professor in the history of medicine, suggests that European physicians were more tolerant of lay analysis because they stood less in awe of themselves generally. In Central Europe, a whole host of titles, such as Herr Hofrat, Herr Geheimrat, Herr Professor, and Herr General were in usage before Herr Doktor, whereas in the United States M.D.s were at the top of the pecking order. E. Shorter, *A History of Psychiatry* (New York: Wiley, 1997), p. 371.

6. See R. S. Wallerstein, *Lay Analysis: Life inside the Controversy* (Mahwah, N.J.: Analytic Press, 1998).

7. Correspondence of Mar. 8, 1968, from George E. Hall, member of the Law Division of the American Medical Association. The psychotherapist-patient privilege in the law of evidence covers communications with a wide range of psychotherapists. See, e.g., Calif. Evidence Code, sec. 1010. Testimonial privilege is discussed in volume 1, chapter 4.

8. J. S. Handler, supra note 1. A similar but shorter definition of *psychotherapy* is that "it is an interaction between two people, one of whom knows what he is talking about—and hopefully that person is the therapist." G. D. Goldman & D. S. Milman (eds.), *Innovations in Psychotherapy* (Springfield, Ill.: Thomas, 1972), p. 235. Dr. Robert Michels notes that psychotherapy has been called the "talking cure," and he suggests that it might better be called the "listening cure." Fundamental to listening is thinking, and it is what makes psychotherapy different from simple friendship. As he puts it, the psychotherapist thinks about what the patient has disclosed about past and present, the story of the problem and of the life that preceded and continues during it. The therapist thinks about what is said, and avoided, during the session. The therapist thinks about his own thoughts and feelings, both those that seem relevant to the therapy and those that don't. Finally, the therapist thinks about theories, the concepts that link the other thoughts together and that generate ideas about what the therapist will say when the listening cure shifts to become a talking cure. R. Michels, "Thinking While Listening," address at the annual meeting of the American Psychiatric Association on May 16, 2000, in Chicago.

9. T. S. Szasz, "Psychiatry, Psychotherapy, and Psychology," *Arch. Gen. Psychiatry* 5 (1959): 455. See also A. Fischer, "Non-Medical Psychotherapists," *Arch. Gen. Psychiatry* 5 (1961): 7; P. E. Huston, "The Relations of Psychiatry and Psychotherapy," *Am. J. Psychiatry* 110 (1954): 814.

10. S. M. Mirin, "Predictions about the Financing and Delivery of Care," in S. Weissman, M. Sabshin, & H. Eist (eds.), *Psychiatry in the New Millennium* (Washington, D.C.: American Psychiatric Press, 1999), p. 321.

11. Final Report of Joint Commission on Mental Illness and Health, *Action for Mental Health* (1961).

12. R. R. Holt (ed.), *New Horizon for Psychotherapy: Autonomy as a Profession* (New York: International Universities Press, 1971); L. S. Kubie, "Need for a New Sub-Discipline in the Medical Profession," *Arch. Neur. & Psychiatry* 78 (1957): 283; Symposium, "Qualifications for Psychotherapy," *Am. J. Orthopsychiatry* 26 (1956): 35.

13. J. D. Frank, *Persuasion and Healing: A Comparative Study of Psychotherapy* (Baltimore: John Hopkins University Press, 1961).

14. S. Blakeslee, "Placebos Prove So Powerful Even Experts Are Surprised," *New York Times,* Oct. 13, 1998, p. D-1; J. Horhan, "Placebo Nation," *New York Times,* Mar. 21, 1999, p. WK-15.

15. *New Introductory Lectures on Psychoanalysis (Standard Edition)* (London: Hogarth, 1960), vol. 22.

16. See R. Shyrock, *Medical Licensing in America, 1950–1965* (Baltimore: John Hopkins Press, 1967); F. Auman, "The Growth and Regulation of the Licensing Process in Ohio," *J. Can. L. Rev.* 21 (1931): 97.

17. The right of the states to regulate the practice of medicine or other regulation is based on constitutional grounds and traditional interpretations of states' rights. As the power to regulate the health professions was not specifically entrusted to Congress, the Tenth Amendment reserves the power to the states and the people. Under the police power, states have the authority to pass regulations to protect the public health and safety of their citizens. In Dent v. West Virginia, 129 U.S. 114 (1889), the U.S. Supreme Court upheld the state's right to require licensure to engage in medical practice, holding that the establishment of minimum standards for licensure did not violate an individual's property rights as protected under the Fourteenth Amendment. Critics charge that through the establishment of cumbersome licensure processes, the mobility of competent professionals is unfairly restricted. Balancing the interests of access to care and public protection has now come to the fore in regard interstate telemedicine licensure and cybermedicine. See R. D. Silverman, "Regulating Medical Practice in the Cyber Age: Issues and Challenges for State Medical Boards," *Am. J. Law & Med.* 26 (2000): 255; see also B. Shartel & M. L. Plant, *The Law of Medical Practice* (Springfield, Ill.: Thomas, 1959), p. 195.

As a prefatory comment, the Florida legislature set out the intent of the legislation regulating professions and occupations: "The Legislature finds that as society becomes increasingly complex, emotional survival is equal in importance to physical survival. Therefore, in order to preserve the health, safety, and welfare of the public, the Legislature must provide privileged communication for members of the public or those acting on their behalf to encourage needed or desired psychological services to be sought out. The Legislature further finds that, since the psychological services assist the public primarily with emotional survival, which in turn affects physical and psychophysical survival, the practice of psychology and school psychology by unqualified persons presents a danger to public health, safety, and welfare." Fla. Stat. Ann., vol. 15c, sec. 490.002.

In Lawrence Kasdan's comedy film *Mumford*, the hero is a charlatan with no therapeutic training. The credentials on his office wall are bogus. While the film appears to be enthusiastically protherapy, it is also antitherapist in its implication that any sensitive person who is a good listener could conceivably establish a successful practice without the benefits of training or certification. The film is reviewed in S. Holden, "Sure the Doctor Is In: In Demand and in Trouble," *New York Times*, Sept. 24, 1999, p. B-9.

Prophecy is not exempt from medical licensure when a clairvoyant attempts not only to predict the future but also to alter the future. In Bibber v. Simpson, 59 Me. 181 (1871), an action to recover compensation for healing services, the court held that the services rendered were medical in their character. The court noted, "True, the plaintiff does not call herself a physician, but she visits her sick patients, examines their condition, determines the nature of the disease, and prescribes the remedies deemed by her most appropriate." In Rushman v. City of Milwaukee, 959 F.Supp. 1040 (E.D.Wis. 1997), the court held that free speech guarantees protection of a person's predicting the future without a license, even if it is the future of a person's health. Fraudulent deceit, however, is actionable, as for example when a con artist predicts that the client must turn over money to the con artist (or an accomplice) based upon the client's fortune. See Spiritual Science Church of Truth v. City of Azusa, 39 Cal.3d 501, 703 P.2d 1119 (1985).

18. See W. Graves, "Professional and Occupational Restrictions," *Temp. L.Q.* 13 (1939): 334.

19. J. Baron, "Business and Professional Licensing: California, A Representative Example," *Stan. L. Rev.* 18 (1966): 640.

20. See D. B. Hogan, *The Regulation of Psychotherapists* (Cambridge: Bollinger, 1979); J. S. Lloyd & D. G. Langsley (eds.), *Evaluating the Skills of Medical Specialists* (Evanston Ill.: American Board of Medical Specialties, 1983); S. Rottenberg (ed.), *Occupational Licensure and Regulation* (Washington: American Enterprise Institute for Public Policy Research, 1980).

21. Fla. Stat. Ann. 458.305 defines the *practice of medicine* as "the diagnosis, treatment, operation, or prescription for any human disease, pain, injury, deformity, or other physical or mental condition." One who takes blood pressure tests only and announces the result without giving advice or prescribing treatment is not a "medical practitioner." Lambert v. State *ex rel.* Mathis, 77 So.2d 869 (1955). The use of the word *therapy* by a hearing aid dealer in a newspaper ad containing the statement "hearing and speech therapy" indicated the dealer "held himself out" as being able to perform or treat matters embraced within the definition of the practice of medicine. Op. Atty. Gen., 064-115 (Aug. 10, 1964). The state board of medical examiners is authorized to prevent unlicensed medical practice of "psychosomatic therapy" and "medical hypnosis" where such treatment invades the field of medical practice. Op. Atty. Gen., 056-12 (Jan. 13, 1956).

Fla. Stat. Ann., sec. 490.003 defines the *practice of psychology* as

the observations, description, evaluation, interpretation, and modification of human behavior, by the use of scientific and applied psychological principles, methods, and procedures, for the purpose of describing, preventing, alleviating, or eliminating symptomatic, maladaptive, or undesired behavior and of enhancing interpersonal behavioral health and mental or psychological health. The ethical practice of psychology includes, but is not limited to, psychological testing and the evaluation or assessment of personal characteristics such as intelligence, personality, abilities, interests, aptitudes, and neuropsychological functioning, including evaluation of mental competency to manage one's affairs and to participate in legal proceedings; counseling, psychoanalysis, all forms of psychotherapy, sex therapy, hypnosis, biofeedback, and behavioral analysis and therapy; psychoeducational evaluation, therapy, remediation, and consultation; and use of psychological methods to diagnose and treat mental, nervous, psychological, marital, or emotional disorders, illness, or disability, alcoholism and substance abuse, and disorders of habit or conduct, as well as the psychological aspects of physical illness, accident, injury, or disability, including neuropsychological evaluation, diagnosis, prognosis, etiology, and treatment.

22. See D. G. Langsley (ed.), *Legal Aspects of Certification and Accreditation* (Evanston, Ill.: American Board of Medical Specialties, 1983). In Abramson v. Gonzalez, 949 F.2d 1567 (11th Cir. 1992), where a First Amendment challenge was made to Florida's licensing and certification scheme, the majority of the court took the view that the public will not be misled if noncertified practitioners are permitted to use the title "psychologist," with the designation "certified psychologist" being reserved for those who are certified by the state. The dissent argued that reserving the use of the title "psychologist" to those who are certified advances a legitimate state interest in avoiding confusion on the part of the public as to those who do and those who do not meet the state's certification requirements.

23. American Psychological Association, Committee on Legislation, "A Model for State Legislation Affecting the Practice of Psychology, 1967," *Am. Psychol.* 22 (1967): 1097; commonly referred to as APA Model Statute Report.

24. American Association of Marriage Counselors, Report on Conference on the State Regulation of Marriage Counselors, Sept. 1964, p. 5; commonly referred to as AAMC 1964 Report.

25. Florida expressly regulates the use of the title "psychotherapist." Florida Code, sec. 490.012.

26. Correspondence (May 7, 1968) from Edward J. Rydman.

27. See, e.g., Calif. Bus. & Prof. Code 6.6:2900.

28. E.g., United States v. Cardiff, 344 U.S. 174 (1952); Connally v. General Const. Co., 269 U.S. 385 (1926).

29. State v. Errington, 355 S.W.2d 952 (Mo. 1962).

30. J. Sharkey, "Philosophers Ponder a Therapy Gold Mine," *New York Times*, Mar. 8, 1988, sec. 4, p. 1.

31. P. Koestenbaum, *The New Image of the Person: The Theory and Practice of Clinical Philosophy* (Westport, Conn.: Greenwood Press, 1978). Lou Marinoff, Ph.D., a philosophy professor at City College of New York and one of one hundred members of the fledgling American Philosophical Practitioners Association, seeks to put philosophers and psychiatrists in the same counseling status. Their approach may reduce road rage, school violence, and other by-products of an unexamined life, devotees say. See L. Marinoff, *Plato, Not Prozac!: Applying Philosophy to Everyday Problems* (New York: Harper Collins, 1999); see also A. de Botton, *The Consolations of Philosophy* (New York: Pantheon, 2000). Socrates has been called the first psychotherapist, given the self-examination inherent in the Socratic "Know thyself." R. Chessick, "Socrates: First Psychotherapist," *Am. J. Psychoanalysis* 42 (1982): 71.

32. *Pilot Project in Training Mental Health Counselors*, Public Health Service Publication No. 125 (1965); "Mothers Good Candidates as Counselors," *Clinical Psychiatry News*, Oct. 1979, p. 32.

33. See, e.g., R. Cohen, "The Oldest Profession Seeks New Market in West Europe," *New York Times*, Sept. 19, 2000, p. 1.

34. See A. Abbott, *The System of Professions: An Essay on the Division of Expert Labor* (Chicago: University of Chicago Press, 1988); S. B. Benatar, "The Meaning of Professionalism in Medicine," *South Africa Med. J.* 87 (1997): 427; J. Goldstein, "Foucault among the Sociologists: The 'Disciplines' and the History of Professions," *History and Theory* 23 (1984): 170.

35. Goldfarb v. Virginia State Bar, 421 U.S. 773 (1975).

36. 421 U.S. at 788 n. 17.

37. R. E. Lee, "Application of Antitrust Laws to the Professions," *J. Legal Medicine* 1 (1979): 143.

38. Shaw's comment is oft-quoted. See, e.g., M. Coady & S. Bloch, *Codes of Ethics and the Professions* (Melbourne: Melbourne University Press, 1996), pp. 29, 203.

39. American Medical Ass'n v. Federal Trade Commission, 638 F.2d 443 (2d Cir. 1980), *aff'd*, 455 U.S. 676 (1982); L. Greenhouse, "Justices Uphold Right of Doctors to Solicit Trade," *New York Times*, Mar. 24, 1982, p. 10.

40. *American Psychiatric Glossary* (Washington, D.C.: American Psychiatric Press, 7th ed. 1994), p. 170. On the development of the profession of psychiatry, see F. G. Alexander & S. T. Selesnick, *The History of Psychiatry: An Evaluation of Psychiatric Thought and Practice from Prehistoric Times to the Present* (New York: Harper & Row, 1966); L. Gamwell & N. Thomes, *Madness in America: Cultural and Medical Perspectives of Mental Illness Before 1914* (Ithaca: Cornell University Press, 1995); G. N. Grob, *Mental Illness and American Society, 1875–1940* (Princeton: Princeton University Press, 1985); R. Hunter & I. Macalpine (eds.), *Three Hundred Years of Psychiatry 1535–1800: A History Presented in Selected English Texts* (London: Oxford University Press, 1963); A. A. Rogow, *The Psychiatrists* (New York: Putnam, 1970); A. Scull (ed.), *Madhouses, Mad-Doctors, and Madmen: The Social History of Psychiatry in the Victorian Era* (Philadelphia: University of Pennsylvania Press, 1981); E. Shorter, *A History of Psychiatry: From the Era of the Asylum to the Age of Prozac* (New York: Wiley, 1997); M. H. Stone, *Healing the Mind: A History of Psychiatry from Antiquity to the Present* (New York: W. W. Norton, 1997). Dr. Marcia Goin, president-elect of the American Psychiatric Association, urges renaming the APA to the American Psychiatric Medical Association because of the "vast number of people who remain unaware of the fact that psychiatrists are graduates of medical school." K. Hausman, "Goin Is Members' Choice to Be Next President-Elect," *Psychiatric News*, Mar. 15, 2002, p. 1.

41. See S. Weissman, M. Sabshin, & H. Eist (eds.), *Psychiatry in the New Millennium* (Washington, D.C.: American Psychiatric Press, 1999); M. Reiser, "Are Psychiatric Educators' Losing their Mind?" *Am. J. Psychiatry* 145 (1988): 148. Robert Whitaker, author of articles on the mentally ill and the drug industry that have won several awards, debunks the alleged benefits of antipsychotic medication. In a recent book he writes:

> Prescribing a medication is *the* ritual that defines modern medicine, and thus psychiatry, eager to see itself as a medical discipline, needed to have at its disposal a "safe and effective" drug for schizophrenia. Psychiatrists also compete with psychologists for patients, and their one competitive advantage is that because they are medical doctors, they can prescribe drugs, whereas psychologists can't. They could hardly lay claim to superior curative prowess if their neuroleptics were not just ineffective but brain damaging. Finally, by the early 1970s, all of psychiatry was in the process of being transformed by the influence of drug money. Pill-oriented shrinks could earn much more than those who relied primarily on psychotherapy (prescribing a pill takes a lot less time than talk therapy); drug-company sales representatives who came to their offices often plied them with little gifts (dinners, tickets to entertainment, and the like); and their trade organization, the APA, had become ever more fiscally dependent on the drug companies. Thirty percent of the APA's annual budget came from drug advertisements in its journals, and it also relied on industry "grants" to fund its educational programs.

R. Whitaker, *Mad in America* (Cambridge: Perseus, 2002), p. 205. See also P. R. Breggin, *Toxic Psychiatry* (New York: St. Martin's Press, 1991); T. Szasz, *Pharmacracy: Medicine and Politics in America* (Westport, Conn.: Praeger, 2001). Dr. E. Fuller Torrey notes that psychiatry and neurology are moving ever closer together, and he predicts that the National Institute of Mental Health and the National Institute of Neurological Diseases and Stroke (NINDS) will soon be merged into a National Institute of Brain Research, and that psychiatry and neurology will ultimately become a single profession. E. F. Torrey, "The Year Neurology Almost Took Over Psychiatry," *Psychiatric Times*, Jan. 2002, p. 1. The prophecy is not new. In the nineteenth century, T. Meynert believed that psychiatry would and should be absorbed into neurology. T. Meynert, *Psychiatry: Clinical Treatise on Diseases of the Forebrain* (1884), trans. B. Sachs (New York: G. P. Putnam's Sons, 1885). See also E. F. Torrey, *The Death of Psychiatry* (New York: Penguin, 1974).

42. See L. Freeman, *Celebrities on the Couch: Personal Adventures of Famous People in Psychoanalysis* (Los Angeles: Ravena Books, n.d.). Seymour Kety, a renowned scientist and one of the most visible of those working toward a biological explanation of mental illness, was named in 1951 the first scientific director of the fledgling National Institute of Mental Health. As head of group studying mental illness, he was told that he really should have firsthand knowledge of the most formidable tool in the psychiatrist's arsenal—he himself should be psychoanalyzed, at government expense. This was a striking demonstration of the prestige of psychoanalysis, but he was ambivalent. After some thought he agreed, considering

that the government would pay the cost. His wife rebuked him, "If they said they'd take your appendix out for free, would you let them?" E. Dolnick, *Madness on the Couch* (New York: Simon & Schuster, 1998), p. 71.

43. See N. Hale, *The Rise and Crisis of Psychoanalysis in the United States* (New York: Oxford University Press, 1995); J. Lear, *Open Minded* (Cambridge: Harvard University Press, 1998).

44. Quoted in R. M. Restak, "Psychiatry in America," *Wilson Q.* 7 (Autumn 1983): 95.

45. Ibid. See also P. Brooks & A. Woloch (eds.), *Whose Freud?: The Place of Psychoanalysis in Contemporary Culture* (New Haven: Yale University Press, 2000). When the once prosperous Argentina turned to bankruptcy, it was observed: "Buenos Aires is said to have the heaviest per capita concentration of psychoanalysts of any city in the world, and even with the country in ruins, fliers continue to be posted on walls here inviting the depressed to group therapy sessions that teach how to 'live with joy and little money.'" Marcos Aguinis, a former minister of culture, said, "Instead of investing in technology and science, the effort was put into training psychiatrists and lawyers because that was easier and didn't require as much expense." L. Rohter, "Argentina Paying Heavily for Squandering Blessings," *New York Times*, Feb. 8, 2002, p. 1.

46. Calif. Bus. & Prof. Code 6.6:2903. The Michigan licensing law on psychology (M.C.L.A., sec. 18201) defines the practice of psychology as "the rendering to individuals, groups, organizations, or the public of services involving the application of principles, methods, and procedures of understanding, predicting, and influencing behavior for the purposes of the diagnosis, assessment related to diagnosis, prevention, amelioration, or treatment of mental or emotional disorders, disabilities or behavioral adjustment problems by means of psychotherapy, counseling, behavioral modification, hypnosis, biofeedback techniques, psychological tests, or other verbal or behavioral means. The practice of psychology shall not include the practice of medicine such as prescribing drugs, performing surgery, or administering electro-convulsive therapy."

Tables enumerating the states having psychology regulatory statutes and the scope of the various statutes are provided in *The Psychologist and Voluntary Health Insurance* (Washington, D.C.: American Psychological Association, 1968). On the development of the profession of psychology, see F. R. J. Fields & R. J. Horwitz, *Psychology and Professional Practice* (Westport, Conn.: Quorum Books, 1982). See also B. R. Fretz & D. H. Mills, *Licensing and Certification of Psychologists and Counselors* (San Francisco: Jossey-Bass, 1980); A. Combs, "Problems and Definitions in Legislation," *Am. Psychol.* 8 (1953): 247; 1953; A. Ellis, "Pros and Cons of Legislation for Psychologists," *Am. Psychol.* 8 (1953): 596; I. Kayton, "Statutory Regulation of Psychologists: Its Scope and Constitutionality," *St. John's L. Rev.* 33 (1959): 249; J. Meltreger, "Legal Limitations of the Practice of Psychology," *Ill. Cont. Legal Ed.* 5 (1967): 85.

47. Four types of licenses are granted by the Michigan Board of Psychology, three of which fall under categories of limited licensure: (1) Temporary Limited License Psychologist (TLLP) under Rule 2, (2) Limited License Psychologist (LLP) under Rule 7, (3) LLP under Rule 10, (4) Limited Psychologist (LP) under Rule 6. An LLP may not advertise and requires supervision by a fully licensed psychologist, who may include the name of an LLP in advertising. Since 1991 the Michigan Psychology Association has engaged in efforts to change the Michigan Public Health Code (the state law) in order to allow LLPs to advertise their services, but at the present time no changes have occurred.

48. See P. Coleman & R. A. Shellow, "Prescribing Privileges for Psychologists: Should Only 'Medicine Men' Control the Medicine Cabinet?" *J. Psychiatry & Law* 18 (1990): 269; R. B. Karel, "Psychologists Press Harder to Prescribe," *Psychiatric News*, Aug. 5, 1994, pp. 1, 25; T. Svensson, "Prescribing for Psychologists," *Clinical Psychiatry News*, Jan. 1998, p. 18.

49. C. Lehmann, "Psychologists' Bid to Be 'Physicians' Comes to Dead End in Florida," *Clinical Psychiatric News*, May 21, 1999, p. 4.

50. Virginia Academy of Clinical Psychologists v. Blue Shield of Virginia, 624 F.2d 476 (4th Cir. 1980). In California Association of Psychology Providers v. Rank, 51 Cal.3d 1, 270 Cal. Rptr. 796, 793, P.2d 2 (1990), the court construed a state statute to require that psychologists be accorded hospital admission privileges equal to those of psychiatrists.

51. N.Y. Stat., sec. 7701.

52. D. Goleman, "Social Workers Vault into a Leading Role in Psychotherapy," *New York Times*, Apr. 30, 1985, p. C-1.

53. A. Gribbon, "Shoddy Counseling," *National Observer*, Oct. 30, 1971, p. 1. In an unreported case, a New York judge ordered the closing of an unlicensed psychotherapy clinic

following disclosures by the state attorney general's office that the party operating the clinic had misled his clients into believing that he was a licensed psychologist. The injunction closing the clinic ordered the party to cease "engaging in the private practice of psychotherapy, marriage, family, or child counseling in the State of New York." *New York Times*, Oct. 4, 1972, p. 41.

54. The Michigan licensing law was enacted by Act 369 of 1978. See MCL, sec. 333.18105.

55. F. Perls, *The Gestalt Approach and Eyewitness to Therapy* (New York: Bantam Books, 1973); discussed in M. T. Singer & J. Lalich, *"Crazy" Therapies: What Are They? Do They Work?* (San Francisco: Jossey-Bass, 1996), pp. 14–15.

56. See L. P. Bradford et al. (eds.), *T-Group Theory and Laboratory Method* (New York: Wiley, 1964); A. Burton (ed.), *Encounter: Theory and Practice of Encounter Groups* (San Francisco: Jossey-Bass, 1969).

57. The First Amendment's prohibition against judicial review of ecclesiastical disputes does not bar a claim against a pastoral counselor for malpractice or breach of fiduciary duty. A minister who holds himself out as a professional marriage counselor is judged by a professional, rather than religious, standard of care. Sanders v. Casa View Baptist Church, 134 F.3d 331 (5th Cir. 1998). Numerous religious sects preach faith healing and at times reject the use of modern medicine. For some, *faith* and *healing* are not easily separable, and this may become problematical since "faith" is protected by the Constitution, but "healing" may be subject to regulation. The healing may be regulated as soon as it takes on any appearance of medical practice. When the believer in faith healing, or his child, becomes ill and does not engage what the majority of society considers what is proper to be cured, he may find himself in a conflict between freedom of religion and the sanctity of life. The state may intervene and, in its role as *parens patriae*, declare the child "neglected," and turn the child over for treatment, regardless of the parents' religious beliefs. Parents who treat sick children only with prayer may be subjected to criminal penalties. People v. Walker, 47 Cal. 3d 112, 253 Cal. Rptr. 1, 763 P.2d 852 (1988). A healer who does any act within the meaning of the term *practicing medicine* may be liable in tort or found guilty of homicide, most likely involuntary manslaughter, in the event of death. C. W. Laughran, "Religious Beliefs and the Criminal Justice System: Some Problems of the Faith Healer," *Loy. L.A. L. Rev.* 8 (1975): 396.

The case of *Nally v. Grace Community Church of the Valley* is discussed in volume 1, chapter 2, on boundaries of legal and ethical forensic practice, and is the subject of the book by Mark A. Weitz, *Clergy Malpractice in America* (Lawrence: University Press of Kansas, 2001). The counselor in the case had no formal training and freely acknowledged that some of the people he had been counseling had severe emotional and mental problems. The biblical counseling literally meant using the Bible as the tool for resolving both spiritual and mental health problems. Prior to *Nally*, the notion of suing a priest, clergyman, or a church would have been almost sacrilegious for the vast majority of Americans throughout the two-hundred-year history of the country. Ken Nally committed suicide, and a wrongful death claim was filed, alleging clergy malpractice, negligence, and outrageous conduct. The concept that became the thread that wove its way throughout the claimant's entire argument and across the eight-year life of the case was: "This is not about religion, or religious beliefs, it is about the minimum standard of conduct that anyone who purports to counsel mentally ill people should have to adhere to." Weitz, p. 58. The church argued that the relationship that existed between Nally and the church, its counselors, and its ministers fell far below what was necessary to create a legal duty between the defendants and the decedent. Weitz, p. 90. Following years of litigation, the California Supreme Court concluded that the plaintiffs had not met the threshold requirements for imposing on defendants a duty to prevent suicide. The court said, "Plaintiffs failed to persuade us that the duty to prevent suicide (heretofore imposed only on psychiatrists and hospitals while caring for a suicidal patient) or the general professional duty of care (heretofore imposed only on psychiatrists when treating a mentally disturbed patient) should be extended to a nontherapist counselor who offers counseling to a potentially suicidal person on secular or spiritual matters. In the present case, the Court of Appeals erroneously created a broad duty to refer, and to hold defendants potentially accountable for Nally's death based on their counseling activities would place blame unreasonably and contravene existing public policy." In a footnote, the court said, "Our opinion does not foreclose imposing liability on nontherapist counselors, who hold themselves out as professionals, for injuries related to their counseling activities." 47 Cal. 3d 278, 253 Cal. Rptr. 97, 763 P.2d 948 (1988).

The *Nally* litigation was the first case to test the clergy malpractice theory. Supporters of church liability argued that the Grace Church defendants held themselves out to the public as competent therapists, which they were not, to handle mental, rather than spiritual, problems. The insurance industry now offers clergy counseling liability insurance, and clergy associations (such as the American Association of Pastoral Counselors) have stepped in to fill the regulatory voice with standards of their own. The California Supreme Court noted that insurance is now available for clergy malpractice, and that may make a difference in which to recognize and enforce this theory of liability. Without liability, insurance companies would collect premiums without risk of loss. See R. J. Basil, "Clergy Malpractice: Taking Spiritual Counseling Conflicts beyond Intentional Tort Analysis," *Rutgers L.J.* 19 (1988): 419.

Over the door of a church-based drug treatment center in Houston, a sign announces, "Drug Addiction Is Not a Disease, It's a Sin." "We have to respect the different methods," said Don Willett, a policy adviser to then-governor Bush. "In the view of faith-based providers, addiction is indicative of sinful behavior; it's at root a moral problem that requires a moral solution, as opposed to the therapeutic notion that it's a disease." Under rules adopted in Texas in 1997, churches that once merely gave advice or pastoral care can now advertise themselves as drug treatment programs, simply by signing up with the state. Counselors in religious programs avoid the training required of state-licensed therapists. H. Rosin, "Bush Puts Faith in a Social Service Role," *Washington Post*, May 5, 2000, p. 1.

58. P. Steinfels, "The Week of the Calendar: A New Year's Rhythms," *New York Times*, Jan. 4, 1997, p. 8. In Ireland it is written: "Counseling is the new religion. As our church pews are emptying, so the counseling couches are filling up. The demise of confession where faltering stories were whispered in the dark has seen a corresponding growth in therapy." T. Martin, "Counselling: Why It's Becoming the New Confession," *Irish Independent*, June 22, 2000, p. 13.

59. Jaffee v. Redmond, 527 U.S. 123 (1999).

60. See R. Kaufman, *Inside Scientology* (New York: Olympia, 1972).

61. Founding Church of Scientology v. United States, 409 F.2d 1146 (D.C. Cir. 1969); United States v. "Hubbard Electrometer," (D.C. July 30, 1971). Compare Church of Scientology v. Richardson, 437 F.2d 214 (9th Cir. 1971). See P. Cooper, *The Scandal of Scientology* (New York: Tower, 1971); R. Kaufman, *Inside Scientology* (New York: Olympia, 1972).

62. W. Reich, *The Function of the Orgasm* (New York: Farrar, Straus & Giroux, 1973); see R. Gilman, "Organization Man," review of M. B. Higgins (ed.), *American Odyssey: Letters and Journals, 1940–1947, by Wilhelm Reich* (New York: Farrar, Straus & Giroux 1999), *New York Times Magazine*, Sept. 5, 1999, sec. 7, p. 13.

63. Baron Richard von Krafft-Ebing (1840–1902), German physician and neurologist particularly known for his studies of sexual deviance and the published collection of case histories *Psychopathia Sexualis* (1886).

64. See. J. Marmor, "In Defense of Masters and Johnson," *World*, Jan. 30, 1973, p. 24; see also "Repairing the conjugal Bed," *Time*, May 25, 1970, p. 39.

65. N. Shainess, "How 'Sex Experts' Debase Sex," *World*, Jan. 2, 1973, p. 21.

66. See generally V. L. Bullough, *Science in the Bedroom: A History of Sex Research* (New York: Basic Books, 1994).

67. R. K. Wallace & H. Benson, "The Physiology of Meditation," *Sci. Am.* 226 (1972): 85.

68. See E. Graham, "Transcendent Trend," *Wall Street Journal*, Aug. 31, 1972, p. 1. For a somewhat disenchanted view of Indian Yoga, see Arthur Koestler's *The Lotus and the Robot* (New York: Macmillan, 1961).

69. M. J. Rioch et al., "National Institute of Mental Health Pilot Study in Training Mental Health Counselors," *Am. J. Orthopsychiatry* 33 (1963): 678. See also Report, *Utilization of Paraprofessionals in Three Mental Health Settings* (New York: Institute for Child Mental Health, 1972).

70. E. F. Torrey, *The Mind Game: Witchdoctors and Psychiatrists* (New York: Emerson Hall, 1972); condensed version, "What Western Psychotherapists Can Learn from Witchdoctors," *Am. J. Orthopsychiatry* 42 (1972): 69.

71. Ibid. In an interesting case at the Tulane University Department of Psychiatry and Neurology, which the author observed, a young woman who had been treated in psychotherapy without much result was suddenly and dramatically healed by a faith healer who cast out demons from within her. After the healing, which included five exorcism sessions over a

period of a month, the health of the patient was remarkably improved, her symptoms had disappeared, and she began to function with mature self-confidence. This individual had grown up in a hypermoralistic environment and previously had not been able to resolve many conflicted feelings. She now knew, she reported, that God loved her. The faith healer who worked with her has a group who sings, chants, and prays in the background as he performs the exorcism. He addresses each devil by name (e.g., Jeremiah) and carries on a heated conversation with each one. The situation builds up to fever-pitch excitement. "Come out, Jeremiah, I know you're in there! Come out! Come out, Jeremiah! Come on out!" The bedeviled has explosive coughs. As each devil is coughed out, the healer expels him across the ocean to Israel. The devils, several in number, are thus defeated (although they might return). In this concrete manner, devils are blamed for the individual's past wrongdoings, real or imagined, and they are exorcised, freeing the possessed from bondage. This faith healer feels that exorcism and psychotherapy have many similarities, the only real difference being the extent to which the patient is directed and the means by which the psychic problems are symbolically represented. The techniques of exorcism, especially as represented in this case history, support the contention that faith healing, hypnotic suggestion, thought reform, and psychotherapy have some similarities. J. A. Knight, *Conscience and Guilt* (New York: Appleton-Century-Crofts, 1969), p. 59.

72. On the pros and cons of the composition of the board, it may be noted that those who favor nonprofessional representation on the boards argue that, as these are public agencies whose primary function is to safeguard the public welfare, it is logical that the public should be represented on them. "Federation and Uniform Licensing Laws," *Fed. Bull.* 51 (1964): 1. It is contended that nonprofessional members might act as observers to see that the boards function properly and do not engage in improper practices. As one study puts it, prostitution of the licensing function occurs because the licensing function is transferred to the profession being licensed. See J. Baron, "Business and Professional Licensing: California, A Representative Example," *Stan. L. Rev.* 18 (1966): 640.

73. Calif. Bus & Prof. Code 6.6:2943 (West 1990).

74. La. Rev. Stat. 37:2356(D) (West Supp. 2000).

75. Husband v. Cassel, 130 So.2d 69 (Fla. 1961).

76. People v. Zimmerman, 391 Ill. 621, 63 N.E.2d 850 (1945).

77. APA Model Statute Report, supra note 23, p. 1100.

78. E.g., La. Rev. Stat. 37:2365(3) (West 1990).

79. R. A. Oppel, "Judge Says Texas Can't Act on H.M.O. Doctor's Ruling," *New York Times*, Sept. 19, 2000, p. C-29.

80. Illustrative of the process to withdraw a license where the practitioner is found to have violated an ethical or legal norm is Mississippi State Board of Psychological Examiners v. Hosford, 508 So.2d 1049 (Miss. 1987) (breach of confidentiality). Then, too, of course, a professional organization may suspend or dismiss a member (not all practitioners are members of a professional or specialty organization so that remedy would not be available). In a first-of-its-kind ruling, the Seventh Circuit U.S. Court of Appeals ruled that a professional society may discipline a member on account of testimony presented at trial that is deemed not up to standards. In Austin v. American Association of Neurological Surgeons, 253 F.3d 967 (7th Cir. 2001), the court said, "Although [the expert witness] did not treat the malpractice plaintiff for whom he testified, his testimony at her trial was a type of medical service and if the quality of his testimony reflected the quality of his medical judgment, he is probably a poor physician. His discipline by the association therefore served an important public policy exemplified by the federal Health Care Quality Improvement Act." 253 F.3d at 975. See P. S. Appelbaum, "Policing Expert Testimony: The Role of Professional Organizations," *Psychiat. Serv.* 53 (2002): 389.

81. The code of ethics condemns an opinion by a psychiatrist or psychologist without an examination. Several psychologists were threatened with state disciplinary action because they speculated in newspaper interviews about Kitty Dukakis's depression and alcohol abuse. She was the wife of then presidential candidate Michael Dukakis. *New York Times*, Nov. 22, 1989, p. 11; see R. Slovenko, "Psychiatric Opinion without Examination," *J. Psychiatry & Law* 28 (2000): 103.

82. B. Shartel & M. L. Plant, supra note 17, at p. 222. Physician addiction to alcohol or narcotics is a widespread problem. J. Emschwiller, "Heal Thyself," *Wall Street J.*, Dec. 7, 1972, p. 1; D. Shepardson, "State Struggles with Drinking Doctors," *Detroit News*, Sept. 15, 1999, p. 1.

83. See Rule 1101, Federal Rules of Evidence; Mississippi State Board of Psychological Examiners v. Hosford, 508 So.2d 1049 (Miss. 1987).

84. See H. R. Hansen, *An Analysis and Evaluation of State Medical Licensure* (Group Health Association of America, 1962).

85. Note, "Regulation of Psychological Counseling and Psychotherapy," *Colum. L. Rev.* 51 (1951): 474.

86. Okla. Rev. Stat. 59-492 (West 1989).

87. S.D. Laws, ch. 106-14.

88. N.C. Gen. Stat. Ann., sec. 90-18 (West 1999); Minn. Stat. Ann., sec. 147.081 (West 1999).

89. Tenn. Code Ann., sec. 63-6-204; Ohio Code Ann., sec. 4731.34 (West 1999).

90. Calif. Bus. & Prof. Code 6.6:2902 (Deering's 1999).

91. Op. Calif. Atty. Gen. 49:104.

92. Rev. Rul. 55-261, 1955-1 CB 307 (Jan. 1, 1955). Under section 213 of the code, the Internal Revenue Service allows expenses for "medical care" even when the practitioner who performs the service is not required by law to be—or is not (even though required by law)—licensed, certified, or otherwise qualified to perform the service.

93. In a landmark decision, Jenkins v. United States, 307 F.2d 637 (D.C. 1962), the District of Columbia Court of Appeals held that a psychologist is not barred as a matter of law from giving expert testimony about mental illness. Following *Jenkins,* most states have provided by statute or case law that doctoral-level clinical psychologists may offer opinions on insanity as well as on other issues concerning the mentally disordered. See R. Gass, "The Psychologist as Expert Witness: Science in the Courtroom," *Md. L. Rev.* 38 (1979): 539. Some states, however, still do not allow psychologists to testify as fully as psychiatrists. In insanity cases, for example, some courts restrict psychologists to interpretations of psychological tests. State v. Bricker, 321 Md. 86, 581 A.2d 9 (1990). Many civil commitment statutes have provisions which restrict the role of expert exclusively to physicians. T. Hafemeister & B. Sales, "Responsibilities of Psychologists under Guardianship and Conservatorship Laws," *Prof. Psychol.* 13 (1982): 354. Research indicates, however, that nonpsychiatrists are even more competent in addressing many forensic issues. G. Dix & N. Poythress, "Propriety of Medical Dominance of Forensic Mental Health Practice: The Empirical Evidence," *Ariz. L. Rev.* 23 (1981): 961.

94. *New York Times,* Nov. 28, 1972, p. 55.

95. The author was a member of the committee.

96. I. Peterson, "State Finds Quacks in Mental Therapy," *New York Times,* Dec. 7, 1972, p. 1.

97. *New York Times,* Apr. 11, 1973, p. 32.

98. Apr. 11, 1973, p. 32.

99. *New York Times,* Apr. 13, 1973, p. 52; Apr. 24, p. 38.

100. D. Satcher, "Mental Health: A Report of the Surgeon General," U.S. Public Health Service, 1999.

101. The film is reviewed in A. O. Scott, "Two Lives Torn by a Child Abuse Case," *New York Times,* Mar. 3, 2000, p. B-25.

102. *New York Times,* Apr. 12, 1992, p. 22.

103. Papers presented in 1994 at an FMS Foundation conference entitled "Memory and Reality: Reconciliation; Scientific, Clinical and Legal Issues of False Memory Syndrome," appear in *J. Psychiatry & Law* 23 (1995): 347–484. See also J. Acocella, *Creating Hysteria* (San Francisco: Jossey-Bass, 1999), excerpted in "The Politics of Hysteria," *New Yorker,* Apr. 6, 1998, p. 64; M. Johnston, *Spectral Evidence: The Ramona Case* (New York: Houghton Mifflin, 1997); S. Taub (ed.), *Recovered Memories of Child Sexual Abuse* (Springfield, Ill.: Thomas, 1999); E. Loftus, "Memory Distortion and False Memory Creation," *Bull. Am. Acad. Psychiatry & Law* 24 (1996): 281. In support of recovered memories, see D. Brown, A. W. Scheflin, & C. L. Whitfield, "Recovered Memories: The Current Weight of the Evidence in Science and in the Courts," *J. Psychiatry & Law* 27 (1999): 5.

104. Dr. Orne's research on memory and undue suggestion has been cited by the U.S. Supreme Court and more than thirty state supreme courts. His expertise in hypnosis played a key role in the trial of Kenneth Bianchi, the former security guard who confessed to killing five women in the Hillside Strangler case. The defense argued that Bianchi had multiple personalities.

105. Bert Peterson of Rockport Insurance Associates advises: "Our professional liability policy is not being offered to those practitioners who *intentionally* [emphasis by Peterson] set out to recover failed or repressed memories through hypnotherapy. We are aware that, as a result of hypnotherapy, the possibility does exist that such an event may occur. The use of hypnotherapy is not specifically excluded from the policy." Letter of June 13, 1996.

106. D. Koontz, *False Memory* (New York: Bantam, 1999), p. 384.

107. Personal communication (Jan. 14, 2001).

108. See E. R. Kandel, "A New Intellectual Framework for Psychiatry," *Am. J. Psychiatry* 155 (1998): 457; P. McHugh, "Psychiatry Awry," *American Scholar* 63 (1994): 17.

109. Cybermedicine (or cyberpsych) is in contrast to the more widely discussed issue of *telemedicine,* which typically refers to technologies, primarily preconvergence telephony, satellite, and video, used to cover geographical areas for health care. In contrast, *cybermedicine* is a broader concept, encompassing not only the technology and legal issues of telemedicine, but also a greater array of nontraditional and unique, technology-enabled interactions among health care providers and consumer-patients. It includes marketing, relationship creation, advice, prescribing and selling drugs and devices, and as with all things in cyberspace, levels of interactivity as yet unknown.

By the late 1980s, military and correctional institutions began experimenting with telecommunication systems designed to meet specific needs in situations where transporting patients to specialty providers would be both difficult and expensive. Slowly, other state and federal agencies dealing with health care began experimenting with telehealth systems across wide geographic areas. K. M. Kirby & D. W. Nickelson, "Telehealth and the Evolving Health Care System: Strategic Opportunities for Professional Psychology," *Prof. Psychology: Research & Practice* 29 (1998): 527. CyberDocs, a Web site currently available on the Internet, offers a sophisticated integration of the available technology. Web site address *www.cyberdoc.com.* CyberDocs apparently avoids controversy with state medical licensing laws by listing for each state only those physicians licensed to practice medicine in each state. Several state medical boards and some state legislatures have decreed that prescribing drugs online without a face-to-face consultation is in violation of state medical practice acts and constitutes inappropriate conduct subject to disciplinary sanctions including loss of licensure. Because it is common for patients to become particularly attached to their mental health professionals, cyberpsych may be especially helpful for patients who find it necessary to terminate therapy early for reasons such as job relocation, childcare difficulties, or postsurgical restrictions.

Whether a physician-patient relationship exists is the threshold question when it comes to discussing liability for providers using the Internet as a means of delivering care. There is apparently no case law to date directly on point, but it is predicted that the courts will use the traditional tort model of malpractice when the cases arise. In Weaver v. University of Michigan Board of Regents, 506 N.W.2d 264 (Mich. App. 1993), the court held that a telephone call to schedule an appointment with a physician did not establish a physician-patient relationship where the caller had no ongoing relationship with the physician and where the caller did not receive medical advice during the telephone conversation.

To avoid a physician-patient relationship, some practitioners of cyberpsych have chosen to limit their practice over the Internet to chat rooms, a form of group therapy where participants drop in and out of e-mail conversations with many people. No actual medical advice is given, and the Web sites have liability disclaimers stating the participating physicians are not practicing medicine. For example, one Web site, called "Ask the Doc," will not diagnose illness, prescribe medication, keep a medical record of the conversations, or even reveal the physician's identity.

In 1996, the Federation of State Medical Boards developed model legislation that allows a state to create and administer a limited telehealth license, but only six states have adopted versions of the model legislation (Alabama, California, Montana, Oregon, Tennessee, and Texas). The American Medical Association has taken the position that limited licensure is not enough and has adopted a policy stating that physicians of any discipline who practice telehealth across state lines should be required to hold full and unrestricted licenses in both states. Most states have adopted the AMA's approach, but they have always recognized certain limited exceptions to the licensing requirement, such as the traditional informal physician-to-physician consultation, where the treating physician consults on an irregular basis with a colleague for no compensation. Malpractice insurance coverage is restricted to jurisdictions where the physician is licensed to practice.

In forensic telepsychiatry, civil commitment is an area of great potential use of telecommunications. Evaluation of issues such as PTSD, emotional distress, and psychiatric disability may also be done by telepsychiatry. Evaluation of issues such as parental competence, juvenile court waiver, and school violence risk assessment may be done by telepsychiatry. In all of these situations body language is missing in making an evaluation. The most frequent use to date of forensic telepsychiatry has been in correctional psychiatry; 30 percent of all telemedicine consults in 1998 were in correctional settings. Legal challenges may arise in regard informed consent, a suicidal patient, the *Tarasoff* duty to warn or protect in the case of a patient who poses a danger, and patient misrepresentation. A patient with an addiction might appear more reasonable when requesting medications online. It may be more difficult to detect the signs of malingering over the Internet. See, in general, C. Erdman, "The Medicolegal Dangers of Telephone Triage in Mental Health Care," *J. Legal Med.* 22 (2001): 553; P. F. Granade, "Medical Malpractice Issues Related to the Use of Telemedicine: An Analysis of the Ways in Which Telecommunications Affects the Principles of Medical Malpractice," *N.D. L. Rev.* 73 (1997): 65; R. L. Scott, "Cybermedicine and Virtual Pharmacies," *W. Va. L. Rev.* 103 (2001): 407; N. P. Terry, "Cyber-Malpractice: Legal Exposure for Cybermedicine," *Am. J. Law & Med.* 25 (1999): 327; R. Wiesemann, "On-line or On-call? Legal and Ethical Challenges Emerging in Cybermedicine," *St. Louis U. L.J.* 43 (1999): 1119. See also K. Gelein, "Are Online Consultations a Prescription for Trouble? The Uncharted Waters of Cybermedicine," *Brook. L. Rev.* 66 (2000): 209; D. Pergament, "Internet Psychotherapy: Current Status and Future Regulation," *Health Matrix: Journal of Law-Medicine* 8 (1998): 233; R. Silverman, "Regulating Medical Practice in the Cyber Age: Issues and Challenges for State Medical Boards," *Am J. Law & Med.* 26 (2000): 255. Dr. Paul McHugh, University Distinguished Service Professor of Psychiatry and Behavioral Science at Johns Hopkins School of Medicine, carried on psychotherapy with author Tom Wolfe by telephone. Wolfe dedicates his book *A Man in Full* (New York: Farrar, Straus & Giroux, 1998): "With immense admiration the author dedicates *A Man in Full* to Paul McHugh, whose brilliance, comradeship, and unfailing kindness saved the day. This book would not exist had it not been for you, dear friend."

110. E. R. Kandel, "Biology and the Future of Psychoanalysis: A New Intellectual Framework for Psychiatry Revisited," *Am. J. Psychiatry* 156 (1999): 505.

111. Dr. Jerome D. Frank points out that although persons come to psychotherapy for relief of specific symptoms or disabilities, their primary reason for seeking help is that they are more or less demoralized and the effect of psychotherapy is to restore morale. The effectiveness of any form of psychotherapy hence depends on its ability to restore the individual's morale. Psychotherapy may help combat the individual's sense of isolation, inspire his hopes for relief, reduce his confusion, and teach him more effective ways of coping with his feelings and the external world, thereby increasing his sense of self-control and mastery. The hypothesis implies that the major determinants of outcome are not therapeutic procedures per se, but rather personal qualities of therapist and patient and the degree of concordance between the patient's belief as to what will help him and the therapeutic method. This depends primarily on the source to which he attributes his symptoms, in turn a function of his education and cultural status and the views of the therapist he happens to encounter. Thus, highly structured concrete procedures such as crisis management and behavior therapies may be especially suited to less highly educated patients, while interview therapies appeal to the verbally skilled who attribute their symptoms and abilities to inner conflicts. J. D. Frank, *Persuasion and Healing: A Comparative Study of Psychotherapy* (Baltimore: Johns Hopkins University Press, 1991). See also W. Gaylin, *Talk Is Not Enough: How Psychotherapy Really Works* (Boston: Little, Brown, 2000).

112. See D. Middlebrook, *Anne Sexton: A Biography* (Boston: Houghton Mifflin, 1991), p. 64.

113. See A. M. Ludwig, *How Do We Know Who We Are? A Biography of the Self* (New York: Oxford University Press, 1997); D. P. Spence, *Narrative Truth and Historical Truth: Meaning and Interpretation in Psychoanalysis* (New York: Norton, 1982).

Appendix 1: Highlights in the History of Law and Psychiatry

Alcohol and Drug Addiction

Alcohol and drug addiction may be the basis in some states for civil commitment, but in cases of alcohol or drug-precipitated crimes, a defense of drunkenness or addiction does not result in exculpation of the accused. However, it may sometimes result in diminished responsibility. The following landmark cases deal with the attempt to criminalize the *condition* of drunkenness or addiction.

Robinson v. California

The U.S. Supreme Court struck down a California statute that made it a criminal offense to use, be under the influence of, or "be addicted to the use of narcotics." The accused was not under the influence of narcotics at the time of his arrest and did not manifest withdrawal symptoms thereafter. Justice Stewart, speaking for the majority, and Justice Douglas, concurring, referred to addiction as an illness. Justice Douglas said: "If addicts can be punished for their addiction, then the insane can also be punished for their insanity. Each has a disease and each must be treated as an ill person. . . . This prosecution has no relationship to the curing of an illness. Indeed, it cannot, for the prosecution is aimed at penalizing an illness, rather than with providing medical care for it. We would forget the teachings of the Eighth Amendment if we allowed sickness to be made a crime and permitted sick people to be punished for being sick. This age of enlightenment cannot tolerate such barbarous action." The Supreme Court noted that mental illness, leprosy, and venereal diseases, all of which were at one time thought to be problems of morality and therefore criminal, could not now constitutionally be made criminal offenses. The Court reasoned that narcotic addiction is in the same category as those other diseases and held the California statute unconstitutional. 370 U.S. 660 (1962).

Powell v. Texas

The U.S. Supreme Court was asked to apply the *Robinson* doctrine to prohibit a state from punishing a chronic alcoholic for public drunkenness. In a 5–4 decision, the Court held that a showing of alcoholism alone is not a sufficient defense. Five Justices, however, were prepared to strike down such a conviction where the defendant could show that he appeared in public not by his own volition but under a compulsion that was part of his chronic alcoholic condition; that is, when the alcoholism is "caused and maintained by something other than the moral fault of the alcoholic." Leroy Powell had been convicted of being in a state of intoxication in a public place. In affirming the conviction, Justice Marshall, speaking for the majority, said that one could not "conclude, on the state of this record or on the current state of medical knowledge, that chronic alcoholics in general, and Leroy Powell in particular, suffer from such an irresistible compulsion to drink and to get drunk in public that they are utterly unable to control their performance of either or both of these acts and thus cannot be deterred at all from public intoxication." Moreover, he said, *Robinson* stands only for the proposition that an individual cannot be punished for mere status but must engage in some behavior or commit some act before criminal sanctions can be invoked against him. The Texas statute, he said, met this requirement since its sanctions were directed at socially offensive behavior. In a concurring opinion, Justice White suggested that punishment of a chronic alcoholic for public intoxication might constitute punishment for the underlying condition of chronic alcoholism and therefore be unconstitutional where "it was not feasible for him to have made arrangements to prevent his being in public when drunk." That is, a homeless alcoholic would not be accountable for being drunk in public. Since Powell had made no showing that he was unable to stay off the streets on the night in question and had a home to which he could go, Justice White concurred in affirming the conviction. 392 U.S. 514 (1968). In a dissenting opinion, Justice Fortas said that most commentators, as well as experienced judges, are in agreement that "there is probably no drearier example of the futility of using penal sanctions to solve a psychiatric problem than the enforcement of the laws against drunkenness" (quoting from Guttmacher & Weihofen, *Psychiatry and the Law* (1952)). 392 U.S. at 565.

Ferguson v. City of Charleston

The U.S. Supreme Court in this case addressed the lengths that the police can go in using medical personnel to provide information for criminal prosecution purposes. In response to an increase in the number of prenatal patients who were found to be abusing narcotics, a South Carolina public hospital instituted a policy of testing urine obtained from certain expectant mothers for the presence of narcotics. The policy was intended to protect unborn children by threatening their mothers with criminal prosecution for the use of narcotics (if the use was detected early in the pregnancy) or for child endangerment (if the use was detected late in the pregnancy). Only patients who fell within nine criteria were tested. The testing policy was instituted after earlier programs, which only referred patients who tested positive for narcotics to abuse counseling, failed to stem the abuse of narcotics by expectant mothers. Patients were notified that all positive test results would be forwarded to the police for possible criminal prosecution. Several women who were arrested after testing positive sued the hospital and police officials for Fourth Amendment violations. The Supreme Court ruled that the policy violated the Fourth Amendment reasonableness requirement because it constituted an unjustified warrantless search. The Court decided that the urine test, as administered under the policy, was a search as defined by the Fourth Amendment, and was therefore subject to the Fourth Amendment reasonableness requirement. The Supreme Court rejected the ruling of the Fourth Circuit Court of Appeals that the policy was reasonable under the Fourth Amendment because "special needs" justified the testing to serve non-law-enforcement ends. The Court ruled that, despite the hospital's assertions that it only desired to curtail prenatal narcotics abuse, the primary purpose of this testing was law enforcement. Absent probable cause and a warrant, or consent or exigent circumstances, such governmental conduct is prohibited by the Fourth Amendment. It is to be noted that the Court did not prohibit the use of all medical test results in criminal prosecutions. When such testing is done in private hospitals, not acting at governmental direction, or for primarily medical purposes, or pursuant to an exigent need (such as drawing blood from someone when there is a reasonable belief that the use of alcohol contributed to a motor vehicle collision), or pursuant to the patient's voluntary consent, the test results may be used by law enforcement for criminal prosecution in compliance with the Fourth Amendment. 121 S. Ct. 1281 (2001).

VOLUNTARY INTOXICATION EXCLUSION

The law is beyond doubt that voluntary intoxication that lowers one's inhibitions does not exculpate. Glanville Williams, the noted English authority, is critical: "If a man is punished for doing something when drunk that he would not have done when sober, is he not in plain truth punished for getting drunk?" G. Williams, *Criminal Law* (London: Stevens & Sons, 1961). The courts have drawn exceptions to the voluntary intoxication exclusion; for example, where "consumption of drugs causes a mental disease or defect, apart from the addiction itself." Commonwealth v. Sheehand, 376 Mass. 765, 383 N.E.2d 1115 (1978). Another example is where consumption of alcohol "activated" a "latent mental disease or defect." Commonwealth v. Shelley, 381 Mass. 340, 409 N.E.2d 732 (1988). The exclusions pertain only if the defendant voluntarily consumed substances without knowing that mental disease or defect would result. The Iowa Supreme Court in State v. Booth, 169 N.W.2d 869 (1989) said, "A distinction is made when prolonged extensive use of alcohol damages the brain and 'settled or established' insanity results therefrom. This is treated the same as insanity from any other cause." Moreover, iatrogenic narcotics addiction alone may constitute a mental disease or defect sufficient to support the defense of insanity in a criminal prosecution. United States v. Lyons, 731 F.2d 243 (5th Cir. 1984).

People v. Conley

William Conley was convicted of murder for having shot and killed a woman with whom he had been romantically involved and who had told him that she would get a divorce and marry him but who was now leaving him to rejoin her husband. He killed her and her husband after having told his friends what he was going to do and having bought a rifle to do it. His friends dismissed the remark as "just the booze talking." The California Supreme Court held that he had been wrongly convicted of murder because he had been drunk enough to reduce his capacity to understand fully his obligation to obey the law. A medical expert testified that some of the medication prescribed to relieve the pain of his back injury and ulcer could have increased the effect of alcohol. A psychologist testified that in his opinion he was in a disassociative state at the time of the killings and because of personality fragmentation did not function with his normal personality. The court said, "Unconsciousness is ordinarily a complete defense to a criminal charge [but] if the state of unconsciousness is caused by voluntary intoxication, it is not a complete defense. Intoxication can so diminish a person's mental capacity that he is unable to achieve a specific state of mind requisite to a crime, but, even if it is sufficient to destroy volition, it cannot excuse homicide. Unconsciousness caused by voluntary intoxication . . . is not a defense when a crime requires only a general criminal intent." 49 Cal. Rptr. 815, 411 P.2d 911 (1966). Professor James Q. Wilson criticizes the reversal of the conviction of murder, as it was, he says, a deliberate, premeditated crime. *Moral Judgment* (New York: Basic Books, 1997).

BURDEN OF PROOF DEFENSES

There are basically two types of defenses in criminal cases. The first serves to negate an element of the offense charged, e.g., alibi in a robbery case and consent in a rape case. The second goes beyond negating an element of the crime and instead proves additional facts that exculpate or excuse the defendant or mitigate the severity of the punishment, e.g., duress, necessity, self-defense, and entrapment. Such defenses are commonly called "affirmative" defenses and the defendant may have the burden of persuasion (usually by a preponderance of the evidence). Some courts hold that a defendant can be required to bear the burden of persuasion with respect to the defense of intoxication even though evidence of intoxication is offered to negate intent.

Long v. Brewer

The Eighth Circuit set out the state of the law: "Voluntary intoxication, if it eliminates the intent to kill, reduces the severity of the crime, but it does not excuse the defendant from the consequences of other gradations of homicide. In that respect, the defense is similar to that of extreme emotional disturbance which, if established, would reduce the crime from first degree murder to a lesser degree of homicide." The court noted that like the defense of extreme emotional disturbance, the burden of persuasion may be placed on the defendant to prove intoxication. The court had difficulty with the distinction (made by the Supreme Court in the two types of cases). It took comfort in Holmes's dictum that "The life of the law has not been logic; it has been experience." 667 F.2d 742 (8th Cir. 1982). See Mullaney v. Wilbur, 421 U.S. 684 (1975); Patterson v. New York, 432 U.S. 197 (1977).

Americans with Disabilities Act

United States law does not recognize an individual right to employment, but numerous statutes and programs implement work disability policies. The United States has now a web of antidiscrimination statutes, such as the Americans with Disabilities Act, that aim to facilitate equal access to employment; vocational rehabilitation statutes that provide rehabilitative services; and a system of insurance and social welfare legislation that guarantees benefits to people with disabilities who are unable to work.

Accommodating mental disabilities under the ADA ranks as one of the most important employment issues. Signed into law in 1990, effective 1993, it has proven to be one of the most complex employment laws in recent American history. Charges of discrimination based on emotional or psychiatric disabilities constitute approximately one-quarter of ADA claims.

Litigation prompted the Equal Employment Opportunity Commission, the administrative agency responsible for enforcing the ADA, in 1997 to publish a forty-page set of guidelines that the commission hoped would clarify—and in some cases, assert—the workplace rights of the mentally ill. The guidelines are not binding on the courts and judicial reception has been tepid at best. Many commentators have offered explanation for the controversy and confusion. The line between a poor performer and a person with a mental disability in need of an accommodation is a difficult one to discern. Moreover, in contrast to persons protected under other fair employment statutes, individuals with mental disabilities may move in and out of protected status.

The EEOC Compliance Manual suggests that an "impairment" is "substantially limiting" if it lasts for more than several months and significantly restricts the performance of one or more life activities during that time. "Working" is cited in the regulations as a major life activity; other examples include thinking, breathing, concentrating, interacting with others, caring for oneself, speaking, walking, performing manual tasks, and sleeping. The ADA requires employers to accommodate disabled workers if they can do so without undue hardship. The act defines disability as an impairment that "substantially" limits one or more "major life activities."

The determination of "impairment" is made with regard to the corrective effects of medication or other devices. Thus, an individual who is taking medication for a mental impairment does not have an ADA disability if there is evidence that the mental impairment, when treated, does not substantially limit a major life activity.

In one hypothetical case, the EEOC said an employer should tolerate disheveled appearance and curt conversation from a mentally disabled worker whose only job was to load boxes in a warehouse. That's a license to behave badly, critics charge, but in practice, courts have not issued that license.

In an Illinois case, a social-service caseworker was dismissed after being accused of threatening to kill her supervisor. The caseworker sued, arguing that she suffered depression paranoia. The Seventh U.S. Circuit Court of Appeals in Palmer v. Circuit Court of Cook County, 117 F.3d 35 (1997), affirmed summary judgement for the employer, saying: "It would be unreasonable to demand of the employer either that it force its employees to put up with this or that it station guards to prevent the mentally disturbed employee from getting out of hand." The First Circuit in Soileau v. Guilford of Maine, 105 F.3d 12 (1997), recognized that "the ability to get along with others" is a skill to be prized but, the court ruled, it is too nebulous and too subjective to constitute a major life activity under the ADA. In Fenton v. Pritchard Corp., 926 F.Supp. 1437 (1996), a federal district court held that a "quick temper" did not qualify as a disability.

In all likelihood, the Supreme Court will address some of the developing issues, such as the definition of a *mental disability*, and in particular, to what extent "chronic, episodic conditions" should be afforded protection under the ADA. Moreover, the issue of the type and scope of a "reasonable accommodation" for mental disability needs to be resolved. One critic has suggested a padded cell. See R. J. Bonnie & J. Monahan (eds.), *Mental Disorder, Work Disability, and the Law* (Chicago: University of Chicago Press, 1997); Symposia, "Persons with Disabilities," *Behavioral Sciences & Law*, Winter 1996, vol. 14, no. 1; "The Americans with Disabilities Act: A Ten-Year Retrospective," *Alabama Law Review* 52 (2000): 1–423. See also S. Stefan, *Unequal Rights* (Washington, D.C.: American Psychological Association, 2001).

Olmstead v. L.C.

The U.S. Supreme Court held that, under appropriate circumstances, the ADA and its regulations require states to move mentally retarded individuals out of institutions and into community settings. In the opinion of qualified experts, the complainants, two mentally retarded women who were in institutional settings, could be provided treatment in community-based settings, but the state system was slow to place them in such settings. The complainants claimed that the ADA has a mainstreaming principle that requires that an individual with a disability should be placed in the most integrated setting appropriate to the person's needs. The Supreme Court adopted the basic principle in holding that "Unjustified isolation . . . is properly regarded as discrimination based on disability." The Court went on to recognize, however, "[t]he States' need to maintain a range of facilities for the care and treatment of persons with diverse mental disabilities, and the States' obligation to administer services with an even hand." The Court noted that "nothing in the ADA or its implementing regulations condones termination of institutional settings for persons unable to handle or benefit from community settings." The Court remanded the case for further proceedings. 119 S. Ct. 2176 (1999).

Breach of Confidentiality (Invasion of Privacy).
See also Duty to Warn or Protect in the Outpatient Setting

WRITING ABOUT A PATIENT

Roe v. Doe
The U.S. Supreme Court in this case accepted for review an action initiated by a psychiatric patient to prevent the publication of a book by her therapist. The patient, a university social work professor, claimed that the publication of the book, which appeared briefly before the suit was filed, violated her right of privacy and the confidential nature of the doctor-patient relationship. The issue as presented to the Supreme Court was the propriety of a prior restraint on free expression in order to protect privacy or confidential information. In a relatively unusual action, after hearing oral arguments, the Supreme Court decided not to resolve the dispute. No reason was given for the dismissal, other than the usual recital that the order accepting the case had been "improvidently granted." 420 U.S. 307 (1975); discussed in R. Slovenko, *Psychotherapy and Confidentiality* (Springfield, Ill.: Thomas, 1998).

MANAGED CARE

Under managed care therapists must disclose more information about a patient than under traditional insurance coverage. They must file reports about their patients to case managers, who review the clinician's observations and recommend a treatment plan before approving insurance benefits. Therapists also must submit frequent progress reports, and sometimes even share their notes about what patients have confided to them. Due to the stigma that attaches to mental illness, some individuals will decide not to seek treatment because a third party will be privy to the therapy. When a managed care company is associated with an employer's human resource department, the employee is even less likely to seek treatment because the information may leak to the employer. K. Corcoran & V. Vandiver, *Maneuvering the Maze of Managed Care* (New York: Free Press, 1996); K. Corcoran & W. Winslade, "Eavesdropping on the 50 Minute Hour: Managed Mental Health Care and Confidentiality," *Behavioral Sciences & Law* 12 (1994): 351. *See* Malpractice

Capital Punishment

The imposition of the death penalty involves a two-phase process, a decision-making phase and then another phase for the carrying out of the penalty. In imposing the penalty, a jury must first decide on guilt or innocence, and, second, after a guilty verdict, the jury must choose between the death penalty and life imprisonment. In doing that, they must consider mitigating circumstances such as age and background and aggravating circumstances such as brutality of the crime and future dangerousness. In the posttrial phase, or the carrying out of the penalty, the condemned must be "competent to be executed." By and large, psychiatrists protest participating in the process, in particular the execution stage. The General Assembly of the World Psychiatric Association Congress in 1996 passed a declaration: "Under no circumstances should psychiatrists participate in legally authorized executions nor participate in legally authorized executions nor participate in assessments of competence to be executed." See Forum, "Psychiatrists and the Death Penalty: Some Ethical Dilemmas," *Current Opinion in Psychiatry* 11 (1998): 1–15; J. C. Schoenholtz, A. M. Freedman, & A. L. Halpern, "The 'Legal' Abuse of Physicians in Deaths in the United States: The Erosion of Ethics and Morality in Medicine," *Wayne L. Rev.* 42 (1996): 1505.

IMPOSITION OF THE DEATH PENALTY

Furman v. Georgia
The U.S. Supreme Court found the death penalty statutes of Texas and Georgia unconstitutional because they were applied in an arbitrary and irrational manner. Justice Brennan wrote, "When a country of over 200 million people inflicts an unusually severe punishment no more than 50 times a year, the inference is strong that the punishment is not being regularly and fairly applied. To dispel it would indeed require a clear showing of nonarbitrary infliction . . . [otherwise] it smacks of little more than a lottery system." 408 U.S. 238 (1972).

Woodson v. North Carolina
To avoid the discriminatory application of the death penalty, states made it mandatory upon conviction of certain crimes—but the Supreme Court struck down mandatory imposition. The Court called for the exercise of discretion. The Court found that the imposition of a compulsory death sentence without regard to the character of the defendant and the circumstances of the crime to be "inconsistent with the fundamental respect for humanity that underlies the Eighth Amendment." 428 U.S. 280 (1976).

Proffitt v. Florida
The Supreme Court upheld a statute listing aggravating and mitigating circumstances to be considered in imposing sentence. As a result, the typical capital sentencing statute sets out a list of aggravating and mitigating factors, but without telling the decision maker how to balance these circumstances. The statutes are phrased in terms that invite

psychiatric participation. 428 U.S. 242 (1976). California's death penalty scheme defines *death eligibility* so broadly that it apparently creates a greater risk of arbitrary death sentences than the pre-Furman death penalty schemes. S. F. Shatz & N. Rivkind, "The California Death Penalty Scheme: Requiem for *Furman?*" *N.Y.U. L. Rev.* 72 (1997): 1283.

Estelle v. Smith

May an examiner who evaluates the defendant's competency to stand trial later testify during the sentencing stage? In this case, Ernest Smith, who was charged with murder of a store clerk in a robbery, was deemed competent to stand trial, and was subsequently convicted. At the sentencing Dr. James Grigson, who had evaluated him for triability, testified that he was a "very severe sociopath" who would commit other acts of violence. The jury concluded that Smith met the criteria for the imposition of the death penalty. On writ of habeas corpus, a U.S. District Court in Texas vacated the sentence on the ground that the trial court made a constitutional error in admitting Dr. Grigson's testimony. The Supreme Court as well as the Fifth Circuit affirmed the district court's ruling. Writing for the majority, Chief Justice Burger dismissed the state's argument that the Fifth Amendment privilege against self-incrimination was inapplicable to the penalty phase of a trial. When examining the accused for triability, Dr. Grigson had not warned the accused about the possible use of the evidence for another purpose; hence, the Court held, the state violated his constitutional rights. 451 U.S. 454 (1980).

Barefoot v. Estelle

The Supreme Court upholds the constitutional validity of statutes mandating as an aggravating circumstance an affirmative prediction of future dangerousness, notwithstanding the difficulty of predicting it. 463 U.S. 880 (1983). At trial the state introduced into evidence the record of the defendant's prior convictions and his reputation for lawlessness. The state called on James Grigson, who, in response to hypothetical questions, testified that the defendant would probably commit further acts of violence and represent a continuing threat to society. Dr. Grigson testified that he could diagnose the defendant "within reasonable psychiatric certainty" as an individual with "a fairly classical, typical, sociopathic personality disorder." And he testified that whether the defendant was in society at large or in a prison society there was a "one hundred percent and absolute" chance that the defendant would commit future acts of criminal violence that would constitute a continuing threat to society. (The testimony was based on hypothetical questions as the defendant declined an examination.) In an amicus brief the American Psychiatric Association argued that psychiatric predictions of future dangerous behavior ought to be excluded from death penalty proceedings as a matter of law, because the empirical data indicate a large margin of error. Justice White defended Dr. Grigson's testimony, saying that psychiatrists are not always wrong with respect to future dangerousness, and he added, "We are unconvinced, at least as of now, that the adversary process cannot be trusted to sort out the reliable from the unreliable evidence and opinion about future dangerousness, particularly when the convicted felon has the opportunity to present his own side of the case." 463 U.S. at 901.

In dissent, Justice Blackmun took issue with the validity of psychiatric predictions of violence. He wrote, "Psychiatric predictions of future dangerousness are not accurate; wrong two times out of three, their probative value, and therefore any possible contribution they might make to the ascertainment of truth, is virtually non-existent. . . . Indeed, given a psychiatrist's prediction that an individual will be dangerous, it is more likely than not that the defendant will not commit further violence." 463 U.S. at 928 (emphasis by Blackmun). See B. J. Ennis & T. R. Litwack, "Psychiatry and the Presumption of Expertise: Flipping Coins in the Courtroom," *Calif. L. Rev.* 62 (1974): 693; P. C. Giannelli, "'Junk Science': The Criminal Cases," *J. Crim. L. & Criminology* 84 (1993): 105. In response, Professor Christopher Slobogin wrote: "While it cannot be denied that mental health professionals using clinical prediction techniques are not very accurate at determining who is violence prone, they are not nearly as inept at the task as many would suggest. In fact knowledgeable clinicians are much better at predicting dangerousness than the random selection process suggested by the coin-flipping analogy." C. Slobogin, "Dangerousness and Expertise," *U. Pa. L. Rev.* 133 (1984): 97. See J. Monahan & H. Steadman (eds.), *Violence and Mental Disorder: Developments in Risk Assessment* (Chicago: University of Chicago Press, 1994); K. Tardiff, *Assessment and Management of Violent Patients* (Washington, D.C.: American Psychiatric Press, 1989); G. P. Palermo et al., "On the Predictability of Violent Behavior: Considerations and Guidelines," *J. Forensic Sciences* 36 (1991): 1435. See also K. B. Dekleva, "Psychiatric Expertise in the Sentencing Phase of Capital Murder Cases," *J. Am. Acad. Psychiatry & Law* 29 (2001): 58.

Penry v. Lynaugh

Two issues were before the U.S. Supreme Court: (1) Does a judge's failure to instruct a jury about mitigating evidence constitute a violation of the Eighth Amendment, and (2) does the Eighth Amendment prohibit the execution of the mentally retarded? Penry was charged with rape and murder. He was deemed competent to stand trial, and was found criminally responsible. He was mildly to moderately retarded, with IQ scores between 50 and 63. To decide on the death penalty, under the Texas statute, the jury had to assess deliberateness and future dangerousness. The defense objected to the trial court's failure to instruct the jury in regard to discretion based on mitigating circumstances. The Supreme Court, in an opinion written by Justice O'Connor, ruled that when mitigating evidence has been presented, the jury must be given instructions that make it possible to give effect to the mitigating evidence. On the second issue, the Court declined to prohibit the execution of retarded offenders under any circumstances. In a dissent, it was maintained that Justice O'Connor's opinion would give juries "unbridled discretion" to bring in all mitigating factors, which the dissenters considered to be just the kind of unpredictability that the Court had attempted to curtail. 492 U.S. 302 (1989).

Victim Impact Evidence

Payne v. Tennessee

The Supreme Court, overruling two of its earlier decisions, held that the Eighth Amendment is not a bar prohibiting a capital sentencing jury from considering victim impact evidence. The Court said: "A state may legitimately conclude that evidence about the victim and about the impact of the murder on the victim's family is relevant to the jury's decision as to whether or not the death penalty should be imposed. There is no reason to treat such evidence differently than other relevant evidence is treated." 501 U.S. 808 (1991).

Carrying Out the Death Penalty

Solesbee v. Balkom

The U.S. Supreme Court stated that postponement of execution because of postconviction insanity bears a close affinity not to trial but to reprieves of sentences, which is an executive power, and "seldom, if ever, has this power of executive clemency been subjected to review by the courts." 339 U.S. 9 (1950).

Caritativo v. California

The U.S. Supreme Court, extending its decision in *Solesbee,* upheld a procedure whereby the initiation of proceedings to determine the sanity of a condemned man is made by the warden in his sole judgment. Justice Harlan said, "Surely it is not inappropriate for [the state] to lodge this grave responsibility in the hands of the warden, the official who beyond all others had had the most intimate relations with, and best opportunity to observe, the prisoner." 357 U.S. 549 (1958). But Justice Frankfurter, joined by Justices Brennan and Douglas, strongly dissented: "Now it appears that [the determination of the sanity of a man condemned to death], upon which depends the fearful question of life or death, may be made on the mere say-so of the warden of a state prison, according to such procedure as he chooses to pursue, and more particularly without any right on the part of a man awaiting death who claims that insanity has supervened to have his case put to the warden. There can hardly be a comparable situation under our constitutional scheme of things in which an interest so great, that an insane man not be executed, is given such flimsy procedural protection, and where one asserting a claim is denied the rudimentary right of having his side submitted to the one who sits in judgment." 357 U.S. at 552.

Ford v. Wainwright

The issues before the U.S. Supreme Court were: (1) Does the Eighth Amendment prohibiting cruel and unusual punishment bar the execution of the insane, and (2) does Florida's procedure satisfy the requirements of due process? As to the first issue, the Court held that the Eighth Amendment prohibits executing a prisoner who is insane. On the due process issue, the Court held that Florida's procedure failed to ensure a fundamental right to be heard. The governor of Florida had an announced policy of excluding any "advocacy" on the issue of competence to be executed, and the entire determination of the issue was carried out within the executive branch. The Court ruled that the denial of *any* opportunity for the condemned person to challenge state witnesses resulted in an inadequate assurance of accuracy in the proceeding. Justice Rehnquist, joined by Chief Justice Burger, dissented, arguing that the executive has the responsibility to determine the sanity of the condemned as the governor is the "prisoner's custodian." 477 U.S. 399 (1986).

Perry v. Louisiana

The U.S. Supreme Court granted certiorari to consider the assertion of a right to refuse antipsychotic medication by a death row inmate who had been found incompetent to be executed. Louisiana had attempted to treat the prisoner with the medication so that he could be executed. After oral argument, the Court vacated the state court's decision ordering forced medication for reconsideration in light of its decision in the same year in *Washington v. Harper* (*see* Right to Refuse Treatment). 498 U.S. 38 (1990). On remand, the Louisiana Supreme Court found *Harper* distinguishable and held that involuntary administration of antipsychotic medication for restoring a prisoner to competency for the purpose of execution violated the state and federal constitutions. Louisiana v. Perry, 610 So.2d 746 (La. 1992). Louisiana now provides that if the state elects to treat the prisoner's incapacity, it can never carry out the death sentence. In Maryland and South Carolina, the sentence of a seriously mentally ill death row inmate who requires treatment is commuted to life imprisonment without parole. Louisiana Governor Earl Long once remarked, "Who in the hell wouldn't go mad on death-row?" The rule on "competency to be executed" is a ploy to avoid the carrying out of the penalty.

Singleton v. Norris

The Eighth Circuit reduced a death row inmate's sentence to life imprisonment without parole, declaring that his frequent slips into psychosis since 1987 even while on psychotropic drugs indicated that no one could be certain he was competent to be executed. The court said, "It is therefore time to bring this case to an end and grant a permanent stay of execution." 267 F.3d 859 (8th Cir. 2001). Dissenting, Chief Judge Roger Wollman wrote that the key problem was the lack of a definitive answer to the question of whether the inmate currently is competent under *Ford*, stating that further proceedings to obtain this answer would be appropriate. 267 F.3d at 871.

Child Abuse

Landeros v. Flood

The statutory duty to report suspected child abuse is construed to allow a malpractice action by the child against the physician who fails to report it. The child in this case claimed that she suffered harm as a proximate result of the defendant's negligence in failing to make a diagnosis and in failing to report the suspected abuse as required by state law. The California Supreme Court ruled that the statute gives rise to a duty under tort law. The court determined that an intervening act (the mother's continued beating of the child) did not relieve the defendant of liability, if the injury was reasonably foreseeable. Foreseeability was deemed a question of fact for the jury. The plaintiff was entitled to prove by expert testimony that the defendant should have reasonably foreseen that her mother would resume the abuse. 17 Cal.3d 399, 551 P.2d 389 (1976). See R. Slovenko, "Child Abuse and the Role of the Physician in the Proof of a Case," *J. Psychiatry & Law* 17 (1989): 477.

Child Custody

By and large, jurisdictions determine custody on the basis of the best interests of the child and legislation sets out factors to be considered in determining best interests. The weight to be accorded the factors is left to judicial discretion. See M. G. Goldzband, *Custody Cases and Expert Witnesses: A Manual for Attorneys* (Clifton, N.J.: Prentice Hall, 1988).

Painter v. Bannister

In a case extensively commented upon, the Iowa Supreme Court rejected the natural parent and awarded custody of a seven-year-old boy to the maternal grandparents. The court noted that the grandparents provided a stable, conventional, middle-class home whereas the father was "unstable, unconventional, arty and Bohemian." The boy's mother had died in an automobile accident. 258 Iowa 1390, 140 N.W.2d 152, *cert. denied*, 385 U.S. 949 (1966).

Civil Commitment. *See also* Right to Refuse Treatment, Right to Treatment

Hospitalization of Mrs. E. P. W. Packard

Modern-day civil commitment codes have their genesis in the campaign by Mrs. E. P. W. Packard for the adoption of mental health codes. In 1860 her husband, the Reverend Theophilus Packard, stating that he could not "manage" her at home, had her institutionalized in a mental hospital. To accomplish this, he utilized a state statute that provided that married women could be involuntarily committed on the request of the husband without the evidentiary standard applicable in other cases. Upon her discharge, by writ of habeas corpus, she went on a crusade for the adoption of mental health codes. Barbara Sapinsky has written a book sympathetic to Mrs. Packard, *The Private War of Mrs. Packard* (New York: Paragon House, 1991). See A. Deutsch, *The Mentally Ill in America* (New York: Columbia University Press, 2d ed. 1949); G. N. Grob, *Mental Institutions in America: Social Policy to 1875* (New York: Free Press, 1973).

In re Brewer

In denying a jury in a civil commitment proceeding, the Iowa Supreme Court in 1937 stated the purposes of commitment in these words: "The purpose of an inquisition of insanity is to aid and assist the individual, to provide means whereby the state may protect its unfortunate citizens, to furnish hospitalization so that the insane will have an opportunity to rehabilitate and readjust themselves into useful and happy citizens.

It is not a criminal proceeding in any way. The restraint placed upon them is only until they have recovered so that they may again take their places in the communities from which they came. The confinement is not intended as punishment, but solely and only to provide the mentally sick with that environment which may possibly cure the disease and return them to society as useful citizens." 224 Iowa 773, 276 N.W. 766 (1937). In dissent, Justice Mitchell said, "The question which confronts us is an all-important one. It involves depriving a citizen of her liberty without a trial by jury. It gives to the court the right to pass upon a fact question, namely, the sanity of an individual, rather than having that question determined by a jury." 276 N.W. at 769.

Discussion

Michigan Probate Court Judge Arthur E. Moore in an article in 1947 recommended enforced hospitalization in the case of: "A person who now is or with reasonable probability or certainty soon will become mentally ill to a degree which will so lessen the capacity of such a person to use his customary self-control, judgment and discretion in the conduct of his affairs and social relations as to make it advisable for him to be under medical and hospital treatment, care, supervision, or control, either for the protection of society or of the individual." A. E. Moore, "Improved Legal Procedure for the Care of the Mentally Ill," *J. Am. Judicature Soc.* 31 (1947): 47.

In a paper published in 1869 the renowned Isaac Ray wrote: "In the first place, the law should put no hindrance in the way to the prompt use of those instrumentalities which are regarded as most effectual in promoting the comfort and restoration of the patient. Secondly, it should spare all the necessary exposure of private troubles and all unnecessary conflict with popular prejudices. Thirdly, it should protect individuals from wrongful imprisonment. It would be objection enough to any legal provision that it failed to secure these objects in the completest possible manner." I. Ray, "Confinement of the Insane," *Am. L. Rev.* 3 (1869):193, 208, reprinted in *Contributions to Mental Pathology* (Boston: Little, Brown, 1873). See also M. A. Peszke, *Involuntary Treatment of the Mentally Ill* (Springfield, Ill.: Thomas, 1975); D. H. Melaney, "Commitment of the Mentally Ill: Treatment or Travesty," *U. Pittsburgh L. Rev.* 12 (1950): 52.

Lessard v. Schmidt

The U.S. District Court in Wisconsin invoked criminal justice procedures in the civil commitment process: notice and hearing, right to counsel, proof beyond a reasonable doubt, the privilege against self-incrimination, and the criterion of dangerousness as the basis for commitment. The decision being that of a lower court, its application was limited to the jurisdiction of that court but it had an impact nationwide. 349 F.Supp. 1078 (E.D. Wis. 1972).

Discussion

During the tumultuous 1960s and 1970s, the focus of civil commitment changed from *parens patriae* to police power. Not only were criminal justice criteria invoked in civil commitment, mental hospitals were closed and jails became the site of the mentally ill. See P. S. Appelbaum, *Almost a Revolution: Mental Health Law and the Limits of Change* (New York: Oxford University Press, 1994); R. J. Isaac & V. C. Arnot, *Madness in the Streets: How Psychiatry and the Law Abandoned the Mentally Ill* (New York: Free Press, 1990); J. Q. La Fond & M. L. Durham, *Back to the Asylum: The Future of Mental Health Law and Policy in the United States* (New York: Oxford University Press, 1993); A. A. Stone, *Mental Health and Law: A System in Transition* (Rockville, Md.: National Institute of Mental Health, 1975); E. F. Torrey, *Nowhere to Go: The Tragic Odyssey of the Homeless Mentally Ill* (New York: Harper & Row, 1988); R. Slovenko, "The Hospitalization of the Mentally Ill Revisited," *Pacific L.J.* 24 (1993): 1107; R. Slovenko, "Criminal Justice Procedures in Civil Commitment," *Wayne L. Rev.* 24 (1997): 1; R. Slovenko & E. D. Luby, "On the Emancipation of Mental Patients," *J. Psychiatry & Law* 3 (1975): 191.

Addington v. Texas

In order to render civil commitment more difficult if not impossible, the Mental Health Law Project urged the court to incorporate the proof beyond a reasonable doubt standard of criminal justice into the civil commitment process. Chief Justice Warren Burger recognized that a standard of proof beyond a reasonable doubt to establish the criteria for civil commitment—"mental illness" and "dangerousness" or "gravely disabled"—would be well-nigh impossible, and as a consequence, would do away with involuntary commitment. Writing the opinion of the Court, he said, "Given the lack of certainty and the fallibility of psychiatric diagnosis, there is a serious question as to whether a state could ever prove beyond a reasonable doubt that an individual is both mentally ill and likely to be dangerous." The chief justice called for a clear and convincing evidence standard in commitment hearings, which is a higher standard than the preponderance of the evidence standard of the ordinary civil case and less than the proof beyond a reasonable doubt standard of criminal cases. 441 U.S. 418 (1979).

Do instructions to the jury on burden of proof make a difference? Justice Burger mused: "Candor suggests that, to a degree, efforts to analyze what lay jurors understand concerning the differences among these three tests or the nuances of a judge's instructions on the law may well be largely an academic exercise; there are no directly relevant empirical studies. Indeed, the ultimate truth as to how the standards of proof affect decision making may well be unknowable, given that fact finding is a process shared by countless thousands of individuals throughout the country. We probably can assume no more than that the difference between a preponderance of the evidence and proof beyond a reasonable doubt probably is better understood than either of them in relation to the intermediate standard of clear and convincing evidence. Nonetheless, even if the particular standard-of-proof catchwords do not always make a great difference in a particular case, adopting a 'standard of proof is more than an empty semantic exercise.' [citation]. In cases involving individual rights, whether criminal or civil, '[t]he standard of proof [at a minimum] reflects the value society places on individual liberty.'" 441 U.S. at 424–25.

Justice Burger went on to say: "The subtleties and nuances of psychiatric diagnosis render certainties virtually beyond reach in most situations. The reasonable-doubt standard of criminal law functions in its realm because there the standard is addressed to specific, knowable facts. Psychiatric diagnosis, in contrast, is to a large extent based on medical 'impressions' drawn from subjective analysis and filtered through the experience of the diagnostician. This process often makes it very difficult for the expert physician to offer definite conclusions about any particular patient. Within the medical discipline, the traditional standard for 'factfinding' is a 'reasonable medical certainty.' If a trained psychiatrist has difficulty with the categorical 'beyond a reasonable doubt' standard, the untrained lay juror—or indeed even a trained judge—who is required to rely upon expert opinion could be forced by the criminal law standard of proof to reject commitment for many patients desperately in need of institutionalized psychiatric care. Such 'freedom' for a mentally ill person would be purchased at a high price." 441 U.S. at 430. See P. Chodoff, "The Case for Involuntary Hospitalization of the Mentally Ili," *Am. J. Psychiatry* 133 (1976): 496; J. Monahan & D. Wexler, "A Definite Maybe: Proof and Probability in Civil Commitment," *Law & Human Behavior* 2 (1978): 37.

Parham v. J.R.

The traditional presumption of parental beneficence along with the role of the admitting physician as a "neutral fact finder" have been deemed sufficient to protect minors in decisions about commitment to a mental institution. This case presented the question of what process is constitutionally due a minor child whose parents or guardian seek state-administered institutional mental health care for the child and specifically whether an adversary proceeding is required prior to or after the commitment. Chief Justice Burger, writing for the majority, said: "Due process has never been thought to require that the neutral and detached trier of fact be law-trained or a judicial or administrative hearing officer. . . . Surely, this is the case as to medical decisions, for neither judges nor administrative officers are better qualified than psychiatrists to render psychiatric judgments." 442 U.S. 584 (1979). The decision has been severely criticized by advocates for children's rights. Abuse in the treatment of minors is described in J. Sharkey, *Bedlam* (New York: St. Martin's Press, 1994). See also S. Jaworoski & A. Zabow, "Involuntary Psychiatric Hospitalization of Minors," *Medicine & Law* 14 (1995): 635.

Zinermon v. Burch

Over the years mental health professionals have urged voluntary mental hospitalization in preference to involuntary civil commitment. Admission practices urged individuals to sign themselves into the hospital as voluntary patients (they were known as "coerced voluntaries"). The process would avoid the stigma of civil commitment as well as the need to satisfy the legal criteria for commitment, the right to legal representation, and adjudication by a court. But in 1990 in *Zinermon,* the U.S. Supreme Court ruled that patient competency must be considered in regard to hospital admission as well as treatment.

Darrell Burch was seen bruised and bloodied, wandering on a Florida highway without shoes. He was brought by a concerned citizen to a community mental health service. He was hallucinating, confused, and disoriented. He thought that he was entering heaven. He signed a form for voluntary admission and another form authorizing treatment. After three days of treatment with psychotropic medication, he was transferred to Florida State Hospital, where he again signed voluntary admission and treatment forms. As a voluntary patient, he was presumably free to leave at any time. He remained there for about five months.

Upon discharge, he complained that he had been improperly admitted to both facilities and had thus been confined and treated against his will. He claimed that because he was not competent to sign any legal documents, he had a constitutional right to a judicial commitment before being admitted and treated and that since there had been no such hearing, he had been deprived of his liberty without due process of law. The Supreme Court agreed. In a 5–4 ruling, the Court held that, before being admitted and treated, he was entitled to a judicial hearing or at least some other hearing that would be a safeguard against arbitrary action by the state, to determine either that he was competent to consent to admission or that he met the statutory standard for involuntary commitment. The Court acknowledged that persons who are mentally ill and incapable of giving informed consent to admission would not necessarily meet the statutory standard for involuntary placement, which requires either that they are likely to injure themselves or others, or that their neglect or refusal to care for themselves threatens their well-being. The Court said: "The involuntary placement process serves to guard against the confinement of a person who, though mentally ill, is harmless and can live safely outside an institution. Confinement of such a person not only violates Florida law, but also is unconstitutional. . . . Thus, it is at least possible that if Burch had had an involuntary placement, [he] would not have been confined at FSH. Moreover, even assuming that Burch would have met the statutory requirements for involuntary placement, he still could have been harmed by being deprived of other protections built into the involuntary placement procedure, such as the appointment of a guardian advocate to make treatment decisions, and periodic judicial review of placement."

The case has been widely criticized because most patients coming to psychiatric facilities are in such a condition that their competence to admit themselves voluntarily or to consent to treatment is questionable. As a result of the decision, a psychiatric facility faces liability for false imprisonment if it admits an individual of questionable competence on a voluntary basis without providing some procedure, possibly an adversarial judicial hearing. Actually, other than his liberty having been deprived without due process, there was little in the way of damages to Burch, and he had been helped by his hospitalization. Accordingly, a nominal settlement was negotiated, giving Burch some money, and making a contribution to his lawyer. 494 U.S. 113 (1990).

Kennedy v. Schafer

Because a voluntary mental patient does not enjoy the same due process protections as an involuntary patient, it is prudent for a patient to enter a hospital via the involuntary route. In this case, the Eighth Circuit ruled that a teenage patient who committed suicide while under treatment at a state psychiatric facility did not have a constitutionally protected liberty interest in a safe and humane environment under the due process clause of the Fourteenth Amendment. Because the patient was voluntarily admitted to the state facility by her parents, the court held that she was not entitled to the same due process right to a safe and humane environment as would a patient under the same circumstances who had been involuntarily committed to the facility. Her parents brought suit under 42 U.S.C., sec. 1983, for infringement of rights conferred by the Constitution.

The due process clause of the Fourteenth Amendment ensures that "[n]o *State* shall . . . deprive any person of life, liberty, or property, without due process of law" (emphasis added). As the U.S. Supreme Court said in *DeShaney v. Winnebago Cty. Dept. Soc. Servs.*, 489 U.S. 189 (1989), the "deprivation of liberty" that triggers "the protection of the Due Process Clause" is "the State's affirmative act of restraining the individual's freedom to act on his own behalf—through incarceration, institutionalization, or other similar restraint of personal liberty." Thus, from the perspective of both the hospital and the patient, the involuntary route is preferable. 71 F.3d 292 (8th Cir. 1995). See also Wilson v. Formigoni, 832 F.Supp. 1152 (N.D.Ill. 1993).

Foucha v. Louisiana

The U.S. Supreme Court ordered the release of a person acquitted by reason of insanity who had since been diagnosed as an antisocial personality and, according to the state's doctors, was no longer mentally ill. A plurality of the Supreme Court held that because Foucha had not been convicted and could not be committed (due to the absence of mental illness), he had to be released. The Court said that to rule otherwise "would be only a step away from substituting confinement for dangerousness for our present system which, with only narrow exceptions and aside from permissible confinements for mental illness, incarcerates only those who are proved beyond reasonable doubt to have violated a criminal law." 504 U.S. 71 (1992). However, in Kansas v. Hendricks, 117 S. Ct. 2072 (1997), the Court held that convicted sex offenders who have a "mental abnormality" or "personality disorder" may be confined indefinitely even if not treatable. *See* Sex Offenders

Heller v. Doe

A Kentucky statute on the civil commitment of individuals with mental retardation was challenged because it had a lower standard of proof for committing mentally retarded people than that used for others, and because it allowed parents and others to participate in the proceedings as if they were parties to the proceedings. Mental disability organizations filed amici briefs arguing that mentally retarded individuals should be entitled to the same procedural protections given to people with other disabilities. The U.S. Supreme Court upheld the statute, but the Court did not accept the state's invitation to hold that the mentally retarded were entitled to no procedural protections. 509 U.S. 312 (1993).

Competencies in the Criminal Trial Process

Various legal competencies are involved in the criminal process: competency to confess, competency to plead guilty, competency to refuse an insanity defense, competency to waive the right of an attorney, competency to stand trial, competency to represent oneself, and competency to testify. For competency regarding execution, *see* Capital Punishment.

COMPETENCY TO CONFESS

Leyra v. Denno

The police interrogated the defendant for several days in connection with the murder of his parents. Then, having promised to obtain a physician to relieve the defendant from the severe pain of a sinus attack, the police summoned a psychiatrist who, rather than providing medical assistance, questioned the defendant for over an hour, using both suggestive and hypnotic techniques. Aside from any issue of coercion, the Court determined that the psychiatrist's interrogation was fundamentally unfair considering the way that society traditionally has viewed the physician-patient relationship. The evidence was thus excluded. 347 U.S. 556 (1954). The deception is to be distinguished from the police use of jail plants and other informants to gain information from defendants. See J. D. Grano, *Confessions, Truth and the Law* (Ann Arbor: University of Michigan, 1993).

Colorado v. Connelly

Despite Miranda warnings that he need not talk, the accused insisted on giving the police self-incriminating details of a murder. In seeking to exclude the confession, the defense offered the testimony of a psychiatrist that although the accused understood his right to remain silent, he had been "compelled" to confess by "command delusions" from God. The Supreme Court held that neither the requirement of voluntariness nor Miranda called for the exclusion of the evidence, because there was no police conduct causally related to the confession. The defendant was not so cognitively impaired that the right to remain silent was not understood. 479 U.S. 157 (1986).

COMPETENCY TO PLEAD

At a preliminary proceeding, known as the arraignment, the accused is called upon to answer to the indictment: guilty, not guilty, or not guilty by reason of insanity. At one time, a refusal to plead (standing mute) deprived the court of capacity to hear the case, but did not provide an escape for a defendant. Pressure was literally applied: increasingly heavier weights were placed on the defendant's chest until he answered. (Hence the expression "pressed for an answer.") A brave or obstinate defendant might allow himself to be pressed to death in order to avoid conviction and consequent forfeiture of his property to the crown, which would leave his family destitute. Nowadays, standing mute is considered the equivalent of pleading not guilty.

Because a guilty plea is a waiver of constitutional rights (privilege against self-incrimination, the right to a jury trial, and the right to confront one's accusers), the judge must set out on the record the defendant's competency to plead (that is, to waive these rights). The question has been posed whether the standard for competency to plead guilty is higher, lower, or the same as competency to stand trial. Obviously, a high standard for competency to plead would frustrate the common practice of plea bargaining. Holding a defendant incompetent to plead but competent to stand trial would result in forcing the defendant into a trial that the defendant would rather avoid to obtain a more favorable negotiated sentence. The Supreme Court ruled that the standard for competency to plead guilty is the "same" as competency to stand trial but that formulation obfuscates the different matters that the defendant must understand.

Godinez v. Moran

The U.S. Supreme Court rejected the argument that the Constitution requires separate evaluations of different competencies. The majority opinion held that "there is no reason to believe that the decision to waive counsel requires an appreciably higher level of mental functioning than the decision to waive other constitutional rights." An amicus brief filed by mental health and mental retardation organizations argued against a unitary all-or-nothing approach as did the dissenting opinion: "The majority's monolithic approach to competency is true to neither life nor the law. Competency for one purpose does not necessarily translate to competency for another purpose." The defendant Moran was sentenced to death after waiving his right to be represented by counsel and pleading guilty to murder. His waiver and plea came shortly after he had attempted suicide and while he was substantially medicated. The Court of Appeals for the Ninth Circuit reversed his sentence on the ground there had not been a determination of whether he was competent to waive counsel and plead guilty. 509 U.S. 389 (1993).

COMPETENCY TO WAIVE THE RIGHT TO COUNSEL AND TO REPRESENT ONESELF

Westbrook v. State of Arizona

The U.S. Supreme Court for the first time drew a distinction between a defendant's competency to stand trial and his competency to waive counsel and represent himself. It ruled that competence to stand trial with the assistance of counsel does not suffice for self-representation, although it is the threshold to a proper determination of competency for self-representation. In *Westbrook*, a case involving a charge of murder, the trial judge ruled that the defendant was competent to stand trial (it was the unanimous opinion of three examining psychiatrists), and thereupon the defendant insisted upon representing himself. He was convicted of first-degree murder with the penalty set at death. On appeal, he argued that he was mentally incompetent to represent himself at trial; that is to say, he claimed ineffective assistance of counsel. The Arizona Supreme Court held that the trial court was not required "to set a hearing to determine whether the defendant through insanity or mental deficiency was not able to conduct his own defense." On certiorari, the U.S. Supreme Court said in a brief per curiam opinion: "Although petitioner received a hearing on the issue of his competence to stand trial, there appears to have been no hearing or inquiry into the issue of his competence to waive his constitutional right to the assistance of counsel and proceed, as he did, to conduct his own defense. . . . [A] protecting duty imposes the serious and weighty responsibility upon the trial judge of determining whether there is an intelligent and competent waiver by the accused." 384 U.S. 150 (1996).

State v. Kolocotronis

The Washington Supreme Court stated, "[*Westbrook v. Arizona*] holds unequivocally that an adjudication by the trial court that an accused is capable of going to trial and aiding his counsel, is not a determination of his competency to act as his own counsel. When the accused demands his constitutional right to act as his own counsel, the trial court is faced with the necessity of making a factual determination of the competency of the accused to: (1) intelligently waive the services of counsel, and (2) act as his own counsel." 73 Wash.2d 92, 436 P.2d 774 (1968).

Government of Virgin Islands v. Niles

A federal district court in the Virgin Islands held, "As for defendant's competency to waive counsel, the court is of the opinion that one who may be suffering from paranoid delusions should not be entrusted with the sole conduct of his defense." 295 F.Supp. 266 (D.V.I. 1969). In 1995, we recall, Colin Ferguson, charged with carrying out a massacre on the Long Island Railroad, was allowed to represent himself, and he turned the trial into a circus. He wanted no part of the "black rage" defense being prepared for him by his lawyers; he insisted instead that he simply was not the killer. "Obviously," said his one-time defense lawyer, "we should not allow an insane man to represent himself." See G. B. Palermo & E. M. Scott, *The Paranoid* (Springfield, Ill.: Thomas, 1997); R. L. Goldstein, "Paranoia in the Legal System: The Litigation Paranoid and the Paranoid Criminal," *Psychiatric Clinics of North America* 18 (1995): 303.

Faretta v. California

In 1975 the U.S. Supreme Court held that a criminal defendant has a constitutional right to self-representation. The Court acknowledged that in most criminal prosecutions the accused could better defend with counsel's guidance than by his own unskilled efforts, but the Court noted, "Personal liberties are not rooted in the law of averages." In dissent, Justice Blackmum quoted the proverb that "one who is his own lawyer has a fool for a client." He needled the majority by stating that the court "now bestows a constitutional right on one to make a fool of himself." He argued that "representation by counsel is essential to ensure a fair trial."

The essence of the ruling in *Faretta* is the right of autonomy. Because it is the defendant, not the lawyer, who will suffer the consequences of a conviction, it is the accused's personal right to decide whether counsel is a benefit or a detriment. Justice Stewart explained, "Whatever else may be said of those who wrote the Bill of Rights, surely there can be no doubt that they understood the inestimable worth of free choice. Even if the defendant's freely-willed decision is ultimately to his own detriment, the choice must be honored out of that respect for the individual which is the lifeblood of the law." Because self-representation is an independent right, and not simply a waiver of the right to counsel, a defendant who wishes to represent himself must be permitted to do so as long as he is mentally competent to understand the basic nature of the right that he is waiving. Specifically, the Court stated that a defendant "should be made aware of the dangers and disadvantages of self-representation, so that the record will establish that 'he knows what he is doing and his choice is made with eyes open.'" At the same time the Court stated that a trial court may, even over the objection of the defendant, appoint "standby counsel." The purpose of standby counsel is limited: to aid the defendant if and when he requests help, and to take over the case in the event self-representation must be terminated. 422 U.S. 806 (1975). See also United States v. Farhad, 190 F.3d 1097 (9th Cir. 1999).

McKaskle v. Wiggins

In 1984 the Supreme Court said that the right of self-representation is not violated unless standby counsel substantially interferes with "significant tactical decisions" of the defendant, "controls the questioning of witnesses," speaks in defendant's place against his wishes "on matters of importance," or in some other way "destroys the jury's perception that the defendant is representing himself." As a corollary, the court stated, as it did in *Faretta*, a defendant who exercises his right to appear *pro se* cannot thereafter complain that the quality of his own defense amounted to a denial of "effective assistance of counsel." Once a court determines that a competent defendant of his own free will has "knowingly and intelligently" waived the right to counsel, the dictates of *Faretta* are satisfied, the inquiry is over, and the court will not inquire further into whether the defendant could provide himself with a substantively qualitative defense, for it is within the defendant's rights, if he so chooses, to sit mute and mount no defense at all. 465 U.S. 168 (1984). See A. R. Felthous, "Competency to Waive Counsel: A Step Beyond Competency to Stand Trial," *J. Psychiatry & Law* 7 (1979): 471.

COMPETENCY TO REFUSE A PLEA OF NOT GUILTY BY REASON OF INSANITY

The appellate courts are divided on the question of the judiciary's authority or duty to impose an insanity defense on a mentally disabled defendant. A defendant may prefer confinement in a prison rather than in a mental institution, or may wish to avoid the stigma associated with mental disorder. At the same time the state has a duty to see that justice is served. The issue is discussed in R. Arens, "Due Process and the Rights of the Mentally Ill: The Strange Case of Frederick Lynch," *Catholic U. L. Rev.* 13 (1964): 3; A. Krash, "The Durham Rule and Judicial Administration of the Insanity Defense in the District of Columbia," *Yale L. J.* 70 (1961): 905; R. Miller et al., "Forcing the Insanity Defense on Unwilling Defendants: Best Interests and the Dignity of the Law," *J. Psychiatry & Law* 24 (1996): 487; H. A. Samuels, "Can the Prosecution Allege That the Accused Is Insane?" *Crim. L. Rev.* 1960: 453. See also M. R. Damaska, *Evidence Law Adrift* (New Haven: Yale University Press, 1997), p. 115.

Whalem v. United States

The District of Columbia Circuit Court of Appeals appeared to establish a duty on trial judges to impose an insanity defense when the defense would be likely to succeed. The court said: "One of the major foundations for the structure of the criminal law is the concept of responsibility, and the law is clear that one whose acts would otherwise be criminal has committed no crime at all if because of incapacity due to age or mental condition he is not responsible for those acts. . . . In the courtroom confrontations between the individual and society, the trial judge must uphold this structural foundation by refusing to allow the conviction of an obviously mentally irresponsible defendant, and when there is sufficient question as to a defendant's mental responsibility at the same time of the crime, that issue must become part of the case. Just as the judge must insist that the *corpus delecti* be proved before a defendant who has confessed may be convicted, so too must the judge forestall the conviction of one who in the eyes of the law is not mentally responsible for his otherwise criminal acts." 346 F.2d 812 (1965).

People v. Redmond

In moving for withdrawal of a not guilty by reason of insanity plea, defense counsel stated that it was his client's wish to accept criminal punishment consisting of a county jail sentence, which at most was six months, rather than an indefinite noncriminal commitment to a mental hospital. The trial court expressed its view that such a disposition would result in defendant's getting a criminal record, albeit for a misdemeanor, in face of "overwhelming" or "very, very strong" evidence in the record that defendant was not criminally responsible for the crime because of his insanity. It stated to defense counsel that under the circumstances, defense counsel (in its opinion) was not acting in the best interests of his client. It also expressed concern about compliance with the penal code provision: "A person cannot be tried, adjudged to punishment, or punished for a public offense, while he is insane." It denied defendant's motion to withdraw his insanity plea and ordered the issue to be tried over defense objections. The California Court of Appeals stated: "The accommodation between humanitarian principles which absolves a convicted criminal of guilt because of insanity and provides for his hospitalization and the necessity of protecting the community at the same time against violent crimes and injuries on innocent people perpetrated by insane persons is neither simple nor easy. We also seek in this accommodation to respect even the mentally ill person's dignity as an individual to the utmost extent permissible with due regard for the protection of the public." 16 Cal. App.3d 931, 94 Cal. Rptr. 543 (1971).

Frendak v. United States

In another line of cases, as illustrated by this case, the defendant's decision on raising the insanity defense is to be followed provided the defendant is competent to make the decision. The court said, "Respect for a defendant's freedom as a person mandates that he or she be permitted to make fundamental decisions about the course of the proceedings." 408 A.2d 364 (D.C. App. 1979). See R. Arens, *Make Mad the Guilty* (Springfield, Ill.: Thomas, 1969).

Competency to Stand Trial

Dusky v. United States

As a legal definition of *competency to stand trial,* the U.S. Supreme Court held that "the test must be whether [the defendant] has sufficient present ability to consult with his attorney with a reasonable degree of rational understanding and whether he has a rational as well as factual understanding of the proceedings against him." 362 U.S. 402 (1960).

United States v. Ezra Pound

When World War II ended in 1945 Ezra Pound was taken into custody by American troops in Italy and returned to the United States where he was charged with treason because of his broadcasts from Rome during the war. It was decided, jointly by the government and by the defense, that Pound be declared mentally unfit to stand trial and that he be hospitalized in St. Elizabeths Hospital, where he spent thirteen years. In 1958, with the consent of the government, the indictment against him was dismissed. He returned to Italy, where on arrival, he greeted reporters with a Fascist salute and announced that "all America is an insane asylum." The case is often cited as an illustration of the triability plea as a device to avoid a trial or to achieve a preventive detention. See T. S. Szasz, *Law, Liberty, and Psychiatry* (New York: Macmillan, 1963); E. F. Torrey, *The Roots of Treason: Ezra Pound and the Secret of St. Elizabeths* (New York: McGraw-Hill, 1984).

Discussion

In many countries a person found incompetent to stand trial is confined "at His Majesty's pleasure" and the "pleasure" is usually that the individual remain confined for the rest of his life. Such is the case, e.g., in South Africa of Demitrio Tsafendas, who assassinated Prime Minister Hendrik Verwoerd, the founder of apartheid. On September 6, 1966, Tsafendas, dressed in his parliamentary messenger's uniform strode between the benches on the floor of Parliament, shouldered aside a cabinet minister, and plunged a knife four times into the prime minister, killing him. Was he a madman, or a man with a mission? Was it a political assassination? It has been an article of faith among most South Africans that an imaginary tapeworm in his stomach ordered him to assassinate Verwoerd. The trial judge said, "I can as little try a man who has not at least the makings of a rational mind as I could try a dog or an inert implement. He is a meaningless creature." He remains in a mental hospital, some thirty years later, now old and enfeebled. As often the case, nontriability, like the insanity defense, saves an individual from the death penalty. Insanity, of course, takes many forms, and it is now asked whether it was Verwoerd who was insane. D. Beresford, "The Madness of Demitrio Tsafendas," *Mail & Guardian* (South Africa), Oct. 31, 1997, pp. 23–25 (an extended version submitted to the Truth and Reconciliation Commission).

Pate v. Robinson

When there are signs to indicate incompetency to stand trial, the trial court on its own initiative has responsibility to order an examination of the defendant. Supreme Court Justice Clark, in writing for the majority, recounted the defendant's long history of erratic behavior. Hence, the issue of competency may be raised on motion either by the prosecution or the defense, or by the court *sua sponte* (on its own motion). 383 U.S. 375 (1966).

Drope v. Missouri

Again in this case, the Supreme Court ruled that the trial court on its own initiative should have ordered an examination. The defendant's wife testified about the "strange behavior" of the defendant, and on the second day of trial he shot himself in an attempted suicide. The threshold for an evaluation on the issue of competency is not very high, for the Court said: "Evidence of a defendant's irrational behavior, his demeanor at trial, and any prior medical opinion on competence to stand trial are all relevant in determining whether further inquiry is required, but even one of these factors standing alone may, in some circumstances, be sufficient. There are, of course, no fixed or immutable signs which invariably indicate the need for further inquiry to determine fitness to proceed; the question is often a difficult one in which a wide range of manifestations and subtle nuances are implicated. That they are difficult to evaluate is suggested by the varying opinions trained psychiatrists can entertain on the same facts." 420 U.S. 162 (1975).

Wilson v. United States

The defendant fractured his skull while being chased by the police following an assault and robbery. He had no memory of the incidents with which he was charged, and he was deemed unlikely ever to regain his memory. The U.S. Court of Appeals for the District of Columbia Circuit ruled that amnesia of itself does not bar prosecution, but issued the following guidelines to assist the trial court in determining triability: (1) the extent to which the amnesia affected the defendant's ability to consult with and assist his lawyer; (2) the extent to which the amnesia affected the defendant's ability to testify in his own behalf; (3) the extent to which evidence to the crime itself as well as any reasonably possible alibi could be extrinsically reconstructed in view of the defendant's amnesia; (4) the extent to which the government assisted the defendant and his counsel in that reconstruction; (5) the strength of the prosecution's case—"most important here will be whether the Government's case is such as to negate all reasonable hypotheses of innocence. If there is any substantial possibility that the accused could, but for his amnesia, establish an alibi or other defense, it should be presumed that he would have been able to do so"; and (6) any other facts and circumstances that would indicate whether the defendant had a fair trial. 129 U.S. App. D.C. 107, 391 F.2d 460 (1968).

State v. McClendon

While holding that the defendant was competent to stand trial without violating his right to due process, the Arizona Supreme Court emphasized that each case of amnesia must be considered on its own merits and that no absolutes may be justified without investigation. 103 Ariz. 105, 437 P.2d 421 (1968).

Jackson v. Indiana

The defendant, deaf and mute, was unlikely ever to be competent to stand trial. The Supreme Court ruled that the disposition of the defendant—indefinite if not lifelong commitment to a mental facility—violated constitutional equal protection and due process guarantees. The Court said, "A person charged by a State with a criminal offense who is committed solely on account of his incapacity to proceed to trial cannot be held more than a reasonable period of time necessary to determine whether there is a substantial probability that he will attain the capacity in the foreseeable future. If it is determined that this is not the case, then the State must either institute the customary civil commitment proceedings that would be required to commit indefinitely another citizen or release the defendant." 406 U.S. 715 (1972). In the course of the opinion, the Court stated, "Considering the number of persons affected, it is perhaps remarkable that the substantive constitutional limitations [on a state's commitment] power have not been more frequently litigated." This comment prompted litigation on civil commitment. See R. Slovenko, "The Hospitalization of the Mentally Ill Revisited," *Pacific L.J.* 24 (1993): 1107.

Illinois v. Allen

To maintain decorum in the courtroom, the Supreme Court said that a judge may use *any* means to restrain an unruly defendant or witness, including handcuffs, gags, or removal from the room. Justice Black wrote, "Although mindful that courts must indulge every reasonable presumption against the loss of constitutional rights . . . we explicitly hold today that a defendant can lose his right to be present at trial if, after he has been warned by the judge that he will be removed if he continues his disruptive behavior, he nevertheless insists on conducting himself in a manner so disorderly, disruptive, and disrespectful of the court that his trial cannot be carried on with him in the courtroom." The Court ruled as it did notwithstanding the questionable mental competence of the defendant. 397 U.S. 337 (1970). See D. Paull, *Fitness to Stand Trial* (Springfield, Ill.: Thomas, 1993); R. Slovenko, "The Developing Law on Competency to Stand Trial," *J. Psychiatry & Law* 5 (1977): 165.

United States v. Davis

The D.C. Circuit Court of Appeals observed that because of the proximity to client and case, "counsel's firsthand evaluation of a defendant's ability to consult on his case and to understand the charges against him may be as valuable as expert psychiatric opinion on his competency." 511 F.2d 355, 360 (1975). Might assessment of competency to stand trial be left to defense counsel? After all, the defense attorney is not only in close and continuing communication with a client, but also knows the extent to which defenses may turn on the client's ability to understand them and assist counsel in advancing them. Or why not leave the assessment to the judge or to another attorney? See D. Woychuk, *Attorney for the Damned* (New York: Free Press, 1996); R. Slovenko, "Assessing Competency to Stand Trial," *Psychiatric Annals* 25 (1995): 392.

INVOLUNTARY TREATMENT TO ACCOMPLISH TRIABILITY

Riggins v. Nevada

The Supreme Court ruled that due process was violated when the defendant was forced to stand trial while on a heavy dose of an antipsychotic drug (Mellaril), which he claimed had negatively affected his demeanor and his ability to participate in the proceedings. The Court's decision turned on the absence of sufficient evidence to justify continuing medication over the defendant's objection. Reiterating that antipsychotic medication intrudes on a significant liberty interest, the Court restated the standard set out in *Washington v. Harper* (1990) as requiring that the state show both an "overriding justification" for the treatment and that it is "medically appropriate." 504 U.S. 127 (1992).

COMPETENCY OR CREDIBILITY OF A WITNESS/HYPNOSIS

Hypnosis may enhance recollection but it also presents significant dangers. Hypnotized subjects may confabulate facts that never occurred and they are highly suggestible. They also may become "hardened" in their memories, thereby presenting an aura of confidence in their statements as well as undercutting the right of cross-examination. Because of these dangers, special rules have been established regulating the admissibility of hypnotically refreshed testimony. See K. M. McConkey & P. W. Sheehan, *Hypnosis, Memory, and Behavior in Criminal Investigation* (New York: Guilford Press, 1995); A. W. Scheflin & J. L. Shapiro, *Trance on Trial* (New York: Guilford Press, 1989).

State v. Hurd

In this seminal case, the New Jersey Supreme Court set out procedural safeguards to the admission of posthypnosis testimony: The hypnosis must be done by a licensed physician or psychologist trained in hypnosis; the hypnotist must be independent of the parties in the case; only written information should be given to the hypnotist prior to the hypnosis; the hypnotist should independently obtain the subject's recollection of the facts prior to initiating hypnosis; all contacts by the hypnotist with the witness should be recorded; and only the hypnotist should be present during the interview. 86 N.J. 525, 432 A.2d 86 (1981). See M. T. Orne, "The Use and Misuse of Hypnosis in Court," *Int'l J. Clin. Exp. Hypnosis* 27 (1979): 311. Dr. Michael T. Orne testified as an expert witness in the case.

People v. Shirley

California and a number of other states have (or had) a per se rule barring admission of hypnotically refreshed testimony. Under this view, even a rape victim, as in this case, is not allowed to testify about the rape if she had undergone hypnosis for any reason. The witness is deemed "polluted" for any testifying purpose. The California Supreme Court was influenced by the testimony of Dr. Bernard Diamond who maintained that hypnosis undercuts the right of cross-examination. 31 Cal.3d 18, 181 Cal. Rptr. 243, 641 P.2d 775, *cert. denied,* 103 S. Ct. 13 (1982). See B. Diamond, "Inherent Problems in the Use of Pretrial Hypnosis on a Prospective Witness," *Calif. L. Rev.* 68 (1980): 313. More recent California cases have retreated from *Shirley,* allowing a once-hypnotized witness to testify to events recalled and related prior to the hypnotic session. People v. Hayes, 49 Cal. 3d 1260, 265 Cal. Rptr. 132, 783 P.2d 719 (1989). In many jurisdictions, the courts have established procedural prerequisites for admissibility in order to reduce the risks associated with hypnosis. Perhaps the leading case in this line is *State v. Hurd,* the aforementioned New Jersey case.

State of Louisiana v. Clay Shaw

Enhancing memory of a witness by hypnosis is not carried out in the courtroom and the adversary may be unaware that it has occurred. In the trial of Clay Shaw in New Orleans for his alleged participation in the assassination of President John F. Kennedy, prosecutor Jim Garrison, unbeknown to the defense, had a principal witness, Perry Russo, hypnotized every morning prior to his testimony, presumably to relax him. R. Slovenko, "Jim Garrison's Pursuit of Justice Often Veered off the Beaten Track," *Detroit Legal News,* Jan. 15, 1992, p. 1. (Slovenko was a senior assistant district attorney under Jim Garrison but was not involved in the case.)

Rock v. Arkansas

With four justices dissenting, the U.S. Supreme Court ruled that a state may not bar the testimony of an accused (unlike that of the hypnotically refreshed testimony of an ordinary witness). The majority opinion was based on recognition of an accused's "constitutional right to testify in [his] own defense." It said, "A State's legitimate interest in barring unreliable evidence does not extend to *per se* exclusions that may be reliable in an individual case. Wholesale inadmissibility of a defendant's testimony is an arbitrary restriction on the right to testify in the absence of clear evidence by the State repudiating the validity of all posthypnosis recollections." 483 U.S. 44 (1987).

Consent to Treatment

Schloendorff v. Society of New York Hospital

In this oft-quoted decision, Judge Benjamin Cardozo wrote, "Every human being of adult years and sound mind has a right to determine what shall be done with his own body; and a surgeon who performs an operation without his patient's consent commits an assault, for which he is liable in damages." The patient had consented to an examination under anesthesia, but did not consent to the subsequent removal of a tumor while anesthetized. Judge Cardozo called the wrong an assault, but strictly speaking it would be a battery. 211 N.Y. 125, 105 N.W. 92 (1914).

Parham v. J.R.

The U.S. Supreme Court ruled on the right of a parent to consent on behalf of a minor, over the objection of the minor, for hospitalization in a mental institution. 442 U.S. 584 (1979). *See* Civil Commitment

Zinermon v. Burch

The U.S. Supreme Court ruled on one's competency to consent to voluntary hospitalization. 494 U.S. 113 (1990). *See* Civil Commitment

INFORMED CONSENT

Under the usual formulation, a physician has a legal obligation to disclose risks associated with the proposed treatment and its reasonable alternatives. Under the traditional doctrine of consent, the physician is obliged to disclose *what* is to be done, but under the more recently developed doctrine of informed consent the physician is also obliged to supply information as to *whether* it should be done. The theory of informed consent allows a cause of action when there is a poor outcome notwithstanding the standard of care. The allegation is made that the risk of the procedure was not made known. The action is based on negligence (covered by liability insurance) rather than a battery.

Patients suing under a theory of informed consent must prove that: (1) the defendant physician failed to inform adequately of a material risk; (2) if they had been informed of the risks they would not have consented to the treatment; and (3) the adverse consequences that were not made known did in fact occur and they were injured as a result of the treatment. There must be a showing, under the consensus view, that "the reasonable patient" would have made a different choice about treatment, or would have foregone the treatment, had the allegedly withheld information been given. The late Dr. Gerald L. Klerman argued for full disclosure of the doctor's approach to therapy. Recent developments indicate that the doctrine may require information not only about the treatment but also about the physician. There is also modification in the requirement of proof of a causal nexus between the lack of informed consent and injury. See R. Slovenko, "Psychotherapy and Informed Consent: A Search in Judicial Regulation," in W. E. Barton & C. J. Sanborn (eds.), *Law and the Mental Health Professions* (New York: International Universities Press, 1978), pp. 51–70.

Information about the Physician

Behringer Estate v. Princeton Medical Center

The hospital informed patients that the plaintiff physician, a plastic surgeon, had AIDS. The physician was also a patient at the hospital. He brought suit against the hospital, claiming invasion of privacy and breach of confidentiality. As a result of the disclosure, his practice declined. He argued (1) the risk of transmission of HIV from surgeon to patient is too remote to require informed consent, and (2) the law of informed consent does not require disclosure of the condition of the physician. The court ruled that the hospital had not only the right but the duty to disclose. It said: "It is axiomatic that physicians performing invasive procedures should not knowingly place a patient at risk because of the physician's physical condition. . . . The policy adopted by the medical center barring 'any procedures that pose any risk of virus transmission to the patient' appears to preclude, on its face, the necessity of an informed consent form; if there is 'any risk' the procedure cannot be performed. . . . The doctrine of informed consent, as an adjunct to the adopted medical center 'any risk' policy, provides the necessary element of patient control which is lacking from the policy standing alone." While recognizing that the risk of transmission of the virus from a provider to patient is low, the court saw other risks such as the risk of extended uncertainty and testing for a patient

927

exposed to a surgical accident involving a surgeon with AIDS. 249 N.J. Super. 597, 592 A.2d 1251 (1991). See J. F. Sullivan, "Should a Hospital Inform Patients If One of Its Surgeons Has AIDS?" *New York Times*, Dec. 12, 1989, p. 15.

Hidding v. Williams

In this Louisiana case, the failure of the physician to disclose his chronic alcohol abuse was held to have vitiated the patient's consent to surgery. There was a poor outcome, but the report of the case does not indicate that the physician was under the influence of alcohol at the time of surgery, or that his hands trembled, or that the care fell below acceptable standards. Nonetheless, the Louisiana Court of Appeals said, "Because this condition creates a material risk associated with the surgeon's ability to perform, which if disclosed would have obliged the patient to have elected another course of treatment, the fact-finder's conclusion that nondisclosure is a violation of the informed consent doctrine is entirely correct." 578 So.2d 1192 (La. App. 1991). See R. H. Coombs, *Drug Impaired Professionals* (Cambridge: Harvard University Press, 1997).

Discussion

Medical consumers are not informed and do not have access to malpractice data about a physician. In a full-page advertisement in the *New York Times* (Dec. 7, 1997) promoting an article in *Worth*, it was stated: "In 1986, Lena Katz-Grossman died during a business trip to New York, of complications related to pregnancy. Her condition, preeclampsia, is routinely diagnosed and virtually always manageable. So what went wrong? Her doctor failed to recognize the classic, life-threatening symptoms. By the time she was rushed to the hospital, it was too late for her and her baby. How was Lena to know that her highly recommended Manhattan ob/gyn, on staff at a famous teaching hospital, had numerous malpractice suits against him? Then as now, it's impossible for the ordinary consumer to find out a doctor's legal history. Even today, when data on payment made to settle malpractice suits is collected by a federal agency, the patient is kept unaware. Why? Because the AMA has made sure such information is available only to the medical profession." E. Grossman, "The Best Medicine," *Worth*, Dec./Jan. 1998, pp. 98–122. The case of Libby Zion made clear that too much responsibility is vested by the hospital in interns and residents and patients are unaware of it. See B. M. Bell, "Greenhorns in White," *New York Times*, Feb. 9, 1995, p. 15; B. Rensburger, "Patients Unaware Surgeon May Be a Beginner," *New York Times*, Feb. 1, 1978, p. 38. Physicians have a code of silence about medical errors that makes even the police "blue code" relatively garrulous. L. K. Altman, "Getting To the Core of Mistakes In Medicine," *New York Times*, Feb. 29, 2000, p. D-1; S. G. Stolberg, "Breaking Down Medicine's Culture of Silence," *New York Times*, Dec. 5, 1999, sec. 4, p. 1; J. R. Wilder, "Give Doctors Tougher Rules," *New York Times*, Dec. 10, 1999, p. 31.

PSYCHOSURGERY

Kaimowitz v. Department of Mental Health

As a taxpayer, claiming a misuse of public funds, Gabe Kaimowitz (an attorney) brought a suit on behalf of taxpayers to halt an experimental psychosurgery procedure in a state facility on one Louis Smith, an individual who had been institutionalized as a dangerous sex offender and who ostensibly consented to the procedure. The facility did not challenge Kaimowitz's standing to bring suit, as it was interested in having the court set out standards of procedures. District Court Judge Horace Gilmore ruled that as a matter of law an individual involuntarily committed cannot consent to a high-risk/low-benefit procedure: "The involuntarily detained [individual] is in an inherently coercive atmosphere even though no direct pressures may be placed upon him." Civ. No. 73-19434-AW (Cir. Ct. Wayne County, Mich., July 10, 1973), excerpted at 42 U.S.L.W. 2063 (1973).

See S. I. Shuman, *Psychosurgery and the Medical Control of Violence: Autonomy and Deviance* (Detroit: Wayne State University Press, 1977); R. Slovenko, *Psychiatry and Law* (Boston: Little, Brown, 1973), pp. 270–72. The court was opposed to psychosurgery, and it used the concept of consent as the rationale for its decision. It did not mention that Smith and other inmates were in the process of discharge by virtue of the fact that the sexual psychopath law under which they were committed had been repealed. As Smith reported to a consent committee in the project, he did not want to return to the free world fearing that he would act out aggressively again. See R. Slovenko, "On Psychosurgery," *Hastings Center Report* 5 (Oct. 1975): 19.

SUBSTITUTED JUDGMENT

Superintendent of Belchertown State School v. Saikewicz
Saikewicz, a 67-year-old severely retarded incompetent man with a mental age of three, contracted leukemia for which his physician recommended chemotherapy, but the record showed that chemotherapy was only 30 to 50 percent effective. With treatment, he could probably live another year but with extreme pain; without treatment, he would live a few painless months. His advanced age, probable side effects of the treatment, his low chance of remission, and his immediate suffering were found to outweigh any benefit he possibly could receive. In other words, the treatment was found to be high risk/low benefit. The court ruled that he should not be subjected to it. 373 Mass. 728, 370 N.E.2d 417 (1977).

In the Matter of Eichner
The New York Court of Appeals was confronted with the issue of whether a court should respect an incompetent individual's previously expressed views as to removing him from life-supporting treatment. Brother Fox, an 83-year-old priest, stated prior to becoming comatose that he did not wish to be kept alive by extraordinary means. He communicated his wish on at least two occasions to members of his religious order. After lapsing into a permanent vegetative state with little hope of recovery, Brother Fox's guardian asked to be allowed to remove him from his respirator. The court found clear and convincing evidence that he did not want his life extended by extraordinary means. 52 N.Y.2d 363, 420 N.E.2d 64 (1981).

Continuing Confinement of Offenders. *See also* Sex Offenders

Baxstrom v. Herold
The U.S. Supreme Court explored the issue of due process owed prisoners facing civil commitment at the expiration of their sentences. The Court ruled that the denial of a review proceeding available to persons civilly committed was not consistent with the equal protection clause of the Fourteenth Amendment. It rejected the state's attempt to distinguish the civilly insane from the criminally insane. 383 U.S. 107 (1966).

McNeil v. Director, Patuxent Institution
The defendant, upon conviction of two assaults, was sentenced to five years imprisonment, but instead of committing him to prison, the sentencing court referred him to a mental institution for examination to determine whether he should be committed to that institution for treatment under Maryland's Defective Delinquency law. That determination was never made, the state contending that he had refused to cooperate with the examining psychiatrists. The state continued to hold him even after his sentence had expired, arguing that the continuing confinement was analogous to punishment for civil contempt in refusing to cooperate. The Supreme Court held that it was a denial of due process to hold him on the basis of an ex parte order committing him for ob-

servation without first affording him the procedures commensurate with a long-term commitment. Nor was the situation analogous to confinement for civil contempt, given that he had never been held to be in contempt. 407 U.S. 245 (1972).

Contractual Capacity

Faber v. Sweet Style Mfg. Corp.

In apparently the first decision of its kind, a New York court appraised a manic-depressive individual's capacity to enter into a binding contract, and allowed him to rescind a transaction for the purchase of land. Testimony revealed that he had been seeing a psychiatrist because he was in a state of depression, that he ceased doing so, and within three months had entered in numerous business ventures and embarked upon a buying spree. Finding him incompetent to enter into the contract because he "acted under the compulsion of a mental disease or disorder but for which the contract would not have been made," the court granted rescission. This motivational standard of incompetency had never before been applied in a contract case. When, as is generally the case, cognitive capacity is the sole criterion used, the manic person is held competent because manic-depressive psychosis affects motivation rather than ability to understand. The court gave as its reason for departing from traditional law that "the standards by which competence to contract is measured were, apparently, developed without relation to the effects of particular mental diseases or disorders and prior to recognition of manic-depressive psychosis as a distinct form of mental illness." 40 Misc.2d 212, 242 N.Y.S.2d 763 (1963). Cf. Smalley v. Baker, 262 Cal. App.2d 824, 69 Cal. Rptr. 521 (1968).

Credibility of Witnesses

United States v. Hiss

The spectacular trial of Alger Hiss in the early 1950s involved the issue of psychiatric evaluation of a witness. Hiss was chairman of the Carnegie Foundation for Peace and a leading member of the Democratic party. He was accused by Whittaker Chambers of passing secrets to Communists in the 1930s. The defense offered psychiatric testimony designed to impeach the credibility of Chambers. Judge Goddard, ruling the testimony admissible, stated: "It is apparent that the outcome of this trial is dependent, to a great extent, upon the testimony of one man—Whittaker Chambers. Mr. Chambers' credibility is one of the major issues upon which the jury must pass. The opinion of the jury—formed upon their evaluation of all the evidence laid before them—is the decisive authority on this question, as on all questions of fact. The existence of insanity or mental derangement is admissible for the purpose of discrediting a witness. Evidence of insanity is not merely for the judge on the preliminary question of competency but goes to the jury to affect credibility." The psychiatric testimony notwithstanding, Hiss was convicted. 88 F.Supp. 559 (S.D. N.Y. 1950). By and large, to avoid reversal and to give the accused the benefit of the doubt, trial judges tend to allow the defense to introduce evidence that would not be allowed on behalf of the state.

United States v. Lindstrom

The Eleventh Circuit Court of Appeals observed: "Although the debate over the proper legal role of mental health professionals continues to rage, even those who would limit the availability of psychiatric evidence acknowledge that many types of 'emotional or mental defect may materially affect the accuracy of testimony; a conservative list of such defects would have to include the psychoses, most or all of the neuroses, defects in the structure of the nervous system, mental deficiency, alcoholism, drug addiction and psychopathic personality.'" Reversing a conviction, the court said: "The jury was denied any evidence on whether it affects one's perceptions of external reality. The jury was denied any evidence of whether the witness was capable of distinguishing reality from hallucinations." 698 F.2d 1154 (11th Cir. 1983).

State v. Lindsey

The Arizona Supreme Court reversed a conviction of incest because of what it deemed "direct opinion testimony of truthfulness" by the state's expert. The court said: "Opinion evidence on who is telling the truth in cases such as this is nothing more than the expert's opinion on how the case should be decided. We believe that such testimony is inadmissible, both because it usurps the jury's traditional functions and roles and because, when given insight into the behavioral sciences, the jury needs nothing further from the expert. We do not invite battles of opposing experts testifying to opinions about the truthfulness of the prosecution witness as compared to that of the defense witnesses." 720 P.2d 73 (Ariz. 1986). See also Lindsey v. United States, 237 F.2d 893 (9th Cir. 1956). Expert evidence on eyewitness identification is persistently controversial. Traditionally, trial judges tend to balk at exercising their broad discretion to admit it. United States v. Langan, 263 F.3d 613 (6th Cir. 2001).

Discussion

In the Clarence Thomas–Anita Hill hearings before the Senate Judiciary Committee in 1991, Senator Alan Simpson expressed incredulity that Hill would continue to associate in a friendly manner with a man who had allegedly sexually harassed her. She responded, "It takes an expert in psychology to explain how that can happen, but it can happen, because it happened to me." Hill's testimony, hearing 4:36. See A. P. Thomas, *Clarence Thomas: A Biography* (San Francisco: Encounter Books, 2001), p. 415. As she had majored in psychology at college, her "expertise" was solicited on occasion to interpret her own behavior. For example, Senator Leahy questioned her regarding contradictions in her testimony about how many people she had confided in about the alleged harassment. In explaining the discrepancy, she said, "I am really finding that I repressed a lot of things that happened during that time, and I am recalling more, in more detail." Charles Krauthammer, psychiatrist turned political writer, posited his diagnosis, "During my three years as a resident psychiatrist at a Boston hospital, I treated many psychotic and delusional patients. I may be rusty, but Anita Hill showed no signs of delusion." See J. L. Nolan, "The Therapeutic State: The Clarence Thomas and Anita Hill Hearings," *Antioch Rev.* 56 (1998): 5; R. Slovenko, "The Psychologizing of Clarence Thomas and Anita Hill," *Newsletter of Am. Acad. Psychiatry & Law*, Apr. 1992, pp. 27–29. See also M. R. Damaska, *Evidence Law Adrift* (New Haven: Yale University Press, 1997); S. I. Friedland, "On Common Sense and the Evaluation of Witness Credibility," *Case West. L. Rev.* 40 (1989): 165; M. W. Mullane, "The Truthsayer and the Court: Expert Testimony and Credibility," *Me. L. Rev.* 43 (1991): 53.

Criminal Procedure

RIGHT OF AN ACCUSED TO A PSYCHIATRIC EXPERT

Ake v. Oklahoma

The Supreme Court declared the right of an indigent defendant to psychiatric assistance. The Oklahoma Court of Appeals had held that the state had no obligation to provide psychiatric services to indigents even in capital cases. Reversing the conviction of Glen Burton Ake, the Supreme Court ruled that due process requires that the indigent accused be equipped with the "basic tools" to ensure "a proper functioning of the adversary process." To that end, a psychiatric expert is necessary, the Court said, considering "the pivotal role that psychiatry has come to play in criminal proceedings." The Court concluded: "We therefore hold that when a defendant demonstrates to the trial judge that his sanity at the time of the offense is to be a significant factor at trial, the State must, at a minimum, assure the defendant access to a competent psychiatrist who will conduct an appropriate examination and assist in evaluation, preparation, and presentation of the defense. That is not to say, of course, that the indigent defendant has a constitutional right to choose a psychiatrist of his personal liking or to receive funds to hire his own. Our concern is that the indigent defendant have access to a competent psychiatrist ... and as in the case of the provision of counsel we leave to state the decision on how to implement this right." 470 U.S. 68 (1985).

Discussion

In more than a decade since 1985, state courts have construed *Ake* with widely varying results. Some courts restrict the ruling to capital cases, others to psychiatric experts testifying about the insanity defense, and most others require the defendant to show that the denial of an expert witness would produce an unfair trial. According to *Ake,* the accused must make a "preliminary showing" that expert assistance is "likely to be a significant factor at trial." That is likely to be the situation in insanity cases but not in other types of cases.

In the same term as *Ake,* the U.S. Supreme Court in Caldwell v. Mississippi, 105 S. Ct. 2633 (1985), declined to consider a trial court's refusal to appoint fingerprint and ballistics experts because the defendant had "offered little more than undeveloped assertions that the requested assistance would be beneficial." The defendant must establish a reasonable probability that (1) an expert would be of assistance to the defense and (2) the denial of an expert would result in a fundamentally unfair trial. Quite often, out of failure to satisfy the burden, the courts have declined to provide an expert for an indigent defendant. In People v. Leonard, 569 N.W.2d 663 (1997), the Michigan Court of Appeal found no specific showing of need for a DNA expert though the prosecution intended to introduce DNA evidence against him. In State v. Mire, 700 So.2d 566 (1997), the Louisiana Court of Appeals found no error in denying a defense motion to perform certain neurological and neuropsychological exams on a defendant who had pleaded not guilty by reason of insanity. The trial judge commented, "If nothing is found will the defendant ask for more tests until something is found?" The court concluded that he had already been adequately examined. In Dirickson v. State, 953 S.W.2d 55 (1997), an attempted capital murder case in which a defense of mental defect was raised, the Arkansas Supreme Court held that the trial court did not abuse its discretion by denying the defendant's motions for expert funds to hire a neuropsychologist for additional mental evaluation. The court said, "Stated simply, the State is not required to pay for a defendant to shop from doctor to doctor until he finds one who will declare him incompetent to proceed with his trial. In the present case, appellant was examined at the state hospital, and, thus, the requirements under Ake were satisfied." Three justices dissented, saying, "It is clear that appellant made an adequate showing that a denial of expert assistance resulted in an unfair trial, especially in light of the fact that a defense of mental disease or defect was appellant's only viable defense." The consensus of opinion is that the promise of *Ake* remains largely unfulfilled. Generally speaking the courts have read *Ake* narrowly, and have refused to require appointment of an expert unless it is absolutely essential to the defense. And one might add, the courts have read *Ake* narrowly because of the many frivolous requests for assistance. See P. S. Petterson, "Indigent Defense," *Champion,* July 1999, p. 48.

Criminal Responsibility under a Not Guilty Plea

Crimes are defined by the combination of an act *(actus reus)* and a mental state (mens rea). To convict a person of any serious offense, the state must prove that the accused performed some act or omission prohibited by law and that he did so with a certain state of mind. The first element is known as the *actus reus;* the second element, as the mens rea. Involuntary activity may negate *actus reus,* as it requires volition, or it may negate mens rea. The admission of evidence of mental illness as affecting *actus reus* or mens rea without pleading not guilty by reason of insanity is controversial. *See* Post-traumatic Stress Disorder, Syndrome Evidence

PSYCHIATRIC TESTIMONY ON COGNITION (MENS REA)

Rejecting the Testimony

Courts have held that due process is not offended by a rule that a defendant, without pleading NGRI, may not rebut evidence of intent by presentation of psychiatric testimony. To put it another way, experts may speak on abnormality but not on normality. The reasons generally adduced for this is that the testimony is not helpful, that the role of the judge and jury must not be usurped by experts unnecessarily testifying on matters within ordinary knowledge, or that the prosecution must be forewarned that psychiatric testimony is forthcoming.

United States v. Esch

The Tenth Circuit held that, in the absence of any claim of mental disease or defect, the trial judge may exclude expert opinion as to the accused's capacity to form the requisite intent. Moreover, the court said, generalized testimony about the influence of personality traits is excludable as within the common knowledge and experience of lay jurors. 832 F.2d 531 (10th Cir. 1987).

United States v. Bright

The Second Circuit upheld the exclusion of testimony about the defendant's "passive-dependent personality disorder" unaffected by psychosis or neurosis, reasoning that "Couched in simpler language [the psychiatrist] was prepared to testify that the appellant was a gullible person." 517 F.2d 584 (2d Cir. 1975).

Accepting the Testimony

Other jurisdictions permit psychiatric testimony relevant to mens rea, even without an insanity plea, notably on specific intent.

People v. Wells

The accused, charged with an assault with malice aforethought, offered evidence that at the time of the assault he was in a state of tension and, as a result, had an abnormal fear for his personal safety. The California Supreme Court found this evidence relevant and material to establish lack of malice aforethought. 33 Cal.2d 330, 202 P.2d 53, *cert. denied,* 338 U.S. 836 (1949).

People v. Gorshen

Gorshen's foreman had asked him to leave work because of his drinking. He subsequently shot and killed the foreman. Evidence was offered that (1) the accused could not premeditate, and (2) he did not, in fact, premeditate. Dr. Bernard Diamond, testifying for the defense, claimed that the killing was psychologically necessary to prevent a psychotic disintegration. He testified that Gorshen killed not because he was insane, but because he needed to ward off a psychosis that might develop if he were revealed as the totally helpless, impotent, and perverted character described at the time of the fight. The California Supreme Court endorsed the admissibility of Dr. Diamond's testimony and established what was then referred to as the *Wells-Gorshen* doctrine of diminished capacity. 51 Cal.2d 716, 336 P.2d 492 (1959).

People v. Wolff

Fifteen-year-old Ronald Wolff wanted to use his home as a place to have girls to engage in sexual activity. He decided that his mother was an obstacle, so he got an ax handle, hit her over the head, and while she struggled, choked her to death. He entered a plea of not guilty by reason of insanity. The trial court decided that he was sane, and sentenced him to life imprisonment with a recommendation that he be confined in a hospital for the insane. On review the California Supreme Court decided that though Wolff knew the difference between right and wrong, that knowledge was "vague and detached." As a result he was "not fully normal or mature, mentally well person," and so his conviction was reduced to second-degree murder. 61 Cal.2d 795, 40 Cal. Rptr. 271, 394 P.2d 959 (1964). See P. Arenella, "The Diminished Capacity and Diminished Responsibility Defenses: Two Children of a Doomed Marriage," *Colum. L. Rev.* 77 (1977): 827.

People v. Saille

The California legislature in 1981 enacted a statute nullifying the *Wells-Gorshen* decisions. In *Saille*, the California Court of Appeals said: "The special defense of diminished capacity, allowing the defendant to show he is less responsible for his actions, has been abolished. Our state has returned to the 'strict mens rea' approach, only allowing the defendant to show that the requisite mental state was not actually formed due to a mental disorder, thus refuting the prosecution's proof of an element of the offense." The California Supreme Court affirmed in a much awaited decision. 270 Cal. Rptr. 502, 221 Cal. App.3d 280 (1990), *aff'd*, 54 Cal.3d 1103 (1991).

PSYCHIATRIC TESTIMONY ON CONTROL (ACTUS REUS)

The thesis that there can be no criminal offense without the doing of a voluntary act is explored in M. S. Moore, *Act and Crime: The Philosophy of Action and Its Implications for Criminal Law* (Oxford: Clarendon Press, 1993). Of the many writings on voluntariness, see R. A. Duff, *Criminal Attempts* (Oxford: Clarendon Press, 1996); J. Viorst, *Imperfect Control* (New York: Simon & Schuster, 1998); W. W. Cook, "Act, Intention, and Motive in the Criminal Law," *Yale L.J.* 26 (1917): 645; S. L. Halleck, "Which Patients Are Responsible for Their Illnesses?" *Am. J. Psychotherapy* 42 (1988): 338; L. J. West, "Psychiatric Overview of Cult-Related Phenomena," *J. Am. Acad. Psa.* 21 (1993): 1. An individual who goes on another's land to answer the call of nature intends to trespass but the act may be said not to be voluntary. See Bass v. Aetna Ins. Co., 370 So.2d 511 (La. 1979) (answering the call of God). Suppose an individual experiences an intense drive to set fires and cannot control his compulsion to do so? The individual presumably does not have a defense under *M'Naghten* (insanity is limited to cognitive impairment), but may have an irresistible impulse defense. Pedophiles (though not claiming insanity) often claim inability to control impulses.

Policeman at the Elbow Test

Some jurisdictions accepting the irresistible impulse defense add a qualification known as the "policeman at the elbow test" and the jury is instructed: "If the accused would not have committed the act had there been a policeman present, he cannot be said to have acted under an irresistible impulse." Query: Does a defendant's ability to desist from a criminal act when a police officer is present show that he also could desist in other circumstances if he really wanted to?

Bizup v. People

In this Colorado case it was contended that the trial court erred in allowing the district attorney to propound questions upon cross-examination to the defense psychiatrist and upon direct examination to his own expert witnesses concerning the policeman at the elbow test. Specifically the district attorney inquired from the experts whether they believed the defendant would have shot his victim if there had been a policeman at his elbow at the time of the shooting. The purpose of the question was to determine whether the defendant was reacting to an irresistible impulse at the time of the shooting, as the defense psychiatrist had testified he was. No objection was made to this line of questioning, and both sides indulged in numerous questions concerning this test. The answer given by the psychiatrist for the defense was that they were dealing with a person with an insane mind who "could have" or "might have" shot the victim even if there were policemen at both elbows. The Colorado Supreme Court ruled that as a result of the answers given, no prejudice resulted to the defendant from these questions asked of the psychiatrist for the defense. Questions in the same vein propounded on both direct examination and cross-examination of the psychiatrists who testified for the prosecution resulted in answers that an insane person might or might not kill if a policeman were at his elbow. The court ruled that the answers were not prejudicial to the defendant and in effect they tended to demolish the state's theory that there could be no "irresistible impulse" if the person alleged to be acting under the same would not have so acted if others were present. Perceiving no prejudicial error, the court affirmed the judgment. 150 Colo. 214, 371 P.2d 786 (1962). See also Henderson v. United States, 360 F.2d 514 (D.C. App. 1965), where psychiatrists testified that the defendant would have committed the alleged robbery even if a policeman had been at his elbow.

Automatism

McClain v. State

Indiana among other states recognizes automatism and insanity as separate defenses, allowing a defendant to present evidence on automatism bearing on the voluntariness of his actions without pleading insanity. 678 N.W.2d 104 (Ind. 1997). See also People v. Martin, 87 Cal. App.2d 581, 197 P.2d 379 (1948), where the California Court of Appeals stated, "The defense of insanity is one thing, and the defense of unconsciousness is another." In a defense of (sane) automatism or unconsciousness, the defendant does not give notice to the state of the contention being made, and commitment to an institution does not follow an acquittal.

Homosexual Panic

People v. Huie

The defendant, charged with murder, claimed that the victim had made a sexual advance toward him and sought to introduce evidence that the alleged advances triggered a violent "pseudohomosexual panic." The trial court excluded the defense. On appeal, defense counsel argued that his experts were not going to testify "that the defendant at the time of this alleged incident was suffering from any mental disease or disorder, defect or illness," but that they were going to address events in his childhood that constituted a "compelling trauma" ostensibly relevant to the formation of the necessary criminal intent. The defense also contended that expert testimony would show that the defendant "actually lacked the mental state necessary to support the charged offense of murder" as a result of childhood events that bore "directly upon his state of mind at the time of the incident." But because the California Penal Code excludes evidence of mental condition except where it reveals a mental disease, defect, or disorder, the trial court's exclusion of the evidence was upheld. Calif. Court of Appeals, 1st App., Div. 5, No. A042962, 1989. Most cases do not use gay panic as part of an insanity defense but as part of a diminished capacity evaluation. See R. B. Mison, "Homophobia in Manslaughter: The Homosexual Advance as Insufficient Provocation," *Calif. L. Rev.* 80 (1992): 133; B. W. Wall, "Criminal Responsibility, Diminished Capacity, and the Gay Panic Defense," *J. Am. Acad. Psychiatry & Law* 28 (2000): 454.

Hypnotic Suggestion

California v. March

The defendant escaped from prison and claimed as a defense that his escape "was not his voluntary act but was caused by a hypnotic suggestion given him by a fellow inmate." Allegedly, the fellow inmate studied hypnotism, had hypnotized hundreds of persons, and hypnotized the defendant over a dozen times. While the defendant was under hypnosis, the fellow inmate suggested that he "go back where he was having a good time." The fellow inmate claimed he merely suggested "age regression," but the defendant interpreted it as a suggestion to return to his former neighborhood. The trial court allowed expert testimony on the hypnotism defense, but the jury convicted. On appeal the court did not rule on the validity of the claim of hypnotism as "negating a conscious or volitional act" because the defendant did not lack an opportunity to present the defense or proper jury instruction. 170 Cal. App.2d 284, 338 P.2d 495 (1959). See M. C. Bonnema, " 'Trance on Trial': An Exegesis of Hypnotism and Criminal Responsibility," *Wayne L. Rev.* 39 (1993): 1299.

CHARACTER EVIDENCE/INCONSISTENT PERSONALITY

There is some support for allowing psychiatric testimony on inconsistent personality, and there is also substantial opposition to it. The attitudes of judges toward propensity evidence are not altogether different from that of the ordinary citizen. See M. Damaska, "Propensity Evidence in Continental Legal Systems," *Chi.-Kent L. Rev.* 70 (1994): 55; M. A. Mendez, "The Law of Evidence and the Search for a Stable Personality," *Emory L.J.* 45 (1996): 221.

People v. Jones

The California Supreme Court allowed the defense to submit expert psychiatric opinion evidence of the personality traits of the defendant as bearing on the unlikelihood that he had committed the crime of sexual abuse of a nine-year-old child. This was also one of the first cases in which a psychiatrist was allowed to testify to an opinion based in part on a narcoanalysis interview with the defendant. The court said, essentially, that if expert testimony could be used to diagnose someone as a sexual psychopath under the sexual psychopath law (psychological assessments are used to evaluate sex offenders), it could be used to say that a person has no such disposition. The evidence submitted by the defendant was negative diagnosis—that is, that he was *not* a sex deviate or sexual psychopath. 42 Cal.2d 219, 266 P.2d 38 (1954).

State v. Cavallo

The defendant, charged with rape, sought to introduce expert psychiatric testimony that he did not have psychological traits common to rapists. In rejecting the proposed testimony, the court said: "The danger of prejudice through introduction of unreliable expert testimony is clear. While juries would not always accord excessive weight to unreliable expert testimony, there is substantial danger that they would do so, precisely because the evidence is labeled 'scientific' and 'expert.' " The court noted that the testimony was based on two unproven and unreliable premises: (1) rapists have particular mental characteristics, and (2) psychiatrists can, by examination, determine the presence or absence of these characteristics. 88 N.J. 508, 443 A.2d 1020 (1982).

United States v. MacDonald

The defendant, Captain Jeffrey MacDonald, physician, was on trial for the murders of his wife and daughters. The trial judge excluded, as confusing and misleading psychiatric testimony that the defendant's "personality/emotional configuration" was inconsistent with violent crime. The defense sought to offer the testimony of leading forensic psychiatrists who contended that MacDonald's personality was inconsistent with the crime. Dr. Seymour Halleck observed at the end of a 24-page report: "On the basis of my clinical experience as a psychiatrist and criminologist and on the basis of my knowledge of theories and research into the area of violence, I would conclude that there is only an extremely remote possibility that a person of his type would commit a crime of this type. Certainly, no one with Dr. MacDonald's personality organization has ever been known to commit such a crime." 485 F.Supp. 1087 (E.D. N.C 1979), 688 F.2d 224 (4th Cir. 1982), *cert. denied,* 459 U.S. 1103 (1983).

Criminal Responsibility under a Plea of Not Guilty by Reason of Insanity

Rex v. Arnold

This case has been interpreted as precedent for the wild beast test according to which in order to be excused from criminal responsibility as insane, the accused must not know what he is doing, "no more than an infant, a brute, or a wild beast." In this case Edward Arnold was tried for the attempted murder of Lord Onslow. 16 How. St. Tr. 695 (1724).

Rex v. Hadfield

James Hadfield planned firing a pistol in the direction of King George III as he entered the Drury Lane Theatre. He did not wish to commit suicide, which was a sin, nor did he wish to harm the king, whom he admired. Knowing that attempted regicide was a capital offense, he fired close to the king, feigning an attempt on the king's life, as a means to his own demise. The intent, it can be said, was insane and he was found NGRI. He was represented by the prominent jurist Thomas Erskine, who was able to recast the insanity defense in terms of the effects of disease processes, a shift from a test of cognitive understanding or moral knowledge. 27 St. Tr. 1281 (1800).

Daniel M'Naghten's Case

The most important legal definition of insanity (criminal responsibility) is the so-called right-or-wrong test formulated by the House of Lords in 1843. The test is often called the *M'Naghten* test, commemorating one Daniel M'Naghten, who shot and killed Edward Drummond, private secretary to the prime minister, Sir Robert Peel. Under this test, a defendant is insane if and only if, at the time of the crime, he was "laboring under such a defect of reason, from disease of the mind, as not to know the nature and quality of the act he was doing; or, if he did know it, that he did not know he was doing what was wrong." 10 Cl. & Fin. 200, 8 Eng. Rep. 718 (1843). See B. R. Kirwin, *The Mad, the Bad, and the Innocent* (Boston: Little, Brown, 1997); T. Maeder, *Crime and Madness* (New York: Harper & Row, 1985); R. J. Simon, *The Jury and the Defense of Insanity* (Boston: Little, Brown, 1967); R. Slovenko, *Psychiatry and Criminal Culpability* (New York: Wiley, 1995); G. Williams, *Criminal Law* (London: Stevens & Sons, 2d ed. 1961); R. J. Bonnie, "The Moral Basis of the Insanity Defense," *A.B.A.J.* 69 (1983): 194; A. L. Halpern, "The Fiction of Legal Insanity and Misuse of Psychiatry," *J. Leg. Med.* 2 (1980): 18. The dichotomy is usually made between "evil" and "sick," a dichotomy called "a simplistic approach to criminality in mentally disordered offenders," says Dr. Abraham L. Halpern, who sets out four types of individuals: non–mentally ill good persons, non–mentally ill bad persons, mentally ill good persons, and mentally ill bad persons. Ltr., "Kaczynski Could Be Both 'Sick' and 'Evil,'" *Gannett Newspapers,* Jan. 10, 1998, p. 10. See B. Bursten, *Beyond Psychiatric Expertise* (Springfield, Ill.: Thomas, 1984).

State v. Felter

In this case a farmer by the name of Felter was on trial for killing his wife. His defense was "homicidal mania." He smashed his wife's skull, mutilated her, and tried to burn down the house. Their young daughter saw the crime: "It was because she poured the buttermilk out. I left because he was going to kill me." He then tried to slit his throat with a razor, but failed. The appellate court reversed his conviction, because the trial court had used the right-or-wrong test: medicine and law, the opinion said, "now recognizes the existence of such mental disease as homicidal insanity"; the trial court should have instructed the jury about the defense of "irresistible impulse." 25 Iowa 67 (1868).

State v. Pike

Josiah Pike, accused of murdering one Thomas Brown with an ax, claimed to be suffering from "a species of insanity called dipsomania." In a much-noted instruction, Judge Charles Doe told the jury they had the right to acquit Pike by reason of insanity if the killing was the "offspring or product of mental disease in the defendant." Judge Doe also told the jury that there was no single rigid test of "mental disease"; rather, "all symptoms and all tests of mental disease are purely matters of fact" for the determination by the jury. The jury convicted Pike anyway. In his opinion Judge Doe said that "insanity has been, for the most part, a growth of the modern state of society. Like many other diseases, it is caused, in a great degree, by the habits and incidents of civilized life." He also felt that the law should abandon "old exploded medical theories" and embrace "facts established in the progress of scientific knowledge." 49 N.H. 399 (1869).

United States v. Guiteau

In 1881 Charles Guiteau shot and killed President James Garfield in a train station as he was about to leave on a trip. The trial was a long, drawn-out affair in which psychiatric experts presented conflicting testimony. As in other insanity trials, expert witnesses for the prosecution and defense set out contradictory views. Psychiatrists for the prosecution argued that the defendant understood the nature and consequences of his act, appeared to reason coherently, and hence, following the generally accepted rule of law, was guilty. Psychiatrists for the defense, on the other hand, argued that he might seem rational, even intelligent, and still not be responsible for his actions. The cause of an individual's criminality, they were convinced, often lay in heredity, in a congenital disposition toward lack of moral perceptivity and control. Indeed, they argued, criminality could often be identified through physical stigmata that seemed to accompany hereditary mental illness and criminality. The verdict, though, was almost a foregone conclusion. The jury deliberated only about an hour: guilty as charged. As he stood in front of the gallows, he recited, in a high-pitched child's voice, a hymn he had written hours before, "I am going to the Lordy, I am so glad." Quite likely, he would have escaped the death penalty if he had killed anyone but the president. It was as illogical to kill him, one journalist wrote, "as it is to kill a cave fish for not seeing." Almost every prominent European criminologist and many psychiatrists of that generation referred to Guiteau as evidence for the hereditary origin of criminality. The trial is recounted in C. E. Rosenberg, *The Trial of the Assassin Guiteau* (Chicago: University of Chicago Press, 1968).

Durham v. United States

Monte Durham had a long history of instability—in fact, he spent his entire adult life in and out of jails and mental hospitals. In this case he was charged with housebreaking and the trial judge, sitting without a jury, applied the standard right or wrong test and convicted him. The U.S. Court of Appeals for the District of Columbia Circuit, speaking through Judge David Bazelon, reversed. In a highly controversial and short-lived decision, Judge Bazelon criticized the *M'Naghten* rules for not taking "sufficient account of psychic realities and scientific knowledge." In consultation with leading forensic psychiatrists, he peppered the decision with citations to psychiatric literature. He set out a new test of criminal responsibility, presumably more scientific and enlightened than the older ones: "an accused is not criminally responsible if his unlawful act was the product of mental disease or mental defect." 214 F.2d 862 (D.C. Cir. 1954).

By and large, psychiatrists applauded the decision; under it there is virtually no criminal trial in which psychiatric testimony would not be relevant. Almost any unusual mental state could become a "disease or defect" and almost any action could be a "product" of that "disease." Dr. Karl Menninger, renowned as dean of American psychiatry, called the decision one of the most important in American jurisprudence. See P. Roche, "Criminality and Mental Illness: Two Faces of the Same Coin," *U. Chi. L. Rev.* 22 (1955): 320. The rule, however, proved troublesome and confusing and, in 1972, in United States v. Brawner, 471 F.2d 969, the D.C. Court of Appeals junked it. Professor James Q. Wilson observed, "What had been lost sight of was the commonsense view that people are responsible for their actions unless those actions are caused by a pure reflex or a delusional state utterly beyond rational control." J. Q. Wilson, *Moral Judgment* (New York: Basic Books, 1997), p. 37. See R. Slovenko, "Should Psychiatrists Honor Bazelon or Burger?" *J. Psychiatry & Law* 20 (1992): 635. In the wake of the guilty verdict in the case of Andrea Yates, who killed her five children, the American Psychiatric Association issued a statement (March 15, 2002) that faulted the verdict and urged, in effect, a return to the proposition advocated by Judge Bazelon that acts that are the product of mental illness are not criminal. In Texas, where the trial was held, the question of legal responsibility depends on whether the defendant knew the difference between right and wrong. In a sense, Andrea Yates obviously knew what she was doing when she drowned her five children. The jury concluded that her actions—waiting until her husband had left home, calling the police immediately after she had killed her children—demonstrated that she knew the killings were wrong. But in the grip of a psychosis, she actually thought it was right, believing that she was saving her children from a worse fate in this world and the next. Invariably, in their warped logic, wrongdoers believe their cause is just. See R. F. Baumeister, *Evil: Inside Human Cruelty and Violence* (New York: W. H. Freeman, 1997); R. Slovenko, "The Way of Evil, Its Measurement, and the Role of God," *J. Psychiatry & Law* 29 (2001): 377.

State v. Padilla

The charge was first-degree murder, and the defense asked the trial judge to instruct the jury on diminished capacity—to tell the jury that it might consider second-degree murder (instead of first-degree) if the defendant was "incapable of thinking over the fatal act beforehand with a calm and reflective mind (or with a fixed and settled deliberation and coolness of mind)" because of a "disease or defect of the mind," even if he was not legally insane. The judge refused, and the jury convicted. The New Mexico Supreme Court reversed, holding that the judge should have given the instruction. Under New Mexico law, a defendant could be so drunk or so befuddled with drugs as to be unable to "premeditate" a first-degree murder; so why not the same rule for "mental disorders"? 66 N.M. 289, 347 P.2d 312 (1959).

United States v. Currens

In this 1961 decision, Judge John Biggs Jr. of the Court of Appeals for the Third Circuit stated that criminal responsibility will be imposed on the accused where he was not suffering from a "disease of the mind," or, even though suffering from such mental disease, where he possessed "substantial capacity" to conform his conduct to the requirements of the law at the time of the criminal act. 290 F.2d 751 (3d Cir. 1961). The thrust of the decision was to eliminate the cognitive prong of the ALI test. Quoting from his own book *The Guilty Mind: Psychiatry and the Law of Homocide* (1955), Judge Biggs wrote: "[T]he mental competency of recidivists should be questioned by realistic means at the earliest possible state. So long as the courts judge criminal responsibility by the test of knowledge of right and wrong, psychotics [sic] who have served prison terms or are granted probation are released to commit increasingly serious crimes, repeating crime and incarceration and release until murder is committed. Instead of being treated as are ordinary criminals, they should be confined to institutions for the insane at the first offense and not be released until or unless cured." 290 F.2d at 767.

United States v. McDonald

In this 1963 decision the D.C. Court of Appeals, before it cast aside its ruling in *Durham*, added to the Durham definition by asking: Did the abnormal mental condition, by whatever name it is called, seriously and substantially affect and impair the defendant's capacity to control his conduct so that he could not refrain from doing the act? Because of the vagaries of psychiatric diagnosis, the court suggested a legal definition of *mental disease or defect* and was unwilling, like Lord Chief Justice Tindal in M'Naghten's case, to leave the definition to science only. The court said: "Our purpose now is to make it very clear that neither the court nor the jury is bound by *ad hoc* definitions or conclusions as to what experts state is a disease or defect. What psychiatrists may consider a 'mental disease or defect' for clinical purposes, where their concern is treatment, may or may not be the same as mental disease or defect for the jury's purpose in determining criminal responsibility. Consequently, for that purpose the jury should be told that a mental disease or defect includes any abnormal condition of the mind which substantially affects mental or emotional processes and substantially impairs behavior controls. Thus the jury would consider testimony concerning the development, adaptation and functioning of these processes and controls." 312 F.2d 847 (D.C. Cir. 1962).

ALI TEST OF CRIMINAL RESPONSIBILITY

In 1955, a year after *Durham*, the American Law Institute in its Model Penal Code recommended the following test for nonresponsibility: "A person is not responsible for criminal conduct if at the time of such conduct as a result of mental disease or defect he lacks substantial capacity either to appreciate the criminality (wrongfulness) of his conduct or to conform his conduct to the requirements of law." The next sentence of the ALI test states that repeated criminal or antisocial conduct does not of itself demonstrate mental illness. The ALI test proved popular. Over the next two decades, a majority of the country's jurisdictions adopted it. It contains a cognition and control prong, unlike the *M'Naghten* test, which has only a cognition prong. In the wake of the *Hinckley* case, where the ALI test was used, various jurisdictions returned to *M'Naghten*. See *United States v. Hinckley*.

State v. Guido

Most courts assume that *mental disease* (or defect) for purposes of the insanity defense is a legal, not a medical concept, but then how should the legal concept of disease be defined? Few courts have offered a definition, or even indicated the general criteria that help determine this legal element. The formulation set out in *United States v. McDonald* was not helpful. In *Guido*, the New Jersey Supreme Court said: "[T]he hard question under any concept of legal insanity is, What constitutes a 'disease'? The postulate is that some wrongdoers are sick while others are bad, and that it is against good morals to stigmatize the sick. Who then are the sick whose illness shows they are free of moral blame? We cannot turn to the psychiatrist for a list of illnesses which have that quality because, for all his insight into the dynamics of behavior, he has not solved the riddle of blame. The question remains an ethical one, the answer to which lies beyond scientific truth. . . . We have described the problem, not to resolve it, but simply to reveal the room for disputation." 40 N.J. 191, 191 A.2d 45 (1963).

The American Psychiatric Association proposed the following definition: "[T]he terms mental disease or mental retardation include only those severely abnormal men-

tal conditions that grossly and demonstrably impair a person's perception or understanding of reality and that are not attributable primarily to the voluntary ingestion of
alcohol or other psychoactive substances." The American Bar Association suggested that
mental disease "refers to impairment of mind, whether enduring or transitory, or to
mental retardation which substantially affected the mental or emotional processes of
the defendant at the time of the alleged offense." R. Slovenko, *Psychiatry and Criminal
Culpability* (New York: Wiley, 1995), pp. 51–117; also *ABA Criminal Justice Mental Health
Standards* (1986, 1989), pp. 330, 336.

Herron v. State of Mississippi
"Defense of irresistible or uncontrollable impulse is unavailable unless the uncontrollable impulse sprang from a mental disease existing to such a high degree as to over-
whelm reason, judgment, and conscience so that the accused would be unable to distinguish right and wrong of a matter." 287 So.2d 759 (Miss. 1974).

United States v. Hinckley
In 1982 a federal court jury in the District of Columbia shocked the nation by finding
John W. Hinckley Jr., the would-be assassin of President Ronald Reagan, not guilty by
reason of insanity. 525 F.Supp. 1342 (D.D.C.), *op. clarified, reconsideration denied,* 529
F.Supp. 520 (D.D.C.), *aff'd,* 672 F.2d 115 (D.C. Cir. 1982). Responding to the outcry, the
American Bar Association and the American Psychiatric Association issued statements
calling for a change in the law. They recommended that insanity acquittals be granted
only for impaired cognition (not for impaired control) as a result of a substantial process
of functional or organic impairment. A federal statute adopted in 1984, and copied in a
number of states, provides: "It is an affirmative defense to a prosecution under any
federal statute that, at the time of the commission of the acts constituting the offense,
the defendant as a result of a severe mental disease or defect, was unable to appreciate
the nature and quality or the wrongfulness of his acts. Mental disease or defect does
not otherwise constitute a defense." 18 U.S.C., sec. 20. see R. J. Bonnie, J. C. Jeffries, &
P. W. Low, *A Case Study in the Insanity Defense: The Trial of John W. Hinckley, Jr.* (New
York: Foundation Press, 2d ed. 2000), p. 130.

Compulsive Gambling

United States v. Torniero
A federal district court in Connecticut barred the defense from introducing expert testimony to show that the defendant could not have helped himself because he was a
compulsive gambler. The defendant, John H. Torniero, was charged with the interstate
transportation of stolen goods, a federal offense. He allegedly stole more than $500,000
in jewelry from the store he managed and sold it in another state to finance his compulsive gambling. The judge ruled that the defendant's "alleged gambling is only tan-
gentially related to the offense with which he has been charged." In effect, he ruled,
there was insufficient causal nexus between the alleged mental illness and the crime.
The ruling came on a pretrial motion filed by the prosecutor to deny the use of this
evidence of mental illness. The judge stated that he excluded the evidence in order to
avoid jury confusion. The defendant was charged with the interstate transportation of
stolen goods, it was noted, not with gambling. And pointing out that his ruling applied
only to this case, the judge, Jose A. Cabranes, said he "shares the widespread and growing public concern that new mental disorders appear to be fabricated in unending suc-
cession . . . and that defendants increasingly seek to 'explain' their alleged criminal acts
as somehow compelled by pathologies of vague description and scant relevance." While
ruling that the use of the insanity defense should not be limited, Judge Cabranes said
in dicta that what qualifies as mental illness is not entirely a factual question for the
jury. He said, "It is appropriate for the court to consider whether the type of disease or

defect alleged by the defendant is sufficient to constitute allegation of insanity." 570 F.Supp. 721 (D.C. Conn. 1983). The Connecticut legislature has specifically excluded pathological or compulsive gambling as a mental illness. Conn. Gen. Stat., sec. 53a-139(c).

Multiple Personality Disorder

State v. Rodrigues

The Hawaii Supreme Court summarized the trend in the law on MPD: "The cases dealing with [MPD] can be examined in a similar fashion as other defenses of insanity. If a lunatic has lucid intervals of understanding he shall answer for what he does in those intervals of understanding; he shall answer for what he does in those intervals as if he had no deficiency. The law governs criminal accountability where at the time of the wrongful act the person had the mental capacity to distinguish between right and wrong or to conform his conduct to the requirements of the law." 679 P.2d 615 (Hawaii 1984). See J. R. Kanovitz, B. S. Kanovitz, & J. P. Block, "Witnesses with Multiple Personality Disorder," *Pepperdine L. Rev.* 23 (1996): 387; R. Slovenko, "The Multiple Personality: A Challenge to Legal Concepts," *J. Psychiatry & Law* 17 (1989): 681.

Post-traumatic Stress Disorder

State v. Utter

Claude Utter was charged with the crime of murder in the second degree. His son entered his apartment and shortly thereafter he stabbed his son to death. At trial he introduced evidence on "conditioned response," which was defined by a psychiatrist as "an act or a pattern of activity occurring so rapidly, so uniformly as to be automatic in response to a certain stimulus." The evidence was presented for the purpose of determining whether a "voluntary act" had been committed. The question was not one of mental incapacity so a plea of NGRI would not be required to offer the evidence, said the court. However, the court held that the evidence presented was insufficient to present the issue to the jury of defendant's unconscious or automatic state at the time of the act. The court ruled that there was no evidence, circumstantial or otherwise from which the jury could determine or reasonably infer what happened in the room at the time of the stabbing; the jury could only speculate on the existence of the triggering stimulus. 4 Wash. App. 137, 479 P.2d 946 (1971). The defendant may have suffered from what is now termed *post-traumatic stress disorder.* When an everyday event triggers a memory of the traumatic experience, the person with PTSD may experience dissociative or flashback episodes or hallucinations. Although a claim of unconsciousness under such circumstances is sometimes successful, the disorder is usually raised in the context of an insanity plea. As a practical matter, of course, a defendant would prefer acquittal on the basis of unconsciousness, as no confinement would result as in the case of an acquittal by reason of insanity. See Fulcher v. State, 633 P.2d 142 (Wyo. 1981); R. Slovenko, *Psychiatry and Criminal Culpability* (New York: Wiley, 1995).

Laws v. Armontrout

In a dissenting opinion to the Supreme Court's denial of a petition for a writ of certiorari, Justices Thurgood Marshall and William Brennan noted that the attorney failed to investigate the defendant's service record in Vietnam, and that the failure to consider PTSD, in their view, constituted ineffective assistance of counsel. That view has been followed. They wrote: "The attorney also knew that many of the soldiers who served in the Vietnam conflict suffered severe emotional trauma afterwards, encountering problems of socialization and readjustment. In some cases, they have suffered from post-traumatic stress disorder so severe as to induce violent criminality, a fact recognized by

Congress when it passed the Veterans Health Care Amendment Act. . . . [T]he attorney failed, too, to explore this potential source of mitigating evidence." 490 U.S. 1040 (1989).

Bouchillon v. Collins

The Fifth Circuit Court of Appeals held that failure to investigate a defendant's competency to stand trial or viability of an insanity defense is ineffective assistance of counsel. It was undisputed that the defendant suffered from PTSD, most likely at the time of the offense and at the time he entered a guilty plea. According to the record, the defendant's disorder was such that "he apparently goes through lucid and competent intervals, as opposed to episodes of 'numbing' and black-outs during which he cannot be expected to exercise judgment or reason." In the habeas corpus hearing, the Fifth Circuit felt that the state court's reliance on the defendant's demeanor to show competence was wrong, because "the existence of even a severe psychiatric defect is not always apparent to laymen." 907 F.2d 589 (5th Cir. 1990).

See G. Mendelson, *Psychiatric Aspects of Personal Injury Claims* (Springfield, Ill.: Thomas, 1988); C. B. Scrignar, *Post-Traumatic Stress Disorder: Diagnosis, Treatment, and Legal Issues* (New Orleans: Bruno Press, 3d ed. 1996); R. I. Simon (ed.), *Posttraumatic Stress Disorder in Litigation* (Washington, D.C.: American Psychiatric Press, 2d ed. 2002); R. Slovenko, "Legal Aspects of Post-Traumatic Stress Disorder," *Psychiatric Clinics of North America* 17 (1994): 439. *See* Syndrome Evidence

INSANITY ACQUITTEE DISPOSITION

People v. McQuillan

In the mid-1970s state courts in the United States began to rule, on a principle of equivalence, that the criteria for commitment of an insanity acquittee must be the same as those for an ordinary civil commitment. In a decision that influenced a number of other states, the Michigan Supreme Court in 1974 held that, after an initial period of sixty days, during which the insanity acquittee was to be evaluated, further confinement had to conform with the procedures and standards of the civil commitment process. The Michigan Supreme Court relied on the U.S. Supreme Court's decision in 1966 in *Baxstrom v. Herold*, which involved a prison inmate whose term of imprisonment was about to expire and where the court said that the prisoner could not be subject to a different standard for commitment to a mental institution than a person outside of prison with a criminal record or any other individual. 392 Mich. 511, 211 N.W.2d 569 (1974).

Jones v. United States

Michael Jones, diagnosed as having paranoid schizophrenia, was arrested in 1975 for trying to steal a jacket from a District of Columbia department store. After being found NGRI of an attempted petty larceny charge (on the basis of plea bargaining), he was committed to St. Elizabeths Hospital, where he remained for nearly a decade. If he had been convicted, his maximum sentence would have been a year. Defense counsel argued that it is unconstitutional for a person found NGRI to be confined in a mental institution longer than he would have been in prison if found guilty. The petitioner also argued that it is unconstitutional to apply stricter commitment procedures for insanity acquittees than for ordinary involuntary commitment cases. *Jones* was decided one year after the *Hinckley* verdict; by a 5–4 vote, the Supreme Court rejected the argument. Writing for the majority, Justice Lewis F. Powell said that imprisonment and commitment to a mental hospital serve two different purposes. The purpose of criminal commitment to a mental hospital, he said, is not punishment "but treatment of a mentally ill person and protection of society, from the potential dangerousness." The continued confinement of such a person, Justice Powell said, "rests on his continuing illness and dangerousness." He added: "There simply is no necessary correlation between severity of the offense and length of time necessary for recovery. The length of the acquittee's hypothetical criminal sentence therefore is irrelevant to the purposes of his commitment." 463 U.S. 354 (1983).

The American Psychiatric Association's Council of Psychiatry and Law in 1988 recommended that the continued hospitalization of non–mentally ill personality-disordered persons, who have recovered from their mental illness in a maximum security hospital following acquittal by reason of insanity, is justified on the grounds that "[t]hose who suffer from personality disorders may also benefit from the special management available only in a psychiatric institution where sensitive, comprehensive, unique and imaginative treatment programs can often be developed to assist them in overcoming their destructive behavior." Council of Psychiatry and Law, American Psychiatric Association, *Final Report of the Subcommittee to Review the Insanity Defence* (1988), p. 3. *See* Sex Offenders

Divorce

The law on divorce was long based, like the criminal law, on an offense theory. During the nineteenth century, a divorce usually was allowed only in the case of adultery, the only offense considered serious enough to warrant divorce, and the evidence had to be sufficiently reliable. The offense grounds were various and were variously interpreted in the several states. Some common grounds were adultery (all states), cruelty (46 states), alcoholism (39 states), drug addiction (11 states), imprisonment (18 states), and wife pregnant by another man at time of marriage (11 states).

The allegation of cruelty, which like many other offenses was not a basis for divorce in the nineteenth century, was, during the first half of the twentieth century, the most commonly alleged ground. That so many persons should sin the same way reflected the careful legal tailoring needed to custom-fit a case to the statutes. If eating cauliflower without clothes on were the only acceptable ground, then there would have been a rash of naked eating of cauliflower.

Insanity was not a defense to a complaint of matrimonial cruelty. The aims of matrimonial law were remedial and protective, not punitive, and the fact that the respondent was insane, under the *M'Naghten* rules, was immaterial. The rules on criminal responsibility did not apply. An intent to injure the petitioner was not material in these cases, as long as the conduct of the respondent could be characterized as cruel. Cruelty in matrimonial law depended upon the nature of the conduct, not the state of mind accompanying the acts by the respondent.

While the definition of insanity as disease or illness has been controversial, the message was prophetic for at least a half-century in divorce law. The increasing acceptance of the idea of divorce without fault was responsible, at least in part, for the doubling of the number of states that, during the period between the two world wars, enacted legislation allowing divorce on the ground of mental illness, which could be characterized as divorce without fault. Almost all the states that allowed divorce based on insanity, however, required the condition to be incurable, and that was difficult to establish. By and large, incurability had to be established by medical testimony. Most states allowing divorce based on insanity made provision for the future support of the mentally ill spouse.

Mental illness at the time of the marriage ceremony or prenuptial mental disability was distinguished from postnuptial mental illness. Under the common law, a marriage was (and is) null or void ab initio (considered as though it never existed) if either party at the time of the marriage was "suffering from insanity" to such an extent as to be incapable of understanding the nature of the ceremony or to have insane delusions on the subject. The laws of the states, in varying language, provide that an applicant who is insane or an imbecile shall not be issued a marriage license. As a rule, however, the marriage was simply rendered voidable or annullable if the party complaining did not know of the infirmity (such as evidenced by prior suicide attempts or mental hospital-ization) of the other party. Lack of sexual intercourse since discovery of the alleged facts was often required.

Beginning in California in 1966, with the adoption of no-fault divorce, the justice system was transformed into a divorce mill. It is now easier to end a marriage than to repudiate a contract to buy a kitchen appliance. The only allegation the petitioner in a divorce case is now required to prove is that "there has been a breakdown of the mar-riage relationship to the extent that the objects of matrimony have been destroyed and there remains no reasonable likelihood that the marriage can be preserved." Nothing else is to be stated in the complaint. The sole defense to a divorce action is that there is a reasonable likelihood that the marriage can be preserved. The no-fault divorce eliminates the defense of insanity.

Why marry, many people ask (ironically, homosexual couples seek the bounds of marriage)? Fewer people in the United States are marrying now than ever before, and half of those who do marry will eventually divorce. More couples are living together outside marriage than in the past, and nearly one-third of all births are out of wedlock (the figure is even higher in Europe). In the past, marriage was an economic institution primarily, one that connected families and that was bound by religion. Those ties have now been frayed. E. Feldman, "Till Divorce Do Us Part," *American Heritage,* Nov. 2000, pp. 38–47. See M. J. Ackerman & A. W. Kane, *Psychological Experts in Divorce Actions* (New York: Aspen, 3d ed. 1998); J. Q. Wilson, *The Marriage Problem: How Our Culture Has Weakened Families* (New York: HarperCollins, 2002).

Katherine Spaht, a key figure in Louisiana family law, helped bring no-fault di-vorce to the state in the 1980s, but seeing the devastation walkaway divorce wrought in the lives of women she knew, in 1997 she helped draw up the nation's first covenant-marriage bill, which makes marriage a stronger legal commitment than that allowed by standard no-fault divorce laws. Louisiana became the first state (and Ari-zona quickly the second) to adopt it, but few couples have opted for it. After decades of witnessing the family tragedies wrought by nonsupport following divorce, matri-monial lawyer Diana Du Broff recently founded the National Organization to Insure Support Enforcement (NOISE), which suggests the ideal bridal gift: divorce insurance. Dr. Judith Wallerstein's 25-year study of children of divorce, *The Unexpected Legacy of Divorce* (New York: Hyperion, 2000), says that children pay dearly for their parents' divorce. She and her coauthors, Julia Lewis and Sandra Blakeslee, suggest that parents stay together even if the marriage is not working. In *For Better or for Worse: Divorce Reconsidered* (New York: W. W. Norton, 2002), E. Mavis Hetherington, a psychology professor emeritus at the University of Virginia, and her coauthor John Kelly declare that 75 to 80 percent of children of divorce are functioning well, with little long-term damage. They found that 25 percent of children from divorced families have serious social, emotional, or psychological problems, as opposed to 10 percent of youngsters from intact families.

Juvenile Justice

Until 1898 when Illinois adopted the first juvenile code, juveniles were considered within the general body of criminal law. The idea spread nationwide. In the juvenile court, unlike the criminal court, the state as *parens patriae* would act on *behalf* of youths and provide them with the treatment needed to ensure that they become law-abiding citizens. In the juvenile court a juvenile is not called a defendant, but a respondent; a prosecutor is not called a prosecutor, but a petitioner; a trial is called a fact-finding hearing; a conviction is a finding; sentencing is a dispositional hearing. See C. E. Goshen, *Society and the Youthful Offender* (Springfield, Ill.: Thomas, 1974); F. B. McCarthy & J. G. Carr (eds.), *Juvenile Law and Its Processes: Cases and Materials* (Indianapolis, Ind.: Bobbs-Merrill, 1980).

In re Gault

In this, the most important case in juvenile law, Justice Fortas described juvenile courts as "kangaroo courts" characterized by arbitrariness, ineffectiveness, and the appearance of injustice. The decision established that juveniles were owed at least those elements of due process essential to fundamental fairness (e.g., right to counsel, written and timely notice of the charges, and the privilege against self-incrimination). 387 U.S. 1 (1967). The Supreme Court also addressed the issue of procedures in juvenile delinquency hearings in *In re Kent*, 383 U.S. 541 (1966), and in McKeiver v. Pennsylvania, 403 U.S. 528 (1971), it held that trial by jury is not guaranteed by the Constitution in juvenile proceedings.

With the rise in juvenile crime, various states have provided for the transfer, or waiver, of jurisdiction when the minor is not "mentally retarded or criminally insane" and "community interests require that the minor be put under legal restraint." Unlike in other areas of the law, jurisdiction is in the discretion of the court. There is now substantial ambivalence about the justification for the juvenile court. See J. Sheindlin & J. Getlin, *Don't Pee on My Leg and Tell Me It's Raining* (New York: HarperCollins, 1997).

Malpractice. *See also* Undue Familiarity

A generation ago psychotherapy was rarely the subject of a malpractice suit. There were until then only a few of appellate cases involving psychotherapy. Almost anything seemed acceptable in the so-called talking cure. Dr. David S. Viscott wrote in his book *The Making of a Psychiatrist* (New York: Arbor House, 1972) that it was a standing joke that it did not matter whether a psychiatrist was a quack, because psychiatrists did so little it was unlikely that they could do any harm.

Most litigation involving psychiatrists resulted from physical and not psychic damage to the patient. The few cases against psychiatrists were based on improper certification in commitment proceedings, negligent discharge, the failure to exercise adequate suicidal precaution, breach of confidentiality, or improper administration of medication or electroshock treatment. A study carried out in Southern California for the years 1958–1967 reported that in twelve cases settled out of a total of thirty-seven, the average amount required to settle a psychiatric malpractice suit before trial was $1,034. The literature on the topic, both legal and psychiatric, was sparse and dealt mainly with the areas of patient suicide, electroshock therapy, and involuntary commitment. The literature indicated that the malpractice problem was not substantial, compared to malpractice in other areas. Few, if any, cases involved improper or poor psychotherapeutic or analytic technique. Unless injury to the patient was physical or there had been obvious misconduct (as in the cases of sexual relations with a patient), the patient was in a difficult position to link the harm to the therapy. Even if the patient were to establish causality, it was unlikely that he would be able to establish negligence. Moreover, a cause of action based on breach of contract was also difficult to sustain since the therapist, when treatment commenced, made a point of promising nothing. Also dissuading lawsuits was the important extralegal consideration of a general reluctance to reveal one's personal life in a courtroom. Now that has changed. See J. Cornwell, *The Power to Harm* (New York: Viking, 1996); J. L. Kelley, *Psychiatric Malpractice* (New Brunswick: Rutgers University Press, 1996); R. I. Simon, *Clinical Psychiatry and the Law* (Washington, D.C.: American Psychiatric Press, 2d ed. 1992); R. Slovenko, "Malpractice In Psychiatry and Related Fields," *J. Psychiatry & Law* 9 (1981): 5.

STANDARD OF CARE

Osheroff v. Chestnut Lodge

In 1979, Rafael Osheroff, a 42-year-old physician, entered Chestnut Lodge with symptoms of psychotic depression. In the course of his seven-month stay at the Lodge, he was treated with four sessions a week in intensive psychotherapy and denied medication despite his requests, on the apparent ground of having him regress back to childhood and then "build" from there. His condition worsened, and he obtained a transfer to another clinic, the Silver Hill Foundation, where he was treated with phenothiazines and antidepressants. Within three months, he improved and was discharged, but he found that his world had disintegrated, his wife having left him, his hospital accreditation gone, and his partner having ousted him from their joint practice. In 1982 he sued Chestnut Lodge for malpractice on the ground that he should have been given state-of-the-art treatment with medications of demonstrated efficacy. In 1987 the case was settled, like *Tarasoff*, without a court ruling, but it has had an impact on the practice of psychiatry. Chestnut Lodge now uses medication, fearing that treating major psychiatric illnesses with psychotherapy alone will be held to constitute malpractice. As often said, the *p*-word is no longer *psychoanalysis,* but *Prozac.* The case is debated in G. L. Klerman, "The Psychiatric Patient's Right to Effective Treatment: Implications of *Osheroff v. Chestnut Lodge,*" *Am. J. Psychiatry* 147 (1990): 419; A. A. Stone, "Law, Science, and Psychiatric Malpractice: A Response to Klerman's Indictment of Psychoanalytic Psychiatry," *Am. J. Psychiatry* 147 (1990): 419. Attorney John G. Malcolm has written a book about the case, *Treatment Choices and Informed Consent: Current Controversies in Psychiatric Malpractice* (Springfield, Ill.: Thomas, 1988). See also T. M. Luhrmann, *Of Two Minds: The Growing Disorder in American Psychiatry* (New York: Knopf, 2000), pp. 232–35. The writer Peter Wyden describes his search for an effective cure for his son in *Conquering Schizophrenia* (New York: Knopf, 1998).

ELECTROCONVULSIVE THERAPY

Responding to various patients' rights groups, state legislatures began regulating ECT. In 1967 Utah was the first to pass such legislation, and by 1983, twenty-six states had passed some kind of statute, six others issued administrative regulations, and one state was under federal court order. Legislation enacted in California in 1974 stipulated that, even when a patient volunteered for ECT, it could only be administered with the consent of a review panel appointed by community medical authorities, and only after all other psychiatric remedies had been exhausted. The legislation was challenged in court and did not take effect. In 1982, the Coalition to Stop Electroshock in Berkeley gathered 1,400 signatures necessary to put a measure banning ECT on the ballot; it passed by a wide margin, but again, the ban was overturned. In Texas in 1995 legislation was introduced to ban ECT but it did not pass (despite receiving wide press coverage.) Renewing efforts in Texas from this failed attempt, a bill was introduced in 1997 that would prohibit the use of ECT on persons sixty-five years of age or older. Current Texas law prohibits the administration of ECT on persons younger than sixteen. Nationwide, liability insurance coverage on the use of ECT often makes it prohibitive. In any event, the doctrine of *res ipsa loquitur* that allows a presumption of negligence in the event of a fracture does not apply inasmuch as it may occur even when the treatment is properly administered. See W. J. Winslade et al., "Medical, Judicial, and Statutory Regulation of ECT in the United States," *Am. J. Psychiatry* 141 (1984): 134. For a vigorous advocacy of the use of ECT, see M. Fink, *Electroshock: Restoring the Mind* (New York: Oxford University Press, 1999).

TARDIVE DYSKINESIA

Antipsychotic medications, introduced in the early 1950s, have revolutionized psychiatric treatment. At the same time, medication-related treatment constitutes the greatest potential for harm to patients. Foremost among the side effects that a patient might have as a consequence of taking neuroleptic medication for an appreciable length of time is tardive dyskinesia. Overdosage, failure to monitor, or inappropriate or unnecessary medication is alleged in malpractice litigation.

Faigenbaum v. Cohen

The patient manifested classic tardive symptoms following neuroleptic medication. Misreading her symptoms, the physician advised the patient to seek medical care for what he thought were signs of an inherited disease—Huntington's chorea. According to the court, neuroleptic treatment was poorly monitored. In addition, the diagnosis of tardive dyskinesia was missed by several psychiatrists and a consulting neurologist, leading to a continuation of neuroleptic treatment amid severe dyskinetic movements. A psychiatrist testified at trial that the patient suffered from "one of the worst cases of tardive dyskinesia I've ever seen." The patient was awarded a million dollars, which plus interest amounted to nearly a million and a half. (The attorney for the patient was Geoffrey Fieger, who later represented Dr. Jack Kevorkian.) Subsequently, the malpractice claim against the hospital was reversed on the ground of governmental immunity. The patient's TD symptoms disappeared, but she had her judgment against the physicians. 143 Mich. App. 303, 373 N.W.2d 161 (1985), aff'd, Hyde v. University of Michigan Board of Regents, 426 Mich. 223 393 N.W.2d 847 (1986).

Clites v. Iowa

Timothy Clites, a mentally retarded individual, was confined in 1963 in a state hospital, and by 1970 his behavior had become aggressive and he was given several neuroleptic medications. By 1975, he was diagnosed as suffering from tardive dyskinesia, allegedly caused by the long-term use of neuroleptics. The Iowa Court of Appeals held that the state violated "industry standards" of reasonable care, specifically by using polypharmacy, by failure to obtain consultation, by lack of drug holidays, and by use of neuroleptics to control his behavior. 322 N.W.2d 917 (Iowa 1982). See R. Slovenko, "On the Legal Aspects of Tardive Dyskinesia," J. Psychiatry & Law 7 (1979): 295; id., "Update on Legal Issues Associated with Tardive Dyskinesia," J. Clin. Psychiatry 61 (2000): 45 (supp. 4); id., "Legal Issues Surrounding Tardive Dyskinesia," Psychiatric Times, Aug. 2000, pp. 38–44.

DUTY TO WARN OR PROTECT IN THE OUTPATIENT SETTING

Tarasoff v. Regents of the University of California

In this well-known case, which has been followed in many jurisdictions, the California Supreme Court imposed a duty on psychiatrists or other psychotherapists to protect readily identifiable third parties from potential harm by their patients. The court thereby made the psychiatrist a proper party defendant whenever a patient causes injury to a third party. In jurisdictions following Tarasoff, it became no longer possible for therapists to avoid trial by summary disposition on the ground that they owed no duty in law to the injured party. Under Tarasoff, it is a matter for the jury to decide on the basis of the facts of the particular case whether the third party was readily identifiable and reasonable care was exercised to protect the third party. The case was settled, but had it gone to trial, the court could have found that the therapist, since he had notified the campus police, discharged the duty imposed by the court. The importance of the case despite the settlement is that it imposed a legal duty on therapists to third persons irrespective of the standard of care in treating the patient.

The court held that by virtue of the "special relationship" that a therapist has with a patient, there results a duty of care to third parties who might be injured by the patient. Under this ruling it is immaterial whether or not the treatment of the patient falls below standard of care, or whether there is a causal nexus between the treatment and the injury to the third person. The court said: "Although under the common law, as a general rule, one person owed no duty to control the conduct of another, nor to warn those endangered by such conduct, the courts have carved out an exception to this rule in cases in which the defendant stands in some special relationship *to either the person whose conduct needs to be controlled or in a relationship to the foreseeable victim of that conduct*" (emphasis added).

Innovating, the court ruled that the special relationship with the patient also creates a special relationship with the victim of the patient. Thus, *Tarasoff* and its progeny represents an evolution of the law from no duty, to a duty to those in a special relationship, and now to those who might be harmed by one to whom a duty is owed. In the words of the court: "Although plaintiffs' pleadings assert no special relation between [the victim] and defendant therapists, they establish as between [the patient] and defendant therapists the special relation that arises between a patient and his doctor or psychotherapist. Such a relationship may support affirmative duties for the benefit of third persons." Under this ruling, a third-party victim may bring a claim against a therapist regardless of whether the therapist's care and treatment of the patient constituted malpractice. The focus of concern is the foreseeable risk to a third party (some jurisdictions extend the duty to nonidentifiable victims and some jurisdictions limit the duty of care to a warning). The court rationalized its holding in part by citing earlier decisions holding physicians liable for failing to warn third parties who contracted contagious diseases from their patients. What care to protect potential victims is reasonably necessary, the court said, can be determined only on a case-by-case basis. 17 Cal.3d 425, 131 Cal. Rptr. 14, 551 P.2d 334 (1976).

Florida, Texas, and Virginia have rejected *Tarasoff.* See Boyton v. Burglass, 590 So.2d 446 (Fla. App. 1991); Nasser v. Parker, 249 Va. 172, 455 S.E.2d 502 (1995). See F. Buckner & M. Firestone, "'Where the Public Peril Begins': 25 Years after Tarasoff," *J. Legal Med.* 21 (2000): 187; A. R. Felthous & C. Kachigian, "The Fin de Millenaire Duty to Warn or Protect," *J. For. Sci.* 46 (2001): 1103. See also A. R. Felthous, *The Psychotherapist's Duty to Warn or Protect* (Springfield, Ill.: Thomas, 1989); V. S. Mangalmurti, "Psychotherapists' Fear of *Tarasoff:* All in the Mind?" *J. Psychiatry & Law* 22 (1994): 379; R. Slovenko, "Misadventures of Psychiatry with the Law," *J. Psychiatry & Law* 17 (1989): 115. Fear of *Tarasoff* is set forth in A. A. Stone, "The *Tarasoff* Decision: Suing Psychotherapists to Safeguard Society," *Harv. L. Rev.* 90 (1976): 358.

Lipari v. Sears Roebuck

Ulysses Cribbs was hospitalized at a Veterans Administration Hospital and thereafter he was treated on an outpatient basis at the hospital, during which time he purchased a shotgun from a Sears store in the area. Approximately a month after leaving the program he fired the shotgun into a crowded restaurant, killing Dennis Lipari and wounding Lipari's wife. Suit was filed against Sears, alleging the injuries were caused by the negligence of Sears in selling a gun to someone they "knew or should have known had been adjudged mentally defective or had been committed to a mental institution." Sears impleaded the U.S. government (Veterans Administration), claiming the VA was negligent in its treatment of Cribbs. The government, seeking to avoid liability, claimed a duty is owed only to warn identifiable victims. The federal district court in Nebraska held that the duty was owed not only to specific, readily identifiable victims, but "to those persons foreseeably endangered by the negligent conduct." 497 F.Supp. 1985 (D.C. Iowa 1980).

DUTY TO PREVENT A SUICIDE

The standard of care in suicide prevention varies depending on whether the patient is in outpatient care or is in a medical or mental facility. The duty to monitor or supervise is higher where the patient is in a custodial ward or a medical facility that provides more control over the patient. But in this age of deinstitutionalization and managed care there are an increasing number of lawsuits against psychiatrists or HMOs in regard outpatient suicide. See S. J. Blumenthal & D. J. Kupfer (eds.), *Suicide Over the Life Cycle* (Washington, D.C.: American Psychiatric Press, 1990); D. A. Jobes & A. L. Berman, "Suicide and Malpractice Liability: Assessing and Revising Policies, Procedures, and Practices in Outpatient Settings," *Prof. Psychol. Res. Practice* 24 (1993): 91; M. Flood, "Dallas Lawyer Makes Suicide Focus of Lawsuits," *Wall Street Journal,* Feb. 26, 1997, p. B-2.

Bellah v. Greenson

The patient's parents in this California case brought a wrongful death action against the psychiatrist who had been treating their daughter as an outpatient. She committed suicide. The California Court of Appeals held that the psychiatrist had no duty under *Tarasoff v. Regents of University of California* to warn the parents that their daughter was a danger to herself. It said, "[The California Supreme Court] did not hold that such disclosure was required where the danger consisted of a likelihood of property damage. Instead, the court recognized the importance of the confidential relationship between a therapists and his patient, holding that 'the therapist's obligations to his patient require that he not disclose a confidence unless such disclosure is necessary to avert danger to others.'"

At the same time, while so holding, the court held that a psychiatrist does have a duty to take steps to prevent a possible suicide. The court said, "[A] psychiatrist who knows that his patient is likely to attempt suicide has a duty to take preventive measures." The court went on to say, "Obviously, the duty imposed upon those responsible for the care of a patient in an institutional setting differs from that which may be involved in the case of a psychiatrist treating patients on an out-patient basis." And it found that a cause of action had been stated for the breach of a psychiatrist's duty of care towards a patient. The psychiatrist was aware that the patient was disposed to suicide and had made notes of it during the treatment sessions. The court said, "The nature of the precautionary steps which could or should have been taken by defendant presents a purely factual question to be resolved at a trial on the merits, at which time both sides would be afforded an opportunity to produce expert medical testimony on the subject. From the face of plaintiff's complaint, we are unable to determine whether defendant did or did not take preventive steps which were consonant with good medical practice in the community. However, that question is not before us in the demurrer stage of these proceedings." 81 Cal. App.3d 614, 146 Cal. Rptr. 535 (1978).

Paddock v. Chacko

In this Florida case the patient, a 35-year-old woman, left the home of her parents with whom she had been temporarily residing, ran into a wooded area nearby, and set her clothes on fire with a cigarette lighter after superficially slashing her wrists with her knife. She sued the defendant, a psychiatrist whom she had seen professionally one time some four days earlier, alleging that his negligence proximately caused or contributed to her self-immolation. After a lengthy trial, the jury awarded her $2,150,000. The decision was reversed on appeal. The court noted that neither civil commitment law nor case law provide a basis for imposing a duty on practitioners to seek commitment of patients against their will. It also mentioned that a practitioner initiating a commitment proceeding that results in involuntary detention may in fact be liable for malicious prosecution. The court further noted that imposing liability on practitioners for failing to involuntarily commit suicidal patients "would create an intolerable burden on psychiatrists and the practice of psychiatry."

The court pointed to the history of psychiatry: "The practice of psychiatry has come a long way from the ancient practice of confining persons with aberrant behavior in institutions or asylums. It has been recognized that mental illness may be caused or intensified by institutionalizing mental patients. The basic form of treatment in these asylums was based on restraint and immobilization. . . . Emerging from these roots, the science and profession of psychiatry has burgeoned into a multifaceted social institution. The practice of psychiatry is no longer limited to the institutionalization of the mentally ill. Professionals in the practice of psychiatry and psychology now offer an innumerable variety of remedial therapies to the troubled and ailing souls of modern society." The court went on to say, "[A] psychiatrist has no duty to assume custodial care over his patient. There is some precedent in Florida law for liability predicated upon the negligent failure to safeguard and protect a psychiatric patient with suicidal tendencies. . . . However, in each of these cases, the patients were already committed to the custody of a hospital or mental institution. . . . [The psychiatrist's] failure to prescribe proper amounts of antipsychotic drugs was not shown to be a proximate cause of the plaintiff's self-inflicted injuries." 522 So.2d 410 (Fla. 1988).

Schuster v. Altenberg

The Wisconsin Supreme Court set out an affirmative duty to seek commitment of a patient who poses a danger to self or others. In this case, a manic-depressive patient on psychotropic medication crashed into a tree at sixty miles per hour within an hour of treatment. The patient died, leaving her seventeen-year-old daughter paraplegic. The court remanded the case to the trial court, saying: "In the instant case, if it is ultimately proven that it would have been foreseeable to a psychiatrist, exercising due care, that by failing to warn a third person or by failing to take action to institute detention or commitment proceedings someone would be harmed, negligence will be established." 144 Wis.2d 223, 424 N.W.2d 159 (1988). The trial court found the decedent 80 percent contributorily negligent, the plaintiff 20 percent negligent, and the defendant psychiatrist not negligent. 86-CV-1327 (Cir. Ct. Racine Cty. 1990).

Bates v. Denney

The Louisiana Court of Appeals noted that forcing commitment on a patient may be counterproductive to successful treatment. The court cited the expert testimony presented at trial that involuntary commitment of the patient could have resulted in his becoming less treatable. This result was a probability, the expert testified, because during previous hospitalizations the patient exhibited negativism to the ministrations of the staff. In a hospital environment, the expert explained, the psychiatrist is the therapist as well as the authoritarian controller of the patient's behavior. The expert said, "This pits the psychiatrist and resistant patient against each other in a power struggle. If the power struggle is resolved positively, the patient benefits. If negatively, then the patient remains resistant throughout his hospitalization." Moreover, the court concluded, "[The patient] cannot be hospitalized forever." 563 So.2d 298 (La. App. 1990). For a criticism, see S. Rachlin, "With Liberty and Psychosis for All," *Psychiatric Q.* 48 (1974): 410; D. Treffert, "Dying with Your Rights On," *Prism* 2 (1974): 49.

Gross v. Allen

The California Court of Appeals held that if a patient has demonstrated a history of being dangerous to self, then the original caretaker is legally responsible for informing the new caretaker of this history. In defense, the original caretaker (irrelevantly) argued that *Tarasoff v. Regents of University of California* imposed no such duty because the patient, unlike the patient in *Tarasoff*, posed no threat to a third person, only to self. The Court of Appeals, rejecting the argument, said, "But *Tarasoff* does not state, as the defendant implies, that a therapist may be silent when to speak may save the life of his patient." 22 Cal. App.4th 354, 27 Cal. Rptr.2d 429 (1994); discussed in C. J. Meyers, "Expanding *Tarasoff*: Protecting Patients and the Public by Keeping Subsequent Caretakers Informed," *J. Psychiatry & Law* 25 (1997): 365. Actually, there was no need of the court to cite *Tarasoff*, or to claim that the decision is an expansion of *Tarasoff*. *Tarasoff* was concerned with a duty to third parties, not a duty to the patient. Standard of care of the treatment of a patient calls for communication with other or subsequent caretakers. Suppose the patient in *Tarasoff*, rather than a third party, had sued the therapist in malpractice? See R. Slovenko, "The Therapist's Duty to Warn or Protect Third Persons," *J. Psychiatry & Law* 16 (1988): 139.

Rich v. Peninsula Psychiatric Hospital

The court differentiated between the psychiatrist's and the hospital's duty: "[W]hen a hospital elects to accept a patient with psychiatric disorders and with orders that 'suicide precautions' be taken, the prime responsibility to afford reasonably safe facilities and reasonable attendance to the patient's needs to prevent self injury lies with the hospital and not the physician. The physician is not in constant attendance. The hospital is supposed to be." The psychiatrist had ordered suicide precautions for the patient, but the hospital negligently failed to discover medication that the patient had hidden and that was used to commit suicide. The hospital was held liable for negligence, but not the psychiatrist. Thus, while the psychiatrist has a duty to order precautions, if necessary, for a suicidal patient, the responsibility for implementing those precautions falls on the hospital. 1990 Tenn. App. Lexis 245 (Ct. App. 1990). See I. N. Perr, "The Liability of the Hospital and the Psychiatrist in Suicide," *Am. J. Psychiatry* 122 (1965): 621; I. N. Perr, "Suicide Litigation and Risk Management: A Review of 32 Cases," *Bull. Am. Acad. Psychiatry & Law* 13 (1985): 209; E. V. Swenson, "Legal Liability for a Patient's Suicide," *J. Psychiatry & Law* 14 (1986): 409.

DUTY OF THERAPISTS TO THIRD PERSONS ARISING OUT OF THERAPY

Ramona v. Isabella, Rose & Western Medical Center

Gary Ramona in California in 1994 sued a medical center and a pair of psychotherapists who he claimed created false memories in his daughter of his sexually abusing her as a child. His lawsuit sought damages for emotional suffering from the breakup of his family, and for harm to his career and reputation. The daughter was satisfied with the therapy. She testified against her father, and she filed a lawsuit against him.

In Ramona's suit against the hospital and therapists, the trial court rejected the defense's motion for summary judgment and held that a duty of care was owed to the parent. According to reports, the therapists suggested to the daughter that her eating disorder was caused by childhood sexual abuse the memory of which she had repressed. The father was granted standing to sue the therapist no matter that the daughter had no quarrel with the therapy. Dr. Harrison G. Pope Jr., on the basis of research he had done on bulimia nervosa, testified for the plaintiff that evidence is wanting of a link between sexual abuse (even if it had occurred) and eating disorders. The daughter apparently was also told that if she recovered a memory of abuse under sodium amytal, the memory of abuse would be historically accurate. The plaintiff maintained that the daughter had succumbed to suggestion by manipulative therapists. "The only time she had memories of her father abusing her was when the doctors told her after the amytal," testified Dr. Park Dietz, another expert witness for the plaintiff. "Before the amytal she couldn't remember for sure who it was in those images she was having." The decision to allow an aggrieved family member to sue a therapist sent vibrations throughout the mental health profession. The jury awarded Ramona $500,000. The legal importance of the case is that the judge allowed it to go to the jury.

See M. Johnston, *Spectral Evidence: The Ramona Case* (New York: Houghton Mifflin, 1997); R. Slovenko, "The Duty of Therapist to Third Persons," *J. Psychiatry & Law* 23 (1995): 383. Some argue that third-party liability in these cases is unsound in terms of tort doctrine or in terms of public policy. See P. S. Appelbaum & R. Zoltek-Jick, "Psychotherapists' Duties to Third Parties: *Ramona* and Beyond," *Am. J. Psychiat.* 153 (1996): 457; C. G. Bowman & E. Mertz, "A Dangerous Direction: Legal Intervention in Sexual Abuse Survivor Therapy," *Harv. L. Rev.* 109 (1996): 549.

REVIVAL OF MEMORY OF CHILDHOOD SEXUAL ABUSE

The contemporary scene is marked by fury about revival of memory of childhood sexual abuse. Patients have come out of therapy convinced that their parents had sexually abused them when they were children. Finding that professional organizations and licensing boards were of little or no assistance, consumers of mental health services organized. Pamela Freyd, an education psychologist accused with her husband of unspecified abuse by her estranged daughter, led the way in forming the False Memory Syndrome Foundation in 1992. Hundreds of parents joined. With an advisory board of scientists and scholars, the FMS Foundation gained almost immediate credibility in the media.

In the aforementioned case, Gary Ramona made history when he sued his daughter's therapists for inducing false memories of incest. The court, as noted, held that the therapists owed a duty of care not only to the patient but also to the patient's parents. The litigation helped transform legal and popular attitudes toward recovered memories from broad acceptance to serious doubt. It was a turning point in the recovered memory debate. The experts testifying on behalf of Gary Ramona unfolded a tale of "suggestive mischief" played by "inept therapist" that had led, not to true memories, but to sad fantasies woven into the "obsessional intrusions" of a depressed and bulimic girl.

See F. Crews, *The Memory Wars* (New York: New York Review of Books, 1995); E. F. Loftus & K. Ketcham, *The Myth of Repressed Memory* (New York: St. Martin's Press, 1994); M. Johnston, *Spectral Evidence: The Ramona Case* (New York: Houghton Mifflin, 1997); R. Ofshe & E. Watters, *Making Monsters: False Memories, Psychotherapy, and Sexual Hysteria* (New York: Scribner's, 1994); M. Pendergrast, *Victims of Memory: Incest Accusations and Shattered Lives* (Hinesburg, Vt.: Upper Access Books, 1995); M. T. Singer & J. Lalich, *Crazy Therapies* (San Francisco: Jossey-Bass, 1996); L. Wright, *Remembering Satan: A Case of Recovered Memory and the Shattering of an American Family* (New York: Knopf, 1994); M. D. Yapko, *Suggestions of Abuse* (New York: Simon & Schuster, 1994); R. Slovenko, "'I'm Not a Detective' in 'Revival of Memory,'" in *Scientific Evidence Review* (Chicago: American Bar Association, monograph no. 3, 1998); R. Slovenko, "The Revival of Memory of Child Sexual Abuse: Is the Tolling of the Statute of Limitations Justified?" *J. Psychiatry & Law* 21 (1993): 7.

MANAGED CARE

Managed care liability cases are at the forefront of health care law. Clinicians are confronted with legal duties to appeal adverse decisions of managed care entities, to disclose the impact of managed care on patients' treatment, and in some circumstances, to continue treatment after payment has been denied by the managed care entity. The managed care entity also faces liability. See J. A. Lazarus & S. S. Sharfstein, "Changes in the Economics and Ethics of Health and Mental Health Care," in J. M. Oldham & M. B. Riba (eds.), *Review of Psychiatry* (Washington, D.C.: American Psychiatric Press, 13th ed. 1994), pp. 389–413.

Wickline v. State of California
In this landmark California case, the patient was treated for problems associated with her legs and back and her doctor recommended surgery. Her hospitalization and treatment were covered by California's Medicaid program, Medi-Cal, which performed its own managed care function. Medi-Cal approved the patient's surgery and a ten-day hospital stay. The patient suffered complications after the surgery, and required two additional surgeries. Her physician determined that she should remain in the hospital for eight days beyond the ten that were authorized. The doctor submitted a Medi-Cal form requesting an extension. Medi-Cal approved the four-day extension. The surgeon

discharged the patient when the four-day extension period expired. All three of her treating physicians knew there was a process to appeal the Medi-Cal decision, but none of them pursued an appeal. Nine days after her discharge, the patient was readmitted to the hospital and eventually had to have her leg amputated. The patient brought an action against Medi-Cal, alleging that her injuries were caused by Medi-Cal's negligence in failing to authorize the full eight-day extension.

A jury verdict was entered in the patient's favor, but the court of appeals reversed. The appellate court reasoned that although the state's preauthorization program played a role in the decision to discharge the patient, the decision to discharge was made by the physicians. The court implicitly criticized the physicians for not appealing the Medi-Cal decision that they disagreed with. It imposed a legal duty on managed care providers to advocate for their patients' needs. The court said, "[T] he physician who complies without protest with the limitations imposed by a third-party payor, when his medical judgment dictates otherwise, cannot avoid his ultimate responsibility for the patient's care." 183 Cal. App.3d 1064, 228 Cal. Rptr. 661 (1986), *review granted,* 231 Cal. Rptr. 560 727 P.2d 753 (1986), *review dismissed and remanded,* 239 Cal. Rptr. 805, 741 P.2d 613 (1987).

Wilson v. Blue Cross of Southern California
The same division of the California Court of Appeals that decided *Wickline* held that a utilization review firm and an insurer could be held liable for the wrongful death of an insured where the treating physician's testimony indicated that a denial of benefits for inpatient hospitalization was a substantial causative factor. The trial court, apparently interpreting language in *Wickline* to suggest that civil liability for damages resulting from discharge decisions is limited to the treating physician, entered summary judgment in favor of the defendants. On appeal the court clarified its earlier opinion in *Wickline* by characterizing much of the language in the decision, including the suggestion that the treating physician is solely responsible for discharge decisions, as dicta. The court elected to apply the general rule of joint tort liability, which imposes liability on all parties whose negligent conduct is a substantial factor in bringing about the harm. 222 Cal. App.3d 660, 271 Cal. Rptr. 876 (1990). See W. A. Chittenden, "Malpractice Liability and Managed Health Care: History and Prognosis," *Tort & Ins. L. J.* 26 (1991): 451.

McEvoy v. Group Health Co-Op
HMOs can be sued by subscribers under the common law tort of bad faith often applied to insurance companies. The Wisconsin Supreme Court said, "Public policy supports our decision to equate HMOs and insurers for purposes of applying bad faith tort to HMOs." To prevail on a bad faith tort claim against an HMO, the plaintiff must plead facts sufficient to show an absence of a reasonable basis for the HMO to deny the claim, and that the HMO in denying the claim either knew or recklessly failed to ascertain that coverage or care should have been provided. 570 N.W.2d 397 (Wis. 1997). See also Hughes v. Blue Cross of Northern California, 215 Cal. App.3d 832, 263 Cal. Rptr. 850 (1989).

Legislators around the country are advocating laws to make it easier for patients to sue managed care companies. Texas legislation provides for malpractice suits against managed care companies that fail to exercise "ordinary prudence" in making health care treatment decisions. Texas Gen. Laws, ch. 163 (1997). The lawyer Harvey Wachsman, who represents plaintiffs in malpractice cases, sums up the HMO record: "All they're interested in is profits. They give nothing to education or research, they bypass specialists, and they have no mission for the poor, whom I describe as the young, the old and the sick." See C. G. Benda & F. A. Rozovsky, *Liability and Risk Management in Managed Care* (New York: Aspen, 1997); D. L. Loiter (ed.), *Managed Care Liability* (Chicago: American Bar Association, 1997); P. S. Appelbaum, "Legal Liability and Managed Care," *Am. Psychologist* 48 (1993): 251.

Obscenity and Pornography

The First Amendment protects freedom of speech but not obscenity. (The terms *obscenity* and *pornography* are used synonymously, but strictly speaking, obscenity is the broader term, referring to that which is offensive to modesty and decency, while pornography means depiction of prostitutes.) In Roth v. United States, 354 U.S. 476 (1987), Justice Brennan came up with this test of obscenity: Would "the average person" think that the "dominant theme of the material" appeals "to prurient interest"? In 1973 the Supreme Court said that expert testimony is not a requirement, but it expressly reserved judgment as to "the extreme case," where the material is directed to "a bizarre deviant group that the experience of the trier-of-fact would be plainly inadequate to judge whether the material appeals to the prurient interest." Miller v. California, 93 S. Ct. 2607 (1973); Paris Adult Theater v. Slaton, 93 S. Ct. 2628 (1973). Catherine MacKinnon and other feminists argue that pornography is part of a system of gender oppression. In 1985 the Seventh Circuit Court of Appeals ruled unconstitutional an Indianapolis ordinance that suppressed pornography on that basis. The ordinance, the court said, was an impermissible form of "thought control." American Booksellers Ass'n v. Hudnut, 771 F.2d 323 (7th Cir. 1985). See J. Monahan & L. Walker, *Social Science in Law: Cases and Materials* (Westbury, N.Y.: Foundation Press, 4th ed. 1994), pp. 125–50; R. Slovenko, *Psychiatry and Law* (Boston: Little, Brown, 1973), pp. 173–90.

Psychotherapist-Patient Testimonial Privilege

In re Lifschutz

California's psychotherapist-patient privilege, a copy of the Connecticut statute and a model for the proposed Federal Rules of Evidence (Rule 504), was tested shortly after its enactment in 1965 in a much-publicized case involving Dr. Joseph Lifschutz. When the plaintiff in the case claimed that he had suffered "emotional distress" as a result of the injuries he had suffered, the court held that he thereby waived the privilege under the patient-litigant exception but the records being of ten-year-old therapy were deemed not to be sufficiently relevant. 2 Cal.3d 415, 467 P.2d 577, 85 Cal. Rptr. 829 (1970).

Jaffee v. Redmond

The U.S. Supreme Court ruled that psychotherapists including social workers cannot be forced to testify or provide other evidence about their patients in federal court cases. The Court did not, however, give unequivocal protection to the confidentiality of the psychotherapeutic relationship. In the majority opinion, Justice Stevens wrote, "Although it would be premature to speculate about most future developments in the federal psychotherapist privilege, we do not doubt that there are situations in which the privilege must give way, for example, if a serious threat of harm to the patient or to others can be averted only by means of a disclosure by the therapist." Justice Stevens also wrote, "Because this is the first case in which we have recognized a psychotherapist privilege, it is neither necessary nor feasible to delineate its full contours in a way that would govern all conceivable future questions in this area." 116 S. Ct. 1923 (1996). See R. Slovenko, *Psychotherapy and Confidentiality* (Springfield, Ill.: Thomas, 1998). The decision is discussed in several articles in the *Hastings Law Review* 49 (1998): 945–1005. See also M. L. Nelken, "The Limits of Privilege: The Developing Scope of Federal Psychotherapist-Patient Privilege Law," *Rev. Litig.* 20 (2000): 1.

Note: An expert engaged by an attorney to undertake an evaluation is considered an agent of the attorney and falls under the broad coverage of the attorney-client privilege. City & County of San Francisco v. Superior Court, 37 Cal.2d 227, 231 P.2d 26 (1951).

Regulation of Prescriptions

Whalen v. Roe
At issue in this case was a New York statute which required the state Department of Health to "record, in a centralized computer file, the names and addresses of all persons who have obtained . . . certain drugs" with a physician's prescription. Security measures had been adopted to ensure that only authorized personnel could access the computer files, and public disclosure of information in the files was prohibited by law. A group of physicians and patients who prescribed or used the drugs brought an action for injunctive relief, claiming that the statute violated the Fourteenth Amendment right of privacy. A unanimous U.S. Supreme Court began by stating that New York's patient-identification statute provided a reasonable way to deter violations of state drug laws and to facilitate the investigation of any apparent abuses. The Court acknowledged "the threat to privacy implicit in the accumulation of vast amounts of personal information in computerized data banks," but it found adequate protection against that threat in the legal duty to avoid unwarranted disclosures. 429 U.S. 589 (1977). The decision was the first time that the Court addressed the question whether the constitutional right of privacy protects against government mandated disclosures of health-related information. See N. Vieira, "Unwarranted Government Disclosures: Reflections on Privacy Rights, HIV and Ad Hoc Balancing," *Wayne L. Rev.* 47 (2001): 173.

Right of Privacy

ABORTION

Roe v. Wade
In this highly controversial case the Supreme Court struck down state laws that made abortion a crime—at least as far as abortion in the early months of pregnancy was concerned. The case quickly became intensely political, and it has remained that way. The legal background for the decision led from the *Griswold* decision in 1965. 410 U.S. 113 (1973). Prior to *Roe v. Wade*, abortion was allowed only for specific reasons such as the physical or mental condition of the woman. See R. Slovenko, *Psychiatry and Law* (Boston: Little, Brown, 1973), pp. 379–91.

CONTRACEPTIVES

Griswold v. Connecticut
Connecticut law made it a crime to use "any drug, medicinal article or instrument for the purpose of preventing conception," and it also made it a crime to aid, counsel, or abet anyone to this end. The Supreme Court struck down the statute on the ground that it violated the "right of privacy," a right secreted somewhere in the Constitution, but *where* none of the Justices could precisely say. 381 U.S. 479 (1965).

Eisenstadt v. Baird
Under Massachusetts law, only physicians or druggists could distribute contraceptives, and only to married couples. Baird gave a lecture about contraception, and gave a "package of Emko vaginal foam to a woman in the audience." He was arrested and convicted, but on appeal the Supreme Court overturned the conviction. The Court in this case went a step beyond its holding in *Griswold v. Connecticut*. It dissolved the line between married and unmarried people set out in *Griswold*. 405 U.S. 438 (1972).

UNAUTHORIZED PUBLICATION

Douglas v. Hustler Magazine

The plaintiff, an actress and model, sued *Hustler* magazine for invasion of privacy for unauthorized publication of nude photographs of her. Judgment for the plaintiff was reversed and the case remanded. The Seventh Circuit said, "An expert witness on the issue of *Hustler's* offensiveness accompanied his testimony with a projection of 128 slides showing some of the vilest photographs and cartoons to have been published in *Hustler* over the years. . . . The prejudicial effect of the parade of filth in the slide show so clearly outweighed its probative value as to require exclusion. . . . [B]ad as it is, *Hustler* is not so concentratedly outrageous as the slide show would make a viewer think." 769 F.2d 1128 (7th Cir. 1985). *See* Breach of Confidentiality, Psychotherapist-Patient Testimonial Privilege

Right to Refuse Treatment. *See also* Civil Commitment

Patient rights are based on the following constitutional arguments: (1) the First Amendment protection of freedom of thought and expression; (2) the Eighth Amendment protection from cruel and unusual punishment (an argument used in cases involving prisoners); (3) a right to privacy under the First, Fourth, Fifth, and Ninth Amendments; and (4) the Fourteenth Amendment protection of liberty and equal protection of the law. The medical profession considers that treatment allows the patient to give competent or informed consent to further treatment; put another way, antipsychotic medication often restores internal autonomy by resurrecting the ability to mentate. An extended discussion of the legal arguments appears in B. J. Winick, *The Right to Refuse Mental Health Treatment* (Washington, D.C.: American Psychological Association, 1997). See also S. Gelman, *Medicating Schizophrenia: A History* (New Brunswick: Rutgers University Press, 1999). Testimony of psychiatrists that a hospitalized individual would harm himself by discontinuing medication when discharged supports an order for continued treatment in the hospital. In re J.S., 638 N.W.2d 45 (N.D. 2002).

Rennie v. Klein

After several years of litigation, the U.S. Third Circuit Court of Appeals in New Jersey recognized the right of an involuntarily committed patient to refuse treatment but it ruled that this right could be overridden and antipsychotic drugs administered "whenever, in the exercise of professional judgment, such an action is deemed necessary to prevent the patient from endangering himself or others." The ruling has been followed in the majority of jurisdictions. 462 F.Supp. 1131 (D.N.J. 1978), *modified and remanded*, 653 F.2d 836 (3d Cir. 1981) (en banc), *vacated and remanded*, 458 U.S. 1119 (1983).

Rogers v. Okin

Unlike the decision in *Rennie v. Klein*, the U.S. First Circuit Court of Appeals in Massachusetts concluded that in the absence of an emergency (e.g., serious threat of extreme violence or personal injury), any person who has not been adjudicated incompetent has a right to refuse antipsychotic medication, and incompetent persons have a similar right but it must be exercised through a "substituted judgment treatment plan" that has been reviewed and approved by a court. 634 F.2d 650 (1st Cir. 1980) (en banc), *vacated and remanded sub. nom.* Mills v. Rogers, 457 U.S. 291 (1982). The decision was followed in Rivers v. Katz, 67 N.Y.2d 485, 504 N.Y.S.2d 74 (1986).

INVOLUNTARY TREATMENT IN PRISON

Washington v. Harper

In this case involving forcible administration of antipsychotic medication in a prison facility, the Supreme Court recognized that the Constitution protects a "significant liberty interest" in resisting such treatment but nevertheless upheld the prison's right to administer the medication. The Court determined that the prisoner's liberty interest, although constitutionally protected, was outweighed by the state's police-power interest in maintaining the security of the prison. That interest allowed the state's treatment of the prisoner in order to protect him as well as other prisoners and correctional staff from the risk of danger he presented when not taking the medication, a risk that had been established at an administrative hearing. 494 U.S. 210 (1990).

Right to Treatment. *See also* Civil Commitment

Rouse v. Cameron

Clarence Rouse brought an action pursuant to a District of Columbia statutory provision against the director of St. Elizabeths Hospital, Dr. Dale Cameron. By writ of habeas corpus he claimed that, following an acquittal on misdemeanor charges, he was confined without treatment in the hospital's maximum security unit. Judge Bazelon discharged Rouse on the basis of the statute while recognizing the possibility that continued involuntary institutionalization without adequate treatment portended constitutional infringement of liberty. It was the first decision, though based on a statute, to suggest a constitutional underpinning of the proposed right to treatment. 373 F.2d 451 (D.C. Cir. 1966).

Wyatt v. Stickney

Federal District Court Judge Frank Johnson in Alabama was not asked, as in *Rouse v. Cameron*, to release a patient on a habeas corpus petition but rather was urged to set out minimum constitutional standards for adequate treatment of the mentally ill. The suit was actually welcomed and encouraged by Stonewall Stickney, then Commissioner of Mental Health for Alabama, as a means of requiring the state to take action to improve its institutions. Judge Johnson was known as an activist judge. He ruled that involuntarily committed patients have a constitutional right, as a quid pro quo for their loss of freedom, to receive such treatment as would give them a reasonable opportunity to be cured or to improve their condition. To fulfill this right, there must be (1) a humane physical and psychological environment, (2) qualified staff in sufficient numbers, and (3) individualized treatment plans for each patient. To further these standards, detailed environmental standards were established. 373 F.2d 451 (D.C. Cir. 1966), later known as Wyatt v. Aderholt, 503 F.2d 1305 (5th Cir. 1974), *aff'd in part*, Wyatt v. Stickney, 344 F.Supp. 387 (M.D. Ala. 1971). See R. Slovenko, "The Past and Present of the Right to Treatment: A Slogan Gone Astray," *J. Psychiatry & Law:* 9 (1981): 263.

O'Connor v. Donaldson

During the 1960s some eighteen attempts, all futile, were made to obtain Kenneth Donaldson's discharge by habeas corpus on the grounds that he was not dangerous, did not require institutionalization, and was receiving inadequate treatment. A damage suit was brought against several doctors at the state hospital under the Civil Rights Act (the state of Florida enjoyed sovereign immunity) alleging that his confinement constituted an unconstitutional deprivation of liberty because he was nondangerous and because he had been provided no therapeutic treatment. At the trial, the jury found for Donaldson and awarded him compensatory and punitive damages. On appeal the Fifth Circuit, Judge John Minor Wisdom writing the opinion, upheld the verdict and said that a person involuntarily civilly committed to a state mental hospital has a constitutional right to receive such individual treatment as will give him a reasonable opportunity to be cured or to improve his mental condition. 493 F.2d 507 (5th Cir. 1974).

Thus, the federal appellate court not only recognized a right to treatment as constitutionally required, the first time any appellate court did so, but it approved the award of damages against the doctors as a remedy for the violation of this right. The Supreme Court granted certiorari, its first to deal with the civil rights of an involuntarily committed mental patient who had committed no crime. Adhering to the traditional judicial practice of dealing with the largest questions in the most narrow way, Justice Stewart on behalf of a unanimous court concluded that "the difficult issues of constitutional law dealt with by the Court of Appeals are not presented by this case in its present posture." In vacating the Fifth Circuit's decision, the Supreme Court declared: "A State cannot constitutionally confine without more a nondangerous individual who is capable of surviving safely in freedom by himself or with the help of willing and responsible family members of friends." Commentators muse about the meaning of "without more." In a concurring opinion, Chief Justice Burger rejected the quid pro quo theory as justifying any constitutional right to treatment. He wrote: "[T]here is no historical basis for imposing such a limitation on state power. Analysis of the sources of the civil commitment power . . . lends no support to the notion. There can be little doubt that in the exercise of its police power a State may confine individuals solely to protect society from the dangers of significant antisocial acts or communicable disease. . . . Additionally, the States are vested with the historic *parens patriae* power, including the duty to protect persons under legal disabilities to act for themselves. . . . [But] however the power is implemented, due process requires that it not be invoked indiscriminately. At a minimum, a particular scheme for protection of the mentally ill must rest upon a legislative determination that it is compatible with the best interests of the affected class and that its members are unable to act for themselves." 422 U.S. 563 (1975). See T. S. Szasz, *Psychiatric Slavery* (New York: Free Press, 1977).

Youngberg v. Romeo

In a lawsuit claiming damages, a mentally retarded resident of a state school alleged violation of a constitutional right to protection from harm. He had been injured seriously more than sixty times. The Supreme Court ruled that such persons have substantive constitutional rights to "adequate food, shelter, clothing and medical care," to "personal security," to "freedom from bodily restraint," and to "minimally adequate or reasonable training to ensure safety and freedom from undue restraint." The Court deferred to the profession in determining whether training is "reasonable." The Court said: "Liability may be imposed only when the decision by the professional is such a substantial departure from accepted professional judgment, practice or standards as to demonstrate that the person responsible did not base the decision on such a judgment." 457 U.S. 307 (1982).

Helling v. McKinney

When the state places an individual in custody, "the Constitution imposes upon it a corresponding duty to assume some responsibility for his safety and general well-being." Quoting an earlier decision, the Supreme Court went on to say, "When the State by the affirmative exercise of its powers so restrains an individual's liberty that it renders him unable to care for himself, and at the same time fails to provide for basic human needs—e.g., food, clothing, shelter, medical care, and reasonable safety—it transgresses the substantive limits on state action set by the Eighth Amendment." 509 U.S. 25 (1993).

Scientific Evidence

Frye v. United States

The *Frye* test of 1923, from *Frye v. United States,* has reigned as the standard governing admissibility of scientific evidence. Under the test, expert opinion based on a scientific technique is inadmissible unless the technique is "generally accepted" as reliable in the relevant scientific community. 293 F. 1013 (D.C. Cir. 1923).

Daubert v. Merrell Dow Pharmaceuticals

In 1993 the Supreme Court ruled that general acceptance within the relevant field of science is but only one consideration in ascertaining reliability, thus allowing experts to testify about new techniques in the vanguard of scientific knowledge. Under *Daubert,* the trial judge is also to consider: Is the theory or technique testable, and has it been tested? Has the theory or technique been subjected to peer review and publication? What is the known or potential error rate for the technique? Are there standards controlling the technique's operation? The *Daubert* decision applies to federal courts. 113 S. Ct. 2786 (1993).

Kumho Tire Co. v. Carmichael

The U.S. Supreme Court in this case further explained its decision in *Daubert* regarding the trial court's role as gatekeeper of expert testimony. The main issue in the case was whether *Daubert*'s general holding on the role of the trial judge as a gatekeeper applies to all expert testimony or only that testimony involving science. Yes, the Court ruled, the testimony of nonscientific experts must satisfy the reliability requirements of *Daubert,* but, no, the factors described in *Daubert* as guidelines are advisory only, rather than mandatory, with the trial court at liberty to apply one or more, or none, under "the particular circumstances of the particular case at issue." *Kumho Tire* was a products liability case brought by those injured when a minivan's tire blew out. The expert testimony was "technical" rather than "scientific." 119 S. Ct. 1167 (1999).

Discussion

Most criminal cases are tried, not in federal, but in state courts, which may or may not have adopted the *Daubert* guidelines. Moreover, a number of courts hold that the *Frye* or *Daubert* tests alike do not apply to the soft sciences (psychiatry or psychology). People v. Beckley, 434 Mich. 691, 456 N.W.2d 391 (1990). Declining to follow *Daubert,* the Iowa Supreme Court noted that a *Daubert* analysis can be "time consuming and costly" and it noted that the federal courts themselves were narrowly limiting *Daubert* to "controversial and novel scientific evidence" and are not applying it to expert testimony that is "technical in nature" or to "other specialized knowledge." Johnson v. Knoxville Community School Dist., 570 N.W.2d 633 (Iowa 1997). Of course, one may question whether any guidelines will make a difference in the face of a witness willing to twist the evidence. See M. Angell, *Science of Trial* (New York: W. W. Norton, 1997); J. Goodman-Delahunty, "Forensic Psychological Expertise in the Wake of *Daubert*," *Law & Human Behavior* 21 (1997): 121. *Daubert* and its progeny allow a trial judge to be rather arbitrary in excluding an expert, as he is not likely to be overruled. For a critique of the assumption in *Daubert* that there is a well-documented "scientific method," see S. Jasanoff, *Science at the Bar: Law, Science and Technology in America* (Cambridge: Harvard University Press, 1995).

In early times disputes were settled by ordeal, battle, or wager. None of these processes utilized the testimony of witnesses or any formal fact-finding procedure. All were premised on the notion of divine intervention. By the end of the twelfth century the jury was introduced into the English judicial process, replacing ordeal, battle, or wager. The jury at that time was self-informing. It heard no evidence. The jurors were selected from the locality in which the dispute arose and almost always included some persons with knowledge of the events that were the focus of the controversy. From at least the fifteenth century onward jurors began to rely upon what was presented in court as the basis for their decision. What they could hear was cleared by rules of evidence. While previously they were familiar with the event in controversy, now they were to know nothing but what was presented to them by witnesses. With increasing regularity, experts assumed the position of partisan experts. James C. Mohr traces the evolution of American medical jurisprudence during the nineteenth century in *Doctors and the Law*

(Baltimore: Johns Hopkins University Press, 1993). Historical surveys also appear in S. Landsman, "Of Witches, Madmen, and Products Liability: An Historical Survey of the Use of Expert Testimony," *Behav. Sci. & Law* 13 (1995): 131; id., "A Brief Survey of the Development of the Adversary System," *Ohio St. L.J.* 44 (1983): 713.

Sex Offenders

Laws for the special commitment of sex offenders first appeared in 1930s. By 1960 over half the states had enacted such laws, variously called "Sexual Psychopath Law," "Sexually Dangerous Persons Acts," and "Mentally Disordered Sex Offender Acts." Michigan was one of the first to adopt a sexual psychopath law. Its statute enacted in 1935 provided: "Any person . . . suffering from a mental disorder and [who] is not feeble-minded, which mental disorder is coupled with criminal propensities to the commission of sex offenses, is hereby declared to be a criminal sexual psychopathic person." These statutes authorized the involuntary commitment to psychiatric facilities for control and treatment of individuals charged with or convicted of sex offenses and found to be mentally disordered, dangerous, and in need of treatment. It was believed that the relatively new science of psychiatry was able to identify and treat sexual psychopaths. They reflected the therapeutic optimism of the time. The ABA Criminal Justice Mental Health Standards noted the assumptions underlying this special dispositional legislation: (1) there is a specific mental disability called sexual psychopathy; (2) persons having such a disability are more likely to commit serious crimes, especially dangerous sex offenses, than other criminals; (3) such persons are easily identified by mental health professionals; (4) the dangerousness of these offenders can be predicted by mental health professionals; (5) treatment is available for the condition; and (6) large numbers of persons with the designated disabilities can be cured.

To carry out the legislation the states expended considerable funds for special sex offender programs and facilities, such as at Atascadero in California and Ionia in Michigan. In the 1970s these laws began to fall out of favor. They were called a failed experiment. By 1985 nearly all of these laws were repealed. When repealing its sex offender statute in 1981 the California legislature declared: "In repealing the mentally disordered sex offender commitment statute, the legislature recognizes and declares that the commission of sex offenses is not itself the product of mental disease."

With the demise of indeterminate sentencing generally, the 1990s witnessed a renewed interest in sex offender commitment. Starting in Washington in 1990, at least seven other states have enacted laws for the commitment of sexually violent predators, to wit: persons (1) convicted of a sexually violent offense, (2) about to be released from confinement, and (3) found to be suffering from "a mental abnormality or personality disorder which makes the person likely to engage in predatory acts of sexual violence." These sexual predator laws are different from the earlier sexual psychopath statutes and from ordinary civil commitment laws in several important aspects. First, they do not require a medically recognized serious mental disorder. Second, they do not require any allegation or proof of recent criminal wrongdoing, dangerous behavior, deteriorating mental state, or inappropriate behavior. Third, they require sex offenders to serve their full prison term prior to commitment. Fourth, no bona fide treatment program need be in place.

Specht v. Patterson

The State of Colorado convicted Richard Specht of a sex offense and then invoked its Sex Offenders Act in order to sentence him to an indefinite term of detention. The U.S. Supreme Court ruled that in this situation the Fourteenth Amendment required full rights to due process. 386 U.S. 605 (1967).

Kansas v. Hendricks

In 1997 in a 5–4 decision the U.S. Supreme Court upheld the Kansas Sexually Violent Predator Act, which established civil commitment procedures for individuals with a "mental abnormality" or a "personality disorder" who were likely to engage in "predatory acts of sexual violence." The majority opinion, written by Justice Thomas, held that the Act does not violate the double jeopardy prohibition of the Constitution, and does not violate ex post facto prohibitions. The U.S. Supreme Court reversed the Kansas Supreme Court, which had held that substantive due process was violated because the definition of *mental abnormality* did not satisfy what is perceived to be the definition of *mental illness* required in a context of involuntary civil commitment. The Kansas Supreme Court did not address double jeopardy or ex post facto issues. The Kansas Supreme Court noted that the law targeted individuals who could not be committed under the general civil commitment law. See In the Matter of the Care and Treatment of Leroy Hendricks, 259 Kan. 246, 912 P.2d 129 (1996).

Justice Thomas acknowledged that in addition to dangerousness, "some additional factor" that was causally linked to the dangerous behavior is constitutionally required. However, he wrote, substantive due process does not require that this condition be a mental disorder recognized by treatment professionals: "Not only do psychiatrists disagree widely and frequently on what constitutes mental illness . . . but the Court itself has used a variety of expressions to describe the mental condition of those properly subject to civil commitment." The term *mental illness* does not carry "talismanic significance." He also said, "[W]e have traditionally left legislators the task of defining terms of medical nature that have a legal significance." Because the Kansas statute requires proof that individuals suffer from a volitional impairment rendering them dangerous beyond their control, he concluded, the statute does not allow commitment of individuals based solely on dangerousness.

The majority also concluded that the law was civil in nature rather than punitive in purpose or effect, and thus, it did not violate either double jeopardy or ex post facto prohibitions. Except for Justice Ginsburg, the dissenters agreed with the majority that states have broad authority to define legal mental illness and that the statute's use of "mental abnormality" satisfies substantive due process. However, the minority concluded that the statute was essentially punitive in nature rather than civil, thus violating both double jeopardy and ex post facto prohibitions. Under the law offenders are committed after they have served virtually their entire criminal sentence. Under the earlier sexual psychopath legislation the prosecutor had to choose between conviction in the criminal system or commitment in the civil system.

The Court suggested in dicta that "treatability" is not a constitutionally required element for commitment, although treatment may be required if the state considers the individual amenable to treatment. Moreover, the state can defer such treatment until after the offender had served his full prison term. Justice Thomas wrote, "[U]nder the appropriate circumstances and when accompanied by proper procedure, incapacitation may be a legitimate end of the civil law. . . . We have never held that the Constitution prevents a State from civilly detaining those for whom no treatment is available, but who nevertheless pose a danger to others." 117 S. Ct. 2072 (1997). So now, whether a sentence is imposed as a result of a trial or plea bargain, the defendant at the end of the sentence may be deemed a proper subject for commitment as a "sexually dangerous person."

The Supreme Court's decision has given the green light to the enactment of sex offender legislation. The section of Law and Mental Disability of the Association of American Law Schools at its 1998 annual meeting discussed the therapeutic and antitherapeutic consequences of the *Hendricks* decision. Questions explored were: Has the Supreme Court opened the gates for broad medicalization of deviance, a return to the therapeutic state, and the replacement of criminal law with civil preventive detention? Should the case be read narrowly as a legitimization of specific, focused, and creative efforts to combat sexual violence? See E. S. Janus, "Sex Offender Commitments: Debunking the Official Narrative and Revealing the Rules-in-Use," *Stanford Law & Policy Rev.* 8 (1997): 71.

Syndrome Evidence

As a rule, expert testimony is impermissible on credibility; that is, testimony at the outset may not be given that a witness—the accused, the complainant, or any other witness—is telling the truth. Credibility is an assessment made by the jury. As one court said, "The jury is the lie detector in the courtroom." United States v. Barnard, 490 F.2d 907, 912 (9th Cir. 1973). A marked inconsistency prevails between differing views of the cognitive powers of jurors that undergird different segments of evidence law. As Professor Edmund Morgan put it bluntly years ago, some rules of evidence assume the jurors to be "a group of low grade morons" while other rules take an unduly optimistic view of their mental powers. See M. R. Damaska, *Evidence Law Adrift* (New Haven: Yale University Press, 1997); quotation at p. 34.

A way to circumvent the bar on expert testimony on credibility is by resort to syndrome evidence. In recent years, in civil and criminal cases, expert testimony about various trauma syndromes (incest trauma, battered child, battered spouse, rape trauma) has been allowed to establish, on the basis of the symptoms, that a particular stressor, or crime, actually happened. The admissibility of evidence about the various trauma syndromes to establish that a stressor actually occurred has gained a good deal of attention recently, and is controversial. Since credibility of all witnesses is at issue, defense attorneys (or prosecutors) may seek to introduce testimony to explain behavior unique to a victim. For example, by syndrome evidence, prosecutors may wish to explain why the alleged child victim of sexual assault delayed in reporting or recanted. Professor James Q. Wilson writes: "When a member of [the psychiatric and social science] professions testifies that [an individual] suffers from a 'syndrome,' be on guard—the syndrome may not exist, or it may exist but not be applicable to the [individual], or it may be applicable but the consequences of being affected by it in some predictable fashion may be unknown or uncertain. With some exceptions, syndrome science is suppositional science, which is to say, it is not science at all." J. Q. Wilson, *Moral Judgment* (New York: Basic Books, 1997), pp. 20–21. See also E. Showalter, *Hystories: Hysterical Epidemics and Modern Culture* (New York: Columbia University Press, 1997).

CHILD SEXUAL ABUSE SYNDROME

State v. Myers
In this oft-cited case, the expert described the behavior and symptoms typically exhibited by sexually abused children and the characteristics that the expert had observed in the complainant. The expert then concluded in a roundabout way of attesting to the credibility of the complainant, that, based upon the constellation of symptoms and noted behavior, the child had been abused. 359 N.W.2d 604 (Minn. 1984).

BATTERED WOMAN SYNDROME

Ibn-Thomas v. United States
Beverly Ibn-Tamas shot and killed her husband, Yusef, in his medical office in Washington, D.C. She asserted in her defense that she felt in imminent danger due to his repeated threats and violence. The defense offered the testimony of Lenore Walker, a Denver psychologist, who described the battered spouse syndrome, and elicited her opinion as to whether the defendant fit the pattern of a battered woman. It argued that the testimony would help the jury to determine the credibility of the claim that she perceived herself in imminent danger and shot in self-defense. The trial court excluded

the testimony for three reasons: (1) the jury was not entitled to hear about past violent acts, (2) it invaded the province of the jury in assessing the credibility of the defendant, and (3) the expert necessarily concluded that the victim was battered. Reversing the ruling, a divided District of Columbus Court of Appeals held that the expert testimony here was beyond the ordinary knowledge of the jury, so that its probative value outweighed any prejudicial effect—it was probative of the defendant's perceptions at the time of the killing, a factor central to her claim of self-defense. The court remanded the case for a determination whether the expert's method for evaluating the battered spouse syndrome had achieved general scientific acceptance. 407 A.2d 626 (D.C. 1979). The trial court thereupon held an evidentiary hearing and concluded that the expert had not established that her methodology was generally accepted by experts in the field. A conviction of second-degree murder was upheld. 455 A.2d 893 (D.C. 1983). She served a year in prison.

State v. Kelly

Ivy Gail Kelly was charged with the murder of her husband. An expert testified about the battered woman syndrome as an explanation of her actions under a claim of self-defense. The expert stated that Kelly fit the category of a battered woman. The expert was asked: "What, if any, information did you obtain from Mrs. Kelly which led you to conclude either that she was battered or was not battered, and which behavioral characteristics did she fit?" The expert described behavioral characteristics that Kelly exhibited, namely, frustration, stress disorders, depression, economic and emotional dependence on her husband, hopes that the marital relationship would improve, poor self-image, isolation, and learned helplessness. The evidence was held to be probative of Kelly's state of mind in support of her claim of self-defense. 102 Wash.2d 188, 685 P.2d 564 (1984).

A number of states have enacted legislation specifically to allow expert testimony on the battered woman syndrome. The California law states that the syndrome is "scientifically valid." Calif. Evidence Code, sec. 2901.06(A) 1–2. See A. M. Dershowitz, *The Abuse Excuse* (Boston: Little, Brown, 1994); L. E. Walker, *Terrifying Love: Why Battered Women Kill and How Society Responds* (New York: HarperCollins, 1989); Comment, "Battered Women Who Kill Their Abusers," *Harv. L. Rev.* 106 (1993): 1585.

RAPE TRAUMA SYNDROME

State v. Kim

In a controversial decision, a child psychiatrist was allowed to testify about rape trauma syndrome to establish a rape by a family member. The symptoms demonstrated by the complainant, the expert said, were "consistent with" symptoms in his other cases involving rape of a child by a family member. 64 Hawaii 598, 645 P.2d 1130 (1982).

State v. Saldana

The Minnesota Supreme Court ruled that testimony on rape trauma syndrome may not be introduced "until further evidence of the scientific accuracy and reliability of the syndrome or profile diagnosis can be established." 324 N.W.2d 227 (Minn. 1982).

People v. Bledsoe

The California Supreme Court found inadmissible evidence of rape trauma syndrome introduced by the prosecution to establish that the complainant was raped. The decision, adopted by a number of other courts, distinguished rape trauma syndrome from battered child syndrome, a concept formulated in the early 1960s to describe a clinical condition in young children who had been physically abused. The court said that the rape trauma syndrome is "fundamentally different" from the battered child syndrome because "[the rape trauma syndrome] was not devised to determine the truth or accuracy of a particular past event." Rather, the court said, it is a "therapeutic tool" used by counselors who consciously "avoid judging the credibility of their clients." The California Supreme Court emphasized, however, that testimony on rape trauma syndrome may be used to explain why a delay in reporting has occurred. Promptness in reporting a crime tends to be taken as a sign of reliability, an indication that the accusation is not a concoction. The law of evidence regards spontaneity of a statement as a mark of trustworthiness and makes an exception for it in the rule against hearsay. The California Supreme Court said: "[I]n such context expert testimony on rape trauma syndrome may play a particularly useful role by disabusing the jury of some widely held misconceptions about rape and rape victims, so that it may evaluate evidence free of the constraints of popular myths." 36 Cal.3d 236, 203 Cal. Rptr. 450, 681 P.2d 291 (1984).

The courts are divided more on the admissibility of syndrome evidence in rape cases than in other types of cases. Compare State v. Black, 109 Wash.2d 336, 745 P.2d 12 (1987), with People v. Hampton, 746 P.2d 947 (Colo. 1989). To show lack of consent the Supreme Courts of Arizona, Kansas and Montana have allowed expert testimony on rape trauma syndrome. Annot., "Admissibility at Criminal Prosecution of Expert Testimony," 42 A.L.R.4th 879 (1985). See J. Monahan & L. Walker, *Social Science in Law* (Westbury, N.Y.: Foundation Press, 4th ed. 1998), pp. 494–510.

Testamentary Capacity

In re Arnold's Case

The evidence of psychosis was fairly extensive (loss of memory as a result of chronic alcoholism), yet the court upheld the testament. The case reflects the general tendency of courts to uphold a testament especially when the testator has provided for the natural objects of his bounty. 16 Cal.2d 573, 107 P.2d 25 (1940).

Testimonial Privilege. *See* Psychotherapist-Patient Testimonial Privilege

Tort Law

LIABILITY FOR EMOTIONAL DISTRESS ARISING OUT OF NEGLIGENCE

The original rule in the law of torts was that there is no cause of action for emotional distress without physical impact of injury arising out of negligence (except when the defendant negligently mishandled the corpse of a loved one or negligently sent a message incorrectly announcing the death of a loved one). The first major qualification of the general rule was the impact rule, when the defendant's negligent conduct resulted in some physical impact or injury. Later, with new knowledge of emotional mental injury, the impact rule was replaced with a zone of danger rule, under which the plaintiff could bring an action for negligently caused emotional distress even if there were no impact if the plaintiff was in the zone in which physical injury was threatened, and feared for his safety. That rule, in turn, has been generally discarded.

The science fiction writer Ray Bradbury says that when he was fifteen, he was witness to a car crash on the street near a friend's house, in which six people died within minutes, one was decapitated, the others were torn apart in various ways so horrible he was in shock for days. He writes, "Once you have seen something like that—brain material on the sidewalk—I don't think you ever quite get over it. We forget that one death has repercussions among dozens of other people. My daughter was involved in an accident three years ago which, indirectly, destroyed a dozen lives. A friend of hers was driving drunk, jumped the divider on the freeway and killed a girl in a car going the other way. The girl's parents, learning of her death, were destroyed for the rest of their lives." Communication to Ralph Slovenko (July 7, 1984), quoted with permission.

Mitchell v. Rochester Ry.

The New York Court of Appeals in 1896 decided that no action could lie in negligence for injuries caused by fright in the absence of physical impact. In this case a team of horses pulling one of the defendant's horse cars turned towards the plaintiff as she was standing upon a crosswalk waiting to board another of the defendant's cars. When the horses were brought to a stop "she stood between the horses' heads." The plaintiff "testified that from fright and excitement caused by the approach and proximity of the team she became unconscious, and also that the result was a miscarriage, and consequent illness." There was medical testimony "to the effect that the mental shock which she then received was sufficient to produce that result." The court noted however that the weight of authority was against recovery. It declared, "If the right of recovery in this class of cases should be once established, it would naturally result in a flood of litigation in cases where the injury may be easily feigned and where the damages must rest upon mere conjecture or speculation." 151 N.Y. 107, 45 N.E. 354 (1896). See also Spade v. Lynn & Boston R.R., 168 Mass. 285, 47 N.E. 88 (1897). *Mitchell* and *Spade* became leading cases in establishing what was for a time the general doctrine in the United States that no action would lie for negligent infliction of mental suffering absent some physical impact.

Hambrook v. Stokes Bros.

The requirement that the plaintiff must fear for his own safety was relaxed in this oft-noted English case of 1925. A mother was awarded judgment for shock she sustained from fear for her children's safety from a runaway lorry, though while she was a percipient witness she was outside the zone of danger. [1925] 1 K.B. 141 (C.A.). Suppose the mother witnessed the event on television or later was told about it? Suppose a nonrelative witnessed the event? Later decisions remained ambivalent.

Bourhill v. Young

The House of Lords in 1943 dismissed the claim of a pregnant woman who had a miscarriage on hearing the noise of a collision and afterwards seeing some blood without herself being at all endangered. The record stated: "As an immediate result of the violent collision and the extreme shock of the occurrence . . . the [plaintiff] sustained a very severe shock to her nervous system. Explained [sic] that the [plaintiff's] terror did not involve any element of reasonable fear of immediate bodily injury to herself. The [plaintiff] was about eight months pregnant at the time and gave birth to a child . . . which was stillborn owing to the injuries sustained." In denying the claim, some of the speeches of the House of Lords proceeded simply on the view that the injury was not foreseeable, but others rested on the fact that she was outside the area of impact. That is to say, she was outside that class of persons who could reasonably expect to be injured by the defendant's negligence. [1943] A.C. 92. The same sentiments were expressed by Justice Cardozo in what is probably the best-known case in the American law of torts, Palsgraf v. Long Island R.R. Co., 248 N.Y. 339, 162 N.E. 99 (1928). D. Mendelson, *The Interfaces of Medicine and Law* (Brookfield, Vt.: Ashgate, 1998); D. F. Partlett, "Tort Liability and the American Way: Reflections on Liability for Emotional Distress," *Am. J. Comp. L.* 45 (1997): 171; see also M. Chamallas & L. K. Kerber, "Women, Mothers, and the Law of Fright: A History," *Mich. L. Rev.* 88 (1990): 814.

Dillon v. Legg

The California Supreme Court discarded the zone of danger rule and held that a mother who saw her child run down and killed could bring an action for her emotional distress, though she was herself in a position of complete safety. As a safeguard against fictitious claims and as a limit on liability, the court set out what is termed the *bystander proximity* doctrine: (1) the bystander is located near the scene of the accident—"physical proximity," (2) the bystander personally observes the accident—"temporal proximity," and

(3) the bystander is closely related to the victim—"relational proximity." 69 Cal. Rptr. 72, 441 P.2d 912 (1968).

Thing v. La Chusa

John Thing, a minor, was struck by a car operated by La Chusa. Thing's mother was nearby but neither saw nor heard the accident. She became aware of it only when told by her daughter. She came upon the bloody aftermath. She sued for her emotional distress caused by the defendant's negligence. The question posed for the California Supreme Court was whether the guidelines enunciated by it in *Dillon v. Legg* are adequate, or if they should be refined to create greater certainty in the law. The court observed: "In order to avoid limitless liability out of all proportion to the degree of a defendant's negligence, and against which it is impossible to insure without imposing unacceptable costs on those among whom the risk is spread, the right to recover for negligently caused emotional distress must be limited."

The court concluded that a plaintiff may recover damages for emotional distress caused by observing the negligently inflicted injury of a third person if, but only if, the plaintiff (1) is closely related to the injury victim; (2) is present at the scene of the injury producing event at the time it occurs and is then aware that it is causing injury to the victim; and (3) as a result suffers serious emotional distress—a reaction beyond that which would be anticipated in a disinterested witness and which is not an abnormal response to the circumstances. Therefore, the court held, "The undisputed facts establish that plaintiff was not present at the scene of the accident in which her son was injured. She did not observe defendant's conduct and was not aware that her son was being injured. She could not, therefore, establish a right to recover for the emotional distress she suffered when she subsequently learned of the accident and observed its consequences." 48 Cal.3d 654, 257 Cal. Rptr. 865, 771 P.2d 814 (1989).

Some states continue to adhere to a zone of danger rule while others apply the test in *Thing*, to wit, familial relationship, contemporaneous perception, and normal reaction. The court in *Thing* traced a distinction, albeit rather disapprovingly, between direct victim cases and bystander cases. The court said, "The subtleties in the distinction between the right to recover as a 'bystander' and as a 'direct victim' created what one Court of Appeal has described as an 'amorphous nether realm.' The problem is: how are we to distinguish between 'direct' victim cases and 'bystander' cases? The inference suggested is that a 'direct victim' is a person whose emotional distress is a reasonably foreseeable consequence of the conduct of the defendant. This does not provide criteria which delimit what counts as reasonable foreseeability. It leads into [a] quagmire of novel claims." A few years earlier, in Molien v. Kaiser Foundation Hospitals, 27 Cal.3d 916, 167 Cal. Rptr. 831, 616 P.2d 813 (1980), the court upheld a duty to a husband of a patient as a direct victim of the negligent diagnosis of the patient as having syphilis. *See* Duty of Therapists to Third Parties Arising out of Therapy

Metro-North Commuter R.R. Co. v. Buckley

The question before the U.S. Supreme Court was whether a railroad worker negligently exposed to a carcinogen (here, asbestos) but without any symptom of any disease can recover for negligently inflicted emotional distress under the Federal Employer's Liability Act (FELA). The Supreme Court ruled that the complainant suffered no physical impact (or physical injury); hence any emotional injury fell outside the circumstance in which, as the Court would have it, the FELA permits recovery. On certiorari, the Supreme Court reversed the Second Circuit, which held that the exposure to insulation dust (containing asbestos) was a "physical impact" that permitted a FELA plaintiff to recover for accompanying emotional distress. The Second Circuit interpreted the words *physical impact* as including a simple physical contact with a substance that might cause a disease at a future time, so long as the contact was of a kind that would "cause fear in a reasonable person." However, the Supreme Court disagreed, saying: "The 'physical impact' does not include a simple physical contact with a substance that might cause a disease at a substantially later time."

The Supreme Court went on to say, "The words 'physical impact' do not encompass every form of 'physical contact.' And, in particular, they do not include a contact that amounts to no more than an exposure." Policy reasons militate against an expansive definition of *physical impact,* said the Court, and it specifically cited the following policy concerns: (1) special difficulty for judges and juries in separating valid, important claims from those that are invalid or trivial; (2) a threat of unlimited and unpredictable liability; and (3) the potential for a flood of comparatively unimportant, or trivial claims.

The large number of those exposed and the uncertainties that may surround recovery suggested what the Court called the problem of "unlimited and unpredictable liability." Does such liability mean, for example, that the costs associated with a rule of liability would become so great that, given the nature of the harm, it would seem unreasonable to require the public to pay the higher prices that may result? The Court said, "We do not raise these questions to answer them (for we do not have the answers), but rather to show that general policy concerns of a kind that have led common law courts to deny recovery for certain classes of negligently caused harms are present in this case as well."

In holding that the emotional distress at issue in the case was not a compensable injury, the Court also denied recovery for a different kind of injury, namely, the economic cost of the extra medical check-ups that the plaintiff expected to incur as a result of his exposure to asbestos-laden insulation dust. The Second Circuit had held that "a reasonable jury" could award plaintiff the "costs" of medical monitoring. 117 S. Ct. 2113 (1997).

See G. Mendelson, *Psychiatric Aspects of Personal Injury Claims* (Springfield, Ill.: Thomas, 1988); N. J. Mullany & P. R. Handford, *Tort Liability for Psychiatric Damage: The Law of "Nervous Shock"* (Sydney: Law Book Co., 1993) C. B. Scrignar, *Post-Traumatic Stress Disorder: Diagnosis, Treatment and Legal Issues* (New Orleans: Bruno Press, 3d ed. 1996); G. M. Stern, *The Buffalo Creek Disaster* (New York: Vintage, 1976); R. Slovenko, "Legal Aspects of Post-Traumatic Stress Disorder," *Psychiatric Clinics of North America* 17 (1994): 1439. *See* Post-traumatic Stress Disorder

FEAR OF AIDS

Brzoska v. Olson

In the first fear of AIDS case in Delaware, the Delaware Supreme Court concluded that, as a matter of law, incidental touching of a patient by an HIV-infected dentist while performing ordinary dental procedures is insufficient to sustain a battery claim in the absence of a channel for HIV infection. In so holding, the court adopted an actual exposure test, which requires a plaintiff to show actual exposure to a disease-causing agent as a prerequisite to prevail on a claim based upon fear of contracting a disease. 668 A.2d 1355 (Del. 1995).

Williamson v. Waldman

The plaintiff, a cleaning person, was pricked by a lancet (a surgical knife with a small, sharp-pointed, two-edged blade) while cleaning a common-trash receptacle in the examining room of offices occupied by the defendant doctors. Fearing that she had contracted AIDS from the prick, she sued the doctors to recover damages for her emotional distress. She claimed that as a result of the incident, she became depressed and suffered "lifestyle changes." The New Jersey Supreme Court held that "a person claiming damages for emotional distress based on the fear that she has contracted HIV must demonstrate that the defendant's negligence proximately caused her genuine and substantial emotional distress that would be experienced by a reasonable person of ordinary experience who has a level of knowledge that coincides with then-current, accurate, and generally available public information about the causes and transmission of AIDS." Regarding the facts of the case, the court concluded that the doctors could be held liable for emotional distress damages only for the "window of anxiety" (that is, the six-month to one-year period after exposure, during which the plaintiff was at risk of testing positive for HIV). 150 N.J. 232, 696 A.2d 14 (1997). See R. J. Jenner, "Claims for Fear of AIDS: The Law is Developing," *Trial*, May 1995, p. 38; G. J. Spahn & T. S. Baird, "Closing the Floodgates on Fear of AIDS Claims," *For the Defense*, June 1995, p. 8.

MALINGERING OR SPURIOUS CLAIMS

The concern over malingering or spurious claims alleging emotional distress without physical injury has a long history. As the New York Court of Appeals observed in 1896 in *Mitchell v. Rochester Ry. Co.*, in such actions "a wide field would be opened for fictitious or speculative claims." Not long ago Mukesh Rai in California sued Taco Bell, claiming he suffered extreme distress because he was served a beef burrito. "He clearly repeated the order twice so that he would be ensured of not receiving a burrito with meat," the complaint stated. He realized the mistake when he bit into it. "Eating the cow, it was a really devastating experience," he said. "So much so that I had to go to a psychiatrist. I couldn't sleep." He traveled to England for a religious purification with Hindu masters. His lawsuit sought damages for emotional distress, medical expenses, and loss of wages. Associated Press news release, Jan. 30, 1998.

On the detection of malingering, see G. B. Melton, J. Petrila, N. G. Poythress, & C. Slobogin, *Psychological Evaluations for the Courts* (New York: Guilford Press, 2d ed. 1997); P. J. Resnick, "Malingering of Posttraumatic Disorders," in R. Rogers (ed.), *Clinical Assessment of Malingering and Deception* (New York: Guilford Press, 1988); D. J. Schretlen, "The Use of Psychological Tests to Identify Malingered Symptoms of Mental Disorder," *Clin. Psychology Rev.* 8 (1988): 51. The metamorphosis of malingering from the imitation of illness to mental illness is explored by Thomas S. Szasz in his classic book *The Myth of Mental Illness* (New York: Harper Row, 1974).

DUTY TO MINIMIZE DAMAGES

Under well-settled principles of law, a person who has been injured has the duty to minimize those injuries. This includes the duty to timely obtain proper medical rehabilitative care. The factors to be considered in determining whether an injured person has a duty to mitigate damages by undertaking treatment includes the risk involved in the treatment, the probability of success, and the expense or effort required. In the event an injured person unreasonably refuses to minimize his damages by accepting nondangerous and customary medical treatment, the damages against a tortfeasor may be limited to that which the injured person would reasonably obtain if he had undergone the recommended treatment. Treatment of post-traumatic stress disorder shortly after exposure to the stressor is particularly efficacious. See, in general, E. Kelly, "Refusal of Surgery in Mitigation of Damages," *Clev. Mar. L. Rev.* 10 (1961): 421; S. D. Solomon, E. T. Gerrity, & A. M. Muff, "Efficacy of Treatments for Posttraumatic Stress Disorder: An Empirical Review," *JAMA* 268 (1992): 633. A plaintiff is not obliged to undertake electroshock treatment though recommended by a physician. *Dohmann v. Richard*, 282 So.2d 789 (La. App. 1973).

Tort Liability of the Mentally Ill

The general rule is that the mentally ill are held to the standard of care of the reasonable and prudent person. In tort law there is no principle of not liable by reason of insanity. Mental infirmities pose measurement and verifiability problems to a much greater degree than physical infirmities. Moreover, in any event, a physical limitation may not warrant departure from the standard of care of the average reasonable person when that physical limitation should have led the person to take precautions different from or additional to those expected of a reasonable person without that physical infirmity (thus a blind person should take special precaution in crossing the street). The same logic is applied to those with a mental infirmity. Consequently, as a rule, unless there is a sudden and unexpected mental breakdown, mentally ill persons are held to the standard of care of the average reasonable person.

Breunig v. American Family Ins. Co.

The defendant thought that she and her car could fly "because Batman does it." To her surprise she was not airborne before striking the truck of the plaintiff. A psychiatrist testified that she was suffering from "schizophrenic reaction, paranoid type, acute" and that "she had no knowledge or forewarning that such illness or disability would likely occur." The Wisconsin Supreme Court reasoned that people who suffer delusions have periods of lucidity and during such periods, the court reasoned (unreasonably), it is negligent not to take action to prevent oneself from causing harm while delusional. The court considered whether the defendant had any warning or knowledge that would occur and be such as to affect her driving an automobile. It concluded that, notwithstanding the testimony of the psychiatrist that in his opinion she did not, there was sufficient evidence of her past conduct to permit the jury to believe otherwise, and the court left the question to the jury. 45 Wis.2d 536, 173 N.W.2d 619 (1970).

Johnson v. Lombotte

The defendant was under observation by court order and was being treated for "chronic schizophrenic state of paranoid type." On the day in question, she escaped from the hospital and found an automobile with its motor running a few blocks from the hospital. She drove off, having little or no control of the car, and soon collided with the plaintiff. As in *Breunig,* the Colorado Supreme Court said this was not a case of sudden mental seizure with no forewarning. The court said, "The defendant knew she was being treated for a mental disorder and hence would not have come under the nonliability rule [in cases of sudden attack]." 147 Colo. 203, 363 P.2d 165 (1961).

Gould v. American Family Mutual Insurance Co.

The Restatement of Torts (sec. 283C) provides: "If the actor is ill or otherwise physically disabled, the standard of conduct to which he must conform to avoid being negligent is that of a reasonable [person] under like disability." But what is a "physical disability"? Which ones should be taken into account? What if the individual is suffering from Alzheimer's disease? Is that to be treated as a mental illness (no exception made) or as a physical condition (the reasonable person with Alzheimer's)? In this case a patient disabled by Alzheimer's injured a nurse who was caring for him in an institutional setting. The Wisconsin Supreme Court rejected the defendant's argument that the patient could not be negligent because he did not have the capacity to understand and control his actions. The court reaffirmed its commitment to the "widely accepted rule in most American jurisdictions that mentally disabled adults are held responsible for the torts they commit regardless of their capacity to comprehend their actions; they are held to an objective reasonable person standard." The court did, however, carve out a narrow exception that resulted in no liability under the facts of this case: "[W]e hold that a person institutionalized, as here, with a mental disability, and who does not have the capacity to control or appreciate his or her conduct cannot be liable for injuries caused to caretakers who are employed for financial compensation." 523 N.W.2d 295 (Wis. App. 1994).

HARM TO A CARETAKER

Early decisions in various jurisdictions imposed liability on a mentally ill person harming a caretaker, but today the courts tend to say in cases where the defendant is institutionally confined and the injured party is employed to care for or control him, that such imposition of responsibility would serve no purpose in cases of defendants "with no control over [their] actions and [who are] thus innocent of any wrongdoing in the most basic sense of the term." Even in the event of the killing of a caretaker there is usually neither a civil nor a criminal proceeding. See R. Slovenko, *Psychiatry and Criminal Culpability* (New York: Wiley, 1975), pp. 227–28; S. K. Hoge & T. G. Gutheil, "The Psychiatric Patients for Assaults on Staff: A Preliminary Empirical Survey," *Hosp. & Community Psychiatry* 38 (1987): 44. See also S. Jauhar, "Learning to Cope When Hospital Patients Turn Violent," *New York Times,* Mar. 12, 2002, p. D-6.

LIABILITY OF A CARETAKER

For harm done to others by the mentally ill person, the caretaker may be held responsible arising out of their custody and supervision. Even if a mentally ill person is said to lack the ability to form the intent to commit a tort, an action based on negligent supervision may lie against persons responsible for caring for the mentally ill person. According to circumstances, the hospital, the psychiatrist, or the parents or guardian who looks after the individual may be held responsible.

In the past decade or two there has been considerable litigation related to the failure of psychiatrists to predict that patients will harm themselves or others and subsequent failure to do anything to prevent these harms. The majority of suits imposing liability on the psychiatrist or hospital involve the suicide of a patient in the inpatient setting. *See* Duty to Warn or Protect in the Outpatient Setting

Transfer from Prison to a Mental Institution

Vitek v. Jones
During his term of imprisonment, Jones was transferred to a mental hospital. He challenged a state statute that permitted the director of correctional services to transfer a felon to a mental hospital if a designated physician or psychologist found that the prisoner was suffering from a mental disease or defect that could not be given proper treatment in prison. The trial court held that before such a transfer could take place, due process required adequate notice, an adversary hearing before an "independent decision maker," a written statement by the fact finder of the evidence relied on and the reasons for the decision, and "qualified assistance" (it need not be provided by a lawyer). The Supreme Court affirmed the decision of the trial court, saying that it had properly identified and weighed the relevant factors in arriving at its judgment. The Court noted the "stigmatizing consequences" of a transfer to a mental hospital. 445 U.S. 480 (1980). *Vitek* did not address the procedure necessary to place an inmate in a treatment program within the same institution. In Bills v. Henderson, 631 F.2d 1287 (6th Cir. 1980), the court suggested that when a decision to segregate an inmate is based upon a clinical "predictive judgment" concerning "general behavior" rather than a specific rule infraction, the only procedural requirement is that the inmate be told the reasons for the segregation. Though correctional programs may compel inmates to participate in treatment, some clinicians regard compelled treatment as inconsistent with professional ethics. T. Ayllon & M. A. Milan, *Correctional Rehabilitation and Management: A Psychological Approach* (New York: Wiley, 1979).

Undue Familiarity

The profession has been outraged by members who engage in sexual misconduct with patients. It is embarrassed by the litigation, but it makes no pretension that the litigation is unwarranted. Suing for sexual misconduct is of fairly recent origin and is much publicized. The impetus to sue on this account in more recent times can be attributed to the decreased stigma associated with being a psychotherapy patient and, certainly, media reports of high damage awards. In 1985 the American Psychiatric Association excluded coverage for undue familiarity from its member malpractice insurance program. Most members of the APA board of trustees thought that dropping coverage for unethical sexual behavior would help deter its occurrence. A women's committee took a strong stand, to no avail, in favor of retaining insurance coverage "to compensate victims for their distress." To be sure, were the concern primarily about the harm sustained by patients, rather than the reputation of the profession, one should logically desire a source of compensation for the victims of sexual misconduct. See R. Slovenko, "Liability Insurance Coverage in Cases of Psychotherapy Sexual Abuse," *J. Psychiatry & Law* 21 (1993): 277.

See generally S. B. Bisbing, L. M. Jorgenson, & P. K. Sutherland, *Sexual Abuse by Professionals: A Legal Guide* (Charlottesville, Va.: Michie, 1995).

Simmons v. United States

The transference phenomenon is construed as unique to the psychotherapist-patient relationship and as validation of emotional injury when sexual relations occur. The Ninth Circuit Court of Appeals explained: "We note that courts do not routinely impose liability upon physicians in general for sexual contact with patients. . . . The crucial factor in the therapist-patient relationship which leads to the imposition of legal liability for conduct which arguably is no more exploitative of a patient than sexual involvement of a lawyer with a client, a priest or minister with a parishioner, or a gynecologist with a patient is that lawyers, ministers and gynecologists do not offer a course of treatment and counseling predicated upon handling the transference phenomenon." 805 F.3d 1363 (9th Cir. 1986).

Rowe v. Bennett

The Maine Supreme Court held that a patient may maintain an action for negligent infliction of mental distress against a therapist who became involved with the patient's sexual companion, having learned of the companion through the course of psychotherapy. The court said, "We hold that because of the nature of the psychotherapist-patient relationship, an action may be maintained by a patient for serious mental distress caused by the negligence of his therapist despite the absence of [physical impact to the patient]." 514 A.2d 802 (Me. 1986).

Workers' Compensation

It is frequently charged that the original intent of workers' compensation has been perverted and that it has become social sickness insurance, the cost of which is being borne unfairly by industry and the consumer. In a larger sense, the problem is a dilemma of modern society: how to provide a needed social service without at the same time having the individual lose a sense of responsibility. Years ago Dr. Norman Q. Brill made an observation that remains pertinent: "The concept of workmen's compensation for employees with industrial accidents has been so expanded that it includes many disorders in which the causal relationship between the special hazards of employment and the illness becomes increasingly obscure." N. Q. Brill, "Workmen's Compensation for Psychiatric Disorders," *JAMA* 193 (Aug. 2, 1965): 95.

Carter v. General Motors

In this landmark decision, the Michigan Supreme Court ruled that psychiatric disability is as much compensable under workers' compensation law as physical injury. Psychiatric testimony was given that the constant emotional pressures of the job were the cause of the disability, but it was not associated with any physical injury, accident, specific event, or unusual stress or incident. A Southerner named James ("Jimmie")

Carter, an assembly-line worker in a GM auto plant, claimed that he suffered a mental breakdown, not from any single traumatic event but as a result of emotional pressures encountered daily in the performance of his work. The defense attorneys called no expert witnesses. The court ruled that the evidence established a causal connection between the pressure of the workplace and the illness, even though he was not subjected to any pressures different from the pressure on other workers. 361 Mich. 577, 106 N.W.2d 105 (1961).

Linskey v. W.C.A.B. (City of Philadelphia)

The claimant, a firefighter who was assigned periodic emergency rescue squad duties, filed a workers' compensation claim with his employer, the Philadelphia Fire Department. During a rescue squad shift, he responded to a call and found a man who had hanged himself. He was so traumatized by this incident that he began seeing a psychologist. A judge assigned to adjudicate such cases upheld his claim; namely, that his rescue squad duties led to his psychiatric disability. On appeal the decision was overturned on the ground that the stressors that caused his disability were not unique to him. The Commonwealth Court of Pennsylvania held that a claimant must prove by objective evidence that he sustained a psychiatric injury *and* that this injury is other than a subjective reaction to normal working conditions. The applicable statute limits claims for injuries to those subjected to "abnormal working conditions" for the job in question. Since the job was itself inherently stressful, and the claimant was subjected to the same conditions as other fire rescue workers, recovery was barred. 699 A.2d 818 (Pa. Cmwlth. 1997).

Discussion

Had the firefighter in the Pennsylvania case received physical injuries, he would presumably have been eligible for benefits, even though the working conditions were not abnormal. The Pennsylvania decision or statute seems to be a trend away from rulings in various states in recent years allowing disability payments in cases where severe anxiety, depression, or other mental problems are linked however tenuously to work stress. The most common clear-cut case is compensation for the shock suffered when a worker sees a coworker fall to his or her death. Some states have a presumption that "heart disease or illnesses resulting therefrom are deemed to arise out of and in the course of employment in the absence of evidence to the contrary." See, e.g., Mich. Comp. Laws, sec. 418.405. See R. C. Landess, "Stress: How It's Straining the Workers' Compensation System," *The Brief: Tort & Insurance Practice Section of the ABA*, Fall 1987, p. 17; M. J. McCarthy, "Stressed Employees Look for Relief in Workers' Compensation Claims," *Wall Street Journal*, Apr. 7, 1988, p. 27. The Wyoming Supreme Court has held that its state statute denying workers' compensation benefits for mental injury unrelated to compensable physical injury does not violate equal protection. In re Frantz, 932 P.2d 750 (Wyo. 1997). Ultimately, the issue reduces to a social choice between expense cutting and social support for disabled individuals.

Appendix 2: American Academy of Psychiatry and the Law Ethics Guidelines for the Practice of Forensic Psychiatry

Adopted May, 1987—Revised October, 1989, 1991, and 1995 (1995 Revisions for grammatic and syntactic changes only).

I. Preamble

The American Academy of Psychiatry and the Law is dedicated to the highest standards of practice in forensic psychiatry. Recognizing the unique aspects of this practice which is at the interface of the professions of psychiatry and the law, the Academy presents these guidelines for the ethical practice of forensic psychiatry.

COMMENTARY

Forensic Psychiatry is a subspecialty of psychiatry, a medical specialty. Membership in the American Psychiatric Association, or its equivalent, is a prerequisite for membership in the American Academy of Psychiatry and the Law. Hence, these guidelines supplement the Annotations Especially Applicable to Psychiatry of the American Psychiatric Association to the Principles of Medical Ethics of the American Medical Association.

The American Academy of Psychiatry and the Law endorses the Definition of Forensic Psychiatry adopted by the American Board of Forensic Psychiatry, Inc.: "Forensic psychiatry is a subspecialty of psychiatry in which scientific and clinical expertise is applied to legal issue in legal contexts embracing civil, criminal, correctional or legislative matters: forensic psychiatry should be practiced in accordance with guidelines and ethical principles enunciated by the profession of psychiatry." (Adopted May 20, 1985)

The forensic psychiatrist practices this subspecialty at the interface of two professions, each of which is concerned with human behavior and each of which has developed its own particular institutions, procedures, values and vocabulary. As a consequence the practice of forensic psychiatry entails inherent potentials for complications, conflicts, misunderstandings and abuses.

In view of these concerns, the American Academy of Psychiatry and the Law provides these guidelines for the ethical practice of forensic psychiatry.

II. Confidentiality

Respect for the individual's right of privacy and the maintenance of confidentiality are major concerns of the psychiatrist performing forensic evaluations. The psychiatrist maintains confidentiality the extent possible given the legal context. Special attention is paid to any limitations on the usual precepts of medical confidentiality. An evaluation for forensic purposes begins with notice to the evaluee of any limitations on confidentiality. Information or reports derived from the forensic evaluation are subject to the rules of confidentiality as applied to the evaluation, and any disclosure is restricted accordingly.

COMMENTARY

The forensic situation often presents significant problems in regard to confidentiality. The psychiatrist must be aware of and alert to those issues of privacy and confidentiality presented by the particular forensic situation, Notice should be given as to any limitations. For example, before beginning a forensic evaluation, psychiatrists should inform the evaluee that although they are psychiatrists, they are not the evaluee's "doctor." Psychiatrists should indicate for whom they are conducting the examination and what they will do with the information obtained as a result of the examination. There is a continuing obligation to be sensitive to the fact that although a warning has been given, there may be slippage and a treatment relationship may develop in the mind of the examinee.

Psychiatrists should clarify with a potentially retaining attorney whether an initial screening conversation prior to a formal agreement will interdict consultation with the opposing side if the psychiatrist decides not to accept the consultation.

In a treatment situation, whether in regard to an inpatient or to an outpatient in a parole, probation, or conditional release situation, psychiatrists should be clear about any limitations on the usual principles of confidentiality in the treatment relationship and assure that these limitations are communicated to patients. Psychiatrists should be familiar with the institutional policies in regard to confidentiality. Where no policy exists, psychiatrists should clarify these matters with the institutional authorities and develop working guidelines to define their role.

III. Consent

The informed consent of the subject of a forensic evaluation is obtained whenever possible. Where consent is not required, notice is given to the evaluee of the nature of the evaluation. If the evaluee is not competent to give consent, substituted consent is obtained in accordance with the laws of the jurisdiction.

COMMENTARY

Consent is one of the core values of the ethical practice of medicine and psychiatry. It reflects respect for the person, a fundamental principle in the practices of medicine, psychiatry and forensic psychiatry. Obtaining informed consent is an expression of this respect.

It is important to appreciate that in particular situations, such as court ordered evaluations for competency to stand trial or involuntary commitment, consent is not required. In such a case, the psychiatrist should so inform the subject and explain that the evaluation is legally required and that if the subject refuses to participate in the evaluation, this fact will be included in any report or testimony.

With regard to any person charged with criminal acts, ethical considerations preclude forensic evaluation prior to access to, or availability of legal counsel. The only exception is an examination for the purpose of rendering emergency medical care and treatment.

Consent to treatment in a jail or prison or other criminal justice setting must be differentiated from consent to evaluation. The psychiatrists providing treatment in these settings should be familiar with the jurisdiction's rules in regard to the patient's right to refuse treatment.

IV. Honesty and Striving for Objectivity

Forensic psychiatrists function as experts within the legal process. Although they may be retained by one party to a dispute in a civil matter or the prosecution or defense in a criminal matter, they adhere to the principle of honesty and they strive for objectivity. Their clinical evaluation and the application of the data obtained to the legal criteria are performed in the spirit of such honesty and efforts to attain objectivity. Their opinion reflects this honesty and efforts to attain objectivity.

COMMENTARY

The adversarial nature of our Anglo-American legal process presents special hazards for the practicing forensic psychiatrist. Being retained by one side in a civil or criminal matter expose forensic psychiatrist to the potential for unintended bias and the danger of distortion of their opinion. It is the responsibility of forensic psychiatrist to minimize such hazards by carrying out their responsibilities in an honest manner striving to reach an objective opinion.

Practicing forensic psychiatrists enhance the honesty and objectivity of their work by basing their forensic opinions, forensic reports and forensic testimony on all the data available to them. They communicate the honesty of their work, efforts to attain objectivity, and the soundness of their clinical opinion, by distinguishing, to the extent possible, between verified and unverified information as well as among clinical "facts," "inferences" and "impressions."

While it is ethical to provide consultation to an adversary in a legal dispute as a testifying or reporting expert, honesty and striving for objectivity are required. The impression that psychiatrists in a forensic situation might distort their opinion in the service of the party which retained them is especially detrimental to the profession and must be assiduously avoided. Honesty, objectivity and the adequacy of the clinical evaluation may be called into question when an expert opinion is offered without a personal examination. While there are authorities who would bar an expert opinion in regard to an individual who has not been personally examined, it is the position of the Academy that if, after earnest effort, it is not possible to conduct a personal examination, an opinion may be rendered on the basis of other information. However, under such circumstances, it is the responsibility of forensic psychiatrists to assure the statements of their opinion and any reports of testimony based in those opinions, clearly indicate that there was no personal examination and the opinions expressed are thereby limited.

In custody cases, honesty and objectivity require that all parties be interviewed, if possible, before an opinion is rendered. When this is not possible, or if for any reason not done, this fact should be clearly indicated in the forensic psychiatrist's report and testimony. Where one parent has not been interviewed, even after deliberate effort, it may be inappropriate to comment on that parent's fitness as a parent. Any comments on that parent's fitness should be qualified and the data for the opinion be clearly indicated.

Contingency fees, because of the problems that these create in regard to honesty and efforts to attain objectivity, should not be accepted. On the other hand, retainer fees do not create problems in regard to honesty and efforts to attain objectivity and, therefore, may be accepted.

Treating psychiatrists should generally avoid agreeing to be an expert witness or to perform evaluations of their patients for legal purposes because a forensic evaluation usually requires that other people be interviewed and testimony may adversely affect the therapeutic relationship.

V. Qualifications

Expertise in the practice of forensic psychiatry is claimed only in areas of actual knowledge and skills, training and experience.

COMMENTARY

As regards expert opinions, reports and testimony, the expert's qualifications should be presented accurately and precisely. As a correlate of the principle that expertise may be appropriately claimed only in areas of actual knowledge, skill, training and experience, there are areas of special expertise, such as the evaluation of children or persons of foreign cultures, or prisoners, that may require special training and expertise.

VI. Procedures for Handling Complaints of Unethical Conduct

Complaints of unethical conduct against members of the Academy will be returned to the complainant with guidance as to where the complaint should be registered. Generally, they will be referred to the local district branch of the American Psychiatric Association (APA). If the member does not belong to the APA, the complainant will be referred to the state licensing board or to the psychiatric association in the appropriate country. If the APA, American Academy of Child and Adolescent Psychiatry, or the psychiatric association of another country should expel or suspend a member, AAPL will also expel or suspend the member upon notification of such action regardless of continuing membership status in other organizations, AAPL will not necessarily follow the APA or other organizations in other actions.

COMMENTARY

It is the present policy of the American Academy of Psychiatry and the Law not to adjudicate questions of unethical conduct against members or nonmembers.

General questions in regard to ethical practice in forensic psychiatry are welcomed by the Academy and should be submitted for consideration to the Committee on Ethics.

The Committee will issue opinions on general or hypothetical questions but will not issue an opinion on the ethical conduct of a specific forensic psychiatrist or about an actual case.

Should a specific complaint against a member be submitted to the Academy, it will be referred to the Chair of the Ethics Committee. The Chair will, in turn, generally direct the complainant to the ethics committee of the local district branch of the American Psychiatric Association, to the state licensing boards or ethics committees of psychiatric organizations of ethical conduct as they relate to forensic psychiatric issues.

Appendix 3: Specialty Guidelines for Forensic Psychologists

Source: Prepared by the Committee on Ethical Guidelines for Forensic Psychologists, Division 41, American Psychological Association, and the American Board of Forensic Psychology. Reprinted by permission of Kluwer Academic/Plenum Publishers.

Introduction

The *Specialty Guidelines for Forensic Psychologists,* while informed by the *Ethical Principles of Psychologists* (APA, 1990) and meant to be consistent with them, are designed to provide more specific guidance to forensic psychologists in monitoring their professional conduct when acting in assistance to courts, parties to legal proceedings, correctional and forensic mental health facilities, and legislative agencies. The primary goal of the *Guidelines* is to improve the quality of forensic psychological services offered to individual clients and the legal system and thereby to enhance forensic psychology as a discipline and profession. The *Specialty Guidelines for Forensic Psychologists* represent a joint statement of the American Psychology-Law Society and Division 41 of the American Psychological Association and are endorsed by the American Academy of Forensic Psychology. The Guidelines do not represent an official statement of the American Psychological Association.

The Guidelines provide an aspirational model of desirable professional practice by psychologists, within any subdiscipline of psychology (e.g., clinical, developmental, social, experimental), when they are engaged regularly as experts and represent themselves as such, in an activity primarily intended to provide professional psychological expertise to the judicial system. This would include, for example, clinical forensic examiners; psychologists employed by correctional or forensic mental health systems; researchers who offer direct testimony about the relevance of scientific data to a psycholegal issue; trial behavior consultants; psychologists engaged in preparation of *amicus* briefs; or psychologists, appearing as forensic experts, who consult with, or testify before, judicial, legislative or administrative agencies acting in an adjudicative capacity. Individuals who provide only occasional services to the legal system and who do so without representing themselves as *forensic experts* may find these *Guidelines* helpful, particularly in conjunction with consultation with colleagues who are forensic experts.

While the *Guidelines* are concerned with a model of desirable professional practice, to the extent that they may be construed as being applicable to the advertisement of services or the solicitation of clients, they are intended to prevent false or deceptive advertisement or solicitation, and should be construed in a manner consistent with that intent.

I. Purpose and Scope

A. Purpose

1. While the professional standards for the ethical practice of psychology, as a general discipline, are addressed in the American Psychological Association's *Ethical Principles of Psychologists,* these ethical principles do not relate, in sufficient detail, to current aspirations of desirable professional conduct for forensic psychologists. By design, none of the *Guidelines* contradicts any of the *Ethical Principles of Psychologists;* rather, they amplify those *Principles* in the context of the practice of forensic psychology, as herein defined.

2. The *Guidelines* have been designed to be national in scope and are intended to conform with state and Federal law. In situations where the forensic psychologist believes that the requirements of law are in conflict with the *Guidelines,* attempts to resolve the conflict should be made in accordance with the procedures set forth in these *Guidelines* [IV(G)] and in the *Ethical Principles of Psychologists.*

B. Scope

1. The *Guidelines* specify the nature of desirable professional practice by forensic psychologists, within any subdiscipline of psychology (e.g., clinical, developmental, social, experimental), when engaged regularly as forensic psychologists.

a. "Psychologist" means any individual whose professional activities are defined by the American Psychological Association or by regulation of title by state registration or licensure, as the practice of psychology.

b. "Forensic psychology" means all forms of professional psychological conduct when acting, with definable foreknowledge, as a psychological expert on explicitly psycholegal issues, in direct assistance to courts, parties to legal proceedings, correctional and forensic mental health facilities, and administrative, judicial and legislative agencies acting in an adjudicative capacity.

c. "Forensic psychologist" means psychologists who regularly engage in the practice of forensic psychology as defined in I(B)(1)(b).

2. The *Guidelines* do not apply to a psychologist who is asked to provide professional psychological services when the psychologist was not informed at the time of delivery of the services that they were to be used as forensic psychological services as defined above. The *Guidelines* may be helpful, however, in preparing the psychologist for the experience of communicating psychological data in a forensic context.

3. Psychologists who are not forensic psychologists as defined in I(B)(1)(c), but occasionally provide limited forensic psychological services, may find the *Guidelines* useful in the preparation and presentation of their professional services.

C. Related Standards

1. Forensic psychologists also conduct their professional activities in accord with the *Ethical Principles of Psychologists* and the various other statements of the American Psychological Association that may apply to particular subdisciplines or areas of practice that are relevant to their professional activities.

2. The standards of practice and ethical guidelines of other relevant "expert professional organizations" contain useful guidance and should be consulted even though the present *Guidelines* take precedence for forensic psychologists.

II. Responsibility

A. Forensic psychologists have an obligation to provide services in a manner consistent with the highest standards of their profession. They are responsible for their own conduct and the conduct of those individuals under their direct supervision.

B. Forensic psychologists make a reasonable effort to ensure that their services and the products of their services are used in a forthright and responsible manner.

III. Competence

A. Forensic psychologists provide services only in areas of psychology in which they have specialized knowledge, skill, experience and education.

B. Forensic psychologists have an obligation to present to the court, regarding the specific matters to which they will testify, the boundaries of their competence, the factual bases (knowledge, skill, experience, training, and education) for their qualification as an expert, and the relevance of those factual bases to their qualification as an expert on the specific matters at issue.

C. Forensic psychologists are responsible for a fundamental and reasonable level of knowledge and understanding of the legal and professional standards which govern their participation as experts in legal proceedings.

D. Forensic psychologists have an obligation to understand the civil rights of parties in legal proceedings in which they participate, and manage their professional conduct in a manner that does not diminish or threaten those rights.

E. Forensic psychologists recognize that their own personal values, moral beliefs, or personal and professional relationships with parties to a legal proceeding may interfere with their ability to practice competently. Under such circumstances, forensic psychologists are obligated to decline participation or to limit their assistance in a manner consistent with professional obligations.

IV. Relationships

A. During initial consultation with the legal representative of the party seeking services, forensic psychologists have an obligation to inform the party of factors that might reasonably affect the decision to contract with the forensic psychologist. These factors include, but are not limited to:

1. the fee structure for anticipated professional services;
2. prior and current personal or professional activities, obligations and relationships that might produce a conflict of interest;
3. their areas of competence and the limits of their competence; and
4. the known scientific bases and limitations of the methods and procedures which they employ and their qualifications to employ such methods and procedures.

B. Forensic psychologists do not provide professional services to parties to a legal proceeding on the basis of "contingent fees," when those services involve the offering of expert testimony to a court or administrative body, or when they call upon the psychologist to make affirmations or representations intended to be relied upon by third parties.

C. Forensic psychologists who derive a substantial portion of their income from fee-for-service arrangements should offer some portion of their professional services on a *pro bono* or reduced fee basis where the public interest or the welfare of clients may be inhibited by insufficient financial resources.

D. Forensic psychologists recognize potential conflicts of interest in dual relationships with parties to a legal proceeding, and they seek to minimize their effects.

1. Forensic psychologists avoid providing professional services to parties in a legal proceeding with whom they have personal or professional relationships that are inconsistent with the anticipated relationship.

2. When it is necessary to provide both evaluation and treatment services to a party in a legal proceeding (as may be the case in small forensic hospital settings or small communities), the forensic psychologist takes reasonable steps to minimize the potential negative effects of these circumstances on the rights of the party, confidentiality, and the process of treatment and evaluation.

E. Forensic psychologists have an obligation to ensure that prospective clients are informed of their legal rights with respect to the anticipated forensic service, of the purposes of any evaluation, of the nature of procedures to be employed, of the intended uses of any product of their services, and of the party who has employed the forensic psychologist.

1. Unless court ordered, forensic psychologists obtain the informed consent of the client or party, or their legal representative, before proceeding with such evaluations and procedures. If the client appears unwilling to proceed after receiving a thorough notification of the purposes, methods, and intended uses of the forensic evaluation, the evaluation should be postponed and the psychologist should take steps to place the client in contact with his/her attorney for the purpose of legal advice on the issue of participation.

2. In situations where the client or party may not have the capacity to provide informed consent to services or the evaluation is pursuant to court order, the forensic psychologist provides reasonable notice to the client's legal representative of the nature of the anticipated forensic service before proceeding. If the client's legal representative objects to the evaluation, the forensic psychologist notifies the court issuing the order and responds as directed.

3. After a psychologist has advised the subject of a clinical forensic evaluation of the intended uses of the evaluation and its work product, the psychologist may not use the evaluation work product for other purposes without explicit waiver to do so by the client or the client's legal representative.

F. When forensic psychologists engage in research or scholarly activities that are compensated financially by a client or party to a legal proceeding, or when the psychologist provides those services on a *pro bono* basis, the psychologist clarifies any anticipated further use of such research or scholarly product, discloses the psychologist's role in the resulting research or scholarly products, and obtains whatever consent or agreement is required by law or professional standards.

G. When conflicts arise between the forensic psychologist's professional standards and the requirements of legal standards, a particular court, or a directive by an officer or the court or legal authorities, the forensic psychologist has an obligation to make those legal authorities aware of the source of the conflict and to take reasonable steps to resolve it. Such steps may include, but are not limited to, obtaining the consultation of fellow forensic professionals, obtaining the advice of independent counsel, and conferring directly with the legal representatives involved.

V. Confidentiality and Privilege

A. Forensic psychologists have an obligation to be aware of the legal standards that may affect or limit the confidentiality or privilege that may attach to their services or their products, and they conduct their professional activities in a manner that respects those known rights and privileges.

1. Forensic psychologists establish and maintain a system of record keeping and professional communication that safeguards a client's privilege.

2. Forensic psychologists maintain active control over records and informa-

tion. They only release information pursuant to statutory requirements, court order, or the consent of the client.

B. Forensic psychologists inform their clients of the limitations to the confidentiality of their services and their products (see also Guideline IV-E) by providing them with an understandable statement of their rights, privileges, and the limitations of confidentiality.

C. In situations where the right of the client or party to confidentiality is limited, the forensic psychologist makes every effort to maintain confidentiality with regard to any information that does not bear directly upon the legal purpose of the evaluation.

D. Forensic psychologists provide clients or their authorized legal representatives with access to the information in their records and a meaningful explanation of that information, consistent with existing federal and state statutes, the *Ethical Principles of Psychologists*, the *Standards for Educational and Psychological Testing*, and institutional rules and regulations.

VI. Methods and Procedures

A. Because of their special status as persons qualified as experts to the court, forensic psychologists have an obligation to maintain current knowledge of scientific, professional and legal developments within their area of claimed competence. They are obligated also to use that knowledge, consistent with accepted clinical and scientific standards, in selecting data collection methods and procedures for an evaluation, treatment, consultation or scholarly/empirical investigation.

B. Forensic psychologists have an obligation to document and be prepared to make available, subject to court order or the rules of evidence, all data that form the basis for their evidence or services. The standard to be applied to such documentation or recording *anticipates* that the detail and quality of such documentation will be subject to reasonable judicial scrutiny; this standard is higher than the normative standard for general clinical practice. When forensic psychologists conduct an examination or engage in the treatment of a party to a legal proceeding, with foreknowledge that their professional services will be used in an adjudicative forum, they incur a special responsibility to provide the best documentation possible under the circumstances.

1. Documentation of the data upon which one's evidence is based is subject to the normal rules of discovery, disclosure, confidentiality and privilege that operate in the jurisdiction in which the data were obtained. Forensic psychologists have an obligation to be aware of those rules and to regulate their conduct in accordance with them.

2. The duties and obligations of forensic psychologists with respect to documentation of data that form the basis for their evidence apply from the moment they know or have a reasonable basis for knowing that their data and evidence derived from it are likely to enter into legally relevant decisions.

C. In providing forensic psychological services, forensic psychologists take special care to avoid undue influence upon their methods, procedures and products, such as might emanate from the party to a legal proceeding by financial compensation or other gains. As an expert conducting an evaluation, treatment, consultation or scholarly/empirical investigation, the forensic psychologist maintains professional integrity by examining the issue at hand from all reasonable perspectives, actively seeking information which will differentially test plausible rival hypotheses.

D. Forensic psychologists do not provide professional forensic services to a defendant or to any party in, or in contemplation of, a legal proceeding prior to that individual's representation by counsel, except for persons judicially determined, where appropriate, to be handling their representation *pro se*. When the forensic services are pursuant to court order and the client is not represented by counsel, the forensic psychologist makes reasonable efforts to inform the court prior to providing the services.

1. A forensic psychologist may provide emergency mental health services to a pretrial defendant prior to court order or the appointment of counsel where there are reasonable grounds to believe that such emergency services are needed for the protection and improvement of the defendant's mental health and where failure to provide such mental health services would constitute a substantial risk of imminent harm to the defendant or to others. In providing such services the forensic psychologist nevertheless seeks to inform the defendant's counsel in a manner consistent with the requirements of the emergency situation.

2. Forensic psychologists who provide such emergency mental health services should attempt to avoid providing further professional forensic services to that defendant unless that relationship is reasonably unavoidable [see IV(D)(2)].

E. When forensic psychologists seek data from third parties, prior records, or other sources, they do so only with the prior approval of the relevant legal party or as a consequence of an order of a court to conduct the forensic evaluation.

F. Forensic psychologists are aware that hearsay exceptions and other rules governing expert testimony place a special ethical burden upon them. When hearsay or otherwise inadmissible evidence forms the basis of their opinion, evidence or professional product, they seek to minimize sole reliance upon such evidence. Where circumstances reasonably permit, forensic psychologists seek to obtain independent and personal verification of data relied upon as part of their professional services to the court or to a party to a legal proceeding.

1. While many forms of data used by forensic psychologists are hearsay, forensic psychologists attempt to corroborate critical data which form the basis of their professional product. When using hearsay data that have not been corroborated, but are nevertheless utilized, forensic psychologists have an affirmative responsibility to acknowledge the uncorroborated status of that data and the reasons for relying upon such data.

2. With respect to evidence of any type, forensic psychologists avoid offering information from their investigations or evaluations that does not bear directly upon the legal purpose of their professional services and that is not critical as support for their product, evidence or testimony, except where such disclosure is required by law.

3. When a forensic psychologist relies upon data or information gathered by others, the origins of those data are clarified in any professional product. In addition, the forensic psychologist bears a special responsibility to ensure that such data, if relied upon, were gathered in a manner standard for the profession.

G. Unless otherwise stipulated by the parties, forensic psychologists are aware that no statements made by a defendant, in the course of any (forensic) examination, no testimony by the expert based upon such statements, nor any other fruits of the statements can be admitted into evidence against the defendant in any criminal proceeding, except on an issue respecting mental condition on which the defendant has introduced testimony. Forensic psychologists have an affirmative duty to ensure that their written products and oral testimony conform to this Federal Rule of Procedure (12.2[c]), or its state equivalent.

1. Because forensic psychologists are often not in a position to know what evidence, documentation or element of a written product may be or may lead to a "fruit of the statement," they exercise extreme caution in preparing reports or offering testimony prior to the defendant's assertion of a mental state claim or the defendant's introduction of testimony regarding a mental condition. Consistent with reporting requirements of state or Federal law, forensic psychologists avoid including statements from the defendant relating to the time period of the alleged offense.

2. Once a defendant has proceeded to the trial stage, and all pretrial mental health issues such as competency have been resolved, forensic psychologists may include in their reports or testimony any statements made by the defendant that are directly relevant to supporting their expert evidence, providing that the defendant has

"introduced" mental state evidence or testimony within the meaning of Federal Rule of Procedure 12.2(c), or its state equivalent.

H. Forensic psychologists avoid giving written or oral evidence about the psychological characteristics of particular individuals when they have not had an opportunity to conduct an examination of the individual adequate to the scope of the statements, opinions or conclusions to be issued. Forensic psychologists make every reasonable effort to conduct such examinations. When it is not possible or feasible to do so, they make clear the impact of such limitations on the reliability and validity of their professional products, evidence or testimony.

VII. Public and Professional Communications

A. Forensic psychologists make reasonable efforts to ensure that the products of their services, as well as their own public statements and professional testimony, are communicated in ways that will promote understanding and avoid deception, given the particular characteristics, roles, and abilities of various recipients of the communications.

　1. Forensic psychologists take reasonable steps to correct misuse or misrepresentation of their professional products, evidence and testimony.

　2. Forensic psychologists provide information about professional work to clients in a manner consistent with professional and legal standards for the disclosure of test results, interpretation of data, and the factual bases for conclusions. A full explanation of the results of tests and the bases for conclusions should be given in language that the client can understand.

　　a. When disclosing information about a client to third parties who are not qualified to interpret test results and data, the forensic psychologist complies with Principle 16 of the *Standards for Educational and Psychological Testing*. When required to disclose results to a non-psychologist, every attempt is made to ensure that test security is maintained and access to information is restricted to individuals with a legitimate and professional interest in the data. Other qualified mental health professionals who make a request for information pursuant to a lawful order are, by definition, "individuals with a legitimate and professional interest."

　　b. In providing records and raw data, the forensic psychologist takes reasonable steps to ensure that the receiving party is informed that raw scores must be interpreted by a qualified professional in order to provide reliable and valid information.

B. Forensic psychologists realize that their public role as "expert to the court" or as "expert representing the profession" confers upon them a special responsibility for fairness and accuracy in their public statements. When evaluating or commenting upon the professional work product or qualifications of another expert or party to a legal proceeding, forensic psychologists represent their professional disagreements with reference to a fair and accurate evaluation of the data, theories, standards and opinions of the other expert or party.

C. Ordinarily, forensic psychologists avoid making detailed public (out-of-court) statements about particular legal proceedings in which they have been involved. When there is a strong justification to do so, such public statements are designed to assure accurate representation of their role or their evidence, not to advocate the positions of parties in the legal proceeding. Forensic psychologists address particular legal proceedings in publications or communications only to the extent that the information relied upon is part of a public record, or consent for that use has been properly obtained from the party holding any privilege.

D. When testifying, forensic psychologists have an obligation to all parties to a legal proceeding to present their findings, conclusions, evidence or other professional products in a fair manner. This principle does not preclude forceful representation of the data and reasoning upon which a conclusion or professional product is based. It does, however, preclude an attempt, whether active or passive, to engage in partisan distortion or misrepresentation. Forensic psychologists do not, by either commission or omission, participate in a misrepresentation of their evidence, nor do they participate in partisan attempts to avoid, deny or subvert the presentation of evidence contrary to their own position.

E. Forensic psychologists, by virtue of their competence and rules of discovery, actively disclose all sources of information obtained in the course of their professional services; they actively disclose which information from which source was used in formulating a particular written product or oral testimony.

F. Forensic psychologists are aware that their essential role as expert to the court is to assist the trier of fact to understand the evidence or to determine a fact in issue. In offering expert evidence, they are aware that their own professional observations, inference and conclusions must be distinguished from legal facts, opinions and conclusions. Forensic psychologists are prepared to explain the relationship between their expert testimony and the legal issues and facts of an instant case.

Case

Index

Name

Index

DeBoers, J., 504
DeBoers, R., 504
DeBotton, A., 893
DeBracton, H., 218
Deftos, L. J., 853
DeGrandpre, R., 179
Deitz, S., 148
Dejowski, E. F., 532
Dekleva, K. B., 358, 912
Delgado, R., 677, 683
Delin, R. C., 506
DeLipsey, J. M., 150
DeMartino, N., 493
DeMille, C. B., 529
Demosthenes, 408
Denenberg, R. V., 152, 184
Dennis, D., 582
Derecho, D. V., 265
DeRose, D., 759
Dershowitz, A. M., 9, 77, 115, 218, 234, 237, 238, 239, 964
DeSaussure, S., 184
Deters, J. T., 201
Deutsch, A., 120, 563, 573, 914
DeWine, M., 579
DeWitt, C., 94
Diamond, B., 15, 125, 133, 208, 238, 249, 273, 275, 276, 281, 285, 286, 387, 926, 933
Dickens, C., 104, 556, 573
Dickerson, E., 275
Didion, J., 670
Diesenhouse, S., 756, 762
Dietz, P., 114, 261, 606, 952
Dimitrius, J. E., 119, 132, 168, 182
Dincin, J., 579
Dinwiddie, S. H., 237
Diogenes, 138
Disch, E., 756
Disney, W., 172
Ditman, K. S., 322
Dix, D., 556
Dix, G. E., 580, 612, 899
Dobbins, J. E., 318
Doe, C., 249, 250, 938
Doerner, W. G., 482
Doherty, M., 301
Doige, J., 243
Dolan, A. K., 338
Doll, W., 607
Dolnick, E., 180, 665, 669, 895
Domenici, T., 428
Donaldson, K., 607, 958
Donaldson, L., 821

Dooling, R., 428
Dorfman, D. A., 612
Dorr, D., 262
Dorris, D., 85, 86
Dorsey, J., 128, 133, 100
Dosrtzev, D., 670
Dostoyevsky, F., 511, 527, 820
Dougherty, D. M., 264
Douglas, A., 408
Douglas, J., 152
Douglas, M., 441
Douglas, W. O., 309, 348, 604, 905, 913
Dowdy, L., 286
Downey, J. I., 854, 856
Doyle, A., 634
Drescher, J., 420, 428
Dressler, J., 234, 237, 425, 427
Drew, C., 131
Driver, J., 110, 111, 308
Droegemueller, W., 177
Drogin, E. Y., 16, 237
Drought, E., 527
Drukteinis, A. M., 156, 177
Drummond, E., 218, 937
D'Souza, D., 471
DuBroff, D., 945
Duff, R. A., 934
Duggan, M., 376
Dukakis, M., 422, 898
Dukeminier, J., 548, 550
Dulles, J. F., 698
Dunne, D., 154
Durfee, E., 551
Durham, M. L., 7, 583, 915, 938
Durkheim, E., 820
Dutton, D. G., 153, 266
Dvoskin, J., 606
Dworkin, G., 717, 730, 733
Dwyer, J., 131
Dyer, F. J., 504
Dyer, J., 13

E

Eads, L. S., 150
Eagleton, T., 692
Easter, D., 308
Easton, N. J., 531
Eastwood, C., 168
Eaton, B., 676, 683
Ebert, R., 527
Edelstein, L. N., 150, 704
Edwardes, C., 470
Edwards, H. T., 36
Edwards, W., 405

Ehrenzweig, A., 353, 361, 446
Eichmann, A., xxv, 236
Eichwald, K., 734
Einbinder, S. D., 42
Einstein A., xx, 262
Eisdorfer, C., 820
Eisenberg, M. M., 578
Eisnitz, A. J., 820
Eissler, K. R., 468, 890
Eist, H., 891, 894
Eizenstat, S., 206
Ekman, P., 167, 168, 182
Eldredge, L. H., 446
Eldridge, W. B., 337
Elias, M., 821
Elkins, B. E., 238
Elliot, C., 140, 426
Ellis, A., 895
Ellis, H., 878
Ellis, J. W., 243, 446, 447
Ellison, J., 637
Ellsberg, D., xxv
Ellsworth, P. C., 152, 502
Emerson, I. I., 426
Emschwiller, J., 898
Engle, B., 573
English, D. M., 98
Engster, D., 582
Ennis, B. J., 57, 63, 558, 588, 604, 911
Entzeroth, L., 356, 358
Epstein, E., 545, 551, 552
Epstein, J., xxvii, 756
Epstein, R. A., 445
Epstein, R. S., 754, 756
Ericsson, S. E., 38
Erikson, E., 11, 15, 860
Erlich, L. B., 334
Erlinder, C. P., 261
Erskine, J., 547
Erskine, T., 937
Ervin, S., 558, 585
Eskridge, W. N., 423
Essig, L., 427
Estrich, S., 127, 237, 290
Eth, S., 748
Etherington, E. D., 14
Etzioni, A., 706
Evans, P., 184
E. W., 569
Ewing, C. P., 581, 609
Ewing, M., 558

F

Faden, R. R., 729
Faderman, L., 428
Faigman, D. L., xxviii, 13, 59

Subject
Index

About the Author

Ralph Slovenko is Professor of Law and Psychiatry at Wayne State University in Michigan. He received B.E., LL.B., M.A., and Ph.D. degrees from Tulane University. He was editor-in-chief of the *Tulane Law Review* and a varsity sports letterman at Tulane University. He served as law clerk to the Louisiana Supreme Court and as senior assistant district attorney under Jim Garrison in New Orleans. He was a Fulbright scholar to France. A professor of law at Tulane University from 1954 to 1964, he was also a member of the faculty of the Tulane University Department of Psychiatry and Neurology. At the invitation of Dr. Robert G. Heath, chairman of the Tulane University Department of Psychiatry and Neurology, he did a residency in psychiatry, one of two persons to do so without a medical degree.

He held a joint appointment, from 1965 to 1968, at the Menninger Foundation and the University of Kansas School of Law. Since then, he has been at Wayne State University. He has lectured widely in the United States and also in Australia, Canada, France, Israel, Japan, Russia (Soviet Union), and South Africa. He was visiting professor in South Africa in 1976 and 1989, and he occupied the Rood Eminent Scholar Chair in 1991 at the University of Florida College of Law. He has been a frequent visitor to Lithuania, Poland, Russia, and South Africa, and has written extensively about them. He has frequently served as an expert witness.

He is a member of the American, Kansas, Louisiana, and Michigan Bar Associations, and a scientific associate of the American Academy of Psychoanalysis and amicus of the American Academy of Psychiatry and Law. He is the author of numerous books and articles. His book *Psychiatry and Law* (Boston: Little, Brown, 1973) received the Manfred Guttmacher award of the American Psychiatric Association and was a selection of the Behavioral Science Book Club. He collaborated with Dr. Karl A. Menninger on the book *The Crime of Punishment* (New York: Viking Press, 1966). He is a regular commentator in the *Journal of Psychiatry and Law* and is editor of the American Series in Behavioral Science and Law. He is on the board of editors of the *International Journal of Offender Therapy and Comparative Criminology, Journal of the American Academy of Psychiatry and Law, Journal of Psychiatry and Law,* and *Medicine and Law.* For years he wrote a weekly column in the *Detroit Legal News.* His articles have appeared in the *New York Times, Wall Street Journal,* and other publications. His writings have been frequently cited by the U.S. Supreme Court and other appellate courts.